PARENTAL BELIEF SYSTEMS:
The Psychological Consequences for Children (Second Edition)

PARENTAL BELIEF SYSTEMS:
The Psychological Consequences for Children (Second Edition)

Edited by

Irving E. Sigel
Educational Testing Service

Ann V. McGillicuddy-DeLisi
Lafayette College

Jacqueline J. Goodnow
Macquarie University

 LAWRENCE ERLBAUM ASSOCIATES, PUBLISHERS
1992   Hillsdale, New Jersey   Hove and London

Lawrence Erlbaum Associates, Inc., Publishers
365 Broadway
Hillsdale, New Jersey 07642

Library of Congress Cataloging-in-Publication Data

Parental belief systems : the psychological consequences for children
/ edited by Irving E. Sigel, Ann V. McGillicuddy-Delisi, Jacqueline
J. Goodnow. — 2nd ed.
   p.   cm.
Includes bibliographical references and index.
ISBN 0-8058-0652-0
1. Parent and child. 2. Child psychology. 3. Child rearing.
4. Parents — Attitudes. 5. Social values. I. Sigel, Irving E.
II. McGillicuddy-De Lisi. III. Goodnow, Jacqueline J.
BF723.P25P28 1992
155.9′24 — dc — 20   91-25515
                                           CIP

Printed in the United States of America
10 9 8 7 6 5 4 3 2

Contents

Introduction to the First Edition

Irving E. Sigel
Educational Testing Service

Studies of parent–child relationships have a long history among developmental psychologists. The reason for such interest is obvious: The child is the father of the man or the mother of the woman and the child's parents are a primal source of genetic, social, and psychological influence. With this guiding belief, thousands of studies have been reported over the past 50 years. What is of particular interest is that all these studies clearly reflect the prevailing psychological theories that have guided research in social and personality development. In the 1920s and 1930s the parent–child research studies that prevailed focused on parent discipline, attitudes, etc., research paradigms common to behavioral science research in general. However, behavior-type theories dominated the psychological literature, with their attendant emphasis on so-called objective methods of experimentation. Critics decried the parent–child studies done in naturalistic settings as imprecise, nonconceptual, etc. After all, experimentation was the critical method for scientific respectability in the behavioral sciences, in spite of the respectability of nonexperimental research among such descriptive sciences as astronomy and botany. The pervasiveness of experimentation tended to relegate parent–child studies to the least desirable category. In spite of these conflicts a major observational study, well executed and meeting all the criteria of scientific rigor, was the early work of Baldwin, Kalhorn, and Breese (1945). Numerous studies followed, using behavioristic, psychoanalytic, and social learning perspectives as theory, each testing the relationship between parental attutides or feelings or disciplinary techniques and children's personal–social and/or intellectual development (Baumrind, 1971; Becker, 1964; Sigel, Dreyer, & McGillicuddy-DeLisi, 1984).

During the 1960s, interest in parent–child research waned; this was especially true of research involving middle-class families with children of preschool age or older. Attention turned to studies of infant development, and interest grew in psychosocial and cognitive development among children in low-income and minority groups (Sigel, Secrist, & Forman, 1973). The paradigm of research, both conceptual and methodological, still tended to be consistent with a logical positivist mold focusing on behavior. The growing interest in infancy continued, with studies on infant responsiveness, learning, and subsequently, cognition. Concurrently, interest was generated in emotional aspects of behavior, in the guise of a quasi-ethological orientation expressed in the attachment literature. While the research efforts included the parent (usually the mother), the attachment paradigm was developed (Ainsworth, 1973), and there was an upsurge of interest in this phenomenon. But behavioral criteria were still used with attachment concepts to describe the child's response to different adults in the attachment situation. The mothers were described as objects in that situation also.

Other developments in social psychology were going on, which during the 1970s and 1980s were to have a significant impact on research in parent–child relations (Sigel, 1981).

This volume of essays reflects the various threads in parent–child research over the past 40 years. The articles demonstrate a reconceptualization of human nature — because the domains of interest, assumed to be significantly affecting the quality of parent–child research relationships, have changed. A major shift is the increased emphasis on cognitive processes and information processing. Although not necessarily ascribing to a particular cognitive theory or the traditional information-processing model, implicitly the perspectives are here. And although affective aspects are among the concerns of the investigators, basically, as will be seen, a cognitive perspective prevails.

As we discover as we go through the volume, there is considerable diversity in the investigators' cognitive orientation. For example, the very concept of "belief" does not afford a general agreement. Whether to rejoice or to despair because of the diversity is a moot point. On the one hand, there is cause for rejoicing, because among the many perspectives reflected in this volume are sophisticated, creative efforts at theory building, methodological strategies, in regard to important dimensions of parent-child relationships. On the other hand, in spite of all the advances, there is still confusion as well as disagreement in regard to theory, method, and problem studied. Perhaps this state of affairs should not surprise us, as it has been endemic to psychology since the beginning of the science. This is not the place to dwell on the whys and wherefores of such diversity or confusion. (For discussion of that issue, see Sigel, 1981.) Rather, the objective in this volume is to present a set of papers that in an overarching way share a common interest; namely, in defining and investigating determinants of parents' behaviors relative to their children.

Even though the papers focus on parent–child interactions in developmental contexts, each reflects the influence of various current psychological and theoretical perspectives. For example, Sameroff and Feil derive their conceptualization from a Piagetian framework; Holloway and Hess work within the attribution theoretical model.

The research presented in this volume is not isolated from a basic psychological perspective, but rather, is an application of that perspective to a particular issue: namely, the study of determinants of parent behavior and the consequences of such behavior on the relationships as well as on each of the participants – parent and child.

During the last decade, with the growing interest in cognition, it is not surprising that those investigators interested in parent–child relationships have employed conceptual models drawn from social, clinical, and developmental psychology.

In this volume, investigations representing various cognitive approaches are presented. Holloway and Hess, and Dix and Grusec represent attribution theory. Applegate et al., McGillicuddy-DeLisi, and Johnson reflect Kellyian personal construct theory. Sameroff and Feil employ a Piagetian model of cognition. Schaefer and Edgerton represent a more comprehensive view without a clearly defined cognitive model – rather, they deal with the belief issue in the terms of a broader cultural perspective. Goodnow represents an intersect between culture and cognition. Skinner's paradigm is different in that hers combines constructivism and contingency analysis.

Finally, Sigel grapples with the *belief* construct as discussed among some of the leading theorists as well as in these chapters. The goal is to differentiate beliefs from values and attitudes.

All but one of the chapters in the volume are empirical studies where data are collected to test specific hypotheses derived from theory. Each of these studies provides its author with sufficient confidence to continue following through with the model he or she has elected to work with. The confidence of the investigators persists because they do obtain meaningful results. Applegate and his colleagues, working within a personal construct system, amplified by Wernerian constructs, generate supportive data for the personal construct idea; Holloway and Hess also produce positive results. To be sure, the findings from these studies only accounted for a relatively small proportion of the variance – small in psychological terms, but statistically significant. We also know that the sum of these studies will not produce the comprehensive coverage we seek to give the "total" answer. Then what do they tell us beyond the obvious and trite statement that human behavior is complex?

From the theoretical perspective, we can ask two questions: one, what are the differences among the theoretical perspectives; and two, how close is the theory–behavior connection? Or to put it another way: Is their overlap at each level between what the concept is and what is being measured?

Let me select just two of the studies as exemplars. Applegate et al. contend they work in a constructivist framework. Personal constructs are defined as bipolar—that individuals "develop and use to interpret, anticipate, and evaluate the thoughts and behaviors of others" (Applegate et al., chapter 5). Dix and Grusec develop an attributional model, where essentially attribution theory is an information-processing approach. It stresses that social behavior depends on people's ongoing assessment of persons and behavior. It emphasizes, in particular, that behavior depends on people's inferences about what is causing the events around them, about what motives and traits characterize those in interaction, and about what properties are inherent in social situations (Dix & Grusec, chapter 8). Personal constructs and attributions may be said to serve a similar function; they influence or direct *how* individuals in social contexts interpret what goes on around them. Are the differences among these basic constructs so different? Unfortunately for us each of these investigators has selected a different set of dependent measures, so we are not able to compare the findings consequent to the different belief systems.

Nevertheless, it is possible to discern some descriptive similarities among these authors' definitions of the cognitive domains of interest. In a sense, they each describe cognitive activity in social contexts with similar properties—the purpose of such cognitions is minimally to make sense of the behavior of others. I shall not develop this argument here, but discuss some of it in the final chapter. The only point here is to articulate the potential of conceptual and/or methodological overlap. For an example of such overlap, let us examine the Applegate et al. and the Dix and Grusec studies.

Applegate et al. evaluated parents' construct systems, yielding a definition of how parents construed traits, disposition, and motivation of others. The next question involved methods of study. Parents were asked to describe explicitly what they would say to their child in situations that involved typical parent–child communication interactions, e.g., getting the child to go to bed, or a child refusing to go to school. Dix and Grusec also presented parents with vignettes, but these were of child misconduct. Parents were to rate the causes of misconduct (i.e., attributing a cause to the child's behavior), whereas Applegate et al. rated parents' communicative level. To carry this exercise in comparison a but further, we can ask what is the relationship between personal constructs and attribution? Do personal constructs comprise the parent's cognitive structure, which in turn influences parental attributions? What if Dix and Grusec assessed parental constructs as predictors of parental attribution?

It can be argued that I am mixing models. Is it not perhaps interrelating theoretical concepts that at the manifest level are complementary, not antagonistic?

In these introductory comments my intention is to pose the issue: Is there not greater potential compatibility among investigators than seems to be the case? I feel the diversity represented in this volume might generate sufficient cognitive conflict among readers to attempt to consider interrelationships. Of course, it may well be that the discrepant material will be rejected. But at least the reader will have been exposed to some of the central perspectives. The articles in the volume offer substantive material that should foster cross-fertilization across the various perspectives. If this volume succeeds in stimulating further research in the role of beliefs as important determinants, particularly of parent behavior, it will have served its purpose.

REFERENCES

Ainsworth, M. D. S. (1973). The development of infant–mother attachment. In B. M. Caldwell & H. N. Ricciuti (Eds.), *Review of child development research* (Vol. 3). Chicago: University of Chicago Press.

Baldwin, A. L., Kalhorn, J., & Breese, F. (1945). Patterns of parent behavior. *Psychological Monographs, 58* (3, Whole No. 268).

Baumrind, D. (1971). Current patterns of parental authority. *Developmental Psychology Monographs, 4*(1, Part 2).

Becker, W. C. (1964). Consequences of different kinds of parental discipline. In M. L. Hoffman & L. W. Hoffman (Eds.), *Review of child development research* (Vol. 1). New York: Russell Sage Foundation.

Sigel, I. E. (1981). Child development research in learning and cognition in the 1980s: Continuities and discontinuities from the 1970s. *Merrill–Palmer Quarterly, 27,* 347–371.

Sigel, I. E., Dreyer, A. S., & McGillicuddy-DeLisi, A. V. (1984). Psychological perspectives of the family. In R. D. Parke (Ed.), *Review of child development research* (Vol. 7, pp. 42–79). Chicago: University of Chicago Press.

Sigel, I. E., Secrist, A., & Forman, G. (1973). Psychoeducational intervention beginning at age two: Reflections and outcomes. In J. C. Stanley (Ed.), *Compensatory education for children, ages two to eight: Recent studies of educational intervention.* Baltimore, MD: Johns Hopkins University Press.

Introduction to the Second Edition

Irving E. Sigel
Educational Testing Service

Ann V. McGillicuddy-DeLisi
Lafayette College

Jacqueline J. Goodnow
Macquarie University

In 1985, the volume *Parental Belief Systems: The Psychological Conse-quences for Children,* was published (Sigel, 1985). The preface from that book, reprinted in this volume (see Introduction to the First Edition) stated that the purpose of that collection of essays was to identify the field of parent beliefs, or parent cognition, as a major and legitimate area for empirical study. Research on this topic has increased tremendously since that time.

Some of the authors who contributed to the 1985 edition are represented by their recent work in this edition. In addition, we invited others to join the effort. Our goal was to have this volume reflect some of the new directions that research on parent cognition has taken. This is particularly evident in the increased number of chapters dealing with the consequences of parent cognition as compared to the 1985 edition.

In this volume, as in the previous one, we continue to find considerable diversity in constructs used to identify parents' thoughts about their children. No one term is accepted by all of the writers. Some refer to *beliefs,* others to *thoughts, constructs, theories, ideas,* and *attributions.* Still others refer to *perceptions* and *goals.* To simplify communication in this intro-duction, we have elected to use a generic term, *parent cognition,* as it encompasses much of the meaning of each term used in this volume.

The chapters can be differentiated on the basis of the research design and the focus employed by the authors. Two types of research design charac-terize the studies. One type links parent cognition to child outcomes, with no description of the intervening parent behavior. A second type includes studies in which parent cognitions are linked to parent behaviors, which in turn influence the child. In the former case, the parent cognitions are direct sources of influence, whereas in the latter case their influence is indirect, that is, moderated bya behavioral set of events. Of particular importance is that in both of these research types investigators are reporting significant findings relating parent cognition to child outcomes. We still need to seek the conduits that will explain the linkage between parent cognition and child outcomes.

The chapters are arranged on the basis of focus rather than on conceptual or methodological criteria. Each type, while investigating the role of parent cognition as a central issue in the parenting process, approaches the investigation with different constructs, methods, and procedures. The research strategies seem to be dictated by the theoretical and methodological preferences of the investigator, rather than by the problem. Hence, a variety of research strategies is found within each set of chapters, organized by focus.

The first type includes studies concerned with normally developing populations — primarily young children. A second type deals specifically with parents of adolescents. The third type of research addresses issues of troubled children and families. The fourth type is explicitly engaged in building models to apply to families in general. Finally, two chapters focus exclusively on cultural issues.

The first set is comprised of the chapters by Applegate, Burleson, and Delia; Rubin and Mills; Palacios, González, and Moreno; Martin and Johnson; McGillicuddy-DeLisi; and Holden and Zambarano. These authors focus on parent cognitiions in families with young children.

Different aspects of the parent–child interaction using different theoretical perspectives and methods are represented within the chapters in this section. Applegate and his colleagues represent a communication model and are interested in messages parents send to their children. They examine the perspective-taking skills of the children as bases for evaluating the effects of the parent communication approach. Rubin and Mills are developing an information-processing model that is interactive, dealing not only with parental perceptions of their children, but also how these perceptions influence their behavior with their children. Children, however, are studied independently of the parents. Hence, the characterizations of the children are based on researchers' observations, not on parents' ratings or judgments. These studies focus on individual differences among parents, whereas Palacios and his colleagues created a typology of Spanish parents on the basis of their perceptions of how children develop. They identify three types of parents: modern, traditional, and paradoxical. The modern parents are more liberal and autonomy-granting. The traditional parents are more conservative and controlling. The paradoxical parents seem to be transitional and attempt to incorporate the old with the new. The authors report child-rearing differences among these three ideological types that account for eventual differences in the children's social cognitive competencies. Whether such a typology can be created in other societies is an open question.

Rubin and Mills as well as Palacios and colleagues provide us with information about the stability of parent beliefs and practices, albeit over a short time span. These authors are among the first to provide us with very important longitudinal information that can help define the course of influence of parent cognition. Longitudinal studies are sorely needed, but not undertaken very often in developmental research.

Martin and Johnson address beliefs and their influence on children's judgment of their own competence, as well as parent cognition. Using teachers as the "reality" base for assessing their elementary school-aged children, these investigators used questionnaires to determine parents' beliefs and related them to children's sense of personal competence. Their findings lend support to the notion that there is a positive relationship between mothers' cognitive developmental belief and children's positive sense of self. The use of teachers as third-party judges of children's competence is also adopted by McGillicuddy-DeLisi. She identified seven different theories parents have about children's personal social development, among them biological theories and constructivist theories. Her chapter exhibits strong interest in gender differences in various combinations of gender relations in the family, for example, mother–father relations, father–son relations, and so on. In addition to the identification of particular beliefs and their relationship to school performance, McGillicuddy-DeLisi identifies a belief structure that has the potential of generating analyses of beliefs as systems rather than as isolated cognitions.

Another topic within the first set of chapters concerns the intergenerational transmission of parents' beliefs to children's beliefs. (These are issues addressed conceptually by Goodnow as well as empirically by Holden and Zambarano. A conceptualization of Goodnow's transmission model is discussed later when we describe the chapters in the fourth set.) Holden and Zambarano report research that sought to demonstrate the degree to which parents and their children share perceptions on the use of physical punishment. One of the challenges raised by Holden and Zambarano is the determination of the dynamics of the transmission process and its measurement.

A second set of chapters extends the study of parent cognitions to focus on parents of adolescents and examines the role they play in the relationships between parents and children during this transitional period. The chapters by Collins and by Youniss, DeSantis, and Henderson, although dealing with different topics, attest to the fact that the importance of parent cognition is not limited to just young children. Collins provides a comprehensive approach to the study of parent cognition as a source of influence on development outcomes and then conceptualizes the relationships between parents' ideas and transition to adolescence. He introduces some of the major theoretical questions beginning with a review of some empirical studies. His concerns are with the linkages between parent cognition and the dynamic changes in the relationship between parents and children that occur during this period. In this way he extends our understanding of the continuous role parent cognition plays in the relationship between parent and child.

Youniss and his colleagues focus on a specific set of issues that are inherent in the socialization of adolescents at this time. They address beliefs about their children's coping with friendship, alcohol, and school. Their findings reveal the values and trust that parents place in their teenage children. The study provides some specific information about the way parents perceive their teenagers and the emphasis they place on their children's coping with issues in these robust categories.

The third set of chapters brings together work with atypical populations. In the 1985 volume, parent cognitions were studied, primarily among typical or *normally* functioning populations. In this volume, increasing attention is paid to the place of cognitive processes along with affect among troubled families as evidenced in the work of Bugental, Holloway, and Machida as well as Iverson and Segal. Bugental deals with clinical populations and brings a systems conceptualization to the study of parent cognitions as a source of influence on the child and family functioning. She proposes that parent cognitions function on two levels, automatic and controlled, where the latter is under voluntary control. She blends in affect as an important filter or stage setter as influencing the parent–child interaction. Here is an interactive system and she identifies ingredients of that system. She works with children from clinical populations, employing experimental manipulations as a method to assess the functioning of the participants. This approach is unique among the research covered in this volume. Most researchers tend to use paper-and-pencil procedures, face-to-face interviews, or nonmanipulative observations as their data source. The ingenuity of Bugental's experiments attests to the feasibility of employing experimental procedures in testing the effect of parent cognitions and the degree to which affect is involved.

Holloway and Machida's study moves into a new arena. They examine divorced mothers' coping with separation and the transition to single-family status. The authors present an interactive model incorporating the multiple sources of influence on the quality of mothers' coping. Parent cognitions are central to the model because they influence the mother's coping skills as well as those of the children. They find that both mothers and children benefit when the mother's sense of empowerment is sufficiently robust to give her confidence in her ability to guide and control her life and that of her child.

The influence of the interaction of mothers with their problem children is the theme of the Iverson and Segal chapter. They use a Q-sort type measure to examine how parents' cognition is related to their own observations of mother and child in interactive situations as well as in peer contexts.

Although several of the previously discussed chapters are derived from a particular model of parent cognition, model building is not the main concern. It is, however, at the core of the enterprise in the fourth set of chapters by Goodnow, Sameroff and Fiese, and Dix (Collins' chapter is a further example).

Each model extends the role of parent cognition by examining a variety of conceptual and methodological issues that serve to enhance the power of the role played by parent cognition in developing the child's competencies. Goodnow builds an interactive model utilizing some concepts from social psychology. The core of her chapter is an interest in the processes involved in the convergence or divergence of parent and child ideas about various life events (e.g., household chores). She continues her conceptualization using two process models in which the two processes are the perceptions of a parent's message (a perception that may or may not be accurate) and the acceptance or rejection of the perceived message. The model she proposes is embedded in an interaction communication context, and it is in this context that intergenerational transmission of ideas about children are revealed. Finally, Goodnow offers insights into sources of conflict between parents and their children. She outlines both methodological and conceptual issues that provide an organizational framework for further study.

Another perspective that emphasizes the interest of investigators in interactions between parents and children is Dix's focus on the role of empathic goals as setting the stage for the quality of the parent–child relationship. He discusses components of the empathic goal-setting model and points out the variations in outcome for children whose parents do not manifest empathic goal setting with their children. He also reports individual differences in such goal-setting and raises the question regarding sources of variation among parents. Because empathic goal-setting serves as a regulating mechanism, Dix implies that regulation of the child's action with empathic goal-setting parents would be a positive force in the child's development.

Sameroff and Fiese reflect a family-oriented focus and direct attention to the family as a system where myths and rituals are important regulating features of the system. Consideration of the family as a unit is frequently ignored by students of developmental psychology although it certainly should be of crucial concern to them in view of their interest in parent–child interactions. Sameroff and Fiese provide a functional model dealing with the family as a quasi-cultural unit.

Attention to the degree to which parent cognitions are reflective of cultural beliefs and values is often underemphasized. It is only recently that developmental psychologists have begun to pay systematic attention to how cultural belief systems are instantiated in parent cognition and actions. The final chapters reflect this trend. Harkness and Super, and Lightfoot and Valsiner, each offer an approach and a method by which to identify how culture could become a framework for the study of parent cognitions and their sequelae. Harkness and Super worked with families in Kenya and in the United States. They have developed both a concept and method for studying common features in each culture. They are interested in parents' conceptions of intelligence and personality. The method Harkness and Super use to obtain such information is to interview the parents and then to assess how these meanings and definitions are instantiated in the cultures. This procedure allows for a proximal determination of concept and social action. Lightfoot and Valsiner have developed theoretical models for coping with issues related to the way the culture contributes to the parents' cognitions. They contend that parents' beliefs emerge from the collectivity in a society. They discuss beliefs as a semiotic phenomenon and use this conceptualization to examine how cultural forces work to create both a collective and personal belief system. They show that belief systems do not emerge de novo, but rather, are reflections or internalization of the messages emanating from the broader milieu, especially the mass media. The use of advertising as their data source reveals how pervasive certain beliefs are and how we often are unaware of that source of influence.

Even within the mainstream culture, however, we need to be alert to within-culture variations. The work of Brody and Stoneman—the final chapters in the volume—offers a poignant example to that effect. They studied isolated rural Black families and noted a unique cultural context replete with its own values and momentum. Their analysis demonstrates that our concern for culture's contribution to parent cognition must not be limited to observing its impact in foreign countries. Rather, cultural contexts need to be included in all our research—whether we deal with subgroups in our own population, with people located at different stages of the life span, with people in different conditions and locations as well as with citizens living in foreign, and perhaps exotic, countries.

In the last chapter, Sigel addresses the methodological issue of how to evaluate the influence of parents' beliefs regarding children's acquisition of knowledge on their teaching strategies. Although the issue of linkage between belief and action is framed within his own reasearch questions, he also alludes to the question of linkage as a general problem for the field.

Understanding how beliefs are instantiated, he argues, helps to explain the bases of parents' actions. The data Sigel uses are derived from interviews of parents and from observations of parents teaching their children. His findings reveal some consistencies with his distancing theory model, but these are not as robust as he would like. He discusses these results, offering some conceptual and procedural suggestions for enhancing the predictability of parents' beliefs to their actions.

SUMMARY AND CONCLUSIONS

In summary, the chapters in this new edition have much in common with the chapters in the first edition. In particular they share a common concern for the part played by parental cognitive processes in developing or hampering the child's cognitive growth. However, in contrast to the 1985 edition, we are now in a far better position when it comes to choices in models we wish to adopt. We are also better able to understand the complexities of parent cognitions as well as the difficulties these pose for the designing of relevant research strategies. We can safely say that progress has been made. Much, however, still needs to be accomplished. It is to this last point — the unfinished task — that we now turn.

Although the field may not yet be in a position to offer a systematic, integrated theory of parent cognitions, it seems, nonetheless, that by now we have advanced sufficiently to take steps in that direction and that a good first step in the next round of research could be the clarification of terms, perhaps even some agreement on common nomenclatures.

A second issue warranting particular attention in the next round has to do with the authors represented in this volume. Irrespective of the label they give to their constructs, all share the conviction that parental cognitions *do* matter. In that respect, they are very much in tune with the growing emphasis on cognition in general psychology. That up-to-datedness notwithstanding, developmental psychologists' preferred methods of investigation have remained surprisingly traditional. Most of the methods described in this volume, for example, are similar to those used in mainstream nonexperimental psychological research. They rely heavily on interviews, questionnaires, observations, standardized tests, and the like. Actual observations of parent–child cognitive interactions — whether in the laboratory or at home — are infrequently used methods, and this volume reflects that tendency as well. Data analysis procedures also are consistent with mainstream quantitative techniques, with heavy reliance on correlational analyses, especially regression and multivariate analyses. The use of such traditional methodologies prompts us to wonder whether respondents, given the opportunity to give free-floating and far-reaching narratives, might conceivably structure the topic quite differently and add dimensions not anticipated by the researcher.

Finally, the choice of participants in our studies must be broadened. Concern with families in different walks of life and different cultures are important as bases for clarifying the particular way cultures play themselves out in family contexts. Consistent attention to gender differences between children, as well as parents, is also needed.

Within this group of a studies it will be noticed that the basic informant in all but two of them are women (mothers and female teachers). In most studies fathers are not included. The need to include fathers in their studies is evident from the work of McGillicuddy-DeLisi as reported in this volume and the work of Sigel, Stinson, and Flaugher (1991). It may well be that the story of how parent cognitions function in the family context and in the culture generally cannot be fully understood until attention is paid to the role of fathers in particular and to gender in general.

This new edition of *Parental Belief Systems: The Psychological Consequences for Children,* by offering a greater variety of topics, gives evidence of the intellectual concerns that now engage researchers in the field and also testifies to the ever expanding scope of their interests. As we reflect on the individual contributions in the new edition, we cannot help but be struck by the way in which researchers who vary so much among themselves, both in the constructs they employ and the theoretical "schools" to which they subscribe, nonetheless managed to reach quite similar conclusions regarding the role of parent cognitions. All of them (as we have said several times already) are in agreement that mental processes count and that parent cognition influences not only how the child develops, but also how the parent behaves and how parent and child interact with each other. Such agreement attests eloquently to the progress that the field has made. If it encourages the reader to discover even more common threads than those to which we have alluded, the volume will have served its purpose well.

REFERENCES

Sigel, I. E. (Ed.). (1985). *Parental belief systems: The psychological consequences for children.* Hillsdale, NJ: Lawrence Erlbaum Associates.

Sigel, I. E., Stinson, E. T., & Flaugher, J. (1991). Socialization of representational competence in the family: The distancing model. In R. J. Sternberg & L. Okagaki (Eds.), *Directors of development: Influences on the development of children's thinking* (pp. 121–144). Hillsdale, NJ: Lawrence Erlbaum Associates.

I Focus on Normal Families of Young Children

Reflection-Enhancing Parenting as an Antecedent to Children's Social-Cognitive and Communicative Development

1

James L. Applegate
University of Kentucky

Brant R. Burleson
Purdue University

Jesse G. Delia
University of Illinois at Urbana-Champaign

INTRODUCTION

In the first volume of *Parental Belief Systems* (Applegate, Burke, Burleson, Delia, & Kline, 1985), we reported an investigation of individual differences in parenting strategies grounded in a constructivist theory of communication. That investigation provided a systematic analysis of a range of parental communication behaviors that we argued had functional significance for children's social-cognitive and communication development. We defined these variations in terms of the reflection-enhancing quality of parenting strategies. Reflection-enhancing parenting strategies were presented as realizations of a more general *person-centered* orientation to communication identified in our previous research as a salient dimension of individual difference in communicative development for children and adults across a variety of contexts (see reviews in Applegate, 1990; Burleson, 1989).

Briefly, reflection-enhancing messages encourage recipients to consider the causes and consequences of their own and others' actions. These messages also encourage recipients to see how actions both grow out of and create psychological and affective states. Our study found that although socioeconomic status (SES) and social-cognitive ability both contributed to mothers using reflection-enhancing messages, the strongest and most direct associations were between individual levels in social cognition and uses of reflection-enhancing communication. These empirical associations suggested a more general analysis of the relations between cultural factors, cognition, and individual differences in communicative behavior.

This chapter further elaborates our analysis of relationships between cognition and communication. Although our previous study examined how individual differences in social cognition contributed to differences in communicative behavior, this chapter considers how differences in the communicative practices of parents may affect children's social-cognitive and communicative abilities. Specifically, we report an investigation of the impact of variations in reflection-enhancing parental communication on individual differences in children's social-cognitive and communicative development. The background to our general approach and the rationale for our expectations in this investigation can be briefly sketched by considering three topics: (a) the relationship of our work to traditional analyses of parental discipline and nurturance, (b) the processes through which we believe reflection-enhancing parental communication facilitates children's social-cognitive and communicative development, and (c) the specific socialization model tested in the present investigation.

Reflection-Enhancing Communication in Disciplinary and Nurturance Contexts

Many theorists have suggested that the manner in which parents interact with their children is one of the most powerful determinants of children's social competencies (see Maccoby & Martin, 1983). Although few studies have examined how parental behaviors affect the development of specific functional communication competencies, parental behavioral styles have been found to predict children's competencies related to prosocial and antisocial behavior (Feshbach, 1975; Zahn-Waxler, Radke-Yarrow, & King, 1979), moral reasoning and moral conduct (Brody & Shaffer, 1982), and general social-cognitive and interactional skills (Parke, MacDonald, Beitel, & Bhavnagri, 1988). Virtually all of these studies focused on either parental disciplinary or nurturant behavior.

Several conceptual systems have been used in characterizing types of parental discipline (e.g., power-assertive/inductive, authoritarian/authoritative, position-centered/person-centered, parent-centered/child-centered, punishment-oriented/reasoning-oriented; see the review by Rollins & Thomas, 1979). Of the various analyses of parenting strategies expressing these distinctions, our analysis of "reflection-enhancing" communication embodies much of what Baumrind (1989) identified as differences between authoritarian and authoritative parenting and Hoffman (1977) described as power-assertive and inductive parenting. Power assertion/authoritarian parenting refers to the use of physical punishment or the exercise of material power over the child (e.g., threatening loss of privileges), and induction/authoritative parenting is reflected in offering reasons to the child for changes in conduct (particularly reasons concerning the consequences of action). Thus, power-assertive/authoritarian parenting seeks to control the child's behavior through the use of negative reinforcement whereas inductive/authoritative parenting seeks to influence the child's behavior through the use of reasoning, especially reasoning about how acts (or their consequences) affect others. Numerous studies indicate that the frequent use of power assertion is associated with increased aggression by children whereas the frequent use of induction is associated with the internalization of self-guiding moral principles and the display of altruistic behavior (see the reviews by Brody & Shaffer, 1982; Maccoby & Martin, 1983).

Applegate and colleagues (1985) integrated Hoffman's discussion of parental discipline with Bernstein's (1974) more general analysis of interaction within family systems. Bernstein suggested that different modes of interaction both express and are organized by the assumption of similarity or uniqueness in the psychological experiences underlying social relations. The communicative style Bernstein termed the *elaborated code* both reflects and fosters the assumption that the motivations, intentions, and feelings of individuals are, at least to some extent, unique. This style thus "presupposes a sharp boundary or gap between self and others which is crossed through the creation of speech which specifically fits differentiated others" (Bernstein, 1974, p. 147). In contrast, the communicative style Bernstein termed the *restricted code* both reflects and fosters the assumption that the identities of others and the meanings of their actions are given in socially defined roles occupied in particular contexts. This latter style thus discourages language use that expresses or adapts to the unique perspectives of others. Instead, communication is based on culturally shared definitions of situations that specify the legitimate roles of participants, authority relations inhering in these roles, and behavioral norms governing conduct between role occupants (e.g., parent and child, teacher and student).

Applegate and colleagues (1985) extended Bernstein's analysis and suggested that parental disciplinary efforts can be scaled on a continuum for the extent to which they embody the pursuit of goal structures that encourage children to reflect on the nature of their transgressions, the consequences of their actions, and how their conduct might affect others psychologically. As in much of our other work, messages defined as more sophisticated within Applegate et al.'s hierarchic system were those with more differentiated and complex sets of goals responsive to the array of exigencies present in the situation addressed (for general discussions see Applegate, 1990; Burleson, 1987, 1989; O'Keefe & Delia, 1982). Applegate and colleagues found the level of "reflection-enhancing" disciplinary strategies associated appropriately with measures of mothers' social class and

social-cognitive development and unassociated with such potentially confounding variables as verbal fluency and verbal intelligence (see Applegate
et al., 1985).

The general framework articulated by Applegate and colleagues provides
a parallel approach for the analysis of parents' nurturant behavior.
Although nurturance has not received as intensive study as discipline as an
antecedent to children's communicative competencies, several recent studies
suggest its potential importance (e.g., Finnie & Russell, 1988; Roberts &
Strayer, 1987; see the review by Radke-Yarrow & Zahn-Waxler, 1986).
However, parental nurturance is an even less differentiated concept than
control or discipline. Broad definitions, including provision of praise, help,
endearments, encouragement, and positive affection, provide categorical
distinctions similar to those employed in the study of parental control (such
as power assertion vs. induction). The distinctions drawn in work on
nurturance are generally less specific and focused (e.g., warm/cold or
accepting/rejecting). Although these global dimensions may capture the
general tenor of parental behavior, they do little to specify the constituents
of "warm," "accepting," or "nurturant" behavior. Further, these global
dimensions are not sensitive to the functional context in which nurturance
is manifested by parents as they pursue specific interactional goals with
their children.

Applegate and colleagues (1985) argued that nurturance can be examined
by identifying a class of situations faced in the normal routine of parenting
in which nurturance plays a central role and then deriving an abstractive
principle and set of categories for identifying and ordering the goal
configurations expressed in messages produced in addressing specific
situations within the class. They investigated situations in which the parent
must deal with the emotional distress of the child (as, e.g., when the child
has not been invited to a classmate's party). The possibility of nurturing the
child through comforting is a manifest feature of these events. Messages
addressing such contexts can be conceptualized as varying in the extent to
which they acknowledge and legitimize the child's feelings and encourage
the child to seek an understanding of his or her feelings. Applegate and
colleagues developed a hierarchically ordered coding system for the goal
structures evidenced in parents' comforting messages. The system scores
such messages for the extent to which they grant legitimacy to the distressed
child's feelings and encourage the child to reflect upon and seek an
understanding of his or her feelings and the circumstances producing them.
The construct validity of this approach to the analysis of comforting
behavior was supported by Applegate et al.'s (1985) finding that maternal
use of messages legitimizing and encouraging reflection on feelings is
positively associated with indices of social-cognitive development and

unassociated with the potentially confounding factors of verbal fluency and verbal intelligence.

The Impact of Reflection-Enhancing Communication on the Child

There are several reasons for believing that the message qualities indexed by our analyses of reflection-enhancing parenting should affect children's social and communicative development. Some reasons are obvious from mainstream psychological research on social development. Baumrind (1989), Hoffman (1977), and Sigel (1985; Sigel & McGillicuddy-DeLisi, 1984) have examined particular features of parental communication for their effects on specific qualities of children's cognitive development. Sigel (1985) and his colleagues, for example, focused on the impact of "distancing" behaviors of parents (demanding the children mentally separate themselves from their environment) on children's representational abilities (i.e., the abilities to anticipate outcomes, de-center, and so on). Other research has singled out the inductive and reflection-enhancing quality of strategies as related to development of (a) specific role-taking and problem-solving abilities, (b) development of consequential thinking, and (c) general level of social skill and peer acceptance (Hart, de Wolf, Royston, Burts, & Thomasson, 1990; Hart, Ladd, & Burleson, 1990; Jones, Rickel, & Smith, 1980; Pettit, Dodge, & Brown, 1988; Putallaz, 1987).

The perspective guiding our own work also suggests effects for parental communication on children but differs from the previous approaches in its conception of (a) the key features of parental messages that are of interest, (b) the structures in the child being affected by the parental messages, and (c) the process through which parenting communication affects children. First, as was just detailed, parental communication is studied as reflecting differential goal configurations. The analysis of these goal configurations involves considering not just context-defining instrumental goals, but also the extent and manner through which subsidiary goals involving instrumental, identity, or relational concerns are addressed. Identification of the complexity of strategic behavior is a central aspect of our analysis of reflection-enhancing parental communication. Person-centered and reflection-enhancing messages are not simply more "inductive" or "authoritative"; they are more functionally and structurally complex forms of behavior (see O'Keefe & Delia, 1982).

For example, the command, "Go to bed right now!" issued by a parent to a recalcitrant child is a relatively simple form of behavior in that it is oriented to a single goal: getting the child to go to bed. In contrast, what we have termed *person-centered* and *reflection-enhancing* messages would, in this situation, not only pursue the goal of getting the child to go to bed, but also might reflect the goals of eliciting the child's reasons for wanting to remain up, getting the child to understand why he or she needs rest, helping the child envision consequences likely to be experienced if he or she doesn't get sufficient rest, and so-forth. Reflection-enhancing messages thus constitute more complex forms of behavior. In addition to pursuing a primary instrumental goal, such messages also encourage the child to reflect on his or her own conduct, envision consequences of this and alternative courses of conduct for him or herself and others, explain the psychological states (feelings and perspectives) of others, bolster the child's self-concept, and so forth.

As complex behavioral configurations, reflection-enhancing messages reflect the desire not simply for the child to act a certain way (in disciplinary situations) or feel a certain way (in comforting situations), but rather to understand the situation in a broadened way and to see that courses of action should follow from consideration of relevant situational features and enduring values. In summary, "person-centered" or, more specifically for parenting, "reflection-enhancing" messages are functionally and structurally more complex forms of behavior that present greater accommodative challenges to the child by calling upon the child to reason about situations and select behaviors based on considered needs, wants, and responsibilities.

We believe that sustained exposure to these more complex forms of behavior will have their primary influence on the child's interpersonal cognitive structures rather than directly on behavior (through, e.g., presenting an available model of a specific response pattern). Parental communication generally does not present the child with ready-made behavioral routines and scenarios that can be executed appropriately in accord with the norms or requirements of particular situations. Rather, the child is pointed toward certain features of contexts that might be addressed and oriented to particular "solutions" to the difficulties and conflicts presented by giving attention to these features of the context. For example, reflection-enhancing messages make salient the desirability of maintaining a positive face for oneself and others across situations, the significance of identity and relationship management in complex social situations, and the importance of considering long-term as well as immediate consequences of actions. Thus, in being exposed to reflection-enhancing messages, the child does not learn a specific set of beliefs or routines, but rather acquires a generalized orientation or interpretive logic that guides the temporally emergent assessment and management of situations.

We thus align ourselves with those who see families not simply as behavioral systems, but as social structures organized around deeply tacit, and in part culturally rooted, beliefs about the nature of language and the social world—beliefs that are themselves maintained in significant measure through patterns of familial communication (Applegate & Delia, 1980; Bernstein, 1974; Gecas, 1979; Grotevant, 1989; Lepper, 1983; Levine, 1989). Such family-based systems of belief provide the child with what Youniss (1989), following Coleman (1987), called "social capital." As Youniss said, "Children need capital if they are to enter society with the shared viewpoint most adults hold" (p. 379). Within the frame of this metaphor, we argue that the most significant effect of parents, and in fact of families as a whole, on children is not the specific forms of capital they provide (i.e., various beliefs, values, and behavioral norms). Most significantly, families (and parents within them) play a large role in imparting a logic—parallel to an economic theory, if you will—of how the social system works: of what social knowledge the child needs to acquire and how social knowledge, once acquired, can and should be used. A central part of any such logic is the component defining the degree of attention to be granted to the other's psychological perspective, the relevance of events temporally distant from the present context, and the salience and importance of future consequences to present actions.

These and several related interpretive premises are foundational to the substantial individual differences in social cognition and "person-centered" communication we have identified in our previous research (see Applegate, 1990; Burleson, 1987; O'Keefe & Delia, 1982; also see O'Keefe, 1988, for a related analysis of premises organizing patterns of communicative means–ends reasoning). These sets of premises define very general interpretive orientations that are sustained and extended through the development of more or less complex systems of interpersonal constructs, patterns of social reasoning, and the goal configurations and behavioral structures they support (see Applegate & Delia, 1980; Bernstein, 1974; O'Keefe, 1988).

To account for the effects of parental communication on the emergence of individual differences in children's social-cognitive development, we invoke ideas of semiotic mediation, social learning, and the concept of accommodation from cognitive-developmental theory. In our view, socialization outcomes occur through processes of social learning and cognitive development in a context that is semiotically mediated by the parents' communication. As parents (and other socializing agents) code and direct attention to particular features of social contexts (e.g., the intrapsychic experiences of others), the child is naturally led to acquire constructs for representing and making inferences about those contextual features. The person-centered parent codes, and makes more easily accessible, a wider range of interpersonal and intrapsychic features of contexts than does the position-centered parent. The child's world is made more complex by the very fact that constructs are appropriated for representing these "precoded" features of the social world. This complexity is underscored by the continual "re-presentation" of complexity to the child in the parents' behavior and expanded by the child's increasing capacity to represent that complexity through the constructs that have already been acquired.

The child raised by person-centered parents is continually confronting an interpersonal world that is presented in the parents' behavior as intrinsically complex. Moreover, this world is increasingly construed by the child as more complex through cognitive structures acquired in this distinctively mediated context. In traditional cognitive-developmental terms, the child's development is channeled toward the elaboration of an interpersonal construct system sufficient in complexity to accommodate to and manage the complexity of the world the child is recurrently confronting. Over time, exposure to behaviorally complex, reflection-enhancing parenting and the person-centered interpretive premises it expresses should promote the child's development of more complex, psychologically centered social thinking.

This emerging interpretive orientation, in turn, forms the scaffold from which person-centered modes of communication can be elaborated for addressing the common and distinct complexities that present themselves within this interpretive horizon in different functional contexts. Within a person-centered orientation, linguistic communication itself is increasingly organized as a system of practices and strategies that addresses the distinctiveness of individual belief systems and sustains the autonomy of individual action. Consequently, within the person-centered orientation, communication increasingly comes to be dominated by symbolic vehicles for restructuring social contexts, maintaining and altering the situated social identities of the participants within them, and aligning and coordinating the interactants' shared and competing goals. Within the person-centered orientation, communication can be expected to be integrated in terms that less and less reflect its function as either a simple vehicle of expression or a conventional sign and discourse system, and more and more as a system of practices and lines of action serving processes of strategic rhetorical construction, negotiation, and consensus building (O'Keefe, 1988; Samter, Burleson, & Basden-Murphy, 1989).

Focus of the Study: Testing a Model of Socialization

Detailing the mechanisms through which parental communication affects the developing child's cognitive and behavioral skills has both theoretical and practical significance. At a theoretical level, such models can better explain the communicative practices of parents that simultaneously express a particular orientation to the social world and promote that orientation in children (e.g., reflection-enhancing communicative practices both expressing and promoting a person-centered cognitive orientation). Pragmatically, models of the mechanisms through which parental communication affects children are important because training efforts designed to improve parental discipline and nurturance must be built upon understanding of the specific aspects of parental behavior that result in particular developmental outcomes.

There are two distinct, albeit related, issues embedded in questions about the mechanism(s) by which parental communication affects children. The first involves the "locus of effect" in the child: What specific features of the child's cognitive structures, reasoning processes, values, self-concept, behavioral routines and so on are primarily acted upon by parental communication? The second issue concerns the "active ingredients" of parental communication behavior. What particular dimension(s) of parental messages affect features of the child's cognition and behavior, and how are these effects achieved?

Clearly, answers to these two questions should complement one another. That is, if a model stipulates that parental communication relates to a particular outcome in the child then the model also must specify the feature of parental communication capable of producing the specified effect. In short, adequate models of the nature of parental effects on children require an integrated understanding of parental behavior, child cognition and behavior, and socialization effects. In the study that follows we test one specific model of the mechanism through which parental communication affects specific cognitive and behavioral competencies of children. The essential features of our analysis have been outlined already. We wish here, however, to make the model we are testing explicit.

The basic structure of our model is as follows. First, our model is a unidirectional one in which influence flows from the parent to the child. In this regard, our focus is similar to that traditionally taken by parenting researchers who have set as a central goal understanding how differences in parenting behavior affect children. Although we recognize the significance and importance of research on the bidirectionality of influence between parents and children (e.g., Grotevant, 1989; Hess, 1981), our theoretical analysis points to the impact of differences in the reflection-enhancing quality of parental disciplinary and comforting strategies on children's development. Moreover, this analysis is consistent with research on the family, parenting, and children's development generally.

Second, our model posits a strong positive relationship between the quality of reflection-enhancing parental communication exhibited in both disciplinary and comforting contexts. We believe, with Rollins and Thomas (1979), that it is important to consider patterns of parenting across functional domains (e.g., discipline and nurturance). Moreover, we think it is important that parental communication be studied in a variety of specific behavioral contexts. This broadened focus permits us to consider whether parental behavior is functionally similar across domains and contexts. Our theoretical analysis and previous research with our behavioral coding systems point to underlying similarities in the person-centered quality of messages produced by an individual across situations and domains. This similarity reflects, we hypothesize, ties between the behavioral complexity of messages produced in the various situations and enduring features of the message producer's social-cognitive orientation (e.g., increased cognitive differentiation and psychological-centeredness of interpersonal constructs). The social-cognitive orientation is elaborated in a system of interpersonal constructs that serve the message producer in the ongoing task of identifying and interpreting relevant features of contexts. The theoretical analysis underlying this aspect of our framework places emphasis on aspects of the interpersonal construct system involving development and elaboration along a variety of developmental axes derived from Wernerian developmental theory (globality/differentiation, diffuseness/integration, concreteness/abstractness, egocentrism/perspectivism, and lability/flexibility; see Applegate, 1982; Delia, O'Keefe, & O'Keefe, 1982; Werner, 1957; Werner & Kaplan, 1963).

Third, as was detailed previously, more reflection-enhancing forms of parental communication should promote the development of more complex social-cognitive orientations in children (e.g., greater differentiation and psychologically centered construing, more advanced social and affective perspective-taking skills). These developments in the child's social-cognitive system are predicated on the operation of processes of semiotic mediation, social learning, and cognitive accommodation.

Fourth, enhanced social-cognitive development in the child, as in the parent, is seen as enabling the child to develop more person-centered communication abilities (e.g., general skill at individuating messages to the needs and perspectives of receivers in making requests, use of more receiver-focused persuasive strategies and more sensitive and sophisticated comforting skill). Contexts involving persuasion, comforting, and making requests are intrinsically person focused. They are all contexts where communication focuses on the dispositions, beliefs, values, and affective states of others (e.g., considering potential objections or advantages that a persuasive request poses for a peer requires understanding his or her wants and beliefs). These functional communication contexts also make salient the child's ability to acknowledge and address the autonomy of the peer and his or her own reasoning ability. Thus, the development of a repertoire of strategies to respond to such situations in more skilled ways must build directly upon the child's social-cognitive abilities. Even if there are close parallels in the functional communicative domains assessed in the parent and the child, the path of influence thus should be from parental communication to the child's social-cognitive abilities and, then, to the child's communicative abilities.

The full model we set out to test thus can be depicted very simply as follows:

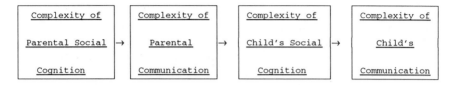

FIG. 1.1   Model of communication development.

In Applegate et al. (1985) we demonstrated the clear relation between parental social-cognitive and communication development. In this study our focus is on the relation of reflection-enhancing parental communication and the child's social-cognitive and communicative development.

In testing this model we also considered the effects of social class on children's development. Our previous study (Applegate et al., 1985) showed direct effects for social class on the mothers' social-cognitive development but no direct effects on their communication. However, the social-cognitive differences strongly affected the quality of maternal communication. Although we are primarily interested here in the impact of parenting on children, the effects of social class on children's development are explored to facilitate our long-term efforts to offer a more complete model of the ways culture, parental social cognition and communication, and children's social-cognitive and communicative development are related.

METHOD

Participants and General Procedures

Participants in the study were 51 school children (28 first graders: 12 males and 16 females; and 23 third graders: 10 males and 13 females) and their mothers. The children were enrolled in a parochial grammar school located in a moderate-sized midwestern community. The mothers and their children represented a variety of social class levels and backgrounds.

Taped interviews with the mothers were conducted in the privacy of their homes. Mothers completed tasks assessing reflection-enhancing regulative and comforting communication skills, social-cognitive ability, and several personality traits. They also answered questions concerning family size, birth order of children, occupations, and educational levels. Analyses of relationships between mothers' communication, social cognition, and social class have been reported previously (see Applegate et al., 1985).

Taped interviews were conducted with the children in a quiet room at the parochial school during which they responded to tasks assessing communication and social-cognitive abilities (see following). In addition, they completed a sociometric questionnaire about classmates (analyses of the children's friendship patterns were reported separately; see Burleson, Delia, & Applegate, 1990). One year later, all the children still enrolled in the school were reinterviewed. Attrition reduced the sample during the second year to 44 subjects (24 second graders: 11 males and 13 females; and 20 fourth graders: 9 males and 11 females). Children responded to the same measures of communication and social-cognitive abilities.

Reflection-Enhancing Quality of Maternal Regulative and Comforting Communication

Tasks and procedures described by Applegate et al. (1985) were used to assess mothers' ability to use reflection-enhancing regulative and comforting messages with their children. Briefly, mothers responded to seven hypothetical situations, five involving discipline and two involving comforting. For each situation, mothers were instructed to state exactly what they would say to their children.

To assess the reflection-enhancing character of the mothers' communication, two parallel six-level hierarchical coding systems, one for disciplinary messages and one for comforting messages, were developed and used. Applegate et al. (1985) described these coding systems in detail. Disciplinary messages were coded for the extent to which they fostered the child's development as a responsible and autonomous agent by encouraging the child to modify his or her behavior as a function of reflecting on and reasoning through the nature and consequences of his or her transgression for himself or herself and others. Comforting messages were coded for the extent to which they granted legitimacy to the child's feelings and encouraged the child to reflect upon his or her feelings and the circumstances generating these feelings. The specific levels of the two coding systems are described and exemplified in Table 1.1. The highest level strategy used for each situation was retained for purposes of analysis.

Coding reliability was assessed by having two judges independently score message sets for 15 subjects (i.e., 30% of the data) for highest-level strategy use. Interrater reliability coefficients, by intraclass correlation, were .85 for the disciplinary messages and .90 for the comforting messages. Internal consistencies, as assessed by Cronbach's alpha, were .90 for the five-item

TABLE 1.1
Coding Systems Used in Scoring Mothers' Disciplinary and Comforting
Messages (Adapted from Applegate et al., 1985)

Regulative Strategies	Comforting Strategies
Mother's regulative strategies were scored for the extent to which they promoted the development of the child as a responsible and autonomous agent by encouraging the child to modify his or her behavior through reflecting on and reasoning through the nature and consequences of the sanctionable behavior for him- or herself and other parties.	Mother's comforting strategies were scored for the extent to which they granted legitimacy to the child to reflect upon and seek understanding of his or her feelings and the circumstances producing them.

I. Discouragement of Reflection

1. Explicit discouragement of the child's self-definition as a responsible and autonomous agent relying on threats, simple commands, physical punishment, and other tactics failing to provide any reason for modification of behavior other than avoidance of punitive sanctions.
    A. "I'd tell him to take it back to the store and ground him."
    B. "Jackie, go to bed. If she didn't go I'd just take her by the hand and put her there."
2. Implicit discouragement of the child's self-definition as a responsible and autonomous agent by forwarding and demanding acceptance of rules *assumed by the parent* to be self-evident, necessary, and sufficient reasons for modification of behavior.
    A. "Taking people's things without asking is wrong. Now go apologize for taking the flower."
    B. "All children must go to school and you are no exception."
3. Implicit encouragement of the self-definition as a responsible and autonomous agent by providing an emergent opportunity for social reasoning through offering minimal, preemptive justifications for rules invoked to modify the child's behavior.

1. Explicit discouragement of the child's understanding of his feeling by condemning or by asserting the inappropriateness of his or her feelings.
    A. "Stop being such a baby about the party. She whines and I just put a stop to it when she does."
    B. "You're being disrespectful to your father. Now apologize to him. He has no right to treat his fater that way."

2. Implicit discouragement of the child's understanding of his or her feelings by asserting how the child *should* feel or act in the situation.
    A. "I'd just tell him we're all human and forget things. He should forgive and forget."
    B. "She can't expect to be invited to every party. She should just put it out of her mind. There'll be other parties."

3. Implicit encouragement of the child's understanding of his or her feelings by providing an emergent acknowledgment of those feelings through the use of diversionary tactics intended to ease the child's distress.

(continued)

TABLE 1.1 *(Continued)*

Regulative Strategies	Comforting Strategies

II. Implicit Encouragement of Reflection

A. "As a child you have to go to school. It's your job like I have to do my job. Now get the clothes on or you'll be late."

B. "Stealing is wrong. It's against the law and you can end up in jail if you keep doing it."

4. Implicit encouragement of the child's self-definition as a responsible and autonomous agent by requiring the child to deal with parent-controlled concessions, contingent rewards, or sanctions as reasons for modification of behavior.

A. "They usually say they're sick and I'd tell him if he was sick he didn't have to go to school but he would stay in bed all day with no friends and no going outside so he could get better. Then I'd ask him if he still wanted to stay home."

B. "I know you want to stay up but it's a school night. You go to bed and maybe you can stay up for a special show on the weekend."

A. "Oh, I'd probably just take her out shopping or to a movie to get her off it. There's not much else you can do."

B. "I'd tell her Daddy or I would make it up to her with another surprise."

4. Implicit encouragement of the child's understanding of his or her feelings through an explicit acknowledgment of those feelings (may be coupled with the invocation of clichés intended to "explain away" the child's behavior.)

A. "I know you're disappointed about the surprise, I would be too, but these things happen sometimes though and we have to understand."

B. "I'd tell her I know she was hurt. Sometimes I wasn't invited to things when I was little but the hurt goes away in a little while."

III. Explicit Encouragment of Reflection

5. Explicit encouragement of the child's self-definition as a responsible and autonomous agent by (1) encouraging the child to think about *parent-articulated* general causes or consequences of his or her behavior, and (2) viewing these typical causes or consequences of his or her behavior as reasons for the modification of behavior.

A. "When people hurt us we want to call them names. It doesn't do any good though. Next time why don't you tell them you're angry at what they did. Then maybe they won't do it again. If they do, then just don't play with them. Just calling someone a name doesn't make you feel better or your friend."

5. Explicit encouragment of the child's understanding of his or her feelings by explaining and attempting to alleviate those feelings in terms of mitigating features of the situation or general principles cited by the parent.

A. "I'd probably tell him that most people don't have houses big enough to invite everybody to parties. That his friend's mother probably told him he could only invite so many and he just invited his very closest friends. That when people don't invite you to one party there can be a lot of reasons and it doesn't mean they don't like you."

(continued)

16

TABLE 1.1 *(Continued)*

Regulative Strategies	Comforting Strategies
B. "When people work hard to have things (flowers) they usually want to keep them to appreciate them. Mrs. Jones might have given you a flower if you'd asked, but taking things from people without asking upsets them a lot."	B. "When people are very busy they can forget things even when they don't mean to. Everyone forgets sometimes and when they do it it doesn't mean they meant to make anyone feel bad, just that they got too busy."
6. Explicit encouragement of the child's self-definition as a responsible and autonomous agent by (1) encouraging the child to articulate in his or her own terms the causes and consequences of his behavior, (2) helping the child to articulate how these causes and consequences (a) are relevant to a broader context involving past or future experiences of the child, or (b) impact on the perspectives of other people salient to the child, and (3) teaching the child to view these factors as reasons for the modification of behavior.	6. Explicit encouragment of the child's understanding of his or her feelings by actively eliciting the child's definition of his or her feelings and the causes of them and encouraging the child to see the situation producing the distressful feelings in a broader context involving specific past or future experiences or the perspectives of other people salient to the child.
A. "First, I'd get him to tell my why he called his friend a name like that. You know, talk about why he felt that way. He's had names thrown at him, in fact not long ago. I'd ask him how he felt when it happened and tell him his friends felt the same way. If he wants to have his friend to play with at school he probably should apologize and tell his friend why he did it. Otherwise he might lose his friend. Is that what he wants?"	A. "Well he can't invite everyone in the class to his parties. I'd remind him of his birthday party and ask him who he invited and why. Did that mean he didn't like the other people? He forgot one of his friends then too. I'd ask him if the boy was one he invited to his party. And I'd encourage him not to exclude this friend from his parties since he knows how it feels now. Let him figure this out for himself so he can deal with it when it happens again, like it will."
B. "If that [refusing to attend school] happened now, she's practicing for the Christmas play, so I'd say she'd miss seeing her friends [in the play] and exchanging Christmas cards. Jackie [a friend] won't get a card from you and she'll be sad. I think she'd react to that. Her friends are important to her."	B. "I'd ask him why he wasn't talking to his dad. Depending on what he said I'd probably remind him of the times he's forgotten to do things he promised to me. He forgets to make his bed a lot. I'd ask him if I treat him like he's doing. He knows his dad feels sorry about it and I'd just ask him to go talk about it with him so they'd both feel better."

measure of regulative communication and .80 for the two-item measure of comforting communication.

An overall assessment of reflection-enhancing maternal communication was formed by summing the standardized scores for the regulative and comforting indices. Summing these indices was warranted by the substantial correlation between them ($r = .85, p < .001$). The high correlation between the two forms of maternal communication suggests that the ability to produce reflection-enhancing messages may be a unitary construct. However, because of the close conceptual tie in the present study between the forms of maternal communication examined and some of the child communication measures (e.g., mother's regulative skill and child's persuasive skill, mother's comforting skill and child's comforting skill), our data analyses examined associations between all of the skill assessments obtained from the children and the three indices of maternal communication skill (i.e., regulative skill, comforting skill, and the combined reflection-enhancing index).

The validity of our approach to the study of maternal communication is supported by the results of research recently reported by Kochanska, Kuczynski, and Radke-Yarrow (1989). These authors had mothers suggest disciplinary strategies they might employ with respect to several hypothetical situations; the mothers were subsequently observed in a naturalistic setting for 90 minutes and all actual disciplinary efforts were recorded. Analyses revealed significant similarities in the strategies mothers reported they would use in response to the hypothetical situations and the strategies they actually used when disciplining their children (also see Burleson, 1984b, for analysis of the appropriateness of constructed interview responses in comforting contexts particularly). Applegate (1980) similarly found strong parallels between day-care teachers' reliance on person-centered or position-centered strategies in response to hypothetical situations posed in an interview format and in their everyday behavior with children in the day-care center in which they worked.

Assessments of Social Class

Information about the occupational and educational levels of parents in the home was obtained during the interview to create an index of family by SES. The index of SES used was derived using Hollingshead and Redlich's (1958) procedure for quantifying the SES of the family head-of-household. This procedure yields a weighted sum of standardized scores for the head-of-household's educational level and occupational status. Scores ranged from 3 to 12 ($x = 7.96$; $SD = 2.72$) indicating reasonable variation in SES.

Assessments of Children's Social-Cognitive Ability

Construct Differentiation. Each child was asked to describe orally four individuals in as much detail as possible: a liked peer, a disliked peer, the child's mother, and the child him- or herself. After completing their spontaneous descriptions of each figure, the children were probed to see if they could add anything else about the figure. Each description was scored for construct differentiation (cognitive complexity) or the number of different interpersonal constructs it contained, by following the slightly modified coding procedures of Crockett, Press, Delia, and Kenny (1974). According to Crockett et al.'s scoring rules, constructs referring to others' physical characteristics, behaviors, and social roles are not counted. However, because children's impressions are often dominated by such constructs, they were included in the differentiation codings. Extensive evidence supports the validity of this approach to assessing interpersonal construct differentiation (see Burleson & Waltman, 1988; O'Keefe & Sypher, 1981).

Coding reliabilities for all measures completed by the children were determined by having two independent judges score responses produced by 15 subjects. These interrater reliabilities are summarized in Table 1.2.

TABLE 1.2
Measures Completed by the Child Sample and Associated Reliabilities

Measure	Coding Reliability[a]	Year 1 Internal Consistency[b]	Year 2 Internal Consistency[b]	Test–Retest Reliability[c]
Social-Cognitive Assessment				
Construct differentiation	.92	.87	.86	.51
Construct abstractness	.91	.72	.77	.71
Social perspective-taking skill	.94	.70	.51	.69
Affective perspective-taking skill[d]	—	.52	.57	.65
Social-cognitive index	—	.71	.83	.79
Communication Assessments				
Persuasive skill	.91	.78	.69	.52
Comforting skill	.93	.77	.69	.28
Listener-adapted skill	.97	.75	.75	.31
Communication skill index	—	.77	.79	.60

[a]Intraclass correlation coefficients or Cohen's *kappa*.

[b]Cronbach's *alpha*.

[c]Pearson correlation.

[d]Coding reliabilities are not reported here for the affective perspective taking measure due to the number of different codings made with respect to this measure (three different coding systems for each of four different situations). Coding reliabilities for this task are available from the authors on request.

Internal consistencies for multi-item or multi-situation measures are also reported in Table 1.2. The longitudinal nature of the study provided a context for examining the stability (i.e., test–retest reliability) of the assessed skills. These test–retest reliabilities are also reported in Table 1.2.

Construct Abstractness (Psychologically Focused Construing).   Each Each construct identified in the differentiation codings was further subjected to a bipolar coding as being either concrete or abstract. Abstract constructs produce psychologically focused construing. They refer to the dispositions, attitudes, affective qualities, and motivational qualities of others. Concrete constructs pertain to the physical, behavioral, and role-based aspects of others. Construct abstractness has been found to be a good indicator of advanced social-cognitive functioning (see Applegate et al., 1985).

Social Perspective-Taking Skill.   Social perspective-taking skill was assessed through a version of Hale and Delia's (1976) Social Perspectives Task modified for use with children (see Burleson, 1982, 1984a). This measure is designed to assess the extent to which the child is able to recognize and coordinate multiple viewpoints in affectively charged situations and understand the recursive nature of social perspectives (i.e., that ego can think about an alter's thoughts about ego, etc.). Participants were asked to think about two situations: an actual instance in which a liked person did something that hurt or disappointed the participant and a hypothetical instance in which a classmate of the participant failed to invite him or her to a party. For each situation, the child was asked to explain why the offending party acted as he or she did and what the offending party was thinking and feeling about the situation. Responses to these questions were coded for the extent to which they exhibited the ability to distance the self from personal feelings and realistically represent the offending party's point of view (a detailed description of coding procedures is presented in Burleson, 1980).

Affective Perspective-Taking Skill.   Affective perspective-taking skill, or the ability to recognize and understand the causes for another's emotional state, was assessed through a task developed by Rothenberg (1970). Children listened to four brief taped vignettes of emotionally charged interactions. After hearing each vignette, the child was asked to (a) identify the emotional state displayed by a target character, (b) explain why the target character was experiencing that emotion, and (c) specify the cues used to infer the emotional state of the target character. Responses to each of these questions were scored within an appropriate hierarchical system (see Burleson, 1982, 1984a; Rothenberg, 1970).

Index of Social-Cognitive Ability.   To provide a more general and stable measure of children's social-cognitive ability, scores on the four measures (construct differentiation, construct abstractness, social perspective-taking skill, and affective perspective-taking skill) were combined into a single index. Scores for each of these indices were standardized (i.e., converted to z-scores) and then summed. In constructivist theory, social-cognitive processes such as perspective taking are viewed as occurring through the application of interpersonal constructs (see Burleson, 1982; Hale & Delia, 1976). Thus, our combined index of social-cognitive ability reflects the character of both cognitive structures and processes. To assess the unidimensionality of these measures of social-cognitive ability, a principal axis factor analysis was carried out on the four measures for each year of data. Strong unidimensional solutions were obtained for both years: Year 1 eigen value = 2.85, loadings ranged from .63 to .93; Year 2 eigen value = 2.70, loadings ranged from .52 to .87. Internal consistencies for the four-measure index of social-cognitive ability are reported in Table 1.2.

Assessments of Children's Communication Skills

Persuasive Communication.   Children responded to two hypothetical situations designed to elicit persuasive messages. One situation had the child imagine persuading a parent to host an overnight party and the other had the child envision persuading a neighbor to take in a stray dog. Children's messages were coded within a nine-level hierarchical system developed by Delia, Kline, and Burleson (1979) for the extent to which they reflected recognition of and adaptation to the perspectives of persuasion targets. Messages coded in the low levels of the hierarchy exhibited concern only with the needs and desires of the persuader, those coded in the middle levels provided implicit recognition of the target's perspective by modifying the request or responding to expected counterarguments, and messages coded in the highest levels of the hierarchy made the perspective of the target primary, for example, by showing the target how compliance with the request would further the target's own goals. The highest level message produced in response to each situation was retained for purposes of analysis.

Comforting Communication.   Messages reflecting children's comforting abilities were elicited by having them respond to two peer-oriented hypothetical situations. In one, a friend was upset about not receiving an invitation to a classmate's party and in the other a friend was upset about having failed an important test in school. Coding procedures developed by Applegate (1978) and refined by Ritter (1979) were used to evaluate children's comforting messages for the extent to which they acknowledged, helped articulate, and legitimized the feelings and perspective of the distressed peer.

A number of studies have demonstrated the representational validity of our analytic systems for evaluating comforting strategies. People perceive person-centered comforting as more sophisticated and accept and respond more positively to those who use them (see Burleson & Samter, 1985). Our coding systems for comforting thus seem valid methods for describing and tapping developmentally ordered individual differences in comforting-strategy production (see the reviews of Applegate, 1990; Burleson, 1984b, 1985, 1987, 1990; also see Applegate et al., 1985).

General Listener-Adapted Communication.   Procedures introduced by Alvy (1973) and refined by Delia and Clark (1977) were used to assess the child's ability to recognize and functionally adapt to the communication-relevant characteristics of listeners. Participants viewed three pairs of cartoon figures; each pair of figures differed in some communicatively relevant way (e.g., a pleasant looking man versus an angry looking man). For each pair of figures, the child was given a specific communicative objective to accomplish (e.g., ask each man to retrieve a ball that had been kicked into his backyard). Messages were scored for the extent to which the communicatively relevant characteristic (e.g., the man's affective state) was recognized and adapted to. A nine-level hierarchy, described at length by Delia and Clark (1977), was used in making these codings.

Index of Person-Centered Communication Skill.   To provide a parsimonious representation of children's general skill at person-centered communication, scores on the three measures of communication ability were combined into a single index. Scores on each of the three measures were standardized (i.e., converted to z-scores) and then summed. To assess the unidimensionality of this three-measure index of communication skill, a principal axis factor analysis was carried out for each year of data. Strong unidimensional solutions were obtained for both years: Year 1 eigen value = 2.03, loadings ranged from .60 to .90; Year 2 eigen value = 2.11, loadings ranged from .68 to .86. Internal consistencies for the index of communication skill are reported in Table 1.2.

RESULTS

The results of the study are presented in the following order: First, we discuss relationships between maternal communication, social class, and children's cognitive and communicative abilities. Next, relations between children's cognitive and communicative skills are reported. Finally, we report simple path analyses assessing whether maternal communication primarily affects children's cognitive or communicative abilities.

Effects of Maternal Communication on Children's Cognitive and Communicative Abilities

Relationships between maternal communication and children's social-cognitive and communicative abilities were assessed initially through partial correlation analysis; the effect of children's chronological age was partialled out to control for its potentially confounding influence. Table 1.3 reports the age-partialled correlations between the indices of maternal reflection-enhancing communication, social class, children's social-cognitive ability, and children's communication skill during both years of the study.

As the partial correlations in Table 1.3 show, the indices of maternal reflection-enhancing communication were associated with most measures of children's social-cognitive and communicative functioning during both years of the study. In particular, during the Year 1 of the study, maternal communication predicted children's construct differentiation, overall level of social-cognitive development, persuasive skills, comforting skills, and overall receiver-focused communication skill. All of these relationships were replicated during Year 2 of the study. In addition, during Year 2 maternal communication further predicted children's construct abstractness, affective perspective-taking skills, and listener-adapted communication skill. These results provide substantial support for the hypothesized effect of maternal communication on children's cognitive and communicative abilities.

Table 1.3 also reports age-partialled correlations between maternal social class and children's social-cognitive and communicative abilities. Social class was significantly related only to children's affective perspective-taking skill ($r = .26$, $p < .05$, and $r = .40$, $p < .01$, during Years 1 and 2 of the study, respectively). Surprisingly, none of the other associations between social class and children's abilities reached statistically significant levels.

It is possible that relationships between maternal communication and children's cognitive and communicative abilities may be moderated by factors other than social class. Thus, to further evaluate the robustness of the relationships between maternal communication and children's cognitive and communicative abilities, a series of partial correlation analyses were undertaken. In these analyses, the effects of social class, family size, and the child's age, gender, and birth order were partialled from relationships between maternal reflection-enhancing communication and the summary indices of children's social-cognitive and communicative abilities. These

TABLE 1.3
Age-Partialled Correlations between Social Class, Maternal Reflection-Enhancing Communication, and Children's Social-Cognitive and Communicative Skills

	Maternal Communication and Social Class Indices			
Children's Indices	Regulative Communication	Comforting Communication	Overall Index	Social Class
Year 1				
Construct differentiation	.43***	.39**	.43***	− .05
Construct abstractness	.19+	.20+	.20+	− .07
Social perspective-taking skill	.13	.19	.17	.06
Affective perspective-taking skill	.20	.13	.17	.26*
Cognitive index	.40**	.41**	.42**	.01
Persuasive skill	.25*	.21+	.24*	.14
Comforting skill	.33*	.41**	.390**	.21+
Listener-adapted skill	.19+	.26*	.23+	.12
Communication index	.34*	.42**	.40**	.19
Year 2				
Construct differentiation	.39**	.33*	.37**	− .00
Construct abstractness	.37**	.34*	.37**	− .01
Social perspective-taking skill	.28*	.10	.20	− .10
Affective perspective-taking skill	.76***	.60***	.71***	.39**
Cognitive index	.58***	.47**	.55***	.03
Persuasive skill	.28*	.16	.23+	.02
Comforting skill	.35*	.22+	.30*	.04
Listener-adapted skill	.47***	.30*	.40**	.24+
Communication index	.47**	.28*	.39**	.11

$+p < .10$; $*p < .05$; $**p < .01$; $***p < .001$.

TABLE 1.4

Fifth-Order Partial Correlations between Mothers' Reflection-Enhancing
Communication and Children's Social-Cognitive and Communication Skills
(Controlling for Social Class, Family Size, Age, Sex, and Birth Order)

Mother Communication	Children's Abilities			
	Year 1		Year 2	
Indices	Social Cognition	Receiver-Focused Communication	Social Cognition	Receiver-Focused Communication
Regulative communication	.46**	.29**	.70***	.56***
Comforting communication	.49**	.40**	.61***	.37*
Communication index	.50**	.36*	.69***	.48**

*$p < .05$; **$p < .01$; ***$p < .001$.

fifth-order partial correlations are reported in Table 1.4. (Note: Due to missing data, these analyses were based on sample sizes of 40 for Year 1 and 35 for Year 2.)

Interestingly, most of the fifth-order partial correlations are somewhat higher than the first-order partials reported in Table 1.3. This suggests that some of the controlled variables may exert modest suppressor effects with respect to relationships between maternal communication and children's cognitive and communicative abilities. In any event, the fifth-order partials reported in Table 1.4 indicate the robustness of the effect of maternal communication on children's social cognition and person-centered communication.

Relationships Among Children's Social-Cognitive and Communication Skills

As discussed in the first part of this chapter, a central assumption of our theoretical framework is that individual differences in social-cognitive ability contribute to individual differences in functional communication skills. Positive relationships between indices of social cognitive ability and communication skill have been found regularly (see Burleson, 1987; Delia, O'Keefe, & O'Keefe, 1982). Indeed, in our earlier analysis of the mothers reported here (Applegate et al., 1985), we found substantial associations between measures of interpersonal construct system development and the ability to generate reflection-enhancing messages.

The measures obtained from the children in the present study afforded the opportunity to explore further potential relationships between social cognition and communication. Table 1.5 reports the age-partialled correlations between the children's social-cognitive and communicative indices during both years of the study.

The age-partialled correlations in Table 1.5 provide strong support for the notion that individual differences in social cognition are associated with individual differences in functional communication skills. With only one exception, all social-cognitive indices are moderately related to all communicative indices in both years of the study. The exception involves construct abstractness (psychologically focused construing) during Year 1: Construct abstractness failed to relate to any of the communication indices (and, for that matter, most of the other social-cognitive indices). Previous research (e.g., Burleson, 1984a; Delia, Kline, & Burleson, 1979) found that young children often have few abstract constructs; thus, construct abstractness is often a poor index of social-cognitive development until later childhood.

Maternal Effects on Children: Cognition or Communication?

Our final analysis was designed to determine whether maternal communication primarily influenced children's social cognition or children's communication skills. If our constructivist analysis of the effects of reflection-enhancing maternal communication is correct, the primary effect of mothers' communication should be on children's social-cognitive abilities. On the other hand, if maternal communication primarily functions to model communication strategies to children, as would be maintained by social learning theory, the strongest influence for mothers' communication will be on children's communication skills.

Simple path analyses utilizing hierarchical regression (see Biddle & Marlin, 1987) were employed to ascertain whether maternal communication exerted primary influence on children's cognitive or communicative abilities. For each year of the study, two regression equations were computed: One equation partialled the effects of maternal communication from the relationship between the summary indices of children's social-cognitive and communicative skills and the other equation partialled the effects of children's social-cognitive abilities from the relationship between maternal communication and children's communication skills. Biddle and Marlin (1987) recommended this comparative procedure as a way of testing whether proper intervening variables have been chosen and correct causal paths have been specified. In all equations, children's ages were entered first to control for their confounding effects. The results of this analysis are reported in Table 1.6.

The results of the regression analyses were very clear. In both years of the

TABLE 1.5
Age-Partialled Intercorrelations Among Children's Social-Cognitive and Communicative Assessments

Variables	(1)	(2)	(3)	(4)	(5)	(6)	(7)	(8)	(9)
(1) Construct differentiation	—	.41**	.55***	.25+	.84***	.53***	.47***	.44***	.62***
(2) Construct abstractness	.68***	—	-.02	-.20	.56***	.12	.10	-.00	.18
(3) Social perspective-taking skill	.60***	.71***	—	.49***	.71***	.48***	.54***	.48***	.62***
(4) Affective perspective-taking skill	.42**	.42**	.28*	—	.53***	.39**	.43**	.45***	.53***
(5) Cognition index	.84***	.88***	.81***	.66***	—	.66***	.60***	.52***	.77***
(6) Persuasive skill	.61***	.52***	.65***	.64***	.76***	—	.47***	.27*	.78***
(7) Comforting skill	.59***	.46**	.51***	.43**	.60***	.51***	—	.43**	.83***
(8) Listener-adapted skill	.48***	.59***	.68***	.51***	.71***	.64***	.40**	—	.74***
(9) Communication index	.70***	.64***	.76***	.64***	.84***	.88***	.76***	.84***	—

Note. Coefficients above the diagonal are for Year 1, those below the diagonal are for Year 2.
+$p < .10$; *$p < .05$; **$p < .01$; ***$p < .001$.

TABLE 1.6

Summary of Regression Analyses Assessing the Mediational Effects of Mothers' Communication on the Relationship Between Children's Cognitive and Communicative Abilities

Dependent Variable: Children's Communication Index, Year 1

Equation 1

Step	Variable Entered	β	R^2 Change	Overall R^2
1	Child's age	.56***	.31***	.31***
2	Child cognition index	.87**	.41**	.72***
3	Mother communication	.08	.00	.72***

Equation 2

Step	Variable Entered	β	R^2 Change	Overall R^2
1	Child's age	.56***	.31***	.31***
2	Mother communication	.34*	.11*	.42***
3	Child cognition index	.83***	.30**	.72***

Dependent Variable: Children's Communication Index, Year 2

Equation 1

Step	Variable Entered	β	R^2 Change	Overall R^2
1	Child's age	.40**	.16**	.16**
2	Child cognition index	.83**	.59***	.75***
3	Mother communication	−.09	.01	.76***

Equation 2

Step	Variable Entered	β	R^2 Change	Overall R^2
1	Child's age	.40**	.16**	.16**
2	Mother communication	.30*	.13*	.29**
3	Child cognition index	.86***	.47***	.76***

$*p < .05; **p < .01; ***p < .001.$

study, controlling for the effects of children's social-cognitive abilities reduced the correlation between maternal communication and children's communication to zero. In contrast, although controlling for the effects of maternal communication somewhat reduced the magnitude of the association between children's social-cognitive abilities and their communication skills, a very substantial association between these latter two variables remained (see Table 1.6). This pattern of results is consistent with the view that maternal communication primarily affects children's social-cognitive abilities and influences their communication skills largely through the mediation of social cognition.

DISCUSSION

In discussing results we first highlight the important findings and then qualify and place the study in the context of current issues in research on parenting and family communication. For reasons of space, we focus on the summative indexes of mothers' and children's social-cognitive and communication development. The indexes were justified given the high intercorrelations of the multiple indices for social cognition and communication, respectively.

Reflection-Enhancing Parental Communication as an Antecedent to Development

The general theoretical orientation that underlies our broad research program has only been presented in highly abbreviated and piecemeal fashion here. Our "constructivist" approach to communication research (see Applegate, 1990; Burleson, 1989; Delia, O'Keefe, & O'Keefe, 1982) emphasizes the centrality of interpretive processes in guiding behavior and of the role of interpersonal construct systems in channeling social cognition and behavior. Given their psychological focus, a danger for interpretivist and constructivist perspectives is that they give too little regard to social and behavioral processes. We trust that the present study makes clear that our commitments, while clearly emphasizing the importance of social-cognitive development, place central importance on the ways social-cognitive orientations are expressed in and shaped through behavior. Ours is a social constructivism that seeks to illuminate the deep interpenetration of social and cognitive processes.

Given this focus, we believe that our most important finding is that reflection-enhancing parenting is a strong predictor of children's social-cognitive development. In turn, social-cognitive ability is powerfully related to children's ability to communicate in more person-centered ways with peers in persuasive and comforting contexts. This pattern appears, if anything, to be somewhat stronger among the older children. The path of influence here supports our argument that reflection-enhancing parenting should primarily encourage children to think in terms of individual feelings, dispositions, and perspectives, a form of thinking that should, in turn, highlight and enhance the ability to construct person-centered communication strategies. This is especially true in those contexts in which individual perspectives are a focus. Persuasion and comforting are two such functional communicative contexts. The results encourage us to continue to believe that a significant role is played by underlying social-cognitive orientations (i.e., the "theories" or "logics" embedded in the social capital that families give children) as these are developed and concretely realized in specific functional communication contexts.

Because we examined children's communicative strategies in functional contexts paralleling those assessed for the parents (regulative/persuasive and comforting/comforting), behavioral modeling could be suggested as an explanation for our findings. However, the paths of influence observed argue against that. Mothers' communication exerted no significant direct effect on children's communication during either year of our study. Rather, maternal communication primarily affected children's social cognition. This suggests that maternal use of reflection-enhancing strategies imparts a person-centered orientation to social relations to children. As in adults, this orientation to social relations encourages the development of more complex, receiver-oriented constructs to address the complexities of a person-centered world. These social-cognitive developments in the child then serve as necessary, but not sufficient, causes for related developments in person-centered communication skills. In this sense the results suggest a path from social cognition (parent) to communication (parent) to social cognition (child) to communication (child) (also see Applegate et al., 1985).

One perplexing finding was the lack of a relationship between reflection-enhancing parenting and children's affective perspective-taking at Time 1, with a substantial and significant relationship between these variables at Time 2. The inconsistent relationship suggests an important general point for this type of developmental research. We found younger children to be lacking abstract, psychologically focused constructs for perceiving others. Hence, we suspect that these younger children were not fully capable of accessing the complexity presented them by more reflection-enhancing parenting strategies. Only as they became more developmentally "ready" were the older children able to access the more complex view of persons presented by those strategies in a way that enhanced their affective perspective taking skills. We assume that such skills are related to the acquisition of psychologically focused abstract constructs.

The important and broader issue here concerns tying parental antecedents to complementary developments in children as those might be expected to emerge given the child's general level of social-cognitive development. Reflection-enhancing parenting should have differential effects depending on the child's own stage of development.

The paths of influence evidenced here (as well as our theoretical approach) also strongly argue for thinking in terms of a parent-to-child directional influence for person-centered development. Person-centered parental communication as an antecedent is tied to an enduring individual difference in the adult's social-cognitive and communication development. It is a difference tied, we believe, to fundamental variations in orientations to social relations that are reinforced by the general cultural environment.

Although we cannot rule out the possibility that, over the course of years, adults could regress to a more position-centered orientation or advance to a more person-centered orientation to communication as a result of the influence of children, such a possibility seems less likely for the cognitive structures focused upon here than for many other variables (e.g., changes in parent beliefs specifically tied to child rearing). Moreover, our results show differences among the children paralleling those evidenced in their mothers' communication, parallels that we cannot believe were caused by children at this young age. Finally, the relationship between social-cognitive and communicative development is stable and strong for both mothers and children across sampling periods and age groups. The paths of influence remain from mother's social cognition to mother's communication to child's social cognition to child's communication. There is no evidence that the child's level of person-centered communication skill is serving as a change agent for the mother's social cognition or communication. The stability of the relationships and the direction of influence from mother to child also is suggested by the continuing significant relationship between the mother's communication at Time 1 with the children's social-cognitive development at Time 2.

In attempting to account for the socialization of cognitive and communicative orientations in children, we believe it is reasonable to assume that differences in parents' communication skills play a causal role in promoting the emergence of differences in children's cognitive and communicative skills. We make this assumption fully cognizant of the evidence on the bidirectionality of influence between parents and children in socialization contexts (e.g., Grotevant, 1989; Hess, 1981). Although children's behavior surely influences the character and quality of parents' behavior in nontrivial ways, it is also the case that the parent comes to parent–child encounters with well-elaborated and reasonably stable beliefs and behavioral orientations that are repeatedly expressed—albeit with variation and inconsistency—across the myriad contexts of everyday life. Thus it is in no way surprising that most developmental researchers interested in issues of socialization begin with the assumption that the parent's beliefs and behavior shape those of the child. Inquiring into how and to what extent the child's development is channeled into the pattern presented by the parent is an important and useful general point of departure for investigating intergenerational influences on development.

Despite all this, it should be noted that we do not have a large sample and the 2-year time frame is brief. Thus, we must temper our claims for directionality of influence. We agree with those who contend that family research should attend (as it has more recently) to the possibility of bidirectional and interactive patterns of influence. However, the nature of the differences examined here and the pattern of results encourage us to continue to think in terms of enduring individual differences in parental communicative orientations influencing the development of similarly stable differences in children's social-cognitive and communicative development.

The Social Cognition–Communication Relationship

The current research also detected stable relationships between children's social-cognitive abilities and their communication skills. We previously argued (Applegate et al., 1985) for the wisdom of identifying specific and conceptually linked axes of development in trying to draw connections between social cognition and communication development. We documented the greater success of this approach in research with adults and, in a more limited way with children, when compared to most other research investigating the social-cognition/communication relationship. The latter research frequently has relied on global (and probably multidimensional) indices of "empathy" or "social competence." To have our more differentiated approach validated in the study of the social-cognitive and communicative development of children across age groups in a longitudinal design is particularly encouraging.

The age-partialled correlations at Time 1 and Time 2 also provide us with a type of test–retest reliability check on these relationships. The results here are satisfying as well. The pattern of relationships between variables for the most part was stable at each time. Psychologically focused construing (construct abstractness) did assume a more important role in predicting communication quality among the older children. As older children become capable of more psychologically focused construing, such construing, in turn, becomes a better predictor of person-centered communication.

An additional point relevant to the social cognition–communication relationship deserves mention: The relationship between social cognition and communication in the children parallels that found in the mothers (see Applegate et al., 1985) but is significantly stronger. There are two possible reasons for this finding. First, the use of multiple measures to create the summary child indexes made those measures more reliable. Second, one general direction of development is for areas of social functioning to become more differentiated from one another and more internally differentiated and articulated (see Werner, 1957). Hence we might expect a weaker general relationship between social-cognitive and communicative development in adults than in younger children.

Social Class and Family Communication

We previously reported the relation of social class to our assessments of these mothers' social cognition and communication (Applegate et al., 1985).

Social class was significantly related to the quality of social perceptions with middle-class mothers' utilizing more complex, psychologically oriented constructs to define social situations. These construct system indices strongly predicted reflection-enhancing parenting but, when controlling for level of social-cognitive development, social class itself did not. Thus, the influence of social class on the mothers' communication was indirect. We take this as a promising result for our contention that culture influences communication in families at the level of basic interpretive orientations. The situated daily communication behavior of families may only imperfectly and in a fragmented way replicate the surface norms, values, and beliefs of their culture. Culture's effect is best seen in the orientation it provides for defining social contexts.

Here we found the effect of culture (as imperfectly indexed by social class) on children's development exerted primarily through its realization in parental communication. We found no direct relationship between social class indices and children's social-cognitive or communicative development. Socioeconomic status is, of course, a crude measure of culture. However, paired with our previous analyses of SES' significant relationship to the mother's social-cognitive development we only can say that, for the specific qualities of social cognition and communication indexed here for this age group, the primary avenue for transmission of cultural effects on children is through culture's relationship to development of the social-cognitive foundations for reflection-enhancing parental communication.

Controlling for the effects of social class (as well as a variety of other important variables referenced in research on antecedents [i.e., birth order, family size, child gender]) did not diminish the relationship between reflection-enhancing parental communication and the indices of children's development. (We also controlled for the age of the child in this analysis.) This argues for an important and distinctive influence for maternal communication on children's development. We also think there is value in exploring directly how family structure variables affect the relationships found here. Are firstborns more influenced than others? Is the antecedent influence of parental communication on children's social development diluted in large families or simply channeled from parents to older children to younger children? Do female children more consistently elicit the reflection-enhancing skills of parents than male children?

Our results raise still other questions. When does the child's own peer group begin to exert an independent influence on the aspects of social-cognitive and communicative development on which we have focused? Do family and peer group influences shape development in different directions? Or do the parental/family influences described here produce peer group and related social choices by children that reinforce the parental/family influence through encouraging participation in groups and contexts that reflect the orientation to social relations of the parents (see Berndt, 1989; Hartup, 1983)?

Qualifications and Future Directions

Several qualifications are called for given the design of this study. First, we have offered a unidirectional linear model of influence. We do not mean to imply by this that the family should not be treated as an interactive system with many important areas of mutual influence among members (Grotevant, 1989; Hess, 1981; Lytton, 1980). Nevertheless, we believe we have tapped a fundamental orientation to communication that should be expected to inform that system as a whole. Further, as noted, we think this system is most logically seen as arising initially from parents. We have coded concrete strategic behaviors in ways that reflect the underlying logic of the social relations that they embody. Neither message strategies nor their underlying logic can be seen as possessing the same level of susceptibility to mutual influence as, say, reciprocal smiling behavior or more general affective reciprocity variables of the type most typical of mutual influence research.

A second qualification must be made in this paradoxical age of, on the one hand, more single families headed by women parents and, on the other hand, suggestions of greater paternal involvement in child rearing in other family types. We studied only mothers' communication in families generally characterized by a very traditional model of family roles (the lack of ethnic and racial diversity is an obvious qualification as well, of course). However, recent work has applied our reflection-enhancing message coding systems to the regulative communication of both mothers and fathers. This research has found only mothers' communication to predict assessments of the child's social competence (Hart et al., 1990). Nevertheless, recent evidence of different socializing roles for fathers and mothers (e.g., Youniss & Ketterlinus, 1987) and possible cultural differences in the valuation of the qualities of person-centered communication suggest that research on more diverse populations may require elaborations and modifications of the substance if not the structure of the model supported in this study.

Finally, it should be noted that we relied on in-depth, open-ended interview data from the mothers. One obviously could prefer behavior obtained in response to real rather than hypothetical situations. However, several studies, including some using our own measures, have compared responses obtained to hypothetical situations with data based on field observation of child-rearing practices (e.g., Applegate, 1980, 1982; Kochanska, Kuczynski, & Radke-Yarrow, 1989). These studies demonstrated considerable correspondence between interview reports and observed behavior in naturalistic contexts. In fact, we believe that using a number of ecologically valid situations in the interviews provides a valuable means of tapping the mothers' guiding social orientation as it is expressed across functionally similar, but concretely different, parenting contexts.

Obviously, future research must address the limitations in the scope of this study: More diverse populations, fathers, lengthier sampling times, and naturalistic methods to observe parent and child communication all need to be included. As importantly, the antecedent influences indexed here and the differences they help produce in children must be directly linked to important outcome variables for families and children. We have preliminary evidence that the communication skill differences in children found here relate to their acceptance by peers, whereas position-centered parenting is tied to isolate status for the children (Burleson, Delia, & Applegate, 1990). Similar findings have been reported by other researchers (e.g. Hart et al., 1990; Putallaz, 1987). If such findings continue to be borne out, the importance of person-centered parenting and the use of reflection-enhancing strategies will become even clearer.

The tie of our conceptual distinctions to concrete strategic behavior in functional communicative contexts also should facilitate the development of educational programs for parents and children. We suspect that the actual form of such educational programs when fully developed will look similar to those already being suggested by researchers such as Shure (1989), Selman (e.g., Selman, 1980; 1989) and, within our research group, Clark (Clark, Willinghanz, & O'Dell, 1985). One difference from current psychologically oriented educational programs perhaps will be a stronger emphasis on teaching communication strategies. Although parent and child beliefs and social-cognitive abilities are necessary to the kinds of communicative development studied here, the logic of our approach and the present results clearly suggest that social-cognitive developments are not sufficient causes for communication development.

Our theoretical orientation also suggests that efforts to improve parent–child communication narrowly focusing only on parenting contexts will be less effective than educational programs aimed at more general enhancement of communicative skills (e.g., persuasive, comforting, negotiation, referential skills). Similarly, analysis of children's development should be tied to a general understanding of the nature of communicative development and its relation to particular dimensions of social-cognitive development (both as cause and effect).

If one idea is to be carried away from this study it is the need to take seriously concrete communication behavior as enacted in functional contexts. Communicative behavior can be studied fruitfully both developmentally and in relation to culture and cognition without making it epiphenomenal to them. Parental communication must be studied this way and in relation to the parent's general communication abilities expressed in the other roles played in everyday life (e.g., in personal and work relationships). It was, after all, the communication of parents that directly affected their children. This result reinforces a general point of this report: Communication and social-cognitive development, although related, are neither isomorphic nor always similar in their relation to important developmental outcomes.

REFERENCES

Alvy, K. T. (1973). The development of listener adapted communication in grade-school children from different social class backgrounds. *Genetic Psychology Monographs, 87,* 33–104.

Applegate, J. L. (1978). *Four investigations of the relationship between social cognitive development and person-centered regulative and interpersonal communication.* Unpublished doctoral dissertation, University of Illinois at Urbana-Champaign.

Applegate, J. L. (1980). Person- and position-centered communication in a day care center. In N. K. Denzin (Ed.), *Studies in symbolic interaction* (Vol. 3, pp. 59–96). Greenwich, CT: JAI Press.

Applegate, J. L. (1982). The impact of construct system development on communication and impression formation in persuasive contexts. *Communication Monographs, 49,* 277–289.

Applegate, J. L. (1990). Constructs and communication: A pragmatic integration. In R. Neimeyer & G. Neimeyer (Eds.), *Advances in personal construct psychology* (Vol. 1, pp. 197–224). Greenwich, CT: JAI Press.

Applegate, J. L., Burke, J. A., Burleson, B. R., Delia, J. G., & Kline, S. L. (1985). Reflection-enhancing parental communication. In I. E. Sigel (Ed.), *Parental belief systems: The psychological consequences for children* (pp. 107–142). Hillsdale, NJ: Lawrence Erlbaum Associates.

Applegate, J. L., & Delia, J. G. (1980). Person-centered speech, psychological development, and the context of language usage. In R. St. Clair & H. Giles (Eds.), *The social and psychological contexts of language* (pp. 245–282). Hillsdale, NJ: Lawrence Erlbaum Associates.

Baumrind, D. (1989). Rearing competent children. In W. Damon (Ed.), *Child development today and tomorrow* (pp. 349–378). San Francisco: Jossey-Bass.

Bernstein, B. (1974). *Class, codes, and control: Theoretical studies toward a sociology of language* (Rev. Ed.). New York: Shocken.

Berndt, T. J. (1989). Friendships in childhood and adolescence. In W. Damon (Ed.), *Child development today and tomorrow* (pp. 332–348). San Francisco, CA: Jossey Bass.

Biddle, B. J., & Marlin, M. M. (1987). Causality, confirmation, credulity, and structural equation modeling. *Child Development, 58,* 4–17.

Brody, G. H., & Shaffer, D. R. (1982). Contributions of parents and peers to children's moral socialization. *Developmental Review, 2,* 31–75.

Burleson, B. R. (1980). The development of interpersonal reasoning: An analysis of message strategy justifications. *Journal of the American Forensic Association, 17,* 102–110.

Burleson, B. R. (1982). The affective perspective-taking process: A test of Turiel's role-taking model. In M. Burgoon (Ed.), *Communication yearbook 6* (pp. 473–488). Beverly Hills, CA: Sage.

Burleson, B. R. (1984a). Age, social-cognitive development, and the use of comforting strategies. *Communication Monographs, 51,* 140–159.

Burleson, B. R. (1984b). Comforting communication. In H. E. Sypher & J. L. Applegate

(Eds.), *Communication by children and adults: Social-cognitive and strategic processes* (pp. 63–104). Beverly Hills, CA: Sage.

Burleson, B. R. (1985, April). *Communicative correlates of peer acceptance in childhood.* Paper presented at the biennial meeting of the Society for Research in Child Development, Toronto.

Burleson, B. R. (1987). Cognitive complexity. In J. C. McCroskey & J. A. Daly (Eds.), *Personality and interpersonal communication* (pp. 305–349). Newbury Park, CA: Sage.

Burleson, B. R. (1989). The constructivist approach to person-centered communication: A research exemplar. In B. A. Dervin, L. Grossberg, B. J. O'Keefe, & E. Wartella (Eds.), *Rethinking communication, Vol. 2: Paradigm exemplars* (pp. 29–46). Newbury Park, CA: Sage.

Burleson, B. R. (1990). Comforting as everyday social support: Relational consequences of supportive behaviors. In S. Duck (Ed.), *Personal relationships and social support* (pp. 66–82). London: Sage.

Burleson, B. R., Delia, J. G., & Applegate, J. A. (1990). *Effects of mothers' disciplinary and comforting strategies on children's communication skills and acceptance by the peer group.* Paper presented at the annual meeting of the International Communication Association, Dublin, Ireland.

Burleson, B. R., & Samter, W. (1985). Consistencies in theoretical and naive evaluations of comforting messages. *Communication Monographs, 52,* 103–123.

Burleson, B. R., & Waltman, M. S. (1988). Cognitive complexity: Using the role category questionnaire. In C. H. Tardy (Ed.), *A handbook for the study of human communication* (pp. 1–35). Norwood, NJ: Ablex.

Clark, R. A., Willinghanz, S., & O'Dell, L. (1985) Training fourth graders in compromising and persuasive strategies. *Communication Education, 34,* 331–342.

Coleman, J. S. (1987). Families and schools. *Educational Researcher, 16,* 32–38.

Crockett, W. H., Press, A. N., Delia, J. G., & Kenney, C. J. (1974). *The structural analysis of the organization of written impressions* Unpublished manuscript, Department of Psychology, University of Kansas, Lawrence.

Delia, J. G., & Clark, R. A. (1977). Cognitive complexity, social perception, and the development of listener-adapted communication in six-, eight-, ten- and twelve-year-old boys. *Communication Monographs, 44,* 326–345.

Delia, J. G., Kline, S. L., & Burleson, B. R. (1979). The development of persuasive communication strategies in kindergartners through twelfth graders. *Communication Monographs, 46,* 241–256.

Delia, J. G., O'Keefe, B. J., & O'Keefe, D. J. (1982). The constructivist approach to communication. In F.E.X. Dance (Ed.), *Human communication theory* (pp. 147–191). New York: Harper & Row.

Feshbach, N. D. (1975). The relationship of child-rearing factors to children's aggression, empathy, and related positive and negative behaviors. In J. deWit & W. W. Hartup (Eds.), *Determinants and origins of aggressive behaviors* (pp. 422–436). The Hague: Mouton.

Finnie, V., & Russell, A. (1988). Preschool children's social status and their mothers' behavior and knowledge in the supervisory role. *Developmental Psychology, 24,* 789–801.

Gecas, V. (1979). The influence of social class on socialization. In W. R. Burr, R. Hill, F. I. Nye, & I. L. Reiss (Eds.), *Contemporary theories about the family* (Vol. 1, pp. 365–404). New York: Free Press.

Grotevant, H. D. (1989). Child development within the family context. In W. Damon (Ed.), *Child development today and tomorrow* (pp. 34–51). San Francisco, CA: Jossey Bass.

Hale, C. L., & Delia, J. G. (1976). Cognitive complexity and social perspective-taking. *Communication Monographs, 43,* 195–203.

Hart, C. H., de Wolf, D. M., Royston, K. E., Burts, D. C., & Thomasson, R. H. (1990, April). *Maternal and paternal disciplinary styles: Relations with behavioral orientations and sociometric status.* Paper presented at the annual meeting of the American Educational Research Association, Boston, MA.

Hart, C. H., Ladd, G. W., & Burleson, B. R. (1990). Children's expectations of the outcomes of social strategies: Relationships with sociometric status and maternal disciplinary styles. *Child Development, 61,* 127–137.

Hartup, W. W. (1983). Peer relations. In E. M. Hetherington (Ed.), *Handbook of child psychology: Vol. 4. Socialization, personality, and social development* (pp. 103–196). New York: John Wiley.

Hess, R. D. (1981). Approaches to the measurement and interpretation of parent–child interaction. In R. W. Henderson (Ed.), *Parent–child interaction: Theory, research, and prospects* (pp. 207–234). New York: Academic Press.

Hoffman, M. L. (1977). Moral internalization: Current theory and research. In L. Berkowitz (Ed.), *Advances in experimental social psychology* (pp. 85–133). New York: Academic Press.

Hollingshead, A. E., & Redlich, F. C. (1958). *Social class and mental illness.* New York: Wiley.

Jones, C. C., Rickel, A. U., & Smith, R. Z. (1980). Maternal child-rearing practices and social problem-solving strategies among preschoolers. *Developmental Psychology, 16,* 241–242.

Kochanska, G., Kuczynski, L., & Radke-Yarrow, M. (1989). Correspondence between mothers' self-reported and observed child rearing practices. *Child Development, 60,* 56–63.

Lepper, M. (1983). Social control processes and the internalization of social values: An attributional perspective. In E. T. Higgins, D. N. Ruble, & W. W. Hartup (Eds.), *Social cognition and social development* (pp. 294–330). New York: Cambridge University Press.

Levine, R. A. (1989). Cultural environments in child development. In W. Damon (Ed.), *Child development today and tomorrow* (pp. 52–68). San Francisco, CA: Jossey Bass.

Lytton, H. (1980). *Parent–child interaction.* New York: Plenum Press.

Maccoby, E. E., & Martin J. A. (1983). Socialization in the context of the family: Parent–child interaction. In E. M. Hetherington (Ed.), *Handbook of child psychology, Vol. 4: Socialization, personality, and social development* (pp. 1–101). New York: Wiley.

O'Keefe, B. J. (1988). The logic of message design. *Communication Monographs, 55,* 80–103.

O'Keefe, B. J., & Delia, J. G. (1982). Impression formation and message production. In M. E. Roloff & C. R. Berger (Eds.), *Social cognition and communication* (pp. 33–72). Beverly Hills, CA: Sage.

O'Keefe, D. J., & Sypher, H. E. (1981). Cognitive complexity measures and the relationship of cognitive complexity to communication. *Human Communication Research, 8,* 72–92.

Parke, R. D., MacDonald, D. B., Beitel, A., & Bhavnagri, N. (1988). The role of the family in the development of peer relationships. In R. Peters & R. J. McMahon (Eds.), *Marriage and families: Behavioral treatments and processes* (pp. 17–44). New York: Brunner-Mazel.

Pettit, G. S., Dodge, K. A., & Brown, M. M. (1988). Early family experience, social problem solving patterns, and children's social competence. *Child Development, 58,* 324–340.

Putallaz, M. (1987). Maternal behavior and children's sociometric status. *Child Development, 58,* 324–340.

Radke-Yarrow, M., & Zahn-Waxler, C. (1986). The role of familial factors in the development of prosocial behavior: Research findings and questions. In D. Olwens, J. Block, & M. Radke-Yarrow (Eds.), *Development of antisocial and prosocial behavior* (pp. 207–233). Orlando, FL: Academic Press.

Ritter, E. M. (1979). Social perspective-taking ability, cognitive complexity, and listener-adapted communication in early and late adolescence. *Communication Monographs, 46,* 40–51.

Roberts, W., & Strayer, J. (1987). Parents' responses to the emotional distress of their children: Relation with children's competence. *Developmental Psychology, 23,* 415–422.

Rollins, B. C., & Thomas, D. L. (1979). Parental support, power, and control techniques in the socialization of children. In W. Burr, R. Hill, R. I. Nye, & I. L. Reiss (Eds.), *Contemporary theories about the family* (Vol. 1, pp. 317–364). New York: Free Press.

Rothenberg, B. B. (1970). Children's social sensitivity and the relationship to interpersonal competence, intrapersonal comfort, and intellectual level. *Developmental Psychology, 2,* 335–350.

Samter, W., Burleson, B. R., & Basden-Murphy, L. (1989). Behavioral complexity is in the eye of the beholder. *Human Communication Research, 15,* 612–629.

Selman, R. L. (1980). *The growth of interpersonal understanding: Developmental and clinical analyses.* New York: Academic Press.

Selman, R. L. (1989). Fostering intimacy and autonomy. In W. Damon (Ed.), *Child development today and tomorrow* (pp. 409–436). San Francisco, CA: Jossey Bass.

Shure, M. B. (1989). Interpersonal competence training. In W. Damon (Ed.), *Child development today and tomorrow* (pp. 393–435). San Francisco, CA: Jossey Bass.

Sigel, I. E. (1985). A conceptual analysis of beliefs. In I. E. Sigel (Ed.), *Parental belief systems: The psychological consequences for children* (pp. 345–371). Hillsdale, NJ: Lawrence Erlbaum Associates.

Sigel, I. E., & McGillicuddy-DeLisi, A. V. (1984). Parents as teachers of their children: A distancing behavior model. In A. D. Pellegrini & T. D. Yawkey (Eds.), *The development of oral and written language in social contexts* (pp. 71–92). Norwood, NJ: Ablex.

Werner, H. (1957). The concept of development from a comparative and organismic point of view. In D. B. Harris (Ed.), *The concept of development* (pp. 125–146). Minneapolis: University of Minnesota Press.

Werner, H., & Kaplan, B. (1963). *Symbol formation: An organismic–developmental approach to language and the expression of thought.* New York: Wiley.

Youniss, J. (1989). Parent-adolescent relationships. In W. Damon (Ed.), *Child development today and tomorrow* (pp. 379–392). San Francisco, CA: Jossey Bass.

Youniss, J., & Ketterlinus, R. D. (1987). Communication and connectedness in mother- and father–adolescent relationships. *Journal of Youth and Adolescence, 16,* 265–280.

Zahn-Waxler, C., Radke-Yarrow, M., & King, R. A. (1979). Child rearing and children's prosocial initiations toward victims of distress. *Child Development, 50,* 319–330.

2

Parents' Thoughts About Children's Socially Adaptive and Maladaptive Behaviors: Stability, Change, and Individual Differences

Kenneth H. Rubin
Rosemary S. L. Mills
University of Waterloo

To some, the study of parental beliefs, ideas, or cognitions represents little more than researchers' recent attempts to join a revivalist movement. Early in the study of child development, and especially in the 1950s, it was common procedure to interview parents or to provide them with questionnaires in order to discover information about socialization practices, parent–child relationships, and the home environment (e.g., Dameron, 1955; Miller & Swanson, 1958; Sears, Maccoby, & Levin, 1957; Stolz, 1967). The advantages of these procedures were obvious. Parents know their children and how they think about and interact with them better than anyone else. Their knowledge bases cut both across time and across social contexts. On the downside, however, parents' self-reports may be distorted by "the intrusion of nonfocal personal characteristics via mechanisms of self-deception, self-defense, and impression management" (Messick, 1983, p. 487). Furthermore, parents may not even be aware of much of their behavior, unless it concerns highly salient events or interactions (Maccoby & Martin, 1983), and, of course, it has been reported that parents' memories are faulty and cannot be relied on when retrospection is required (Robins, 1963). And then there is the problem of the verbal report-observed behavior disconnection. Correlations between what parents report that they do with their children and what observers report that parents do with their children are in the miniscule-to-moderate range (Miller, 1988).

Given these latter problems, it is not surprising that graduate students in the 1960s and 1970s were being warned against interviewing or questioning parents. What *is* surprising is that many of those warned have become revivalists. Did we not learn our lessons well? Is our behavior merely a reflection of continuities in rebelliousness from young- to mid-adulthood?

It is our opinion that asking parents about their children and their relationships and interactions with them provides psychologists with a wealth of important information. After all, the disconnection between self-report and observed behavior is common to almost all areas of study in psychology. Sometimes it is referred to as the attitude–behavior problem and at other times we use terms like the competence–performance distinction. On these grounds alone, there is no need to begin each manuscript on parental beliefs, ideas, or cognitions with apologetic statements concerning the choice of interviews or questionnaires over observational data. Besides, there is good reason to discount the advice of our mentors. For example, few have argued that the study of social-cognitions and social perceptions in children or in college sophomores is an inane exercise. Books have been published on the subject, and there is even a respected journal devoted entirely to the study of *Social Cognition*! So, why not study the social cognitions of parents (Goodnow, 1988)?

Furthermore, the apparent disconnection between cognition/self-report and behavior remains an important mystery that we need to unravel. Some have explained the disconnection by referring to problems of methodology. It appears, for example, that miniscule relations become moderate and often statistically significant when the questions asked of parents deal with concrete, here-and-now encounters or interactions with their children and when the behaviors observed are tied conceptually and are matched specifically with those being asked about. In a recent study, for example, Kochanska, Kuczynski, and Radke-Yarrow (1989) reported reliable correspondence between self-reported beliefs regarding child-rearing behaviors and actual socialization practices. They attributed their findings to the facts that the interview items matched the content of action observed and that the data from both the interview questions and the observed behaviors were aggregated to produce conceptually meaningful and statistically robust clusters.

Others attempt to solve the mystery of disconnection by referring to factors that may mediate between thought and behavior. For example, parents may be able to tell us countless seemingly competent ways to deal with their child's aggressive behavior and yet may not use any of these means during naturalistic interaction. Researchers have begun to suggest that factors like felt affect or social context may intervene to weaken the verbal report–social behavior relation (e.g., Goodnow, 1988; Rubin & Krasnor, 1986).

The bottom line is that our research has been driven, in part, by Goodnow's (1988) astute comment that "to focus only on a behavior ignores the fact that parents are thinking creatures who interpret events and whose interpretations influence their actions and feelings" (p. 287). Indeed, the *raison d'etre* for our research program stems from *our* beliefs that the ways in which parents think about their children's behaviors and their relationships with their children are linked intimately to the ways they feel about and interact with them. Moreover, we are of the opinion that this complex interplay of parental beliefs, affect, and behavior determines, in part, the quality of the parent–child relationship. All of these factors, in turn, may conspire to predict behavioral "outcomes" for children.

In this chapter, we first provide a rationale for our focus on social development and social competence. We then describe a conceptual model that has provided the basis for our research program on parental beliefs. Subsequently, we review recent findings concerning how parents report that they think and feel about the development of children's adaptive and maladaptive social behaviors. We also report what it is that parents indicate they would do to promote the development of social skills and to discourage the development of maladaptive social behaviors.

We then address three critical questions not previously dealt with in the parental beliefs literature concerning social skills. First, we consider whether meaningful relations can be shown to exist between the ways in which parents report thinking and feeling about social development and their children's actual social behaviors. Second, we consider whether parental beliefs are stable over time and across different periods of child development. Third, we consider what forces operating within and outside of the home may be associated with and predictive of variability in parental beliefs about social development.

Why Social Development?

The ways in which children acquire social competence and develop forms of less competent social behavior are highly significant issues in the study of human development. Because social relationships are of such central importance in everyday life, there may well be no skills more important than those required to sustain relationships. Thus, the acquisition of socially competent behaviors must be considered critical to adaptive development. Indeed, it is known that children who lack social competence usually evidence a variety of other difficulties and are considered to be at risk for maladjustment later in life. For example, aggression and social withdrawal are two very different forms of maladaptive behaviors that not only tend to persist in childhood but also tend to predict personal and social maladjustment in later years (e.g., Parker & Asher, 1987; Rubin, Hymel, & Mills, 1989).

Given the significance of social competence, it is critical to explore its origins and consequences. Parents are undoubtedly among the most important sources of the development of their children's socially adaptive and maladaptive behaviors. Indeed, from our reading of the literature extant, it appears as if almost all major psychological theories that deal with the development of social competence place primary responsibility on parental attributes and behaviors. For example, from a *learning theory* perspective, it is the case that parents shape specific social behaviors through conditioning and modeling (Bandura, 1977; Sears, 1961). Children's tendencies to imitate adult communicative, prosocial, and aggressive behaviors have been reported consistently in the literature; in addition, many social behaviors have been described as responsive to reinforcement principles (Radke-Yarrow & Zahn-Waxler, 1986).

From both *ethological* and *psychoanalytic* perspectives, the quality of an infant's attachment with his or her primary caregiver is thought to have its roots in maternal competence, responsiveness, and sensitivity to the child. Security of attachment, in turn, has been posited to predict positive relationships amongst peers, and insecurity of attachment has been hypothesized to forecast peer rejection (see Rubin, Hymel, Mills, & Rose-Krasnor, 1991; and Sroufe, 1983, for relevant reviews). These links have been attributed to the child's development of an internal working model or cognitive representation that interpersonal relationships are loving and comforting or, alternatively, are rejecting or neglectful (Bowlby, 1973).

Empirically, there has been a recent accumulation of studies demonstrating the relations between parental behaviors and the quality of children's extrafamilial social relationships. For example, mothers of popular children appear to be less demanding, less disagreeable, and more likely to use positive verbalization than mothers of less popular children (Putallaz, 1987). Ladd and Golter (1988) showed that popular preschoolers are more likely than their unpopular age-mates to have mothers who provide opportunities for them to interact with peers and who monitor indirectly their children's peer interactions.

Researchers have also demonstrated significant associations between parenting styles and those behaviors that are likely to predict negative peer relationships in childhood. For example, Stevenson-Hinde, Hinde, and Simpson (1986) reported that the frequency of mothers' positive interactions with their children at home is inversely related to the frequency of the child's production of negative peer-directed behaviors at preschool. Attili (1989) showed that the degree to which mothers disconfirm and attempt to control their children without providing them with appropriate rationales for their authoritarian actions is associated with the frequency of children's hostile behaviors with peers.

Taken together, sufficient data exist to suggest that parenting behaviors are associated, perhaps causally so, with the quality of children's peer relationships as well as with the development of their social skills. One question that deserves attention, however, concerns what it is that may lead parents to interact with their children as they do. It is this question that has led us to our current program of research.

Factors That May Influence Parenting Behaviors

Our research has been guided by an information-processing model of parenting behavior (Rubin, Mills, & Rose-Krasnor, 1989) that postulates links between parental beliefs, socioecological factors, and personal-social setting conditions (see Fig. 2.1). We briefly describe this model next.

An Information-Processing Model of Parental Behavior. Parenting behaviors are undoubtedly the product of a highly complex mix of factors. For one, it is likely that *parental beliefs* influence parenting behaviors. The

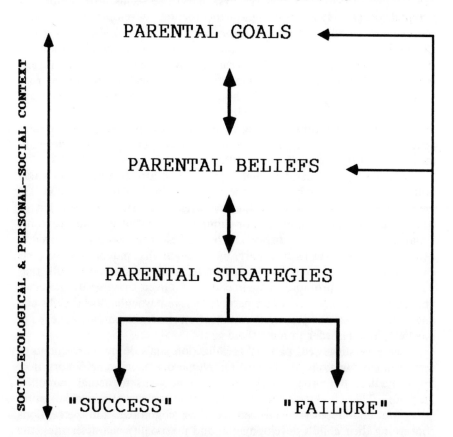

FIG. 2.1   Processing Model of Parenting (from Rubin, Mills, & Rose-Krasnor, 1989).

beliefs that parents have concerning developmental timetables and causes of development, the importance that they attach to certain aspects of development, and cognitions they have about how children should best be socialized, are all likely to be intimately associated with the child-rearing strategies they choose. In fact, researchers have examined such issues as when it is that parents believe particular milestones should be reached *(timetables)* (Goodnow, Knight, & Cashmore, 1986), what characteristics parents consider most important for their children to develop *(values)* (Emmerich, 1969; Stolz, 1967), why it is that these characteristics do or do not develop on time *(causal attributions)* (Dix & Grusec, 1985), and how it is that parents believe they can foster these characteristics *(socialization strategies)* (Emmerich, 1969). To date, most of this research has concerned the development of physical-motor and cognitive skills; there has been a notable lack of relevant data concerning social development (see Goodnow, 1988; Miller, 1988, for recent reviews). Yet there seems little doubt that parental belief systems are significant for the development of social competence. Surely, if parents have inaccurate perceptions concerning when it is possible for children to understand the perspectives of others, or if they believe that maladaptive social behaviors derive from biological factors, or if they believe in folkloristic homilies such as "spare the rod, spoil the child," then such beliefs should have some influence on the ways in which they interact with their children and, in turn, the quality of the relationship that develops between them. We propose, then, that parental beliefs have an *indirect* effect on children's social and emotional development through their impact on parental behavior.

In our model, we postulate that cognitive and affective processes guide both parents' *proactive* behavior (the strategies they use to promote skilled or competent social behavior in their children) and their *reactive* behavior (the strategies they use to modify or eliminate the unskilled or unacceptable behaviors their children display). We suggest that *proactive* parental behavior is guided, at least in part, by the *goals* that parents set for their children's social development. For example, what are the social skills that parents aspire to promote in their children? Given these goals, it seems important to ask *when* it is that parents believe particular social skills can and should be learned and *what* socialization *strategies* parents believe are most effective in order to meet these goals.

As we have suggested, parents' socialization goals do not correspond to their behaviors in a one-to-one fashion. Numerous intervening factors most likely mediate the processes linking parental goals to actual parenting behaviors. The actual strategies they choose for achieving their socialization goals are undoubtedly influenced by their cognitions and perceptions concerning their child's developmental and personality characteristics, the quality of the affective relationship they have with their child, their own or their child's affective wellness, and/or dispositional characteristics of themselves or their child.

In our model, we also consider information processes that may guide the *reactive* strategies parents use when their proactive goals are not met. If desirable behaviors do not enter the child's repertoire "on time" or if undesirable, maladaptive social behaviors are displayed, how do parents react affectively? To what do they attribute these problematic behaviors? What strategies do parents think they would use to modify maladaptive behaviors and can these reactive strategies be predicted by parents' feelings and attributions about the behaviors?

Finally, as with proactive socialization, the actual behavioral outcomes of these reactive information processes are undoubtedly influenced by a variety of intervening factors including socioecological and personal-social setting conditions, dispositional characteristics of the child or the parent, and the quality of the parent–child relationship. For example, a parent who is under a great deal of stress may consider aggressive behavior very upsetting but nevertheless choose to ignore it for fear of losing control.

With regard to *socioecological* setting factors, there is growing evidence that life conditions may set the stage for positive and negative developmental "outcomes" by influencing the quality of parent–child interaction. Thus, being economically disadvantaged, unemployed, or poorly housed may produce sufficient stress in the family to interfere with the ability of a parent to be sensitive and responsive to the needs of a child (e.g., Belsky, 1984; Belsky, Robins, & Gamble, 1984; Booth, Rose-Krasnor, & Rubin, 1991). Researchers have shown, for example, that economic poverty and the stress that often accompanies it are associated with parental conflict (Elder, Caspi, & Burton, 1988) and with parental anger, inconsistency, and punitiveness in child-rearing (Conger, McCarty, Yang, Lahey, & Kropp, 1984; Radke-Yarrow, Richters, & Wilson, 1988).

There is also evidence that parental belief systems interact with socioecological factors to facilitate or inhibit the quality of parent–child interaction. For example, it has been found that parents of higher socioeconomic status are more likely than their counterparts of lower status to believe that children learn best by being active processors rather than passive recipients of direct instruction (McGillicuddy-DeLisi, 1982). In addition, psychologists have often reported that parental teaching styles that involve direct instruction are associated with poor child performance on a variety of cognitive measures; more perspectivistic or "distancing" teaching styles, on the other hand, are associated with competent performance (e.g., Hess & Shipman, 1965; Sigel, 1982). Given that beliefs may mediate parental behaviors and may themselves be influenced by socioecological factors, there is a high probability that these phenomena play a role in the development of *social* competence.

With regard to *personal-social* setting factors, which may be comprised of stressors stemming from inter- and intraindividual sources, again there is growing evidence that these factors affect the parent–child relationship. Thus, the development of children's social competence may be influenced by factors such as maternal age and psychological functioning, marital conflict or breakdown, or the lack of a supportive social network (Booth et al., 1991). We know, for example, that older mothers interact more sensitively with their infants than younger mothers (Ragozin, Basham, Crnic, Greenberg, & Robinson, 1982), that infants' attachment relationships with the mother may prove to be insecure when she is or has been depressed (Radke-Yarrow, Cummings, Kuczynski, & Chapman, 1985; Spieker & Booth, 1988), and that mothers with more committed occupational identities and less role conflict report more confidence as parents and evidence more positive perceptions of their children (Frank, Hole, Jacobson, Justkowski, & Huyck, 1986). We know also that mothers who experience affectionate and relatively conflict-free marital relationships feel competent in their parenting roles and are observed to be sensitive, affectionate parents (Engfer, 1988). Finally, the availability of social support from one's relatives, friends, and spouse is negatively related to maternal restrictiveness and punitiveness (Colletta, 1979; Desfossés & Bouchard, 1987).

Furthermore, the socioecological and personal-social setting conditions described can interact with one another. For example, high-risk mothers who are single and poor and who lack social support are more likely to have insecure relationships with their infants than those who have the support of a partner as well as extrafamilial social support (Spieker & Booth, 1988). Similarly, mothers who are poor feel less stress and are less authoritarian in their relationships with their preschoolers when they receive socioemotional support from their mates and relatives (Zur-Szprio & Longfellow, 1981).

Guided by this information-processing model, we began the research program we describe next.

Parental Beliefs About Children's Social Development

We started by posing a number of simple questions concerning parental beliefs about social development. How is it that mothers of preschoolers believe their children acquire such social skills as getting acquainted with or accepted by unfamiliar peers? How would they feel if their children consistently displayed two forms of maladaptive behavior — aggression and social withdrawal? To what would they attribute these behaviors and what, if anything, would they do about them? We provide initial answers to these questions below.

Mothers' Proactive Beliefs Concerning the Development of Social Skills.
Our first efforts at tapping maternal beliefs about the development of
social competence had a descriptive, normative focus. We studied 122
mothers, each of whom had a 4-year-old child attending day care or
preschool. Mothers were given a set of short descriptions of four social
skills (getting acquainted with someone new, resolving peer conflicts,
getting accepted into an ongoing play group of unfamiliar peers, persuading
others to do what she or he wants), each of which was followed by a list of
eight influences (taken from Elias & Ubriaco, 1986) that could contribute to
the development of these skills:

1. Being rewarded for appropriate behavior and punished for inappropriate behavior.
2. Observing what other children do.
3. Being told exactly how to act.
4. Experiencing interactions with others.
5. Being taught and encouraged at school.
6. Observing what adults do.
7. Being told why one should act in a certain way.
8. Experiencing the feelings that arise when being with someone.

The mothers were asked to choose the three most likely developmental
influences, among the eight presented to them, and to rank them in order of
importance. Scores of 3, 2, and 1 were assigned to ranks of 1, 2, and 3
respectively, so that higher scores would represent greater importance, and
a score of 0 was assigned to each influence not ranked among the top three.
Scores were then summed across pairs of similar influences to reflect the
perceived importance of four general proactive strategies: (a) the child's
personal experiences in the social milieu (*personal experiences* = Strategies
4 and 8 from the preceding list); (b) imitation of parents and peers
(*observational learning* = Strategies 2 and 6); (c) receipt of explanations
offered by adult socializing agents (*explanations* = Strategies 5 and 7); and
(d) parental commands and use of reinforcement contingencies (*directive
teaching* = Strategies 1 and 3). These summary scores could range from 0
to 5.

The results of our data analyses revealed that mothers thought that
preschoolers best learn the four relevant social skills through personal
experiences; thereafter, the mothers were most likely to suggest the importance of observational learning, followed by the use of adult explanations
or inductive techniques. Mothers were most reticent to suggest the use of
directive teaching. The resultant numerical means for each of the strategies
described were significantly different from each other.

Interestingly, the only significant interaction found was between the social skill of being able to resolve conflict and type of strategy. Mothers were *more* likely to suggest adult explanations or inductive techniques, and *less* likely to suggest observational learning as the means by which to socialize conflict resolution than they were for the skills of getting acquainted with others or persuading others to do what they wanted. Thus, it appeared that when the behavior to be socialized involved the possibility of conflict, a more hands-on approach was advocated by the mothers.

Given that directive teaching was the least preferred proactive socialization method of maternal choice, we considered it to be non-normative. We then asked what kinds of factors may be associated, predictively, with this authoritarian form of parenting. Naturally, we drew from our information processing model, to seek evidence concerning the extent to which the maternal choice of these non-normative, directive socialization strategies could be predicted from indices of stress and perceived social support. Multiple regression analyses revealed that the choice of *directive* strategies for the socialization of getting acquainted with others, resolving conflicts, and persuading others could be significantly predicted by socioeconomic hardship. The use of directive strategies for the socialization of getting acquainted with others was significantly predicted by both economic hardship and the recent experience of many negative life events. These findings are clearly consistent with our model; stressors impinging on the family appeared to have some influence on the ways that mothers thought about the socialization of their children's social skills. Specifically, it appeared that the experience of stress could be used to predict whether mothers choose to use non-normative authoritarian techniques to proactively socialize their children's social skills.

To summarize, mothers believed that self-mediated learning was the primary means by which children learn to be socially competent. Direct tutelage was believed to be a relatively poor strategy. These findings may reflect the parental assumption that "good things" are best learned in a painless, self-directed fashion and that children might think more poorly of these "good things" (i.e., socially competent behaviors) if they were taught in a directive, authoritarian fashion. This seems like a plausible argument, and it sets up our next assumption that parents' ideas about proactive socialization may differ significantly from their notions about how best to react to children's maladaptive behaviors. More specifically, we expected that mothers' ideas about how they would react to their children's displays of *incompetent* social behavior would be more directive than their ideas about how they should best proactively socialize social competence.

Mothers' Reactive Beliefs Concerning Aggression and Withdrawal.   As with our investigation of mothers' proactive beliefs, our attempts to examine mothers' reactive beliefs about maladaptive social behaviors had a descriptive, normative focus (Mills & Rubin, 1990a). The mothers of those preschoolers whose ideas about the proactive socialization of social skills comprised the data base for the study described earlier responded individually to four hypothetical scenarios involving their own preschool-aged child. Two of the scenarios involved their children behaving consistently in an aggressive manner; two scenarios described their children behaving consistently in an anxious, withdrawn manner. The mothers were asked how they would react *affectively* if their preschooler consistently displayed these social behaviors. We also asked them to what causes they would attribute these behaviors, and what strategies they thought they would use to modify them.

When we began our program of research, we knew little about parents' judgments of children's social behaviors; however, we did know that parents expect their children to have developed some control over aggression and some skill at social participation by early childhood (Goodnow, Cashmore, Cotton, & Knight, 1984). We knew also that by middle childhood, if not sooner, aggression and social withdrawal are perceived by parents as problematic (Bacon & Ashmore, 1985). Thus, we considered parents' *emotional reactions* to be an important facet of their response to these behaviors. In our first study, we speculated that when parents are cognizant of their children's aggression and/or withdrawal, their emotional response would be, in some way, negative. Drawing from Grusec, Dix, and Mills (1982), who showed that antisocial acts such as aggression make parents feel more angry than other types of transgressions, we postulated that anger would be the predominant reaction to aggression and a stronger reaction to aggression than to social withdrawal. Given the total lack of similar information about emotional reactions to withdrawal, we asked simply what the predominant affective response is. Finally, we examined whether the reported affective responses differed for aggression and withdrawal.

Our second focus concerned the beliefs parents have about the *causes* of their children's social behaviors. As Dix and his colleagues (Dix & Grusec, 1985; Dix, Ruble, & Zambarano, 1989) suggested, it may well be that parents' attributions about the causes of their children's behaviors influence their choice of parenting strategies. Because norms for what is or is not appropriate social behavior change with the age of the child, it may be that parents attribute few of these behaviors to traits or enduring dispositions. Thus, it did not seem likely to us that parents of preschoolers would attribute either aggression or withdrawal to traits or permanent dispositions in the child. We asked, then, to what causes parents attribute these behaviors, and whether there are any differences between aggression and withdrawal in the types of causes that predominate in parents' thinking.

Our third focus concerned the *influence strategies* parents believe they would use in responding to aggression and withdrawal in early childhood. Grusec and her colleagues (Grusec, Dix, & Mills, 1982; Grusec & Kugyndin, 1980) reported that parents suggest the use of more force with antisocial acts than with other types of transgressions. Consequently, we predicted that parents would report more highly power assertive strategies for dealing with aggression than for dealing with social withdrawal. But we also wanted to know specifically what it is that parents think they would do about each of these behaviors, that is, what kinds of power assertive strategies they would use with aggression, and what sorts of reactions they would have to social withdrawal.

The results of this study indicated clearly that mothers' predominant emotional reaction to their children's aggressive behavior was concern. Next, mothers reported being angry and disappointed. In response to the consistent display of social withdrawal, mothers most frequently reported that they would feel concerned and puzzled. Not surprisingly, mothers reported feeling more angry in response to aggression than withdrawal and more puzzled about withdrawal than aggression.

Both aggressive and solitary behaviors were attributed, for the most part, to transient emotional states such as mood or fatigue. However, mothers were more likely to explain aggression than withdrawal on the basis of age or age-related factors (e.g., a stage or phase that she will grow out of).

Finally, mothers suggested that they would most likely react to their child's aggression with moderately power assertive strategies (e.g., reasoning, use of gentle instructions) and to withdrawal with low power assertive techniques (e.g., redirecting the child). Interestingly, mothers were more likely to advocate high and moderate power assertion in response to aggression than to withdrawal, and to suggest low power assertive strategies in reaction to withdrawal than aggression. Taken together, the data demonstrated that by early childhood, mothers respond more negatively and coercively to aggressive behavior than to withdrawal.

Another major concern of our first study was the question of *why* it is that parents may differ from one another in their reactive socialization beliefs. This is an important question to address if one speculates that parental beliefs about their choice of socialization strategies is the cognitive variable most closely related to their actual socialization behavior. Drawing from our information processing model, we postulated that strategy choice may be influenced by parents' emotional reactions to and causal attributions about their children's problematic behaviors, and that these emotions and attributions, in turn, are influenced by the socioecological and personal-social setting conditions under which parenting occurs. To explore these relations, evidence was sought concerning the extent to which parental choice of socialization strategies could be predicted from parental emotional responses and causal attributions and indices of stress and perceived social support.

One specific hypothesis we tested was that the choice of *directive or coercive* reactions to problematic social behaviors could be predicted by negative maternal feelings about these behaviors. We found clear support for this hypothesis; the choice of coercion was, indeed, associated with more intense negative emotional responses (anger, disappointment, embarrassment) to *both* aggression and social withdrawal. This finding supported the link often drawn between angry emotional climates and abusive and coercive parental behavior toward children (e.g., Patterson, 1982). In this earlier work, the presence of anger in family environments has been inferred rather than measured directly, and the contribution of emotions other than anger has generally been neglected. Our data suggested that a complex *mix* of negative emotions best predict parental choice of power assertion.

But what other factors lead mothers to choose high power assertive strategies in reaction to aggression and withdrawal? As our model suggested, we discovered that the prediction of maternal choice of high power or coercive strategies could be further improved when life circumstances were taken into account. Specifically, low socioeconomic status was associated with stronger negative emotional reactions *and* the choice of more coercive strategies in reaction to both aggression and withdrawal. This was especially true when mothers perceived that they had little social support available to them. Thus, the availability of a social support network appeared to buffer the choice of coercive reactive strategies for modifying their children's unskilled social behaviors. Finally, we found that if mothers experienced difficult life circumstances, they would choose high power assertive strategies, but only in those cases in which they responded to withdrawal with anger. In short, anger mediated the relation between difficult life circumstances and the choice of power assertive responses to withdrawn behavior.

From our descriptive data analyses, we learned that mothers sometimes choose *not* to respond to their children's maladaptive social behavior, particularly when it takes the form of social withdrawal. This finding prompted us to test a second hypothesis, which was concerned with the prediction of a maternal reactive choice of "no response." We hypothesized that the choice of not responding to socially maladaptive behavior could best be predicted by (a) the belief that the behavior is caused by dispositional factors and by (b) the presence of unfavorable life circumstances. That is, it might be that parents who believe that a child is predisposed to behaving in a given fashion will think that there is little they can do to alter the child's behavior. The impact of stress might also predict a response of maternal inaction insofar as this response may indicate perceptions of helplessness while under stress. This hypothesis was confirmed, and held true regardless of the availability of social support. However, the hypothesis was confirmed only for social withdrawal but not for aggression.

In summary, our findings attest not only to the impact of socioecological circumstances on parental emotions, attributional beliefs, and influence strategies, but also to the fact that maternal reactions differ for aggression and withdrawal. Not only did the mothers' emotions, causal attributions, and influence strategies differ depending on whether the behavior displayed was aggression or social withdrawal, but the cognitive-affective processes involved in mothers' choice of influence strategies also differed for these two types of behavior. This finding raises the question of why mothers differentiate between aggression and withdrawal. For example, why were mothers more likely to say they would intervene to modify social withdrawal when they attributed it to a trait (usually shyness) than when they did not? Could it be that mothers intervene less with this type of behavior because they share culturally acquired beliefs that shyness is the manifestation of a trait and that traits are not malleable? It is possible that behaviors believed to be impervious to social influence are attributed to dispositional causes (Kelley, 1971). The finding that mothers were more puzzled about social withdrawal than aggression suggests that they may be uncertain about how to influence this behavior and, consequently, they may perceive themselves as having little influence over it. This belief may, then, become self-fulfilling, engendering the inference that social withdrawal is the product of a trait in the child and hence that it is futile to try to change it. With aggression, on the other hand, our data hint at the possibility that considerations of malleability do not enter into the decision to intervene.

Whatever the reasons may be for mothers' distinctions between aggression and social withdrawal, the fact that they differentiate between these behaviors has important implications with regard to the differential socialization of aggression and social participation. As we have just suggested, for example, mothers may be somewhat inclined, for good or ill, to let social participation skills unfold without their intervention. Of course, this presupposes that mothers' ideas and feelings about aggression and social withdrawal do not change over time. Because our information-processing model postulates that parental behavior is guided by parental beliefs, it would seem logical to suggest that changes in beliefs should be associated with changes in behavior. Furthermore, given that changes may occur over time with regard to any of the factors affecting parental beliefs, it follows that beliefs may also change. Interestingly, however, we know next to nothing about the degree to which parents actually do change their beliefs and attitudes in response to changing conditions, what kinds of changes affect parental beliefs and what kinds do not, or what processes underlie change and continuity (Goodnow, 1988).

Given the developmental nature of social behavior, changes associated with the age of the child are obvious ones to consider (e.g., Dix, Ruble, Grusec, & Nixon, 1986; Dix, Ruble, & Zambarano, 1989). For example, it is well known that children become less aggressive (Parke & Slaby, 1983) and more sociable (e.g., Rubin, Watson, & Jambor, 1978) with age. Thus, the display of either aggressive or socially inhibited behavior in 6-year-olds may elicit a different set of parental reactions and beliefs than such displays in 4-year-olds. Do parents really think as much like social developmentalists as we might imagine; that is, do age-related changes in children affect parents' ideas about social behavior? In our next study, we addressed this question by recontacting our original sample of mothers 2 years later in order to assess the continuity of maternal beliefs across the transition period from early to middle childhood (ages 4 to 6).

Continuity in Maternal Proactive and Reactive Beliefs.   Of the original sample, 45 mothers (of 21 girls and 24 boys) participated in a second phase of the study by completing the same set of questionnaires that they had before (Mills & Rubin, 1990b). They were asked to rank-order four general proactive strategies (personal experience, observations of others, receiving explanations, directive teaching) in terms of their importance for the development of four social skills (getting acquainted with someone, getting accepted into an ongoing play group, resolving peer conflicts, and persuading other children to carry out one's wishes). The hypothetical incidents of peer-directed aggression and withdrawal that had been presented to mothers when their children were 4 years old were considered equally appropriate for 6-year-olds; consequently, the identical descriptions were presented to mothers. Mothers were asked to indicate their emotional reactions to, causal attributions about, and likely behavioral responses to these incidents. As in the initial study, the mothers completed questionnaires concerning recent negative life events, the availability of social support, and socioeconomic status.

Data analyses assessing changes over the 2-year interval in mothers' beliefs about the importance of the four general proactive strategies for teaching children social skills revealed that mothers continued to consider personal experience to be the most important strategy and directive teaching to be the least important, with observational learning and explanation being ranked as intermediate. However, mothers were significantly more likely at Time 2 than at Time 1 to advocate observational learning as a means by which children learn social skills. On the other hand, inductive teaching or the use of adult explanation was less often advocated as a socialization method of choice at Time 2.

There were also minimal amounts of change in the strategies mothers said they would use to deal with their children's *maladaptive* social behaviors. The modal strategy was still moderate power assertion for dealing with aggression and low power assertion for dealing with social withdrawal; it was still the case that high and moderate power strategies were suggested more frequently for aggression than for social withdrawal, and low power techniques, information-seeking, and planning strategies were suggested more frequently for withdrawal than for aggression. Despite these similarities, a number of changes were found. For example, there was a significant increase in the extent to which low-power strategies were reported in reaction to both withdrawal and aggression, a decrease in reported information-seeking in response to both withdrawal and aggression, and a decrease in choice of "no response" to displays of social withdrawal. In short, as their children increased in age, mothers were more likely to suggest that they would deal firsthand with their children's maladaptive behavior and less likely to suggest that they would ignore it.

Similarly with causal attributions, mothers continued to attribute both aggression and withdrawal most often to transient internal states and least often to acquired habits, and to distinguish between aggression and withdrawal by citing age-related factors more as the cause of aggression than of social withdrawal. The only change found over time was a decrease in the extent to which mothers attributed either of these types of behavior to age-related factors.

Mothers' emotional responses also showed relatively little change. At both times, they reacted to aggression primarily with concern, and secondarily with anger, surprise, and disappointment; they reacted to social withdrawal primarily with concern and puzzlement, and secondarily with surprise; and they reported feeling more angry about aggression than withdrawal and more puzzled about withdrawal than aggression. They also reported stronger reactions to withdrawal if their child was a girl than if their child was a boy. The only change found over time occurred with aggression: Mothers' *negative* emotional reactions to aggression increased in strength if the child was a girl, and decreased if the child was a boy, such that by Time 2, mothers of girls felt significantly more negative about displays of aggression than mothers of boys.

In summary, there were no dramatic changes in mothers' proactive or reactive beliefs over the transition from early to middle childhood. The changes observed may be attributed to several different factors, and few of them appear to have been responsive to the perception of developmental changes in the child. The assignment of more importance to observational learning and less importance to explanation, and the reporting of more low-power influence strategies all may be taken to reflect mothers' awareness of advances in their children's ability to think abstractly and to regulate their own behavior with less "hands-on" direction. This particular finding is also suggestive of the significance of parents' *perceptions* of the zone of proximal development (Palacios, Gonzales, & Moreno, 1987; Wertsch,

1984). In other words, the belief in less directive parenting strategies with the increasing age of the child may be an indication that parents anticipate an increase in self-regulation with age.

Other changes found in the study seem attributable to maternal "timetables" with respect to the acquisition of certain skills. For example, maternal expectations about the age by which children should have acquired control over aggressive impulses and the ability to participate socially may be responsible for the decrease in mothers' tendency to attribute these behaviors to age-related factors, and for their tendency to respond more to social withdrawal (that is, to choose low-power solutions rather than not to respond at all). Thus, our data suggest that aggression and withdrawal may be more easily excused as reflecting immaturity, or a passing phase, in early childhood than at school entry.

Not surprisingly, parental timetables are often moderated by gender-related expectations; these expectations may explain why mothers became more upset about aggression over time when it was displayed by daughters and less upset when it was displayed by sons. If these changes were indeed based on timetables, then they likely originated more from culturally acquired expectations than from expectancies formed as a result of developmental changes perceived to have occurred in the child.

Finally, one change may have been the result of the *mothers'* growing knowledge of their children's characteristic behavior patterns. Over time, mothers reported less information-seeking in response to displays of aggression and withdrawal, suggesting to us that they may have felt more knowledgeable about the contextual factors governing their child's displays of aggressive and withdrawn behaviors.

In our first set of longitudinal data analyses, we examined the extent to which mothers, as a group, changed their reactive and proactive beliefs. These analyses, however, tell us nothing about the relative consistency or stability of beliefs over time. To address this question, we computed a series of correlational analyses to examine whether there was any relation between mothers' earlier and later beliefs. Analyses assessing the stability of mothers' beliefs about the importance of the four general proactive strategies for teaching children social skills revealed, by and large, that these beliefs were moderately stable across the 2-year interval (correlation coefficients ranged from .34 to .50). Consistent with this finding, there was also moderate stability across time in maternal directiveness (choice of high-power strategies) for dealing with aggression, $r = .41$, $p < .01$, and moderate-power strategies for dealing with social withdrawal, $r = .30$, $p < .05$. Other influence strategies suggested by mothers (low power assertion, planning strategies, and no response) were also significantly stable, but only for social withdrawal (rs ranged from .27 to .78).

There was also greater stability for social withdrawal than for aggression in mothers' attributions about the causes of their children's maladaptive social behaviors. For social withdrawal, there was moderate stability in the extent to which mothers made attributions to traits, transient states, and situational factors (rs ranged from .27 to .56); for aggression, there was stability only in attributions to situational factors ($r = .31$). Emotional responses, on the other hand, were generally quite stable for both types of behavior (rs generally in the .40 to .50 range), the most noteworthy exception being that anger was stable for aggression ($r = .37$) but not for social withdrawal.

On the whole, then, there was statistically significant, albeit modest, stability in mothers' proactive and reactive beliefs across the 2 years. Thus, although mothers may have changed their beliefs somewhat from one time period to the next, their relative standing within the sample remained fairly stable vis-à-vis their reported emotions, attributions, and strategies.

Next, we attempted to determine whether there was stability across time in the concurrent relations between mothers' choices of high-power strategies and their other beliefs and life circumstances. First, we assessed the extent to which mothers' choice of high-power strategies for dealing with displays of *aggression* at Time 2 could be predicted from the following Time 2 variables: the strength of mothers' negative emotions about aggression, socioeconomic status, perceived social support, and the multiplicative interaction between socioeconomic status and social support. The results of this analysis indicated that the choice of highly power-assertive strategies for dealing with aggression was significantly predicted by socioeconomic status ($R^2 = .10$) as well as by the multiplicative interaction of socioeconomic status and perceived support ($R^2 = .09$). Low socioeconomic status was more strongly related to the choice of high-power strategies when mothers perceived that they had little social support available to them. Thus, just as we had found 2 years earlier, the availability of a social support network appeared to buffer mothers' choices of coercive reactive strategies for modifying their children's unskilled social behaviors.

We then assessed the extent to which mothers' choice of high-power strategies for dealing with *social withdrawal* at Time 2 could be predicted from the following Time 2 variables: the strength of mothers' negative emotions about social withdrawal, socioeconomic status, perceived social support, and the multiplicative interaction between socioeconomic status and social support. "High power" for dealing with social withdrawal was defined as the choice of high- or moderate-power strategies, as low-power strategies were the modal choice for this type of behavior. The results of the analysis indicated that the choice of high-power strategies for dealing with social withdrawal was significantly predicted by the presence of strong negative emotional reactions to displays of social withdrawal ($R^2 = .13$), low socioeconomic status ($R^2 = .09$), and the multiplicative interaction between socioeconomic status and social support ($R^2 = .12$). Again, socioeconomic status was more strongly related to the choice of high-power strategies when perceived support was low than when it was high.

Next, we assessed the extent to which the importance mothers placed on *proactive* strategies relatively high in power assertion (directive teaching and explanation) could be predicted concurrently from mothers' life circumstances. At Time 1, mothers' beliefs could be predicted from low socioeconomic status ($R^2 = .17$). At Time 2, they could be predicted from the multiplicative interaction between socioeconomic status and perceived support ($R^2 = .53$); socioeconomic status was more strongly related to the choice of high-power strategies when perceived support was low than when it was high.

In summary, these analyses suggest that there is continuity in the factors that concurrently predict mothers' choice of high-power reactive and proactive strategies. High-power strategies were most likely to be suggested by mothers experiencing low socioeconomic status and reporting a low level of social support.

Finally, we attempted to determine whether mothers' choice of high-power reactive and proactive strategies at Time 2 could be predicted from their beliefs and/or life circumstances at Time 1. With regard to mothers' choice of high-power reactive strategies, we found that there were predictive relations for aggression but not for social withdrawal. Regression and partial-correlation analyses indicated that there was a predictive relation between mothers' earlier socioeconomic status and their later choice of high-power strategies for dealing with aggressive behavior, and that this relation was more attributable to the temporal stability of mothers' strategy choices than it was to the stability of socioeconomic status over time. With regard to mothers' beliefs about the importance of high-power *proactive* strategies, the analyses indicated that earlier occupational status significantly predicted later beliefs. Once again, the relation could not be attributed simply to the stability of socioeconomic status over time.

Taking all the findings together, there appears to have been some stability across the 2 years in mothers' proactive and reactive beliefs and in the relations between their socioeconomic status and their choice of high-power reactive and proactive strategies. Moreover, earlier socioeconomic status could predict later beliefs, and these predictive relations could not be attributed simply to the stability of socioeconomic status over time. Because, in one case, earlier beliefs could explain the predictive relation, we are inclined to think that maternal cognitions may play an important role in mediating relations between parents' earlier life circumstances and their later beliefs.

According to our information-processing model, maternal cognitions are associated not only with socioecological and personal-social setting conditions but also with dispositional or other characteristics of the child. To investigate this aspect of our model, we also examined maternal cognitions in subgroups of mothers of extremely aggressive, extremely anxious/ withdrawn, and average preschool-age children.

Proactive and Reactive Beliefs of Mothers Whose Children are Aggressive or Withdrawn. Up to now, there has been a limited focus on individual differences in parenting beliefs (Goodnow, 1988). Given neglect of this issue, and given our interest in the characteristics of children that may allow us to distinguish between *maternal* belief systems, we identified small groups of extremely aggressive and extremely withdrawn children, as well as a larger comparison group of average children. Subsequently, we compared the mothers of these children with regard to their proactive beliefs about how socially competent behaviors are acquired and their reactive beliefs concerning the origins of aggression and withdrawal in childhood (Rubin & Mills, 1990).

The study began with approximately 120 four-year-olds. Two methods were used to evaluate children's social adaptation: observations of free play and teacher ratings of social behaviors. Following procedures described by Rubin (1982, 1986), each child was observed during free play for 30, nonconsecutive 10-sec time samples each day over a period of 5 nonconsecutive days. The frequencies of isolate behavior (ISOPLAY, defined as the *total* frequency of solitary play + unoccupied behavior + onlooker behavior) and negative behavior (PNEGINT, defined as the proportion of all social behavior coded as negative) were of particular interest. Teacher ratings were obtained using the *Preschool Behavior Questionnaire,* a 30-item scale that best yields two factors for preschoolers and elementary-school children (Moller & Rubin, 1988): an internalizing factor (TRINT) consisting of items describing fearfulness, anxiety, and solitude, and an externalizing factor (TREXT) consisting of items describing hostile-aggressive and impulsive-distractible behaviors. Each child received two factor scores (TRINT and TREXT). Higher factor scores were indicative of greater internalizing and externalizing difficulties.

From the observational and teacher rating data we used a multimethod, extreme groups targeting procedure to identify three groups of children: *Aggressive-Externalizing (A-E)* children, *Withdrawn-Internalizing (W-I)* children, and *Average (AVG)* children (Rubin & Mills, 1990). This procedure resulted in the identification of 6 *W-I* children (5% of the sample), 10 *A-E* children (8% of the sample), and 60 *AVG* children (50% of the sample). Forty-five children could not be classified using this procedure (37% of the sample). By and large, this group was composed of children whose scores exceeded the criteria on only one of the two measures.

Information concerning mothers' proactive and reactive beliefs about social development was obtained in a manner identical to that described previously.

Proactive Teaching Strategies.   For each of the four social skills — getting acquainted with someone new, getting accepted into an ongoing play group of unfamiliar peers, resolving conflicts with peers, and persuading other children to do what one wants — scores reflecting the *importance* of each of four general proactive strategies — directive teaching, observational learning, explanation, and personal experience — were computed. The results indicated a significant effect of target group for only one of the four proactive strategies: The mothers of W-I children placed significantly more importance on *directive teaching* than did the mothers of A-E children. Both these groups of mothers considered directive teaching to be significantly more important than did the mothers of AVG children.

Reactive Strategies to Withdrawal and Aggression.   Mean proportions reflecting the extent to which mothers reported *high* and *low coercion* for dealing with aggression and social withdrawal, and the extent to which they reported *indirect or no-response strategies* (those which did not involve an immediate reaction to the child's behavior, such as seeking information, arranging opportunities for peer experience, or simply choosing not to respond) were first computed. Subsequent data analyses revealed that for both social withdrawal and aggression, mothers of W-I children were more likely to report highly coercive strategies than the mothers of either the A-E or the AVG children. Conversely, the mothers of W-I children were *less* likely to report indirect–no-response strategies than were the mothers of either the A-E or the AVG children. Mothers of A-E children did not differ from mothers of AVG children in the extent to which they reported highly coercive strategies, but they were more likely to report indirect–no response strategies than mothers of AVG children. Mothers of AVG children were more likely to report the use of low power coercion than the mothers of either W-I or A-E children.

Emotional Reactions to Withdrawal and Aggression.   Our data analyses revealed that mothers of AVG children were more puzzled about displays of withdrawal and aggression than the mothers of A-E and W-I children. Mothers of both A-E and W-I children, however, reported that they would feel more angry about these behaviors than mothers of AVG children. Moreover, mothers of W-I children suggested that they would feel more disappointed, embarrassed, and guilty than mothers of both A-E and AVG children. There were nonsignificant differences between the two latter groups.

Causal Attributions About Withdrawal and Aggression.   We found a significant effect of Target Group (W-I, A-E, AVG) for two of the five types of attribution: attributions to a *trait* in the child and to *age-related factors.* Mothers of W-I children were significantly more likely to attribute both aggression and withdrawal to a trait in the child than did mothers of AVG children. Mothers of A-E children did not differ from either of the other two target groups.

For attributions to *age-related factors,* a significant interaction was found between target group and type of behavior. Subsequent analyses revealed that mothers of A-E children were more likely to attribute aggression to age-related factors than mothers of either the W-I or the AVG children; the two latter groups did not differ significantly. There were no differences between any of the three target groups in the extent to which mothers attributed social withdrawal to age-related factors.

Summary.   Despite the relatively small number of children in each of the two extreme groups identified on the basis of multiple criteria, we found, nevertheless, that a coherent pattern of significant differences existed in the ways that the mothers of Aggressive-Externalizing (A-E), Withdrawn-Internalizing (W-I), and Average (AVG) children thought about adaptive and maladaptive social development.

Mothers of W-I children placed greater importance than did mothers of AVG children on the directive teaching of social skills. They were also more likely to choose high power strategies for dealing with unskilled behaviors than the other mothers. These findings suggest that mothers of W-I children believe strongly in a directive approach to the *proactive* teaching of social skills, and in their *reactive* strategies they may be described as overcontrolling. Interestingly, our data fit well with the conclusion drawn by others that anxious withdrawal in childhood is associated, and perhaps causally so, with parental overcontrol (e.g., Hetherington & Martin, 1986). To our knowledge, however, this link between parental overcontrol and anxious withdrawal had not been reported previously as an empirical finding.

The findings concerning maternal emotional reactions to and causal attributions about social withdrawal and aggression provide some initial clues to explain why mothers of anxious-withdrawn children may be overcontrolling. Mothers of W-I children were significantly more likely than other mothers to blame themselves when their children displayed unskilled social behaviors. They felt not only more angry and disappointed in their children than mothers of AVG children but also more guilty and embarrassed. These responses of guilt and embarrassment suggest that mothers of W-I children may provide them with a significant and highly salient model for an internalizing style of emotional regulation. Such emotions may also provoke an overdirective pattern of parenting behavior in order to assure the production of adaptive behavior or the negation of maladaptive behavior. Obviously, at this time, we cannot be certain that these factors actually contribute to their children's development of an internalizing style, but they would undoubtedly help to perpetuate any tendency these children may already have to internalize their emotions and to behave in an anxious-withdrawn manner. In summary, our data provide an initial empirical hint that anxious-withdrawn children are exposed to a rather complex mix of conflicting emotions and attributions in their mothers, and that mothers of internalizing children may feel overidentified with and somewhat ambivalent toward their child (Levy, 1943; Parker, 1983).

Mothers of Aggressive-Externalizing (A-E) children were quite different than those of W-I children vis-à-vis their pattern of beliefs and feelings. Although these mothers believed more strongly than mothers of AVG children in taking a directive approach to the proactive teaching of social skills, and although their children were highly aggressive and they indicated that this kind of behavior certainly made them feel angry, they were nevertheless *more* inclined than the other groups of mothers to choose very *indirect* strategies or *no strategies at all* to deal with both aggression and withdrawal. Thus, for mothers of A-E children there was some disparity between their proactive beliefs, which suggested a preference for highly directive parenting styles, and their choice of reactive strategies, which suggested a preference for a laissez-faire style.

What may explain this apparent disparity? Our best guess, at this time, is that the laissez-faire response to their children's aggression stems from their attribution of aggressive behaviors to age-related factors. Thus, it may be that these mothers' attempts to teach social skills directively may be unsuccessful; moreover, they may be somewhat intimidated by their child's aggressiveness. Perhaps they attribute their child's behavior and their own lack of success to short-lived age-related factors and choose less direct strategies in order to lessen their anxiety, avoid confrontation, and wait out what they hope will be a passing phase. It seems to us, then, that these mothers are attempting to normalize their children's behavior despite the fact that it makes them feel quite angry. Such conflicting emotions and attributions could perpetuate a high level of aggression in the child in precisely the way Patterson and his colleagues have found; that is, by initiating an erratic pattern of behavioral interchanges in which undesirable behavior is sometimes rewarded or ignored as the parent attempts to avoid confrontation, and desirable behavior is sometimes, out of frustration, dealt with in an authoritarian fashion (Patterson, 1982; 1986).

The scenario we have described for mothers of A-E children is admittedly highly speculative. Given that our data were correlational in nature, it is clearly impossible to determine the direction of causality for the relations found. Thus, we cannot tell whether mothers' beliefs evolved in response to their children's behaviors or whether children's behaviors developed as a result of maternal beliefs. Most probably, the relation was bidirectional. One implication of the reciprocal association between maternal cognitions and child behavior may be that it makes the pattern of parent–child interaction a complementary one. The findings from our first study of individual differences help to call attention to the kind of information that is needed to further our understanding of the complementary patterns of parent–child interaction associated with the development of socioemotional difficulties in childhood.

CONCLUSIONS

We began this chapter by indicating why it is that the study of parental beliefs and ideas about children's social development represents an important and timely area of psychological enquiry. Drawing from an information-processing perspective, we suggested that parental beliefs are likely influenced by socioecological and personal-social circumstances, and in turn, that these beliefs are influential in determining parental behavior and child development. The data we have described herein provide an initial snapshot of the relations between different aspects of our guiding model. For example, we have demonstrated meaningful linkages between parental attributions, emotions, and their choice of socialization strategies. The influence of socioecological and personal-social settings factors on parental beliefs was also ascertained. Thus, mothers who reported difficult life circumstances were more likely to suggest that they would respond to their children's maladaptive social behaviors with coercion; as expected, however, the suggested use of such reactive strategies was qualified by the availability of social support. Finally, we have provided an initial data base for the examination of the stability of parental beliefs and for the relations between beliefs and children's behaviors. These data provide a productive beginning for our programmatic research on the relations between parental beliefs, parenting behaviors, and children's social competence.

But it must be acknowledged that we are only a small step into our research program. As of this writing, we are investigating the relations between maternal proactive and reactive beliefs as assessed in an interview and maternal socialization strategies as observed in the research laboratory. The situations we are observing in the lab are designed to mirror the scenarios described in the beliefs interviews. For example, we are asking the mothers what, if anything, they would do to help their children initiate friendships or to resolve object conflicts. The lab situations involve the meeting of an unfamiliar same-age peer and the presentation of a limited number of toys to the children in the presence of the mother. We expect that these situations will "pull for" maternal action of one sort or another; whether the actions correspond to the mother's words is a question remaining to be answered. At the same time, we are also examining possible developmental differences in the relations between beliefs and behaviors; furthermore, these relations are being studied in a sample of mothers of extremely aggressive, extremely anxious and withdrawn, and average 6-, 8-, and 10-year-old children. These small steps thus carry us well beyond our initial studies of beliefs and cognition in mothers of preschool age children.

Our ongoing studies, however, are limited in two important respects. First, we currently have no idea whether the findings reported herein would bear any resemblance to those found in identical studies conducted in non-North American, non-Western cultures or in nonmiddle-class North American samples. To this end, we have initiated a new set of maternal beliefs studies in The People's Republic of China as well as in a high-risk sample of young, mostly unmarried, and poor mothers residing in Seattle, Washington.

Perhaps the major omission in our work has been our systematic neglect of 50% of the parenting unit. Despite a good deal of lip service paid to the need for studying the roles and contributions of fathers vis-à-vis child development, researchers have not done well to advance our knowledge base. Although it is true that the study of fathers may muddle up the relationships picture, and although the inclusion of both mothers and fathers will make it more difficult to analyze and interpret our data about the significance of parental beliefs and parental behaviors for child development, it is nevertheless time to stop neglecting fathers. On this last note of admitted ignorance, the reader has a hint about where we plan to take our research program in the 1990s.

ACKNOWLEDGMENTS

Preparation of this chapter was aided by a Killam Research Fellowship to author Rubin and by a Social Sciences and Humanities Research Council of Canada Postdoctoral Fellowship to author Mills. The research described herein was supported by grants from the Social Sciences and Humanities Research Council of Canada. We would like to thank Veronica Kallos, Melanie Mann, Karen McEwan, and Margo Rubin for their help in the collection and coding of data.

REFERENCES

Attili, G. (1989). Social competence versus emotional security: The link between home relationships and behavior problems in preschool. In B. Schneider, G. Attili, J. Nadel-

Brulfert, & R. Weissberg (Eds.), *Social competence in developmental perspective* (pp. 293–312). Holland: Kluwer.

Bacon, M. K., & Ashmore, R. D. (1985). How mothers and fathers categorize descriptions of social behavior attributed to daughters and sons. *Social Cognition, 3,* 193–217.

Bandura, A. (1977). *Social learning theory.* Englewood Cliffs, NJ: Prentice-Hall.

Bell, R. Q., & Chapman, M. (1986). Child effects in studies using experimental or brief longitudinal approaches to socialization. *Developmental Psychology, 22,* 595–603.

Belsky, J. (1984). The determinants of parenting: A process model. *Child Development, 55,* 83–96.

Belsky, J., Robins, E., & Gamble, W. (1984). The determinants of parental competence: Toward a contextual theory. In M. Lewis (Ed.), *Beyond the dyad* (pp. 251–279). New York: Plenum.

Booth, C. L., Rose-Krasnor, L., & Rubin, K. H. (1991). Relating preschoolers' social competence and their mothers' parenting behaviors to early attachment security and high risk status. *Journal of Social and Personal Relationships, 8,* 363–382.

Bowlby, J. (1973). *Attachment and loss, Vol. 2. Separation.* New York: Basic.

Colletta, N. (1979). Support systems after divorce: Incidence and impact. *Journal of Marriage and the Family, 41,* 837–846.

Conger, R. D., McCarty, J. A., Yang, R. K., Lahey, B. B., & Kropp, J. P. (1984). Perception of child, child-rearing values, and emotional distress as mediating links between environmental stressors and observed maternal behavior. *Child Development, 55,* 2234–2247.

Dameron, L. E. (1955). Mother–child interaction in the development of self-restraint. *Journal of Genetic Psychology, 86,* 289–308.

Desfossés, E., & Bouchard, C. (1987, April). *Using coercive behaviors with children: Stressors, conflictual relationships and lack of support in the life of mothers.* Paper presented at the Biennial Convention of the Society for Research in Child Development, Baltimore.

Dix, T. H., & Grusec, J. E. (1985). Parent attribution processes in the socialization of children. In I. E. Sigel (Ed.), *Parental belief systems: The psychological consequences for children* (pp. 201–233). Hillsdale, NJ: Lawrence Erlbaum Associates.

Dix, T. H., Ruble, D., Grusec, J. E., & Nixon, S. (1986). Social cognition in parents: Inferential and affective reactions to children of three age levels. *Child Development, 57,* 879–894.

Dix, T. H., Ruble, D. N., & Zambarano, R. J. (1989). Mothers' implicit theories of discipline: Child effects, parent effects, and the attribution process. *Child Development, 60,* 1373–1391.

Elder, G. H., Caspi, A., & Burton, L. M. (1988). Adolescent transition in developmental perspective: Sociological and historical insights. In M. R. Gunnar & W. A. Collins (Eds.), *Minnesota Symposia on Child Psychology* (Vol. 21, pp. 151–179). Hillsdale, NJ: Lawrence Erlbaum Associates.

Elias, M., & Ubriaco, M. (1986). Linking parental beliefs to children's social competence: Toward a cognitive-behavioral assessment model. In R. Ashmore & D. Brodzinsky (Eds.), *Thinking about the family: Views of parents and children* (pp. 147–179). Hillsdale, NJ: Lawrence Erlbaum Associates.

Emmerich, W. (1969). The parental role: A functional cognitive approach. *Monographs of the Society for Research in Child Development, 34,* (8, Serial No. 132).

Engfer, A. (1988). The interrelatedness of marriage and the mother–child relationship. In R. Hinde & J. Stevenson-Hinde (Eds.), *Relations between relationships within families* (pp. 104–118). Oxford: Oxford University Press.

Frank, S., Hole, C. B., Jacobson, S., Justkowski, R., & Huyck, M. (1986). Psychological predictors of parents' sense of confidence and control and self- versus child-focused gratifications. *Developmental Psychology, 22,* 348–355.

Goodnow, J. J. (1988). Parents' ideas, actions, and feelings: Models and methods from developmental and social psychology. *Child Development, 59,* 286–320.

Goodnow, J. J., Cashmore, J., Cotton, S., & Knight, R. (1984). Mothers' developmental timetables in two cultural groups. *International Journal of Psychology, 19,* 193–205.

Goodnow, J. J., Knight, R., & Cashmore, J. (1986). Adult social cognition: Implications of parents' ideas for approaches to development. In M. Perlmutter (Ed.), *Cognitive perspectives on children's social and behavioral development, Vol. 18, The Minnesota Symposia on Child Psychology* (pp. 287–329). Hillsdale, NJ: Lawrence Erlbaum Associates.

Grusec, J. E., Dix, T., & Mills, R. (1982). The effects of type, severity, and victim of children's transgressions on maternal discipline. *Canadian Journal of Behavioural Science, 14,* 276–289.

Grusec, J. E., & Kugyndin, L. (1980). Direction of effect in socialization: A comparison of the parent versus the child's behavior as determinants of disciplinary techniques. *Developmental Psychology, 16,* 1–9.

Hess, R. D., & Shipman, V. C. (1965). Early experience and socialization of cognitive modes in children. *Child Development, 36,* 869–886.

Hetherington, E. M., & Martin, B. (1986). Family factors and psychopathology in children. In H. C. Quay & J. S. Werry (Eds.), *Psychopathological disorders of childhood* (3rd ed., pp. 332–390). New York: Wiley.

Kelley, H. H. (1971). Attribution in social interaction. In E. E. Jones, D. E. Kanouse, H. H. Kelley, R. E. Nisbett, S. Valins, & B. Weiner (Eds.), *Attribution: Perceiving the causes of behavior* (pp. 1–26). Morristown, NJ: General Learning Press.

Kochanska, G., Kuczynski, L., & Radke-Yarrow, M. (1989). Correspondence between mothers' self-reported and observed child-rearing practices. *Child Development, 60,* 56–63.

Ladd, G. W., & Golter, B. S. (1988). Parents' management of preschooler's peer relations: Is it related to children's social competence? *Developmental Psychology, 24,* 109–117.

Levy, D. M. (1943). *Maternal overprotection.* New York: Columbia University Press.

Maccoby, E. E., & Martin, J. A. (1983). Socialization in the context of the family: Parent–child interaction. In E. M. Hetherington (Ed.), *Handbook of child psychology, Vol. 4, Socialization, personality, and social development* (pp. 1–102). New York: Wiley.

McGillicuddy-DeLisi, A. (1982). The relationship between parents' beliefs about development and family constellation, socioeconomic status, and parents' teaching strategies. In L. M. Laosa & I. E. Sigel (Eds.), *Families as learning environments for children* (pp. 261–299). New York: Plenum.

Messick, S. (1983). Assessment of children. In W. Kessen (Ed.), *Handbook of child psychology, Vol. 1, History, theory, and methods* (pp. 477–560). New York: Wiley.

Miller, S. A. (1988). Parents' beliefs about children's cognitive development. *Child Development, 59,* 259–285.

Miller, D. R., & Swanson, G. E. (1958). *The changing American parent.* New York: Wiley.

Mills, R. S. L., & Rubin, K. H. (1990a). Parental beliefs about problematic social behaviors in early childhood. *Child Development, 61,* 138–151.

Mills, R. S. L., & Rubin, K. H. (1990b). *Continuity and change in maternal beliefs about adaptive and maladaptive social behaviors.* Manuscript under review.

Moller, L., & Rubin, K. H. (1988). A psychometric assessment of a two factor solution for the Preschool Behavior Questionnaire in mid-childhood. *Journal of Applied Developmental Psychology, 9,* 167–180.

Palacios, J., Gonzalez, M. M., & Moreno, M. C. (1987). Ideas, interaccion, ambiente educativo y desarrollo. *Infancia y Aprendizaje, 39,* 159–169.

Parke, R. D., & Slaby, R. G. (1983). The development of aggression. In E. M. Hetherington (Ed.), *Handbook of child psychology: Vol. 4, Socialization, personality, and social development* (pp. 547–641). New York: Wiley.

Parker, G. (1983). *Parental overprotection: A risk factor in psychosocial development.* New York: Grune & Stratton.

Parker, J. G., & Asher, S. R. (1987). Peer acceptance and later personal adjustment: Are low-accepted children "at risk?" *Psychological Bulletin, 102,* 357–389.

Patterson, G. R. (1982). *Coercive family processes.* Eugene, OR: Castilia Press.

Patterson, G. R. (1986). Maternal rejection: Determinant or product for deviant child behavior? In W. Hartup & Z. Rubin (Eds.), *Relationships and development.* Hillsdale, NJ: Lawrence Erlbaum Associates.

Putallaz, M. (1987). Maternal behavior and children's sociometric status. *Child Development, 58,* 324–340.

Radke-Yarrow, M., Cummings, E. M., Kuczynski, L., & Chapman, M. (1985). Patterns of attachment in 2- and 3-year-olds in normal families and families with parental depression. *Child Development, 56,* 884–893.

Radke-Yarrow, M., & Richters, J., & Wilson, W. E. (1988). Child development in a network of relationships. In R. A. Hinde & J. Stevenson-Hinde (Eds.), *Relationships within families; mutual influences* (pp. 48–67). Oxford: Clarendon Press.

Ragozin, A. S., Basham, R. B., Crnic, K. A., Greenberg, M. T., & Robinson, N. M. (1982). Effects of maternal age on parenting role. *Developmental Psychology, 18,* 627–634.

Robins, L. N. (1963). The accuracy of parental recall of aspects of child development and child-rearing practices. *Journal of Abnormal and Social Psychology, 33,* 261–270.

Rubin, K. H. (1982). Nonsocial play in preschoolers: Necessarily evil? *Child Development, 53,* 651–657.

Rubin, K. H. (1986). Play, peers and social development. In A. Gottfried & C. Caldwell Brown (Eds.), *Play interactions: The contribution of play materials and parental involvement to child development.* (pp. 163–174). Lexington, MA: Heath.

Rubin, K. H., Hymel, S., & Mills, R. S. L. (1989). Sociability and social withdrawal in childhood: Stability and outcomes. *Journal of Personality, 57,* 238–255.

Rubin, K. H., Hymel, S., Mills, R. S. L., & Rose-Krasnor, L. (1991). Conceptualizing different developmental pathways to and from social isolation in childhood. In D. Cicchetti & S. Toth (Ed.), *Rochester Symposium on Developmental Psychopathology: Vol. 2. Internalizing and externalizing expressions of dysfunction* (pp. 91–122). Hillsdale, NJ: Lawrence Erlbaum Associates.

Rubin, K. H., & Mills, R. S. L. (1990). Maternal beliefs about adaptive and maladaptive social behaviors in normal, aggressive, and withdrawn preschoolers. *Journal of Abnormal Child Psychology, 18,* 419–436.

Rubin, K. H., Mills, R. S. L., & Rose-Krasnor, L. (1989). Maternal beliefs and children's social competence. In B. Schneider, G. Attili, J. Nadel-Brulfert, & R. Weissberg (Eds.), *Social competence in developmental perspective* (pp. 313–331). Holland: Kluwer.

Rubin, K. H., Watson, K., & Jambor, T. (1978). Free play behaviors in preschool and kindergarten children. *Child Development, 49,* 534–536.

Sears, R. R. (1961). Relation of early socialization experiences to aggression in middle childhood. *Journal of Abnormal and Social Psychology, 63,* 466–492.

Sears, R. R., Maccoby, E., & Levin, H. (1957). *Patterns of child rearing.* Evanston, IL: Row, Peterson.

Sigel, I. E. (1982). The relationship between parents' distancing strategies and the child's cognitive behavior. In L. M. Laosa & I. E. Sigel (Eds.), *Families as learning environments for children* (pp. 47–86). New York: Plenum.

Spieker, S. J., & Booth, C. L. (1988). Maternal antecedents of attachment quality. In J. Belsky & T. Nezworski (Eds.), *Clinical implications of attachment* (pp. 95–135). Hillsdale, NJ: Lawrence Erlbaum Associates.

Sroufe, L. A. (1983). Infant–caregiver attachment and patterns of adaptation in preschool: Roots of maladaptation and competence. In M. Perlmutter (Ed.), *Minnesota symposia on child psychology* (Vol. 16, pp. 41–83). Hillsdale, NJ: Lawrence Erlbaum Associates.

Stevenson-Hinde, J., Hinde, R., & Simpson, A. (1986). Behavior at home and friendly or hostile behavior in preschool. In D. Olwens, J. Block, & M. Radke-Yarrow (Eds.), *Development of antisocial and prosocial behavior* (pp. 127–145). Orlando, FL: Academic Press.

Stolz, L. M. (1967). *Influences on parent behavior.* Stanford, CA: Stanford University Press.
Wertsch, J. V. (1984). The zone of proximal development: Some conceptual issues. In B. Rogoff & J. V. Wertsch (Eds.), *Children's learning in the "zone of proximal development."* San Francisco: Jossey-Bass.
Zur-Szprio, S., & Longfellow, C. (1981, April). *Support from fathers: Implications for the well-being of mothers and their children.* Paper presented at the Biennial Meeting of the Society for Research on Child Development, Boston.

3 Stimulating the Child in the Zone of Proximal Development: The Role of Parents' Ideas

Jesús Palacios
María-Mar González
María-Carmen Moreno
University of Seville

The purpose of this chapter is to investigate the relationship between three different types of parents as defined by their ideas about child development and education, and their educational behavior towards their children, as well as to analyze the relations between those two domains (parents' ideas, parents' educational behavior) and developmental outcomes in the child.

Previous studies with our longitudinal sample have allowed us to differentiate three different classes of parents: traditional, modern and paradoxical. The main features of each type of parents are as follows (Palacios, 1988, 1990):

Traditional parents: Parents with a low educational level (primary education or less) living in rural areas. Their developmental expectations are pessimistic, with an innatist concept of the origins of their children's psychological features, a pessimistic perception of their own ability to influence the child and his or her development, educational attitudes of an authoritarian nature, and stereotyped ideas about differences in the social-ization of boys and girls.

Modern parents: Parents with a high educational level (university) living in an urban environment. Their developmental expectations conform, generally, to those of developmental psychologists; they have a concept of the origin of psychological features as arising from the nature–nurture interaction; they see themselves as being able to influence the child and his or her development; their educational attitudes are authoritative and they do not have stereotyped ideas with respect to differences in socialization between boys and girls.

Paradoxical parents: With either a low or medium educational level, these parents reside in both rural and urban areas. Their developmental expectations are very optimistic, and sometimes not realistic; nevertheless, paradoxically, the plans of action with the child that they envisage do not take advantage of such precocity. They are strongly environmentalist, but, strangely, they evince a relatively low estimation of their personal ability to influence the child, and reveal this attitude by frequently attributing to other people rather than to themselves the ability to shape the child's development. Their ideas are sometimes stereotyped and at other times opposed to stereotypes.

The connection between what parents think and their behavior toward the child has been explored in a number of studies. Recent literature reviews (Goodnow, 1988; Goodnow & Collins, 1990; Miller, 1988; Palacios, 1988; Sigel, 1985, 1986) have emphasized the complexity of this connection. Thus, Goodnow (1988) indicated that the ideas–behavior concordance is likely to be variable, occurring more often with some people than with others, under certain conditions, and in some spheres rather than in others.

The ideas–behavior connection has been investigated in at least two different domains: in educational situations where a parent tries to teach something to his or her child, and in the way parents structure and organize the child's daily life at home. In the first instance, we refer to "direct influences" (i.e., the strategies that parents use to motivate the child, to explain the problem they are going to deal with, to help him or her when facing a difficulty, and so on), as opposed to the more "indirect influences" in the second realm (i.e., daily routines of the child, objects in the household, contacts with other adults and children, and so on).

STIMULATION OF THE REPRESENTATIONAL COMPETENCE

A number of studies have been done in order to identify the types of teaching strategies that parents use and so to be in a position to evaluate the effects of these strategies. The teaching tasks that have been used are selected for theoretical and practical purposes. One of the major shared concerns among researchers is that the task chosen be age appropriate. Moreover, the selected task needs to be compatible with the conceptual frame inspiring the analysis of parent–child interactions. For our study, we selected a book-reading task (in our case, the reading of a picture book, because the children were about 2 years of age at the time of the data collection). This is a very well-known task, frequently used in developmental research with children of different ages, including infants (e.g.,

DeLoache & DeMendoza, 1987; Goodsitt, Raitan, & Perlmutter, 1988; Ninio, 1980, 1983; Sigel, McGillicuddy-DeLisi, & Johnson, 1980; White-hurst et al., 1988).

Book-reading tasks are easy to analyze in terms of the distancing theory that we would like to adopt as the framework for the analysis of interactions. The distancing theory has been described by Sigel in several articles (Sigel, 1970, 1982; Sigel & Cocking, 1977; Sigel & McGillicuddy-DeLisi, 1984; Sigel, Stinson, & Flaugher, 1991). According to Sigel's definition, distancing demands are verbal interactions that force the child to distance him or herself (through representation) to a greater or lesser extent from the immediately present and observable context. Within the context of parent–child interaction, what the parent tells or asks the child activates in him or her mental processes whose content may be linked to a greater or lesser extent to what is immediately perceptible. When parent and child look at a book and the parent says to the child, "The bird is drinking water," the distance between the picture they both have in front of them and the mental processes the child must use is minimal: All the child has to do is look at the bird in the picture. When the parent points out the bird in the book and a dog which is also in the picture, and tells the child "The bird has got feathers but the dog hasn't; the dog's got hair," the parent is asking the child to do something more than simply look; now he or she has to look at the picture of the bird and the dog and make a comparison relating to the selected feature. The comparison is not made in the picture, and the mental process that the child must carry out is based on what is in the picture (but he or she only needs to look at what is in the picture). Finally, when the parent asks the child: "What will the bird do when it has finished drinking water?," the actual image is only an excuse to activate representation in the child. Sigel has classed these three levels of separation between what is actually present and the representations activated in the child as low, medium, and high distancing demands.

Obviously, the high-level distancing demands are those that most stimu-late the representational capacities of the child. However, the stimulation value of distancing demands made by parents cannot be considered in the abstract, but must be viewed in relation to the child's level of development. Thus, as Sigel and McGillicuddy-DeLisi (1984) pointed out, demands with a low level of distancing ("That's a tree."; "The dog has a tail."; "Look at the roof of the house.") aimed at a 2-year-old child can be considered to have a high stimulation value, because such activities as teaching verbal labeling, classification of objects, demands for attention, and so forth are implicit in their content.

In the distancing theory, not only is the content of verbal interactions important, but also the form adopted by these interactions is of interest. Following Sigel's proposals, the fundamental distinction in this area is between "telling" and "asking." In the case of "telling," the child is given information which it is hoped he or she will pay attention to and assimilate. In the case of "asking," the child is being asked to carry out a mental process that moves from the question asked to the answer expected. Thus, the "asking" form is more stimulating for representational activities than the "telling" form, always assuming, of course, that the content of the message is geared to the child's capacity for comprehension.

The research developed by Sigel and McGillicuddy-DeLisi at Educational Testing Service (McGillicuddy-DeLisi, 1980, 1982, 1985; Sigel, McGillicuddy-DeLisi, & Johnson, 1980), was summarized by Sigel (1986). They have explored the relationship between parents' beliefs and their distancing strategies. Direct correspondences between a particular belief and a behavior were infrequent when examined by correlations. Regression analyses, however, revealed a relationship between sets of beliefs and distancing strategies. For example, fathers who believed that children develop through exploration, experimentation, and active learning tended to use high-level distancing strategies, whereas fathers who viewed the child as passive tended to use low-level distancing strategies.

CHILD'S DAILY EXPERIENCES AND LIFE ORGANIZATION

In our attempt to explain how parents exert an influence on the development of their children, we developmental psychologists devote a great deal of effort to the analysis of adult–child educational interactions of the type examined by Sigel and McGillicuddy-DeLisi. One complementary line of research pays attention to the form in which adults organize the everyday context in which children develop: the routines organized for them, the objects put at their disposal, the degree to which social contacts outside the nuclear family are encouraged, and so on. The fact that developmental psychologists tend to pay little attention to this type of influence does not imply, however, that it is less important. On the contrary, one may think that many of our observations of parent–child interactions are closely determined by the nature of the task and the characteristics of the context in which it is carried out. This is clearly shown, for example, in the ETS research program referred to previously: The findings for the task of paper-folding differ from those of book-reading. Conversely, when we analyze the child's everyday life, the contexts in which he or she grows up, the stimuli that surround him or her, and the routines he or she follows, and so on, we are attempting to capture influences over and above those of concrete situations, because we are referring rather to the usual context in which the child develops, to the material and social scenario for the various interactive situations in which we are most frequently interested. In any case, the child's development can be seen to be influenced by both types of stimulation, as Valsiner (1988) showed: The organization of child development is cumulative, with the effects of the organization of the surroundings combining with the effects of direct stimulation.

Various authors (e.g., Goodnow & Collins, 1990; Lautrey, 1980; McGillicuddy-DeLisi, 1985; Seginer, 1983) have defended the existence of a relationship between the ideas held by parents on the child's development and education, and the manner in which they arrange their children's lives, their surroundings, and their daily routines. This relationship has been confirmed in research projects using the HOME scale to examine the relationship between parental ideas and structuring of the family educational environment (Parks & Smeriglio, 1986; Reis, Barbera-Stein, & Bennett, 1986; Stevens, 1984). In general, parents who have a greater knowledge of child development and the factors that influence it obtain higher HOME scores than those who show less knowledge.

A MODEL OF INFLUENCES

We study the ideas of parents, their interactions with the child, and the way in which they organize their everyday life because we believe that all these aspects are crucial determinants of the child's development. The translation of stimulation into development can be understood particularly well within a conceptual framework like that of Vygotsky (1978) who maintained that the higher psychological processes observed in the child are the internalized version of experiences of social interchange that have been adjusted to certain procedures and rules, like the scaffolding processes and the contingency rule described by Wood (Wood, 1980; Wood, Bruner, & Ross, 1976; Wood & Middleton, 1975). Thus, we expect the cognitive-linguistic development of the children in our study to bear some sort of relation to the quality of the stimulation given by the parents within the book-reading task. Parents who give more encouragement to the representational abilities of their children, or who induce complex symbolic processes in them more frequently, will create a more favorable situation for their children to develop these psychological contents, provided that such stimulation is tuned to the children's developmental capacities and helps them to build these up a little further. More specifically, parents who encourage *distancing* from what is immediately present in their children at an appropriate level will be helping them to develop more mature cognitive-linguistic processes. Equally, those who most frequently use the "asking" form in their interactions will be demanding their children to play a more active role in the interaction, thereby stimulating their representational development in a more positive fashion.

The same argument can be used to justify our hypothesis that the HOME score bears some relationship to the children's development scores, because what such score reflects is the richness, variety, and accessibility of physical and social stimuli in the child's life, as well as the suitability of such stimuli to the developmental possibilities of the child, and all these factors, including his or her experiences with objects and experiences with people, form part of his or her everyday life.

The role played by parental ideas in the whole process of influencing child development fits well within this interpretative framework. When an adult and a child interact, they do so in the context of a specific task. This adult–child interaction involves a certain "definition" or "representation of the situation" (Wertsch, 1984) both on the part of the adult and on that of the child. But, at the same time, it also involves, on the adult's part, a certain definition of what a child is, how his or her development and education come about, how and to what extent it is possible to help him or her to attain new achievements. The Zone of Proximal Development does not exist in the child waiting for the adult to discover it, but is created in the course of social interaction and arises from the previous developmental level of the child and the adult's interaction strategies. In order to create it, the adult should be capable of recognizing that the possibility of development exists, that he or she can contribute to making this possibility take effect, and that this involves the utilization of certain strategies. What we are talking about is the parents' representation of the child, of his or her present and potential development, and of their capacity to influence him or her and to do so in the best possible way. From the Vygotskyan standpoint, the interaction that generates development is that which is situated within the Zone of Proximal Development. The concept of fitness is crucial in this respect, because, obviously, it refers to the adjustment of what the child can already do and the stimulation that makes him develop a little further.

One hypothesis that guides this study is that modern parents' interactions with their children will be productive as a result of the following factors: their developmental calendar is correct, they see themselves as capable of influencing the child — though not to an unlimited degree, their educational attitudes are "authoritative," which implies the presence of some control, but also a certain spirit of autonomy. Conversely, we hypothesize that traditional parents, who have pessimistic developmental expectations, do not see themselves as capable of exerting an active influence on the child's development, are restrictive, and so forth, may be expected to be less liable to promote development through their interactions. We can expect paradoxical parents to present a more mixed pattern of results, because, on the one hand, their over-precocious developmental expectations shown in the first stage of our study could give rise to interactions that are beyond the child's capabilities, whereas their conception of relatively low capability of influence on the child could lead to a degree of passivity. Paradoxical parents are not halfway between modern and traditional parents, but are sometimes nearer to one class, and sometimes nearer to the other one (Palacios, 1990).

Our predictions relating to indirect stimulation through the richness and variety of the physical and social environment lead in the same direction, as we believe that such stimulation will also bear some relation to various aspects of parental ideas. The richness of the daily scenario in which the child normally moves will vary, depending on the importance given to the child's social contacts, the value ascribed to toys and the suitability of toys to the child's capabilities, and the importance given to conducts such as talking to the child, praising his achievements, showing affection, and so on. Our hypotheses predict that modern parents, with their greater consciousness of the child's psychological needs, of his or her capabilities and of the importance of the environment, will obtain high scores in this area. Paradoxical parents will obtain lower scores than modern parents, followed by traditional parents.

If our predictions are correct, richer and more suitable stimulation should be reflected in higher development scores in children of modern parents. Children of paradoxical parents and traditional parents, in that order, will have lower development scores than those of modern parents. We expect these differences to appear both in the general measurements of child development and in the more specific measurements of verbal behavior during the telling of the story.

Our model therefore predicts a connection between what parents think, the way in which they organize the child's life and stimulate the child in learning situations, and the child's development scores. We believe that if some previous studies have not always successfully demonstrated such connections, this may be due to the fact that they explored one-to-one correspondences between certain ideas and certain behaviors. As Sigel (1985) suggested, wider categories may produce stronger relationships. In this sense, our three classes of parents (traditional, paradoxical, and modern) are more comprehensive than the more fragmented classifications sometimes found in the literature.

METHOD

Subjects

The sample consists of 139 individuals (67 couples, 4 women, and 1 man). The children were on average $22\frac{1}{2}$ months old, varying from 21;18 to 24;09.

Of the families, 38% lived in rural areas and 62% in urban areas in the south of Spain. Of the 139 subjects, 37% had a low educational level at the time of the study (primary education or less), 33% had a high level (university education), and 30% had an educational level that was between these two groups. Out of our 72 families, 48% were single-child families. All the families in this sample are intact families in which parents and children live together.

For this chapter, we chose couples in which the father and the mother have been classified as traditional, paradoxical, or modern. Our choice of parent-pair with concordant ideas is governed by the fact that some of the scores we use in our study cannot be strictly applied only to the father or only to the mother. This occurs in the case of the HOME scores, which are scores of home environment, and with the child's development scores, which result from the set of family environment influences acting upon the child. The concordance of parental ideas resolves this problem and more-over enables us to analyze the characteristics of each class of parents with greater clarity. As indicated in the following, concordant ideas were presented in the case of 36 of the couples from our sample.

Materials

Parents' Ideas Questionnaire.   Starting from the Parents' Ideas Ques-tionnaire (PIQ) used in the first phase of the longitudinal study (Palacios, 1988), questions that did not discriminate significantly between parents were eliminated and new questions were introduced. The PIQ has 114 questions dealing with a wide variety of contents: the parents' use of channels of information and support networks in connection with problems presented by the development and upbringing of the child; capabilities attributed to the fetus, the baby, and the child; influence of nature and nurture on various psychological factors; mother–child relationship during pregnancy; the role of the father; practices concerned with upbringing and education (discipline, control, and acceptance of the child's behavior, etc.); ideas on cognitive-linguistic stimulation and sociopersonal development of the child; attributions; values, expectations, aspirations; ideas about nursery schools and schooling; perception of themselves as parents and of the influence of their experience as parents on their ideas.

The parents' responses were coded by a system of categories which allowed for encompassing the wide range of answers to the PIQ. There is a considerable overlap between this system and the system developed in the previous utilization of the PIQ. Three coders scored the PIQ. Disagree-ments among them were infrequent, but when they did occur, the final decision was resolved through discussion.

Family Educational Environment.   The infants' version (0–3 years) of Caldwell and Bradley's HOME scale (1984) was used to assess the family environment. The information was collected on its 45 items. Each parent in the study was interviewed and observed using the HOME scale items as bases for these procedures.

Parent–Child Interaction.   Parents and children were recorded on video while interacting looking at a picture book. Two different books were involved: one used by the fathers and another by the mothers, showing everyday scenes of a rainy day and a trip to a park, respectively. Although we could have counter balanced the use of the books by both fathers and mothers, our initial uncertainty regarding the number of fathers we might get for our sample (given their greater initial resistance to being observed) made it seem advisable to us to have all the mothers at least use the same book. As it turned out, we were also able to observe practically all the fathers.

The categories used for the coding of interactions are shown in Table 3.1. The parent–child interactions revolving around the book were analyzed using an event-sampling procedure. For some analyses, our main interest lies in what the parent says to the child (low, medium, high distancing demands) or in how the parent says it to the child (asking versus telling); in these instances, our unit of analysis is the *turn of intervention* (each verbal

TABLE 3.1
Coding System Used for the Analysis of Interaction

Distancing Demands

- *Low distancing demands:* Utterances that require a minimum separation from the immediate environment, as they can be answered by observation or association (denomination, description, recognition): "This boy has a hat and a coat."; "What do you call this?"
- *Medium distancing demands:* Utterances elaborating on the immediate context; all the elements involved in the operation are present, but not the relationship linking them (putting into sequence, comparing, categorizing, relating, reproducing): "Which of these flowers is the biggest?"; "They've closed the umbrella because it's stopped raining."
- *High distancing demands:* Utterances that formulate or make the child formulate rational hypotheses or elaborations that completely transcend what is perceived in the immediate environment (inferring, concluding, planning, reconstructing): "These shoes must have got wet, and that's why the boy's taking them off."; "How do you think they filled this dump truck with sand?"

Form of Utterances

- *Telling statements:* Utterances in the form of positive or negative statements: "This is an umbrella."
- *Asking:* Utterances formulated as questions that demand a response from the child: "What do you call this thing we use when it rains?"

---

unit of a parent which terminates when a change in the topic of conversation occurs, when the child intervenes, or when there is a lapse of 3 sec or more between two utterances). For other analyses, we are mainly interested in the dialogue between parent and child; the unit of analysis is then the *cycle of interaction* (all consecutive parent–child interventions revolving around the same illustration of the story).

The coding was carried out independently by two observers, with an average reliability index of 88%.

Level of Child Development.   The child development level was ascertained in two different ways. First, the child's performance throughout the reading of the book was noted. For this, the child's utterances were analyzed using the SALT program (Miller & Chapman, 1985) which analyzes the level of linguistic development using Brown's rules (1973) as adapted for the Spanish language by Vila (1984) to calculate the morphemes. Number of different roots and Total number of words were selected as criteria to estimate the child's level.

Furthermore, the child's development was evaluated using the 1977 Spanish version of the mental development subscale of the Bayley scale for babies (1969).

Procedure

The families were contacted by mail and by telephone. All the data collection was carried out in the family homes by two researchers. Two sessions were normally necessary to complete the data collection. The first visit began with the questions connected with the organization of the everyday life of the child (HOME questions), which built up a relaxed climate of conversation between parents and researchers. From then on, the exploration of the ideas and interactions of the fathers and the mothers was carried out separately; for example, in the first visit to the home one researcher interviewed the mother using PIQ, while the other recorded the father interacting with the child in three different situations. In this report we concentrate on the picture-book reading (the other two tasks were the construction of a tower or a pyramid and playing with ordinary household materials); in the second session the father was interviewed while the mother was recorded on video.

Regarding the adult–child interaction, the situation was presented to the parents explaining that we were interested in observing the child in different situations. One of these was a book-reading situation. The parents were asked to behave with the child as they normally did when looking at books, stories, magazines, or photographs with the child.

The evaluation of the child's development level took place either at the end of the first or the second visit.

RESULTS

Parents' Ideas on the Development and Education of Children

The analysis of the parents' answers to PIQ was carried out using Multiple Correspondence Analysis (MCA) followed by a cluster analysis. The MCA (Lebart & Morineau, 1984; Lebart, Morineau, & Fenelon, 1982; Lebart, Morineau, & Warwick, 1984) allows us to discover the dimensions or factors by which we can group items. The use of automatic classification techniques then permits the forming of clusters containing those individuals who are similar on the basis of the previously established factors. The process uses a hierarchical type of algorithm for classification that goes on forming and adding groups according to their likeness. We know, in the case of each of the classes thus formed, to which of the previously detected factors it is related.

Of the various factors with an eigen value above .059 (criterion value established using the method recommended by Benzecri for MCA: Lebart & Morineau, 1984), we are particularly interested in the two that are relevant for the classes of subjects described on pages 82 and 83.

The first of these two factors (eigen value .251) seems to be easily interpretable in terms of modernity–traditionalism. In fact, at one of its extremes we find contents that reveal a lack of information on pregnancy, development, and education; low awareness of the psychological side of certain relationships or behaviors (there is no mother–fetus relationship, or else it is strictly physical; infantile play is used only to amuse the child or pass the time); innatist concepts of development; low personal capacity to influence the child's future and development; pessimistic forecasts of the developmental calendar; valuing children's dependence on the parents as a desirable trait in children. At the other extreme of this factor, we find contents which are in opposition to those above: a high level of information; a defense of the nature–nurture interaction to explain development; a high perception of personal influence on the development and future of the child; sensitivity to the psychological side of the relationship with the child; optimistic forecasts of the child's developmental calendar; valuing children's independence from their parents as a desirable trait.

The second of the factors relevant to our comprehension of groups of parents (eigen value .137) seems to be definable by the paradoxical nature of its contents: parents state that they have carried out various activities in their search for information on child development and education but are incapable of remembering anything concrete learned as a result of these activities; environmentalist explanations of interindividual differences which contrast with the low educational value assigned to activities such as going for trips or playing, combined with the belief that parents can only partly influence the child's linguistic development; valuing the child's dependence on parents.

Of the classes defined on the basis of these factors, the first corresponds — following the previous data in this research — to what is classed as *traditional parents:* very little or no information on pregnancy, development, and education (76% state that they have not read anything about these matters); scarcely any emphasis on the psychological aspects of various experiences and situations (89% only mention pregnant women looking after their physical health; 87% see children's play as mere entertainment); a tendency toward innatist interpretations of interindividual differences (68% believe that the differences between boys and girls are due to hereditary factors); low perception of their personal influence on the child and its development (37% believe that nothing can be done to make a shy child less so); pessimistic expectations in developmental forecasts (55% believe that infantile language is not comprehensible to strangers until the child is 3–4 years old); stereotyped ideas (89% believe that being an only child is a bad thing). This class comprises 38 parents of our sample (27% of the total).

The second class of parents, in contrast with those just described, and again showing continuity with the previous study, is that of *modern parents.* Among the characteristics defining its components the following stood out: a high degree of information about pregnancy, development, and upbringing (87% had read something about these topics); awareness of the psychological aspects of different situations and experiences (83% view infantile play as a source of learning; 73% believe that holding the child helps to strengthen attachment); interpretation of interindividual differences in terms of nature–nurture interaction (67% attribute the differences in children's intelligence to this interaction); a high perception of their influence on different facets of the child's development, both cognitive and social (97% believe that they can influence the child's language development); optimistic developmental expectations (90% think that a 7-month-old fetus can hear); ideas that are only slightly stereotyped (70% do not think it is desirable for boys to be very masculine and girls to be very feminine). There are 30 parents in this class (22% of the total).

The third of our classes requires some comment before we go on to expound its contents. The subject classification at the end of MCA provides us with a list of answers that are characteristic of each of the classes. The longer the list and the more elements it contains, the more clearly defined is the class with which it deals. This occurs in the case of the traditional parents (the 32 types of answers that characterize them — with a significance equal to or greater than .01 — give a quite unequivocal picture of what the identity marks are as far as ideas are concerned), and also in the case of modern parents (whose 28 types of answers reach values with a significance of over .01). The fact that with respect to the third class only eight types of answers reach significant values means two things: first, that we are dealing with a class in which there is a greater degree of heterogeneity than in the previous two, as there are fewer identifying features; second, that it is more difficult to define its features.

However, the fact that the types of answers that are characteristic of the third class sometimes approach modern and at other times traditional patterns, as well as the fact that the class is defined by the second of the factors just mentioned, allows us to label these parents as *paradoxical* according to the terms of the previous phase of this research. These paradoxical parents resemble modern parents in that they state that they have followed a number of different lines in their search for information on pregnancy, development, and upbringing (79% say that they read about the subject), although there is also a considerable proportion (39% of these) who did not remember any specific content learned as a result of this search for information, or who had only a vague memory. They are close to modern parents in their awareness of psychological aspects (72% believe that children's happiness is derived from the climate existing within the family). However, they also resemble traditional parents in the way they stimulate the child (35% believe that it is not worth giving explanations to children until they are about 3 years old) and in their view of their personal influence on development as limited (18% believe that their influence on language development is limited). This class is composed of 71 subjects, representing 51% of the sample. Hence the term *paradoxical*.

The chi-square analyses in which membership of the various classes is related to a diversity of sociodemographic variables show the important role played by educational level (68% of traditional parents have a low level; 77% of modern parents have a high level; paradoxical parents are divided, with 34%, 37%, and 29% in the low, medium, and high levels, respectively). The difference in educational level across groups is statistically significant: χ^2 (4, $N = 139$) = 49.13, $p < .001$.

There is also a significant relationship between classes of parent and rural or urban habitat (90% of modern parents are urban, compared with 63% of paradoxical parents and 37% of traditional parents): χ^2 (2, $N = 139$) = 20.22, $p < .001$. The various classes of parents also differ in their level of previous experience of parenthood (70% of modern parents have only one child as opposed to 41% of paradoxical parents and 42% of traditional parents): χ^2 (2, $N = 139$) = 7.79, $p < .05$. Gender bears no relation to the classes of parents, because the components of each class are divided almost 50% between men and women.

The concurrence between parents was found in 8 couples of traditional parents, 20 couples of paradoxical parents, and 8 couples of modern parents. Of the 16 traditional parents, 12 have a low educational level, and 4 have a medium level. All the modern parents have a high educational level, except one who has a medium level. Paradoxical parents are divided almost equally between those with a low level of education (12 subjects), those with a medium level of education (13 subjects) and those with a high level of education (15 subjects).

In the following analyses, the ideas of these concordant parents will be related to their behavior in the task of book-reading, with the HOME score obtained and with the child's development scores. In all the analyses, the variable of the parental educational level is introduced systematically, given its relevance in the literature on parent–child interactions.

Parents' Ideas-Stimulation in the Interaction

With the aim of analyzing the role of parents' ideas in the development of their interaction with their children, one-way ANOVAs were carried out on the three classes (traditional, paradoxical, and modern) with the measurements of stimulation in the situation of reading the book. As can be seen from Table 3.2, there was no difference between the types of parents in the total number of utterances with low-distancing, $F(2, 69) = 1.48, p = .23$, whereas there were significant differences between the various groups in the case of interventions with a medium or high level of distancing, included here in a single category given the scarceness of their occurrence, $F(2, 69) = 4.32, p < .05$. In this case, the Tukey means contrasts reveal that it is

TABLE 3.2
Stimulation Received by Children of Traditional, Paradoxical, and Modern Parents

	Low Distancing (Total)	Medium + High Distancing (Total)*	Low Distancing (Asking)*	Cycles With Asking*	HOME**
Traditional	17.62	2.31	6.62	6.06	26.12
	(9.30)	(2.82)	(4.44)	(3.35)	(3.40)
Paradoxical	21.55	4.90	7.82	7.20	30.75
	(8.12)	(3.14)	(5.52)	(4.81)	(4.21)
Modern	22.00	2.87	11.06	10.06	32.25
	(7.92)	(4.24)	(5.05)	(4.40)	(3.25)

Note. Group standard deviations are in parentheses.
*p ($df = 2,69$) < .05; **p ($df = 2,69$) < .001.

paradoxical parents who present a greater volume, significantly different from traditional parents, t (54) $=$ 2.68, $p < .01$, but not from modern parents.

The data present a different pattern when distancing demands formulated as a question or request (asking) are analyzed specifically. Leaving aside the questions that involve medium or high distancing (their presence is very scarce: the mean is lower than 0.50 for medium distancing and lower than 0.25 for high distancing), the three groups of parents differ significantly in the case of questions involving demands with a low level of distancing, $F(2,69) = 3.24$, $p < .05$. The Tukey means contrasts show that modern parents differ significantly from traditional parents in this respect, $t(30) =$ 2.64, $p < .05$, and from paradoxical parents, $t(54) = 2.03$, $p < .05$. Very similar findings are obtained when the number of cycles that contain questions addressed to the child are analyzed (the majority of these have low levels of distancing, as shown previously): The differences between the groups of parents are significant, $F(2, 69) = 3.57$, $p < .05$, and once again modern parents differ significantly from traditional parents, $t(30) = 2.89$, $p < .01$, as well as from paradoxical parents, t (54) $= 2.06$, $p < .05$. This demonstrates that modern parents ask their children more questions and do so more consistently in the course of the reading of the story.

ANOVAs of 3 (classes of parents) × 3 (level of studies) × 2 (gender of parent) were carried out, taking the total number of utterances with high or medium distancing and the number of cycles featuring questions as dependent variables, in an attempt to disentangle the effect of each of the variables as well as the effect of the interaction between them, by isolating their influence from each other. Neither the educational level nor gender were found to be significant in any of the cases, and the same was true of the interaction of these variables with parents' ideas, whereas the ideas maintained their significance in the two dependent measures.

To evaluate whether the child's gender exerted any influence on the type of interactions developed by the parents, one-way ANOVAs were carried out with the gender of the child on the various stimulation measures in the interaction, but these all gave values that were not significant. When ANOVAs of 2 (gender of child) × 3 (classes of parents) were carried out, on the stimulation measurements in the interaction, significant indices of the interaction between both variables were not obtained either, which demonstrates that neither traditional parents nor paradoxical parents nor modern parents altered their behavior on the basis of whether they were dealing with a boy or a girl.

Parental Ideas – Structuring of the Home (HOME)

A one-way ANOVA was carried out and established, as shown in Table 3.2, the significance of the differences in the HOME scores in the three classes of parents in function of their ideas, $F(2, 69) = 11.571, p < .001$. Modern parents are the ones with the highest HOME score, with significant differences from the traditional parents, $t(30) = 5.20, p < .001$, but not from paradoxical parents.

Another ANOVA of 3 (classes of parents) $\times$ 3 (educational level), with the HOME scores as a dependent variable was carried out. Neither the effect of the parental educational level, nor that of the interaction between educational level and ideas reached significant values, while parents' ideas maintained their significance.

Parental Ideas—Developmental Level of the Children

As mentioned previously, the evaluation of the child was carried out in two different ways: the scores of Bayley's subscale of mental development and the child's verbal performance in the course of the book-reading task (Number of different roots, Total number of words) (see Table 3.3). The one-way ANOVAs showed that the differences between the children's Bayley scores in function of parents' ideas were significant, $F(2, 69) = 5.69$, $p < .01$. The Tukey means contrasts showed that children of modern parents had a level of development significantly higher than that of traditional parents' children, $t(30) = 3.26, p < .01$, whereas there were no significant differences between the former and children of paradoxical parents.

The verbal performance of the children during the book-reading task also proved to be significantly different in function of parents' ideas, both in the case of Number of different roots, $F(2, 69) = 4.21, p = .01$, and in the case of Total number of words, $F(2, 69) = 4.87, p = .01$. The Tukey means contrasts again showed that children of modern parents had a significantly better level of verbal production than children of traditional parents [for

TABLE 3.3
Scores of Children of Traditional, Modern, and Paradoxical Parents

	Mental Development (Bayley)**	Number of Different Roots*	Total Number of Words**
Traditional	103.37	13.62	26.62
	(15.19)	(6.86)	(15.93)
Paradoxical	114.60	21.15	39.95
	(15.91)	(14.58)	(30.46)
Modern	122.62	25.50	54.75
	(18.07)	(6.28)	(18.02)

Note. Group standard deviations are in parentheses.
*p ($df = 2,69$) $< .05$; **p ($df = 2,69$) $< .01$.

Total number of words, $t(30) = 4.68$, $p < .001$; for Number of different roots, $t(30) = 5.10$, $p < .001$], but there was no significant difference between the former and children of paradoxical parents (in this last case, this was doubtless due to the size of the standard deviations of children of paradoxical parents, inasmuch as the differences in the case of the mean value are appreciable).

The ANOVA of 3 (classes of parents) × 3 (level of studies) with the children's scores as dependent variable showed that the relation between parents' ideas and Bayley mental development score lost significance when the influence of the level of studies was taken into consideration, but the significant relationship between parents' ideas and child's verbal production during the reading of the story was maintained.

Relationship Between Direct Stimulation in the Interaction and Structuring of the Home with Developmental Level

Correlations were carried out between parental scores in the various stimulation categories, Bayley values, and verbal performance of the children. These values are shown in Table 3.4, and as can be observed, neither the total low-distancing utterances nor the total medium–high distancing utterances were correlated to the Bayley score or to the linguistic performance of the children. On the contrary, low-distancing asking and the number of cycles featuring questions addressed to the child were positively correlated to the Bayley scores, and to the verbal performance scores. With regard to the HOME scores, the correlation with the children's values were significant in all cases as can be seen in Table 3.4.

TABLE 3.4
Correlations Between Stimulation Scores and Scores of Development

	Mental Development (Bayley)	Number of Different Roots	Total Number of Words
Low distancing (total)	.19	.26	.23
Medium–high distancing (total)	.13	.06	.01
Low distancing (asking)	.39**	.43**	.44**
Cycles with asking	.41**	.46**	.47**
HOME	.68**	.38**	.35*

$*p < .01$; $**p < .001$.

DISCUSSION

As had already been seen in our longitudinal sample, ideas held by parents on the development and education of their children have a certain degree of internal coherence. The knowledge and the representation adults have concerning the world around them do not consist merely of a succession of impressions and heterogeneous beliefs, but possess an internal organization that gives them coherence. A similar idea may be said of parents' ideas about their children. The organized coherent character of these ideas can be seen very clearly in the case of traditional and modern parents where notions of the origin of interindividual differences (e.g., the importance attached to nature and nurture) are closely related to the role each person feels he can play in the process of child development (low in the case of those with innatist ideas, high in the case of the interactionists). The case of paradoxical parents is different, because their chief characteristic is lack of internal coherence in their ideas.

With regard to the ideas–educational conducts relationship, our data are quite clear and consistent. In the book-reading situation, modern parents are the ones who seem to be better at managing the stimulation of the cognitive-linguistic development of their children. They are not always the ones who stimulate *the most,* but they appear to be the ones who do it *best.* In fact, as the data in Table 3.2 show, it is paradoxical parents who obtain higher frequencies in utterances with a medium–high level of distancing. But these medium–high distancing interactions are probably in many cases beyond the representational capabilities of children under 2.

Modern parents seem to be capable of employing their stimulation where it can be most productive: frequent and stable low-distancing demands formulated as questions. Low-distancing suits these small children, who, before they can distance themselves from what is immediately observable, need to be able to observe, label, organize, and articulate it. But the children seem to acquire such a capacity more readily when their mental processes are activated through questions that push them to think and solve small problems than when they are presented with statements that give the solution to these problems.

This thesis fits in particularly well with the notion of interaction in the Zone of Proximal Development. With their lesser tendency to present the child with questions throughout the interaction, traditional parents provide little stimulation for the cognitive-linguistic capabilities of their children. The higher proportion of medium–high distancing demands found in the case of paradoxical parents is not proximate to the present capabilities of the children. Modern parents' interactions seem to be capable of adapting to what is within the child's capabilities and at the same time stretching these through stimulation.

What is the role played by parents' ideas in the development and education of children in all this? As our hypotheses predicted, traditional parents, who have pessimistic expectations of the developmental calendar, who see themselves as having little influence on the development of the child, are those whose stimulation is poorer. At the other extreme, modern parents, with correct predictions of the child's capabilities and a positive perception of their role as educators, provide rich and well-adapted stimulation. The behavior of paradoxical parents corresponds in part to our hypothesis: Their over-precocious developmental expectations make them stimulate the children beyond what is developmentally possible for them. These parents are not passive, as we predicted on the basis of their rather negative perception of personal influence: They stimulate, but do not adjust this stimulation sufficiently to the children's requirements. As regards their interaction with their children in the situation of reading a book, paradoxical parents are closer to modern parents in some aspects (total number of utterances with low and medium–high level distancing), whereas they are more like traditional parents in others (number and persistence of questions with low distancing). What this indicates is that with regard to paradoxical parents we can say the same of their behavior as we have already said of their ideas: They are not halfway between traditional and modern, but at times closer to one or the other.

Researchers who have used the reading of a story in their longitudinal studies on babies have often indicated that as the children grow up, the mothers change their interaction style from the informative mode to the interrogative mode, from telling to asking (DeLoache & DeMendoza, 1987; Goodsitt, Raitan, & Perlmutter, 1988; Ninio, 1980, 1983), indicating that telling is used more when it is believed that a child does not know the word in question. As the child's knowledge of labels increases, the mother changes from a fundamentally informative style to a more interrogative style. Thus, given that the children in our sample are all about the same age, it could be argued that modern parents use interrogatives more because their children have a wider vocabulary, as the data in Table 3.3 show. But it is obvious that these children were not born with a wider vocabulary, but that in all probability they acquired it (and were still acquiring it even while we were collecting our data) in the course of interactions in which the parents could make maximum use of the child's capabilities at every point. If, in accordance with data from the literature on reading books with babies, the affirmatives are characteristic of interactions with younger babies, and interrogatives are more typical of interaction with older babies, it seems as if traditional and paradoxical parents—with their lower frequency of interrogatives—were addressing smaller children and as if modern parents were interacting with older children. Certainly that is not what is happening, because they are all interacting with children of similar ages. Quite simply, the modern parents are situating their interaction within the higher limit of their children's capabilities—but still in an area within their reach—whereas traditional and paradoxical parents are working more at the level of what is present, rather than what is possible. When paradoxical parents move away from this point they go out of the reach of the representational competence of the child, using medium-high distancing demands that are beyond the child's capabilities. They lack the fine calibration required by interaction in the Zone of Proximal Development.

Our data are compatible with Sigel's distancing theory, but they also emphasize, empirically prove, and qualify McGillicuddy-DeLisi's and Sigel's statement (Sigel & McGillicuddy-DeLisi, 1984) that contents with low-distancing can be stimulating for 2-year-olds. This may be so, of course, and possibly the fact that the ETS group has worked especially with preschool children has led them to emphasize the stimulating character of higher level distancing demands more frequently. What our data show is that it is not just low-level distancing utterances that are very stimulating for 2-year-old children. They also show that it is low-level distancing utterances *in interrogative form* that are particularly stimulating, and this is where children of modern parents have the advantage.

However, children of modern parents do not benefit merely from more stimulating interaction strategies. They also grow in a domestic environment that is richer, as the HOME scores in Table 3.2 demonstrate. The difference here is to be found between modern and traditional, not between modern and paradoxical. As other researchers have shown, it seems that a greater knowledge of children and their developmental processes is associated with greater richness of the scenario of their everyday life.

As our data show, the educational influence of the environment on the child—whether we are dealing with interactions in the strictest sense, or with the organization of everyday life—affects his development level and his verbal performance. The greatest differences are to be found, clearly, between children of traditional parents and children of modern parents, and the latter always appear with higher scores. In fact, in the different outcomes analyzed, the scores continue to increase from children of traditional parents to paradoxical to modern. The high standard deviations found in the verbal performance scores of children of paradoxical parents, however, prevent the differences between these and the children of modern parents from being significant, despite the obvious differences in the means.

It is notable that the child's gender introduces no significant difference in the behavior of traditional parents, whose ideas lie close to old gender stereotypes. It is difficult to know if this absence of differences is due to the fact that these stereotypes are increasingly diluted in Western society, or to the fact that the task chosen did not lend itself much to the appearance of these stereotypes, or whether the age of the children did not yet encourage the appearance of stereotypes which may become obvious as the children get older. It is also notable that no significant differences have appeared in the behavior of fathers and mothers in the book-reading task, despite the fact that this is probably an activity in which mothers are more involved than fathers. Possibly the concordance of ideas that we used as a criterion for the formation of the sample in our study may lessen the gap between fathers' and mothers' behavior, behavior which various studies have demonstrated differs significantly (see, for example, McGillicuddy-DeLisi, 1982).

One of the facts that we find most interesting is that in all the analyses of the data used in this chapter, it is parents' ideas and not their educational level that are associated with the different dependent measures used, whether we are talking about distancing demands, HOME scores, or the children's development scores (the only exceptions are the Bayley scores, whose significant association with parents' ideas disappears when educational level is also introduced to the analysis). Although the educational level of the parents very frequently appears to be associated with deter-mined styles of interaction in the literature, as regards the tasks and dependent measurements we used, and in the case of small children, the evidence is not so copious. In the case of reading books, "middle-class mothers" are often referred to in the literature, a classification that does not leave room for comparison in function of educational level (Ninio's study, 1980, is an exception, although the mothers used in the study varied not only in their educational level, but also in their membership of cultural groups with varying child-rearing practices). In the case of HOME, Caldwell and Bradley (1984) and Bradley, Caldwell, and Elardo (1977) showed that in a sample of 3-year-olds, the quality measures of the family environment (HOME) are more closely associated with cognitive develop-ment than the social status measures (assessed, amongst other variables, by the level of studies of the father and the mother).

Our classes of parent bear some relation to the educational level but there is not a perfect correspondence between these two variables, especially because very similar proportions between low, medium, and high educa-tional levels are found in the class of paradoxical parents. The grouping of our subjects in function of their ideas has turned out to be more predictive of the different dependent variables analyzed than the use of groupings on the basis of educational level.

This shows that, at least in the case of the tasks and subjects analyzed here, our knowledge of parents' ideas on the development and education of children helps us to understand why parents behave as they do and why children develop differently in function of the stimulation they receive.

The set of data presented in this chapter shows the importance and usefulness of the concept of the Zone of Proximal Development, an importance and usefulness already demonstrated by many other researchers. What our data possibly add to this is that in the creation of this Zone, parents' ideas on the development and education of their children play a role worthy of consideration.

ACKNOWLEDGMENT

This chapter has been translated from Spanish into English by Catriona Zoltowska.

REFERENCES

Bayley, N. (1969). *Manual for the Bayley Scales of Infant Development.* New York: The Psychological Corporation. (Spanish translation in Madrid: TEA.)

Bradley, R. H., Caldwell, B. M., & Elardo, R. (1977). Home environment, social status, and mental test performance. *Journal of Educational Psychology, 69,* 697–701.

Brown, R. (1973). *A first language: The early stages.* Cambridge, MA: Harvard University Press.

Caldwell, B. M., & Bradley, R. H. (1984). *Home Observation for Measurement of the Environment: Administration Manual* (rev. ed.). Little Rock, AR: University of Arkansas at Little Rock.

DeLoache, J. S., & DeMendoza, O. A. P. (1987). Joint picturebook interactions of mothers and 1-year-old children. *British Journal of Developmental Psychology, 5,* 111–123.

Goodnow, J. J. (1988). Parents' ideas, actions, and feelings: Models and methods from developmental and social psychology. *Child Development, 59,* 286–320.

Goodnow, J. J., & Collins, W. A. (1990). *Development according to parents: The nature, sources and consequences of parents' ideas.* Hillsdale, NJ: Lawrence Erlbaum Associates.

Goodsitt, J., Raitan, J. G., & Perlmutter, M. (1988). Interaction between mothers and preschool children when reading a novel and familiar book. *International Journal of Behavioral Development, 11,* 489–505.

Lautrey, J. (1980). *Classe sociale, milieu familial et intelligence* [Social class, family environment and intelligence]. Paris: Presses Universitaires de France.

Lebart, L., & Morineau, A. (1984). *S.P.A.D.* Paris: CESIA.

Lebart, L., Morineau, A., & Fenelon, J. P. (1982). *Traitement des donnés statistiques* [Statistical data analysis]. Paris: Dunod.

Lebart, L., Morineau, A., & Warwick, K. M. (1984). *Multivariate descriptive statistical analysis. Correspondence analysis and related techniques for large matrices.* New York: Wiley.

McGillicuddy-DeLisi, A. V. (1980). The role of parental beliefs in the family as a system of mutual influences. *Family Relations, 29,* 317–323.

McGillicuddy-DeLisi, A. V. (1982). Parental beliefs about developmental processes. *Human Development, 25,* 192–200.

McGillicuddy-DeLisi, A. V. (1985). The relationship between parental beliefs and children's cognitive level. In I. E. Sigel (Ed.), *Parental belief systems: The psychological consequences for children* (pp. 7–24). Hillsdale, NJ: Lawrence Erlbaum Associates.

Miller, J. F., & Chapman, R. S. (1985). *Systematic Analysis of Language Transcripts (SALT).* Language Analysis Laboratory, University of Wisconsin.

Miller, S. A. (1988). Parents' beliefs about children's cognitive development. *Child Development, 59,* 259–285.

Ninio, A. (1980). Picture-book reading in mother-infant dyads belonging to two subgroups in Israel. *Child Development, 51,* 587–590.

Ninio, A. (1983). Joint book reading as a multiple vocabulary acquisition device. *Developmental Psychology, 19,* 445–451.

Palacios, J. (1988). *Las ideas de los padres sobre el desarrollo y la educación de sus hijos* [Parents' ideas about children's development and upbringing]. Sevilla: Instituto de De-Sarrollo Regional.

Palacios, J. (1990). Parents' ideas about the development and education of their children: Answers to some questions. *International Journal of Behavioral Development, 13,* 137–155.

Parks, P. L., & Smeriglio, V. L. (1986). Relationships among parenting knowledge, quality of stimulation in the home and infant development. *Family Relations, 35,* 411–416.

Reis, J., Barbera-Stein, L., & Bennett, S. (1986). Ecological determinants of parenting. *Family Relations, 35,* 547–554.

Seginer, R. (1983). Parents' educational expectations and children's academic achievements: A literature review. *Merrill-Palmer Quarterly, 29,* 1–23.

Sigel, I. E. (1970). The distancing hypothesis: A causal hypothesis for the acquisition of representational thought. In M. R. Jones (Ed.), *Miami Symposium on the prediction of behavior, 1968: Effect of early experience* (pp. 99–118). Coral Gables, FL: University of Miami Press.

Sigel, I. E. (1982). The relationship between parents' distancing strategies and the child's cognitive behavior. In L. M. Laosa & I. E. Sigel (Eds.), *Families as learning environments for children* (pp. 47–86). New York: Plenum.

Sigel, I. E. (1985). A conceptual analysis of beliefs. In I. E. Sigel (Ed.), *Parental belief systems: The psychological consequences for children* (pp. 345–371). Hillsdale, NJ: Lawrence Erlbaum Associates.

Sigel, I. E. (1986). Reflections on the belief-behavior connection: Lessons learned from a research program on parental belief systems and teaching strategies. In R. D. Ashmore & D. M. Brodzinsky (Eds.), *Thinking about the family: Views of parents and children* (pp. 35–65). Hillsdale, NJ: Lawrence Erlbaum Associates.

Sigel, I. E., & Cocking, R. R. (1977). Cognition and communication: A dialectic paradigm for development. In M. Lewis & L. A. Rosenblum (Eds.), *Interaction, conversation and the development of language* (pp. 207–226). New York: Wiley.

Sigel, I. E., & McGillicuddy-DeLisi, A. V. (1984). Parents as teachers of their children: A distancing behavior model. In A. D. Pellegrini & T. D. Yawkey (Eds.), *The development of oral and written language in social contexts* (pp. 71–92). Norwood, NJ: Ablex.

Sigel, I. E., McGillicuddy-DeLisi, A. V., & Johnson, J. E. (1980). *Parental distancing, beliefs and children's representational competence within the family context* (ETS RR 80–21). Princeton, NJ: Educational Testing Service.

Sigel, I. E., Stinson, E. T., & Flaugher, J. (1991). Socialization of representational competence in the family: The distancing paradigm. In L. Okagaki & R. J. Sternberg (Eds.), *Directors of development: Influences on the development of children's thinking* (pp. 121–144). Hillsdale, NJ: Lawrence Erlbaum Associates.

Stevens, J. H. (1984). Child development knowledge and parenting skill. *Family Relations, 33,* 237–244.

Valsiner, J. (1988). *Developmental Psychology in the Soviet Union.* Brighton, Sussex: Harvester Press.

Vila, I. (1984). La competencia comunicativa en los dos primeros años de vida [Communicative competence in the first two years of life]. Unpublished doctoral dissertation, University of Barcelone.

Vygotsky, L. S. (1978). *Mind in society: The development of higher psychological processes.*

Cambridge, MA: Harvard University Press.

Wertsch, J. V. (1984). The Zone of Proximal Development: Some conceptual issues. In B. Rogoff & J. V. Wertsch (Eds.), *Children's learning in the Zone of Proximal Development* (pp. 7–18). San Francisco, CA: Jossey-Bass.

Whitehurst, G. J., Falco, F. L., Lonigan, C. J., Fischel, J. E., DeBaryshe, B. D., Valdez-Menchaca, M. C., & Caulfield, M. (1988). Accelerating language development through picture book reading. *Developmental Psychology, 24,* 552–559.

Wood, D. J. (1980). Teaching the young children: Some relations between social interaction, language and thought. In D. R. Olson (Ed.), *The social foundations of language and thought* (pp. 280–296). New York: Norton.

Wood, D. J., Bruner, J. S., & Ross, G. (1976). The role of tutoring in problem solving. *Journal of Child Psychology and Psychiatry, 17,* 89–100.

Wood, D. J., & Middleton, D. (1975). A study of assisted problem-solving. *British Journal of Psychology, 66,* 181–191.

Children's Self-Perceptions and Mothers' Beliefs About Development and Competencies

Carole A. Martin
Rutgers University

James E. Johnson
The Pennsylvania State University

The family environment typically is the first setting in which developing children not only learn and practice new competencies but also soon come to understand and evaluate their own level of competence. Undoubtedly, a major responsibility for this early development within families is due to specific parental behaviors and beliefs, particularly maternal behaviors and beliefs in the case of very young children. Various parental manifestations with their supporting ideational and attitudinal bases significantly impact developing children's competencies and sense of competence.

Recently, Harter (1988) explicitly drew attention to the psychological interplay between children's global self-awareness and their self-evaluation in specific domains, such as in peer relations or in academic areas of mastery. A basic assumption is that children's motivation overall, and classroom motivation as a particular case, depends on children's sense of competence and self-worth as well as their mood states that are transient and situational. Parental factors are implicated in a chain or ring of relations involving beliefs, attitudes, and behaviors of significant others on the one hand, and children's outcomes and inputs on the other hand. Moreover, few would dispute the benefits of healthy (i.e., accurate, positive) self-perceptions in children's development and socialization.

Leichter (1974) identified the process of evaluating and labeling in the home as one dimension to consider when viewing the family as an educational system. Other dimensions listed and discussed included how time and space are organized in the family setting, how language is used, how memories are evoked in interactive contexts, and how educational experiences within and outside the family system are mediated. Certainly evaluative features apply to each dimension listed and they touch a variety of spheres that pervade the social life of children on a day-to-day basis. Although many are informal and fleeting, other evaluations are raised to a conscious formal level as in explicit parent–teacher discussions of school behavior or progress. In each case evaluations are important in their cumulative effect upon children's self-definitions and sense of competence. The process of evaluating and labeling must be taken into account in theory construction pertaining to the family as educator. Evaluative processing needs to be understood with reference to values and beliefs of the primary actors within the family system. How parents construct and interpret their children's development and their evaluation of children's accomplishments give meaning to family interaction in general and to educational encounters in particular. These parental factors have considerable potential consequences for children's psychological development.

With the secular trend in many quarters toward raising developmental expectations and standards of accomplishment for young children, it would be revealing to learn more about how well or not so well parents and kindergarten teachers match in their views of competence for children. Assuredly, any divergence in views reflects the different knowledge base possessed by parents and teachers of young children. Not only do parents and teachers interact with young children around different tasks and objectives in home and school settings, but they also typically bring to bear markedly contrasting perceptions of the children in question, given the teachers' normative focus and parents' ipsative focus. The likelihood, then, is to encounter a gulf between teachers' and parents' assessments of developmental status and ideals during the early years, the extent of discontinuity dependent upon family demographic variables such as educational level.

In our previous publication (Johnson & Martin, 1985) we reported the theoretical framework and the results of a large project investigating the relationship between family environment and children's cognitive skills in rural Wisconsin families. We have maintained, along with McGillicuddy-DeLisi (1990) and Sigel (1990), that distancing theory is a useful approach toward conceptualizing and operationalizing the beliefs and practices of parents within diverse family environments relevant to the socialization of competence and the development of representational thought in young children. Both proximal and process variables, as well as demographic variables, must be included in research designed to investigate the educational role of families. Accordingly, we have examined parental beliefs and practices and child outcomes across varied family contexts determined by geographic location, socioeconomic status (SES), and family structure. The focus is on the kindergarten-age child.

Here we report the results of a specific study from the larger project that examined the relationship among several mother, child, and family variables. More specifically, we were interested in mother's perceptions of the child's physical and cognitive abilities, the child's self-perceptions in these same competence domains, maternal beliefs about development, and select demographic characteristics of families (gender of child, ordinal position of child, mother's education, family's geographic location). A central question is: To what extent are demographic variables and maternal beliefs about development and competencies related to the congruence between the kindergarten child's actual and perceived abilities?

METHODOLOGY

Subjects

The mothers and children in this sample participated in a larger study of rural Wisconsin families. Fifty mother–child dyads from intact families were recruited through kindergarten classrooms in three rural communities. Approximately 47% of those contacted agreed to participate in the study.

The sample included 23 girls and 27 boys, ranging in age from 60 to 81 months ($M = 69.4$ months). Of the target children, 40% were first-borns or only children. Family size varied from one to eight children, with the modal family structure being the two-child family (40%).

Mothers' ages ranged from 23 to 41 years ($M = 32.4$ years). Approximately half (52%) of the mothers had completed some education beyond high school. Efforts were made to include fathers in the larger study, but a poor response rate from the lower SES fathers was cause for concern. In an effort to maintain a socioeconomically diverse sample, this investigation narrowed its focus to mothers.

Because one variable of interest was geographic location as it related to the relative isolation of the family residence, information regarding the location of the home was collected. Only 22% of the families lived in neighborhoods in towns or villages; the majority lived in rural areas with no close neighbors. Most families were long-time residents of their respective communities; only 20% had moved into the area during the preceding 3 years.

Child and family characteristics are summarized in Table 4.1.

Procedure

Information from the mothers was obtained using two questionnaires that were distributed by mail. In earlier phases of the larger study, instruments were piloted to determine how to get the most accurate information from

TABLE 4.1
Sample Characteristics (*N* = 50)

Variable	Category	Frequency	Percentage
Sex of target child	Boy	27	54
	Girl	23	46
Ordinal position of	Only child	6	12
target child	First-born	14	28
	Later-born	30	60
Number of children	One	6	12
in family	Two	20	40
	Three	16	32
	Four	5	10
	Five	1	2
	Eight	2	4
Mother's level of	Part high school	1	2
education	High school/GED	23	46
	Part college	13	26
	College	10	20
	Grad school	3	6
Geographic location of	Town/village	11	22
family home	Rural (nonfarm)	27	54
	Rural (farm)	12	24
Length of time residing	More than 6 yrs	33	66
in community	Three to 6 yrs	7	14
	Less than 3 years	10	20

rural families if investigators were restricted to mail contact. Our initial questionnaires included open-ended questions requiring essay-type answers — a format that was biased in favor of those whose writing skills were more developed. Using these responses to gain a better understanding of parents' thinking, a forced-choice format was developed that incorporated the wording and explanations commonly expressed by mothers. Random phone contact with mothers indicated that they understood the questions and felt comfortable with the forced-choice format. Of those who had initially consented to participate, 86% returned the questionnaires.

Children were assessed at their schools. These evaluations took place during the first 3 months after the child's entry into kindergarten. Two 15-minute sessions were conducted with the child to collect the data necessary for this study and the larger project.

Teacher ratings of the child's competence were obtained through questionnaires that were distributed when the researcher visited. Teachers completed these rating forms and returned them to the researcher within 2 weeks of the date that the children were interviewed at their schools.

Mothers and teachers were paid $5 for their participation in this study.

Measures

The research questions required investigators to find or develop ways of assessing children's perceptions of competence, children's actual abilities, maternal beliefs about child development, and maternal perceptions of their children's abilities. The instruments chosen are described next.

Beliefs About Development Scale. This instrument was developed for the larger study and represents an attempt to assess parents' general beliefs regarding the nature of children and how they change over time. The 30-item scale (see Appendix A) asks the respondent to explain children's changing abilities by rank ordering three possible explanations to situations involving young children (e.g., "How do children come to know why some things float and others sink?"). The response options represent learning, maturational, and cognitive-development perspectives. These three theories seemed appropriate choices because they are the guiding assumptions upon which many early educational models are based (Peters, Neisworth, & Yawkey, 1985).

Using actual parent responses to open-ended questions from earlier phases of this study and from previous work by Sigel, McGillicuddy-DeLisi, and Johnson (1980), the three different theoretical positions, worded in everyday language, were presented in a forced-choice format. During the development of the instrument, child development professionals assisted in evaluating face validity by indicating which responses represented learning, maturational, and cognitive-developmental perspectives. Appendix B includes the definitions of the theories that were used in developing and validating the instrument. The strictest criterion was applied and only items that generated 100% agreement were kept from the original item pool.

Three subscale scores were computed for each mother using a principal components factoring method to weight raw scores before summing (Lord, 1958). When internal consistency reliabilities were computed on the subscale scores, the alphas on the learning, maturation, and cognitive-developmental subscales were well within the acceptable range: .81, .85, and .74, respectively.

Pictorial Scale of Perceived Competence and Acceptance for Young Children. Children's perceptions of personal competence were measured with a scale developed by Harter and Pike (1984). This 24-item scale includes four subscales: cognitive competence, physical competence, peer acceptance, maternal acceptance. The present study used individual item scores on six cognitive items and five physical items, as well as total scores for these two subscales. Harter and Pike reported internal consistency reliability, alpha = .61, on the combined competence subscales.

The Pictorial scale was administered as part of a battery of tests given to children who participated in the larger study. For each item, the child is presented with two pictures and is read a statement about each. One picture represents a child who is competent at a particular task and the other picture shows a child who is not very skilled. On the basis of the child's response to the question "Which child is most like you?" and follow-up questions, the item is scored on a 4-point ordinal scale.

Teacher Rating Form. Harter and Pike suggested a procedure for assessing the child's actual competence. The teacher is asked to rate the child on the same dimensions and items to which the child responds. Teachers in this study were given a brief description of each cognitive and physical skill and were asked to rate the child's ability on a 4-point scale. Insofar as the teacher could make an accurate assessment of the child's ability in the six cognitive and five physical domains, these scores enabled the researcher to assess the degree of convergence between the child's actual and perceived competence, as well as the degree of convergence between the mother's perceptions of her child and her child's actual abilities.

Family Questionnaire. This questionnaire was designed by the researcher to gather demographic data and to determine the mother's perception of her child's competence. A section of the Family Questionnaire is similar to the Teacher Rating Form just described in that it asks mothers to assess their children in the competence domains on a 4-point scale. These scores were interpreted as the mother's perceptions of or beliefs about the child's competence.

RESULTS

The means, standard deviations, and ranges for the perception and beliefs variables are presented in Table 4.2. These univariate statistics provide a global description of the way in which the sample responded to the measures.

The relationships among beliefs variables (developmental and accuracy), continuous demographic variables (mother's education and ordinal position of the child), and child outcomes (perception of competence) were evaluated using Spearman-rank correlation coefficients. These correlations are presented in Table 4.3.

The relationship between dichotomous variables (geographic location, sex of target child) and beliefs variables were evaluated using *t* tests and a test statistic based on the Welch–Aspin degrees of freedom.

TABLE 4.2
Descriptive Statistics for Perceptions and Beliefs Measures (*N* = 50)

Variable	Mean	SD	Range
Child perceptions			
Cognitive	21.12	2.28	12–24
Physical	16.76	2.74	11–20
Mother perceptions			
Cognitive[a]	21.94	2.25	12–24
Physical	16.94	2.92	8–20
Teacher ratings			
Cognitive	16.32	3.20	6–20
Physical	21.40	2.90	11–24
Child accuracy			
Cognitive	3.68	2.18	1–10
Physical	3.44	2.35	0–9
Maternal accuracy			
Cognitive[a]	2.69	1.91	0–7
Physical	3.58	2.05	1–8
Beliefs			
Learning	19.64	4.71	9.90–28.41
Maturation	7.83	5.70	0–27.63
Cog.-devel.	14.83	3.67	5.12–21.93

[a]*N* = 48

TABLE 4.3
Correlations of Maternal Accuracy on Competence Subscales with Child Accuracy and Demographic Variables (*N* = 48)

	Maternal Inaccuracy	
	Cognitive	Physical
Demographic variables		
Mother's education	−.15	.18
Child's ordinal position	.02	.10
Child's inaccuracy		
Cognitive	.33*	.06
Physical	.20	.57**
Child's actual competence		
Cognitive	−.53**	−.25*
Physical	−.35**	−.56**
Mother's developmental beliefs		
Learning	.02	.01
Maturational	.14	.10
Cognitive-developmental	−.30*	.00

*p < .05; **p < .01.

Child Accuracy.   There is a significant positive relationship between the mother and child accuracy variables related to the cognitive subscale (r = .33, p < .05) and the physical subscale (r = .57, p < .01). That is, children with accurate self-perceptions in the cognitive and physical domains have mothers who more accurately evaluate their children's competencies.

There were significant positive relationships between the child's actual ability (as reported by the teacher) and child accuracy (cognitive subscale: r = − .48, p < .01; physical subscale: r = − .53, p < .01).

Maternal Accuracy.   The association between maternal perceptions and teacher perceptions was first measured using Spearman-rank correlation coefficients. A significant positive relationship between these variables was found on the physical subscale (r = .35, p < .01), but not on the cognitive subscale. Thus, mother and teacher rankings of the child's physical skills were more similar than their rankings of cognitive skills.

For most of the analyses, maternal accuracy was computed from discrepancy scores derived from mother and teacher ratings of the child. A two sample t test was used to examine maternal accuracy differences when the sex of target child varied. The results indicated that mothers of daughters tended to be more accurate in assessing cognitive competence than were mothers of sons (t = 2.12, df = 43). However, mothers of daughters overestimated their daughters physical competence. This was determined by computing a point-biserial correlation between the child's sex and the mother's perceptions while removing the effects of the child's actual competence. The resulting partial correlation was significant (r = .26, p < .05).

The geographic location of the family home was a predictor of maternal accuracy. Mothers who lived in towns and villages were more accurate than mothers who lived in outlying rural farm areas (t = 2.61, df = 21).

Maternal Beliefs About Development.   Mothers with higher cognitive-developmental beliefs were more accurate in evaluating their children's cognitive competence (r = − .30, p < .05).

Developmental beliefs were unrelated to mother's education, geographic location of the family home, family size, or child competence. However, gender of the target child did predict beliefs. The girls in this sample had mothers who rated the learning subscale higher than mothers of boys did (t = 2.18, df = 46). Cognitive-developmental beliefs were significantly higher for mothers of boys than they were for mothers of girls (t = 2.21, df = 44).

DISCUSSION

This study investigated the way in which the young child's competencies and self-perceptions are related to beliefs variables. The assumption underlying this research is that the child's perceptions of self can influence motivation and that accurate self-perceptions enhance development. Children's faulty notions about competencies may interfere with their efforts to improve their skills. If their self-perceptions are unrealistically optimistic, they may not be motivated to improve performance. Conversely, an unrealistically pessimistic self-appraisal can undermine self-confidence and lead to giving up on a task prematurely. Although children's inaccurate perceptions of personal abilities are often attributed to their limited cognitive development, the present research attempted to identify family environment variables that might account for some of the variance. More specifically, this study focused on the maternal beliefs, cognitions that guide mother's interpretations of child behavior. This study examined two types of parental beliefs, developmental beliefs and accuracy of child-related perceptions. Figure 4.1 presents a model for understanding the way in which maternal beliefs are related to these child outcomes.

Child Accuracy. Why do children vary in the accuracy of their self-perceptions? The correlation between maternal inaccuracy and child inaccuracy suggests that children learn (or fail to learn) standards of evaluation in the home. The mother who is accurately monitoring her child's skill development may also be relating that information to the child. For example, the accurate mother and child both know about the child's ability to do puzzles because they have both noted this progress together. Similarly, the mother and child who are both inaccurate may have shared standards related to competence that do not match the teacher's standards. An alternate explanation is that the home environment may not be providing any information regarding the child's competence. If this is the case, the child's perceptions might be random, rather than based on either family or school norms.

The highest ability children (as rated by the teachers) were also the most

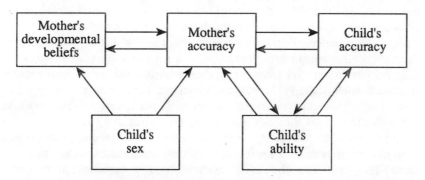

FIG. 4.1   Proposed model of relationship between maternal beliefs (developmental and accuracy) and child outcomes (ability and accuracy).

accurate in their assessments of competence. Three possible explanations for this finding are presented. First, brighter children may be more perceptive and may have the cognitive capacity necessary to make accurate ability estimates. This explanation is supported by the work of Nicholls (1978, 1979) and Stipek (1981). It is also possible that lower ability children are inaccurate because of a desire to present themselves favorably to others. Higher ability children do not have a need to distort reality. A third possibility is that the ability–accuracy correlation does not reflect real differences between children's responses. If all children give high self-ratings, only those whose actual ability is high will be classified as accurate using our operational definition. Therefore, the ability–accuracy correlation may be an artifact of the measurement used and the pattern of high self-ratings.

The data from this study do not suggest that kindergarten children have adopted either home or school standards exclusively. Although they had limited experience in the formal school setting and extensive experience in the home setting, children in this sample did not always evaluate their competence in the same way that their mother did. It is possible that children acquire their perceptions of competence through interactions and experiences in multiple settings, some of which exclude the mother.

Maternal Accuracy. The discrepancy between mother and teacher ratings was assumed to be an index of maternal inaccuracy. If this assumption is correct, the lack of agreement can be explained in several ways. As noted previously, evaluators have different standards of attainment. For example, mothers' evaluative framework might be based on the changes they have observed over time. As there is rapid, steady growth during early childhood, the mother could easily view the child as becoming progressively more competent and overlook inadequacies based on absolute standards.

Different norms for abilities might exist because the mother lacks the knowledge about the school setting that is needed to make accurate judgments. If the mother does not know what the "average" kindergarten child is expected to know how to do, she will be unable to evaluate her own child (Vandeventer, 1969). Some parents have a better sense of the distribution the teacher uses in grading, and some are more attentive to the information they receive from the teacher regarding the child's performance (Entwistle & Hayduk, 1978). Although the data for this study were collected soon after school entry in order to minimize school effects, it is possible that some mothers based their perceptions on teacher information.

There are biases associated with both mother and teacher ratings. For example, mothers might be influenced by their emotional attachment to the child. They may rate the child's abilities high in the hope of fostering positive self-esteem. It is also true that mother ratings are often noncomparative, whereas teachers compare the child with others in the same age group (Entwistle & Hoyduk, 1978).

This study found mothers living in outlying rural areas to be less accurate in assessing child competence than their counterparts in small towns were. The relative isolation of the family can influence the mother's understanding of norms outside the family. One might speculate that there are social network differences between the mothers in the two geographic areas. If mothers who live in more populated areas have more extensive contacts with friends and neighbors, they might have been informally exposed to school standards prior to the child's kindergarten year.

If teacher ratings do reflect reality, mothers of boys are more inaccurate than mothers of girls. This finding suggests that mothers of boys may have difficulty placing their sons' abilities on a continuum of normative standards. This tendency toward inaccuracy for sons can be juxtaposed with the finding that mothers of girls overestimate their daughters' physical abilities. The reason for this finding might be that mothers have lower standards or expectations for girls in the physical domain. That is, when a girl is able to perform a certain motor skill, she is rated higher than if a boy performed at the same level.

Mothers are more accurate in evaluating high-ability children. Four possible explanations can be presented for this finding. First, if mothers' ratings are influenced by feelings of pride in their children, mothers of high-ability children have less to lose by being honest. That is not to suggest that mothers of low-ability children are dishonest; rather, they may be trying to present the child in the best possible light. Another interpretation of the finding is related to the "overestimation bias" — all mothers are kind in evaluating their children, so ratings are high across the sample. For mothers of high-ability children, a high rating is an accurate response; for mothers of low-ability children, this response bias is an inaccurate response. In their study of this issue, Miller, Manhal, and Mee (1989) demonstrated that this tendency is not merely a statistical artifact. They suggested that, because there is a correlation between maternal intelligence and child intelligence, higher ability children may have smarter mothers who make more accurate assessments of their children. However, in our study, mother's educational level did not correlate with maternal accuracy. Finally, the Hunt and Paraskevopoulos (1980) explanation might be appropriate. These authors postulated that the mother who is more aware of her child's abilities is more likely to be providing the child with challenging experiences that will enhance intelligence and lead to skill mastery.

Our index of maternal accuracy is not sensitive to the fact that mothers and teachers come to know children in different settings. Mothers and teachers may experience the child differently because the contextual reality is not constant. Possible context effects must be considered when interpreting the findings related to maternal accuracy in this study.

Beliefs About Development.   Developmental beliefs represent the psychology that parents use to explain child behavior in everyday situations. Although some parents may have a somewhat sophisticated understanding of child development theories and learning, most employ a "naive psychology" to interpret their observations of growth and change. This study revealed a significant relation between maternal perceptions of child competence and maternal beliefs about development. More accurate mothers tend to have stronger cognitive-developmental beliefs. Although the interactional perspective is related to the mother's knowledge of child abilities, these data allow us only to speculate about the possible causal relations that exist between the two variables. Perhaps mothers who are more observant of their children simultaneously acquire knowledge about the child's competence and an appreciation for the child as an active learner. However, it is also possible that a cognitive-developmental belief system encourages the mother to be more observant of the child, rather than concentrating on maternal teaching.

The beliefs literature suggests that parental cognitions may be influenced by family demographics and child characteristics (e.g., McGillicuddy-DeLisi, 1990; Miller, 1988). These hypotheses were not supported by the present study. Mother's education, geographic location of the family home, number of children in the family, and child ability were unrelated to maternal beliefs about development. The lack of significant differences between mothers of different educational levels with respect to beliefs about development is noteworthy. Although previous research has found that more educated mothers make greater use of parenting literature (Clarke-Stewart, 1978), it has also been noted that less educated mothers acquire child rearing information in more informal ways (MacPhee, 1983). The present results indirectly suggest that the content of beliefs is not affected by these different acquisition processes. The Beliefs Questionnaire was developed on the assumption that all three alternatives represent plausible explanations, not varying degrees of "correctness." As more educated mothers did not favor a particular theoretical perspective, this assumption appears to have been met.

One child characteristic, the child's gender, was associated with maternal beliefs about development. Mothers of girls rated learning beliefs higher than mothers of boys did. In contrast, stronger cognitive-developmental beliefs were expressed by mothers of boys. Bell (1979) offered a paradigm for interpreting these findings. He suggested that a learning perspective leads parents to assume that they are exclusively responsible for the child's behavior. The cognitive-developmental theory, however is more child-centered and respects the child as an active learner. With this in mind, the gender-related differences in maternal beliefs seem congruent with literature that describes mothers as less restrictive with their sons than they are with their daughters (Maccoby & Jacklin, 1974).

Future research in this area should attend to methodological concerns raised by this study. First, during the administration of the Pictorial Scale for Children, it was apparent was that stimulus pictures were evoking child responses that would not be evoked by the verbal statements to which mothers and teachers responded. Although the measures for child, teacher, and mother are comparable, they are not identical. These differences may have affected the data.

Second, the findings related to the children's actual abilities must be viewed in the context of this study. This research assumed that teacher ratings reflected "reality," and based maternal and child accuracy scores on these standards. In fact, parents and teachers experience children in different settings and, therefore, their appraisals of children may be functionally different. Although using a school-based reality seems justified in a study that examines individual differences in children's self-perceptions at school entry, the measure has limitations because teacher ratings are associated with certain biases. Future studies also might incorporate behavioral measures of competence into the research design. If trained testers administered a more "objective" assessment of actual abilities to all children, additional insight into parent–teacher–child perceptions might be gained.

Finally, although the questionnaires used to evaluate maternal beliefs in this study appear valid and reliable, future studies might explore developmental beliefs and accuracy issues by interviewing mothers. The questionnaires were well-suited for use with the rural population discussed here, but interviews with parents would enable follow-up probes that could enhance our understanding of belief systems.

In summary, the data presented in this chapter support the notion that the cognitive aspects of parenting are important because they relate to child outcomes. The results suggest moderate positive correlations between maternal cognitions and individual differences in the accuracy of children's self-perceptions. The implications raised by these results can guide those interested in facilitating children's motivation and performance. If parents understand the way in which they impact the child's ability to make an accurate assessment of competence, they may be more attentive to these details. Also, parent educators might focus training on some of the cognitive aspects of parenting, rather than giving situation-bound remedies for child-rearing problems. Beliefs appear to have a pervasive influence on the parenting experience and, consequently, on child outcomes.

APPENDIX A: BELIEFS ABOUT DEVELOPMENT SCALE
(MARTIN, 1983)

The purpose of this questionnaire is to determine your beliefs about the development of young children. We are interested in your opinions. There are no right or wrong answers.

Directions: Assume that all questions refer to preschool children who are 4–5 years old. Read each item and decide which answers you think are most important. Number your choices as follows:

1 = best answer
2 = second best answer

1. What makes two preschool children friends?
_____ They are encouraged to spend time together.
_____ They are about the same age and same size.
_____ They think about things in similar ways.

2. Where do children's misconceptions about the world come from?
_____ Television and other children present confusing information.
_____ Misconceptions are a natural part of childhood.
_____ Children interpret their observations incorrectly.

3. Why do children's misconceptions about the world eventually change?
_____ As they get older, they outgrow immature ideas.
_____ Adults or older children present the correct information.
_____ Their curiosity motivates them to test their ideas.

4. How do children come to understand the parent's viewpoint?
_____ They figure out how the parent thinks from everyday experiences with the parent.
_____ Parents must explain their viewpoint to children.
_____ When they reach a certain stage, they are able to understand the parent's viewpoint.

5. How do children come to know why some things float and others sink?
_____ Parents or teachers must explain the concept to them.
_____ They discover the concept by experimenting with objects.
_____ They know why things float when they reach a certain stage.

6. What good does playing with others serve for young children?
_____ They have an opportunity to test and develop their ideas.
_____ Playmates teach each other new ideas and behaviors.

_____ During play children demonstrate the skills that are appropriate for their age.

7. What makes children act independently?

_____ They reach a stage when they can do things alone.

_____ Parents praise them for doing things on their own.

_____ They have a desire to experiment with new ideas and actions.

8. When do children usually follow rules?

_____ When they want the approval of others or they fear punishment.

_____ When the rules are appropriate for their age level.

_____ When children understand the reasons for the rules.

9. How do young children make decisions?

_____ They make decisions by weighing all the alternatives.

_____ They rely on adults to help them decide.

_____ They decide on the basis of what a child their age usually knows.

10. How do young children become able to plan things ahead of time?

_____ When children are ready, they are able to plan.

_____ They discover through daily experiences that planning is important.

_____ Parents emphasize the importance of planning ahead.

11. How do young children come to realize that older children may feel different than they do?

_____ Teachers and parents teach children to recognize different feelings.

_____ Their curiosity leads them to think about the feelings of others.

_____ Some children seem to naturally understand that others have different feelings.

12. What makes a child come to realize that some things are alive and others are not?

_____ Adults describe and label the important characteristics for them.

_____ At a certain age they know the distinction naturally.

_____ The child discovers the concept by observing and thinking about different things.

13. How do children become able to resolve conflicts with their playmates?

_____ Some children are naturally more agreeable or cooperative than others.

_____ They discover that cooperation reduces playtime conflicts.

_____ They are encouraged by parents to get along.

14. How do young children come to understand the differences between plants and animals?

_____ The distinction is obvious to children at a certain age.

_____ They formulate the concept by observing and thinking about living things.

_____ They are taught the important characteristics of each group.

15. How do young children become able to find their way home from school on their own?

_____ They are given directions by others and then practice the skill with supervision.

_____ Children's sense of direction improves as they grow older.

_____ Children's abilities to observe and reason strongly influence this skill.

16. How do children know that a candy bar broken into pieces is still the same amount of candy?

_____ While playing with objects, children think about the relationship of parts and wholes.

_____ Adults keep reminding them that the amounts are equal.

_____ Children begin to know this when they reach a certain age.

17. How do children come to realize that parents cannot control the times of TV programs?

_____ Parents must explain this to children a number of times before it sinks in.

_____ They figure this out by observing parents' limitations.

_____ As they get older, they outgrow such confusion.

18. How do children come to know that TV commercials are different from regular shows?

_____ This understanding comes naturally as children develop.

_____ Repeated exposure and explanation from others helps them learn the difference.

_____ They gradually formulate the concept as they observe the difference.

19. Why are children able to make up imaginative stories?

_____ Make believe is a natural part of childhood.

_____ Teachers and parents encourage and foster the child's imagination.

_____ As children play with others and think about objects, their imagination develops.

20. How do children become able to read a clock?

_____ They must develop the concept of time and know their numbers.

_____ They reach a stage when they are ready to learn.

_____ They are taught by parents or teachers.

21. How do young children come to understand that cartoon characters are not real?

_____ Parents tell them that these stories are make-believe.

_____ At some point, the difference is obvious to children.

_____ Their everyday experiences help them realize that cartoon characters cannot be real.

22. Why do children begin to take care of their toys and other belongings?

_____ Parents continually remind them that this is important.

_____ They realize that they will have toys longer if they take care of them.

_____ Some children seem to have a natural tendency to be neat and orderly.

23. How do children come to know when to follow rules and when to be independent?

_____ If children know why the rules exist, they will know when to follow them.

_____ The natural balance between rules and independent action emerges spontaneously.

_____ Adults explain when rules must be followed.

24. How do children overcome irrational fears?

_____ They rely on adults to calm their fears.

_____ Most children outgrow the stage when they are susceptible to such fears.

_____ Thinking processes lead to the discovery that the fears are unfounded.

25. What makes young children be cautious in dangerous situations?

_____ They naturally fear danger.

_____ They are taught to recognize danger.

_____ They observe danger signals and regulate themselves.

26. How do children get the desire to do their best?

_____ Some children seem to be born with a desire to succeed.

_____ They imitate adults who work hard.

_____ Their curiosity motivates them to keep testing their ideas.

27. When are children best able to deal with sad feelings?

_____ When they are comforted by adults.

_____ When they understand what has caused the sadness.

_____ When they are mature enough to cope with the sad situation.

28. How do children form opinions?

_____ Opinions develop naturally as children grow older.

_____ Children's insights into everyday experiences are the basis of their opinions.

_____ They take on the opinions of their parents and peers.

29. How do children become able to solve everyday problems?
    _____ Parents demonstrate the solutions for them.
    _____ They relate past experiences to new situations.
    _____ The necessary problem-solving skills emerge spontaneously as children mature.
30. How do children come to realize the consequences of their actions?
    _____ Children gradually become more aware of how things happen as they grow older.
    _____ They think about possible outcomes of their actions.
    _____ Adults praise their good behavior or ignore their bad behavior.

APPENDIX B: DEFINITIONS

Learning
Changes in the child are shaped by the social environment (parents, teachers, peers) and the physical environment (toys, situations). The mechanisms that lead to change are direct instruction, association, reinforcement, reward, punishment, imitation, and modeling.

Cognitive-Developmental
The dynamic interaction between the child's existing knowledge and the environment is the key to development. Knowledge is the result of active processing on the child's part. The primary mechanisms responsible for learning and development (curiosity, exploration, discovery, self-regulation, experimentation) are internal to the child.

Maturational
Characteristics of the child emerge spontaneously as a result of a natural biological growth. The gradual unfolding of genetically based potential is the key to the child's readiness. The timing and patterning of behavior changes are independent of training or experience.

REFERENCES

Bell, R. Q. (1979). Parent, child, and reciprocal influences. *American Psychologist, 34,* 821–826.
Clarke-Stewart, K. A. (1978). Popular primers for parents. *American Psychologist, 33,* 359–369.
Entwistle, D. R., & Hayduk, L. A. (1978). *Too great expectations: The academic outlook of young children.* Baltimore, MD: Johns Hopkins University Press.
Harter, S. (1988). Developmental processes and the construction of self. In T. Yawkey & J. Johnson (Eds.), *Integrative processes and socialization: Early to middle childhood* (pp. 45–78). Hillsdale, NJ: Lawrence Erlbaum Associates.

Harter, S., & Pike, R. (1984). The pictorial scale of perceived competence and acceptance for young children. *Child Development, 55,* 1969-1982.

Hunt, J. M., & Paraskevopoulos, J. (1980). Children's psychological development as a function of the inaccuracy of their mother's knowledge of their abilities. *Journal of Genetic Psychology, 136,* 285-298.

Johnson, J. E., & Martin, C. (1985). Parents' beliefs and home learning environment: Effects on cognitive development. In I. E. Sigel (Ed.), *Parent belief systems: The psychological consequences for children* (pp. 25-50). Hillsdale, NJ: Lawrence Erlbaum Associates.

Leichter, H. J. (1974). Some perspectives on the family as educator. In H. Leichter (Ed.), *Family as Educator* (pp. 1-42). New York: Teachers College Press.

Lord, F. M. (1958). Some relations between Guttman's principal components of scale analysis and other psychometric theory. *Pschometrika, 23,* 291-296.

Maccoby, E. E., & Jacklin, C. N. (1974). *The psychology of sex differences.* Stanford, CA: Stanford University Press.

MacPhee, D. (1983, April). *The nature of parents' experiences with and knowledge about infant development.* Paper presented at the Biennial Meeting of the Society for Research in Child Development, Detroit, MI.

Martin, C. A. (1983). *Children's self-perceptions in relation to mothers' developmental beliefs and mothers' perceptions of the child.* Unpublished doctoral dissertation, University of Wisconsin, Madison.

McGillicuddy-DeLisi A. (1990). Parental beliefs within the family context: Development of a research program. In I. E. Sigel & G. E. Brody (Eds.) *Methods of family research: Biographies of research projects. Vol. 1: Normal families* (pp. 53-85). Hillsdale, NJ: Lawrence Erlbaum Associates.

Miller, S. A. (1988). Parents' beliefs about children's cognitive development. *Child Development, 59,* 259-295.

Miller, S. A., Manhal, M., & Mee, L. (1989, April). *Parental beliefs, parental accuracy, and children's development: A search for causal relations.* Paper presented at the Biennial Meeting of the Society for Research in Child Development, Kansas City, MO.

Nicholls, J. G. (1978). The development of the concepts of effort and ability, perceptions of academic attainment, and the understanding that difficult tasks require more ability. *Child Development, 49,* 800-814.

Nicholls, J. G. (1979). Development of perceptions of own attainment and causal attributions for success and failure in reading. *Journal of Educational Psychology, 71,* 94-99.

Peters, D. L., Neisworth, J. T., & Yawkey, T. D. (1985). *Early childhood education: From theory to practice.* Monterey, CA: Brooks/Cole.

Sigel, I. E. (1990). Journeys in serendipity: The development of the distancing model. In I. E. Sigel & G. E. Brody (Eds.), *Methods of family research: Biographies of research projects. Volume I. Normal Families* (pp. 87-120). Hillsdale, NJ: Lawrence Erlbaum Associates.

Sigel, I. E., McGillicuddy-DeLisi, A. V., & Johnson, J. E. (1980). *Parental distancing beliefs, and children's representational competence within the family context.* Princeton, NJ: Educational Testing Service.

Stipek, D. (1981). Children's perceptions of their own and their classmates' ability. *Journal of Educational Psychology, 73,* 404-410.

Vandeventer, M. (1969, May). Mothers' conceptualization of children's thinking. Research Bulletin, Princeton, NJ: Educational Testing Service.

5 Parents' Beliefs and Children's Personal-Social Development

Ann V. McGillicuddy-DeLisi
Lafayette College

My 4-year-old was practicing "pumping" himself on the swing and didn't want me distracting him, so I sat on a swing myself and watched the Frisbee game that two fathers were having around their two 3-year-old sons. One of the little boys was getting all excited. He yelled "Hi-yahhh!" and kicked karate-like at the other boy, who ran away laughing. One father threw the Frisbee to the karate kid, who spun around until he was dizzy and then released it. The fathers then went back to their Frisbee game and the two little boys ran around, making contact occasionally, falling and laughing, and then separating again.

The little kicker was getting more excited and more physical and aggressive with each interlude, however. I thought "That's the difference between mothers and fathers. A mother would see that this behavior is escalating and someone is bound to get hurt. She'd intervene now." I was wondering why mothers and fathers seem to react so differently to the same behavior from a child. The father called to the boy who had just connected a kick to his playmate's leg and threw the Frisbee again. The kid missed the Frisbee, ran to it and then ran off with it. The father caught him, wrestled playfully with him, took it away and resumed the steady back and forth toss with the other father.

Suddenly there were screams. The karate kid was sitting on his friend, swinging his little fists, pummeling his friend, and laughing while the other boy screamed. The father ran over, pulled the aggressor off the other child and spanked him hard, three times. He shouted, "I told you never to hit! Now say you are sorry!" I was thinking, "Boy, this guy never heard of Bandura." I was about to go into a daydream concerning the beliefs parents hold about their children, and how this might affect their child-rearing strategies, when a neighbor on the swing next to me said, "It's really amazing, isn't it? I knew that kid was going to go wild." Aha . . . a kindred spirit who knew that this man behaved the way he did because he believed in negative feedback as a means of conveying messages regarding appropriate behavior . . . giving little importance to the role of imitation, identification, and so forth in children's personal-social development. I said (in my best distancing voice), "Why do you think he did that?", looking for my neighbor's rationale for the father's behavior. My neighbor answered, "Boys are just so aggressive and physical. They can't help it."

Parental beliefs about the nature of children and their ideas about how children develop are complex and fascinating. I wanted to be *inside* that father's mind to understand how he interpreted his child's behavior and why he handled the situation with a spanking and reprimand. I also wanted to be in the neighbor's mind. She watched exactly the same interactions as I did, and yet her construction of the event was different. I saw the child's activity level and physical aggressiveness as a learned behavior that continued to escalate as a result of the intermittent reinforcement of his father's attention following aggressive acts, as well as through imitation of the father's own physical aggressiveness with the boy. The neighbor saw the same behavior as an expression of an inborn trait that is characteristic of boys. She and I would have reacted to the child's behavior differently because we differed in our beliefs about the source to which the behavior was attributed. I am not sure why the father acted as he did, but I am pretty sure that he would not have referred to imitation and rewards as responsible for children's growth and development in social development and self-control.

How will this little boy turn out? Within the construction just described, it is likely that I would predict that he will continue to act out aggressively because he is exposed to physical and punitive behaviors that will be incorporated into his own behavioral repertoire. It is likely that the father, as well as the neighbor who commented on the nature of boys, would each anticipate that the child would learn self-control, gaining the ability to harness his own impulsive nature as a result of the negative consequences that follow such behaviors.

In the late 1960s, Baumrind (1967) began a series of investigations that described mothers' control or management strategies, and how different strategies were related to the development of children's social responsibility. She was essentially asking, "What do parents do that affects how their children develop in the personal-social domain?." She reported that mothers who use authoritative discipline strategies (e.g., firm control coupled with rationales and warmth) had children who were more achievement-oriented, persevering, independent, friendly, and so forth than parents who were authoritarian (strict, but without give and take and/or warmth), nonconforming, or permissive (Baumrind, 1967, 1971; Baumrind & Black, 1967). These relationships between parental control strategies and children's personal-social development have been replicated over the years, sometimes using Baumrind's taxonomy and sometimes using others. For example, children's self-esteem has been linked to authoritative parenting styles (Coopersmith, 1967; Loeb, Horst, & Horton, 1980; Openshaw, Thomas, & Rollins, 1984), and Hoffman (1975) tied a similar classification of parenting strategies to children's moral development.

Many investigators have asked why these parents are different from one another. Why do some parents spank, others provide explanations for the rules, and still others allow a child to explore and regulate their own behavior? It is important to ask this question about the sources of individual differences in parental child-rearing strategies if we want to understand human behavior—how it is organized, how we can predict it, and how cognitions and behavior are related to one another. It is important if we want to educate parents to provide optimal experiences both to enhance their own development as parents and to enable them to attain their parenting goals vis-á-vis their children. And it is important because the child-rearing environment created through the management strategies used by parents has great potential impact on the personal-social development of the child.

Baumrind addressed the issue of sources of individual differences only briefly in her early work. She suggested that the authoritarian, the nonconforming, and the permissive parent might each have an unrealistic view of the child (Baumrind, 1971, 1983). The authoritarian parent might see the child as impulsive and deficient. The parent's job is therefore centered on the control of behavior, to impose a regulatory force. The nonconforming or permissive parent might also view the child as impulsive, but reveres the free and natural state of the child, or trusts in the self-regulatory properties that individuals develop on their own through maturation. These parents might hesitate to regulate the child's behaviors through firm controls because the imposition of such structure in the child's life could interfere with the natural order of development or crush the child's individualistic spirit.

Although there have been many studies of the types of discipline, control, or management *strategies* used by parents, there has been little investigation of parents' *beliefs* about child development in the personal-social domain. Interest in parents' attitudes, beliefs, and attributions has increased in recent years as investigators have sought to explain adult cognitions about children and/or consequences of beliefs on children's development (see Miller, 1988). With some exceptions, these investigations have focused on parents' views of children's cognitive development and intellectual expectations/capabilities. These studies have met with some success in terms of relating beliefs about children's cognitive development to parental teaching strategies (McGillicuddy-DeLisi, 1982a), and uncovering many aspects of individual differences, including differences between mothers and fathers (see Miller, 1988), differences that occur with educational level, cultural or ethnic background of the parents (Goodnow, 1988), and experience as a parent (Holden, 1988). Do parents also differ from one another in their view of the nature of the child's personality and social development? If they do, are such differences related to children's personal-social development in the areas of achievement, self-concept, moral reasoning, and so on?

Although the area of parental beliefs concerning children's personal-social development has been neglected, two recent studies of the social competence of preschool children included assessment of mothers' beliefs about the development of social skills (Mills & Rubin, 1990; Rubin, Mills, & Rose-Krasnor, 1989). For example, mothers were asked how they believed three social skills or behaviors (e.g., making friends, aggression) are developed and what the source of those social skills are. Mothers who believed that social skills were based on external and direct causes had children who engaged in fewer attention-seeking and more social action initiation goals. That is, when the parent believed that the development of social skills was influenced by direct instruction, as opposed to the child's nature, for example, the child was more socially mature. The authors concluded that parental beliefs about children's social development are subject to individual variation and are related to the development of children's social competence during the preschool years (Rubin, Mills, & Rose-Krasnor, 1989).

The preschool years are marked by great changes in personal-social development. Are parental beliefs likely to be related to children's development in the personal-social domain during elementary school years? Are beliefs of parents of older children also subject to individual variability? What particular types of beliefs are likely to characterize parents' accounts of development during this period? That is, do parents believe that developmental progress is due to imitation of role models, or to the child's social constructions or attributions? Is the child's personality and social competence seen as limited by genetic factors and by maturation or is it affected by a pattern of rewards and negative consequences? Are parents somewhat eclectic in their beliefs and, if so, is there variability in the extent to which they espouse one cause of behavior over another? There is little information available regarding how parents think children develop in the personal-social domain during this age period. The results of the Rubin et al. study are encouraging, however, precisely because they suggest that parents have developed complex beliefs about children's social development during the preschool years, and these appear to be related to the child's actual behavior and competence. Parents can be expected to continue to think about these issues and sources of abilities and skills as their children grow into the school years (Murphy, in press).

We have begun to gather some information regarding the nature of parents' beliefs about school-age children's personal-social development. What types of processes do parents posit as responsible for children's growth in this domain? Are there individual differences? If so, do beliefs vary with parent gender, child gender, and other descriptive characteristics of the family? What is the relationship, if any, between the beliefs of spouses? Are these beliefs related to children's personal-social development? If so, in which areas? We have just begun to explore some of these questions in a sample of two-parent families from a middle-class suburban community in the northeast part of the United States.

THE STUDY

Participants

Each family with a child in the elementary school of a small, middle-class suburban town in New Jersey received a letter describing the purpose and requirements of the study. Volunteers were asked to complete a short form that indicated their willingness to discuss the study and solicited the ages of the children, and the address and the phone number of the family. Over 100 replies out of the initial mailing of about 500 were received. All of the children in these families were assessed, but only 74 of the mothers and 68 of the fathers completed all aspects of data collection. The number of boys and girls in each grade are presented in Table 5.1. Because the ratio of males and females varied within grades it was necessary to group the children into three grade levels, Grades 1 and 2, Grades 3 and 4, and Grades 5 and 6, in order to conduct analyses of trends that occur with children's development. The participant families were White and both parents were living in the home with the child. Level of education and income were within the middle to upper middle-class range for all families. The mean level of education was 16.06 years for mothers (range = 12–21) and 17.28 years for fathers

TABLE 5.1
Number of Participant Families by Grade Level and Child Gender

	Grade Level		
Child Gender	Grades 1–2	Grades 3–4	Grades 5–6
Boys	11	20	11
Girls	12	7	13

(range = 12–26). Median family income was $90,000 per year (range = 33–395 thousand). Mean ages of fathers and of mothers were 41.76 and 39.66 years respectively (range = 29–55 years for fathers and 31–52 years for mothers). The average number of children per family was 2.65 (range = 1–6). Only one child from each family was included in the study.

Parents' Personal-Social Development Beliefs

A new measure was developed to assess beliefs about children's personal-social development. Previous investigations have used either interviews or questionnaires or both. Interviews provide more depth of information in general, but are time-consuming and require some expertise in both administration and scoring. As a result, we decided to develop a questionnaire that would be appropriate for the sample of parents available. Most questionnaires used in previous studies do not focus on beliefs regarding the nature of the child and of developmental change in a manner that is consistent with our view of beliefs. Beliefs about the child are viewed as constructions based upon experience, which are used to explain and predict the child's behavior. This theoretical framework is derived from Kelly (1955) and can be applied to parents' beliefs about the personal-social nature of children as well as about the nature of the child's cognitive development (cf. McGillicuddy-DeLisi, 1982b).

Development of the Parent Belief Questionnaire. A 53-item questionnaire designed to assess parents' beliefs about children's personal-social development was developed. Five undergraduate child development textbooks with a topical approach served as the source of the item content. Two students and two professors went through the chapters on personality, emotional, social, gender-role, and moral development. Over 600 statements representing social learning theory, attribution theory, psychoanalytic theory, biological/genetic theories, constructivist theories, operant learning theory and assumptions regarding gender differences in development were composed in this manner. These statements were randomly ordered and presented to a class of 45 undergraduate college students who had completed the child and adolescent development course. These students were asked to classify each statement as representative of one of the seven theoretical perspectives just listed. The theoretical perspectives were labeled but were not further defined. Those items for which there was 99% agreement regarding the theoretical basis for the statement among the 45 judgments were retained. A total of 53 items comprised the final questionnaire. There were eight items representing the constructivist perspective, eight from social learning, eight from attribution theory, eight from biological theories, seven items representing the psychoanalytic perspective, seven from operant conditioning, and seven items representing beliefs in gender differences. These were randomly ordered and each item was accompanied with a 6-point Likert-type scale.

Administration Procedure. Parents were instructed to indicate the degree to which they thought each of the 53 statements was true of children's personal-social development in general by circling one of the six numbers on the scale. The Likert scale was presented in the following manner: 1 = strongly disagree, 2 = disagree, 3 = moderately disagree, 4 = moderately agree, 5 = agree, 6 = strongly agree. Cronbach alphas computed on the items comprising each category indicated moderate to good internal consistency (biological = .76; constructivist = .75; attribution = .72; psychoanalytic = .66; operant = .69; social learning = .64; gender differences = .52). Each parent received a score in each of the seven theoretical categories that was the mean of their responses across the relevant items. The questionnaire items are presented in Table 5.2.

The questionnaires were mailed to the parents with a cover letter that instructed the two parents to complete the questionnaire separately and without discussion between spouses. The questionnaires were collected by a research assistant who made home visits to assess the child. If the questionnaires were not completed by that time, a stamped return envelope was left with the parent.

The Nature of Parent Beliefs About Children's Personal-Social Development. There is little information available regarding how parents view the nature of children's personal-social development and the mechanisms responsible for social competence and maturity. The first task was therefore to explore which constructs parents endorsed most frequently as an explanation of children's social development. The mean (and *SD*) scores for the 142 participants of the study were as follows (possible range = 1–6): Constructivist theory = 4.60 (.49); Attribution theory = 4.59 (.46); Operant learning theory = 4.57 (.47); Social Learning theory = 4.51 (.45); Biological theories = 4.37 (.61); Gender differences = 4.00 (.53); Psychoanalytic theory = 3.99 (.61).

Parents were most likely to endorse constructivist theories or children's attributions as sources of growth in the personal-social domain. Parents also rated principles of operant and social learning theories as factors that explain children's development, and endorsed explanations based on psychoanalytic theories and inherent gender differences less often. There are two aspects of parents' thinking that are readily apparent. First, the parents view children's personal-social development more in cognitive (e.g., constructivist and attribution concepts are endorsed) terms than affective (e.g., psychoanalytic) terms. Second, parents view the child as active in his or her

TABLE 5.2
Items Comprising the Parent Questionnaire About Children's Personal-Social
Development

Constructivist Items

---

1. Children mentally organize their experiences to make sense out of their social world.
2. Experiences that are just a little more advanced than the child's current level of understanding provide "food for thought" for the child.
3. Children formulate ideas that help them explain and predict events in their world.
4. Children develop ideas about social relationships through play with peers.
5. Children's early ideas about people and relationships change because of experiences that contradict those ideas.
6. Children's social and personality development depends on the child's level of thinking about their social experiences.
7. Children, as they grow, develop an appreciation that other people have perspectives and feelings different from their own.
8. Children's ability to interpret other people's personalities and actions increases with age.

Psychoanalytic Items

---

1. Children have basic drives that they need to learn to control.
2. Children first develop a close relationship with their mothers and later with their fathers.
3. Much of a child's behavior is caused by inner forces of which they are not aware.
4. Children reach a stage where they want to be like their mothers or like their fathers.
5. Children are aggressive, but learn self-control through their parents' enforcement of social values.
6. Without adult controls, children would be naturally wild and unruly.
7. Children identify with a parent because they perceive that parent as powerful.

Social Learning Items

---

1. Children take in much of what they see and the behavior occurs later in play or interactions with other people.
2. Children will copy complex behaviors of other simply because it is fun.
3. Children learn that certain behaviors are appropriate through their observation of adults.
4. Children's behavior is guided by the consequences they anticipate for their actions.
5. Children will copy other children who are successful or are rewarded for their performance.
6. Children will behave toward others the same way they see their parents behave towards others.
7. Children imitate people whom they admire.
8. Chilren learn social behaviors because they imitate grown men and women.

Attribution Items

---

1. Children form ideas about the kind of person they are, based on judgments about other peoples' behavior toward them.
2. Children seek explanations for other people's behavior.
3. Children conclude that they are a certain type of person by comparing their behavior to that of other people
4. Children's feelings of pride or failure determine whether they will try new activities or ideas.

(continued)

TABLE 5.2 *(Continued)*

Attribution Items (Continued)

5. A child who expects to succeed is more likely to do well than a child who expects to do poorly.
6. Children show the personality traits they are told they possess.
7. Children create theories about themselves and others in order to make sense out of what they see.
8. As children have social experiences, they form and revise their conceptions of themselves.

Biological Items

1. Children differ in their inborn motivation to master activities or ideas.
2. Almost from birth, differences in children's personalities can be seen.
3. Personality characteristics have a strong genetic component.
4. Children's preferences for certain kinds of toys and activities develop no matter how they are raised.
5. Some children are more sociable than others by nature.
6. Few differences in personality or social development are biologically rooted (reverse coded).
7. Sex hormones may play a role in differences in children's behavior.
8. Personality is largely inborn.

Operant Learning Items

1. Unacceptable behaviors become less likely if rewards or privileges are taken away when those behaviors occur.
2. Time-out (i.e., removing the child to a quiet place) teaches that certain behaviors will not be allowed or rewarded.
3. Children learn that being kind and nice to others brings its own rewards.
4. Direct rewards and punishments are responsible for children's knowledge of appropriate conduct.
5. Firm enforcement that backs up rules leads to good behavior.
6. Children behave well to please their parents and other authorities.
7. Praise helps develop pleasant behavior and personality in a child.

Gender Differences Items

1. Boys are more active than girls from birth.
2. Children learn that certain behaviors are appropriate for girls and others are appropriate for boys by watching adults.
3. Children generate their own ideas about appropriate behavior for males and females.
4. Little girls wants to be like their mothers and little boys want to be like their fathers.
5. Girls like different toys and activities than boys.
6. Sex hormones may be important in producing differences in boys' and girls' behaviors.
7. Children learn masculine and feminine behavior through imitation of men and women.

own personal-social development (as indicated in the endorsement of constructivist and attribution concepts), rather than passive in either a maturational (biological and psychoanalytic) sense, or in terms of being molded by environmental forces (operant and/or social learning theory).

Individual Differences in Parents' Beliefs.   Previous studies of parents' beliefs about processes responsible for children's intellectual development have sometimes revealed no relationship between mothers' and fathers' beliefs (McGillicuddy-De Lisi, 1982a), whereas other studies have suggested both similarity and complementarity of beliefs between spouses (Miller, 1988). Beliefs about children's intellectual development and expectancies for behavioral abilities have been reported to vary with social class (McGillicuddy-De Lisi, 1982b), with parenting experience (Holden, 1988), and with ethnic group membership and culture (Goodnow, Cashmore, Cotton, & Knight, 1984).

Once the issue of individual differences in parental beliefs is raised, the function and the origin of beliefs become intertwined in any attempt to explore those differences. For example, the observation of the Frisbee game presented at the opening of the chapter led to my conclusion that a mother would intervene at an earlier point in the children's interaction than a father would. This conclusion reflected a perhaps unwarranted assumption that mothers have more experience with children's behavior as a result of more frequent exposure to children, and a greater salience is attached to the parenting role by mothers as girls are socialized into nurturant roles. One could argue, as a learning theorist might, that mothers have learned that aggressive child behaviors lead to negative outcomes, and that early intervention into the peer interaction averts those negative outcomes. The mother is a respondent and differs from the father in that she has a different learning history than he has. She has had more experiences with children and has been more likely to attend to children's behavior as a result of her different socialization experiences. She therefore responds differently to this child behavior of aggressive peer interaction. The individual difference is behavioral, not cognitive.

On the other hand, if her experiences with children lead her to develop personal constructs that are used to explain and predict children's behavior—and those experiences differ for men and women because of role expectations and socialization—then the content of her cognitions about children become important. It suggests that parents organize their experiences cognitively. The content and structure of that organization becomes at once a reflection of their experiences with children and a source of subsequent behaviors with children as expectations and predictions arise from those beliefs. This, in turn, raises questions about the origins of beliefs.

It has been argued that parents do not construct beliefs, but adopt them ready-made from the culture. Variation in beliefs across culture and lesser interindividual differences that have been observed to occur with social class and gender within cultures have been used as support for this view (see Goodnow, 1988). Within a constructivist perspective, however, the beliefs are not constructed in isolation from the culture or society, but must necessarily be embedded within the cultural ethic. The assumptions about children that are a part of the society necessarily form boundaries for beliefs about children's development. The cultural norms and views of change and capabilities provide the very basis for experiences with children, and are themselves constructed as part of the process of building beliefs out of the experiences one has growing into the parent role throughout both childhood and adulthood. If beliefs are constructed, at once reflecting and producing differences in experiences, we expect beliefs to vary among individuals to the extent that the experiences of those individuals differ. Within a particular culture, then, individual differences should be observed that parallel different levels and types of experiences, while acknowledging that the culture indeed provides a common context that should be reflected as commonality.

The social class, ethnicity, and parenting experience of parents in the present sample are relatively homogeneous, leaving experiences as a male or a female as the most salient dimension for experiences that may have led to individual differences in beliefs about children. The responses of mothers and of fathers to the belief questionnaire were first compared to see if there was a pattern of differences that was attributable to parent gender. Then the correlations between mothers' and fathers' scores were inspected to determine if either similarity or complementarity were revealed in the pattern of positive and negative correlations between spouses.

The mean ratings of mothers and fathers for each of the six categories of beliefs are displayed in the total columns of Table 5.3. Comparisons of the scores of mothers and fathers revealed that mothers' agreement with each type of explanation for children's social development exceeded that of the fathers, with the exception of beliefs in psychoanalytic constructs (based upon a $3 \times 2 \times 2$ MANOVA involving child gender and grade level as well as parent gender; $ps < .02$ in all cases). In that area, mothers and fathers did not differ from one another. The higher rate of endorsement might reflect a positive response bias on the part of women. On the other hand, it could indicate that mothers reflect upon and accept alternative explanations of development more than fathers do. This would be consistent with the greater salience of the mother role than the father role within the socialization of boys and girls.

A consistent pattern of relationships between scores of mothers and fathers is possible regardless of the reason underlying the differences

TABLE 5.3

Mean (and SD) Belief Ratings for Fathers and for Mothers of Boys and Girls

| | Parent Gender and Child Gender | | | | | |
| | Fathers | | | Mothers | | |
Belief	Sons	Daughters	Total	Sons	Daughters	Total
Constructivist	4.44	4.57	4.49	4.66	4.77	4.71*
	(.50)	(.59)	(.54)	(.39)	(.44)	(.41)
Psychoanalytic	3.95	3.91	3.93	4.06	4.01	4.04
	(.58)	(.74)	(.64)	(.60)	(.54)	(.57)
Social learning	4.35	4.52	4.42	4.53	4.69	4.60*
	(.41)	(.44)	(.43)	(.49)	(.42)	(.46)
Attribution	4.41	4.60	4.48	4.71	4.66	4.69*
	(.43)	(.44)	(.44)	(.44)	(.49)	(.46)
Biological	4.25	4.21	4.23	4.50	4.49	4.50*
	(.63)	(.80)	(.70)	(.53)	(.46)	(.50)
Operant	4.40	4.46	4.42	4.70	4.71	4.71*
	(.38)	(.54)	(.44)	(.47)	(.46)	(.46)
Gender	3.94	3.90	3.92	4.04	4.09	4.06*
	(.44)	(.57)	(.49)	(.60)	(.46)	(.55)

$*p < .02$

between mothers' and fathers' belief scores. Significant relationships were found for three of the seven theoretical approaches to personal-social development. That is, if mothers tended to endorse constructivist views, psychoanalytic constructs, or biological constructs as responsible for children's personal-social development, their husbands were also likely to endorse these particular constructs (rs = .27, .26, and .37 for the three categories, respectively). In addition, the relationship between mothers' ratings of constructivist items and fathers' rating of attribution items was significant (r = .29). It should be noted that mothers' scores for beliefs in constructivist and attribution processes varied with education level, and mothers' and fathers' education levels were significantly correlated with one another. The significant relationships between beliefs of spouses were maintained when education was partialled out, however. None of the remaining correlations between mothers' and fathers' belief scores approached significance.

Thus it appears that the middle-class parents in this sample believed that the children's cognitive processes were responsible for a large part of their personal social development, although principles consistent with learning theory (e.g., rewards, punishments, and modeling) were also endorsed. Psychoanalytic, biological, and gender differences held somewhat less explanatory power for these parents. Mothers and fathers differed from one another in that mothers tended to rate nearly all developmental constructs higher than their husbands did. There was some degree of consistency between spouses in their beliefs in constructivist processes, children's attributions, and biological factors as determinants of children's personal-social development. This was the extent of the pattern of significant relationships between the beliefs of spouses, suggesting a modest relationship at best.

How coherent were these beliefs of mothers and fathers? Each parent was asked to indicate the extent of their agreement with statements that were representative of the seven theoretical perspectives. As a result, these scores do not reflect a typology or provide a way to classify parents, for example, as constructivists versus psychoanalytic in their beliefs. These perspectives exist within several dimensions which may be reflected in the pattern of parental responses. For example, constructivist and attribution approaches each have a strong cognitive component. Psychoanalytic views are theoretically linked to maturational stages and therefore have a biological component. Operant conditioning and observational learning share an assumption that external reality shapes the acquisition of social behaviors and personality. The intercorrelations among the seven theoretical perspectives — presented in Table 5.4, above the diagonal for mothers and below the diagonal for fathers — reveal patterns that are consistent with underpinnings shared by these theoretical perspectives. Scores for attribution and for constructivist views are strongly related for both mothers and fathers, as are scores for beliefs in social learning and operant conditioning explanations of personal-social development. The pattern of relationships differs slightly for mothers and fathers in several instances. The endorsement of psychoanalytic concepts is strongly related to constructs from operant learning and gender differences for fathers, for example.

An exploratory principal component analysis was conducted on the scores of mothers and on the scores of fathers in order to examine the interrelationships among the seven theoretical approaches. Seventy percent of the variance was accounted for by the first two factors extracted for

TABLE 5.4
Correlation Coefficients for Mothers' Beliefs (Above Diagonal) and Fathers' Beliefs (Below Diagonal)

	Belief Variable						
	Constr	Psych	Soc lnx	Attrib	Bio	Operant	Gender
Constructivist	.27*	.03	.63*	.51*	.23*	.30*	.22*
Psychoanalytic	.33*	.26*	.46*	.16+	.26*	.25*	.41*
Social learning	.42*	.47*	.15	.53*	.27*	.52*	.34*
Attribution	.68*	.23*	.61*	.10	.42*	.41*	.23*
Biological	.33*	.45*	.02	.06	.37*	.26*	.53*
Operant	.57*	.53*	.50*	.33*	.38*	.07	.34*
Gender	.35*	.67*	.37*	.21+	.55*	.50*	.22+

Note. Diagonal entries are the correlations between mothers' and fathers' belief scores.
*p < .05; +p < .10

fathers and 69% for the mothers. The factor loadings are presented in Table 5.5. The pattern was similar for fathers and mothers. Beliefs in biological factors, psychoanalytic concepts, and gender differences formed the first factor, reflecting an emphasis on innate and maturational individual differences (accounting for 49% and 41% of the variance in fathers' and mothers' scores, respectively). The second factor had a strong cognitive component, and was comprised of constructivist concepts, attribution theory, and observational learning. Beliefs in operant learning were loaded about equally on both factors. Thus there appears to be some degree of coherence among the different types of beliefs expressed as responsible for children's personal-social development, and this pattern is similar for mothers and fathers.

The Relationship of Parental Beliefs to Child Gender and Age Characteristics. The beliefs of parents of sons and daughters were compared to determine if child gender is related to the nature of parents' beliefs in different developmental processes. The mean ratings of each category of developmental constructs are also presented for sons and for daughters in Table 5.3. There were no reliable main effects for child gender.

There were, however, several instances in which significant child gender × grade level interactions occurred. Previous researchers have reported that parents' expectancies and behaviors each change as the child passes from preadolescence to adolescence. This period is also marked by great developmental change in the child, which may be a major source of shifts in parental views of that child (see, e.g., Collins, in press). There have been few studies that investigated the possibility of variation in parental beliefs about children's personal-social development that occur as boys and girls progress through middle childhood. For this reason, we examined the responses of parents with children at three different grade levels — Grades 1

TABLE 5.5
Results of Principal Component Analyses of Mothers' and Fathers' Belief Scores

	Fathers		*Mothers*	
	Factor 1	*Factor 2*	*Factor 1*	*Factor 2*
Belief				
Constructivist	.30	.75	−.19	.80
Attribution	−.01	.90	.28	.73
Social learning	.18	.80	.43	.73
Psychoanalytic	.77	.30	.72	.05
Biological	.82	−.06	.67	.21
Operant learning	.58	.53	.47	.49
Gender differences	.84	.22	.81	.09

and 2, Grades 3 and 4, and Grades 5 and 6—looking for patterns that might differ for sons versus daughters at these grade levels. There were no significant differences in beliefs between parents of children in the lower, middle, and upper grades unless child gender was considered simultaneously with grade level. Significant interactions between grade and child gender occurred for psychoanalytic, biological, and gender difference beliefs. These effects were obtained through an application of Wilk's criteria to the $3 \times 2 \times 2$ MANOVA described earlier. Significant results are depicted in Table 5.6.

As the means depicted in Table 5.6 show, parents of daughters in Grades 5 and 6 were less likely than parents of sons in those grades to believe in constructs derived from psychoanalytic theory, biological explanations of development, or gender differences. Parents of daughters and sons in the lower grades did not differ from one another with respect to biological and gender difference beliefs. Parents of daughters in Grades 3 and 4 were more likely than parents of sons to endorse psychoanalytic concepts as a source of personal-social development. Thus, there is support for the notion that parents' beliefs vary with children's age during the later grades of elementary school for girls, and this trend seems to be restricted to particular types of beliefs. The gender difference may reflect the earlier maturation rates for girls as psychoanalytic, biological, and gender differences are each tied to

TABLE 5.6
Mean (and SD) Belief Ratings for Parents of Sons and Daughters at Three Grade Levels

| | Child Gender and School Grade | | | | | |
| | Grade 1–2 | | Grade 3–4 | | Grade 5–6 | |
Belief	S	D	S	D	S	D
Constructivist	4.57	4.65	4.55	4.66	4.57	4.71
	(.41)	(.46)	(.43)	(.52)	(.59)	(.59)
Psychoanalytic*	4.16	4.07	3.81	4.23	4.20	3.72
	(.47)	(.61)	(.62)	(.39)	(.57)	(.69)
Social learning	4.53	4.62	4.34	4.65	4.52	4.59
	(.43)	(.44)	(.52)	(.37)	(.30)	(.48)
Attribution	4.62	4.56	4.50	4.73	4.61	4.65
	(.33)	(.38)	(.48)	(.39)	(.53)	(.57)
Biological*	4.35	4.57	4.31	4.48	4.52	4.11
	(.56)	(.49)	(.64)	(.29)	(.56)	(.82)
Operant	4.65	4.67	4.48	4.73	4.58	4.46
	(.38)	(.53)	(.48)	(.45)	(.47)	(.51)
Gender*	4.01	4.16	3.92	4.21	4.10	3.75
	(.59)	(.49)	(.56)	(.46)	(.38)	(.55)

Note. S = Sons; D = Daughters
*Child gender $\times$ school grade interaction $p < .05$

maturational factors in some way. A shift in parental beliefs in such constructs may occur for boys during later grades or it may occur only for parents of daughters. It is somewhat surprising that the direction of change is a downward trend in parental beliefs in biological factors, psychoanalytic constructs, and gender differences as daughters approach the end of middle childhood. Perhaps the shift in beliefs in such constructs reflects an awareness that biological changes are occurring for the earlier maturing girls (as compared with the later maturing boys) during this period, but these physical changes are not viewed as the major source of change in personal-social areas. Thus, parents of older daughters reject these notions more than parents of younger daughters and of sons who have not yet begun some of the changes which occur with maturation during Grades 5 and 6.

Children's Personal Social Development

Information regarding the child's classroom behavior, academic achievement, self-concept, concepts of distributive justice, and sex-role identity was obtained through a survey of the classroom teacher, standardized test results obtained from the school with parent permission, and individual assessments that took place in the child's home. Only data regarding classroom behavior, achievement, and self-esteem have been analyzed in relation to parental beliefs at this time.

Classroom Behavior.   The classroom teacher of each child received a request to complete Schaefer's (Schaefer, 1961; Schaefer & Edgerton, 1978) Classroom Behavior Inventory, which consists of 42 items, accompanied by a copy of a permission form signed by a parent. The teachers indicated, using a 5-point Likert-type scale, the degree to which the child displayed 10 different categories of behavior (extroversion, creativity, distractibility, independence, hostility, intelligent behavior, task orientation, introversion, considerateness, and dependence) in the classroom. Nearly all the teachers complied with this request for a rating of the child's behavior. Internal consistency reliability estimates ranged from .71 to .94. Mean ratings were computed over items comprising each subscale to yield 10 scores for each child. In addition, the teacher was asked to rate the child's behavior in five different areas: science, arithmetic, social studies, language, and social understanding. Teachers placed the child's classroom performance for each of these five areas on a four-point continuum relative to the rest of the class.

The first question explored dealt with the relationship between teacher ratings of child behaviors and parental beliefs about how the child develops in the personal-social domain. Are there any significant relationships and if so, which constructs of parents form the basis for the associations? For example, a child might score high for introversion based upon the teachers' ratings. Is this behavior related to parental beliefs in gender differences, in psychoanalytic concepts, social learning, or biological forces?

Mothers' and fathers' beliefs in gender differences were significantly related to children's classroom behavior in a number of areas. In addition, fathers' beliefs in biological processes and principles of operant conditioning were related to teacher ratings of some of their children's classroom behavior. Correlations for these belief variables are presented for mothers in the left half of Table 5.7 and in the right half of the table for fathers.

For mothers, beliefs in gender differences were negatively related to children's ratings in science, arithmetic, social studies, and language. Mothers who believed that the course of development is different for boys and for girls had children who were rated more poorly in every academic area polled. Teachers did not rate boys and girls differently in any of these areas, and the magnitude of the correlations was essentially the same for mothers of sons and for mothers of daughters (although the significance levels changed because of the smaller number of subjects included in the

TABLE 5.7
Pearson Correlation Coefficients for Selected Parental Beliefs and Children's Classroom Behavior

| | Parent Gender and Belief Construct | | | |
| | Mother | | Father | |
Classroom Behavior	Operant	Gender Differences	Operant	Gender Differences
Science	− .14	− .34*	− .20 +	− .14 +
Arithmetic	− .06	− .22*	− .22*	− .25*
Social Studies	− .14	− .33*	− .14	− .18
Language	− .10	− .23*	− .28*	− .29*
Extroversion	− .05	− .08	.22*	− .03
Creativity	− .27*	− .27*	− .04	− .05
Distractibility	− .07	− .08	.30*	.31*
Independence	− .09	− .11	− .19	− .25*
Hostility	− .08	− .19 +	.16	.23*
Intelligent behavior	− .18	− .30*	− .14	− .13
Task orientation	− .01	− .00	− .23*	− .30*
Introversion	− .12	.02	− .09	.11
Consideration	.06	.16	− .13	− .23*
	Iowa Achievement Scores			
Reading	− .19 +	− .20 +	− .09	− .14
Vocabulary	− .05	− .20 +	− .21 +	− .27*
Language	.23*	− .15	− .22 +	− .18
Math	− .15	− .24*	− .13	− .22 +
Complete	− .20 +	− .23*	− .20 +	− .20

*p < .05; +p < .10

analyses when boys and girls were considered separately). As a result, it is unlikely that the association between mothers' beliefs in gender differences and children's classroom performance in these areas reflect the mothers' accurate appraisal of gender differences in ability or achievement. In addition, mothers' beliefs in biological processes as responsible for development were also negatively related to their children's rating in science by the teacher ($r = -.23$; $p < .05$). It appears, then, that maternal beliefs in immutable traits or characteristics are not conducive to children's classroom performance in any of these four very different domains.

Mothers' beliefs in gender differences were also negatively related to children's creativity (e.g., "says interesting and original things" and "wants to know more about things presented in class") and intelligence (e.g., "has a good fund of information for a child his/her age" and "can draw reasonable conclusions from information given to him/her") ratings. Analysis of variance indicated that there were no gender differences in teachers' ratings of the children on these characteristics, reducing the likelihood that the mothers' beliefs in gender differences were due to an accurate observation of gender differences in behavior that was also observed by the teachers. These two types of classroom behavior are the ones most closely related, theoretically, to academic performance, creating a consistent pattern of negative relationships between characteristics associated with intellectual activity and mothers' beliefs in gender differences.

Mothers' beliefs in psychoanalytic concepts ($r = -.22$) and in operant learning principles (see Table 5.7) were also negatively related to the children's ratings for creativity. Beliefs in psychoanalytic concepts were also correlated with children's introversion scores ($r = .27$). Psychoanalytic concepts included in the questionnaire focus on drives, maturation, and inner states whereas the operant principles focus on external consequences as responsible for development (see Table 5.2). These have in common a lack of self-regulation and activity that may be seen as part of creativity. Similarly, the child's tendency to be introverted can be derived directly from psychoanalytic concepts. Thus the pattern of relationships between mothers' beliefs and children's classroom performance is consistent with expectations.

Fathers' beliefs in gender differences were negatively related to children's arithmetic and language performance ratings by teachers (see right half of Table 5.7), as was the case for mothers' beliefs. In addition, the fathers' beliefs in gender differences were positively correlated with teachers' ratings of the children's distractibility and hostility, and were negatively related to children's independence, task orientation, and considerateness. Although causal relationships cannot be determined, there is a consistent pattern that indicates that parents who believe in gender differences have children who tend to be rated higher in less desirable classroom behaviors and lower in desirable classroom behaviors.

Fathers' beliefs in principles of operant conditioning essentially paralleled the associations between their beliefs in gender differences and children's classroom behavior. As was the case for beliefs in gender differences, fathers' operant conditioning beliefs were negatively related to children's arithmetic and language performance, and to children's task orientation. Beliefs in operant learning were positively correlated with children's distractibility in the classroom. In addition, fathers' beliefs in operant principles were positively correlated with children's ratings for extroversion.

Fathers' beliefs in biological processes as a source of personal-social development were associated with ratings of children for extroversion and for distractibility ($rs = .22$ and $.23$, respectively; $ps < .05$). Beliefs in psychoanalytic processes were positively related to children's ratings for hostility ($.29$) and negatively related to their considerateness ($-.25$).

To summarize thus far, parents' beliefs in gender differences and in operant learning principles were the parent constructs that were most consistently related to children's classroom behavior. The pattern of relationships was generally negative in two ways. First, parents who endorsed the view that boys and girls develop in different ways had children who performed at lower levels, in the teachers' eyes, on a variety of school subjects. Language and arithmetic, stereotypically viewed as female and male subject areas respectively, were each subject to this pattern when either mothers' or fathers' beliefs were considered. This pattern, coupled with a lack of gender differences in both the teacher ratings and the parents' beliefs (i.e., parents of sons and of daughters did not differ from one another in their beliefs regarding gender differences) suggests that gender stereotypes regarding superiority of boys versus girls in different school subjects are not the source of this association between beliefs and children's behavior.

Second, parental beliefs in these constructs were negatively correlated with the more desirable classroom behaviors that were assessed (e.g., independence, creativity, task orientation) and positively correlated with less desirable classroom behaviors (e.g., distractibility, hostility). In both cases, the cause of the association cannot be determined. It is likely that for some of the child behavior variables, the child evidences behavior that the teacher notices and that has also affected parents' beliefs about personal-social development in general. This is most likely, for example, when one considers behaviors like distractibility. Parents might indeed conclude that a child who is often distracted is that way "by nature" (a biological process) because of his/her gender (a belief in gender differences), and realize that this behavior is modifiable through reinforcement and negative consequences (operant principles). On the other hand, it is also possible that the parent who believes that children are passive in their own personal-social development will view the child as both a passive recipient of genetic programming and of behavior management based upon rewards and punishments. At home, the environment might be structured and controlled by the parent with these beliefs. This child does not then develop self-regulatory mechanisms similar to his or her peers who do not experience as much structure and control at home. The teacher therefore finds the child quite distractible in school when the expectation for self-regulation on the part of the child is not met. Thus, it is possible to argue that children's behaviors have an effect on the development of parents' beliefs, in effect modifying them as the parent experiences his or her own child. But the data can also be construed as support for the position that the content of the parent's beliefs affects the course of the child's personal-social development.

It is not clear why children's behavior was related almost exclusively to beliefs in gender differences and operant learning concepts. For example, children's creativity and independence were expected to be related to parental beliefs in constructivist processes. Introversion and extroversion were expected to be related to psychoanalytic views. The variance for each of the seven belief variables was similar, which indicates that range restriction did not reduce the possibility for correlations for any particular sets of variables.

Academic Achievement.   Parents gave written permission to the school system for the release of the children's test scores on the Iowa Test of Achievement. Subscale scores for reading and for vocabulary, total scores for language and for math, and the complete Iowa scores were available for children at all grade levels. A correlational analysis of the parents' belief scores and the children's achievement test scores was conducted to determine if standardized achievement test scores were related to parent beliefs in a manner that was similar to the teacher ratings of classroom performance in academic areas and classroom behavior.

As was the case for classroom behaviors, beliefs in gender differences and in operant learning principles were related to children's scores most consistently. This was true for both mothers and fathers. The correlation coefficients are presented in the lower portion of Table 5.7. Mothers' beliefs in gender differences were negatively correlated with the children's reading, vocabulary, math, and complete scores. Beliefs in operant principles were negatively related to language scores and approached significance levels for reading and complete scores. In addition, beliefs in psychoanalytic concepts were correlated negatively with children's vocabulary scores ($r = -.23$).

Fathers' beliefs in gender differences were also negatively related to children's vocabulary scores and approached significance for math and complete scores as well. Beliefs in operant conditioning were negatively related to vocabulary and language scores, and approached significance for the complete scores. Thus, similar patterns of relationships between beliefs and children's school performance were obtained using teacher reports of classroom performance and standardized achievement test scores.

These data, too, are nonexperimental, and do not allow conclusions regarding direction of effects. If, however, the parents' beliefs are influenced by information regarding children's achievement rather than vice versa, then a positive relationship should exist between grade level and parental beliefs. That is, parents of children in the Grade 1 group had not seen any Iowa scores for their children until after the data regarding beliefs had been gathered. Those in Grade 2 had seen only one report, and parents of children in Grades 5 and 6 had seen many years of relatively stable achievement scores. If the parents constructed beliefs at least in part on this information, the belief scores should be related to grade, serving as a proxy variable for amount of available information regarding achievement. Correlational analyses revealed that grade was not significantly related to any of the mother belief variables, and was negatively correlated with fathers' beliefs in operating principles ($-.26$), gender differences ($-.20$), psychoanalytic concepts ($r = -.26$), and biological processes ($-.22$), precisely those constructs related to children's achievement. That is, the less available information regarding academic achievement was to the parent, the more likely the father was to believe in these views of development. If the relationship between parent beliefs and children's standardized achievement scores is in part due to alteration of parental beliefs in response to information regarding children's school achievement, it is most likely to be due to sources other than standardized test scores, for example, from test grades, feedback from teachers, children's own reports of their performance, and so forth. In addition, the children's further progress remains open to influence from the content of parents' beliefs, especially in the areas of operant principles and gender differences.

Several previous studies that focused specifically on antecedents to achievement in boys and in girls suggest that parental beliefs are not based on children's actual performance, at least in the domain of mathematics. For example, Parsons (Eccles), Adler, and Kaczala (1982) studied parents' perceptions of their children's math ability in relation to school grades and standardized achievement test scores in math. They found that parents' views of math ability varied more with child gender than with the child's actual performance in math. Furthermore, these parental beliefs were stronger predictors of the children's own views of their math ability than the children's actual prior math performance. Subsequent studies led to a model in which Eccles (1987) proposed that parental expectancies influence children's preferences and performance in mathematics. These findings relate to the present data in three ways. First, they suggest that parent belief–child achievement associations are probably not simply due to an accurate evaluation of the child's ability by the parent. Second, they suggest that parents' beliefs continue to persevere even when contradictory information may exist or, at the very least, there is little information that validates a particular parental belief or perception. Third, parents can and do differentiate beliefs about children's aptitude according to gender.

The findings of the present study suggest that parents vary in the degree to which they believe gender differences exist in the general domain of personal-social development, and these gender difference beliefs are not restricted to the special case of mathematics ability. These beliefs in gender differences in personal-social development are associated with differences in a variety of achievement areas. Children's language, vocabulary, social studies, and science achievement were each related to parents' beliefs that boys and girls develop differently. In light of Eccles' work as well as these current findings, it seems likely that parents have organized beliefs regarding personal-social development along gender lines. Specific information about their own child's performance might not affect that gender differentiation, and those parental beliefs may indeed affect the child's self-concept and view of his or her ability to achieve. It is important to note that the present study focused on beliefs concerning constructs of developmental change, not perceptions of child ability in a particular domain, and yet a pattern of relationships that is congruent with Eccles' data regarding parents' perceptions of ability in the area of children's mathematics was obtained. With respect to the structure of beliefs, this raises the possibility that perceptions of ability and expectations of success might have their origin in a more general construction of the nature of children and of developmental processes. To the extent that those more basic beliefs are differentiated by gender, one would find differential expectancies and attributions for success and failure for boys and for girls.

Self-Esteem.   The Piers-Harris Self-Concept Test was administered to all children in the study. This test consists of six scales (behavior; school; physical appearance; anxiety; popularity; and happiness & satisfaction). A score is assigned for each of these areas of self-esteem and a total score is assigned based on all items.

The usual administration procedure is a questionnaire format in which 60 statements are presented in written form to the child, who responds "yes" (it is true of me) or "no" (it is not true of me) to each statement. The test is not used often with first and second graders and the procedure was therefore altered for the present study in accordance with suggestions in the administration manual. A research assistant read each statement aloud as the child went through the questionnaire. The child marked "yes" or "no" in the standard questionnaire booklet as the child and research assistant went through each question in the usual sequence. Estimates of internal consistency were acceptable for all grade levels (Cronbach alpha = .79 for Grades 1 and 2, .88 for Grades 3 and 4, and .82 for Grades 5 and 6). Correlations between the 6 self-esteem scores and the 14 parents' belief scores (7 for mothers and 7 for fathers) yielded only two significant coefficients. Mothers' beliefs in psychoanalytic constructs correlated − .22 with children's anxiety scores and fathers' beliefs in psychoanalytic constructs correlated .24 with children's positive feelings about their intellectual and school status.

It was surprising to find no reliable relationship between children's esteem and parental beliefs. Anecdotal reports from the parents indicated that this was one area in which they felt that parents have great potential impact on their children, and previous studies reported associations between children's self-concept and parenting (e.g., Coopersmith, 1967). There was considerable variability in the children's self-esteem scores (range = 3–17 across the scales). In addition, self-esteem scores correlated with achievement scores in a predictable fashion, that is, about .22–.30 and in a positive direction. It is therefore unlikely that the lack of relationship is a result of the lack of variability or an unusual distribution of self-esteem scores.

SUMMARY AND CONCLUSIONS

Specific findings were discussed as they were presented. However, there are some general issues regarding beliefs about children's personal-social development that are tied directly to the manner in which beliefs are conceptualized. For example, we began by asking what is the nature of parents' beliefs about children's personal-social development. A pattern of preference for explanations of developmental change that focus on children's cognitive processes, followed by constructs derived from learning approaches, and in which biological/dispositional explanations were least favored was found. This pattern is consistent with Rubin and Mills' (this volume) report that mothers attribute children's social-skill acquisition to children's personal experiences first, followed by observational learning and then by direct verbal instruction. The Rubin and Mills study differs from the present one in several important ways. These differences, considered in conjunction with the similar patterns of parental responses, lead to several conclusions. The studies differ in that the Rubin and Mills sample included only mothers, whereas the present study sampled fathers as well. The former study focused on preschool age children, whereas the latter included children aged 6–12 years. The samples of parents were from different parts of the United States and were recruited in different ways. Parents ranked explanations in one case and indicated the extent of agreement with theoretical constructs using Likert-type scales in the other. Similar patterns of preferences across such methodological differences provide some sense of convergent validity, and suggest that there are some shared beliefs that predominate among middle-class parents at this point in the history of our society.

The studies differ in another important way, however. The assessments of Rubin and Mills (this volume), Mills and Rubin (1990), and Rubin, Mills, & Rose-Krasnor (1989) are closely tied to *socialization practices* in that parents are asked what experiences influence the development of children (e.g., being told exactly how to act). This approach to assessment of parental beliefs reflects the theoretical basis of their research program. An information processing model has been developed, within which parental beliefs are linked to attributions regarding observed child behaviors. In the present study, the focus was upon *constructs of development* that parents see as truths about the nature of children. The methods for assessments of beliefs differ because they reflect the differences in the theoretical under-pinnings of the research, but there are other differences that are far more important than the differences in methodological approaches. Differences in theoretical underpinnings of the research may lead the investigator to ask different questions, focus on different outcomes in both parents and children, and affect the interpretation of results. For example, timetables, expectancies, child development goals, and particular types (e.g., adaptive vs. maladaptive) of social behavior are an integral part of the information-processing model of beliefs.

Within a constructivist perspective, these are domains to which constructs of development apply, but they do not define the notion of belief itself. Thus there is a fundamental difference in the conceptualization of beliefs and in assumptions about the effects on parent behavior and child outcomes. The utility of multiple theoretical perspectives is evidenced when findings converge, as in the case of patterns of preferences for different explanations of children's abilities. Information about the organization, function, and interrelationships among different types of beliefs as well as their content can then be explored. In addition, the findings can comple-ment, challenge, and extend those that are derived from a different approach and a different paradigm in a manner that would not be possible within a unitary or generally accepted model. For example, questions derived from a model of beliefs as personal constructs are likely to focus on what aspects of children's experience lead parents to posit personal experi-ences as the source of children's social skills. Data from the present study suggest that parents believe that children make attributions and reflect upon those personal experiences in a manner that leads the child to think, interpret, and organize those experiences. The child's own cognition, then, forms the basis for social development. Thus information from the present study can be used to help interpret what "personal experience" might have meant to the parents in the Rubin and Mills study. The diversity of conceptualizations of beliefs, of their functions, of their relation to parental behavior as well as to different domains of child behavior is therefore a positive aspect of current work in the area of beliefs and serves to add both breadth and depth to our understanding of the form and function of parental cognition about children and development.

The second issue of importance concerns interindividual differences in parental beliefs. Mothers and fathers differed from one another in a consistent manner in that mothers expressed greater agreement with nearly all theoretical constructs of development assessed. This was discussed in terms of socialization differences for men and women, resulting in greater salience of child development issues for women and therefore greater reflection and more acceptance of alternative explanations of behavior. In addition, parents' beliefs did not vary directly with the age of their children, but parents of older daughters were less accepting of psychoanalytic, biological, and gender difference concepts as sources of social development than parents of children in Grades 1 to 4. Finally, the pattern of intercorrelations among the seven constructs was coherent and consistent with underlying assumptions of theoretical frameworks. The strong and consistent patterns of intercorrelations was similar for mothers and fathers, but the beliefs of spouses were not consistently and strongly related to one another. The focus on variability and similarity of beliefs was discussed in terms of both the origin and the function of beliefs. There are currently three explanations of origins of beliefs: (a) They are adopted, ready-made, from the culture; (b) they are constructed gradually out of reflection on experiences with children; or (c) they are momentary rationales for one's own or other's behavior, tied to specific behaviors and contexts in which the individual is involved. The explanation for origins of beliefs accepted by a particular investigator affects the conceptualization of their function, the way they are assessed, and the manner in which differences and coherent patterns are analyzed. For example, if beliefs are seen as constructions of developmental processes that guide behavior, form the basis of predictions about behavior, and are used to interpret experiences with children, one does not expect to see changes in beliefs unless the parent encounters child behaviors that are very discrepant with core constructs about the nature of the child and developmental processes. The constructs focus on *processes* of change, not the ability level or state of the child at any single point in the child's development. As such, these beliefs are used to anticipate and explain changes in the child as she passes from Grade 1 to Grade 5. The parent can acknowledge change in the child, can alter behavior in accordance with those observed changes, but beliefs in the *processes* that effected those changes do not need to be altered as long as the changes in the child are congruent with the processes held to be true.

If, however, beliefs are not conceptualized as general truths about the nature of child development processes, but as attributions for the causes of particular child behaviors/abilities at a specific point in development, when the child changes, the content of those beliefs will be expected to change. This is not to say that investigators of beliefs must choose one position or the other with respect to constructivism or attribution, or that one position will eventually be accepted and the other rejected. Parental beliefs are known to be complex, and to relate to behavior and to situational constraints in complex ways. Beliefs may exist in different forms, and we must be aware of the multiple functions that they may fulfill for the parent. Constructions of developmental processes may form a basic and global view of humanity from which attributions about child behavior in different domains and in different contexts arise (see, e.g., Sigel, 1986). One needs only to read the chapters in this volume to see how many different ways beliefs are conceptualized, how the definitions affect assumptions regarding their origin, openness to change, general versus specific nature, and relationship to both parental practices and child behaviors.

Finally, the relationship between parental beliefs and children's development continues to be an area of focus. This interest is derived from concern about children's welfare, that is, how to optimize outcomes for children, but also from a desire to understand the nature of the relationship between parent beliefs and child outcomes. How do parental beliefs affect child development directly as well as indirectly, that is, through parenting practices that may be derived from those beliefs? Does the relationship vary with domain, that is, are beliefs about the child's intellectual ability/development related to child outcomes in a different manner or to a different degree than beliefs about personal-social development? Does the relationship of parental beliefs and child outcomes vary with the child's age as other socialization agents become important? In the area of personal-social development, there is little known about the beliefs of parents regarding the causes of growth and maturity in these domains, and the parents' views of their role in the process. It is generally assumed that parents do have an impact, and that this influence is transmitted through parental control or management strategies that have been associated with positive child outcomes in previous studies. Our conceptualizations of adult cognitions about children's personal-social development will become more complex and will contribute to our understanding of parental beliefs in general as studies conducted from a variety of theoretical perspectives continue to focus on these issues.

ACKNOWLEDGMENTS

Research reported in this chapter was supported in part by a grant from the Committee on Advanced Scholarship and Research, Lafayette College. The work of Robert Bacino, Kevin LaBar, and Stacey Otstot in data collection, scoring, and analyses and the participation of parents and children are gratefully acknowledged.

REFERENCES

Baumrind, D. (1967). Child care practices anteceding three patterns of preschool behavior. *Genetic Psychology Monographs, 75,* 43–88.

Baumrind, D. (1971). Current patterns of parental authority. *Developmental Psychology Monographs, 4,* (1, Part 2).

Baumrind, D. (1983). Rejoinder to Lewis's reinterpretation of parental firm control effects: Are authoritative families really harmonious? *Psychological Bulletin, 94,* 132–142.

Baumrind, D., & Black, A. E. (1967). Socialization practices associated with dimensions of competence in preschool boys and girls. *Child Development, 38,* 291–327.

Coopersmith, S. (1967). *The antecedents of self-esteem.* San Francisco: W. H. Freeman.

Collins, W. A. (in press). Parent–child relationships in the transition to adolescence: Continuity and change in interaction, affect, and cognition. In R. Montemayor, G. Adams, & T. Gullota (Eds.), *Advances in adolescent development* (Vol. 2). Beverly Hills, CA: Sage.

Eccles, J. S. (1987). Gender roles and achievement patterns: An expectancy value perspective. In J. M. Reinisch, L. A. Rosenblum, & S. A. Sanders (Eds.), *Masculinity/femininity* (pp. 240–280). New York: Oxford University Press.

Goodnow, J. J. (1988). Parents' ideas, actions and feelings: Models and methods for developmental and social psychology. *Child Development, 59,* 286–320.

Goodnow, J. J., Cashmore, J., Cotton, S., & Knight, R. (1984). Mothers' developmental timetables in two cultural groups. *International Journal of Psychology, 19,* 193–205.

Hoffman, M. L. (1975). Altruistic behavior and the parent–child relationship. *Journal of Personality and Social Psychology, 31,* 937–943.

Holden, G. W. (1988). Adults' thinking about a child-rearing problem: Effects of experience, parental status and gender. *Child Development, 59,* 1623–1632.

Kelly, G. A. (1955). *The psychology of personal constructs.* New York: Norton.

Loeb, R. C., Horst, L., & Horton, P. J. (1980). Family interaction patterns associated with self-esteem in preadolescent girls and boys. *Merrill-Palmer Quarterly, 26,* 203–217.

McGillicuddy-De Lisi, A. V. (1982a). Parental beliefs about developmental processes. *Human Development, 25,* 192–200.

McGillicuddy-De Lisi, A. V. (1982b). The relationship between parental beliefs and children's cognitive development. In L. Laosa & I. E. Sigel (Eds.), *Families as learning environments for children* (pp. 7–24). New York: Plenum.

Miller, S. A. (1988). Parents' beliefs about their children's cognitive development. *Child Development, 59,* 259–285.

Mills, R. S. L., & Rubin, K. H. (1990). Parental beliefs about problematic social behaviors in early childhood. *Child Development, 61,* 138–151.

Murphy, D. A. (in press). Constructing the child: relations between parents' beliefs and child outcomes. *Developmental Review.*

Openshaw, D. K., Thomas, D. L., & Rollins, B. C. (1984). Parental influences of adolescent self-esteem. *Journal of Early Adolescence, 4,* 259–274.

Parsons (Eccles), J. E., Adler, T. F., & Kaczala, C. M. (1982). Socialization of achievement attitudes and beliefs: Parental influences. *Child Development, 53,* 310–321.

Rubin, K. H., Mills, R. S. L., & Rose-Krasnor, L. (1989). Maternal beliefs and children's social competence. In B. H. Schneider, G. Attili, J. Nadel, & R. P. Weissberg (Eds.), *Social competence in developmental perspective* (pp. 313–337). Dordrecht: Kluwer Academic Publishers.

Schaefer, E. S. (1961). Converging conceptual models for maternal behavior and for child behavior. In J. C. Glidwell (Ed.), *Parental attitude and child behavior* (pp. 124–146). Springfield IL: Charles C. Thomas.

Schaefer, E. S., & Edgerton, M. (1978). *Child Behavior Inventory.* Unpublished manuscript. University of North Carolina at Chapel Hill.

Sigel, I. E. (1986). Reflections on the belief–behavior connection: Lessons learned from a research program on parental belief systems and teaching strategies. In R. D. Ashmore & D. M. Brodzinsky (Eds.), *Thinking about the family: Views of parents and children* (pp. 35–66). Hillsdale, NJ: Lawrence Erlbaum Associates.

Passing the Rod: Similarities Between Parents and Their Young Children in Orientations Toward Physical Punishment

6

George W. Holden
Robert J. Zambarano
University of Texas at Austin

One conspicuous reminder that parents do indeed affect their children lies in the phenomenon of intergenerational transmission—the adoption by children of beliefs, attitudes, interests, or behavior similar to their parents. Maybe the most striking instances occur when a child follows a parent's vocational interest and both achieve excellence and international recognition. Some of the names of families that illustrate this transmission include Darwin, Bach, Mozart, Freud, Gandi, and Wyeth, to name but a few.

Although those families represent exceptional manifestations, well within everyone's experience are cases of shared family beliefs, attitudes, or behavior patterns. Evidence for this can be found in many autobiographies, as well as in more systematic analyses from researchers. The study of intergenerational transmission now represents a considerable area of research, and has attracted the attention of anthropologists, sociologists, and political scientists, as well as psychologists.

The transmission of psychological characteristics from parent to child has long been recognized as a fundamental process of human development. Early psychological research into this training process was guided by Sigmund Freud's theoretical writings on identification (e.g., Freud, 1923). Robert Sears' investigations into identification and social behavior (Sears, Rau, & Alpert, 1965), and Lawrence Kohlberg's analysis of identification and moral development (Kohlberg, 1963) are but two examples of the attention this process has received from prominent psychological researchers.

In contrast to this early work and a considerable amount of ensuing research that has focused on the psychological effects that parents can have

143

on their children, work into intergenerational transmission has focused on *similarities* between parent and child. In essence, the goal has been to identify the maintenance of individual differences passed from one generation to the next. In a wide variety of domains of thought and action, from aggressive behavior and moral values to divorce and political affiliations, researchers have investigated the extent to which children maintain the differences exhibited by their parents. That focus contrasts with the more general process that has been labeled "socialization," in which the parents guide children to act in accord with the social norms of their culture. Thus, efforts to identify intergenerational transmission — or individual differences maintained from parent to child — are concerned with the process of "parentization."

Parentization represents an extremely important domain of psychological study because through this social process not only do children develop patterns of behavior, but Lamarkian evolution occurs. That is, the characteristics or behavioral patterns acquired by parents are passed on to offspring. Instead of a biological evolutionary mechanism, parentization represents cultural evolution within particular families. What gets passed on can be prosocial or positive characteristics, such as vocational interests and religious beliefs, or harmful beliefs or behavior such as racial prejudices or abusive behavior. For these reasons and others, understanding the processes behind and limits to the cliché "Like father, like son" are consequential.

The transmission from parent to child of thoughts or behaviors occurs through a variety of mechanisms; these vary on the degree of intentionality and subtlety with which the transmission may occur. The three mechanisms most commonly mentioned are child modeling, parental instructing, and child accordance. By far and away, the most common mechanism involves the child modeling the parent. The modeling may be a direct imitation of the parent's action or, more commonly, a more unconstrained modeling of the parent's verbal behavior or prevailing behavioral propensities. This results in what has been called a "slow, informal, and unwitting apprenticeship" (Faris, 1947, p. 159). The outcome of this apprenticeship is commonly identified in measurements of the "similarity" of responses.

A second mechanism of transmission involves parental instruction of beliefs or actions. In this case, parents tutor the child in a direct and intentional fashion. This is likely the case with regard to certain religious values (Hoge, Petrillo, & Smith, 1982). A third type of mechanism deals with the child behaving in accord with the expectations internalized from either parent. Hill (1967) labeled this outcome "accordance" and found evidence for it with boys' conforming to their fathers' expectations concerning attitudes toward mathematics. A fourth mechanism, sometimes discussed in the psychoanalytic research, is that of subconscious transmission (e.g., Miller, 1984). Despite the appeal of differentiating the mechanisms, it should be remembered that they often co-occur and are interrelated.

The preponderance of research into intergenerational transmission has focused on identifying similarities between parent and child, and assumes some type of modeling mechanism. Investigations into the similarity between parents' and children's beliefs or behavior have been published in a wide range of domains. Among these are inquiries into: parental transmission of political and religious attitudes (Acock & Bengtson, 1980; Middleton & Putney, 1963); attitudes toward education, work, and achievement (Cashmore & Goodnow, 1985; Parsons, Adler, & Kaczala, 1982; Rosen, 1964); authoritarian beliefs (Rigby, 1988; Williams & Williams, 1963), values and personality (Troll, Neugarten, & Kraines, 1969); sexual behavior (Shah & Zelnik, 1981); substance abuse (Gaines, Brooks, Maisto, Dietrich, & Shagena, 1988; Lerner, Karson, Meisels, & Knapp, 1975); marital violence and instability (Greenberg & Nay, 1982; Kalmuss, 1984; Mueller & Pope, 1977), and loneliness (Lobdell & Perlman, 1986).

Each of these studies was designed to identify continuities between generations; some were more successful than others. None of the studies listed have explicitly searched systematically for discontinuities. Part of the reason is that a conclusion of discontinuity may be indicative of poor measurement instruments rather than actual discontinuity; in contrast, significant intergenerational correlations of similarity provide some evidence for transmission. But also the emphasis of researchers has been on identifying similarities rather than differences. Interestingly, as early as 1934, researchers into intergenerational transmission of attitudes identified two distinct paths that offspring may take. Some children were found to adopt a "direct imitation" to their mothers' attitudes whereas others chose to "deliberately take the opposite course" (Francis & Fillmore, 1934).

The extant research into intergenerational transmission highlights four recurrent problems relevant to the topic of this chapter. First, parental influence is inadequately assessed. Parental impact appears to depend on a number of variables, including the particular variable in question, the quality of the relationship between the parent and child, the correspondence between the mothers' and fathers' beliefs and actions, and the gender of child and parent (Acock & Fuller, 1984; Cashmore & Goodnow, 1985; Elder, Caspi, & Downey, 1986). Typically, a number of relevant variables are neglected or sampled inadequately. For example, though many studies ostensibly concern parental influence, fathers' input is commonly neglected.

Second, parents are by no means the exclusive source of influence, consequently discontinuity from parental influences can be accounted for by some of these alternative influences. Peers, contextual pressures, schooling, and idiosyncratic intrapersonal variables are four of the major sources of discontinuity (Bronson, Katten, & Livson, 1959). Depending on the age of the child and the type of variable, nonparental sources of information or modeling require attention.

A third type of problem is the common assumption of the direction of influence from parent to child (Bengtson & Troll, 1978). Making the assumption that parental beliefs or actions were preexisting and causally linked to their offsprings' beliefs or actions often has gone unverified because investigations have failed to look at the intergenerational links early in the ontogeny of the offspring. There has been a widespread theoretical and methodological failure of investigators to provide a bidirectional or transactional view of transmission as the interactive process that it is.

Finally, as many researchers have pointed out, the study of intergenerational transmission is laden with methodological pitfalls (Acock, 1985; Jackson & Hatchett, 1986). Ideally, studies addressing intergenerational transmission would use longitudinal data; in fact, only a few such studies exist (e.g., Elder, Caspi, & Downey, 1986). Among the nonlongitudinal studies, a locus of problems has centered around data collection. Collecting data from young children presents various problems and threats to the validity of the data that are not at issue when assessing adults (see Heilbrun, Bateman, Heilbrun, & Herson, 1981). Some studies have failed to collect data from both generations (e.g., Middleton & Putney, 1963). When parents are sampled, some studies gather long-term retrospective memories of parents which are well known to be inaccurate, rather than focusing on concurrent behavior (see McGraw & Molloy, 1941; Yarrow, Campbell, & Burton, 1964). When parents are sampled, their reports are often collected on surveys of attitudes rather than on questionnaires about their behavioral practices; the latter type of instruments are better predictors of behavior than beliefs or attitudes (Holden & Edwards, 1989).

Despite the methodological problems, an increasing amount of attention is being devoted to the study of intergenerational relations. One domain that has of late received an infusion of attention is that of parental transmission of child-rearing attitudes and behaviors. Part of the impetus for such work is the increasing appreciation for the multidetermined nature of parental behavior. Consequently, to understand why parents act the way they do, psychologists must investigate a complex constellation of influences. These include the greater culture, the parent's personality, marital relations, stress and social support, child characteristics, and developmental history such as previous experience with children, or experience in one's family of origin (e.g., Belsky, 1984). Among the experiences occurring within the family of origin is one that is the concern of this chapter – how parents transmit orientations toward parenting.

To date, a relatively small number of studies have been published concerning intergenerational transmission of parenting. Those studies are briefly reviewed next. That is followed by a study examining parent-to-child transmission of one child-rearing behavior — the use of physical punishment as a disciplinary technique. The chapter ends with a more general discussion of the transmission of parenting and orientations toward physical punishment.

TRANSMISSION OF PARENTING BELIEFS, ATTITUDES, AND BEHAVIOR

The adage that children are destined to repeat the child-rearing practices of their parents is a familiar one. In fact, if there was no relation between parents and children's behavior it would call into question some of our most basic theories of development including social learning, operant conditioning, and cognitive development. But a better way of framing the question is not "Does transmission occur?," but rather the related questions of "In what domains is it most likely to occur?," "Under what conditions is it strongest?," and "What variables mediate transmission?."

At this point in time, the study of intergenerational transmission of parenting in humans has focused on three topics: dysfunctional parenting and child abuse, parent–child attachment, and discipline and management. Rutter (1989) recently reviewed much of the work in the area of intergenerational dysfunctional parenting. Despite methodological limitations, such as the reliance on retrospective reports rather than assessing two generations (Carroll, 1977; Herrenkohl, Herrenkohl, & Toedler, 1983), the evidence reveals both continuity and discontinuity. It is clear that continuity of inept parenting is not inevitable and that the quality of parenting, given the appropriate conditions, can show considerable plasticity. Similarly, Elder and his colleagues in a variety of reports (e.g., Elder, Caspi, & Downey, 1986) identified both continuity and discontinuity in family problems across generations using data from the longitudinal Berkeley Guidance Study. Other investigators have found evidence for continuity of dysfunctional parenting in the case of child abuse (Egeland, Jacobvitz, & Papatola, 1987). Two recent reviews summarized the evidence for intergenerational cycles of physical child abuse (Kaufman & Zigler, 1989; Widom, 1989) and conclude that the rate of transmission is 30% ± 5%, a sixfold increase over the base rate.

The second domain that has been studied is intergenerational transmission of mother-child attachment. This topic only began to receive attention in the mid-1980s but is attracting increasing interest. The pioneering investigations of Main, Kaplan, and Cassidy (1985) and Ricks (1985) began to trace how internal representations of mothers' influence affect subsequent attachment relations and thus create one source of continuity. Ricks reviewed the available evidence and concluded that "the quality of a mother's caregiving behavior is strongly related to her memories of child-hood relationships" (p. 226). Presumably, there are also influences not accessible to conscious memory that are also affecting the quality of attachment (see Miller, 1984).

To date, most of the work into intergenerational transmission of parenting has been in the area of child management and discipline. In some studies reported to be investigating intergenerational transmission, children's attitudes are correlated with the children's perceptions of their parents (e.g., Lyle & Levitt, 1955). When researchers did take the trouble to collect data from both generations, college students and their mothers were the sample of choice and attitudes toward parenting have been the topic of choice (e.g., Kell & Aldous, 1960; Woods, Glavin, & Kettle, 1960). A listing of all the studies that we located that have examined some aspect of the transmission of child management or disciplinary practices is provided in Table 6.1.

At least two investigations have assessed the relations between mothers' and grandmothers' attitudes. The first such attitude study was by Staples and Smith (1954), who found some evidence for mothers and their own mothers sharing similar attitudes toward child rearing. But the degree of similarity was mediated by variables such as whether the grandmother resided with the mother and the mothers' education. Furthermore, there is no information about who was influencing whom. In a more recent study of child-rearing attitudes in two generations of mothers, Cohler and Grune-

TABLE 6.1

A Chronological Listing of Empirical Studies Concerning Intergenerational Effects in the Domain of Parenting Discipline and Authority

Author(s)	Date	Sample Size and Type of Children	Parent(s) Assessed	Types of Variables Studied
Radke	1946	43 3–5-yr-olds	both	Authority
Staples & Smith	1954	87 mothers	mothers	Attitudes
Bronson, Katten, & Livson	1959	100 6-yr-old & older	both	Authority, affection, involvement
Kell & Aldous	1960	50 college students	mothers	Values
Woods, Glavin, & Kettle	1960	86 college students	mothers	Attitudes
Williams & Williams	1963	245 college students	both	Authoritarian attitudes
McGahey & Sporakowski	1972	83 college students	mothers	Attitudes
Cohler & Grunebaum	1981	88 mothers	mothers	Attitudes
Wolfe, Katell, & Drabman	1982	15 4–6-yr-olds	mothers	Disciplinary responses
Bush, Gallagher, & Weiner	1982	68 college students	both	Authoritarian attitudes

baum (1981) found reliable relations in three of five subscales on the Maternal Attitude Scale. However the median correlation was modest, $r(88)$ = .31, p < .05.

Though such information is informative about the relations between parental and child attitudes, the reliance on this type of instrument is problematic for understanding the development of orientations toward child rearing. The focus on global, decontextualized child-rearing attitudes has been criticized elsewhere (Holden & Edwards, 1989); such an approach fails to provide information about particular parenting behaviors. A second problem with the use of attitude questionnaires is that by the time children are cognitively advanced enough to be capable of responding to a standard, Likert-type attitude survey, they are elementary or high school students. If the question of interest is parental influence, then investigations that neglect other influences on the children have a serious confound. Third, attitude surveys do not typically contain just attitude statements but rather a mixture of attitudes, beliefs, behavioral intentions, and self-perceptions (Holden & Edwards, 1989). Thus, if continuity is found, little can be inferred about the mechanism of transmission because of the confounded nature of the surveys.

One alternative to the standard child-rearing attitude questionnaires is to use context-specific vignettes (see Sigel, 1987). We located two studies that employed such an approach. Morgan and Gaier (1956) developed a projective device to assess perceptions of aggressiveness expressed by elementary school children and their mothers. Unfortunately, data from individual mother–child dyads were not analyzed so the study provides no information concerning parent–child transmission. The only study that has assessed links between parents' and young children's specific disciplinary responses was conducted by Wolfe, Katell, and Drabman (1982). Fifteen mothers and preschoolers were shown six different videotaped scenes of child misbehavior and asked how they would respond. Based on a reduction of the data to a dichotomous variable, Wolfe and his colleagues found that, across the six scenes, about 77% of the mother–child dyads reported similar behavioral intentions on whether they would use a coercive or noncoercive response.

The study by Wolfe and his colleagues provides a starting point for identifying the origins of parenting by focusing on use of particular responses. However, it is limited by the small sample size, the use of mothers only, and the dichotomized responses. In addition, a number of questions are raised. First, could transmission—or at least similarity of responses—be found in parent–child selection of a specific child-rearing practice rather than just a coercive orientation? How similar would fathers' behavioral intentions be with their sons and daughters? And are behavioral intentions better than attitudes or reports of practices for identifying similarities between parent and child? To address these and other questions the following study was conducted.

A STUDY OF PARENTAL TRANSMISSION
OF PHYSICAL PUNISHMENT

Given the multiple roles inherent in child rearing and the wide range of behaviors that encompass parenting (Holden & Ritchie, 1988; Rutter, 1989), a study into the transmission of parenting must be a circumscribed effort. Therefore, we culled the possible domains of study down to a short list of child-rearing behaviors that might impinge on a preschooler and ones that were salient to both the parent and child. The child-rearing practice that met those criteria and thus was a likely candidate for transmission was parental use of physical punishment.

For several reasons, the study of physical punishment is both a useful and important approach to the transmission of parenting. The practice of spanking, from all accounts, is widespread but also subject to considerable interparent variation. According to various surveys, over 90% of American parents have spanked their children (Gelles, 1978; Wauchope & Straus, 1989). However, the frequency with which spanking is used varies dramatically. For a sample of middle-class parents, the majority of parents (perhaps 60–70%) use it occasionally — maybe once or twice a week — in response to severe misbehavior. Severe misbehavior typically means one of three things to most parents: engaging in defiant disobedience, endangering him/herself or someone else, or being willfully destructive (Holden, 1989). The remaining parents can be placed at either ends of the frequency of use continuum. Some parents (perhaps 10%–15%) rely on physical punishment as a mainstay disciplinary technique and use it almost daily or more. The remaining parents form the third group and report that they never or rarely spank their children.

In addition to having considerable variation, physical punishment is a worthwhile behavior to study because of its significance to parents and children. When it is used, it results in an emotionally charged interaction for both parent and child (Patterson, 1982; Vasta, 1982). There is little room for misinterpretation associated with physical punishment — it is a discrete behavior that requires the use of some object (e.g., hand, paddle) to strike some part of the child's body (e.g., hand, buttocks). Though physical punishment has a number of synonyms (e.g., smacking, slapping, whipping, spanking) there is widespread recognition of its meaning. Together the salience and the well-defined nature of the behavior mean that parents tend to have clear and preexisting attitudes about the use of physical punishment

(Sears, Maccoby, & Levin, 1957; Stolz, 1967) and to display some degree of continuity in the attitude over time (Roberts, Block, & Block, 1984). It is not surprising that questions about physical punishment were found to have among the highest test–retest reliability properties of any questions in a parent questionnaire (Rickard, Graziano, & Forehand, 1984).

Physical punishment is also a useful behavior to study with regard to intergenerational transmission because, with the exception of isolated school experiences, children's experience with it is largely limited to the confines of their home and the hands of their parents. Middle-class parents typically refrain from spanking in public or spanking other people's children (Holden, 1989). As a consequence, most of the lessons children learn about spanking, at least during the first decade of life, come from personal experience at home.

There are other reasons to study physical punishment besides the opportunities it provides for understanding individual differences in parents. A number of researchers have discussed theoretical reasons or provided data linking parental use of physical punishment and subsequent child abuse, spouse abuse, adult violence, or approving attitudes toward violence (see Erlanger, 1979; Feshbach, 1970; Owens & Straus, 1979). It is presumed that the experience children have with violence in the home sets the stage for future violence. In a longitudinal study, Huesmann, Eron, Lefkowitz, and Walder (1984) found that the severity of punishment received by 8-year-old children was reliably related to the ratings of the aggressiveness of those individuals at age 30 [$r(82) = .25, p < .01$].

Despite the importance of the topic of intergenerational transmission of physical punishment, relatively little empirical data is available. What work has been done comes from a variety of perspectives. For example, Radke (1946), in an investigation of child-rearing practices, found that children tend to prescribe the same kind of punishments as they received from their parents. Sears (1951) adopted a psychoanalytic perspective and found that children who were punished the most were most likely to use fantasy aggression. A number of researchers have assessed children's perceptions of parental discipline (e.g., Appel, 1977; Armentrout & Burger, 1972; Carlson, 1986; Goldin, 1969; Tisak, 1986) and their views of the appropriateness of physical punishment as a parental response to certain misbehaviors. Though most studies sample children of elementary school age or older, a few investigations have included children as young as 5 or 6 years old (Haviland, 1979; Siegal & Cowen, 1984). Results from those studies indicate that young children appear to hold more favorable ratings of physical punishment than older children (Siegal & Cowen, 1984), and younger children are less likely to take into account situational variables before prescribing a spank.

One of the common findings concerning children's perceptions of their parents' use of punishment concerns gender differences. For example, Kagan and Lemkin (1960) interviewed 3- to 8-year-old children and found that fathers were perceived to be more frequent spankers than mothers. Others have also found gender effects, both in reviews of parenting practices (Maccoby & Jacklin, 1974; Wauchope & Straus, 1989) and in studies of perceptions of discipline (Herzberger & Tennen, 1985). Generally, females report more negative views of discipline and receive less physical punishment from their parents. However, not all studies find significant differences due to the parents' or children's gender (e.g., Siegal & Cowen, 1984).

Predictions

To review, the intergenerational transmission of physical punishment, as a child-rearing practice, is an understudied topic. The major goal of the study was to collect data concerning parental use of physical punishment in an effort to identify links with children's views about using the disciplinary behavior. We expected that parental use of physical punishment would be positively correlated with children's perceptions of how likely they would be to use that response. To better understand how transmission may occur, our particular focus was to separate out attitudinal items from behavioral intentions and reported practices as has been recommended by researchers into attitude–behavior relations (e.g., Acock & Fuller, 1984; Manfredo & Shelby, 1988), though we expected parental attitudes, behavioral intentions, and reported practices to be at least moderately correlated.

Given that physical punishment is most frequently used with 3- to 5-year-old children (Wauchope & Straus, 1989), it was decided that the study would focus on the use of physical punishment with 5-year-old children. This would then allow 5-year-old children and their parents to report on their concurrent experiences with physical punishment. Because a number of studies have reported age changes in children's perceptions of physical punishment, we included a second age group of 8-year-old children and their parents in a cross-sectional design. We expected the similarity between the 8-year-old children and their parents would be higher with parental attitudes and behavioral intentions variables as the older children might receive more parental instruction (i.e., warnings and discussions) about spanking but have fewer opportunities for direct modeling of the behavior, given the decreasing incidence of that practice with older children.

In sum, we expected to find support for the following four hypotheses: (a) parents will have a coherent system of beliefs and practices with regard to physical punishment such that assessments of attitudes, behavioral intentions, and reported practices are all reliably correlated; (b) parents' beliefs about physical punishment and reported practices will be positively correlated with children's behavioral intentions concerning their likelihood of using the behavior; (c) younger children's intentions will be more closely linked with parental practices and the older children's intentions will be more linked with parental attitudes; and (d) parents of boys, in comparison to parents of girls, will have more positive attitudes, greater behavioral intentions, and higher reported use of physical punishment. Consequently, we expected boys to report that they would be more likely to use physical punishment than girls.

METHOD

Subjects

Participating were 40 children, all of their mothers, and 27 of their fathers from a mid-sized southwestern city in the United States. Twenty of the children were 5 years old and 20 were 8 years old with an equal number of boys and girls. The 5-year-old children averaged 5:5 years (range 5:0 to 5:9) and the 8-year-olds had a mean age of 8:6 (range 8:0 to 8:11). The mean age of the mothers of the younger group of children was 35 years and 38 years for the older group. The level of educational attainment was similar in both groups; 30% of the mothers' highest degree was from high school, 50% graduated from college, and the remaining 20% held graduate degrees. Forty percent of the mothers of the younger children were homemakers in contrast to 15% of the mothers of the older group. About 40% of the mothers in each group were employed full-time and the remaining mothers worked part-time or were students.

Fifteen fathers of 5-year-olds and 12 fathers of the 8-year-olds completed the questionnaires; the remaining fathers either declined to participate or never returned the questionnaires. Neither the fathers' amount of education nor Hollingshead (1975) scores of occupational status differed between the age groups. As with the mothers, the fathers had earned a range of educational degrees. Thirty percent held high school diplomas, 48% had bachelors' degrees, and 25% received graduate degrees. The mean Hollingshead rating was 7.2 (range 3 to 9) indicating an occupational status of small business owner, manager, or some type of professional.

Materials

Three questionnaires were developed to assess parents' attitudes and parents' and their children's behavioral intentions and practices concerning the use of physical punishment as a disciplinary technique.

Attitudes Toward Physical Punishment.   The attitude questionnaire consisted of 10 statements about physical punishment. Parents rated how strongly they agreed or disagreed with each statement on a Likert-type scale from 1 = *strongly disagree* to 7 = *strongly agree*. The statements include both positively and negatively phrased items, and were written in the first person. Examples include: "I believe it is the parents' right to spank their children if they think it is necessary"; "Sometimes a spank is the best way to get my child to listen." This scale of parents' general orientation toward physical punishment was a shorter version of a 30-item questionnaire, based on the results from a factor analysis (Holden, 1989).

Parents of 5-year-olds rated their current attitudes toward physical punishment. Parents of 8-year-olds made two separate ratings. First they were asked to recall their attitudes when their children were 5, and then they were instructed to report on their current attitudes towards spanking.

The 2 week test–retest reliability of the items, assessed in an earlier study, was found to be .76 with a sample of 20 mothers. The coefficient alpha of the 10 items calculated on the data used in the present study was consistently high. Alphas ranged from .92 to .94 depending on whether it was calculated with the mothers' current or retrospective attitude scores or the fathers' current or retrospective attitude scores.

Behavioral Intentions.   Eight vignettes were created that described the misdeeds of a 5-year-old child in a variety of situations. These misdeeds and their situations were developed from information gathered via a series of interviews with mothers on their use of physical punishment. Based on that data and other research (e.g., Dix, Ruble, & Zambarano, 1989; Grusec & Kuczynski, 1980), vignettes were constructed to elicit reports of physical punishment. The misdeeds and settings were as follows:

1. In spite of a specific command to stop, the child splashes in a mall fountain, getting other shoppers wet.
2. After being told twice to come inside, the child responds "I didn't want to so I didn't have to."
3. The child is found playing with matches.
4. The child crosses a street alone to play with the neighbors.
5. The child throws rocks at a cat in a tree.
6. The child hits the mother during a shopping trip.
7. The child breaks an expensive lamp.
8. The child breaks another child's toy after being told to return it.

These eight vignettes were presented, in an elaborated form, to all the subjects. Parents were asked to imagine that the child described in the vignettes was their own child when he or she was 5 years old. Children were asked to imagine a 5-year-old named Kelly whose gender matched their own. Pilot testing revealed that 5-year-old children had difficulty using a rating scale for this task. Therefore, the children were asked to rank order the appropriateness of the following three possible discipline responses: the use of reasoning, a "time out" (defined as removing the child from the immediate situation), or a physical punishment (defined as a spank or slap). All other subjects rated how likely it was that they would use each discipline type for that situation. Ratings were made on a 7-point Likert scale (1 = very unlikely; 7 = very likely).

Behavioral Reports.   Parents also filled out a questionnaire designed to assess the frequency with which they used each of nine different responses to misbehavior over the course of an average week. Response frequency choices ranged from 0 times per week to 11 or more. The nine response types included responses such as reasoning, diverting to another behavior, time-out, spanking, and withdrawal of privileges. Parents of 5-year-olds were asked to report their current rate of responses, though parents of 8-year-olds were asked to recall their response frequency when their children were 5 years old. Retrospective reports were solicited because of the decrease in the rate of spanking of older children (Wauchope & Straus, 1989) and the consequent decrease in variability. In addition, we suspected that prior experiences with spanking should be related to children's current views of spanking younger children.

Children's behavioral reports consisted of indicating how frequently they experienced the three target discipline responses from their parents: reasoning, time-out, and physical punishment. They selected one of six responses from "never" to "once or more a day" for each of the discipline types. Because pilot testing revealed that 8-year-old children had difficulty in judging the frequency of events that had happened 3 years earlier, the older children were also asked to report on how frequently they currently were the recipients of the three different disciplinary responses.

Procedure

The names of children of the appropriate ages were identified from birth records. Mothers were sent an introductory letter followed by a phone call. Of those contacted, 57% agreed to participate. Mothers decided whether they wanted to come to a university research facility to participate or have an investigator come to their homes.

Questionnaires were administered to all participating children by an investigator. Vignettes were read to 5-year-olds. The 8-year-olds had the option of reading the vignettes by themselves or having the vignettes read to them. All subjects were probed after the presentation of each vignette to assess adequate understanding. Five-year-olds were then verbally presented with the three response choices and asked to select the most appropriate: "If you were the parent in charge, what do you think would be the best thing to do?." After an initial response was selected, the two remaining choices were presented and children were asked "What would be the next best thing to do?." In this way the three response types were ranked. The 8-year-olds were guided through the rating scales for the first two vignettes; experimenter assistance with the remaining vignettes depended upon the competency demonstrated by the child on the first two. Children's recollections of the frequency with which they were disciplined was assessed verbally by the investigator.

Mothers were present for the child interviews in all cases, and typically filled out their own questionnaires during this time. Parents were not required to fill out the questionnaires in the presence of the investigator; mailing envelopes were provided. Most fathers filled out the questionnaires within a week of the mothers and mailed them in. All children received $2 for participating.

Analyses

Data were analyzed in three ways. To assess group differences, a 2 (age of child) × 2 (sex of child) × (sex of parent) ANOVA was performed on most of the dependent variables. Indications of parental transmission of spanking as a child-rearing technique was examined in two ways. First, correlations between parent and child spanking scores were computed by summing the rankings or ratings over the eight situations. Due to the differences in the scores of the children's dependent variables, the results from the two age groups were analyzed separately for those variables. An alternative strategy involved dividing the samples into the three parental practices groups (never or rarely, sometimes, and frequently spank) and then examining the children's mean group scores. The classification was based on parents' reports of practices and attitudes toward spanking. Given the small cell sizes, particularly for fathers, the results must be taken as tentative and exploratory.

RESULTS

Parental Attitudes, Behavioral Intentions, and Practices

Parents of 5-year-old and 8-year-old children indicated a wide range of attitudes toward physical punishment. On the 10-item questionnaire assessing parental attitudes, mothers had a mean score of 39.3 ($SD = 16.7$, range 10–70). Fathers' scores were somewhat higher, indicating a tendency for greater approval of physical punishment, with a mean of 45.8 ($SD = 15.9$, range 10–70), however, the difference was not statistically significant. A significant main effect for sex of child on parental attitudes was found. As predicted, parents of boys held attitudes more favorable for the use of physical punishment than parents of girls [$M_b = 47.1$, $M_g = 37.4$, $F(1,59) = 6.01, p < .01$].[1]

Parental behavioral intentions toward spanking, as revealed by their summed likelihood of spanking, indicated a similar story. Mothers had a mean of 31.1 and fathers a mean of 35.5, but again the difference was not reliable. The ANOVA did indicate a significant main effect for sex of child and a trend for age of child. Parents of boys had more frequent intentions to spank their sons ($M_b = 38.9$) than those with daughters [$M_g = 28.8$, $F(1,58) = 8.70, p < .01$]. Parents of the 8-year-olds reported they were less inclined to spank their children (if their children were currently 5) than the parents of the 5-year-olds [$M_8 = 30.3$, $M_5 = 36.4$, $F(1, 58) = 3.44, p = 06$]. The mothers' attitudes and mothers' behavioral intentions were highly correlated, $r[39] = .91, p < .0001$, as were fathers', $r(27) = .83, p < .001$.

The third parental dependent variable was parental reports of the frequency with which they used spanking when their children were 5 years old. The means for mothers and fathers were almost identical, with an average of one to two times a week. Twenty-five percent of the mothers of 5-year-olds reported that they never spanked, as did 20% of the fathers. In contrast, 60% of the mothers of 8-year-olds reported that they never spanked, as did 67% of the fathers. This difference was borne out in the ANOVA: Only a main effect for child's age was found, $F(1,59) = 7.20, p < .01$. Parents of the older children reported that when their children were 5, they spanked their children less frequently than the current practices of the parents of the 5-year-olds ($M_5 = 2.3$, $M_8 = 1.6$).

Maternal reports of spanking practices were reliably correlated with their attitudes, $r(40) = .55, p < .001$, and with their behavioral intentions to spank, $r(39) = .53, p < .001$. Fathers also indicated reliable correlations between reports of spanking practices and attitudes [$r(27) = .54, p < .01$] and reports of spanking and behavioral intentions [$r(27) = .42, p < .05$].

---

[1]To determine whether the mothers and fathers of 8-year-old children perceived changes in their attitudes toward physical punishment, they were also asked to report on their current attitudes concerning spanking their children if they were now 5 years old. In a 2 (sex of parent) × 2 (time: previous or current attitudes) ANOVA, with repeated measures on the last factor, there were no significant main effects nor interactions. Thus, parental reports of their current and retrospective attitudes toward spanking have apparently changed little over the 3-year period. Similarly, when the attitude summary scores are correlated, mothers' attitudes were highly related, $r(20) = .96, p < .0001$, as were the fathers', $r(12) = .84, p < .0001$.

The correspondence between the mothers and fathers on the three types of variables was high. Mothers' and fathers' attitudes were reliably correlated, $r(27) = .65, p < .001$, as were behavioral intentions, $r(27) = .66, p < .001$, and reported practices, $r(27) = .72, p < .0001$. The correlation matrix between the parental variables concerning physical punishment is provided in Table 6.2.

Children's Intentions and Reports About the Frequency of Spanking

Both the younger and older children reported a wide range of views on the appropriateness of spanking. The younger group average sum of ranks was 14.2 ($SD = 3.6$, range 8 to 20). Notice that the range almost covers the possible range of scores, 8 to 24. When the individual vignettes are examined to see how many children ranked spanking as the preferred response, six children ranked spanking first on two of the eight vignettes. At the extremes, one child ranked spanking third on all vignettes and another child ranked spanking first on five vignettes. The summed ranking of intention to spank was negatively correlated to the children's ranking of reasons $[r(20) = -.71, p < .001]$ and negatively related to ranking of use time-outs $[r(20) = -.40, p < .07]$. There was no reliable gender difference on intention to spank, though there was a tendency for the boys to rank it higher than the girls $[M_b = 15.5, M_g = 12.8, F(1, 18) = 3.18, p < .10]$.

Five-year-old children reported getting spanked an average of a few times a week ($M = 4.2, SD = 1.7$, range 1 to 6). Three children reported never getting spanked; four reported daily spankings. No reliable relation was found between the younger children's behavioral intention to use spanking and their reports of their frequency of getting spanked, $r[18] = .19, p = .45$.

TABLE 6.2
Correlations Between Mothers' and Fathers' Variables for Total Sample

	Mothers'			Fathers'		
	Attitudes	Intentions	Practices	Attitudes	Intentions	Practices
Mothers' attitudes	—	.91***	.54***	.65***	.68***	.40*
Mothers' intentions		—	.53***	.64***	.66***	.53***
Mothers' practices			—	.39*	.29	.72***
Fathers' attitudes				—	.83***	.54**
Fathers' intentions					—	.42*
Fathers' practices						—

Note. $n = 40$ for mothers, $n = 27$ for fathers, though some correlations are based on a smaller cell size due to missing data.
*$p < .05$; **$p < .01$; ***$p < .001$.

Eight-year-old children, using a Likert-type rating rather than a simple ranking, also showed a wide distribution in their ratings of their likelihood of spanking. With a possible range of 8 to 56, the 20 children averaged 33.9 ($SD = 14.6$, range 8 to 54). Intentions to use reasoning and time-out were not correlated with intentions to spank [$rs(20) = .10$ to .13], indicating their abilities to differentiate the three techniques. No gender effect on intentions to spank were found, $F(1, 18) = .55, p = .46$.

The older children had almost the identical mean frequency of receiving physical punishment as the younger group ($M = 4.1, SD = 1.4$, range 2 to 6). A positive association was found between their reports of the frequency with which they were spanked and their views of the appropriateness of spanking, $r(20) = .42, p = .06$. Though the magnitude of the correlation missed the conventional level of significance with this sample, it clearly indicated a link between perceived receipt and perceived likelihood of using the technique.

Links Between Parents and Their Children Regarding Spanking

As can be seen in Table 6.3, the intentions of 5-year-old children to use physical punishment did not correlate reliably with maternal or paternal attitudes, behavioral intentions, or practices. The strongest association was between children's likelihood ratings and maternal attitudes, $r(20) = .33, p = .13$. However, the child report variable of how frequently they had been spanked was found to be correlated reliably with maternal attitudes and practices, and to be a trend with maternal intentions and fathers' attitudes, intentions, and practices.

The pattern of correlations from the 8-year-olds indicates some important differences. No longer are the correlations between children's reports and parental variables providing the highest levels of associations. In four of the six correlations, the correlations are lower with the 8-year-old children than the 5-year-olds. The central difference lies in the magnitude of the relations between children's intentions to spank and parents' attitudes, intentions, and practices. The median correlation with the older group is .36, in contrast to .04 for the younger group. The relation between children's intentions and maternal practices approached the conventional significance level, $r(20) = .41, p < .07$. Thus, for those mothers who spanked more, their children had higher likelihood ratings of using physical punishment (see Table 6.4).

The second approach to assessing transmission relied on forming the three groups of parenting practices. For the 5-year-old children, this was done solely on the basis of parents' reports of their current spanking practices. Three families were grouped into the "never or rarely spank"

TABLE 6.3

Correlations Between the Physical Punishment Variables in the 5-year-old Children and Their Parents

	Mothers'			Fathers'			Children's	
	Attitudes	Intentions	Practices	Attitudes	Intentions	Practices	Intentions	Reports
Mothers' attitudes	—	.93***	.42+	.70**	.76**	.37+	.04	.50*
Mothers' intentions		—	.39+	.61**	.76**	.42+	-.07	.46+
Mothers' practices			—	.50*	.37+	.90***	.33+	.50*
Fathers' attitudes				—	.73**	.54*	.15	.48+
Fathers' intentions					—	.50*	.26	.34
Fathers' practices						—	.19	.40+
Children's intentions							—	.19
Children's report of spanking								—

Note. $n = 20$ for mothers, $n = 15$ for fathers, though some correlations are based on a smaller sample due to missing data.
+$p \leq .10$; *$p < .05$; **$p < .01$; ***$p < .001$.

TABLE 6.4

Correlations Between the Physical Punishment Variables in the 8-year-old Children and Their Parents

	Mothers'			Fathers'			Children's	
	Attitudes	Intentions	Practices	Attitudes	Intentions	Practices	Intentions	Reports
Mothers' attitudes	—	.91***	.63**	.60*	.61*	.58*	.36+	.41+
Mothers' intentions		—	.61**	.62*	.56*	.41+	.29	.36+
Mothers' practices			—	.12	.15	.21	.41+	.19
Fathers' attitudes				—	.90***	.42+	-.12	.65*
Fathers' intentions					—	.34	-.09	.47+
Fathers' practices						—	.39	.32
Children's intentions							—	.19
Children's report of spanking								—

Note. $n = 20$ for mothers, $n = 12$ for fathers, though some correlations are based on a smaller sample due to missing data.
+$p \le .10$; *$p < .05$; **$p < .01$; ***$p < .001$.

group, 14 families were placed in the "sometimes spank" group, and three families were in the "frequently spank" group. For the parents of the older children, 12 mothers reported that they had not spanked their children when they were 5 years old. However, 6 of those 12 mothers had moderately positive attitudes toward the use of physical punishment. Therefore, we suspect that their retrospective reports of their practices were not accurate. Thus, we classified those six families in the "sometimes spank" category along with five other families. Another six families were put into the "never or rarely" spank group and the final three families made up the "frequent spank" group.

The mothers' reported practices and attitudes, divided by age of child and use of spanking group are listed in Table 6.5. Also in that table are the mean summed scores for children's intentions to spank. For both ages of children, the parents who never spank had children with the lowest mean intention scores, followed by the parents who sometimes spank, and then the parents who frequently spank. The results are in the predicted direction, though the cell sizes are too small for statistical analysis.

DISCUSSION OF THE STUDY

The results provide evidence indicating that parental attitudes and practices concerning the use of physical punishment as a child-rearing technique can be transmitted to children. Parents generally had a relatively coherent set of beliefs and practices about physical punishment as indexed by the high correlations between measures of attitudes, behavioral intentions, and reported practices. What's more, the parents generally shared similar orientations and practices concerning the use of physical punishment as indicated by the significant correlation between parents' reported frequency of use, $r[27] = .72, p < .001$.

That finding speaks to a somewhat controversial issue about physical punishment: whether the practice is a consequence of an angry outburst from the parent or the behavior represents a more reasoned, instrumental child-rearing technique (see Vasta, 1982). The fact that mothers and fathers had strong correlations between reports of spanking and the two indices of parental cognitions — their attitudes and their behavioral intentions — provides some evidence for the instrumentality of its use. If spanking was predominantly a result from a negative emotional outburst, then we would not expect to find the same magnitude of intercorrelations between mothers and fathers attitudes, intentions, and reported practices ($rs = .42$ to $.91$). Though at times the result of a fit of anger, the data indicate spanking is predominantly a reasoned child-rearing practice.

With the younger group of children, reliable correlations were found only

TABLE 6.5

Children's Intentions to Spank and Two Maternal Variables Divided Into Groups Based on Parents' Reported Frequency of Spanking

Parents' Reported Practices	Children's Intention			Mothers' Practices			Mothers' Attitudes		
	M	*SD*	*range*	*M*	*SD*	*range*	*M*	*SD*	*range*
Never or rarely spank									
5-yr-old (*n* = 3)	12.0	3.4	8–14	1.0	0	1–1	27.3	10.2	20–39
8-yr-old (*n* = 6)	20.3	9.4	8–29	1.0	0	1–1	17.2	4.8	10–24
Sometimes spank									
5-yr-old (*n* = 14)	14.2	3.6	8–20	2.0	.0	2–2	40.4	16.6	11–62
8-yr-old (*n* = 11)	31.9	18.4	14–54	1.5	.5	1–2	44.5	11.7	28–62
Frequently spank									
5-yr-old (*n* = 3)	16.3	3.2	14–20	4.3	1.2	3–5	54.3	2.9	51–56
8-yr-old (*n* = 3)	48.3	6.4	41–53	4.3	.6	4–5	56.7	13.1	42–67

between their reports of how frequently they were spanked and mothers' attitudes and practices. When the children's intentions toward the use of spanking were related to the parental variables, the highest correlation was with maternal practices, $r(20) = .33, p = .16$. More persuasive evidence for the origins of transmission was found when the children were divided into the tripartite grouping of parental spanking practices. Parents who never or rarely spanked had children with the lowest intention scores, followed by the "sometimes spank" group and then the "frequently spank" group. Due to the small numbers of children who fit in the groups, statistical analyses were not possible; an extension of the sample size is needed.

With the 8-year-old children, the links between their behavioral intentions to use spanking and their mothers' attitudes and intentions were stronger, as we had predicted. However, the correlation between child intentions and parental practices was also higher than that of the younger group's. The correlations between children's intentions and mothers' attitudes, intentions, and practices ranged from .29 to .41. The correlations are in the predicted direction but handicapped by the relatively small sample size.

Correlations with paternal measures were less successful and only one index — child intentions — and fathers' reported practices showed a trend $[r(12) = .39, p < .21]$. This suggests that mothers' orientations and practices toward physical punishment have considerably more impact on their young children than the fathers'. One speculation is that this finding is due to the differential amount of involvement that typically distinguishes mothers from fathers. A larger sample is needed to determine whether the influence of parental beliefs or practices is modified by the sex of the child and parent.

When the 8-year-old children were divided into the three parental practice groups, their mean intentions ratings were differentiated. The three children who had parents who frequently spanked them had intention scores, on average, more than twice as high as the six children who were reported to have never been spanked. The mean intention-to-spank score of the "sometimes spanked" group fit almost in the middle of the two other groups. So, 8-year-old children's current views toward the use of physical punishment show some evidence that they have been influenced by mothers' and to a lesser extent fathers' retrospective accounts of their beliefs and practices 3 years earlier. Thus, in partial support of one hypothesis, older children's intentions are relatively less closely linked with parental practices and increasingly linked to parental belief structures than the younger children. Though the magnitude of the correlations is not high, it is in the range that has been found in other studies of parental transmission (e.g., Cohler & Grunebaum, 1981).

As with previous research, a variety of differences based on the sex of the child were found. Parents of boys had more positive attitudes toward the use of physical punishment, had higher intention-to-spank scores, and, for the parents of 5-year-olds, reported that they spanked their children more frequently. Despite those differences, we did not find that boys, at either age, had significantly more favorable ratings toward the use of physical punishment. The relatively small sample size and large variation account for at least some of our inability to find differences.

Studies of intergenerational transmission face various methodological pitfalls (Jackson & Hatchett, 1986), and ours is no exception. Most generally, we relied on a cross-sectional sampling when longitudinal sampling is necessary. With regard to the parents, there were two methodological problems. First, simply getting fathers to participate proved to be difficult; we were able to collect data from only 60% of the fathers of the 8-year-old children. The second methodological limitation was the reliance on self-report data. Given the nature of our inquiry — parents' cognitions and practices — the relatively infrequent occurrence of the target behavior, as well as sensitivity of the topic of our study, we relied on verbal self-reports. Well aware of the potential problems associated with parental self-report measures (see Holden & Edwards, 1989), we took pains to minimize potential reporting bias by couching the focus of the study within other child-rearing techniques, making the reports concrete and specific, having parents report anonymously on paper, and having highly context-specific vignettes. Nevertheless, it could be that parents' evaluation apprehension or social desirability concerns may have affected the accuracy of their reports.

The retrospective reports of parents of the older children appear to be suspect, as many researchers have found (e.g., Yarrow, Campbell, & Burton, 1964). For example, six mothers of 8-year-old children reported that they did not spank their children during an average week when they were 5 years old, but at the same time reported that they held (and still hold) relatively positive attitudes toward the use of physical punishment. In contrast, the mothers of 5-year-old children who held similar attitudes toward physical punishment all indicated that they did spank their children. That suggests that the mothers of the older children did not accurately remember their child-rearing practices and were underreporting the frequency of that unpleasant child-rearing behavior.

Collecting data from young children provided another methodological hurdle. Although the 5-year-old children had no difficulty in understanding the instructions or vignettes, our pilot testing indicated that they did find the use of rating scales to be confusing. Our solution to that problem was to use rankings rather than ratings, at the expense of having comparable data with the older children.

GENERAL DISCUSSION

The study described here provides evidence that parents orient their children toward child-rearing practices. Children as young as 5 revealed that they were adopting positions similar to their parents with regard to spanking. Parents who favor the practice of spanking and report that they frequently use it are passing the rod to their children. In contrast, parents who don't like the practice and report that they don't use it have children who indicate they are not likely to use it as a child-rearing practice. This study extends some of the earlier work on intergenerational transmission of disciplinary behaviors by targeting young children rather than college students or adults, focusing on one behavior, and assessing the influence of both parents.

We have inferred parental transmission by assessing the similarity between parents' attitudes, intentions, and self-reported practices with their children's responses to hypothetical vignettes. The second inference is that the self-reports represent accurate reflections of behavior or behavioral intentions. A third inference is that the mechanism through which parental beliefs and actions were linked to child responses was modeling. The pattern of correlations suggests that children's intentions were most associated with their parents' disciplinary practices. Although it is likely that some explicit instruction about the appropriateness of spanking may well have occurred, we have no information on that. In general, we suspect that the children have begun to internalize "unwittingly" their parents' orientations toward the use of physical punishment.

In order to test those inferences and examine other questions, there are three distinct directions for future work in the area of the transmission of parenting and orientations toward physical punishment. First, a longitudinal study could address some of the initial findings we report here. Specifically, a short-term, cross-longitudinal prospective study could provide more definitive evidence about the veridicality of the retrospective data as well as transmission. Such a study would also yield useful information about the extent and duration of the similarity between parent and child attitudes and behavioral intentions about physical punishment.

A second crucial direction is to focus explicitly on sources and extent of discontinuity. Given that children are not vessels for their parents' beliefs, but rather dynamic and cognizant developing individuals, more attention is needed to identify the ways in which subsequent experiences interfere with the reception of parental transmissions. As children get older, the opportunities for and likelihood of discontinuity increases.

With regard to physical punishment, we suspect that discontinuity will most likely be found in the offspring of frequent spankers. For instance, those children who either found spanking to be embarrassing or humiliating are likely to deliberately adopt alternative child-rearing responses (Francis

& Fillmore, 1934). Discontinuity should also be found in the children of frequent spankers who received certain "remediating" experiences. A prime experience would be work at daycare centers where physical punishment is prohibited. Such individuals would then have to learn substitute disciplinary techniques such as the use of "time-out." Other remediating experiences include witnessing the behavior of parents who don't use the technique, reading child-care articles or books about how to discipline (except a few authors such as Dodson, 1970), or taking classes in child development or parenting. Presumably, it should be possible to chart the ways in which individuals' attitudes, beliefs, and behavioral intentions toward physical punishment diverge from their parents' as a consequence of particular life experiences or exposures.

A third direction for subsequent work is to examine in more detail some of the specific processes at work in parental transmission. One possibility is to experimentally manipulate the type of transmission by having some parents explicitly instruct their children on when physical punishment is appropriate. The children could subsequently be interviewed to test the relative influence of instruction versus modeling.

Another way of revealing how transition works would be to adopt a social information processing model (e.g., Dodge, 1986) to help reveal why children who receive more frequent spanking tend to favor the technique. For example, a child might be more likely to spank either because of a limited repertoire of alternative responses or a bias in evaluating the effectiveness of that response. A social information processing approach could test those and other competing hypotheses by examining how children evaluate and utilize various disciplinary responses in response to other children's misbehavior.

Despite the variety of unanswered questions, some general observations can be made. We have found evidence that, at least by age 5, "parentization" is occurring. Not only are parents socializing their children about how to behave within the culture, but parents are also training their offspring to perpetuate parents' beliefs and practices on their grandchildren. Though we explored only one behavior within one domain, we suspect that the process is similar within a number of other child-rearing domains, such as parental expression of empathy (see Zahn-Waxler, Radke-Yarrow, & King, 1979).

This parentization also serves to instruct children about what is acceptable parenting behavior. The study of the origins of caregiving, with the exception of nurturance (Fogel & Melson, 1986), has gone largely neglected. However, the first place children learn about child rearing is through their own experiences with their parents. How potent this lesson is undoubtedly depends on such variables as the domain, the child's age, and subsequent experiences related to that domain. But efforts to identify the impact of family of origin on parenting and well as other influences including previous caregiving experiences (Holden, 1988) or situational determinants (Grusec & Kuczynski, 1980) are needed. Only with such efforts can we explicate the multidetermined nature of parental behavior (Belsky, 1984).

The most important implication of parental transmission of orientations toward spanking lies in transmission of the acceptance of physical punishment. Seventy-five percent of the mothers and 80% of the fathers reported that they spanked their 5-year-old children at least once a week. These figures are only somewhat lower than those reported by other researchers (e.g., Wauchope & Straus, 1989). Such numbers reveal that, to the chagrin of organizations like EPOCH (End Physical Punishment of Children), many psychologists, and other concerned individuals, the practice of spanking young children in our society appears to be widely accepted and well entrenched. Physical punishment provides children a prelude to the many manifestations of violence in our culture (Miller, 1984).

Intergenerational transmission is a subtle yet potent force in the development of behavior, the transference of individual differences in parents to their children, and the maintenance and evolution of our culture. The data reported here reveal yet another way in which parents' beliefs and actions can affect their children.

ACKNOWLEDGEMENTS

We thank Becky Banasik, David Estrada, and Lisa Marshall for assistance with data collection and reduction. This work was supported by a grant from the University of Texas Research Institute.

REFERENCES

Acock, A. C. (1985). Parents and their children: The study of intergenerational influence. *Sociology and Social Research, 68,* 151–171.

Acock, A. C., & Bengtson, V. L. (1980). Socialization and attribution processes: Actual versus perceived similarity among parents and youth. *Journal of Marriage and the Family, 42,* 501–515.

Acock, A. C., & Fuller, T. (1984). The attitude–behavior relationship and parental influence: Circular mobility in Thailand. *Social Forces, 62,* 973–994.

Appel, Y. H. (1977). Developmental differences in children's perception of maternal socialization behavior. *Child Development, 48,* 1689–1693.

Armentrout, J. A., & Burger, G. K. (1972). Children's reports of parental child-rearing behavior at five grade levels. *Developmental Psychology, 7,* 44–48.

Belsky, J. (1984). Determinants of parenting. *Child Development, 55,* 83–96.

Bengtson, V. L., & Troll, L. (1978). Youth and their parents: Feedback and intergenerational influence in socialization. In R. M. Lerner & G. B. Spanier (Eds.), *Child influences on marital and family interaction: A life-span perspective* (pp. 215–240). New York: Academic Press.

Bronson, W. C., Katten, E. S., & Livson, N. (1959). Patterns of authority and affection in two generations. *Journal of Abnormal and Social Psychology, 58,* 143–152.

Bush, D. F., Gallagher, B. J. III, & Weiner, W. (1982). Patterns of authoritarianism between generations. *Journal of Social Psychology, 116,* 91–97.

Carlson, B. E. (1986). Children's beliefs about punishment. *American Journal of Orthopsychiatry, 56,* 308–312.

Carroll, J. C. (1977). The intergenerational transmission of family violence: The long-term effects of aggressive behavior. *Aggressive Behavior, 3,* 289–299.

Cashmore, J. A., & Goodnow, J. J. (1985). Agreement between generations: A two-process approach. *Child Development, 56,* 493–501.

Cohler, B. J., & Grunebaum, H. U. (1981). *Mothers, grandmothers, and daughters: Personality and childcare in three-generation families.* New York: Wiley.

Dix, T., Ruble, D. N., & Zambarano, R. J. (1989). Mothers' implicit theories of discipline: Child effects, parent effects, and the attribution process. *Child Development, 60,* 1373–1391.

Dodge, K. A. (1986). A social information processing model of social competence in children. In M. Perlmutter (Ed.), *Minnesota symposium on child psychology, Vol. 18* (pp. 77–126). Hillsdale, NJ: Lawrence Erlbaum Associates.

Dodson, F. (1970). *How to parent.* New York: New American Library.

Egeland, B., Jacobvitz, D., & Papatola, K. (1987). Intergenerational continuity of abuse. In R. J. Gelles & J. B. Lancaster (Eds.), *Child abuse and neglect: Biosocial dimensions* (pp. 255–277). New York: Aldine de Gruyter.

Elder, G. H., Jr., Caspi, A., & Downey, G. (1986). Problem behavior and family relationships: Life-course and intergenerational themes. In A. M. Sorenson, F. E. Weinert, & L. R. Sherrod (Eds.), *Human development and the life course: Multidisciplinary perspectives* (pp. 293–340). Hillsdale, NJ: Lawrence Erlbaum Associates.

Erlanger, H. S. (1979). Childhood punishment experience and adult violence. *Children and Youth Services Review, 1,* 75–86.

Faris, R. E. L. (1947). Interaction of generations and family stability. *American Sociological Review, 12,* 159–164.

Feshbach, S. (1970). Aggression. In P. H. Mussen (Ed.), *Carmichael's manual of child psychology,* (3rd ed., pp. 159–259). New York: Wiley.

Fogel, A., & Melson, G. F. (1986). *Origins of nurturance.* Hillsdale, NJ: Lawrence Erlbaum Associates.

Francis, K. V., & Fillmore, E. A. (1934). The influence of environment upon the personality of children. In G. D. Stoddard (Ed.), *University of Iowa studies: Studies in child welfare* (pp. 1–71). Iowa City: University of Iowa.

Freud, S. (1923). *The ego and the id.* London: Hogarth Press.

Gaines, L. S., Brooks, P. H., Maisto, S., Deitrich, M., & Shagena, M. (1988). The development of children's knowledge of alcohol and the role of drinking. *Journal of Applied Developmental Psychology, 9,* 441–457.

Gelles, R. J. (1978). Violence toward children in the United States. *American Journal of Orthopsychiatry, 48,* 580–592.

Goldin, P. C. (1969). A review of children's reports of parent behaviors. *Psychological Bulletin, 71,* 222–236.

Greenberg, E. F., & Nay, W. R. (1982). The intergenerational transmission of marital instability reconsidered. *Journal of Marriage and the Family, 44,* 335–347.

Grusec, J. E., & Kuczynski, L. (1980). Direction of effect in socialization. *Developmental Psychology, 16,* 1–9.

Haviland, J. M. (1979). Teachers' and students' beliefs about punishment. *Journal of Educational Psychology, 71,* 563–570.

Heilbrun, A. B., Jr., Bateman, C. P., Heilbrun, K. L., & Herson, A. M. (1981). Retrospections of mother: The effect of time interval upon perception. *Journal of Genetic Psychology, 138,* 133–142.

Herrenkohl, E. C., Herrenkohl, R. C., & Toedler, L. J. (1983). Perspectives on the intergenerational transmission of abuse. In D. Finkelhor, R. J. Gelles, G. T. Hotaling, & M. A. Straus (Eds.), *The dark side of families: Current family violence research* (pp. 305–316). Beverly Hills: Sage.

Herzberger, S. D., & Tennen, H. (1985). "Snips and snails and puppy dog tails:" Gender of agent, recipient, and observer as determinants of perceptions of discipline. *Sex Roles, 12,* 853–865.

Hill, J. P. (1967). Similarity and accordance between parents and sons in attitudes toward mathematics. *Child Development, 38,* 777–791.

Hoge, D. R., Petrillo, G. H., & Smith, E. I. (1982). Transmission of religious and social values from parents to teenage children. *Journal of Marriage and the Family, 44,* 569–580.

Holden, G. W. (1988). Adults' thinking about a child-rearing problem: Effects of experience, parental status, and gender. *Child Development, 59,* 1623–1632.

Holden, G. W. (1989, April). Parental selection of responses to misbehavior: The case of physical punishment. In T. Dix (Chair), *Beyond belief: Information processing approaches to parents.* Symposium conducted at the biennial meeting of the Society for Research in Child Development, Kansas City.

Holden, G. W., & Edwards, L. A. (1989). Parental attitudes toward child rearing: Instruments, issues, and implications. *Psychological Bulletin, 106,* 29–58.

Holden, G. W., & Ritchie, K. L. (1988). Child rearing and the dialectics of parental intelligence. In J. Valsiner (Ed.), *Children's development within socio-culturally structured environments, Vol. 1: Parental cognition and adult-child interaction* (pp. 30–59). Norwood, NJ: Ablex.

Hollingshead, A. E. (1975). *Four factor index of social status.* New Haven: Yale University.

Huesmann, L. R., Eron, L. D., Lefkowitz, M. M., & Walder, L. O. (1984). Stability of aggression over time and generations. *Developmental Psychology, 20,* 1120–1134.

Jackson, J. J., & Hatchett, S. J. (1986). Intergenerational research: Methodological considerations. In N. Datan, A. L. Greene, & H. W. Reese (Eds.), *Life-span developmental psychology: Intergenerational relations* (pp. 51–76). Hillsdale, NJ: Lawrence Erlbaum Associates.

Kagan, J., & Lemkin, J. (1960). The child's differential perception of parental attributes. *Journal of Abnormal and Social Psychology, 61,* 440–447.

Kalmuss, D. (1984). The intergenerational transmission of marital aggression. *Journal of Marriage and the Family, 46,* 11–19.

Kaufman, J., & Zigler, E. (1989). The intergenerational transmission of child abuse. In D. Cicchetti & V. Carlson (Eds.), *Child maltreatment: Theory and research on the causes and consequences of child abuse and neglect* (pp. 129–150). New York: Cambridge University.

Kell, L., & Aldous, J. (1960). The relation between mothers' child-rearing ideologies and their children's perceptions of maternal control. *Child Development, 31,* 145–156.

Kohlberg, L. (1963). Moral development and identification. In H. W. Stevenson (Ed.), *Child psychology* (pp. 277–332). Chicago: University of Chicago.

Lerner, R. M., Karson, M., Meisels, M., & Knapp, J. R. (1975). Actual and perceived attitudes of late adolescents and their parents: The phenomenon of the generation gap. *Journal of Genetic Psychology, 126,* 195–207.

Lobdell, J., & Perlman, D. (1986). The intergenerational transmission of loneliness: A study of college females and their parents. *Journal of Marriage and the Family, 48,* 589–595.

Lyle, W. H., Jr., & Levitt, E. E. (1955). Punitiveness, authoritarianism, and parental discipline of grade school children. *Journal of Abnormal and Social Psychology, 51,* 42–46.

Maccoby, E. E. & Jacklin, C. N. (1974). *The psychology of sex differences.* Stanford, CA: Stanford University Press.

Manfredo, M. J., & Shelby, B. (1988). The effect of using self-report measures in tests of attitude–behavior relationships. *Journal of Social Psychology, 128,* 731–743.

Main, M., Kaplan, N., & Cassidy, J. (1985). Security in infancy, childhood, and adulthood: A move to the level of representation. *Monographs of the Society for Research in Child Development, 50* (1–2, Serial No. 209).

McGahey, C., & Sporakowski, M. J. (1972). Intergenerational attitudes toward child bearing and child rearing. *Journal of Home Economics, 64,* 27–31.

McGraw, M. B., & Molloy, L. B. (1941). The pediatric anamnesis: Inaccuracies in eliciting developmental data. *Child Development, 12,* 255–265.

Middleton, R., & Putney, S. (1963). Student rebellion against parental political beliefs. *Social Forces, 41,* 377–383.

Miller, A. (1984). *For your own good: Hidden cruelty in child-rearing and the roots of violence.* New York: Farrar Straus Giroux.

Morgan, P. K., & Gaier, E. L. (1956). The direction of aggression in the mother–child punishment situation. *Child Development, 27,* 447–457.

Mueller, C. W., & Pope, H. (1977). Marital instability: A study of its transmission between generations. *Journal of Marriage and the Family, 39,* 83–92.

Owens, D. J., & Straus, M. A. (1979). The social structure of violence in childhood and approval of violence as an adult. *Aggressive Behavior, 1,* 193–211.

Patterson, G. R. (1982). *Coercive family process.* Eugene, OR: Castalia.

Parsons (Eccles), J. E., Adler, R. F., & Kaczala, C. M. (1982). Socialization of achievement attitudes and beliefs: Parental influences. *Child Development, 53,* 310–321.

Radke, M. J. (1946). *The relation of parental authority to children's behavior and attitudes.* Monograph of University of Minnesota, No. 22.

Rickard, K. M., Graziano, W., & Forehand, R. (1984). Parental expectations and childhood deviance in clinic referred and non-clinic children. *Journal of Clinical Child Psychology, 13,* 179–186.

Ricks, M. (1985). The social transmission of parental behavior: Attachment across generations. *Monographs of the Society for Research in Child Development, 50,* (1–2, Serial No. 209).

Rigby, K. (1988). Parental influence on attitudes toward institutional authority. *Journal of Genetic Psychology, 149,* 383–391.

Roberts, G. C., Block, J. H., & Block, J. (1984). Continuity and change in parents' child-rearing practices. *Child Development, 55,* 586–597.

Rosen, B. C. (1964). Family structure and value transmission. *Merrill-Palmer Quarterly, 10,* 59–76.

Rutter, M. (1989). Intergenerational continuities and discontinuities in serious parenting difficulties. In D. Cicchetti & V. Carlson (Eds.), *Child maltreatment: Theory and research on the causes and consequences of child abuse and neglect* (pp. 317–348). New York: Cambridge University.

Sears, R. R. (1951). Effects of frustration and anxiety on fantasy aggression. *American Journal of Orthopsychiatry, 21,* 498–505.

Sears, R. R., Maccoby, E. E., & Levin, H. (1957). *Patterns of child rearing.* Evanston, IL: Row.

Sears, R. R., Rau, L., & Alpert, R. (1965). *Identification and child rearing.* Stanford: Stanford University.

Shah, F., & Zelnik, M. (1981). Parent and peer influence on sexual behavior, contraceptive use, and pregnancy experience of young women. *Journal of Marriage and the Family, 43,* 339–348.

Siegal, M., & Cowen, J. (1984). Appraisals of intervention: The mother's versus the culprit's behavior as determinants of children's evaluations of discipline techniques. *Child Development, 55,* 1760–1766.

Sigel, I. E. (1987). Reflections on the belief–behavior connection: Lessons learned from a research program on parental belief systems and teaching strategies. In R. D. Ashmore & D. M. Brodzinsky (Eds.), *Thinking about the family: Views of parents and children* (pp. 35–65). Hillsdale, NJ: Lawrence Erlbaum Associates.

Staples, R., & Smith, J. W. (1954). Attitudes of grandmothers and mothers toward child-rearing practices. *Child Development, 25,* 91–97.

Stolz, L. M. (1967). *Influences on parent behavior.* Stanford: Stanford University.

Tisak, M. S. (1986). Children's conceptions of parental authority. *Child Development, 57,* 166–176.

Troll, L. E., Neugarten, B. L., & Kraines, R. J. (1969). Similarities in values and other personality characteristics in college students and their parents. *Merrill Palmer Quarterly, 15,* 323–336.

Vasta, R. (1982). Physical child abuse. *Developmental Review, 2,* 125–149.

Wauchope, B., & Straus, M. A. (1989). Physical punishment and physical abuse of American children: Incidence rates by age, gender, and occupational class. In M. A. Straus & R. J. Gelles (Eds.), *Physical violence in American families: Risk factors and adaptations to violence in 8,145 families* (pp. 1–15). New Brunswick, NJ: Transaction.

Widom, C. S. (1989). Does violence beget violence? A critical examination of the literature. *Psychological Bulletin, 106,* 3–28.

Williams, E. I., & Williams, C. D. (1963). Relationships between authoritarian attitudes of college students, estimation of parents' attitudes, and actual parental attitudes. *Journal of Social Psychology, 61,* 43–48.

Wolfe, D. A., Katell, A., & Drabman, R. S. (1982). Parents' and children's choices of disciplinary child-rearing methods. *Journal of Applied Developmental Psychology, 3,* 167–176.

Woods, P. J., Glavin, K. B., & Kettle, C. M. (1960). A mother–daughter comparison on selected aspects of child rearing in a high socioeconomic group. *Child Development, 31,* 121–128.

Yarrow, M. R., Campbell, J. D., & Burton, R. V. (1964). Reliability of maternal retrospection: A preliminary report. *Family Process, 3,* 207–218.

Zahn-Waxler, C., Radke-Yarrow, M., & King, R. A. (1979). Child rearing and children's prosocial initiations toward victims of distress. *Child Development, 50,* 319–330.

II Focus on Normal Families of Adolescents

7

Parents' Cognitions and Developmental Changes in Relationships During Adolescence

W. Andrew Collins
University of Minnesota

This chapter addresses the linkages between parents' cognitions, their adaptation to developmental changes in their *relationships* with their offspring, and the implication of these adaptations for the psychosocial development of the children. This focus stems from both the growing emphasis on the nature and course of relationships as significant determinants of developmental outcomes for children and the concomitant interest in examining the functioning of both parent and children with reference to their relationships (e.g., Hartup & Rubin, 1986; Hinde & Stevenson-Hinde, 1987, 1988). To get at *developmental change* in the linkage between relationships and individual change, I focus particularly on the period of transition from childhood to adolescence. The advantage to choosing a time of such rapid and extensive change as a period for study is that changes in individuals and their relationships are likely to be both frequent and salient enough that we can detect them in comparisons across ages.

The chapter has four main sections. The first focuses on the linkage between parent–child relationships and developmental outcomes, drawing both on the socialization literature and on recent findings emphasizing the developmental impact of early caregiver–child relationships.

The second section reviews some current conceptualizations of relationships and, in particular, the place of cognitive constructs such as ideas, perceptions, and attributions in the processes that comprise relationships. A central premise of this section is the idea that relationships change as a function of ontogenetic changes in children and parents and that such changes constitute adaptations that help to determine the impact of parent–child relationships on the development of offspring.

The third section is organized around a primary question about the linkage between parents' ideas and developmental outcomes in the transition to adolescence (viz., the question of the nature of, and normative changes in, parents' expectancies about the developing child during this period of life and the implications of violations of these ideas for parent–child relationships). This third section describes briefly the first phases of a program of research pertaining to change in relationships during the transition to adolescence, as a way of addressing the question of linkage between individual change and change in relationships.

The fourth and final section is devoted to factors and conditions in the impact of parents' perceptions of violated expectancies on parent–child relationships and their developmental sequelae. Of special interest are considerations for undertaking further research on the role of cognitions about relationships in individual development.

PARENT–CHILD RELATIONSHIPS
AND DEVELOPMENTAL OUTCOMES

A central assumption of this chapter is that patterns of action and affect between parents and children are significant influences on the development of prosocial competence and psychosocial maturity during childhood and adolescence. The question of the contribution of parents' ideas to these conjoint patterns falls at the intersection of two general themes from past research. One is identifying the critical characteristics of the conjoint patterns, with greatest attention to the child-rearing attitudes and actions of parents. The second, and lesser, theme is that of specifying the adaptations in conjoint patterns that are necessitated by the changing characteristics and orientations of the developing child (e.g., Collins, 1990; Hill, 1988; Maccoby, 1984a, 1984b). In this section, evidence on these two themes is reviewed briefly as a basis for considering the possible contributions of parents' ideas to children's developmental outcomes.

Links Between Parent–Child Interactions
and Child Characteristics

Although the study of the correlation between parent child-rearing behaviors and child outcomes began within the perspective of psychodynamic trait psychology, recent findings have shifted from this unidirectional perspective to a focus on patterns of communication, responsiveness, and firmness of socialization demands that emphasizes the qualities of typical exchanges *between* parent and child (e.g., Baumrind, 1989; Maccoby & Martin, 1983). This shift in perspectives has led to the frequently demonstrated linkage between authoritative rearing patterns and prosocial competence throughout the childhood and adolescent years. The research has indicated that patterns of greater independence, achievement orientation, and social responsibility occur in children whose parents have typically articulated clear behavioral guidelines and expectancies and have behaved toward children in a responsive, child-centered manner (Hill, 1988; Maccoby & Martin, 1983; Steinberg, in press).

Maccoby and Martin (1983) suggested that the critical factors in differentiating among characteristics of parenting patterns are a combination of socialization strategies (demanding/controlling vs. undemanding/low in control attempts) and relational style (accepting, responsive, and child-centered vs. rejecting, unresponsive, and parent-centered). Research findings to date are consistent with the inference that parents who are demanding but also accepting, responsive, and child-centered frequently have warm, positive affectional relationships and frequent bidirectional communication with their children; these characteristics of parent–child relationships also tend to be associated with development of social responsibility and interpersonal competence in children (Baumrind, 1989; Hill, 1988; Steinberg, 1991).

These findings are conceptually related to work on the sequelae of qualities of relationships between caregivers and children (Ainsworth, 1973; Bowlby, 1969, 1973, 1980; Sroufe, 1979; Sroufe & Fleeson, 1986). The core of this work has demonstrated the functional significance of variations in relationship qualities for age-appropriate developmental outcomes, both short-term and long-term (for reviews, see Collins & Russell, 1991; Waters, Hay, & Richters, 1986). Although the relational perspective has furthered the study of a variety of relationships, both within and outside of the family, it has been especially influential in broadening the study of parent–child relationships (e.g., Bretherton & Waters, 1985; Grotevant & Cooper, 1985, 1986; Sroufe & Fleeson, 1986).

Changes in Relationships During Adolescence

The relevance of parent–child relationships to psychosocial development during adolescence is well documented. Despite theoretical and popular speculation that parent–adolescent relationships are disrupted and that parents' influence is diminished in adolescence, research evidence points to significant continuity in parent–child relationships during the second decade of life. Studies of reported influence show consistent high regard for parents and differentiation between parents and peers in areas to which their influence is pertinent. Furthermore, differences in families correlate with differences in adolescents in much the same way that family and child differences correlate in earlier periods (see Collins, 1990, for a review).

Research on adolescent–parent interactions (Grotevant & Cooper, 1985, 1986) indicates that parental behaviors that foster both individuation and connectedness in relationships are associated with the achievement of identity and the development of interpersonal skills such as role-taking in adolescent offspring. For example, such characteristics as openness of communication, tolerance of contrary opinions, and willingness to change positions in problem-solving have been found to be associated with more advanced psychosocial status in adolescents (Grotevant & Cooper, 1985, 1986).

At the same time, there are major changes in the nature and content of interactions and in the relative influence of offspring in family decision-making. Decrease in positive affective expression begins in the 10- to 12-year-old period (Papini & Datan, 1983; Papini & Sebby, 1987). In addition, conflictual interactions increase in the early adolescent years (for a review see Montemayor, 1983), and there are increases in assertiveness and attempts at dominance, which appear to be concomitant with pubertal maturation (Hill, Holmbeck, Marlow, Green, & Lynch, 1985a, 1985b; Steinberg, 1981, 1987; Steinberg & Hill, 1978). In short, there are changes in *modes* or *styles* of interaction, combined with apparent continuity in emotional connections to family. Collins (1990) suggested that this balance between continuity and change may reflect a process of transformation that enables families to move gradually toward more symmetrical power structures and different patterns of exchange as their offspring move toward adulthood. Given the pronounced physical, social, and cognitive transitions associated with early adolescence, an examination of parents' ideas about the nature and course of change and implications of those ideas for relationships may offer a useful perspective on how families adapt to the ontogenetic changes of this period. To date, however, parents' ideas and the role of those ideas in this complex process have not been examined.

CLOSE RELATIONSHIPS
AND THE PROCESSES OF CHANGE

How might parents' ideas about relationships be examined? My students and I have adopted an approach that is based on the analysis of *close relationships* proposed by Kelley et al. (1983). The basic premise of this formulation is that close relationships are comprised of highly interdependent action sequences. In the case of parents and children, these interdependencies are natural products of their shared histories and complementary roles in earlier life periods.

Several ideas regarding the study of adaptation in parent–adolescent relationships follow from this premise. The first is that these interdependencies are mediated by *expectancies*. This term refers to complex schemata of thought, action, and emotion that affect the perception and interpretation of behavior and that, therefore, guide actions and reactions in interpersonal relations. The notion of expectancies includes many influential ideas concerning the nature and organization of knowledge about common experiences; constructs such as scripts, prototypes, schemas, behavioral norms, and rules are all examples of the types of representations that we think are relevant. The expectancies that make possible functional relationships between parents and children undoubtedly differ in content and complexity at different times in the lifespan (Maccoby & Martin, 1983). We are especially interested in what happens during the transition to adolescence to produce different expectancies than those that parents and children held for each other in earlier life periods.

The second idea is that, when interdependent sequences are interrupted by behavior inconsistent with expectancies, conflict and emotional arousal occur. In our view perturbations between parents and children in the transition to adolescence are especially likely to be associated with violations of expectancies on both sides that arise from rapid physical, social, and cognitive changes in the child (and, to a lesser extent, the parents as well). We assume that these violations of expectancies serve as an impetus to generate and coordinate new expectancies that are appropriate to the greater maturity of the child and the more symmetrical structures and coregulatory functions that characterize adolescence. Term like *realignment,* or the *reestablishment of equilibrium,* and *transformation* have been used to describe this process. Such changes are virtually continuous in the dynamics of relationships across the life span; for example, the first 2 years of life are a period of marked change. Others occur more subtly and over relatively longer time spans. Late childhood and the very early period of adolescence are opportune for tracing these phenomena, because changes in individuals and their mutual expectancies are likely to be both frequent and salient enough to be detectable in research.

The approach to changes in relationships at adolescence outlined here, then, hinges on the idea that parents and children are frequently violating and modifying expectancies of each other as they move toward an accommodation to altered physical, social, and cognitive characteristics in the child; and these changing expectancies are both the basis for, and the result of, frequent interruptions in the interdependent relationships between them. Thus, in analyzing parents' cognitions, the interest is in examining expectancies and deviations from them. This perspective contrasts with an interest in disagreement between parents and children (see Goodnow, this volume) in that the analysis of expectancy violations is intrapersonal, focusing on parents' but not adolescents' cognitions.

The focus on expectancies implies a model of relationship *change* in response to changes in cognitions about the other. It is intended to show how the perceptions and expectancies of others' behavior are significant mechanisms whereby multiple changes — biological, social, emotional, and cognitive — affect parents' contributions to conjoint functioning with their offspring. Research on ideas pertinent to relationships provides a much-needed perspective on the cognitive dimensions of relationship functioning, to complement the more extensive body of work we now have on the interactional and affective dimensions (for reviews see Collins, 1990; Collins & Russell, 1991). A central question concerns the conditions under which perturbations associated with perceived violations of expectancies have implications for developmental outcomes.

COGNITIONS AND TRANSITION IN PARENT-ADOLESCENT RELATIONSHIPS

A primary question regarding parents' ideas and developmental outcomes in the transition to adolescence is, "To what extent are different expectancies associated with different ages within the transition to adolescence, and to what extent do parents typically perceive violations of these expectancies by their offspring?" If expectancies are extensively violated, parents face a more difficult task in adapting to changes in their offspring than if expectancies and perceptions are more congruent. They may also find it more difficult to contribute to a relational environment that supports optimal psychosocial development during this period.

In our research at Minnesota, we have been examining parental expectancies in connection with the idea that during the transition to adolescence, parents and adolescents must realign their expectancies with respect to each other in order for their relationships to function in the face of changes on both sides. Discrepancies between parents' expectancies and their perceptions of their offspring's behavior contribute to this bilateral process, and we have gathered data on both adolescents and parents to examine this possibility. In keeping with the focus of this volume, I concentrate on the findings from parents.

I now turn to a brief description of this approach to the study of parents cognitions. The research to date has involved a sample of 69 pairs of married parents, recruited from among the parents of 385 students in 5th, 8th, and 11th grades who had participated in an earlier phase of the project. This sample is not representative, in that more than 95% of the families were Caucasian and 81% of the parents were the original marriage partners. This restricted sample was chosen deliberately, in order to get a sense of relational cognitions in conjunction with other information about parent-

–child relationships in different age groups under a relatively limited set of conditions.

The central measure was the Behavior Expectancies Inventory (BEI), an instrument that was developed in the project for assessing expectancies regarding behaviors that are commonly thought to change between the ages of 11 and 16. Three major questions were addressed: Are expectancies different for parents whose oldest children are in the 5th, 8th, and 11th grades? Are the discrepancies between parents' expectancies and their perceptions of children greater in early adolescence (Grade 8) than in preadolescence or middle adolescence? Are discrepancies related to family functioning?

Age-Related Differences in Parents' Expectancies

The first question was whether expectancies were different across groups of parents whose oldest children were in the 5th, 8th, or 11th grades. In factor analyses of the BEI items, three highly similar factors emerged for mothers and fathers. These factors captured three categories of issues that are implicated in most theoretical formulations about parent–child relations in the transition to adolescence: *Compliance, Communicativeness,* and *Task Independence.* The factors were used as the basis for grouping items and computing mean scores.

The results showed that some broad, general dimensions of parent and child perceptions differed from one age period to another, whereas others were quite similar. The pattern depended on whether the information came from mothers or fathers: *Mothers* of 8th graders perceived less communicativeness and less compliance in their own children than did mothers of 5th and 11th graders, whereas *fathers'* perceptions of communication and compliance for these same children were statistically similar at all three grades. Thus, although research on parents' ideas has focused most frequently on mothers, there were quite pronounced differences between mothers and fathers in the degree to which they perceived behaviors at different ages.

Age-Related Patterns of Discrepant Perceptions

The second question was whether *discrepancies* between parents' perceptions of their own offspring and their expectancies of typical and desirable behavior are greater in adolescence than in the preadolescent years. This age-related hypothesis is of special interest, because it gets at the common idea that violations of expectancies are likely to increase during periods of rapid developmental change. For example, it is often suggested that parents would perceive deviation from highly valued socialization goals or behavioral norms as an indication of failure in their parental responsibilities and would, therefore, be more likely to feel dissatisfaction and to be involved in conflict with their children than if their expectancies and perceptions were congruent.

Two categories of expectancies were examined. One was *category-based expectancies,* or normative expectancies associated with membership in a particular age group or social role category. For example, the fact that a 13-year-old is physically mature or has reached a certain age may evoke expectancies about what he or she should or should not do, regardless of whether that person has previously shown a tendency to behave in that way. In some respects, category-based expectancies are similar to the types of behavior assessed in studies of parents' implicit developmental timetables. The second was *value- or goal-based expectancies,* or implicit standards of behavior that are related to general values or goals for socialization, without regard to individual history or the typicality of behavior. An example is the distinction proposed by Kohn (1963) between values of conformity and subordinate behaviors versus values of self-direction.

Categorical and goal-based expectancies were examined by having parents fill out the BEI under two different sets of instructions, with order counterbalanced and intervening activities to break set. On one occasion, they responded with respect to a typical child of the age and gender of their own child to get at categorical expectancies. On the other occasion, the instruction was to respond in terms of an ideal child of the same age and gender, as a way of tapping implicit standards of behavior derived from general values or goals for socialization.

The findings support the hypothesis that perceptions of actual behavior are more likely to violate expectancies about ideal behavior in adolescence than in preadolescence. Three specific points should be noted about the kind and degrees of discrepancies between expectancies and perceptions found with these parents. First, parents' expectancies of ideal youngsters on the communication and the compliance items were generally more positive than their perceptions of actual behavior on those items. Second, for mothers (though not for fathers) the discrepancies were greater at eighth grade than at 5th and 11th grades. Third, at Grades 5 and 11, both mothers' and fathers' perceptions of their own child were more positive than their expectancies regarding the *typical* child of the same age and gender as their own offspring, but perceptions and expectancies at 8th grade were similar to each other and less positive than at the other grades. In short, parents' cognitions regarding the match between their children's actual behavior and their expectancies of typical and ideal behavior are notably different in early adolescence than in preadolescence or middle adolescence.

Linkages Between Discrepant Perceptions and Family Interactions

Now let me turn to our third question: To what extent were parents' cognitions associated with other aspects of their relationships with their children? The data addressing this question are preliminary, but a few suggestive findings have emerged.

Schoenleber and Collins (1988) asked parents in the same sample to complete the Behavior Expectancies Inventory once again, on a separate occasion. They were instructed to indicate how frequently during the past week the behavior described in each item had been associated with two different types of conflict: *overt conflict,* in which arguments actually occurred between themselves and their child; and *covert conflict,* in which they felt dissatisfaction, tension, or anger, but did not engage in an open argument about it. Parents' perceptions of compliance and communicativeness predicted both overt and covert conflict. Not surprisingly, the group that perceived their children to be lowest in compliance and communicativeness were mothers and fathers who showed a pattern of high overt *and* high covert conflict; their conflict scores were significantly higher than those of parents in the other three groups.

This correlation was examined further by considering subsets of BEI items, based on two ratings of the items: (a) a rating by independent judges of whether the behaviors referred to were positive or negative; and (b) a rating by parents of the degree to which items were either of low or high importance to them. The importance of the behavioral items heightened the correlation between negative perceptions and the occurrence of parent--child conflict. When behaviors were rated as important, parents' perceptions of their child on the negative behaviors were high and positively correlated with reported overt and covert conflict; whereas perceptions on positive behaviors were high and negatively correlated with the two conflict measures. For the low-importance behaviors, the correlations were in the same directions, but statistically nonsignificant. These findings were replicated in parallel analyses of a more global measure of family functioning, in which both parents and adolescents rated their families on a variety of process dimensions, not just the incidence of conflict (Collins, 1990).

Although parents' perceptions of their own children are related to family conflicts, the discrepancy between this perception and expectancies regarding typical or ideal members of the category did not account for significant additional variance in the regression analyses. This null finding may reflect several limitations of this first attempt to link cognitive discrepancies of this type to relationship indicators; in particular, it may be due (a) to the impaired power in this small sample, (b) to the restricted range of scores in a sample that was remarkably homogeneous and well functioning or (c) to reliance on very global measures of expectancies and conflict. Longitudinal studies incorporating microanalytic analyses of observed interactions over time are needed to address these limitations.

To summarize, these initial studies have given us three bases for continuing to look at parents' cognitions in connection with changes in parent–child relationships. First, some broad, general dimensions of parents' perceptions differ from one age period to another, with a rather pronounced difference between mothers and fathers in the extent of age-related patterns. Second, these perceptions are associated with self-reported incidence of conflict and with global assessments of family functioning, particularly when behaviors are rated as important, thus providing some evidence of the perceptions as significant components of parent–child relationships. Third, discrepancies between expectancies and perceptions are greater in adolescence than in the preadolescent years, indicating that violations of expectancies are especially likely to increase during periods of rapid developmental change. Similar conclusions can be drawn from our work with adolescents, thus supporting our idea that the processes of interest in studying changes in relationships require some models of bilateral or transactional change, rather than a unidirectional model of the impact of parents' ideas on relationships.

These findings do not, however, address the link between parents' expectancies and specific actions that may affect their ongoing relationships with adolescents. A methodological challenge for future research is discriminative mapping of information about parents' ideas, including their perception of and imputation of significance to violations of expectancies, onto relationship-relevant actions. Taking a cue from the literature on the functional significance of relationships (e.g., Grotevant & Cooper, 1985, 1986), such actions might include parental behaviors that indicate openness to exploration of new, perhaps threatening or controversial issues and expression of opinions different from the parents' views, appropriate involvement of adolescents in decision making, and the like. An essential first step in this mapping process is a clearer understanding of the characteristics of parents' ideas that may make them particularly pertinent to actions that impinge on parent–adolescent relationships.

FACTORS LINKING EXPECTANCY VIOLATION TO DEVELOPMENTAL OUTCOMES

How might parents' perceptions of their offspring and the degree of discrepancy between perceptions and expectancies affect child outcomes? An implicit model for considering the impact of discrepancies is based on the assumption that discrepancies may instigate a response by the parent that disrupts the relational patterns that have been found to foster optimal psychosocial development during adolescence. The frequent finding that the nature and frequency of interactions and the affective quality of parent–child relationships are associated with periods of peak physical change in early adolescence (for reviews, see Collins, 1990; Steinberg, 1991) conceivably reflects the greater occurrence of violated expectancies associated with rapid maturation and intensified social transitions. To date, however, this linkage to ideas has not been tested, nor is information available about the implication of parents' ideas for their reactions to perceived discrepancies. As a starting point for research to fill these gaps, it may be useful to consider what factors influence parents' responses to perceived discrepancies.

Two somewhat different forms of discrepancies offer examples. One is that multiple, rapid changes in the child make past behavior an unreliable basis for predicting actions and responses. For example, take the common case of a preadolescent child who has typically been compliant and easy to manage and now begins to question or seek rationales for parental demands more frequently (Maccoby, 1984a). Parents may see this behavior as resistant and, perhaps, insolent, because it is a departure from the child's usual compliant behavior, and they may respond to it by applying extra pressure for compliance. In this case, expectancies that were prematurely stabilized in periods of relatively slow developmental change are now lagging behind as behavior changes more rapidly in the transition to adolescence, with the result that the relationship between parents and child has been altered, at least temporarily.

Violations of expectancies may come about in a second way, as well. As physical, social, and cognitive changes occur, new expectancies may be formed or instantiated for both parent and child, but these new expectancies — like out-of-date expectancies — may not be appropriate or may not be shared by parents and child. In the example, for instance, the child may interpret the parents' extra pressure for compliance as an unfair or repressive response to questions about parental demands. Her new expectancies may have several sources: For example, they might reflect experiences in other social settings like the middle-school classroom or the peer group, where questioning and challenging are more typical modes of interaction; or they may indicate partial, but not yet fully realized, concepts of reciprocity and mutuality in parent–child relations. Regardless of the reasons, the child's expectancies are violated by parental response, just as parents' expectancies had been violated by the child's assertiveness in the first place. If parents continue to expect unquestioning compliance, the child may form an expectancy that the parent is not open to discussion, and that the child will accordingly avoid communication — and perhaps also devise ways of circumventing the rules, rather than simply complying with them. On the other hand, if the parents' expectancies change, so that they interpret questions as a legitimate and potentially useful socialization opportunity, both communication and compliance may be enhanced. In these examples, perceptions that violate expectancies clearly imply change in parent–child relationships.

In the following we propose that several aspects of parents' ideas may be important in determining the impact of perceived discrepancies on adolescent development. The ideas fall into two broad categories: (a) ideas about development during adolescence, and (b) ideas about the nature and processes of interpersonal relationships. Of particular interest are possibilities for future research that can shed light on the nature of these ideas and their role in changing parent–child relationships during the transition to adolescence.

Ideas About Development During the Transition to Adolescence

Whether discrepancies from expected behavior patterns are functionally significant to the development of adolescents depends partly on the meaning assigned to the discrepant pattern in the context of perceived developmental norms. Three themes in research on parents' ideas about developmental norms in this period are especially relevant: (a) ideas about the goals of child rearing and development in adolescence, (b) inferences that discrepancies signal a deviation from normative timetables for manifestation of specific competencies and psychosocial orientations and (c) attributions regarding the causes of newly appearing behavior patterns.

Parental Goals. Discrepancies that are perceived as threatening parental socialization goals are especially likely to elicit negative parental reactions. These reactions may be inimical to maintaining positive interactions with offspring. The potential for relationship difficulties as a result of perceived violations of goal-based expectancies is suggested by Schoenleber and Collins's (1988) data showing the greatest likelihood of parent–child conflict on behavioral items that were rated as negative, especially if the item was also rated as highly important to the parents. This possibility could be addressed more directly in future research by asking parents to rate importance or centrality of violations of behavioral expectancies to their goals as parents.

The goal of assessing importance is complicated by the need to distinguish between parents' valuing a particular behavioral item and its significance to a more general socialization goal. For example, parents may be alarmed by a failure of a child to keep her own room tidy, less because of the domestic disarray itself than because they regard it as a sign of irresponsibility. Other parents may value tidiness for its own sake or regard it as a sign of the child's sensitivity to and affection for them. Thus, an analysis of the impact of relevance to goals may require a procedure that allows each parent to rate the relevance of a specific behavior to general principles that they have identified as significant socialization goals for them.

For many parents a significant goal of socialization may be to convey to their children the importance of relationships, perhaps especially family relationships. Relationship-relevant goals are discussed further in the subsection on ideas about relationships.

Inference of Off-Time Maturation.   Ideas in this area are likely to affect the impact of perceived discrepancy because of the possibility of inappropriate or unrealistic expectancies regarding adolescent behavior and developmental change. The concern is that such discrepancies may be especially likely to increase demandingness and unresponsiveness to the specific characteristics and needs of offspring.

In highly age-graded societies, such as the United States and most other industrialized nations, perceived discrepancies are most likely to be important to the conduct of relationships when they are perceived to be important to parental goals, but off-time with respect to implicit timetables (Lerner, 1985; Livson & Peskin, 1980). The direction of difference is likely to be more important than the degree of discrepancy, and the significance of directional deviation is likely to depend on the area of behavior in question. For example, parents are likely to view as desirable relatively early assumption of responsibility for household chores, but they will probably also prefer that autonomy with respect to activities outside of the family come somewhat later than the normative time, especially if the activities reflect on the parents' or family's reputation or standing in the community (Collins & Luebker, 1991; Psathas, 1957).

The study of parental expectancies about when children will be capable of and/or oriented toward particular cognitive, social, and behavioral patterns has been largely focused on the early years of life (e.g., Goodnow, Cashmore, Cotton, & Knight, 1984; Hess, Price, Dickson, & Conroy, 1984; Ninio, 1979). Several recent studies indicate, however, that parents and other adults also often hold well-differentiated expectancies about the course of development in the transition from childhood to adolescence and make specific inferences about the implications of these changes for individual functioning (e.g., Collins, Schoenleber, & Westby, 1987; Feldman & Quatman, 1988; also see Hill & Lynch, 1983). For example, Collins, Schoenleber, and Westby (1987) found that expectancies assessed on the Behavior Expectancies Inventory (discussed earlier) followed linear patterns with respect to age. Expectancies for behavior judged typical of 11-

to 12-year-olds and 15- to 16-year-olds were at the extremes and expectancies for 13- to 14-year-olds in the middle. In some categories, adults expected more abrupt changes in behavior within this span of ages. For example, behaviors having to do with communication and sensitivity, like "is moody" and "responds in a surly way to parents' comments," were thought to be characteristic of the older two groups, but not of the younger. A few items, mostly those concerning heterosexual activity and seriousness, were expected for 15- to 16-year-olds, but not the younger two groups. There was, then, quite extensive differentiation of expectancies on the basis of age alone, divorced from any cues about individual physical or personal characteristics. Other studies (Feldman & Quatman, 1988) have documented that parents within cultural groups hold convergent expectancies regarding the attainment of autonomy by adolescents, although their expected age is typically later than that of their teenage offspring.

The problem of perceived violations of expectancies depends to some degree on the degree of differentiation in parents' ideas about the nature and course of development (Goodnow & Collins, 1990). It is likely that attainment of expected behavioral standards varies in timing across different domains of competence and performance. Thus, mature behavior in one setting or task may or may not be correlated with the degree of maturity in another domain. Recognizing the multifaceted nature of developmental change may enable parents to modulate reactions to discrepancy ("She does show good judgment in dealing with pressure from her friends, even though she is maddeningly irresponsible about her chores and homework"), whereas expecting parity across domains in maturity of behavior may intensify negative reactions to perceived violations of expectancies. Similarly, categorizing a discrepant behavior as being largely a matter of personal preference, rather than of morality or conventionality, may make a perceived discrepancy less worthy of parental reaction (Smetana, 1988).

Attributions of Cause and Responsibility for Discrepancies.   In addition to the perception that behaviors represent off-time developmental course, attributions about the causes of discrepancy have been found to affect parental affective responses and preferred reactions to children. For example, age-related changes may elicit different *attributions* about the causes of child behaviors than were made by parents at earlier points in development. Dix, Ruble, Grusec, and Nixon (1986) compared adults' responses to hypothetical misbehaviors by children and adolescents and found that the older the child, the more likely parents were to infer that the child understood that certain behaviors are wrong, that the transgression was intentional, and that the behavior indicated negative dispositions in the child. Furthermore, when parents inferred that the child was capable of self-control and that the misbehavior was intentional, they were more upset with the child, and they thought punishment, rather than discussion and explanation, was a more appropriate response (Dix, Ruble, & Zambarano, 1989). Clearly, perceived transgressions by adolescents have a different significance than transgressions by younger children; they are viewed as violations of expectancies that are attributable to the adolescent's own willfulness or disregard of behavioral standards.

In studies of marital dyads, attributions that negative interpersonal conditions were caused by the spouse and that he or she was responsible for the outcomes of perceived negative events have been found to be associated with subsequent reports of dissatisfaction with the relationship and with the incidence of conflictive interactions (Fincham & Bradbury, 1987). Although implications for parent–adolescent relationships have not been tested, it might be expected that violated expectancies of desired behavior could reduce positive feelings about the parent–child relationship, foster hostility and alienation, and otherwise impede positive interactions. In terms of positive models of parental influence, such modifications in interactions would be inimical to development of interpersonal competence and psychosocial maturity in adolescents.

A related point is that attributions of one's own power to affect the remediation of deficiencies can also affect responses to perceived discrepancies. Low self-attribution of power in dealing with unresponsive or resistant children has been found to be associated with more negative affect toward the child and with more peremptory strategies by adults (Bugental, Blue, & Cruzcosa, 1989; Bugental & Shennum, 1984). In addition, parents report lowest satisfaction with their parental roles when they perceive themselves as incapable of influencing a child's behavior on some characteristic that should, in principle, be open to influence and that other parents seem able to influence (Emmerich, 1969). Bugental (1989) argued that these self-attributions of power and situational attributions for child "difficulty" may serve both to sensitize parents' to discrepancies and to buffer them against the challenge of the child's behaviors.

In summary, during the period of increased unpredictability of behavior associated with the transition to adolescence, parents' implicit ideas about adolescent development and their standards for mature behavior may be important factors in exacerbating or moderating reactions to perceived violation of expectancies. The concomitant implications for the quality of parent–child relationships and for the impact of these relationships on development of offspring have been neglected in research on family influences in adolescence. Understanding the process of parental adaptations to individual changes in their children may be advanced by assessing the pertinence of expectancy violations to parents' socialization goals, their implicit inferences about off-time maturation, and their attributions of the child's role in causing the discrepancy and their own power to rectify it.

Ideas About Relationships and Relationship Processes

The nature of adaptation in relationships with adolescents may also be affected by implicit views of relationships held by both parents and children and by the implications of these views for modifying interpersonal behavior following perceived violations of expectancies. In general, the impact of ideas about relationships in this process depends on the perception that the violation is pertinent to the nature and future functioning of the parent–child relationship itself, rather than seeing it simply as a signal that corrective socialization is needed. The differences between these two categories and the contrasting emotional and behavioral responses of parents to them may help to clarify the implications of parents' ideas for maintaining relationships that support or interfere with optimal psychosocial development.

Three aspects of parents' ideas about relationships pertain to the likely impact of violations of expectancies: (a) inferences that the violation is relevant to the relationships; these inferences are likely to be based on beliefs about the nature of family relationships generally; (b) the extent to which parents consider repair of relationships to be a requirement of the parental role; and (c) the particular methods or strategies that are believed to be necessary and/or available to them in attempting to improve the relationship.

Inferences of Relationship Relevance.   A beginning question is, "What aspects of perceived violations of expectancies signal difficulties with relationships?." Goodnow and Collins (1990) noted several aspects of ideas about family relationships that may be germane to judging relevance:

- The extent to which relationship considerations outweigh concern about personal wants and needs. As examples, studies of Italian families (New, 1988; Soccio, 1977) and Black families in the rural United States (Heath, 1983, 1990) have both documented how culturally based values regarding a sense of concern for family over satisfaction of individual needs affect specific child-rearing practices from infancy onward. For parents in such families, discrepancies that imply self-concern rather than regard for the collective may elicit especially strong reactions.
- The importance of reciprocity based on a communal, rather than an exchange, model (Clark, 1984). Ideas of relationships that are based on obligation to carry out certain actions or to behave in specific ways may be inappropriate to close, caring relationships. Parents who view a child's failure to conform to expectancies as failing to

"repay" them for their nurturance may react to discrepancies in ways that exacerbate relationship difficulties.

- The degree to which boundaries among family members are respected and maintained. This concern is central to family systems formulations (e.g., Minuchin, 1985) in which diffuse boundaries signal inappropriate regard for the other person's rights and needs. Parents who perceive discrepancies in terms of inappropriate boundary violations may react to those expectancies especially strongly.

Little is known about parents' ideas about families or relationships. The few studies now available emphasize the importance of cultural determinants of ideas in this area (Goodnow & Collins, 1990). To understand their implications for the ways in which relationships are conducted and their ramifications of developmental outcomes in offspring requires considerable additional work, both conceptually and empirically.

Parental Responsibilities for Relationship Quality.   The impact of perceived discrepancy in relationship-relevant areas of behavior may be greatest when the parent perceives that responsibility for rectifying the problem falls within the parental role. The degree of perceived role-prescriptiveness would seem to be relevant to the dimension of parenting patterns that foster responsivity and child-centered communication. In families in which parents do not consider this part of their responsibilities, discrepancies may become a persistent obstacle to the kinds of relationships that foster positive psychosocial development during adolescence.

Views that implicitly assign responsibility for relationships to parents have not been clearly delineated. Some suggestive findings, however, have been reported. In a study of Scottish parents, Backett (1982) found that parents considered the need to try to "understand" children to be a fundamental responsibility of parents. This responsibility might be considered to be especially important when a perceived violation of expected behavior signals difficulty in the relationship between them. By contrast, parents may feel that the responsibility for repairing the relationship is as much the child's as the parent's; this belief may increase as a function of the child's age and other aspects of observed change during adolescence. The degree to which children are believed to carry responsibility for the quality of relationships with parents has not been investigated. A common speculation, however, is that one aspect of dysfunctional parenting is the premature expectation that undesired behavior on the part of the child is a signal of rejection or dislike of the parent and, implicitly, disregard of the parent–child relationship (e.g., Emery, 1989; Parke & Collmer, 1975). Parents' ideas about the balance of responsibility for relationships and age-related changes in these ideas should be a priority area for future research.

Methods of Repair. Finally, responses to perceived relationship-relevant violations of expectancies is likely to depend on ideas about how to reach agreement and resolve conflict (Goodnow & Collins, 1990). Little information about specific responses is available with respect to this age period. It might be expected, however, that there would be generally less invocation of specific behavioral expectancies and relatively more articulation of general principles than at younger ages. It may also be that parents give greater attention to means of conveying concern about behavior, choosing to phrase them in ways that minimize potential jeopardy to the relationship (Higgins, 1981).

Goodnow (this volume) noted two broad aspects of ideas that may underlie specific attempts to respond to relationship-relevant violations of expectancies. One relevant aspect of ideas about resolving disputes in families concern the degree to which consensus or joint decision-making is viewed as a characteristic of "good" family relationships. Openness toward others' expression of opinions and respect for others' views may be the most important aspect of an apparent orientation to consensus. Research on family influences indicates that it is these characteristics, rather than equal influence from parents and children, that marks the interactions of families in which adolescents are highest in prosocial competence and psychosocial maturity (Grotevant & Cooper, 1986).

A second pertinent aspect of ideas is the degree to which family members "should" make allowances for one another ("You should overlook her crabbiness; after all she is your sister") (Goodnow & Collins, 1990). These ideas imply a tolerance for behavioral variations that would portend a flexible, responsive family environment, with positive effects on offspring. In addition, they may buffer parents' own tendencies to react to violated expectancies in ways that might impair the quality of the parent–child relationship.

CONCLUSIONS

The question of how families adapt to the changing capacities and needs of their adolescents represents a relatively new perspective in research on individual development in the family context, but it is one with important implications for how families continue to function and to influence offspring in the years after childhood (Collins, 1990; Collins & Russell, 1991). The advances of the past decade in the study of parents' ideas now makes it possible to consider the role of cognitive factors in the nature and functioning of relationships with children. The central proposal of this chapter has been that the impact of parental cognitions about violations of expected behavior as a function of physical, cognitive, and social changes in early adolescence is likely determined in part by a series of parental ideas about development during this life period and about the nature and processes of relationships among family members.

Other moderating influences affect the impact of parents' perceptions of violated expectancies, as well. For example, adult developmental issues that affect parental reactivity, emotional state, and level of distraction from the tasks of parenting may also affect parents' responses to the changes of adolescence (e.g., Aldous, 1978; Rossi, 1987; Silverberg, 1989a, 1989b; Silverberg & Steinberg, 1990). In addition, a number of child factors (see Collins, 1990, for a discussion) need to be added to the focus on parent ideas. Several considerations raised in Goodnow's (this volume) analysis of disagreement are also relevant to children's role in creating and responding to discrepancies and parental reactions to them. Clearly, the conviction that change in parent–child relationships is a bilateral process requires that both parent and child factors in producing outcomes should be considered.

Two intermediate linkages between ideas and developmental outcomes also deserve attention in designing further research. One is the linkage between parents' ideas and specific actions that may impinge on the quality of parent–adolescent relationships. It is likely that relationship-relevant actions are not limited behaviors designed to regulate the child's behavior (Goodnow & Collins, 1990). Such actions may take the form of verbal statements, statements of beliefs, or expressions of affect that, for adolescents, have the pragmatic force that more demonstrative techniques have for younger children. The second linkage is between idea-mediated actions and the qualities of relationships. Thus far, most research involving adolescents has focused on the link between parental actions and individual sequelae, without addressing the role of parental actions in relationship functioning and change. Findings from studies in younger age groups (e.g., Sroufe & Fleeson, 1986) indicate that explicit attention to relationship characteristics may be fruitful in understanding the significance of parental actions for conjoint parent–adolescent functioning, as well.

These considerations imply a model that incorporates the interplay of affective and motivational factors with cognitive processes in both parents and children. The component represented by parents' ideas, as outlined in this chapter, is an important, and newly available, element for better understanding both parents' adaptation to adolescent changes and the concomitant effects on their offspring.

ACKNOWLEDGMENTS

Preparation of the chapter was supported by a grant from the National Institute of Mental Health to the author. Gratitude is expressed to

Jacqueline J. Goodnow for influential discussions regarding the ideas outlined in the chapter and to Coral Luebker and Daniel Repinski for helpful comments on an earlier version of the manuscript.

REFERENCES

Ainsworth, M. (1973). The development of infant–mother attachment. In B. Caldwell & H. Ricciuti (Eds.), *Review of child development, Vol. 3* (pp. 1–94). Chicago: University of Chicago Press.

Aldous, J. (1978). *Family careers: Developmental change in families.* New York: Wiley.

Backett, K. C. (1982). *Mothers and fathers: The development and negotiation of parental behavior.* London: MacMillan.

Baumrind, D. (1989). Rearing competent children. In W. Damon (Ed.), *Child development today and tomorrow* (pp. 349–378). San Francisco: Jossey-Bass.

Bowlby, J. (1969). *Attachment and loss. Vol. 1: Attachment.* New York: Basic Books.

Bowlby, J. (1973). *Attachment and loss. Vol. 2: Separation.* New York: Basic Books.

Bowlby, J. (1980). *Attachment and loss. Vol. 3: Loss, sadness, and depression.* New York: Basic Books.

Bretherton, I., & Waters, E. (Eds.). (1985). Growing points in attachment theory and research. *Monographs of the Society for Research in Child Development, 50*(Serial No. 209).

Bugental, D. B. (1989, April). *Caregiver cognitions as moderators of affect in abusive families.* Paper presented at meetings of the Society for Research in Child Development, Kansas City, MO.

Bugental, D. B., Blue, J., & Cruzcosa, M. (1989). Perceived control over caregiving outcomes: Implications for child abuse. *Developmental Psychology, 25,* 532–539.

Bugental, D. B., & Shennum, W. A. (1984). "Difficult" children as elicitors and targets of adult communication patterns: An attributional–behavioral transactional analysis. *Monographs of the Society for Research in Child Development, 4*(1, Serial No. 205).

Clark, M. S. (1984). Implications of relationship type for understanding compatibility. In W. Ickes (Ed.), *Compatible and incompatible relationships* (pp. 119–140). New York: Springer Verlag.

Collins, W. A. (1990). Parent–child relationships in the transition to adolescence: Continuity and change in interaction, affect, and cognition. In R. Montemayor, G. Adams, & T. Gullotta (Eds.), *From childhood to adolescence: a transitional period?* (pp. 85–106). Beverly Hills, CA: Sage.

Collins, W. A., & Luebker, C. (1991, April). *Change in parent–child relationships: Bilateral processes in the transition to adolescence.* Paper presented at the meeting of the International Society for the Study of Behavioural Development, Minneapolis, MN.

Collins, W. A., & Russell, G. (1991). Mother–child and father–child relationships in middle childhood and adolescence: A developmental analysis. *Development Review, 11,* 99–136.

Collins, W. A., Schoenleber, K., & Westby, S. (1987). *The Behavior Expectancies Inventory: Middle-class adults' expectancies for 11–16 year olds.* Unpublished manuscript, Institute of Child Development, University of Minnesota.

Dix, T., Ruble, D., Grusec, J., & Nixon, S. (1986). Social cognition in parents: Inferential and affective reactions to children of three age levels. *Child Development, 57,* 879–894.

Dix, T., Ruble, D. N., & Zambarano, R. J. (1989). Mothers' implicit theories of discipline: Child effects, parent effects, and the attribution process. *Child Development, 60,* 1373–1391.

Emery, R. E. (1989). Family violence. *American Psychologist, 44,* 321–328.

Emmerich, W. (1969). The parental role: A functional-cognitive approach. *Monographs of the Society for Research in Child Development, 34* (Serial No. 132).

Feldman, S. S., & Quatman, T. (1988). Factors influencing age expectations for adolescent autonomy: A study of early adolescents and parents. *Journal of Early Adolescence, 8,* 325–343.

Fincham, F., & Bradbury, T. (1987). The impact of attributions in marriage: A longitudinal analysis. *Journal of Personality and Social Psychology, 53(3),* 510–517.

Goodnow, J. J., Cashmore, J., Cotton, S., & Knight, R. (1984). Mothers' developmental timetables in two cultural groups. *International Journal of Psychology, 19,* 193–205.

Goodnow, J. J., & Collins, W. A. (1990). *Development according to parents: The nature, sources, and consequences of parents' ideas.* London, England: Lawrence Erlbaum Associates.

Grotevant, H., & Cooper, C. (1985). Patterns of interaction in family relationships and the development of identity exploration in adolescence. *Child Development, 56,* 415–428.

Grotevant, H., & Cooper, C. (1986). Individuation in family relationships. *Human Development, 29,* 82–100.

Hartup, W., & Rubin, Z. (Eds.). (1986), *Relationships and development* (pp. 1–26). Hillsdale, NJ: Lawrence Erlbaum Associates.

Heath, S. B. (1983). *Ways with words: Language, life, and work in communities and classrooms.* Cambridge, England: Cambridge University Press.

Heath, S. B. (1990). The children of Trackton's children: Spoken and written language in social change. In J. Stigler, G. Herdt, & R. A. Shweder (Eds.), *Cultural psychology: The Chicago symposia* (pp. 496–519). New York: Cambridge University Press.

Hess, R. D., Price, G. G., Dickson, W. P., & Conroy, M. (1984). Different roles for mothers and teachers: Contrasting styles of child care. In S. Kilmer (Ed.), *Advances in early education and day care, Vol. 2* (pp. 1–28). Greenwich, CT: JAI Press.

Higgins, E. T. (1981). The "communication game": Implications for social cognition and persuasion. In E. T. Higgins, C. P. Herman, & M. P. Zanna (Eds.), *Social cognition: The Ontario symposium* (Vol. 1, pp. 343–392). Hillsdale, NJ: Lawrence Erlbaum Associates.

Hill, J. (1988). Research on adolescents and their families: Past and prospect. In C. E. Irwin, Jr. (Ed.), Adolescent social behavior and health. *New Directions for Child Development, 37,* 13–31.

Hill, J., Holmbeck, G., Marlow, L., Green, T., & Lynch, M. (1985a). Menarcheal status and parent–child relations in families of seventh-grade girls. *Journal of Youth and Adolescence, 14,* 314–330.

Hill, J. Holmbeck, G., Marlow, L., Green, T., & Lynch, M. (1985b). Pubertal status and parent–child relations in families of seventh-grade boys. *Journal of Early Adolescence, 5,* 31–44.

Hill, J., & Lynch, M. (1983). The intensification of gender-related role expectations during early adolescence. In J. Brooks-Gunn & A. Petersen (Eds.), *Girls at puberty: Biological and psychosocial perspectives* (pp. 201–228). New York: Plenum.

Hinde, R. A., & Stevenson-Hinde, J. (1987). Interpersonal relationships and child development. *Developmental Review, 7,* 1–21.

Hinde, R., & Stevenson-Hinde, J. (1988). *Relationships within families.* Oxford, England: Clarendon Press.

Kelley, H., Berscheid, E., Christensen, A., Harvey, J., Huston, T., Levinger, G., McClintock, E., Peplau, L., & Peterson, D. (Eds.). (1983). *Close relationships.* New York: W. H. Freeman.

Kohn, M. (1963). Social class and parent–child relationships. *American Sociological Review, 68,* 471–480.

Lerner, R. M. (1985). Adolescent maturational changes and psychosocial development: A dynamic interactional perspective. *Journal of Youth and Adolescence, 14,* 355–372.

Livson, N., & Peskin, H. (1980). Perspectives on adolescence from longitudinal research. In J. Adelson (Ed.), *Handbook of adolescent psychology* (pp. 47–98). New York: Wiley.

Maccoby, E. (1984a). Middle childhood in the context of the family. In W. A. Collins (Ed.), *Development during middle childhood: The years from six to twelve* (pp. 184–239). Washington, DC: National Academy of Sciences Press.

Maccoby, E. (1984b). Socialization and developmental change. *Child Development, 55,* 317–328.

Maccoby, E., & Martin, J. (1983). Socialization in the context of the family: Parent–child interaction. In E. M. Hetherington (Ed.), *Handbook of child psychology, Vol. 4: Socialization, personality, and social development* (pp. 1–101). New York: Wiley.

Minuchin, P. (1985). Families and individual development: Provocations from the field of family therapy. *Child Development, 56,* 289–302.

Montemayor, R. (1983). Parents and adolescents in conflict: All families some of the time and some families most of the time. *Journal of Early Adolescence, 3,* 83–103.

New, R. S. (1988). Parental goals and Italian infant care. In R. A. LeVine, P. M. Miller, & M. M. West (Eds.), *Parental behavior in diverse societies* (pp. 51–64). San Francisco: Jossey-Bass.

Ninio, A. (1979). The naive theory for the infant and other maternal attitudes in two subgroups in Israel. *Child Development, 50,* 976–980.

Papini, D., & Datan, N. (1983, April). *Transitions into adolescence: An interactionist perspective.* Paper presented at the biennial meetings of the Society for Research in Child Development, Detroit, MI.

Papini, D., & Sebby, R. (1987). Adolescent pubertal status and affective family relationships: A multivariate assessment. *Journal of Youth and Adolescence, 16,* 1–15.

Parke, R. D., & Collmer, C. (1975). Child abuse: An interdisciplinary analysis. *Reviews of Child Development Research (Vol. 5,* pp. 509–590). Chicago: University of Chicago Press.

Psathas, G. (1957). Ethnicity, social class, and adolescent independence, *American Sociological Review, 22,* 415–423.

Rossi, A. (1987). Parenthood in transition: From lineage to child to self-orientation. In J. Lancaster, J. Altmann, A. Rossi, & L. Sherrod (Eds.), *Parenting across the life span: Biosocial dimensions* (pp. 31–81). New York: Aldine de Gruyter.

Schoenleber, K., & Collins, W. A. (1988). *Parental perceptions, conflict, and family satisfaction in preadolescence and adolescence.* Unpublished manuscript, Institute of Child Development, University of Minnesota.

Silverberg, S. B. (1989a, April). *Parents as developing adults: The impact of perceived distance in the parent–adolescent relationship.* Paper presented at the biennial meetings of the Society for Research in Child Development, Kansas City, MO.

Silverberg, S. B. (1989b, July). *A longitudinal look at parent–adolescent relations and parents' evaluations of life and self.* Paper presented at the Tenth Biennial Meetings of the International Society for the Study of Behavioural Development, Jyvaskyla, Finland.

Silverberg, S., & Steinberg, L. (1990). Psychological well-being of parents with early adolescent children. *Developmental Psychology, 26,* 658–666.

Smetana, J. (1988). Adolescents' and parents' conceptions of parental authority. *Child Development, 59,* 321–335.

Soccio, L. (1977). A family in Italy and Australia. In S. Murray-Smith (Ed.), *Melbourne studies of education* (pp. 1–26). Melbourne: Melbourne University Press.

Sroufe, L. A. (1979). The coherence of individual development. *American Psychologist, 34,* 834–841.

Sroufe, L. A., & Fleeson, J. (1986). Attachment and the construction of relationships. In W. Hartup & Z. Rubin (Eds.), *Relationships and development* (pp. 51–71). New York: Cambridge University Press.

Steinberg, L. (1981). Transformations in family relations at puberty. *Developmental Psychology, 17,* 833–840.

Steinberg, L. (1987). Impact of puberty on family relations: Effects of pubertal status and pubertal timing. *Developmental Psychology, 23,* 451-460.

Steinberg, L. (1991). Interdependency in the family: Autonomy, conflict, and harmony in the parent-adolescent relationship. In S. S. Feldman & G. R. Elliott (Eds.), *At the threshold: The developing adolescent.* (pp. 255-276). Washington, DC: Carnegie Council on Adolescent Development.

Steinberg, L., & Hill, J. (1978). Patterns of family interaction as a function of age, the onset of puberty, and formal thinking. *Developmental Psychology, 14,* 683-684.

Waters, E., Hay, D., & Richters, J. (1986). Infant-parent attachment and the origins of prosocial and antisocial behavior. In D. Olweus, J. Block, & M. Radke-Yarrow (Eds.), *Development of antisocial and prosocial behavior: Research, theories, and issues* (pp. 97-126). New York: Academic Press.

8

Parents' Approaches to Adolescents in Alcohol, Friendship, and School Situations

James Youniss
James P. DeSantis
Sandra H. Henderson
Life Cycle Institute
The Catholic University of America

This chapter is centered around a descriptive report of strategies that parents say they would use in dealing with their adolescent children in situations involving school, friendship, and alcohol. In recent years, theories of adolescence have begun to take account of the positive role that families play in the psychological development of adolescents (Grotevant & Cooper, 1986; Steinberg, 1987; Youniss & Smollar, 1985). Previously, major theories viewed adolescents' development as contingent on movement away from the family. Emphasis was placed on emancipation from parents, self-construction of one's identity, and establishment of an independent adult personality.

This view has given way to the perspective that adolescents and parents collaborate in transforming their relationship, thereby facilitating adolescents' development. This change in perspective is due, in part, to insights from sociological and historical studies that show an essential connection between adolescence, as a stage of life, and social context. Gillis (1981) documented various ways in which parents in Western cultures have historically served as mediators in helping their offspring into roles that allow them to function advantageously in adult society (cf. Kett, 1977). The strategies cover a wide assortment of techniques that vary according to the social circumstances parents and adolescents had to meet; for instance, the apprentice system posed different challenges than the modern structure of schooling. The conclusion that adolescents develop through family mediation suggests that parents are neither oppositional nor passive as their children struggle toward maturity. Rather, parents use their knowledge, power, and status as resources that benefit their sons and daughters (Coleman, 1987; Youniss, 1989).

This perspective has stimulated a search for methodologies that can provide insights into the structure and functions of parent–adolescent relationships. The bulk of data has come from two main sources, adolescents' descriptions of the relationship (Youniss & Smollar, 1985) and on-line studies of parent–adolescent communicative interaction (Grotevant & Cooper, 1986). Adolescents' reports have been useful in pointing to issues about which teenagers have concerns. For instance, many teenagers want communication with parents because they seek validation for their ideas and clarification of their feelings (Hunter & Youniss, 1982; Smollar & Youniss, 1989). Direct studies of interaction have been equally informative by providing behavioral instances of advice-seeking and -giving which involve questions and tentative assertions on one side, and affirmations and further discussion on the other side (e.g., Cooper, Grotevant, & Condon, 1983; Hauser, Powers, Noam, & Jacobson, 1984).

The present chapter offers a view of the relationship from still another perspective, that of parents. Although there is a growing literature about parents' beliefs and rationales for child-rearing practices (McGillicuddy-DeLisi, 1980; Goodnow, 1988; Sigel, 1985), considerably less is known about parents' beliefs and rationales regarding the rearing of adolescents. Kohn (1969) showed that characteristics that parents wish to engender in youth are related to the parents' socioeconomic status. Baumrind (1975) reported that the well-known dimensions of communication clarity, control, nurturance, and maturity demands, which have been studied with parents of children, apply also to parents of adolescents. And several investigators have reported on the disciplinary techniques that parents use to control adolescent behavior (McKenry, Price-Bonham, & O'Bryant, 1981; Smith, 1983).

The present chapter offers data about strategies that parents say they use in situations that impinge on the welfare of their teenage sons and daughters. We collected these data in order to gain insight into the roles that parents assume for themselves in their adolescent sons' and daughters' rearing. Given that so little is known about the role that parents of adolescents assume for themselves, we think it appropriate to begin with descriptive results. As with adolescents' reports, descriptions from parents ought to point to aspects of the relationship that are of central interest to the participants. We propose that these findings can provide a base upon which subsequent work can build and specific questions about the relationship's transformation can be asked.

Because the parents in this study were asked to react to realistic situations that could arise with their sons and daughters, we can use the results also to address a theoretical issue of some interest in the current literature.

Researchers have debated whether parents rear children with consistent styles or whether parents react mainly to the immediate demands of changing situations (Grusec & Kuczynski, 1980). The data appear to show that consistency in style and sensitivity to situational variations may be compatible rather than exclusive aspects of parenting. This is especially evident when one notes that situations vary in degree of seriousness and, therefore, call for modulation of responses. The point is made further through the consideration that wives and husbands may utilize different but complementary strategies in given instances. They thereby can convey a particular point of view while they react adaptively to the situations at hand.

This conclusion fits with two contemporary positions. Grusec and Kuczynski (1980) proposed that rearing is best seen as involving many functions, such as meeting immediate needs while orienting children toward long-range norms. Actions in service of the former may appear "inconsistent" because they necessarily vary according to demands of situations. Actions serving the second function are more likely to look consistent because they emanate from a parent's cognitive position, which is assumed to be coherent and enduring. McGillicuddy-DeLisi (1980, 1982), Sigel (1985), and Goodnow (1988) offered a related but different resolution. They proposed that parents operate from a general belief system that includes presuppositions about ways children develop and learn. Actions would have to be tailored to specific circumstances that come up and would, therefore, appear dissimilar in a material sense. Conceptually, however, the various actions could be consistent because they emanate from a unitary belief system and are directed toward a common purpose.

Both of these views shift focus from parents' actions alone to parents' perspectives on their role in children's development. This orientation meshes with the previously described trend to understand better the character of parent–adolescent relationships. The present study extends this line of work by bringing new data from parents' perspectives of their role and contribution to adolescents' functioning and development. Although our study does not deal directly with outcomes such as ego or identity development (see Enright, Lapsley, Drivas, & Fehr, 1980; Leahy, 1981), it is understood that subsequent research would seek them. A prior task, however, is to plot elemental features of the parental side so that they can be prospectively studied within a clear theoretical framework.

BACKGROUND TO OUR STUDY

An initial sample of parents was obtained in the 1986–1987 school year from two parochial (Catholic) high schools, one in western New York and the other in southeastern Massachusetts. Additions were made to the sample in 1987–1988 of parents from two public high schools, one in central New Jersey and one in a Maryland suburb of Washington, DC. Parents were solicited initially either by mail or by having students carry home the questionnaires. About 550 families were polled through these means and we obtained responses from about an estimated 20% of possible returnees. This figure corresponds with return rates by mail in other surveys (Dillman, 1978). We experienced several difficulties with these procedures. For example, a batch of unanswered questionnaires were returned immediately from the school in which adolescents carried them home. We assumed that several students never delivered them to their homes but simply deposited them in the mail. Hence, data from the additional sample were collected by our directly contacting parents through a snowball technique.

The final sample consisted of 208 parents who returned completely scoreable questionnaires. These parents represented 160 families, 48 in which both a mother and father responded, and 112 in which one parent in the family responded. There were 134 mothers and 74 fathers; 48 of each were matched married couples.

Description of Parents

On the basis of parents' education and occupations, we judged that the sample represents middle to upper-middle SES levels. Most parents were White and all parents were presently living with a spouse. The adolescents about whom parents responded were all enrolled in high school and ranged in age from 14 to 19 years ($M = 16$); 54% were females. No claim is made about representativeness. Given the schools from which we drew parents and the self-selection in response rate, we would depict these parents as living in the northeast, from the middle SES level, and interested in and serious enough about their children's schooling to respond to the question- naire.

Description of Questionnaire

The survey instrument contained several sections; the part of interest to the present chapter contained 15 hypothetical situations, each of which de- scribed a teenager in some potentially problematic state. Parents were instructed to imagine that one of their teenage sons or daughters was in these situations and to write out the action-strategy they were likely to take. For this chapter, we consider 9 of the 15 stories, which are reported in Table 8.1. The 6 stories not presently considered yielded little variation among parents. For example, 3 stories in which adolescents were depicted as

TABLE 8.1
Hypothetical Alcohol, Friend, and School-Related Situations

Alcohol

1. Your teenager appears to be drinking more than he/she should be. What would you be most likely to do?
2. Your teenager's social life seems to involve drinking alcohol instead of involvement in more constructive and productive activities. What would you be most likely to do?
3. Your teenager comes home late one night after a party and you discover that he/she has had too much alcohol to drink. What would you be most likely to do?
4. Your teenager wants to go to a party at someone's house where you have a good idea that kids will be drinking alcohol. What would you be most likely to do?

Friendship

5. Your teenager is hanging around with friends whom you think are troublemakers. What would you be most likely to do?
6. You overhear your teenager on the telephone planning to go out with a group of people whom you don't approve of. What would you be most likely to do?
7. Your teenager wants to go to a party given by friends whom you do not know. What would you be most likely to do?

School-Related

8. Your teenager decides to drop out of high school before graduating. What would you be most likely to do?
9. Your teenager brings home a report card which shows a drop in academic performance. What would you be most likely to do?

achieving something worthwhile generated almost uniform responses of reward or praise.

Of the stories now considered, four dealt with alcohol use, three with friendship, and two with school achievement. We had originally designed stories to vary in degrees of seriousness and immediacy so that a range of parental strategies would be obtained. We considered the story in which a teenager announced she was dropping out of high school as serious and meriting of immediate attention. In contrast, the story in which a teenager showed a drop in grades was presumed to be less serious and, although it might demand attention, the ensuing action might be less drastic than that applicable to an adolescent's dropping out of school. The ordering of results did not consistently fit our scheme as parents attached their own meanings to the stories. Hence, we allowed parents' own statements to define seriousness.

Scoring

We transposed parents' written statements to typescripts and coded them according to content similarity. Data reduction consisted of grouping responses into about 25 categories that accounted for about 85% of all the statements. We then reduced this number to three general categories by combining strategies that seemed conceptually similar. The specific and general categories are listed in Table 8.2.

Category I includes strategies in which parents said they would react by taking direct control in order to produce a change in the adolescent's behavior. Parents either tried to stop behaviors, such as drinking, or to coerce new behaviors, such as improving school grades, to replace undesired behaviors. The subcategories were: forbidding recurrence of a behavior, taking control, getting outside help, punishing or restricting, and forcing an alternate activity to replace the undesirable behavior. Instances of these strategies are exemplified by statements taken from the story regarding a teenager's drinking more than she should. Instances of Category I were: *Getting outside help:* "Get professional help to conquer the problem." *Punish:* "My daughter should not be drinking at all — I'd ground her." *Restrict:* "Take away the car keys." and *Force alternatives:* "Keep her away from places and friends who are serving her alcohol." All instances entail parental intervention that is designed to coerce an alternative, desired behavior.

The strategies in Category II entailed less direct and immediate control. In using strategies within this category, parents expressed disagreement with the adolescent's behavior, as with Category I, but did not directly take charge. Although parents let adolescents know they wanted them to follow a new course of action, they still allowed adolescents decide how to make

TABLE 8.2
Specific and General Categories

Category I	Category II
counseling	disappointment
forbid	disapproval
control	discourage
punish	discuss negative
demand	consequences
say no	caution
call parents	stress responsibility
monitor	
force into an alternative	

Category III
encourage alternatives
determine why
do nothing
trust adolescent
ask for more information

this happen. Specific strategies included: expression of disappointment, stating disapproval discouraging behavior by pointing out negative consequences, cautioning against a behavior, and stressing the adolescent's responsibility to behave properly. Instances are illustrated again with statements from the story involving persistent drinking. *Point out consequences:* "Explain the dangers of early alcohol abuse and relate it to a personal experience." *Disapproval:* "Tell her you don't want her to drink." *Caution:* "Remind her of the dangers of booze — healthwise, driving, and so forth."

Category III included strategies in which parents manifested the least control and gave adolescents the most choice in their subsequent behavior. Illustrations of specific strategies are taken from the same story. *Discussion:* "Discuss her problem of drinking." *Get more information:* "Ask him what kind of problem he could have to want to drink so much and see if we could talk about it." *Trust:* "I trust she will use her head." The dominant strategy was to discuss the issues entailed in the matter at hand with the adolescent.

ANALYSIS

Categories by Situations

Table 8.3 reports percentages of general category use for each of the nine situations. Parents used the most controlling strategies in situations involving alcohol consumption. The story in which alcohol had become a persistent problem engendered the greatest use of direct actions. Of parents' responses, 52% involved direct intervention with the most frequent strategies being getting professional help and forbidding further use of alcohol.

TABLE 8.3
Percentages of Parents' Category Use in Nine Adolescent Situations

	Categories		
Situation	I. Direct Control	II. Less Control	III. Least Direct
1. Drinking more	52	25	23
2. Social life	40	20	40
3. Drunk	38	6	56
4. Alcohol party	44	44	11
5. Friends are trouble	20	59	20
6. Don't approve of friends	34	39	27
7. Don't know friends	24	5	71
8. High school dropout	33	44	23
9. Drop in grades	12	9	70

The other three stories involving alcohol generated from 38% to 44% use of Category I strategies. Direct control strategies were used least in situations involving a drop in grades, hanging around with friends who are trouble-makers, and going to a party given by friends whom the parents do not know. No more than 24%, and at most 12%, of the parents used direct actions for these stories.

For contrast, we direct the reader to use of strategies in Category III which entailed the least parental control. The two situations in which parents exerted the least number of controlling strategies were found to engender the highest usage of noncontrolling strategies. These were a drop in school grades, for which 79% of the responses were noncontrolling, and not knowing the friends with whom the teen was going to a party, for which 71% of the responses were noncontrolling. Category II data constitute the remainder of the responses with four situations yielding 39% or more responses. The chief strategies were stating disapproval or expressing disappointment.

It is not clear whether variations in degree of control reflect parents' concern for the respective domains or reactions to the particular stories. We decided to appraise this question by looking across domains at stories that seemed comparable in severity and form. The two stories about going to a party, one given by friends that parents do not know and the other when parents are not sure whether alcohol will be served, afford an opportunity for such a comparison. Here we might be able to compare parents' concern for friendship and alcohol. We constructed a contingency table for the two stories to assess same and different use of strategies in Categories I, II, and III. Of the 191 scoreable responses for this table, 54 came from responding with the same general strategies to both stories. The remainder of the table suggests that parents were more concerned with the alcohol story than the story about not knowing friends who were hosting a party. There was a net of 39 more Category I responses to the alcohol than the friend story. Further, the friend story yielded 135 more Category III responses than the alcohol story.

The most typical responses to the alcohol story focused on forbidding attendance or calling the other parents. Parents said: "I wouldn't let her go," "Not allow him to go," "Call and see if the parents are aware there will be drinking," and "Call the parents to see if alcohol will be served." In contrast, the most typical response to not knowing about friends was to ask for information but leave the decision to go to the teenager. Parents said: "Let her go after asking her about these friends," "Tell him to use his head if alcohol or drugs are present — I'd pray for the best," "Trust him," and "Ask who they are and get her to tell you about them." These contrasts suggest that parents view alcohol and friends differently. They appear to trust that adolescents' familiar friends will probably not be sources of immediate danger whereas they fear alcohol, which is less predictable and can have harmful consequences. The preceding excerpts also show that part of the concern about unfamiliar friends is connected with fear that alcohol might be served at the party. This result suggests that friendship and alcohol probably are not independent domains in parents' minds.

Stories 2 and 5 provided a second comparison between alcohol and friends. In Story 2, alcohol had become too much a part of the teenager's social life, whereas in Story 5, the teenager was hanging around with peers who were troublemakers. The alcohol story generated 32 more Category I responses than the friend story, whereas the friend story generated 33 more Category II and III responses than its alcohol counterpart. The chief strategies for the alcohol story were to secure professional help and to restrict the teen's activity. Parents said: "Have her attend a teen alcohol program. . . ," "Try counseling services — either professional or through school," "Keep her away from bad influential friends," and "I'd restrict involvement with this group of friends as best I could." One can see in the latter two responses that parents are attributing alcohol use to certain peer associations. This finding supports the preceding suggestion that domains are not independent. In contrast to direct actions, the same parents were less controlling toward the trouble-making friends. Their most common strategies were to express disapproval and point out consequences. Parents said: "I'd tell her I don't like these kids," "Say up front what I think," and "Tell her why I felt this way and what problems could arise."

It seems fair to conclude from these two comparisons that parents in our sample were especially sensitive to teenagers' use of alcohol and reacted with the most direct control to situations involving alcohol. Alcohol constitutes a realistic concern for contemporary parents as 88% of high school students reportedly drink alcohol (Johnston, Bachman & O'Malley, 1979) and alcohol-related traffic accidents are the leading cause of death among 15-24-year-olds (Callen, 1983). This is not to say that parents are unconcerned about peers and school issues. It is more likely that school performance and peer associations reflect established behavior patterns for which parents have expectations and management experience. Because alcohol use enters abruptly during middle or late adolescence, parents need to establish new strategies for dealing with it. This task involves the risk that a single overindulgence can cause unusual harm, as with an automobile accident. By using strategies of direct control, parents may be signalling the significance of alcohol in their experience of rearing contemporary adolescents.

Parent Consistency and the Use of Patterns

It is evident in Tables 8.2 and 8.3 that parents used a variety of tactics to deal with the nine hypothetical situations. We decided to ask whether this range represents sensitivity to situational change and flexibility on parents' part, or whether it denotes the collated effect of different parents, each using a consistent style. We looked for an answer by scoring individual parents across the nine responses. Any parent could have made one category of response to all nine stories, at one extreme, or could have given a mixed array of responses, for example, three from each category. Both options were manifested but very few parents fit exactly into these extremes. We first established criteria that would characterize dominant modes of responding and five patterns resulted. A pattern of *Control* was defined when parents made at least five Category I responses but no more than two Category III responses in the nine situations. A contrasting pattern, called *Democratic,* required at least five Category III responses but not more than two Category I responses. It followed that use of at least five category II responses but no more than two responses in either other category would constitute an *Intermediate* pattern. A total of 31 parents were classified in the Control pattern, 53 were Democratic, and 10 parents were Intermediate.

A further pattern, called *Flexible,* was defined by use of each category two, three, or four times. This pattern denoted that parents shifted responses as situations changed; 64 parents fit this pattern. Finally, a pattern called *Extreme* was defined by parents who used strategies from Categories I and III at least four times each. These parents used the most and least controlling strategies, perhaps reflecting a special case of flexibility to situational variation. Thirty parents used this approach. In sum, 188 parents, or 86% of the sample, fit these patterns.

Pattern Use in Relation to Other Factors

We set out to determine whether factors could be identified that might account for the differential patterns. Two kinds of factors were assessed in the questionnaire. For the adolescents, we had data on sex and age, and on the parents, we had data for sex of parent, education of parent, maternal employment, and birth order of adolescent. The last score was considered a parent variable insofar as it represented parental experience in dealing with adolescence.

Table 8.4 presents contingency tables that display relations between these factors and frequency of parents fitting each pattern. Chi-square tests were run only for Control, Democratic, and Flexible patterns because of cell sizes. Three of the six factors differentiated patterns. One was age of adolescent; parents of younger teenagers were twice as likely than parents of older teenagers to use the Control pattern, and parents of older teenagers were twice as likely than parents of younger teenagers to use the Flexible pattern. Age made no difference for the Democratic pattern.

The second differentiating factor was birth order. We classified adoles-

TABLE 8.4
Cross Classification of Parental Pattern by Adolescent Parent Characteristics

Factor	Control	Democratic	Flexible	Chi Square
Age of adolescent:				
younger	19	24	22	6.35*
older	11	29	40	
Birth order:				
first born	8	27	34	6.53*
later born	22	26	29	
Sex of adolescent:				
female	21	26	37	3.45
male	9	27	27	
Parent's level of education:				
below college	17	13	24	7.50*
college or above	13	37	39	
Sex of parent:				
mother	24	34	44	1.60
father	7	19	20	

*$p < .05$.

cents' birth order as either first-born or later-born. First-born represented the first child whom parents reared as an adolescent, whereas later-born represented parents who had previously faced the tasks of rearing an adolescent. Parents who had previously reared an adolescent were three times more likely than first-time parents to use the Control pattern. Birth order did not differentiate use of the Democratic pattern but had a slight effect for the Flexible pattern in that parents of first-borns were a bit more likely than parents of later-borns to use it.

A third effect was found for education of parent. Education refers to completed years of schooling by the parent who filled out the questionnaire. Education levels allowed categorization into college graduate and noncollege-graduate groups. College graduates were more likely than nongraduates to use either Democratic or Flexible patterns, whereas nongraduates were more likely than graduates to use the Control pattern (cf., Kohn, 1969).

These results for strategies fit with Goodnow's (1988) view that parents' beliefs about rearing are rooted in several sources. In the present case, age of teenager, parents' prior experience rearing adolescents, and parents' educational level differentiated use of patterns. Two of the significant factors are in keeping with the view that parents formulate strategies from the experience of having previously dealt with adolescents. Parents with this experience were more controlling and parents of younger teenagers were also more controlling and less evenly spread across the categories. The effect for education substantiates a fairly well-established finding that parents with more years of schooling tend not to use coercive tactics and are more likely to discuss rationales for desired behavior with their children (Kohn, 1969; Dornbusch, Ritter, Leiderman, Roberts, & Fraleigh, 1987).

Husband-Wife Comparability

Of the 208 parents, 96 were wife-husband pairs. We explored first whether these 48 couples were similar to the overall sample and the answer was affirmative. When use of Control, Democratic, and Flexible patterns in these 48 pairs were assessed as a function of the factors described previously, we found again that adolescents' age, birth order, and parents' education differentiated use of patterns in the same direction as with the full sample; no other factor proved to be significant.

The next question was whether the wife and husband of a couple responded to the nine situations with similar or dissimilar patterns. Each parent's assignment to a pattern had been made without knowledge of the other's assignment. Of the 48 pairs, 45 provided scoreable patterns. Although parents had been instructed to respond for the same target adolescent in their family, 8 of the 48 pairs of parents, in fact, responded for different children in their families. Nevertheless, all 45 scoreable couples are included in the subsequent analyses.

Fifteen of the couples were found to have used the same pattern in their responses whereas members in the other 30 couples responded with unlike patterns. The data were examined to see whether any obvious factor differentiated use of same from unlike patterns, but only one factor came close to having an effect—use of the same pattern was more evident in couples with the same level of education ($N = 10$) than in couples with different levels of education ($N = 5$). The Chi-square test was not significant.

The 30 couples in which wives and husbands had used different patterns were then examined to assess the scatter of combinations they used. Of the possible combinations, only a small number actually occurred. Nearly one half ($N = 14$) of the couples were limited to two combinations; nine couples used Patterns 2 and 4 and five couples used Patterns 2 and 5. The 2–4 and 2–5 combinations provide an interesting view of how parents might divide parenting labor. The parent who used Pattern 2 approached problems by being open to discussion whereas the parent who used Pattern 4 or 5 was open to discussion on some matters but prone to be directive in other matters.

With the remainder of the couples scattered across combinations, and with no other combination being used by more than three parents, we focused on those couples who manifested either 2–4 or 2–5 combinations. Factors that might account for these as opposed to other combinations were statistically explored, but neither adolescent nor parent characteristics showed reliable associations. We therefore looked at these combinations as pragmatic and adaptive ways for mother–father pairs to deal with adolescent problems. With one parent in a family ready to discuss the do's and don'ts of teenage behavior, the adolescent would regularly have an opportunity to express views as well as to hear an adult's perspective. The other parent in the family would also discuss behavior but, at the same time, be ready to demand a specific direction the adolescent's behavior should take when matters required. This couple would, hence, provide direction while encouraging openness to express as well as listen to viewpoints.

Further review of the protocols among the 14 couples who used these two combinations was made to see how precisely parent-couples strategically coordinated their parental roles. It was found that the strategies used by these parents fit our conjecture rather well. The less serious situations, defined by the total sample's use of less controlling strategies, were likely to elicit discussion-type responses from both parents. The more serious situations, on the other hand, were more apt to engender more controlling strategies from one of the parents.

We now illustrate this point by citing statements from three couples who coordinated their strategies rather clearly. Couple 1 was composed of a physician wife and a husband who was a sales manager. Both had responded for a 16-year-old son who was the eldest of their three children. The mother in Couple 2 was a medical assistant and the father worked in sales; they responded for their 18-year-old daughter who was the older of two children. Couple 3 was in their early 30s; the mother was a teacher and the father was an attorney. They focused on their 16-year-old, first-born son.

Recall that Situation 9, which described a drop in grades, had yielded the least controlling strategies for the total sample. We now show that this situation elicited noncontrolling strategies from both parents in the 14 couples under consideration. In the verbatim excerpts that follow, the first quote is from the parent with Pattern 2, and the second from the other parent with Pattern 4 or 5. The father in Couple 1 said: "Discuss [it] with [the] child," and the mother said: "Discuss priorities." The father in Couple 2 said: "Question and try to find out the truth," and the mother said: "Ask her what happened." Finally, the father in Couple 3 said: "Ask what difficulty he is having and why." The mother said: "Discuss with him and his teachers the reason for the drop."

We turn now to the situations that the parents in the total sample considered more serious. In order to illustrate how couples paired their strategies, excerpts are presented from three situations, one each concerning alcohol, friendship, and school. In Story 3, the teenager had come home drunk; in Story 7, the teenager was going to a party given by friends the parents did not know; and in Story 8, the teenager announced he or she was dropping out of high school before graduation.

Couple 1 responded to the three stories as follows. Story 3: The father said: "Wait till morning—then discuss [it]," and the mother said: "Ground them." Story 7: The father said: "Ask teenager for details—who, where, etc." The mother said: "Who's giving the party? Who's supervising? We're driving." Story 8: The father said: "Blow my cool," and the mother said: "Lots and lots and lots and lots and lots and lots and lots of talking."

We now present the statements from Couple 2 for the same story sequence. Story 3: The father said: "Let her know you know and expect [her] to use [her] head." The mother said: "She would be sent to her room because I am so upset." Story 7: The father said: "Ask her who they are and how she met [them]." The mother said: "Ask her if her regular group of friends would be there." And regarding Story 8, The father said: "Ask why and try to understand," and the mother said: "Get hysterical."

Couple 3's responses are as follows. Story 3: The father said: "Ignore it and hope there will not be a repeat occurrence." The mother said: "Talk to him. Point out the evils of alcohol." Story 7: The father said: "Tell him candidly that I overheard, do not approve, and why." The mother said: "Ask about the phone call." And Story 8: The father said: "Express the fact that I am disappointed but encourage him to find a meaningful alternative career." The mother said: "Insist he go back to school."

CONCLUSIONS

This descriptive set of findings allows us to address three issues that bear on questions in the literature and should be pursued in future research. We first consider how results help to clarify the issue of style or consistency. Few parents responded to all nine situations with a single strategy or even strategies within a general category. Nonetheless, about 85% of the parents responded with patterns that had one dominant strategy along with other strategies that reflected adjustment to the details of the nine situations. For instance, parents who were prone to discuss the problems brought up by most situations also reacted with controlling strategies when situations pointed to impending danger to the adolescent.

Goodnow (1988), Grusec and Kuczynski (1980), McGillicuddy-DeLisi (1980, 1982), and Sigel (1985) have developed a perspective that helps account for these results. In rearing children, parents form viewpoints about their roles in socialization and development and express their beliefs through strategies that pertain to the situations faced by children. In contemporary society, adolescence presents parents with the task of dealing with new and varied situations that were not experienced during childhood. Hence, parents of adolescents may be altering beliefs in adjusting to adolescence, while they adapt strategies for the new situations that adolescence brings up. This idea is supported by the finding that birth order, which assessed parents' prior experience with rearing adolescents, in fact, differentiated types of strategies.

We suggest that measuring consistency in parents of adolescents is especially difficult. The beliefs parents form during childhood may be challenged by the abrupt onset of adolescence and the new tasks it brings. Although our a priori design of seriousness was not sustained, results implied that parents differentiated situations according to seriousness and the need for them to intervene. The immediacy of situations is clearly a factor that determines strategies and may be as important as the beliefs that parents hold. This appeared to be the case in situations involving alcohol, which many parents viewed as potentially dangerous. Consider, then, the question of consistency for a parent who believes that adolescents ought to think for themselves. This parent might very well discuss the consequences of a lowered school grade on a report card, thinking a remedy might be had through discussion. That same parent however, might intervene in a coercive way if the adolescent were seen as endangered by alcohol.

In summary on this first point, we agree with the line of thinking that parents are complex agents who have beliefs but who must continually construct strategies to handle the details of situations. Beliefs are formed as parents proceed through the experience of rearing and they include long-term aims as well as strategies by which they can be achieved. Nevertheless, context-specific strategies would come to the fore when circumstances warranted and they would be framed as much by context as by belief. Moreover, in studying parents of adolescents, one is probably seeing a reorganization of beliefs as new situations are confronted and old beliefs apropos childhood are being modified.

The data on couples adds a second point to the discussion of consistency. Most prior research has studied individual parents, so present results on couples put questions about consistency in a new perspective. Readiness to discuss problems on the part of one parent was often accompanied by the other parent's readiness to admonish or make a direct demand. Mother–father pairs who used the combination of openness to discussion and control are particularly interesting because they represent a style that Baumrind (1975), Sigel (1985), and others have found effective in individual parents. Couples who practice this combination are showing how clear limits can be placed on expected behavior while closeness is maintained through communication.

The conception of strategies as expressions of coordinated parenting is also found in family systems theories and studies of communication among adolescents, mothers, and fathers (Bell & Bell, 1983; Grotevant & Cooper, 1986; Hauser, Powers, Noam, & Jacobson, 1984). The conception is congruent further with our previous findings from adolescents who described their parents similarly to parents' own descriptions in the present study (Youniss & Smollar, 1985). Adolescents said that mothers and fathers served different roles in talking, giving advice, asserting discipline, and the like. Often, one parent was very engaged with the adolescent's current experiences and the other parent, usually the father, was less involved in ongoing activities, but functioned to support the other parent. We conclude on this point that mothers and fathers may divide the labor of rearing rather than duplicating each other. This tactic allows them to reach adolescents through different modes of contact and to express complex feelings in clear fashion. For instance, we found expressions of concern along with strict demands and affirmations of warmth coupled with directives for action. These considerations complicate the initial question about consistency but emphasize the value of studying mother–father pairs in their division of parenting labor.

The third theoretical point of interest pertains to the kinds of strategies this sample of parents manifested. The majority of parents avoided direct control but let adolescents know the kind of behavior of which they approved. This conjunction of parental concern with assignment of responsibility to adolescents is reflective of a recently articulated position on adolescent development. Grotevant and Cooper (1986) proposed that parents serve a mediating role in helping adolescents establish themselves as individuals with distinctive character and identifying viewpoints. In traditional theories of adolescence, individuality was established through a hydraulic model wherein increases in self-definition were proportional to declines in dependence on parents. Modifying Blos' (1967) concept of individuation, Grotevant and Cooper proposed that separation and distinctiveness occur, in part, through the parents' agency. Separation proceeds as adolescents learn to express their own ideas to parents, who in turn, listen and discuss these ideas as potentially interesting and valid. Distinctiveness proceeds in like manner as adolescents and parents recognize one another's individuality and accept the possibility of further differentiation and independence (White, Speisman, & Costos, 1983; Youniss, 1988).

Many parents in the present sample used strategies that specified desired behavior but also gave responsibility to adolescents to enact it. These strategies signify the basic workings of the processes that promote individuation. The typical forms found in our data exemplified this point well. Parents said, in effect, "I care that you do not harm yourself with alcohol, will tell you about the risks, and will take more coercive action if necessary." Parents further told adolescents that they expected them to use their heads and to act responsibly. In so doing, parents were contributing to transformation of their relationship with adolescents by acknowledging the end of childhood dependence while encouraging greater self-reliance.

The final issue concerns the place of friendship in these parents' perspectives. We had initially expected that situations involving friends would be potent in generating parents' concern and perhaps controlling strategies. In fact, however, parents were not especially provoked by these stories but responded to them with only moderate control. It appears from responses that parents were rather confident of their teenagers' choices regarding familiar friendships to whom they referred as "regular friends." In current theoretical perspectives, parents view their teenagers' friends as allies rather than competitors in the socialization process (Berndt, 1979; Youniss & Smollar, 1989). It is interesting that parents made a distinction between friends they knew, and presumably trusted, and friends they did not know, about whom they were wary. In the main, parents in the present sample typified current theory by showing confidence in their sons' and daughters' friendships even to the point of viewing them at times as buffers against potential harm.

REFERENCES

Baumrind, D. (1975). Early socialization and adolescent competence. In S. E. Dragastin & G. H. Elder, Jr. (Eds.), *Adolescence in the life cycle* (pp. 117–143). New York: Halstedt.

Bell, D. C., & Bell, L. G. (1983). Parental validations and support in the development of adolescent daughters. In H. D. Grotevant & C. R. Cooper (Eds.), *Adolescent development in the family* (pp. 27–42). San Francisco: Jossey-Bass.

Berndt, T. J. (1979). Developmental changes in conformity to peers and parents. *Developmental Psychology, 15,* 608–616.

Blos, P. (1967). The second individuation process of adolescence. *The Psychoanalytic Study of the Child, 22,* 162–186.

Callen, K. (1983). The secretary's conference for youth on drinking and driving: special report. *Public Health Reports, 98,* 336–343.

Cooper, C. R., Grotevant, H. D., & Condon, S. M. (1983). Individuality and connectedness as a context for adolescent identity formation and role-taking skill. In H. D. Grotevant & C. R. Cooper (Eds.), *Adolescent development in the family* (pp. 43–59). San Francisco: Jossey-Bass.

Coleman, J. C. (1987). Families and schools. *Educational Researcher, 16,* 32–38.

Dillman, D. A. (1978). *Mail and telephone surveys: the total design method.* New York: Wiley.

Dornbusch, S. M., Ritter, P. L., Leiderman, P. H., Roberts, D. F., & Fraleigh, M. J. (1987). The relation of parenting style to adolescent school performance. *Child Development, 58,* 1244–1257.

Enright, R. D., Lapsley, D. K., Drivas, A. E., & Fehr, L. A. (1980). Parental influences on the development of adolescent autonomy and identity. *Journal of Youth and Adolescence, 9,* 529–545.

Gillis, J. R. (1981). *Youth and history: Tradition and change in European age relations.* New York: Academic Press.

Goodnow, J. (1988). Parents' ideas, actions, and feelings: Models and methods from developmental and social psychology. *Child Development, 59,* 286–320.

Grotevant, H. D., & Cooper, C. R. (1986). Individuation in family relationships. *Human Development, 29,* 61-81.

Grusec, J. E., & Kuczynski, L. (1980). Direction of effect in socialization: A comparison of the parent's vs. the child's behavior as determinants of disciplinary techniques. *Developmental Psychology, 16,* 1-9.

Hauser, S. T., Powers, S. I., Noam, G. G., & Jacobson, A. M. (1984). Familial contexts of adolescent ego development. *Child Development, 55,* 195-213.

Hunter, F. T., & Youniss, J. (1982). Changes in function of three relations during adolescence. *Developmental Psychology. 18,* 806-811.

Johnston, L. D., Bachman, J. G., & O'Malley, P. M. (1979). *Monitoring the future.* Ann Arbor, MI: Institute for Social Research.

Kett, J. F. (1977) *Rites of passage.* New York: Basic Books.

Kohn, M. L. (1969). *Class and conformity.* Chicago: University of Chicago Press.

Leahy, R. L. (1981). Parental practices and the development of moral judgment and self-image disparity during adolescence. *Developmental Psychology, 17,* 580-594.

McGillicuddy-DeLisi, A. V. (1980). The role of parental beliefs in the family as a system of mutual influences. *Family Relations, 29,* 317-323.

McGillicuddy-DeLisi, A. V. (1982). Parental beliefs about developmental processes. *Human Development, 25,* 192-200.

McKenry, P. C., Price-Bonham, S., & O'Bryant, S. L. (1981). Adolescent discipline: different family members' perceptions. *Journal of Youth and Adolescence, 10,* 327-332.

Sigel, I. (Ed.). (1985). *Parental belief systems: The psychological consequences for children.* Hillsdale, NJ: Lawrence Erlbaum Associates.

Smollar, J., & Youniss, J. (1989). Transformations in adolescents' perceptions of parents. *International Journal of Behavioral Development, 12,* 71-84.

Smith, T. E. (1983). Adolescents' reactions to attempted parental control and influence techniques. *Journal of Marriage and the Family, 45,* 533-542.

Steinberg, L. (1987). Family processes at adolescence: A developmental perspective. *Family therapy, 14,* 77-86.

White, K. M., Speisman, J. C., & Costos, D. (1983). Young adults and their parents: Individuation to mutuality. In H. D. Grotevant & C. R. Cooper (Eds.), *Adolescent development in the family* (pp. 61-76). San Francisco: Jossey-Bass.

Youniss, J. (1988). *Mutuality in parent-adolescent relationships.* Washington, DC: The William T. Grant Foundation Commission on Work, Family, and Citizenship.

Youniss, J. (1989). Parent-adolescent relationship and social capital. In W. Damon (Ed.), *Child development today and tomorrow* (pp. 379-392). San Francisco: Jossey-Bass.

Youniss, J., & Smollar, J. (1985). *Adolescent relations with mothers, fathers, friends.* Chicago: University of Chicago Press.

Youniss, J., & Smollar, J. (1989). Adolescents' interpersonal relationships in social context. In T. J. Berndt & G. W. Ladd (Eds.), *Peer relationships in child development* (pp. 300-316). New York: Wiley.

III Focus on Atypical Families

9

Affective and Cognitive Processes Within Threat-Oriented Family Systems

Daphne Blunt Bugental
University of California, Santa Barbara

Michelle didn't clean her room again. I told her several times and she still didn't do it. My first thoughts were "This is usual. She doesn't follow directions. She ignores me." I felt a combination of despair and anger. I don't want to keep reminding her over and over again.
> —Excerpt from interview with mother recalling
> a recent problem episode with her child.

Parental response to children involves a complex sequence of intervening events—as suggested by this example. The way this mother interprets her child's behavior acts as an important influence on her affective state, and ultimately on her care-giving strategy. Her thoughts identify the child's behavior as fitting her views of "how Michelle acts" along with implicit inferences about Michelle's motives, that is, she misbehaves intentionally. Additionally, her thoughts convey a sense of her own helplessness in the relationship. The mother's emotional response is consistent with a care-giving schema in which Michelle has a negative, controlling role and the mother is the victim. And her subsequent ruminations about Michelle mirror her affectively tagged understanding of what Michelle does and why she does it.

The representation of care-giving relationships in terms of intervening cognitive variables is consistent with a general trend within the socialization literature (Sigel, 1985). But it is argued here that we need to add more specificity to our conceptualization of the role of cognitions. First, it is suggested that two types of cognitions—automatic and controlled—need to be considered. In the preceding example, we argue that the mother

219

automatically accesses a care-giving schema in which she has a power disadvantage; and that she subsequently engages in reflections and deliberations (*controlled* cognitions) that follow from her automatic categorization of Michelle's behavior. Second, the importance of affect as both cause and consequence of cognitive processes is stressed. And finally, evidence is presented from dysfunctional family systems in support of the proposed model. The model presented incorporates concepts from the fields of both developmental and social psychology.

BACKGROUND

Concern with Cognitions in Care-Giving Relationships

In initial concerns with the reciprocal nature of influences within family systems, the focus was on two-way influences of parent and child *behaviors* (Bell, 1968). More recently, interest has emerged in the social *cognitions* of parents and children as moderators of their responses to each other (e.g., Bugental & Shennum, 1984; Dodge, 1986; Fincham & Bradbury, 1987; Goodnow, 1988). Parental beliefs about their children or about parenting may have a marked influence on the way they interpret and respond to their children's behavior patterns (Bell, 1979; Dix & Grusec, 1985; Goodnow, 1985; Hess, Kashiwagi, Azuma, Price, & Dickson, 1980; Holloway & Hess, 1985; McGillicuddy-DeLisi, 1982). Identical child behaviors may elicit different reactions from different adults based upon the perceived implications of those behaviors, that is, care-giver cognitions act to *moderate* response patterns.[1]

As research on care-giver cognitions has progressed, increasing interest has been shown in the influence of parental cognitions on *affect* — within both normally functioning and distressed families. The essential tenet of such research has been that affect experienced in response to others is determined not only by what the other person does, but also by the

---

[1]The usual distinction is made here between "moderators" and "mediators." "Moderators" refer to intervening variables that act to yield differential response patterns to the same stimuli, that is, a branching operation is implied by a moderator model. For example, a novel stimulus may lead to a fear response for an individual with one temperament pattern or cognitive explanatory pattern; the identical stimulus may lead to interest and approach for someone with a different temperament pattern or cognitive explanatory pattern. Thus we speak of those individual difference variables as "moderators." On the other hand, "mediators" refer to intervening variables that follow a regular sequential course. For example, attentional focus may be found to follow increasing levels of defensive arousal for *all* individuals; thus defensive arousal acts as a "mediator."

interpretation made of that behavior. For example, Dix and his colleagues showed that negative affect on the part of care-givers may follow from the inferences they draw with regard to the basis of the child's behavior, that is, parents respond negatively if they infer that a child's negative behavior is "correspondent with" negative intentions on the part of the child (the child's behavior is freely chosen) (Dix, Ruble, Grusec, & Nixon, 1986; Dix, Ruble, & Zambarano, 1989). In our own initial research, we found that the causal beliefs of care-givers (about the causes of care-giving success and failure) acted to either sensitize to or buffer against the effects of child behaviors; adult expressive behavior was, in turn, found to maintain child behavior that was consistent with adult causal beliefs (Bugental & Shennum, 1984).

Interest in the role of parental cognitions has also extended to their influence on autonomic arousal. Some have argued (e.g., Vasta, 1982) that parents who are prone to unusually high levels of autonomic reactivity may be more prone to "preemptive processing" of care-giving events, that is, bypassing cognitive processing to respond emotionally to eliciting events. Such a process is consistent with the general finding that elevated levels of defensive arousal are associated with narrowing of attentional focus (Easterbrook, 1959). In our own research, we have argued that parental cognitions may have consequences for subsequent autonomic patterns. For example, we found that adults with low perceived control who were anticipating interaction with unresponsive children manifested higher levels of defensive arousal (increased skin conductance and heart rate) than did adults with higher levels of perceived control (Bugental & Cortez, 1988).

Direction of Effect Between Cognitions and Affect

In conceptualizing complex interpersonal systems that involve an interplay between affect and cognition, it is important to look at evidence from social psychology and cognitive psychology as well as developmental psychology. Researchers within these related fields have shown increasing interest in the influences of affect on cognition (e.g., Clark & Fiske, 1982; Ellis, Thomas & Rodriguez, 1984; Isen, 1984) and the influences of cognition on affect (e.g., Abramson, Seligman, & Teasdale, 1978; Fiske & Pavelchak, 1986; Lazarus & Folkman, 1984).

Theorists concerned with the relationship between affect and cognition have differed in the causal influences posited. Some have argued primarily for the causal influences of cognitive processes on subsequent affect. For example, Weiner and his colleagues argued and provided evidence for the effect of causal attributions on subsequent mood states and specific affective responses (Weiner, 1985; Weiner, Russell, & Lerman, 1978). According to this view, the way an event is explained will determine the affective evaluation of that event. For example, if individuals are seen as poor through no fault of their own, they may elicit sympathy; but if they are seen as responsible for their own fate, they may elicit contempt.

Lazarus and his colleagues have written extensively on the role of cognitive appraisal in relationship to emotion (e.g., Lazarus & Folkman, 1984). From this point of view, the emotional impact of eliciting events is determined by the individual's construal of their significance. Events are initially appraised as benign, threatening, or irrelevant for the individual's welfare. In a secondary appraisal process, threatening events are assessed in terms of potential coping options. Both Weiner and Lazarus have been concerned primarily with causal attributions/appraisals in connection with *specific* events.

A third approach—the reformulated learned helplessness model—has been concerned with the role of *chronic* or generalized attributions (Abramson, Metalsky, & Alloy, 1989; Abramson, Seligman, & Teasdale, 1978). The work of Abramson, Seligman, and their colleagues has explored the extent to which a pessimistic explanatory style may ultimately lead to depressive symptomology.

Finally, from the stress and coping literature, it has been shown that individuals whose beliefs are characterized by high perceived control (as a generalized attributional pattern or as an appraisal of a specific situation) tend to cope better with illness and other sources of stress (e.g., Anderson, 1977; Johnson & Sarason, 1978; Lefcourt, Miller, Ware, & Sherk, 1981; Taylor, Lichtman, & Wood, 1984). In a similar vein, Affleck, Allen, McGrade, and McQueeney (1982) observed that maternal coping with serious medical problems in infants is influenced by the mother's interpretation of the causes of the child's condition.

From an alternate point of focus, other researchers have argued for the influences of affect on subsequent processing patterns. Affective states—in particular, negative affective states—have been shown to deplete cognitive resources and thus reduce information-processing capacities (e.g., Ellis, Thomas, & Rodriguez, 1984; Isen, 1984; Nasby & Yando, 1980; Mackie & Worth, 1989). Affect has also been found to increase cognitive access to content and to memories that are consistent with that affect (e.g., Bower, 1981; Gotlib & McCann, 1984).

Automatic Versus Controlled Cognitions in Relation to Affect

A distinction has been made in the adult literature between automatic and controlled cognitions. That is, social cognitions have been seen as involving either intentional, controlled cognitions that are subject to the individual's awareness, or as involving automatic (unaware) processing of social events. These qualitatively distinct cognitive structures may be thought of as involving different levels of processing—levels that may ultimately act to influence one another in processing sequences that occur over time. Controlled cognitions reflect those portions of our interaction that are most subject to our conscious deliberation (e.g., Schneider & Shiffrin, 1977; Shiffrin & Schneider, 1977). At this point, our concern with parental cognitions has most typically been of this type, that is, the conscious appraisal or interpretation that parents make in the care-giving setting. Researchers taking this approach are likely to ask adults for their thoughts about specific care-giving events, for example, why they think a child engaged in a particular behavior, and what they believe would be an appropriate care-giver response to the child. Although the distinction between these automatic and controlled processes has received considerable attention in social psychology (e.g., Bargh, 1982; Devine, 1989; Higgins & King, 1981), it has not as yet been well-incorporated into our understanding of family relationships.

Automatic or precognitive processes have been conceptualized as preceding affect (Epstein, 1984), which in turn may influence subsequent controlled or aware cognitions. Unlike the conscious appraisal or interpretive processes that have been the primary interests of Lazarus, Weiner, and others, initial schematic processing of social stimuli operates very quickly, automatically, and with little or no apparent awareness (e.g., Winter, Uleman, & Cunniff, 1985). Additionally, it appears to operate without depletion of processing capacity (Bargh & Thein, 1985). These automatically accessed structures may then directly access affect that is associated with a schema. Fiske and her colleagues described this process as "schema-triggered affect" (Fiske, 1982; Fiske & Pavelchak, 1986); if a social stimulus matches an existing schema, it will elicit the affect associated with that schema. If, for example, an adult interacts with a child that fits her or his category of a "difficult child," the affect experienced will be consistent with the category label. As noted earlier, the affective state engendered may act to influence, focus, or limit subsequent processing at a higher level of awareness and cognitive complexity, that is, the processing involved in appraisal and planning. Finally, Lewicki and his colleagues (Lewicki, 1986; Hill, Lewicki, Czyzewska, & Boss, 1989) showed that nonconscious encoding biases may ultimately act in a self-perpetuating fashion; what comes to be "known" and "remembered" about social events is a composite of social reality and the biased encoding processes imposed upon reality.

Up to this point, research within the socialization area (including our own) has been mute with regard to the extent to which care-giver cognitions operate at an automatic or a controlled level. It is argued here that care-giver cognitions operate at both levels. Automatic cognitions are, however, expected to act as central organizers of controlled cognitions; and, in line with the thinking of Fiske and Pavelchak (1986), they are also expected to trigger or prime congruent affect. Schematic representations of self and others are typical examples of such structures. The dynamic or causal interrelationship between self and others may also be represented as a schema or script (e.g., Read, 1987). When an individual is confronted with a potentially threatening or ambiguous social interaction, such schematic structures are readily available on a "default" basis. For example, Michelle's mother may be thought of as having a script for "the way bad things happen" in families. If Michelle misbehaves, her mother automatically accesses a relationship schema in which she is the victim and Michelle is the victimizer. In a happier state or with refocused interpretation, she may be capable of other interpretations, but the "victim scenario" represents her "fallback" perception of the event. Once accessed, this schema acts to prime emotional reactions and thoughts that are consistent with this schema. Ultimately, Michelle's mother may even "remember" the events of the day in a way that is more consistent with her schema than with the objective facts.

In Bowlby's terms (1980), schematic constructions about family relationships may be thought of as representing the "working model" that adults have about children and care giving, and which in turn reflect their own early experiences. Relationship schemas, as is true for schematic structures as a whole, may be initially acquired as a function of repeated experiences (Nelson & Gruendel, 1986)—in particular when those experiences are associated with strong affect (Hoffman, 1986). Once acquired, they operate with little or no use of cognitive resources. They may be thought of as analogous to a perceptual filter through which incoming stimuli are screened (Bugental & Shennum, 1984)—an event that is more common under conditions of ambiguity or potential threat.

Concern with the effects of interpersonal schemas on information processing is just beginning to emerge within the developmental literature. For example, Crowell and Feldman (1988) found that mothers' internal models of care-giving relationships (based on their descriptions of their own childhood experiences) were reflected in their parenting behavior as adults. As an ultimate manifestation of this effect, the behavior shown by children corresponded to the mother's "internal model"—even when the effects of maternal behavior were removed.

PROPOSED MODEL

The general model proposed here is concerned with both malfunctioning, self-maintaining care-giving systems and adaptive, self-correcting care-giving systems. The point of focus is on patterns of response to potentially "difficult" child behavior; thus the point of entry to interactive systems is with the behavior of the child. The model (see Fig. 9.1) includes seven steps in the interactional sequence:

1. *Eliciting stimulus:* Stimulus features of the child that pose a potential challenge to care-giving adults (e.g., ambiguous, unusual, or aversive behavior).

2. *Care-giver schema activation:* Automatic processing of stimulus on the basis of care-giver schemas.

3a. *Priming of schema-consistent autonomic/affective responses:* Changes in autonomic arousal and affective state in response to child stimulus, as transformed by care-giver schemas.

3b. *Priming of schema-consistent cognitions:* Controlled cognitive processing (evaluations, ruminations, and/or plans) in response to child stimulus, as transformed by care-giver schemas.

4a. *Uncontrolled expressive behavior:* "Leakage" of state/autonomic information, for example, acoustical features of voice, motoric behavior.

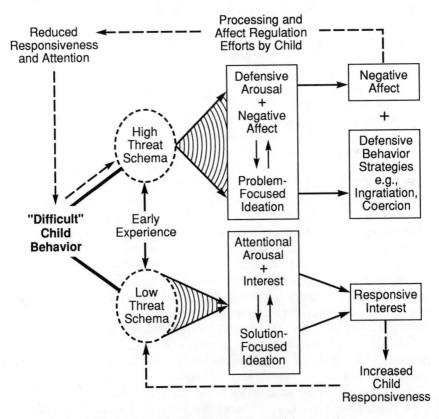

FIG. 9.1   Model of threat-oriented care-giving systems.

4b. *Controlled expressive behavior:* Behaviors such as verbal content (and some facial actions) deliberately directed to child.

5. *Cognitive, affective, and autonomic processing by child:* Information-processing of child as a combined function of stimulus features of adult message and child's developmental level.

6. *Alteration of child's stimulus properties:* Changes in child's attention and/or affective/behavioral responsiveness to adult as a function of child's own emotion regulation efforts.

7. *System maintenance:* Confirmation of adult cognitions.

The child is seen as a potential system stressor as well as the ultimate recipient of parental response patterns. Parenting itself can pose a source of stress (i.e., the system demands introduced by the presence of a child), but stresses are more probable if the child's behavior or needs are problematic. For example, parents of children who manifest hyperactivity (Barkley, 1981; Mash & Johnston, 1983), aggressiveness/conduct disorders (e.g., Patterson, 1976, 1980) or a variety of disabilities (e.g., Kogan, Tyler, & Turner, 1974) may be particularly prone to stress responses. And yet there is also a great deal of variability in the extent to which adverse reactions are shown to such problems. In our initial example, the eliciting behavior of Michelle in not cleaning her room is an offense that might draw strong concern from some parents but little response from others.

It is proposed here that, just as cognitions act to moderate reactions to other types of stress, they also act to moderate reaction to the potential stress that may be induced by children and parenting. Care-giver cognitions are introduced at two levels: (a) at an initial preconscious level, and (b) at an aware or controlled level of cognitive appraisal. Precognitions operate at an automatic, unaware level and may be conceptualized as leading the individual to a "perceptual readiness" to attend to particular aspects of the environment (Bruner, 1957; Shiffrin & Dumais, 1981). Care-giving schemas may be understood as representing this type of cognitive structure. The eliciting stimulus posed by the child, as filtered through precognitive schematic structures, will subsequently influence both affective reactions and more aware or deliberate levels of cognitive processing. The presence of "difficult" child behavior will have different consequences based on differences in these care-giving schemas. More adverse reactions will occur for those parents who have a schematic representation of the care-giving relationship that places the adult at a power disadvantage ("threat-oriented" schema). Such parents focus on the child as a "problem source" and themselves as a helpless victim of that child.

Returning to the initial example of Michelle and her mother, one sees evidence for such a schema. The child's behavior is seen as "usual," as directed at the mother, and as beyond the control of the mother. Ultimately, the mother will lose the battle—confirming her preconceptions. Another parent with a different care-giving schema might show lower levels of reactivity to the same child behavior, and ultimately might be better able to modify the child's behavior.

As the third step in the model, changing inner states are predicted at both the autonomic/affective and controlled cognition level. At the autonomic/affective level, the pairing of "difficult" children with "threat-oriented" adults is expected to lead to autonomic mobilization and increases in feelings of negative affect. Such individuals will increase in physiological responses that are more typically associated with physically active coping (Obrist, 1982), such as increases in heart rate and electrodermal activity. This preparation for action is accompanied by ideation that is threat-focused and pessimistic. Two-way feedback between autonomic/affect and ideational systems can be anticipated. For example, thoughts of failure may lead (initially) to depressed affect (Clark, Beck, & Brown, 1989); at the same time, increases in negative affect and autonomic arousal may lead to negatively focused thoughts. For example, Michelle's mother reported a combination of despair and anger, along with pessimistic ruminations.

As the fourth step in our model, expressive behaviors occur at different levels of controllability. Some behaviors may occur with little conscious awareness or control *(affect leakage)*. Others may reflect deliberately managed response patterns *(strategic behavior)*. Still other behaviors may be only partially controllable. When confronted with a "difficult" child, "threat-oriented" adults may respond with increased arousal; subsequently, information about their altered inner state may be revealed in *unintentional* changes in their behavior, for example, altered vocal intonation. These same individuals may also engage in exaggerated *strategic* efforts (positive or negative) due to their perceived inability to have an influence on the child.

At the fifth step, the child goes through similar processing sequences that reflect a combination of his or her developmental level and earlier experiences (information processing manifested by the child is only briefly discussed within this chapter and is more fully developed elsewhere, e.g., Bugental, Blue, Cortez, Fleck, & Rodriguez, in press). It can be anticipated that the ultimate message shown by "threat-oriented" adults is predominantly negative and possibly confusing—acting to generate negative affect or anxiety in the child. Younger children, in particular, are likely to interpret inconsistent affect as negative (Bugental, Kaswan, & Love, 1970). In coping with their own negative affect, children can be expected (at the sixth step of the model) to respond with increases in avoidance or (apparent) unresponsiveness (Kopp, 1989). This pattern in turn acts to support the adult's relationship schema and confirms the validity of their threat- or problem-focused ideation (final step). Ultimately, the system acts not only in a self-maintaining but also in a potentially escalating fashion. As levels of autonomic arousal and negative affect increase, the system may destabilize and move out of control to expressions of anger or rage (recall that Michelle's mother reported both despair and anger).

Conversely, the postulated sequence of events in "solution-oriented" systems more easily leads to problem reduction. Adults whose relationship schemas do not place them at a power disadvantage will be less easily triggered to action by a potentially "difficult" child. Instead of mobilizing for action, they may respond with increased attention and solution-focused ideation. Their behavior, as a reflection of these inner processes, is likely to reflect a pattern of "interest." Children, in turn, are likely to respond to adult interest with increased responsiveness or attention. In this case, the care-giving system may be thought of as self-correcting.

The postulated sequence of events in "threat-oriented" systems is consistent with notions of either the reformulated model of learned helplessness (Abramson, Seligman, & Teasdale, 1978) or the reformulated frustration-aggression hypothesis (Berkowitz, 1989). It is also consistent with the information-processing model proposed by Dodge and his colleagues to account for the social interactions of aggressive children (e.g., Dodge, 1980; Dodge, Murphy, & Buchsbaum, 1984). In all of these formulations, triggering events are assumed to be cognitively transformed, and to lead to either depressed and/or angry affect. We have attempted to add to existing understanding by specifying the role of both automatic and controlled cognitions within such transformations. Additionally, we are concerned with the ways in which affective and autonomic state changes influence and are influenced by cognitive processes. Finally, we have attempted to move past a focus on single individuals to a concern with *interdependent systems,* and the ways in which dysfunctional and well-functioning systems are maintained. In the present discussion, however, we focus on the development and maintenance of dysfunctional systems.

EVIDENCE FOR MODEL

Evidence for the proposed model focuses on intrapersonal and interpersonal processes that occur in threat-oriented family systems. Attention is directed to processes occuring within coercive or abusive family systems. In order to test component processes, a program of research has been designed that makes use of both *naturalistic observation* and *laboratory analog* studies. The original research that prompted this research direction (Bugental & Shennum, 1984) involved an analog manipulation in which child confederates were trained to produce behaviors that posed a challenge for unrelated adults. It was predicted and confirmed that adults with low perceived control in the care-giving relationship are more reactive to child behavior than are adults with higher levels of perceived control. Adults with low perceived control manifested an ambivalent pattern of affect and a "helpless" style that acted to maintain unresponsive child behavior.

As a follow-up to this research, observations were made of distressed families (families at risk for abuse) in order to test the application of the emerging model of family interaction in a naturalistic setting. In this chapter, attention is focused on naturalistic interactions between children at risk for abuse with their own parents and with strangers (Bugental, Blue, & Cruzcosa, 1989; Bugental, Blue, & Lewis, 1990). This research focused on "eliciting" characteristics of children, care-giving schemas of adults, expressive behavior of adults, and changing response patterns of children (Steps 1, 2, 4, and 6 of the model). Reference is also made to recently completed analog research (Bugental, Blue, Cortez, Fleck, Kopeikin, Lewis, & Lyon, 1990) in which a test was made of autonomic changes and thoughts that occur in response to experimentally controlled child stimuli that pose a potential challenge for adults (Step 3 of the model).

Naturalistic Research with Children "at Risk" For Abuse

Observations were made of interactions between children "at risk" for abuse with their own mothers and with strangers (Bugental, Blue, & Cruzcosa, 1989; Bugental, Blue, & Lewis, 1990). Sibling pairs were selected from 40 families currently in counseling at a child abuse agency. Abuse had been substantiated in half of these families; for the other half of the families, parents were fearful that they might abuse their children but there was no evidence that abuse had occurred. Sibling pairs included one child (target child) who was seen by their own mother as relatively "difficult" and who was subject to more coercive levels of discipline, and a second child (nontarget child) who was seen as relatively "easy" and subject to lower levels of discipline. All children were between the ages of 3 and 13. As far as possible, sibling pairs were balanced for gender and age; additionally, both gender and age were introduced as covariates in statistical analyses.

Children ($N = 40$) were observed during unstructured interactions with their own mothers and with 40 unfamiliar mothers recruited from the general community (not in counseling). Data is based on four sets of dyadic interactions: (a) interactions between 40 target children and their own mothers; (b) interactions between 40 nontarget children and their own mothers; (c) interactions between 40 target children and 40 unrelated mothers drawn from the general community; and (d) interactions between 40 nontarget children and 40 unrelated mothers drawn from the general community. Each child was involved in two interactions (related and unrelated mothers), and each mother was involved in two interactions (target and nontarget sibling pairs drawn from the same family).

These investigations asked an unfolding set of questions:

1. What are the "eliciting" features of children who are at relatively higher risk for coercive discipline or abuse within their own family?
2. Are abusive mothers more likely to have "threat-oriented" schemas than are nonabusive mothers? What evidence do we have that such schemas may be thought of as reflecting chronically accessible constructs?
3. What expressive patterns are shown by strangers who have "threat-oriented" schemas during their interactions with "difficult" (targeted) children?
4. How do children respond to expressive behaviors shown by "threat-oriented" adults?

Observations of mothers with their own children allowed us to determine whether such families showed the system features we anticipated. Observation of strangers (from the general community) with children from distressed families allowed us to test some of the causal inferences made within the model. That is, in the absence of any history between children and strangers, differential patterns of reactivity by adults with different care-giving schemas may be assumed to be due the combined influences of the eliciting behaviors of children and the care-giving schemas of adults. If, for example, threat-oriented strangers show a pattern of high reactivity to child behavior (systematic differences in ways of interacting with target versus nontarget children) and other strangers do not, it may be assumed that these differences occur as a combined function of the initial stimuli posed by children and the care-giving schemas of adults. Ruled out within this design is the possibility (present in related families) that adult attributions have been determined by child characteristics, or that child characteristics (of those that preceded interactions with the stranger) have been determined by adult attributions or behaviors.

Eliciting Features of Children

An extensive analysis was conducted on behavioral differences shown by children seen as relatively "easy" or "difficult" by their own parents (within distressed families). (Statistical tests of these differences are reported in Bugental, Blue, & Lewis 1990; only those results achieving significance at the .05 level of confidence are reported here.) One of the most striking differences between sibling pairs was in the extent to which "difficult" children (who were also at higher risk for abuse) were rated by blind observers as "unusual, odd, or inappropriate" in their behavior patterns. Additionally, their visual responsiveness was distinctive, not only during interactions with their own mothers but also during interactions with strangers. In both of these interactive settings, "difficult" children were more likely to look away from adults when those adults direct gaze towards them; such children were, in turn, seen as more unresponsive during these interactions. To the extent gaze aversion represents an affect regulation strategy, this behavior may reflect a coping mechanism that leads such children to be perceived negatively by adults.

These observations parallel those found by other investigations of abused children. Abused children have been found to be more likely to demonstrate a variety of behavior patterns or characteristics that can pose a potential threat to the care-giving system. Although many of the behavior patterns shown (e.g., social withdrawal, aggression, impulsivity) can readily be understood as potential sequelae to abuse (including the behavior patterns we observed), other patterns can only be understood as antecedents. For example, abused children are more likely to have been premature (Elmer & Gregg, 1967); they have a history of chronic illness that precedes abuse (Sherrod, O'Connor, Vietze, & Altemeier, 1984); they are more likely to have a variety of physical and learning disabilities (de Lissovoy, 1980). In short, features that are more common among abused children may either precede or follow from abuse; but in all cases, such features may act to increase future risk of abuse.

Threat-Oriented Schemas

Even though differences have been found between abused and nonabused children, one cannot imagine that such differences, on their own, account for negative adult reactions. Many children are "difficult," but relatively few adults are abusive. The aversive child features that trigger negative reactions in one adult may be scarcely noticed by another. Wolfe (1985) concluded in a recent review of the literature on abusive parents that they are best characterized by unusually high levels of reactivity to stress. Our concern was with the individual differences between those adults who are more or less reactive to the potential challenge posed by "difficult" child behavior. Our expectation was that care-giving schemas or scripts provide a marker of such differences. That is, those adults who see the care-giving relationship as characterized by "threat" were expected to be maximally reactive to variations in child behavior. If parents believe that they are at a disadvantage in a relationship—that the child has more control over what happens than they do—they are in a vulnerable position. That is, undesired things can happen to them relatively easily. We expected that such individuals would be perceptually vigilant for care-giving problems. Or, stated in other terms, care-giving threats or problems are "chronically accessible" to them. The predicted pattern is consistent with Diener and Dweck's (1978) finding that individuals with "helpless" attributions have ready access to potential causes of failure experiences. The core feature of "threat-oriented" scripts is that of problems instigated intentionally by the child and which the "blameless" care giver is powerless to prevent.

Measurement of Care-Giving Schemas (Parent Attribution Test). The measure employed for the assessment of care-giving schemas or scripts was the Parent Attribution Test (PAT). This instrument was originally formulated within an attributional framework (Bugental & Shennum, 1984; Bugental, Blue, & Cruzcosa, 1989); but, as noted earlier, attributions for the causes of interactional outcomes may be reinterpreted as representing interpersonal schemas or scripts. The PAT assesses the perceived contributions of both adult and child to their *joint* outcomes. Respondents are asked to indicate the importance they assign to various factors as potential sources of influence on interactional success or failure. For example, in accounting for a hypothetical failure in taking care of a neighbor's child, respondents are asked to rate (on a 7-point scale) the relative importance they would assign to such factors as "How well you get along with children in general," "The extent to which the child was stubborn and resisted your efforts," "Whether or not this was a bad day for the child," "What kind of a mood you were in on that day," and so on.

Items were originally divided into dimensions on the basis of multidimensional scaling techniques, that is, a group of mothers sorted causal categories into similarity groups (all statistical procedures are fully described in Bugental, Blue, & Cruzcosa, 1989). Additionally, mother judges rated item groupings based on potential meaning dimensions; for example, one group of items was rated as reflecting causes that were believed to be controllable by adults. On the basis of this analysis, items were divided into dimensions that reflected: (a) high versus low controllability of success by adults, (b) high versus low controllability of success by children, (c) high versus low controllability of failure by adults, and (d) high versus low controllability of failure by children.

Our focus here was on attributions for failure, that is, the extent to which interactional failure is seen as controllable by adults and/or children. Of critical interest was the pairing of low attributed control to adults, and high attributed control to children (over failure). Such respondents would, for example, believe that interaction problems are more influenced by such factors as the adult's bad mood or the adult having a bad day (factors generally seen by naive judges as hard to control) than by the adult's care-giving strategy or care-giving motivation (judged to be controllable factors); at the same time, they would be likely to believe that problems are more influenced by such factors as the child's stubbornness or low effort (controllable by child) than by the child being tired or sick (hard for child to control). This combination represents a relationship schema that is characterized by an unfavorable balance of power and is referred to here as a "threat-oriented" schema. As such, it was expected to predict negative response patterns during interactions with "difficult" children. Further details about psychometric properties of the PAT are described in Bugental, Blue, and Cruzcosa (1989).[2]

A few words may be in order here with respect to attributional dimensions. As Brown and Siegel (1988) noted, the relationship between attributions and negative affective state cannot be fully understood without considering the relative controllability of perceived causes of negative events. In a study of stress and well-being, Brown and Siegel found that internal, stable, and global attributions for negative events attributed to relatively uncontrollable causes were positively related to increased depression, whereas internal and global attributions for negative events that were attributed to controllable causes were found to be inversely related to increases in negative affect. This analysis is similar to that of Janoff-Bulman (1979, 1982) who argued that characterological self-blame for negative events (bad events due to the kind of person one is) is positively related to depression, but behavioral self-blame for negative events (bad events due to controllable acts of self) is negatively related to depression. We would summarize these findings (and other findings in this area) as follows: If bad events are due to features about the self that cannot be easily controlled or to features about others that those others could easily control, negative affect is likely.

Threat-Oriented Schemas as Chronically Accessible Constructs. It has been argued here that low attribution of control to care givers and high attribution of control to children over care-giving failure may be thought of as reflecting a threat-oriented relationship schema. It was expected that individuals who manifested this schematic structure would be found to have easy access to threat-oriented or problem-focused ideation. In recently completed research (Bugental, Cortez, & Lyon, 1990), we explored the

---

[2]Detailed information on the PAT is available in Bugental, Blue, and Cruzcosa, 1989, or by request for additional information to the author. The assignment of subjects to the threat-oriented category reflects a composite of four scores: high attributed control to self over care-giving failure; low attributed score to self over care-giving failure; high attributed control to children over care-giving failure; and low attributed control to children over care-giving failure. The median estimate of reliability, based upon interitem consistency within these scales (Cronbach's alpha) is .69 ($N = 160$). Based on test–retest measures (with a sample of 30 mothers), 83% of subjects categorized as threat-oriented or not threat-oriented remained in the same category over time.

accessibility of problem-focused ideation versus solution-focused ideation among mothers with threat-oriented schemas (high attribution of control to children and low attribution of control to adults over care-giving failure) versus other schematic groupings.

We asked 40 mothers of school-aged children to use a series of cartoon pictures to tell a story about events leading up to a care-giving problem, and then select from a second set of pictures to describe what led to an ultimate solution. It was expected that threat-oriented subjects would show high access to problem ideation but not solution ideation. Primary concern was with the differential processing of problem and solution information. Based upon research concerned with schema accessibility (e.g., Bargh, Bond, Lombardi, & Tota, 1986; Fazio, Sanbonmatsu, Powell, & Kardes, 1986; Higgins, King, & Mavin, 1982; Markus, 1977), respondents may be thought of as being schematic for a particular construct if they (a) show short response latencies and (b) provide many exemplars of a particular construct. On this basis, subjects were measured for latency of response as well as number of pictures selected as causes of problems versus solutions.

Subjects were shown a picture depicting a family-related problem and a second picture depicting a family-related solution. They were then asked to tell a story (and select from pictures offered to them) about events that led up to the problem. Next, they were asked to relate (and select from a second set of pictures) the events that led to the solution. They were asked to tell stories (and select pictures) about events accounting for four problem–solution sequences involving a parent and child (as well as one sequence involving only a child in the problem picture).

In support of our predictions, threat-oriented subjects (in comparison with other subject groupings) were found to show different response patterns to *problem* pictures. The difference between attributional groupings was reflected by both indicators of accessibility: (a) threat-oriented attributors selected a larger number of pictures ($M = 3.79$) than did other groupings ($M = 3.32$) in telling stories about events leading up to conflict between parents and children; and (b) threat-oriented attributors had a shorter average latency ($M = 34$ sec) than did other groupings ($M = 45$ sec) in selecting pictures described as leading up to parent–child conflict. For both variables, a significant interaction was found between attributional grouping and story segment (problem vs. solution). No comparable differences or trends were found between attributional groupings in their description of events leading to resolution of conflict. Additionally, no significant differences or trends were found between attributional groupings and/or story segment for a set of pictures depicting an initial problem shown as involving only the child. These findings support our contention that caregivers who make threat-oriented attributions on the PAT have ready access to problem or threat-focused ideation in the care-giving domain. It is necessary for future research to determine the extent to which the observed effects are domain-specific or reflective of a more general "pessimistic bias" about interpersonal relations.

These findings allow us to think of threat-oriented responses to the PAT as providing a measure of the chronic accessibility of threat or problem ideation. (Ongoing research is being conducted in which construct accessibility is being measured under conditions of cognitive load — an approach that will allow us to further substantiate the automatic role of schematic processing.)

Threat-Orientations of Abusive and Nonabusive Parents. A comparison was made of the PAT responses of three groups of respondents within our observational study of abuse. We compared the care-giving schemas of 21 abusive parents (being seen in counseling at a child abuse agency), 19 nonabusive but "at-risk" parents (being seen at a child abuse agency), and 40 mothers drawn from the general community (unrelated mothers who were observed interacting with children from families in counseling). Abusive mothers were found to differ significantly from either of the other two groups (Bugental, Blue, & Cruzcosa, 1989). As expected, they were more likely to show threat-oriented care-giving schemas. Specifically, they were likely to attribute relatively low control to care givers but relatively high control to children as causes of bad events. That is, they believed that negative outcomes were likely to be caused by hard to control features of the care giver (e.g., her mood) and more controllable features of the child (e.g., his or her stubbornness). This supports the findings of Larrance and Twentyman (1983) who found that abusive parents were more likely to attribute the failures of their children to stable, internal factors than were nonabusive parents.

Caregiver Schemas as Moderators of Response to Children. No causal inferences regarding the direct role of parental attributions within dysfunctional family systems can be drawn from the disproportional presence of threat-oriented attributions among abusive mothers. This relationship is subject to multiple interpretations. It might mean that parental experiences with one or more of their children have fostered a better care-giving schema. Alternately, it might mean that parental attributions have a direct causal effect in producing abuse. And quite reasonably, some causal chain might be posited in which child behaviors and parental attributions have reciprocal influences. Because of the difficulty of unconfounding these correlational patterns, it was necessary to move to a different research strategy in testing our prediction that threat-oriented schemas act to increase the probability of negative response patterns to difficult children. We shifted to the assessment of the responses shown by unfamiliar women to sibling pairs (one relatively difficult child and one relatively easy child) whom they had never met before. If, indeed, threat-oriented care-giver schemas act to sensitize adults to differences in child behavior, we could expect to see differential reactions of threat-oriented women to difficult and easy children. No such differential reactions were expected for more solution-oriented women during these initial interactions.

Women in our previously described group of unrelated mothers were categorized into those who manifested threat-oriented care-giving schemas versus those who did not. Selection was based upon the presence of scores that were above the median for "attributed control to children over failure" and below the median for "attributed control to adults over failure."

Expressive Behaviors Shown by Threat-Oriented Adults to "Difficult" and "Easy" Children

We now shift to consideration of Step 4 in our model (we return later to preliminary evidence from ongoing research that provides support for Step 3). It is suggested in our model that adults with threat-oriented schemas, when confronted with relatively challenging or difficult child behavior, will respond with predictable shifts in both their controlled and their uncontrolled expressive behavior. As described earlier, 40 unrelated mothers interacted with 40 sibling pairs (a relatively difficult and a relatively easy child drawn from the same family).

The affective patterns shown by abusive parents have typically been found to be more negative than that shown by nonabusive parents (e.g., Bousha & Twentyman, 1984; Burgess & Conger, 1978; Oldershaw, Walters, & Hall, 1986; Reid, Patterson, & Loeber, 1982; Trickett & Kuczynski, 1986). Supporting this finding, we observed that abusive mothers showed significantly less facial happiness than did nonabusive mothers who were also in counseling (Bugental, Blue, & Lewis, 1990); abusive mothers showed "felt smiles" (as defined by Ekman & Friesen, 1978) at a rate of 1.3 per min, whereas nonabusive mothers showed felt smiles at a rate of 2.5 per min. But, as we have been arguing, it is impossible to determine the extent to which these affective patterns occurred in response to child elicitors or adult cognitions. For this reason, we moved to consideration of the affective differences shown by unrelated mothers with children drawn from "at-risk" families.

As described earlier, 40 mothers recruited from the general community were videotaped interacting with children selected from distressed families in counseling. Dependent variables measuring their affective responses (happy affect, and sad or depressed affect)[3] included both facial affect and vocal affect. Facial affect was measured on the basis of FACS coding of facial actions (Ekman & Friesen, 1978); voice affect was measured on the basis of judgments of content-filtered speech. Facial affect was interpreted as providing information with regard to both (a) the adult's affective state change in response to the child *(affect "leakage"),* and (b) the adult's *"strategic" use of affective displays* (Ekman, Friesen, & O'Sullivan, 1988). Vocal affect, a less controllable and less reactive communication component (Ekman & Friesen, 1969), was interpreted as primarily providing a source of information on affective state changes (leakage) in response to the child.

Affect Leakage. As predicted by our model, affective state changes were more common among threat-oriented adults (see Fig. 9.2). With target children (children who were seen as more difficult by their own parents who were also the recipients of more coercive care-giving), threat-oriented adults showed increasing levels of dysphoric affect.[4] That is, their nonverbal expressions of affect (facial and vocal) revealed increasing sadness and decreasing happiness. With nontarget children, on the other hand, threat-oriented adults showed exactly the reverse pattern. They manifested increasingly happy affect and decreasingly sad affect. Threat-oriented adults can be seen as showing a marked pattern of affective reactivity. Consistent with their understanding of care-giving relationships, the children with whom they interacted actually did come to control their affective state. Not only

---

[3]Other negative affects (disgust, anger, fear) were measured but occurred too infrequently for reliable measures to be obtained. Four scores (frequency of occurrence of facial actions reflecting happy affect; frequency of occurrence of facial actions reflecting sad affect; proportion of verbal messages accompanied by happy vocal affect; proportion of verbal messages accompanied by sad vocal affect) were converted to standard scores (with sad affect scored in an opposite direction to happy affect). These four standard scores were then compared in a multivariate analysis of variance. In view of the absence of any significant differences in effects due to the four variables, an *average z*-score was used to display the general levels of affect shown by different subject groupings (Fig. 9.2).

[4]In our original analysis (described in detail in Bugental, Blue, & Lewis, 1990) we showed only the change scores of threat-oriented versus other attributional groupings. Additionally, affect shown during three time periods was displayed only for those subjects who attributed high versus low control to children (rather than the specific grouping of subjects who attributed high control to children *and* low control to adults—versus all other attributional groupings). The analysis of variance described here introduced one grouping variable (high vs. low threat-orientation), and three repeated measures (time, target status of child, and affect valence); the only significant effect found was the predicted interaction between threat-orientation, target status of child, and time, $F (2, 76) = 3.16$, $p = .048$. A post hoc t test assessing the difference in affect shown for threat-oriented attributors to target and nontarget children was significant at better than the .05 level of confidence.

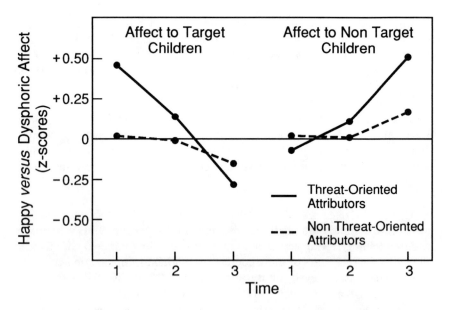

FIG. 9.2   Shifting affect in response to target versus nontarget children as a function of care-giving schemas (z scores were based on the combined affect shown by both related and unrelated mothers; as a result, the average z score shown here is greater than 0).

did "difficult" children have a negative impact on the adult's affective state, "easy" children had a positive impact. These findings are consistent with our earlier experimental research (Bugental & Shennum, 1984), in which we found that unresponsive child confederates elicited negative affect, whereas responsive confederates elicited positive affect from adults with low perceived control.

On the other hand, adults who did not have threat-oriented attributions showed no significant reaction to child characteristics — maintaining an even state that was not characterized by extremes of either happy or sad affect. Again, this is consistent with our earlier experimental findings (Bugental & Shennum, 1984). Adults who did not attribute such high control to children kept an "even keel" across variations in child behavior. In a confirmation of their schematic representation of care-giving relationships, children did *not* have the power to markedly influence adult outcomes (in this case, their affective state).

Several questions may reasonably be asked concerning the pattern of observed changes. Although differences in levels of reactivity between attributional groupings is well-supported, less clear are the implications of the specific pattern of change shown by threat-oriented adults. One such question arises in connection with shifting patterns of response to "difficult" children. Why do threat-oriented adults show an initial response to difficult children that is affectively more positive than that shown to their easier siblings? The most conservative explanation would be that this initial difference is not reliable (initial differences in response to children did not reach statistical significance) and it should be disregarded. Alternately, it may be that this "opening" behavior reflects the combination of a rapid appraisal of the child combined with a strategic effort directed toward ingratiation. In either case, clear support is shown for the *final difference* in response patterns shown to "difficult" versus "easy" children by adults with different care-giving schemas. Threat-oriented adults manifested a rapid fall-off from their initially positive behavior and demonstrated ending affect that was negative in valence. Additionally, the ending affect of threat-oriented adults with target children was significantly more negative than the ending affect of these same individuals with nontarget children. The most supportable conclusion is that threat-oriented adults show rapid decrements in positive affect during their interactions with difficult children, and rapid increases in positive affect during their interactions with easy children.

A question may be also raised concerning the nature of the negative affect that we observed. Why did we find that threat-oriented adults showed increasingly sad or depressed affect rather than angry affect? We would argue that perceived threat may induce either sadness/depression and/or anger. For example, Berkowitz and his colleagues have observed both depressed affect and anger in response to frustration (Berkowitz, 1983; Finman & Berkowitz, 1989). And as Berkowitz noted, depressed individuals are likely to show a surprising degree of aggression (Berkowitz, 1983, 1989). Early bouts involving threat-oriented adults and potentially threatening children may be more likely to be characterized by despair and hopelessness (Abramson, Metalsky, & Alloy, 1989). But as defensive attempts to restore the power base of the adult fail, anger may emerge.

Strategic Affect. Evidence regarding the "strategic" affect shown by threat-oriented adults with difficult children focused on their facial displays. In our earlier experimental research (Bugental & Shennum, 1984) we found that adults with low power attributions employed communication patterns with unresponsive children that could be characterized as ingratiating. Their visual behavior had the quality of communication appropriate for a young child, for example, high use of head tilts, exaggerated smiles. Our observations of the interactions of strangers with children at risk for abuse revealed a parallel pattern. Threat-oriented adults interacting with difficult children showed a high frequency of what may be considered strategic or "unfelt" positive affect (Ekman, Friesen, & O'Sullivan, 1988), that is, smiles that contained cues to their insincerity (Bugental, Kopeikin,

& Lazowski, 1991). For example, they showed a higher frequency of smiles that were not accompanied by eye involvement (crow's feet) or that were accompanied by facial actions that are associated with negative affect (e.g., raising of the inner brows). Threat-oriented women produced "unfelt" smiles at the rate of 1.15 per min during interactions with difficult children but at the rate of only .41 per min during interactions with easy children; for other adult groupings, no differences or trends were found in the occurrence of "unfelt" smiles during interactions with the two child groupings.

Child Reactions to Adult Expressive Behavior

The ultimate combination of expressive behaviors shown by threat-oriented care givers with difficult children poses a complex display pattern. They begin interactions with children with positive vocal and facial qualities which are rapidly replaced by increasing levels of vocal and facial dysphoria. Additionally, much of their positivity suggests insincerity or ingratiation. In past research (Bugental & Shennum, 1984) we observed that unresponsive children were likely to become increasingly unresponsive with adults with "low control" attributions. And in doing so, they were primarily negatively reactive to the ingratiating behavior of those adults (e.g., exaggerated smiles). For this reason, we explored the reactions of "at-risk" children in the present study to the "feigned" positivity more typically shown by threat-oriented women (Bugental, Kopeikin, & Lazowski, 1991).

In our earlier research (Bugental & Shennum, 1984), we assessed children's increasing levels of conversational unresponsiveness in response to facial ingratiation. In our research with the present sample, we explored children's increases in visual unresponsiveness in response to adult facial ingratiation. We found that children (whether difficult or easy) were much more likely ($p > .001$) to break eye contact in the 5 sec following the adult's use of "unfelt" smiles ($p = .91$) rather than following the adult's demonstration of "felt" smiles ($p = .51$). But this pattern was greater among those children who had experienced abuse. This provides support for the notion of a negative feedback loop. That is, the expressive patterns (facial ingratiation) more common among threat-oriented adults act to support the initial behavior (unresponsiveness) of "at-risk" children.

Missing Pieces in the Model

Evidence for our model drawn from naturalistic observations of mothers and strangers interacting with children at risk for abuse must be viewed with considerable caution. The schematic and behavioral patterns shown are consistent with the model but provide information with regard to a limited subset of the processes of interest. In our more recent research, we have shifted to an experimental analog strategy in which the information-processing patterns are assessed in response to controlled social stimuli. Additionally, we are directing our attention to inner state changes and on-line cognitions during challenging interactions.

Autonomic Responses and On-Line Cognitions in Response to Difficult Children (Step 3)

In the first of these investigations (Bugental, Blue, Cortez, Fleck, Kopeikin, Lewis, & Lyon, 1990), we were concerned with the ongoing changes in autonomic responses and thoughts of women (160 mothers of school-aged children) who believed they were teaching a child a computer game via remote contact. Depictions of the "child's" behavior were computer-generated, allowing full control of stimulus inputs. Our interest focused on shifts in autonomic response and thought patterns during "interactions" with responsive and unresponsive "children." As noted earlier, we previously found that adults (undergraduates) with low perceived control—anticipated interaction with "difficult" children with defensive autonomic arousal, that is, elevated skin conductance and elevated heart rate (Bugental & Cortez, 1988). Conversely, adults with higher perceived control are more likely to respond to such children with attentional arousal, that is, elevated skin conductance but decreasing heart rate. Additionally, there is evidence that abusive parents as a whole tend to show higher levels of physiological reactivity to stress, in particular to the potentially stress-eliciting features of children (e.g., Frodi & Lamb, 1978; Wolfe, Fairbank, Kelly, & Bradlyn, 1983). We argue that such elevated levels of reactivity may actually be determined by systematic differences in the ways in which abusive parents interpret potentially challenging situations.

In support of our predictions, we observed that threat-oriented mothers (as measured by the PAT), during interactions with unresponsive "children," were significantly more likely to show increases in heart rate level and electrodermal activity; these findings provided a replication of our earlier analysis of adult responses during *anticipated* interaction with "difficult" children. Thought listing procedures (recall of thoughts in response to video replay of preceding events) also indicated that threat-oriented subjects engaged in more threat-consistent ideation. Further analysis is still underway at this time, but these preliminary results support the general model.

Information-Processing Mechanisms of Children

As noted earlier, Bowlby (1980) proposed that the child forms an initial working model of care-giving relationships from his or her earliest attachment experiences; insecure attachment subsequently has a damaging effect on future relationships as a function of this maladaptive working model. Even in early childhood, children encode their experiences in terms of scripts and schemas that simplify their processing of and accommodation to life events (Mandler, 1984). The traditional view of scripts or schemas is that they are knowledge structures that are acquired gradually as a function of repeated experience, which eventually come to act in an automatic fashion. But it may also be (and Hoffman, 1986, suggested) that this process is *accelerated* by the presence of strong affect or arousal. For example, Fivush and Slackman (1986) found that children manifested well-formed scripts of certain distinctive events (first day of school, a fire drill) after a single instance. When considering the features of relationship schemas, they can be easily understood as having strong affective linkages. The intensity and nature of these linkages will, of course, vary as a function of the early experiences from which they are originally constructed. A schema that is tightly bound to a particular affect may be expected to constrain the affective states, perceptions, cognitions, and behaviors that follow once it is activated. For example, individuals who have experienced maltreatment at the hands of their parents are particularly likely to experience repeated relationships in which they are victimized (e.g., Browne & Finkelhor, 1986).

At an older age, differential experiences may underlay the adequacy of inferences regarding other people's inner thoughts and motives. If threat-oriented representations of relationships have been instantiated, biases in social inferences are probable. In support of this notion, Gnepp (1989) observed that 8-year-olds with less successful interpersonal relationships had more difficulty than other children in making personalized inferences about others on the basis of those individuals' past history. Dodge's research (e.g., Dodge, Murphy, & Buchsbaum, 1984) supports the view that unsuccessful social experiences with others is associated with biased perceptions of the negative intentions of others. And children who have experienced maltreatment differ from nonmaltreated children in their processing of emotional information (Camras, Grow, & Ribordy, 1983) and aggressive stimuli (Rieder & Cicchetti, 1989).

In the future, it will be important to determine the differential histories of abused children who go on to become abusive themselves (and thus may have acquired an unchallenged threat-oriented schema at an early age) versus those abused children who do *not* become abusive parents. The latter group have been found to be more likely to have received emotional support from a nonabusive adult during childhood (Egeland, Jacobvitz, & Sroufe, 1988). By virtue of these alternate socialization experiences, such children may acquire a less rigid (and less affectively constrained) schematic representation of care-giving relationships. Although a history of abuse by no means guarantees that the child will grow up to become an abusive parent, the elevated probability of this occurrence is substantial (Widom, 1989). It may be that relationship schemas provide the bridge for cross-generational maintenance of abuse. Or alternately, of course, they may act as protective buffers against this risk.

CONCLUSIONS

I have proposed here that we need to move beyond simple representations of care-giver beliefs in a number of ways. First, it is useful to think of cognitions about care giving in terms of relationship schemas — schemas that include the control attributed to children relative to the control attributed to adults. To consider cognitions about self only, or cognitions about the child only, is incomplete. Additionally, we need to consider the dual role of both unaware (automatic) and aware (controlled) cognitions in care-giving systems. I have suggested that automatically accessed or unaware cognitions of care givers may act to either amplify or attenuate affective and autonomic responses to potentially threatening child behavior. The ensuing conscious thoughts and strategies of care givers may simultaneously reflect the extent to which they feel out of control and are attempting to regain control. From this disparity a pattern of inconsistent or ambiguous communication may emerge. Such messages pose a confusing, or stress-inducing stimulus for children. As a result, low perceived control by care givers may come to maintain actual lack of control. And ultimately, a dysfunctional care-giving system is maintained.

REFERENCES

Abramson, L. Y., Metalsky, G. I., & Alloy, L. B. (1989). Hopelessness depression: A theory-based subtype of depression. *Psychological Review, 96,* 358–372.

Abramson, L. Y., Seligman, M. E. P., & Teasdale, J. D. (1978). Learned helplessness in humans: Critique and reformulation. *Journal of Abnormal Psychology, 87,* 49–74.

Affleck, G., Allen, D., McGrade, B. J., & McQueeney, M. (1982). Maternal causal attributions at hospital discharge of high-risk infants. *American Journal of Mental Deficiency, 86,* 575–580.

Anderson, C. R. (1977). Locus of control, coping behavior, and performance in a stress setting: A longitudinal study. *Journal of Applied Psychology, 62,* 446–451.

Bargh, J. A. (1982). Automatic and conscious processing of social information. In R. S. Wyer, Jr. & T. K. Srull (Eds.), *Handbook of social cognition, Vol. 3* (pp. 1–43). Hillsdale, NJ: Lawrence Erlbaum Associates.

Bargh, J. A., Bond, R. N., Lombardi, W. J., & Tota, M. E. (1986). The additive nature of chronic and temporary sources of construct accessibility. *Journal of Personality and Social Psychology, 50,* 869–878.

Bargh, J. A., & Thein, R. D. (1985). Individual construct accessibility: The case of information overload. *Journal of Personality and Social Psychology, 49,* 1129–1146.

Barkley, R. A. (1981). Hyperactivity. In E. J. Mash & L G. Terdal (Eds.), *Behavioral assessment of childhood disorders*. NY: Guilford.

Bell, R. Q. (1968). A reinterpretation of the direction of effect. *Psychological Review, 75,* 81–95.

Bell, R. Q. (1979). Parent, child, and reciprocal influences. *American Psychologist, 34,* 821–826.

Berkowitz, L. (1983). Aversively stimulated aggression: Some parallels and differences in research with animals and humans. *American Psychologist, 38,* 1135–1144.

Berkowitz, L. (1989). Frustration–aggression hypothesis: Examination and reformulation. *Psychological Bulletin, 106,* 59–73.

Bousha, D. M., & Twentyman, C. T. (1984). Mother–child interactional style in abuse, neglect, and control groups: Naturalistic observations in the home. *Journal of Abnormal Psychology, 93,* 106–114.

Bower, G. H. (1981). Mood and memory. *American Psychologist, 36,* 129–148.

Bowlby, J. (1980). *Attachment and loss*. New York: Basic Books.

Brown, J. D., & Siegel, J. M. (1988). Attributions for negative life events and depression: The role of perceived control. *Journal of Personality and Social Psychology, 54,* 316–321.

Browne, A., & Finkelhor, D. (1986). Impact of child sexual abuse: A review of the literature. *Psychological Bulletin, 99,* 66–77.

Bruner, J. S. (1957). On perceptual readiness. *Psychological Review, 64,* 123–152.

Bugental, D. B., Blue, J., Cortez, V., Fleck, K., Kopeikin, H., Lewis, J. C., & Lyon, J. (1990). *Information-processing deficits during stressful interactions, as influenced by perceived power disadvantages*. Unpublished paper.

Bugental, D. B., Blue, J., Cortez, V., Fleck, K., & Rodriguez, A. (in press). Influences of witnessed affect on information processing in children. *Child Development*.

Bugental, D. B., Blue, J., & Cruzcosa, M. (1989). Perceived control over care-giving outcomes: Implications for child abuse. *Developmental Psychology, 25,* 532–539.

Bugental, D. B., Blue, J., & Lewis, J. (1990). Care-giver cognitions as moderators of affective reactions to "difficult" children. *Developmental Psychology, 26,* 631–638.

Bugental, D. B., & Cortez, V. (1988). Physiological reactivity to responsive and unresponsive children—as modified by perceived control. *Child Development. 59,* 686–693.

Bugental, D. B., Cortez, V., & Lyon, J. (1990). *Chronic accessibility of threat-focused ideation among adults with low perceived control in care-giving relationships*. Unpublished manuscript.

Bugental, D. B., Kaswan, J. W., & Love, L. R. (1970). Perceptions of contradictory messages conveyed by verbal and nonverbal channels. *Journal of Personality and Social Psychology, 16,* 647–655.

Bugental, D. B., Kopeikin, H., & Lazowski, L. (1991). Children's responses to authentic versus polite smiles. In K. Rotenberg (Ed.), *Children's interpersonal trust* (pp. 58–79). NY: Springer-Verlag.

Bugental, D. B., & Shennum, W. A., (1984). "Difficult" children as elicitors and targets of adult communication patterns: An attributional–behavioral transactional analysis. *Monographs of the Society for Research in Child Development, 49,* (1, Serial No. 205).

Burgess, R. L., & Conger, R. (1978). Family interaction in abusive, neglectful, and normal families. *Child Development, 49,* 1163–1173.

Camras, L. A., Grow, J. G., & Ribordy, S. C. (1983). Recognition of facial expression by abused children. *Journal of Clinical Child Psychology, 12,* 325–328.

Clark, D. A., Beck, A. T., & Brown, G. (1989). Cognitive mediation in general psychiatric outpatients: A test of the content-specificity hypothesis. *Journal of Personality and Social Psychology, 56,* 958–964.

Clark, M. S., & Fiske, S. T. (1982). *Affect and cognition*. Hillsdale, NJ: Lawrence Erlbaum Associates.

Crowell, J. A., & Feldman, S. S. (1988). Mothers' internal models of relationships and children's behavioral and developmental status: A study of mother–child interaction. *Child Development, 59,* 1273–1285.

de Lissovoy, V. (1979). Toward the definition of "abuse-provoking child." *Child Abuse and Neglect, 3,* 341–350.

Devine, P. (1989). Stereotypes and prejudice: their automatic and controlled components. *Journal of Personality and Social Psychology, 56,* 5–18.

Diener, C. I., & Dweck, C. S. (1978). An analysis of learned helplessness: Continuous changes in performance, strategy and achievement cognitions following failure. *Journal of Personality and Social Psychology, 36,* 451–462.

Dix, T., & Grusec, J. E. (1985). Parent attribution processes in the socialization of children. In I. E. Sigel (Ed.), *Parental belief systems: The psychological consequences for children* (pp. 201–234). Hillsdale, NJ: Lawrence Erlbaum Associates.

Dix, T., Ruble, D. N., Grusec, J. E., & Nixon, S. (1986). Social cognition in parents: Inferential and affective reaction to children of three age levels. *Child Development, 57,* 879–894.

Dix, T., Ruble, D. N., & Zambarano, R. J. (1989). Mother's implicit theories of discipline: Child effects, parent effects, and the attribution process. *Child Development, 60,* 1373–1391.

Dodge, K. A. (1980). Social cognition and children's aggressive behavior. *Child Development, 51,* 162–170.

Dodge, K. A. (1986). A social information processing model of social competence in children. In M. Perlmutter (Ed.), *Minnesota symposia in child psychology* (Vol. 18, pp. 77–125). Hillsdale, NJ: Lawrence Erlbaum Associates.

Dodge, K. A., Murphy, R. R., & Buchsbaum, K. (1984). The assessment of intention–cue detection skills in children: Implications for developmental psychopathology. *Child Development, 55,* 163–173.

Easterbrook, J. A. (1959). The effect of emotion on cue utilization and the organization of behavior. *Psychological Review, 66,* 183–201.

Egeland, B., Jacobvitz, D., & Sroufe, L. A. (1988). Breaking the cycle of abuse. *Child Development, 59,* 1080–1088.

Ekman, P., & Friesen, W. V. (1969). Nonverbal leakage and clues to deception. *Psychiatry, 32,* 88–106.

Ekman, P., & Friesen, W. V. (1978). *Manual for the Facial Affect Coding System.* Palo Alto, CA: Consulting Psychologists Press.

Ekman, P., Friesen, W., V., & O'Sullivan, M. (1988). Smiles while lying. *Journal of Personality and Social Psychology, 54,* 414–420.

Ellis, H. C., Thomas, R. L., & Rodriguez, I. A. (1984). Emotional mood, states and memory: Elaborative encoding, semantic processing, and cognitive effort. *Journal of Experimental Psychology: Learning, Memory, and Cognition, 10,* 470–482.

Elmer, E., & Gregg, G. S. (1967). Developmental characteristics of abused children. *Pediatrics, 40,* 596–602.

Epstein, S. (1984). Controversial issues in emotion theory. In P. Shaver (Ed.), *Review of personality and social psychology* (pp. 64–88). Beverly Hills, CA: Sage.

Fazio, R. H., Sanbonmatsu, D., Powell, M. C., & Kardes, F. R. (1986). On the automatic activation of attitudes. *Journal of Personality and Social Psychology, 50,* 229–238.

Fincham, F. D., & Bradbury, T. N. (1987). The impact of attributions in marriage: A longitudinal analysis. *Journal of Personality and Social Psychology, 53,* 510–517.

Finman, R., & Berkowitz, L. (1989). Some factors influencing the effect of depressed mood on anger and overt hostility toward another. *Journal of Research in Personality, 23,* 70–84.

Fiske, S. T. (1982). Schema-triggered affect: Applications to social perception. In M. S. Clark & S. T. Fiske (Eds.), *Affect and cognition: The 17th Annual Carnegie-Symposium on*

Cognition (pp. 55–78). Hillsdale, NJ: Lawrence Erlbaum Associates.

Fiske, S. T., & Pavelchak, M. A. (1986). Category-based versus piecemeal-based affective responses: Developments in schema-triggered affect. In R. M. Sorrentino & E. T. Higgins (Eds.), *Motivation and cognition* (pp. 167–203). New York: Guilford.

Fivush, R., & Slackman, E. A. (1986). The acquisition and development of scripts. In K. Nelson (Ed.), *Event Knowledge: Structure and Functions of Development*. Norwood, NJ: Ablex.

Frodi, A. M., & Lamb, M. E. (1978). Child abusers' responses to infants' smiles and cries. *Infant Behavior and Development, 1,* 187–198.

Gnepp, J. (1989) Personalized inferences of emotions and appraisals: Component processes and correlates. *Developmental Psychology, 25,* 277–288.

Goodnow, J. J. (1985). Change and variation in ideas about childhood and parenting. In I. E. Sigel (Ed.), *Parental belief systems: The psychological consequences for children* (pp. 235–276). Hillsdale, NJ: Lawrence Erlbaum Associates.

Goodnow, J. J. (1988). Parents' ideas, actions, and feelings: Models and methods from developmental and social psychology. *Child Development, 59,* 286–320.

Gotlib, I. H., & McCann, C. F. (1984). Construct accessibility and depression: An examination of cognitive and affective factors. *Journal of Personality and Social Psychology, 47,* 427–439.

Hess, R. D., Kashiwagi, K., Azuma, H., Price, G. G., & Dickson, W. P. (1980). Maternal expectations for mastery of developmental tasks in Japan and the United States. *International Journal of Psychology, 15,* 259–271.

Higgins, E. T., & King, G. (1981). Accessibility of social constructs: Information-processing consequences of individual and contextual variability. In N. Cantor & J. F. Kihlstrom (Eds.), *Personality, cognition, and social interaction* (pp. 69–121). Hillsdale, NJ: Lawrence Erlbaum Associates.

Higgins, E. T., King, G. A., & Mavin, G. H. (1982). Individual construct accessibility and subjective impression and recall. *Journal of Personality and Social Psychology, 43,* 35–47.

Hill, T., Lewicki, P., Czyzewska, M., & Boss, A. (1989). Perpetuating development of encoding biases in person perception. *Journal of Personality and Social Psychology, 57,* 373–387.

Hoffman, M. (1986). Affect, cognition, and motivation. In R. M. Sorrentino & E. T. Higgins (Eds.), *Handbook of motivation and cognition* (pp. 23–63). New York: Guilford.

Holloway, S. D., & Hess, R. D. (1985). Mothers' and teachers' attributions about children's mathematics performance. In I. E. Sigel (Ed.), *Parental belief systems: The psychological consequences for children* (pp. 177–200). Hillsdale, NJ: Lawrence Erlbaum Associates.

Isen, A. M. (1984). Toward understanding the role of affect in cognition. In R. S. Wyer, Jr. & T. K. Srull (Eds.), *Handbook of Social Cognition* (Vol. 3, pp. 179–235). Hillsdale, NJ: Lawrence Erlbaum Associates.

Janoff-Bulman, R. (1979). Characterological versus behavioral self-blame: Inquiries into depression and rape. *Journal of Personality and Social Psychology, 37,* 1798–1809.

Janoff-Bulman, R. (1982). Esteem and control bases of blame: "Adaptive" strategies for victims and observers. *Journal of Personality, 50,* 180–199.

Johnson, J. H., & Sarason, J. C. (1978). Life stress, depression, and anxiety: Internal–external locus of control as a moderator variable. *Journal of Psychosomatic Medicine, 22,* 205–208.

Kogan, K. L., Tyler, N., & Turner, P. (1974). The process of interpersonal adaptation between mothers and their cerebral palsied children. *Developmental Medicine and Child Neurology, 16,* 518–527.

Kopp, C. (1989). Regulation of distress and negative emotions: A developmental view. *Developmental Psychology, 25,* 343–354.

Larrance, D. T., & Twentyman, C. T. (1983). Maternal attributions and child abuse. *Journal of Abnormal Psychology, 92,* 449–457.

Lazarus, R. S., & Folkman, S. (1984). *Stress, appraisal, and coping.* New York: Springer.

Lefcourt, H. M., Miller, R. S., Ware, E. E., & Sherk, D. (1981). Locus of control as a modifier of the relationship between stressors and moods. *Journal of Personality and Social Psychology, 41,* 357-369.

Lewicki, P. (1986). *Nonconscious social information processing.* New York: Academic.

Mackie, D. M., & Worth, L. T. (1989). Processing deficits and the mediation of positive affect in persuasion. *Journal of Personality and Social Psychology, 57,* 27-40.

McGillicuddy-deLisi, A. V. (1982). Parental beliefs about developmental processes. *Human Development, 25,* 192-200.

Mandler, J. M. (1984). *Stories, scripts, and scenes.* Hillsdale, NJ: Lawrence Erlbaum Associates.

Markus, H. (1977). Self-schemata and processing information about the self. *Journal of Personality and Social Psychology, 35,* 63-78.

Mash, E. J., & Johnston, C. (1983). Parental perception of child behavior problems, parenting self-esteem, and mothers' reported stress in younger and older hyperactives and normal children. *Journal of Consulting and Clinical Psychology, 51,* 86-99.

Nasby, W., & Yando, R. (1982). Selective encoding and retrieval of affectively valent information: Two cognitive consequences of children's mood states. *Journal of Personality and Social Psychology, 43,* 1244-1253.

Nelson, K., & Gruendel, J. (1986). Children's scripts. In K. Nelson (Ed.), *Event knowledge: structure and function in development* (pp. 21-46). Hillsdale, NJ: Lawrence Erlbaum Associates.

Obrist, P. A. (1982). Cardiac-behavioral interactions: A critical appraisal. In J. T. Cacioppo & R. E. Petty (Eds.), *Perspectives in cardiovascular psychophysiology* (pp. 265-291). NY: Guilford Press.

Oldershaw, L., Walters, G. C., & Hall, D. K. (1986). Control strategies and noncompliance in abusive mother-child dyads: An observational study. *Child Development, 57,* 722-732.

Patterson, G. R. (1976). The aggressive child: Victim and architect of a coercive system. In E. J. Mash, L. A. Hamerlynck, & L. C. Handy (Eds.), *Behavior modification and families. I. Theory and research* (pp. 267-316). New York: Brunner/Mazel.

Patterson, G. R. (1980). Mothers: The unacknowledged victims. *Monographs of the Society for Research in Child Development, 45,* (5, Serial No. 186).

Read, S. J. (1987). Constructing causal scenarios: A knowledge structural approach to causal reasoning. *Journal of Personality and Social Psychology, 52,* 288-302.

Reid, J. B., Patterson, G. R., & Loeber, R. (1982). The abused child: Victim, instigator, or innocent bystander? In J. Bernstein (Ed.), *Response structure and organization* (pp. 47-72). Lincoln: University of Nebraska Press.

Rieder, C., & Cicchetti, D. (1989). Organizational perspective on cognitive control functioning and cognitive-affective balance in maltreated children. *Developmental Psychology, 25,* 382-393.

Schneider, W., & Shiffrin, R. M. (1977). Controlled and automatic human information processing. I. Detection, search, and attention. *Psychological Review, 84,* 1-66.

Sherrod, K. B., O'Connor, S., Vietze, P. M., & Altemeier, W. A., III (1984). Child health and maltreatment. *Child Development, 55,* 1174-1183.

Shiffrin, W., & Dumais, S. T. (1981). The development of automatism. In J. R. Anderson (Eds.), *Cognitive skills and their acquisition* (pp. 111-140). Hillsdale, NJ: Lawrence Erlbaum Associates.

Shiffrin, R. M., & Schneider, W. (1977). Controlled and automatic human information processing. II. Perceptual learning, automatic attending, and a general theory. *Psychological Review, 84,* 127-190.

Sigel, I. E. (Ed.). (1985). *Parental belief systems: The psychological consequences for children.* Hillsdale, NJ: Lawrence Erlbaum Associates.

Taylor, S. E., Lichtman, R. R., & Wood, J. V. (1984). Attributions, beliefs about control, and adjustment to breast cancer. *Journal of Personality and Social Psychology, 46,* 489–507.

Trickett, P. K., & Kuczynski, L. (1986). Children's misbehaviors and parental discipline strategies in abusive and nonabusive families. *Developmental Psychology, 21,* 115–123.

Vasta, R. (1982). Physical child abuse: a dual-component analysis. *Developmental Review, 2,* 125–149.

Weiner, B. (1985). An attributional theory of achievement motivation and emotion. *Psychological Review, 92,* 548–573.

Weiner, B., Russell, D., & Lerman, D. (1978). Affective consequences of causal ascriptions. In J. H. Harvey, W. J. Ickes, & R. F. Kidd (Eds.), *New directions in attribution research* (Vol. 2, pp. 59–88). Hillsdale, NJ: Lawrence Erlbaum Associates.

Widom, C. S. (1989). Does violence beget violence? A critical examination of the literature. *Psychological Bulletin, 106,* 3–28.

Winter, L., Uleman, J. S., & Cunniff, C. (1985). How automatic social judgments? *Journal of Personality and Social Psychology, 49,* 904–917.

Wolfe, D. A. (1985). Child-abusing parents: An empirical review and analysis. *Psychological Review, 97,* 462–482.

Wolfe, D. A., Fairbank, J. A., Kelly, J. A., & Bradlyn, A. S. (1983). Child abusive parents' physiological responses to stressful and nonstressful behavior in children. *Behavioral Assessment, 5,* 363–371.

10
Maternal Child-Rearing Beliefs and Coping Strategies: Consequences for Divorced Mothers and Their Children

Susan D. Holloway
University of Maryland and Harvard University

Sandra Machida
California State University, Chico

In the mid-1980s, if asked about the effects of divorce on children's development, researchers would have responded that stress created by divorce appears to have a markedly negative – although temporary – effect on parents and children. In the last several years, however, the consensus about divorce and its sequelae appears to be evaporating. On one hand, some writers find even greater dangers associated with divorce than had previously been thought. For example, Wallerstein and Blakesly (1989) have questioned previous conclusions about girls' lesser vulnerability to divorce relative to that of boys, as well as assumptions about the eventual disappearance of stress reactions by children of both sexes. On the other hand, several recent studies comparing children from divorced and intact families have found that family structure accounts for only 3% or less of the variance in many child outcome measures (Allison & Furstenberg, 1989; Slater & Power, 1987). A third set of voices calls for moving away from blanket statements – either positive or negative – concerning the effects of divorce. Hetherington (1989) began her Presidential Address to the Society for Research in Child Development with the following statement, "One of the things that is notable in studies of family transitions is the great diversity in the response of parents and children to divorce and remarriage" (p. 1). Similarly, Demo and Acock (1988) concluded a review of the literature on divorce with the assertion, "It is simplistic and inaccurate to think of divorce as having uniform consequences for children" (p. 642).

In this chapter, we sketch out a model in which the impact of divorce is seen as a function of how the stressors associated with divorce are appraised by family members, and on the availability of resources for coping with these stressors. In our model we consider the possibility that the effects of potential stressors stem not only from objective characteristics of the experience itself, but also from the subjective processes by which individuals analyze the meaning of the experience for them and assess their ability to cope with it. In some theoretical writing, divorce has been reconceptualized in terms of a cognitive model of appraisal and coping (e.g., Hetherington & Camara, 1984; Kurdek, 1988b); however, the empirical work on divorce has not taken advantage of these recent conceptualizations.

We illustrate portions of this model with data from a study recently conducted on divorced mothers and their 4-year-old children. The study highlighted the role of three maternal appraisal processes in mediating the effects of divorce on maternal and child adjustment:

1. Mothers' appraisals of their ability to control the children's behavior as well as their perception of the child's capability for self-control.
2. Mothers' attributions of responsibility for children's misbehavior and good behavior.
3. Mothers' views of their own role versus that of other care-givers in guiding children's learning.

The purpose of our study was to determine whether mothers' appraisal and coping patterns were related to their reported parenting behavior and personal adjustment. We were also interested in whether maternal beliefs and coping patterns were associated with the self-esteem, classroom behavior, cognitive competence, and health symptoms of their children.

MOTHERS' RESPONSE TO DIVORCE-RELATED STRESSORS: THE ROLE OF APPRAISAL AND COPING

In constructing a cognitively based model of appraisal and coping with divorce, it is first necessary to realize that divorce is not a single experience and hence not a single stressor; rather, the occasion of parental divorce increases the likelihood of a number of more particular stressors (Hodges, Tierney, & Buchsbaum, 1984). In this chapter, we focus on child misbehavior as a major stressor that divorcing parents often encounter. In response to marital dissolution, children frequently demonstrate increased negative behavior both at home and at school (e.g., Hetherington, Cox, & Cox, 1985). In the model, we illustrate how mothers' appraisal of children's misbehavior — including who caused it and how successfully it can be controlled — may affect their parenting behavior and perceived distress. The model is presented in Fig. 10.1; the remainder of this introduction describes

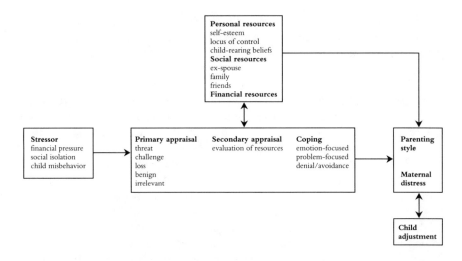

FIG. 10.1   A model of maternal appraisal and coping processes used in dealing with divorce-related stressors.

this appraisal and coping process as it unfolds over time, beginning with appraisal, which is located at the far left side of the figure.

Faced with a child's misbehavior, a parent must first appraise the seriousness of the situation. In the primary appraisal process, the individual judges whether a potential stressor is unimportant, benign, a threat, or a challenge (Folkman & Lazarus, 1985; Lazarus & Folkman, 1984). In the case of a child's misbehavior, parents first make a decision about whether the incident merits further consideration. This appraisal may be based in part upon their view of who is responsible for the child's misbehavior. If a parent attributes misbehavior to her own inadequacies rather than to the child or other external sources, she is more likely to see a given instance of misbehavior as a threat; parents who view misbehavior as caused by external circumstances might be less likely to decide that the behavior merits their attention (Dix & Grusec, 1983, 1985; Dix, Ruble, Grusec, & Nixon, 1986).

If the misbehavior is perceived as meriting a response, the parent must then address the question, "What can I do about the misbehavior?" Coping resources are evaluated as part of this secondary appraisal, including social resources or support systems, psychological resources such as morale or self-esteem, and material resources (Folkman & Lazarus, 1985; Lazarus & Folkman, 1984). In the secondary appraisal process, the individual takes stock of available resources, decides which might be of use in dealing with a particular situation, and determines the likelihood that the resources can be successfully employed in the situation. This process depends partly on the actual resources available but also, importantly, on characteristics of the appraisor such as his or her own self-esteem. Thus, for example, a divorced woman with low self-esteem may be less likely to call on school personnel for help in dealing with a child's misbehavior than would a woman who feels that her family's problem merits the time and effort of school staff.

In the case of divorced women, certain types of resources have been shown to be particularly important in determining their ability, and that of their children, to cope with stressors. These resources are usually seen in the literature as having a direct effect on mothers' and children's adjustment. In our model, their effect is also seen as indirect, depending on how they are appraised by mothers and children. For example, one important category of resources is the family's financial situation. The direct effects of lowered financial resources on a mother's ability to cope with children's misbehavior might include inability to pay for counseling or to reduce her working hours in order to spend more time with the child. Indirect effects may also be found, depending on how mothers appraise the loss of income. For instance, some mothers may feel a great loss of personal status as a result of moving into a lower income bracket, and so may be reluctant to help the child maintain relationships with friends made before the divorce.

The social support available to mothers and children — including relations with the ex-spouse as well as other family members and friends — comprise a second important category of coping resources. The importance of harmonious relations with the ex-spouse and frequent contact between father and child has been underscored in many studies (e.g., Hess & Camara, 1979; Kurdek, 1988a). Predictors of satisfactory social adjustment of divorced mothers include the quality of relationship with friends and family (Pett, 1982). Mothers' sense of pleasure and competence in negotiation with children also appears to be related to their satisfaction with their social network (Bowen, 1982). Social support has been associated with the use of active coping rather than avoidance coping by depressed and nondepressed adults (Holahan & Moos, 1987). Thus, studies on social support emphasize the importance for maternal adjustment of objective measures of social support as well as subjective indicators such as satisfaction with social support.

In addition to financial and social resources, various personal resources have been identified as being related to children's and mothers' adjustment to divorce. For mothers, personality characteristics such as locus of control and self-assurance predict effective coping in divorce and other stressful situations (Lefcourt, Martin, & Saleh, 1984; Parkes, 1984; Thomas, 1982). Mothers' self-efficacy in controlling their children's behavior is likely to be one important determinant of their ability to cope with children's misbehavior. If they perceive themselves as in control, mothers are less likely to evade the situation or deny its importance, and more likely to take effective measures to improve it (Bugental & Shennum, 1988; Bugental, Blue, & Cruzcosa, 1989).

After the individual has evaluated available resources, he or she initiates some type of coping strategy to address the stressor. *Coping* is defined by Lazarus and Folkman (1984) as cognitive and behavioral efforts to master, reduce, or tolerate the internal and/or external demands created by a stressful situation. The efficacy of various types of adult coping strategies in reducing stress has been studied extensively. Most studies find that coping by passive means such as denial or avoidance is not effective. McCrae (1984) argued that more passive strategies such as faith, fatalism, and expression of feelings are more commonly used to cope with a loss—in which category some of the stressors associated with divorce may be placed—than with a threat or challenge. Most studies find that attempts to deal with a problem actively may be the most effective. Two types of active coping strategies have been identified: problem-focused coping and emotion-focused coping (e.g., Billings & Moos, 1984; Pearlin & Schooler, 1978). In problem-focused coping, individuals attempt to deal with a problem by actively managing it. This type of strategy generally works best in situations where the individual has many social, financial, and personal resources available. To the extent that these resources are lacking, a situation is less controllable; in these cases, emotion-focused coping—in which individuals actively manage their cognitive or emotional response to the stressor rather than trying to change the situation—may be most effective (Elman & Gilbert, 1984; Folkman, 1984).

Divorced mothers of preschool children are likely to need both emotion-focused and problem-focused coping strategies in dealing with children's misbehavior and other divorce-related stressors. Evidence on this question is practically nonexistent, although one study examining coping style in divorced women found that the use of both emotion-focused and problem-focused strategies in a variety of situations was related to less anxiety, depression, and stress (with emotion-focused coping as the stronger predictor of the two) (Propst, Pardington, Ostrom, & Watkins, 1986). In one sense, divorced mothers of small children have few resources for dealing with many aspects of their situation. They may have little time to develop social support networks, and may not have the benefit of a cooperative ex-spouse. They are also likely to have limited incomes. To the extent that their situation is uncontrollable, divorced mothers may be better off using emotion-focused coping. On the other hand, there will undoubtedly be many situations involving their children that need to be dealt with actively and for which the necessary resources must be identified; women who are cognizant of this responsibility may engage in problem-focused coping.

Most studies of adults' response to stressors have traced the relationship of coping to their own adjustment. However, others have found that mothers' coping will also be related to the adjustment of their children (Longfellow & Belle, 1984). Compas, Howell, Phares, Williams, and Ledoux (1989) argued that children use parental behavior as a guidepost in assessing the meaning of potentially stressful situations; in their study of young adolescents and their parents, the relationship between major life events and children's emotional and behavioral problems was mediated by fathers' symptoms of distress. The authors of this study also suggested that children's reactions to the stressors associated with divorce are mediated by their own appraisals of the meaning of these events; thus appraisal processes are crucial mediators of both the child's and the parent's responses to divorce. In our model, we indicate that maternal coping, child-rearing practices, and symptoms of distress (as perceived by children) mediate the relationship between child adjustment and the family's financial, social, and personal resources.

In the remainder of this chapter, we explore the relationship between mothers' beliefs during the appraisal processes and (a) their parenting behavior and overall distress level, and (b) their children's adjustment as reflected in self-esteem, classroom behavior, cognitive competence, and health symptoms. Other aspects of the model, including the role of parental harmony, father–child contact, and social support in promoting maternal and child adjustment have been explored elsewhere (Holloway & Machida, 1991; Machida & Holloway, 1991).

SAMPLE

The sample included 58 divorced, single mothers and their preschool-aged children (*M* age = 4.5 years, *SD* = 4.5 months). Three of the mothers were Black; the remaining participants were White. There were 35 boys and 23 girls in the sample. About two thirds of the mothers lived in a university community in Northern California, and the remaining one third were drawn from a suburban community in Maryland.

All mothers worked outside the home or were attending school. Average monthly income was $1,200. Most of the respondents were working in clerical, service, or sales jobs. The average level of schooling was approximately 1 year of post-secondary education (*SD* = 1.57).

On average, mothers had been separated from their ex-husbands for 31 months (*SD* = 15.56) and had been legally divorced for 10 months (*SD* = 13.89 months). Of the mothers, 59% had sole custody and the remaining mothers had either joint legal or joint physical custody of their children. Of the children, 59% were cared for in day-care centers while their mothers were working or attending class; the remaining children were cared for in family day-care homes or by babysitters.

MEASURES

The following information was obtained from questionnaires mailed to mothers: demographic data, perceptions of parenting authoritativeness, level of distress, perceived social support, and ratings of children's psychosomatic problems. Interviews with the children were conducted to assess kindergarten readiness and self-esteem. Caregivers were asked to rate children's level of task orientation, extroversion, and considerateness. These measures are described more fully in the Appendix. Mothers were also interviewed to obtain appraisals of their child-rearing responsibilities and effectiveness. The variables resulting from these interviews are described next.

Maternal Perceived Control.   Mothers were asked to recall their child being involved in five recent positive events (playing well with another child, helping with chores, giving a gift, taking on a challenging task, behaving affectionately) and five negative events (refusing to share, refusing to go to bed, becoming very angry, not telling the truth, refusing to clean up). Then they were asked "How much can you control your child's [cleaning up]?" Responses were indicated on a 6-point scale. Ratings were summed over the 10 events (coefficient alpha = .73).

Maternal Attributions for Positive and Negative Events.   For each of the events described previously, mothers were asked to what they attributed their child's behavior. Their attributions were coded as referring to factors internal or external to the mother. Reliability coefficients (g factor) were .55 and .53 for positive and negative events, respectively.

Parental and Caregiver Guidance.   Mothers were asked to explain their theories of development by responding to eight vignettes that commonly occur when parenting a preschooler (e.g., sharing toys) (McGillicuddy-DeLisi, 1982, 1985; McGillicuddy-DeLisi, Sigel, & Johnson, 1979; Sigel, 1982, 1985). Mothers ranked the importance of parental influences, influences by other caregivers, and child's own personality or ability. A parent guidance score was calculated by summing the ranks of all the parent-initiated or controlled choices (i.e., imitating parent, training by parent, exposure to experiences provided by parent). Coefficient alpha was .72. A care-giver guidance score was calculated by summing the ranks of all care-giver-initiated or controlled choices (i.e., imitating caregiver, teaching by caregiver, exposure to experiences provided by the caregiver). Coefficient alpha was .62.

Maternal Coping.   Maternal coping was assessed using the Ways of Coping (Revised) (Folkman & Lazarus, 1985). Respondents indicated on a

4-point scale, which of 66 behaviors or thoughts they had used since separating from their former husbands. Item scores were summed to create a single index representing baseline frequency of using varied coping strategies (coefficient alpha = .84). Additionally, items were grouped in eight subscales identified by the authors of the scale (Folkman, Lazarus, Dunkel-Schetter, DeLongis, & Gruen, 1986). Five subscales with sufficient internal reliability were retained: distancing (alpha = .72), seeking social support (alpha = .74), escape–avoidance (alpha = .68), planful problem-solving (alpha = .68), and positive reappraisal (alpha = .66).

RESULTS

Association of Maternal Appraisal
to Coping, Parenting, and Distress

The relationship of the three sets of maternal appraisal variables—control beliefs, attributions, and maternal versus caregiver guidance—to coping strategies, authoritative parenting and distress can be viewed in Table 10.1.

Mothers who made internal attributions for children's negative behavior had a higher baseline of varied coping strategies and made more use of problem solving and avoidance as coping strategies.

Women who indicated that they felt in control of their children's behavior had a higher baseline of varied coping strategies and used the strategies of problem solving and positive appraisal more often. They also felt that their children were in control of their own behavior; in other words, control over behavior cannot be viewed as a bipolar dimension in which less control by parents would imply more control by the child.

Correlations regarding the guidance variables indicated that these variables were not related to any of the other maternal variables.

Relation of Maternal Appraisal and Coping
to Children's Adjustment

A second set of correlations examined the association of maternal appraisal and coping to children's adjustment (Table 10.2). Children with higher self-esteem had mothers who did not take credit for children's positive behavior (i.e., they made external attributions), but *did* accept blame for misbehavior. Children with more health and psychological problems had mothers who made internal attributions for misbehavior, had low perceived control, used avoidance coping, and used a greater number of coping strategies. Children rated by teachers as more extroverted had mothers with high perceived control. Children whom teachers rated as considerate were

TABLE 10.1

Relationship of Mothers' Beliefs to Their Coping Strategies and Adjustment

	Coping Strategies						Adjustment	
Beliefs	Distancing	Social Support	Avoidance	Problem Solving	Positive Apprsl.	Total Coping	Authoritative	Distress
Internal attribution/pos	02	08	26*	03	06	23	-04	16
Internal attribution/neg	-01	13	25*	25*	-02	26*	-09	-04
Maternal control	21	16	-04	29*	33**	35**	17	15
Child control	13	02	04	43***	30*	29*	23	18
Parental guidance	17	-14	04	-05	-01	-03	-10	02
Care-giver guidance	-20	-05	08	07	-11	01	09	-04

Note. Pearson product moment correlations reported with decimal points omitted; n = 58.

*p < .05; **p < .01; ***p < .001.

TABLE 10.2

Relationship of Maternal Beliefs and Maternal Coping Strategies to Child Adjustment

	Child Adjustment					
	Self-Esteem	Health Problems	Kindergarten Readiness	Extroversion	Considerateness	Task Orientation
Beliefs:						
Internal attribution/pos	-30*	10	07	09	03	16
Internal attribution/neg	28*	25*	-14	-10	-04	-15
Maternal control	15	-32*	06	26*	-04	15
Child control	01	-12	01	12	07	18
Parental guidance	-02	-08	-09	05	14	16
Care-giver guidance	17	10	04	17	-34**	-35**
Coping:						
Distancing	-01	23	-11	-07	09	09
Social support	-12	17	15	05	-02	10
Avoidance	-01	26*	-03	-14	24	25*
Problem solving	-08	07	19	05	-02	03
Positive appraisal	02	-06	-05	10	12	24
Total coping	-09	26*	11	-05	08	18

Note. Pearson product moment correlations reported with decimal points omitted; $n = 58$.
*$p < .05$; **$p < .01$.

less likely to have mothers who gave high rankings to caregiver guidance. Children rated as highly task-oriented had mothers who gave low rankings to caregiver guidance and used avoidance as a coping strategy.

The strength of these associations after controlling on sex of child, family financial situation, and length of time since parental separation was examined using stepwise multiple regressions. A model for each maternal and child adjustment variable was created by first entering the three control variables; subsequently, the following predictors were allowed to enter: maternal attributions for negative behavior, maternal perceived control, care-giver guidance, coping using problem solving, and total coping.

As Table 10.3 indicates, the models were significant for each outcome except kindergarten readiness and extroversion. Time since separation and financial resources were not significant predictors for any of the child or maternal outcome measures. In general, the maternal appraisal variables contributed from 10% to 29% of the variance in the outcome measures. Mothers who were more authoritative were less likely to take the blame for negative incidents with their children and were more likely to use problem solving as a coping strategy. Mothers who experienced greater distress were also less likely to take the blame for misbehavior, but were less likely to use problem solving and had a higher baseline of varied coping strategies. For children, high self-esteem was associated with mothers' tendency to take the blame for children's negative behavior and to feel in control of children's behavior. Mothers who rated their children as having more health and psychological problems felt less control over children's behavior and used more coping strategies overall. Children rated as considerate by teachers were cared for by mothers who were less likely to view caregivers as a source of guidance and who used more coping strategies. Low ranking of caregivers was also a significant predictor of task orientation, along with higher baseline use of varied coping strategies.

DISCUSSION

A central theme emerging from these data is the importance of the mother's perception of her centrality in her child's life. Some mothers perceived themselves as having a great deal of control over the child's behavior, as being responsible for the child's misbehavior, and as being responsible for guiding the child's learning and development. These beliefs were then put into practice in the form of setting limits on children's behavior and enforcing household rules; mothers with these beliefs also approached their own situations proactively, using active behavioral and cognitive strategies to cope with distress. Other mothers seemed to perceive themselves as out of

TABLE 10.3
Multivariate Association of Maternal Beliefs and Coping Strategies to Mothers' and Children's Adjustment

	Maternal Adjustment		Child Adjustment			
	Authoritativeness	Distress	Self-Esteem	Health Problems	Considerateness	Task Orientation
Control variables:						
Sex of child (1)	ns	23.42* (11.24)	.29+ (.20)	-7.34+ (4.19)	2.95+ (1.53)	ns
Family finances	ns	ns	ns	ns	ns	ns
Time since separation	ns	ns	ns	ns	ns	ns
Beliefs and coping:						
Internal attributions/neg	-.55* (.27)	-24.80+ (15.72)	.99** (.31)	—	—	—
Maternal control	—	—	.05* (.02)	-1.48*** (.38)	—	—
Care-giver guidance	—	—	—	—	-6.25** (2.48)	-7.70* (3.10)
Problem solving	.55*** (.16)	-22.80+ (12.51)	-.43* (.19)	—	—	—
Total coping	—	1.46*** (.34)	—	.34** (.10)	—	—
R² added by beliefs	.20	.29	.20	.26	.10	.07+ (.04)
R² for total equation	.24	.31	.26	.33	.20	.14
F for equation	3.17**	3.81**	2.92*	4.93***	3.25*	2.62*

Note. Nonstandardized betas and standard error at final step reported; dashes indicate beta lower than .15 criterion for entry; $n = 58$.
(1) Sex of child coded (1) male (2) female.
$+p < .15$; $*p < .05$; $**p < .01$; $***p < .001$.

control, or, at best, sitting on the sidelines. These women appeared less able to buffer the negative effects of divorce for themselves or their children.

In the model we have constructed, beliefs about control are seen as influencing behavior. Our cross-sectional data do not permit causal inferences. An alternative possibility is that women whose children are adjusting badly to the divorce feel out of control as result of their children's negative behavior. The potency of perceived control as a causal factor influencing parental responses to misbehavior has rarely been demonstrated, although Bugental and her associates were able to demonstrate the causal precedence of beliefs in experimental studies (Bugental & Shennum, 1988; Bugental, Blue, & Cruzcosa, 1989). Yet another explanation for our findings is that mothers behave in certain ways and then develop beliefs to justify those actions. The possibility that beliefs are epiphenomena rather than causal agents has been raised in the sociological literature (see Goodnow, 1988, for a review).

Accepting responsibility for events involving one's children and maintaining an authoritative parenting style may have psychic costs as well as benefits. In our study, women who blamed themselves for their children's misbehavior rated their children as having more problems. It may be that women who are willing to face their own responsibility for their children's behavior are less likely to deny difficulties that their children may indeed be facing.

The overall finding that problem solving and positive appraisal were associated with positive adjustment falls in line with theoretical predictions. The strength of the total coping variable was more surprising and difficult to interpret. On one hand, mothers who used more coping strategies identified themselves and their children as having more health and psychological symptoms of distress. On the other hand, use of more coping strategies was associated with teacher ratings of considerateness and task orientation. It may be that women who are more conscious of the stress in their lives and are attempting to deal openly and actively with the stressful situations that they are experiencing are likely to report the use of many strategies and are well aware of the psychological discomfort created by the stress. This awareness and willingness to confront the problems actively may facilitate the child's adjustment, as reflected in their more positive teacher ratings.

In the future, the assessment of coping should be conducted in relation to particular incidents that mothers have appraised as stressful. In this study, mothers were asked to indicate use of coping strategies over many situations in the period since separating from their husbands. This global variable has provided a useful first look at the role of coping but it glosses over the changes in coping that occur during this time period as well as the likely differences in coping styles depending on the type of stressor and the resources available to the individual. In effect, coping needs to be viewed less as an attitudinal variable and more in terms of parental information processing, an argument made by others in reference to a variety of parental belief processes (Holden, 1989; Holden & Edwards, 1989).

In conclusion, we came away from this study with a clear understanding of why the debate on divorce and its effects has oscillated between the two poles of "divorce as disaster for children" and "divorce as transitional experience." In conducting our interviews we visited homes so chaotic that one could scarcely find a place to sit that wasn't already occupied by a stack of dirty laundry or an aging peanut butter sandwich. In contrast, other households appeared to be running quite smoothly. Certainly, these observed differences in adjustment resulted in part from differences in financial, social, and personal resources. However, our study indicates that mothers' appraisal of their own role in socializing their children — and particularly their perceived control over behavior — was also predictive of families' adjustment in the wake of divorce. Studying the appraisal processes through which children's behavior was construed provided for us a fascinating insight into the way in which families are impelled along various trajectories — some positive and some negative — following divorce.

APPENDIX: ADDITIONAL MATERNAL AND CHILD MEASURES

Material Resources. Total score on the Financial Well-Being and Sources of Support subscales of the Family Inventory of Resources for Management (McCubbin, Comeau, & Harkins, 1980). Three items judged less relevant for single parents were dropped. Coefficient alpha for the total score was .73.

Social Resources. Social support was assessed by asking mothers about ten situations in which they may have needed information, assistance, or companionship. Two scores were derived: number of different friends mentioned and number of different family members mentioned.

Maternal Authoritativeness. To ascertain their firmness in supervising and controlling their children's behavior, mothers were asked to respond to seven statements about rule-setting and household responsibility (e.g., "I usually give out chores for my child to do."; "I have rules about when my child has to go to bed."). Mothers indicated on a 5-point scale how well each statement described her family. Scores on these items were summed (coefficient alpha = .66).

Maternal Perceived Distress. To assess mothers' symptoms of perceived distress, the SCL-90-R was administered (Derogatis, 1975). Respondents are asked to indicate how much discomfort each of 90 problems has caused them during the past week. They indicated their responses on a 5-point scale. Item scores were summed to create a total score (coefficient alpha = .97).

Kindergarten Readiness. The Cooperative Preschool Inventory (Caldwell, 1970) was administered by the interviewer. It assesses a child's knowledge of body parts, colors, shapes, and other concepts. Coefficient alpha for the scale was .87.

Child's Self-Esteem. Children were administered the Pictorial Scale of Perceived Competence and Social Acceptance (Harter & Pike, 1984). Coefficient alpha for the total score was .81.

Child's Health and Psychological Problems. Mothers were asked to check off on the Child Behavior Checklist any health and psychological problems the child was experiencing (Achenbach, 1984). This scale consists of 112 symptoms which respondents indicate are true, sometimes true, or very true of the child's behavior. Coefficient alpha for the total score was .97.

Task Orientation, Extroversion, and Considerateness. Care givers completed the Child Behavior Inventory, a 30-item scale assessing task orientation, extroversion, and considerateness (Schaefer & Aaronson, 1965). For each item, care givers responded on a 5-point scale ranging from *almost never* to *almost always*. Coefficient alpha for the task orientation, extroversion, and considerateness were .90, .83, and .85, respectively.

REFERENCES

Achenbach, T. M. (1984). *Child Behavior Checklist.* Published Form, University of Vermont.

Allison, P. D., & Furstenberg, F. F., Jr. (1989). How marital dissolution affects children: Variations by age and sex. *Developmental Psychology, 25,* 540–549.

Billings, A. G., & Moos, R. H. (1984). Coping, stress, and social resources among adults with unipolar depression. *Journal of Personality and Social Psychology, 46,* 877–891.

Bowen, G. L. (1982). Social network and the maternal role satisfaction of formerly married mothers. *Journal of Divorce, 5,* 77–83.

Bugental, D. B., Blue, H., & Cruzcosa, M. (1989). Perceived control over care-giving outcomes: Implications for child abuse. *Developmental Psychology, 25,* 532–539.

Bugental, D. B., & Shennum, W. A. (1988). Physiological reactivity to responsive and unresponsive children as moderated by perceived control. *Child Development, 59,* 686–693.

Caldwell, B. M. (1970). *Cooperative Preschool Inventory*. Princeton, NJ: Educational Testing Service.

Compas, B. E., Howell, D. C., Phares, V., Williams, R. A., & Ledoux, H. (1989). Parent and child stress and symptoms: An integrative analysis. *Developmental Psychology, 25,* 550–559.

Demo, D. H., & Acock, A. C. (1988). The impact of divorce on children. *Journal of Marriage and the Family, 50,* 619–648.

Derogatis, L. R. (1975). *The SCL-90-R*. Baltimore MD: Clinical Psychometrics Research.

Dix, T. H., & Grusec, J. E. (1983). Parental influence techniques: An attributional analysis. *Child Development, 54,* 645–652.

Dix, T. H., & Grusec, J. E. (1985). Parent attribution processes in the socialization of children. In I. E. Sigel (Ed.), *Parental belief systems: The psychological consequences for children* (pp. 201–233). Hillsdale, NJ: Lawrence Erlbaum Associates.

Dix, T. H., Ruble, D. N., Grusec, J. E., & Nixon, S. (1986). Social cognition in parents: Inferential and affective reactions to children of three age levels. *Child Development, 57,* 879–894.

Elman, M. R., & Gilbert, L. A. (1984). Coping strategies for role conflict in married professional women with children. *Family Relations, 33,* 317–327.

Folkman, S. (1984). Personal control and stress and coping processes: A theoretical approach. *Journal of Personality and Social Psychology, 46,* 839–852.

Folkman, S., & Lazarus, R. S. (1985). If it changes, it must be a process: Study of emotion and coping during three stages of a college examination. *Journal of Personality and Social Psychology, 48,* 150–170.

Folkman, S., Lazarus, R. S., Dunkel-Schetter, C., DeLongis, A., & Gruen, R. (1986). Dynamics of a stressful encounter: Cognitive appraisal, coping, and encounter outcomes. *Journal of Personality and Social Psychology, 50,* 992–1003.

Goodnow, J. J. (1988). Parents' ideas, actions and feelings: Models and methods from developmental and social psychology. *Child Development, 59,* 286–320.

Harter, S., & Pike, R. (1984). The Pictorial Scale of Perceived Competence and Social Acceptance for Young Children. *Child Development, 55,* 1969–1982.

Hess, R. D., & Camara, K. A. (1979). Post-divorce family relationships as mediating factors in the consequences of divorce for children. *Journal of Social Issues, 35,* 79–96.

Hetherington, E. M. (1989). Coping with family transitions: Winners, losers, and survivors. *Child Development, 60,* 1–14.

Hetherington, E. M., & Camara, K. A. (1984). Families in transition: The processes of dissolution and reconstitution. In R. D. Parke (Ed.), *Review of child development research* (Vol. 7, pp. 398–439). Chicago: University of Chicago Press.

Hetherington, E. M., Cox, M., & Cox, R. (1985). Long-term effects of divorce and remarriage on the adjustment of children. *Journal of the American Academy of Child Psychiatry, 24,* 518–530.

Hodges, W. F., Tierney, C. W., & Buchsbaum, H. K. (1984). The cumulative effect of stress on preschool children of divorced and intact families. *Journal of Marriage and the Family, 46,* 611–617.

Holahan, C. J., & Moos, R. H. (1987). Personal and contextual determinants of coping strategies. *Journal of Personality and Social Psychology, 52,* 946–955.

Holden, G. W. (1989, April). *Parental selection of responses to misbehavior: The case of physical punishment.* Paper presented at the biennial meeting of the Society for Research in Child Development, Kansas City, MO.

Holden, G. W., & Edwards, L. A. (1989). Parental attitudes toward child rearing: Instruments, issues, and implications. *Psychological Bulletin, 1,* 29–58.

Holloway, S. D., & Machida, S. (1991). Child-rearing effectiveness of divorced mothers:

Relation to coping strategies and social support. *Journal of Divorce and Remarriage, 14,* 179–201.

Kurdek, L. A. (1988a). A 1-year follow-up study of children's divorce adjustment, custodial mothers' divorce adjustment, and post-divorce parenting. *Journal of Applied Developmental Psychology, 9,* 315–328.

Kurdek, L. A. (1988b). Issues in the study of children and divorce. *Journal of Family Psychology, 2,* 150–153.

Lazarus, R. S., & Folkman, S. (1984). *Stress, appraisal, and coping.* New York: Springer.

Lefcourt, H. M., Martin, R. A., & Saleh, W. E. (1984). Locus of control and social support: Interactive moderators of stress. *Journal of Personality and Social Psychology, 47,* 378–389.

Longfellow, C., & Belle, D. (1984). Stressful environments and their impact on children. In J. H. Humphrey (Ed.), *Stress in childhood* (pp. 63–78). New York: AMS.

Machida, S., & Holloway, S. D. (1991). The relationship between divorced mothers' perceived control over child rearing and children's post-divorce development. *Family Relations, 40,* 272–278.

McCrae, R. R. (1984). Situational determinants of coping responses: Loss, threat, and challenge. *Journal of Personality and Social Psychology, 46,* 919–928.

McGillicuddy-DeLisi, A. V. (1982). The relationship between parents' beliefs about development and family constellation, socioeconomic status, and parents' teaching strategies. In L. M. Laosa & I. E. Sigel (Eds.), *Families as learning environments for children* (pp. 261–299). New York: Plenum.

McGillicuddy-DeLisi, A. V. (1985). The relationship between parental beliefs and children's cognitive level. In I. E. Sigel (Ed.), *Parental belief systems: The psychological consequences for children* (pp. 7–24). Hillsdale, NJ: Lawrence Erlbaum Associates.

McGillicuddy-DeLisi, A. V., Sigel, I. E., & Johnson, J. E. (1979). The family as a system of mutual influences: Parental beliefs, distancing behaviors, and children's representational thinking. In M. Lewis & L. A. Rosenblum (Eds.), *The child and its family.* (pp. 91–106) New York: Plenum.

Parkes, K. R. (1984). Locus of control, cognitive appraisal, and coping in stressful episodes. *Journal of Personality and Social Psychology, 46,* 655–668.

Pearlin, L. I., & Schooler, C. (1978). The structure of coping. *Journal of Health and Social Behavior, 19,* 2–21.

Pett, M. G. (1982). Predictors of satisfactory social adjustment of divorced single parents. *Journal of Divorce, 5,* 1–17.

Propst, L. R., Pardington, A., Ostrom, R., & Watkins, P. (1986). Predictors of coping in divorced single mothers. *Journal of Divorce, 9,* 33–53.

Schaefer, E. S., & Aaronson, M. R. (1965). *Classroom Behavior Inventory, Preschool to Primary Age.* Unpublished Form, University of North Carolina, Chapel Hill.

Sigel, I. E. (1982). The relationship between parental distancing strategies and the child's cognitive behavior. In L. M. Laosa & I. E. Sigel (Eds.), *Families as learning environments for children* (pp. 47–86). New York: Plenum.

Sigel, I. E. (1985). A conceptual analysis of beliefs. In I. E. Sigel (Ed.), *Parental belief systems: The psychological consequences for children* (pp. 345–371). Hillsdale, NJ: Lawrence Erlbaum Associates.

Slater, M. A., & Power, T. G. (1987). Multidimensional assessment of parenting in single parent families. *Advances in Family Intervention, Assessment and Theory, 4,* 197–228.

Thomas, S. P. (1982). After divorce: Personality factors related to the process of adjustment. *Journal of Divorce, 5,* 19–36.

Wallerstein, J. S., & Blakesly, S. (1989). *Second chances: Men, women, and children a decade after divorce.* New York: Basic Books.

11 Social Behavior of Maltreated Children: Exploring Links to Parent Behavior and Beliefs

Timothy J. Iverson
The Child and Family Institute, Coconut Creek, FL

Marilyn Segal
The Family Center of Nova University

Reports of social deficits with abused and neglected children abound in the maltreatment literature. Maltreated children have been reported to be more aggressive (George & Main, 1979; Hoffman-Plotkin & Twentyman, 1984; Kinard, 1980; Reid, Taplin, & Lorper, 1981; Reidy, 1977), less positive and socially competent (e.g., Howes & Espinosa, 1985; Iverson, Tanner, & Segal, 1987), and less interactive with peers and adults (e.g., Jacobson & Straker, 1982). Neglected children are typically characterized as more withdrawn and less socially interactive with peers (e.g., Hoffman-Plotkin & Twentyman, 1984; Iverson, Tanner, & Segal, 1987).

In addition to the literature describing the social deficits of children who have been neglected and abused, there is an abundance of literature describing differences between maltreating and nonmaltreating parents in terms of both manifest behavior and expressed beliefs and values. Although a transactional model of development would suggest a relationship between parent and child behaviors, the research stops short of exploring these differences in reference to the children's behavior in other social settings. Delineating the relationships between the family or parent variables and the sequelae of maltreatment could inform the development of effective prevention and intervention strategies.

This chapter is devoted to an exploration of the relationships between parent beliefs and patterns of parental behavior, and the social deficits observed in maltreated children. Following a description of parental beliefs and behaviors associated with maltreatment, the authors describe preliminary results from an ongoing research study that explores relationships between beliefs, parent–child interactions, and the peer interaction behav-

267

iors of maltreated children during free play. The primary goal of the chapter is to present a methodology for studying maltreated children's social deficits concurrently with the family variables that may be associated with these deficits. By focusing on the chain of relationships (parent beliefs–parent behaviors–child outcomes), we hope to provide a context for a fuller understanding of the social deficits of maltreated children.

BELIEFS AND BEHAVIORS
ASSOCIATED WITH MALTREATMENT

Investigators of parent beliefs and behaviors share the underlying assumption that differences in child-rearing styles are associated with individual differences in the social and emotional development of children. Caregiver-child relationships provide the earliest experiences in socialization, and these early social experiences help set the stage for subsequent relationships the children will develop. Although each child brings to the world unique temperamental and behavioral predispositions, these predispositions interact with the child's early experiences in the process of social development.

Two separate lines of research with maltreatment and nonmaltreatment samples become relevant when discussing parent variables associated with social deficits in maltreated children. The first relates to differences in parent–child interactions between maltreating and nonmaltreating families, and the second involves differences in attitudes or beliefs between these groups. The two lines of research are integrated in studies that explore the relationship between parent beliefs and the parents' interactions with their children (e.g., Bugental, Blue, & Cruzcosa, 1989). Each of these lines of research is briefly discussed, followed by a presentation of the authors' research which begins to explore the relationship between these parenting factors and children's social behavior with peers.

Parent-Child Interactions in Maltreating Families

Differences between maltreating and nonmaltreating parents in both the quantity and quality of their interactions with their children have been identified in the maltreatment literature. Studies comparing the amount of time abusive or neglectful parents spend interacting with their children show that both abusive and neglectful parents tend to be less interactive with their children than nonmaltreating parents (e.g., Bousha & Twentyman, 1984; Burgess & Conger, 1978; Trickett & Susman, 1988). The qualitative aspects of the parent–child interactions in abusive families have also been shown to differ from nonabusive families, with the abusive parents being more negative (Burgess & Conger, 1978; Trickett & Susman, 1988), more directive and controlling (Mash, Johnston, & Kovitz, 1983; Oldershaw, Walters, & Hall, 1986), and exhibiting less requests and reasoning with their children (Trickett & Kuczynski, 1986).

Studies that focus on the behavior of children during parent–child interactions also demonstrate differences in the interactions of maltreating families. The behavior of abused children during parent–child interactions has been characterized as more aggressive, less compliant, and angrier than that of nonabused children (e.g., Bousha & Twentyman, 1984; Oldershaw, Walters, & Hall, 1986; Trickett & Susman, 1988). Neglected children have been described as being less interactive with their parents than either abused or nonmaltreated children (Bousha & Twentyman, 1984).

The differences in the parent–child interactions between maltreatment and nonmaltreatment families is not surprising, but the parallels between the parent–child interactions and findings regarding the peer interactions of maltreated children are striking. Although the separate studies cannot be directly linked, abuse seems to be associated with more aggressiveness and neglect with less interaction, and these patterns seem to hold with both family and friends. In essence, these studies support the transactional model of development in that behavioral exchanges taking place at one point in time in one setting affect subsequent exchanges at a later point in time and in a different setting.

Parent Beliefs in Maltreating Families

Recognizing that social cognitions have been linked to child-rearing behaviors in the general population, parent beliefs become another probable determinant of children's social interaction styles. Parent beliefs may relate directly to children's social behavior, or indirectly by influencing intermediate factors such as family interactions, opportunities to socialize with friends, and so on. Researchers interested in child maltreatment have compared the belief systems of maltreating parents to the belief systems of parents who have not abused their children across several types of beliefs. In the domain of discipline, maltreating parents are more likely to believe in the value of spanking and less likely to describe reasoning as a discipline technique (Trickett & Susman, 1988). When parent's attributions are the domain of interest, maltreating parents appear to be more negatively biased in rating the behavior of their child (Mash, Johnston, & Kovitz, 1983; Reid, Kavanagh, & Baldwin, 1987) and more likely to attribute their children's transgressions or failures to their child (Larrance & Twentyman, 1983). When the domain of interest is parent expectancies, maltreating parents are reported to have higher expectations regarding their children's capabilities

(Azar & Rohrbeck, 1986; Spinetta, 1978). In general, beliefs in several domains have been shown to differentiate maltreating from nonmaltreating parents.

There is also evidence that parent beliefs relate to differences in parent–child interactions. For example, Bugental, Blue, and Cruzcosa (1989) found that mothers with low perceived balance of control over care-giving failure showed higher levels of coercive care-giving behaviors. Although studies of this nature provide a critical link between beliefs and parent–child interactions, the relationship of these variables to children's behavior outside the family remains uncertain.

Although the research on the behavior and beliefs of maltreating parents has identified common threads that differentiate maltreating from nonmaltreating parents, the assumption cannot be made that these differences relate to differences in the social interactions or behavioral repertoires of the children outside the home. The relationship between parent beliefs, behaviors, and child outcomes is tenuous (Miller, 1988). Developmental psychologists have identified the fact that behavior has multiple determinants, and that just as the behavior of a parent can impact on a child, so can the behavior of a child impact on the behaviors and beliefs of the parent. Similarly, the social interactions of a child with friends outside the home may have an entirely different set of determinants than the child's behavior with his or her parents. Because of the complexities of parent belief–behavior relationships, assumptions about how a particular set of beliefs relates to a class of behavior must be tested empirically.

The remainder of this chapter describes the authors' research designed to clarify the relationship of parents' beliefs and behavior and social interaction styles of maltreated children with their peers. The research originated with an investigation of differences in social behavior between abused, neglected, and nonmaltreated preschoolers, and was subsequently expanded to improve our understanding of family variables in relation to the social differences we found.

To explore the family variables that may be associated with the social deficits observed in maltreated children, an observational measure of parent–child interactions and a Q-sort measure of parent beliefs were included with observations of the children's interactions in free-play with their peers. The measure of parent beliefs focuses on the domain of values; specifically, goals that parents value in regards to their children's behavior and development. The decision to focus on the domain of values in the current study was based on an earlier study conducted by the authors on maternal beliefs and values in the context of an intervention program (Segal, 1985). In this study, parents' ratings of obedience and process goals (e.g., independence, responsibility, imagination) were correlated with low income, being a single parent, and lower parent education. The findings suggested that parents who valued obedience and did not value process goals would use more authoritarian and less interactive or process-oriented teaching strategies when asked to instruct their children. Because the parent belief study is designed to identify associations between beliefs and behaviors, the Q-sort of values was selected as the measure of beliefs.

The research described is preliminary in nature, and several working hypotheses are being tested. These hypotheses involve the peer interactions of the children, the parent–child interaction patterns, the parent beliefs, and the relationship among these three domains. Specifically, the hypotheses that our data address in this chapter are as follows:

Hypothesis Related to Child Behaviors with Peers: Research Hypothesis 1 — In a free-play situation, maltreated children will exhibit less positive peer interactions than nonmaltreated children.

Hypotheses Related to Parent–Child Interactions: Research Hypothesis 2 — Maltreating parents will spend less time interacting with their child during a craft activity than nonmaltreating parents.

Research Hypothesis 3 — Maltreated children will respond less frequently to parents' commands and questions than nonmaltreated children during a craft activity.

Research Hypothesis 4 — Maltreating parents will respond less positively to their child's comments and questions than nonmaltreating parents during a craft activity.

Hypotheses Related to Belief–Behavior Relationships: Research Hypothesis 5 — Parent process goal ratings will be positively correlated with the frequency of parent initiated questions and comments during a parent and child craft activity.

Research Hypothesis 6 — There will be a negative correlation between parents' rating of obedience and children's response to parent questions and comments during a craft activity.

Research Hypothesis 7 — Maltreating parents will place a higher value on obedience and a lower value on process goals than nonmaltreating parents.

METHODOLOGY

The Setting

The Belief/Behavior Study was initiated in an urban child care setting in conjunction with a therapeutic child-care program for preschool children identified as having been physically abused or neglected. In this program, maltreated children who have been identified as abused or neglected are mainstreamed with nonmaltreated children into subsidized child-care settings. Within the child-care settings, therapeutic programs are carried out with the parents and the children in accordance with a comprehensive intervention plan. This intervention plan includes: (a) a parent component designed to reduce the stress of maltreating parents and increase their knowledge of and sensitivity to the physical, intellectual, and emotional needs of their children; (b) a parent–child component where parents have the opportunity to teach their child using supportive techniques; and, (c) a child component designed to reduce aggression and enhance peer interaction skills. The parent and child assessments described in this chapter serve in part as pretests for the evaluation component of the therapeutic intervention program.

Subjects

The sample was comprised of 33 children between the ages of 3 and 5 years and their custodial parents. All children were enrolled in Title XX day-care centers and considered to be of lower socioeconomic status (SES). Nine of these children had been identified by Florida Department of Health and Rehabilitative Services as physically abused and nine as physically neglected. The remaining 15 children were randomly selected from a list of names, stratified by age and race, of children who had no history of maltreatment and who were not considered at risk by the day-care staff. Table 11.1 summarizes the demographic characteristics of the total sample. The abused, neglected, and control children did not differ significantly on the variables of age, sex, race, SES, or intelligence.

TABLE 11.1
Demographic Characteristics of Participating Families

	Abused	*Neglected*	*Control*	*Total*
n	9	9	15	33
Average age (in months)	45.9	40.6	54.1	48.2
Sex	(M) 7	(M) 4	(M) 6	17
	(F) 2	(F) 5	(F) 9	16
Race	(B) 5	(B) 6	(B) 10	21
	(W/other) 4	(W/O) 3	(W/O) 5	12
McCarthy GCI	88.6	83.7	91.6	88.6
SES*	Low	Low	Low	

*All children were enrolled in government funded Title XX day-care centers that require low income to participate.

Instruments

Parent Beliefs.   The *Q*-sort is a 30-item instrument (see Appendix A) that requires parents to prioritize values or goals for their children. The items were selected to represent one of six general values: process goals, obedience, competition, success in school, cooperation, and ethical values.

Prior to using the *Q*-sort in the current study, it was factor analyzed using a sample of 125 low SES parents to provide information on reliability. The results of the factor analyses indicated that four factors had adequate reliability, two of which correlated highly with the a priori factors suggested by Segal (1985). These factors, which were used in the current study, were process goals (alpha = .57) and obedience (alpha = .64). The items comprising the factor of process goals were:

I want my child to be imaginative.
I want my child to be curious.
I want my child to be a good problem solver.
I want my child to be responsible.
I want my child to be an independent learner.

These items were identical to the priori factor of process goals suggested by Segal (1985), except the item "I want my child to be responsible" was included and the item "I want my child to have good communication skills" was excluded.

The items comprising the factor of obedience were:

I want my child to be obedient.
I want my child to do what he is told.
I want my child to get good grades in school.
I want my child to recognize that his parents are the boss.
I want my child to listen to his elders.

These items were identical to the a priori factor of obedience as suggested by Segal (1985), except the item "I want my child to get good grades in school" was included and the item "I want my child to listen to the teacher" was excluded.

These factors correlated respectively with the process goals (r = .83) and obedience factors (r = .90) used in the Segal (1985) study, which were found to be significantly related to marital status, educational level, and ethnicity.

Observational Measures.   The Behavior Observation Record (Iverson & Segal, 1986) was used to assess both parent–child interactions on a puppet-making task, and the social interactions of the children with their peers during free play. The Behavior Observation Record (BOR) is a time/event sampling instrument designed to assess both the presence of various social behaviors and the quality or effectiveness of these behaviors (see Appendix B). The BOR consists of 35 discrete behaviors under four general categories of social behavior: child alone, child approaching others, child being approached, and child interacting with others. When a behavior is observed, it is coded with a plus (+), minus (−), or zero (0). In the categories of child alone and interacting with others, the plus, minus, or zero reflect the affect of the child during the activity. In the approach categories, these ratings reflect the elicited response, thus capturing both the occurrence and consequence of the behavior. The BOR can be used to observe children with peers, parents, teachers, or other adults, thus eliminating variability due to different methods of observation in different settings.

For the current study, observers were trained and they practiced with the BOR until interobserver reliability of .7 to .9 was consistently obtained. Interobserver reliability was measured by the percentage of observation intervals in which the observers agreed.

Procedure

The children in the sample were observed with the BOR during regular daytime hours at the day-care centers they attended. The behavioral observations were conducted during morning free-play on the playground, and consisted of 15-min observations for each child, divided into alternate periods of 10 sec of observing and 5 sec of recording.

The *Q*-sort of parent values and parent–child interactions were conducted in the late afternoon and early evening. The maltreatment groups were assessed during early evening parent training sessions, and the control group was assessed at the end of the working day when picking up their children from day care. After the *Q*-sort of parent values was completed, the parent–child dyad was videotaped completing a puppet-making task. The task involved coloring and cutting out a face, and then gluing it to a stick to make a puppet. The following instructions were given prior to the task: "We'd like you to make a puppet. Color the faces, cut them out, and then glue them onto the stick." The task was presented as something for the child to do with the parent present, with no additional instruction regarding the parent's role in the task. The videotaped interactions were later coded until completion of the task or up to a 10-minute limit. Two observers, blind to the classification of children, rated the videotapes with the Behavior Observation Record.

RESULTS

The data on beliefs and behavior were subject to two levels of analysis. First, group differences in the peer interactions, parent–child interactions, and parent beliefs were explored to determine if there were parallels as suggested by the maltreatment literature. Second, correlational analyses were used to look at relationships between these areas, providing information on how the family variables may relate to the peer interactions of the children. For the following analyses there were a few children for which play observations were not available, but parent–child interactions and parent beliefs were (and vice versa), and the degrees of freedom for each analysis reflect the missing data.

Child–Peer Interactions

The first area of analysis involved the social interactions of the children on the playground. As expected, maltreated children exhibited less positive peer interactions on the playground than nonmaltreated children. During free play on the playground, control children spent significantly more time than neglected children interacting with peers, with abused children falling in between [$F (2, 23) = 7.32, p < .01$]. The mean number of combined verbal and nonverbal play interactions (i.e., time intervals in which these types of interactions were predominant) were 60.4 ($SD = 24.8$) for the nonmaltreated children, 23.3 ($SD = 16.5$) for the neglected children, and 31.5 ($SD = 19.7$) for the physically abused children.

In addition to differences in the amount of time spent interacting, the groups differed in regard to the effectiveness of their social approach behaviors. Abused and neglected children were less effective in their approach behaviors, with neglected children in particular being rejected or ignored more often than the other groups (see Table 11.2). In our previous study using the BOR to assess peer interactions of maltreated children (Iverson, Tanner, & Segal, 1987), the approaches by neglected children also

TABLE 11.2

Frequency of Children's Approach Behaviors on the Playground by Peer's Response and Maltreatment Status

| | | Response to Approach | | | |
		Positive	Negative	No Response	Total
Maltreatment Status	Control	2.7	0	.1	2.8
	Abuse	3.5	0	1.1	4.6
	Neglect	2.3	.8	3.2*	6.3

*Differs from other maltreatment groups, $p < .05$.

failed to elicit a response more often than the other groups; in that study, abused children elicited more negative responses as well, but that pattern was not evident in the current data. Nonetheless, the current data clearly reflect the pattern of less effective social interactions for the maltreated children.

Parent–Child Interactions

The first step in exploring the family variables in relation to the social deficits observed in the maltreated children involved looking at the parent–child interactions on the puppet-making task. All three research hypotheses relating to parent–child interactions were supported by the data. In accordance with our second hypothesis, maltreating parents spent significantly less time than nonmaltreating parents interacting with their children $[F (2, 21) = 8.58, p < .01]$. The mean number of observation intervals in which parent–child interaction was predominant was 33.8 $(SD = 17.7)$ for nonmaltreated children, 6.1 $(SD = 10.8)$ for neglect, and 7.9 $(SD = 5.7)$ for abuse families.

In addition to differences in amount of time spent in ongoing interactions with their children, the groups differed in regard to the approach behaviors noted in the puppet-making task. The approach behaviors reflect comments/questions (e.g., "Here is the scissors," or "Why don't you color the face first?") and directives/limits (e.g., "Don't use so much glue."). The differences were not in the frequency of approaches, but in the response the approaches elicited. Tables 11.3 and 11.4 show the pattern of responses elicited by the parents comments/questions and directives/limits. In accordance with Hypothesis 3, positive responses were elicited much more frequently by the nonmaltreating parents, regardless of whether the stimulus was a comment or directive. In addition, neglected children frequently ignored or did not respond to their parents comments or directives, but this was relatively rare in the abusive or control families.

The converse was also true, with the response the children received to

TABLE 11.3
Frequency of Parent's Comments/Questions on the Puppet-Making Task by Child's Response and Maltreatment Status

		Response by Child			
		Positive	*Negative*	*No Response*	*Total*
Maltreatment Status	Control	10.1*	.1	.1	10.3
	Abusive	1.3	0	.7	2
	Neglectful	3.1	0	3.5*	6.6

*Differs from other maltreatment groups, $p < .05$.

TABLE 11.4

Frequency of Parent's Directives/Limits on the Puppet-Making Task by Child's Response and Maltreatment Status

		Response by Child			
		Positive	Negative	No Response	Total
Maltreatment Status	Control	11.4*	.5	.2	12.1
	Abusive	2.6	1.5	4.3*	8.4
	Neglect	1.3	.5	8.5*	10.3

*Differs from other maltreatment groups, $p < .05$.

their approaches differing by group. As reflected in Table 11.5, the neglected children directed significantly fewer comments and questions toward their parents during the puppet-making task. When comments and questions were directed toward the parents, the control parents typically responded in a positive way, whereas both the abusive and neglectful parents typically ignored or did not respond to the child. None of the parents responded negatively to questions or comments by the children.

Similar to the patterns for peer interactions, the parent–child interactions suggest that both the frequency and quality of interaction was greater in the nonmaltreatment group. Both the abusive and neglectful parents interacted less during the puppet-making task, and the neglectful parents in particular showed more noncontingent interaction, with both parents and children often ignoring verbal approach behaviors by the other.

Similar patterns of interaction were evident in both the peer and parent interactions, so correlational analyses were used to look more specifically at the relationships between these domains. When the parent–child interactions were correlated with the peer interactions, several consistencies were found.

As shown in Table 11.6, the amount of time the children spent interacting with peers was positively related to the percentage of approaches to which the parent responded positively during the puppet-making task ($r = .50$).

TABLE 11.5

Frequency of Children's Comments/Questions on the Puppet-Making Task by Parent's Response and Maltreatment Status

		Response by Parent			
		Positive	Negative	No Response	Total
Maltreatment Status	Control	9.1*	0	.5	9.6
	Abuse	1.8	0	5.9*	7.7
	Neglect	.2	0	2.1*	2.3

*Differs from other maltreatment groups, $p < .05$.

TABLE 11.6

Correlations Between Parent-Child Interactions on the Puppet-Making Task and Children' Social Behavior on the Playground

			Parent–Child Interactions			
	Time Alone	Verbal Inter-action	Positive Response by Parent to Child's Approaches	Criticisms by Parent	No Response to Child's Approaches	Positive Response by Parent to Child's Directives
Time Interacting	−.18	.34	.50**	−.27	−.51**	−.01
Approaches accepted by peers	−.15	.30	.04	.23	−.04	.59**
Approaches rejected by peers	.22	−.26	−.33	.84**	.33	−.06
Approaches ignored by peers	.48*	−.36	−.65**	.43*	.65**	−.10
Aggression	.68**	−.59**	−.47*	.02	.18	−.15

(Left margin label: Children's Behavior with Peers)

*p < .05; **p < .01.

Conversely, the time in peer interactions was negatively correlated with the percentage of approaches to which the parents did not respond during the puppet-making task.

The effectiveness with which the children approached or attempted to initiate social interaction also related to certain aspects of the parent–child behavior. Successful approaches on the playground did not correlate with the overall positive responses by parents, but did relate to positive responses by parents to directives from their children ($r = .59$). Conversely, the frequency of approaches that were not responded to or were ignored by peers correlated with time alone during the parent–child task ($r = .48$), the percentage of approaches to which the parent did not respond ($r = .65$), and the number of criticisms from the parents ($r = .43$) during their interactions with their children. Unsuccessful approaches of this nature also were inversely related to positive responses by parents to their children's approaches ($r = -.65$). In addition, social approaches responded to by rejection on the playground correlated very highly with the number of criticisms by the parents during the parent–child interactions ($r = .84$).

Finally, aggression on the playground was also related to the parent–child interactions during the puppet-making task. Aggression was directly related

TABLE 11.7
Correlations Between Child's Approaches and Parent's Responses on the
Puppet-Making Task

		Parents' Responses			
		Positive Responses to Comments/ Questions	*No Response to Comments/ Questions*	*Positive Response to Directives*	*No Response to Directives*
Child's Approaches	Comments/ Questions	.93**	.10	.10	− .06
	Directives	.08	− .05	.90**	.39*

*$p < .05$; **$p < .01$.

to the amount of time the child spent alone on the parent–child task ($r =$ .68). In addition, aggression on the playground was inversely related to both the amount of parent–child verbal interaction ($r = -.59$) and positive responses by the parent to the child's approaches ($r = -.47$).

The parallels between the social interactions of these children with their parents and with their peers are remarkable. Children who are responded to positively by their parents interact more and are responded to more positively by their peers. Children who are ignored by their parents interact less and are ignored by their peers. Children who experience more parental criticism appear to be rejected more often by their peers.

The consistencies of the interaction styles of the children in the two different settings is impressive, but one cannot tell if behavior patterns are learned in the family and generalized to other social settings or if there are certain traits or characteristics that make certain children prone to ineffective interaction styles in general. A transactional model would suggest that the children are active in eliciting certain responses from both parents and peers, and at the same time parent responses play a role in shaping social interaction styles. A correlational analysis between parent responses and children's approaches on the puppet-making task was run to determine the degree to which a behavioral relationship accounted for the type of approach made by the children.[1] As shown in Table 11.7, positive responses by parents to their children's approaches are clearly associated with an increased frequency of those approaches. Positive responses to comments

---

[1]Because the BOR allowed for simultaneous coding of the parent and child behaviors during the puppet-making task, the behaviors are inherently dependent and correlations would be misleading. The exception to this is the nature of the response to approach behaviors. Parents' approaches can elicit either a plus, minus, or zero response by the child and vice versa, so approach–quality of response comparisons are theoretically independent.

were associated with more comments but not more directives, whereas positive responses to directives were associated with more directives, but not more comments.

These correlations suggest that parents' responses play a very active role in shaping the social styles of their children, and lead us to the next step of looking at beliefs in relation to the interaction styles of parents and children.

Parent Beliefs and Parent Behaviors

A correlation matrix was used to test Hypotheses 5 and 6 related to parent beliefs and parent behaviors on the puppet-making task. Correlational analyses were also used to investigate relationships between parent beliefs and child behaviors on the playground.

In accordance with Hypothesis 5, parents' ratings of process goals were related to their behavior on the puppet-making task (see Table 11.8). Parents who valued process goals, such as imagination, creativity, and independence, were observed to make more comments and ask more questions of their children ($r = .55$) and to spend a greater amount of time interacting with their children ($r = .43$) during the task. In addition, there was a tendency for parents who reported higher process goals to be less critical of their children ($r = -.30$). The factor of obedience did not correlate with any of the parent behaviors on the puppet-making task. Hypothesis 6, that there would be a negative correlation between parents' ratings on obedience and children's positive responses to parents' questions or directives was also not supported by the data. Similarly, parent beliefs as measured by the Q-sort did not correlate with peer interactions of the children during free play.

Interestingly, the final research hypothesis, that maltreating parents will

TABLE 11.8
Correlations Between Q-Sort Factors and Parents' Behaviors on
Puppet-Making Task

		Q-Sort Factor	
		Process Goals	Obedience
Behavior of Parent	Time Interacting	.43*	− .15
	Comments/ Questions	.55*	− .09
	Directives/ Limits	.00	− .24
	Criticism	− .30	− .20

*$p < .05$; **$p < .01$.

place a higher value on obedience and a lower value on process goals than nonmaltreating parents, was not supported by the data. The abusive, neglectful, and comparison parents did not differ on the Q-sort factors of process goals or obedience, suggesting that these groups of parents hold similar values regarding the development of their children. It is possible that the lack of differences may reflect biased reporting by the parents or simply be a function of the small sample size on which the analyses was based. On the other hand, because the maltreating and nonmaltreating parents are from the same low-SES population, it may be that the contribution of SES is so strong that the other sources of variability (e.g., maltreatment status) are masked. This may be particularly true with a Q-sort instrument that has built-in limitations on variability.

In short, the final step of this research provided some evidence that beliefs were related to parent behaviors with their children, although differences according to maltreatment status and relationships between beliefs and the children's peer interactions were not evident.

DISCUSSION

Taken as a whole, the methodology and data presented in this chapter, though preliminary, provide an interesting picture of the chain of relationships from parent beliefs to parent behavior to child outcomes. The small sample and the fact that beliefs and behaviors are measured at only one point in time limit the conclusions that can be drawn from the data, but the fact that beliefs, behavior, and child outcomes were studied concurrently provides a unique glimpse at their interrelationships.

As hypothesized, the strongest relationship identified in the study is the relationship between parent interaction styles on the puppet-making task and the behaviors of their children, both in the teaching situation with the parent, and on the playground with peers. From a behavioral point of view, it appears that children adapt the same interaction style that they have experienced. Parents who do not engage in back and forth conversations during an instructional activity have children who do not engage in conversational interactions either with their parents or with their peers. It can be postulated that this lack of social responsiveness or inability to engage in play interchanges contributes to a dynamic in which children both reject and are rejected. Negative affect associated with rejection may contribute to the heightened aggression of maltreated children.

Although outcomes related to parent–child behaviors in this study supported the research hypotheses, the relationships between parent beliefs and parent behaviors were not as strong as predicted. An unexpected finding was that the Q-sort did not significantly differentiate between maltreating and nonmaltreating parents. This outcome seems inconsistent with the finding that maltreating parents spent less time interacting with their children than nonmaltreating parents, and that parents who placed a relatively high value on process goals asked more questions and made more comments in a parent–child activity than parents who placed a relatively low value on process goals. One possible explanation for these apparent inconsistencies may relate to distinctions in the types of behaviors to which beliefs correlate. For example, certain beliefs may be more strongly related to behaviors or comments initiated by the parent, in comparison to the parent's spontaneous responses to the child.

The results regarding parent beliefs raise several additional questions. Other research (e.g., Bugental, Blue, & Cruzcosa, 1989) has shown that parent beliefs do relate to the potential for abuse, and our data suggest that parent beliefs do relate to parent behaviors. It may be that differences do exist in values or beliefs of maltreating and nonmaltreating families, but that the Q-sort was not a sensitive enough instrument to identify these differences. An equally possible explanation is that maltreating and non-maltreating parents differ significantly in terms of behavior and somewhat in terms of belief, but that differences in behavior are more easily measured or are attributable to factors other than or in addition to the beliefs tapped by the Q-sort.

The issue of measurement may be particularly relevant to studying parent beliefs in abusive or neglectful parents. Parents who have been identified as abusive or neglectful may be very sensitive to the beliefs they report, leading to a positive bias in this data. Similarly, reported beliefs may differ from the beliefs that are more specifically associated with behavior. For example, beliefs may exist on both an explicit and an implicit level, explicit beliefs being those that are consciously formulated and can be talked about, and implicit beliefs being only assumed on the basis of behavior but not having been consciously formulated or verbalized. Instruments used in parent belief studies are designed to measure explicit beliefs. If there are discrepancies between beliefs that people admit to and beliefs that govern their behavior, studies that focus on belief/behavior correspondencies may present an incomplete picture.

The complexity of the belief construct has also given rise to theoretical debates that add to the complexity of measurement issues. A particularly difficult issue revolves around the interaction of feelings and beliefs (Goodnow, 1988). When beliefs are conceptualized as both affecting feelings and being affected by feelings, the study of parent belief relationships becomes more complex.

The research discussed in this chapter suggests that parent beliefs, parent behavior, and child behavior are related. Although the relationships were strongest when looking at parent and child behavior, direct observation of behavior does not present the measurement dilemmas posed by cognitive-constructs such as beliefs. Beliefs may be a much stronger determinant than our data suggests, but additional research with the belief construct, carefully addressing the measurement issues, is needed to clarify the role of parent beliefs.

Finally, the data presented in this chapter point to some guidelines for intervention in maltreatment samples. The finding that the social behaviors of maltreated children are, at least in part, a reflection of the kind of interactions they have experienced with their parents provides guidelines for the design of intervention programs. Early intervention that encourages parents to carry on conversations with their children, and to respond in positive ways to their children's questions and comments, could help children learn positive ways of interacting with parents. If the relationships described in this study hold true, positive interaction patterns experienced by children in the parent context could be reflected in their interaction with peers. Parents' beliefs regarding discipline and goals for their children also need to be addressed, and doing so in the context of teaching positive interaction strategies may not only improve parent–child relations, but may have the additional benefit of improving the peer relationships of the children as well.

Although the current study does not provide conclusive results, several hypotheses and directions for future research are suggested by the data. First, studying beliefs, behavior, and child outcomes simultaneously is methodologically difficult, but provides an enormous amount of information that cannot be derived from studies addressing only a single area of functioning.

Second, the present research suggests the need for longitudinal studies addressing both theoretical and practical issues.

Theoretical questions related to beliefs and behaviors in maltreating families include the following:

1. Are there measures of parent values or aspirations other than the Q-sort that identify critical differences between maltreating and nonmaltreating parents?
2. Are there domains of belief other than values or aspirations that discriminate between maltreating and nonmaltreating parents?
3. Are there measures of parent aspiration that have a stronger relationship to parent–child interaction style than the Q-sort of Values?
4. Are there domains of parent beliefs other than aspirations that relate to child-rearing practices?
5. Are there variables such as degree of stress, affective state, or substance abuse that have greater explanatory power in terms of parent–child interactive style than domains of belief?

Practical questions related to intervention include the following:

1. Are programs that focus on influencing parents' beliefs effective in changing beliefs?
2. Are some domains or levels of belief more easily influenced by intervention than others?
3. Are programs designed to change parent–child interaction patterns effective in changing those patterns?
4. Will interventions designed to change parent beliefs produce changes in related parent–child interactions?
5. Will interventions designed to change parent–child interaction patterns affect parent beliefs?

Although the list of unanswered questions is formidable, controlled research related to beliefs and behaviors holds the promise of increasing our understanding of belief–behavior relationships and of informing our interventions. This kind of research is demanding in terms of time and resources, but child abuse is a complex phenomena and there are no easy answers.

APPENDIX A
Q-SORT

Q-SORT INSTRUCTIONS

Tell the parents(s) you want them to:

1. Divide the stack into three piles with 10 cards per pile. The *right-hand* pile indicates values you hold most *strongly* for your child. The *center* pile indicates those values which are *second* in importance. The *left-hand* pile will indicate the values which are *third* in importance.
2. From the *right-hand* pile, pull out *three* values to which you give top priority and put those three to your extreme right. From the *left-hand* pile, pull out *three* values to which you give the lowest priority and put these three to your extreme left.
There should now be five piles. The pile on the extreme right has 3 cards, next pile 7, middle pile 10, next pile 7, and the extreme left pile 3.
3. Each pile is assigned a number. Starting on the left, all cards in the extreme left pile are assigned the number 1, next pile−2, next pile−3, next pile−4, and the extreme right pile−5.

4. Use the following chart to record the score for each value you sorted.

Lowest				Highest
Pile #1	Pile #2	Pile #3	Pile #4	Pile #5
___	___	___	___	___
___	___	___	___	___
___	___	___	___	
	___	___	___	
	___	___	___	
	___	___	___	
	___	___	___	
		___		
		___		

5. After listing the cards on the above chart, proceed to score them on the chart below: Example: if card #4 was placed in Pile #3, put a 3 next to 4 under Process Goals, and so on. After listing all the numbers, total each column.

Process Goals	Cooperation	Obedience	Success & School	Competition	Ethical Value
4	1	15	3	7	20
5	2	17	6	8	23
13	11	26	10	9	24
22	18	27	14	12	29
25	19	28	21	16	30

TOTAL

Q-SORT ITEMS

PROCESS GOALS

4   I want my child to be an independent learner.
5   I want my child to have good communication skills.
13   I want my child to be imaginative.
22   I want my child to be a good problem solver.
25   I want my child to be curious.

COOPERATION

1   I want my child to be helpful and considerate.
2   I want my child to get along well with other children.
11   I want my child to make friends with culturally different children.
18   I want my child to have the capacity to love and care for other people.
19   I want my child to share.

OBEDIENCE

15   I want my child to listen to his elders.
17   I want my child to be obedient.
26   I want my child to recognize that his parents are the boss.
27   I want my child to do what he is told.
28   I want my child to listen to the teacher.

SUCCESS AND SCHOOL

3   I want my child to achieve at or above the grade level in reading and mathematics.
6   I want my child to get good grades in school.
10   I want my child to be a good student.
14   I want my child to go to college.
21   I want my child to have a good foundation in reading and mathematics.

COMPETITION

7   I want my child to fight his own battles.
8   I want my child to be competitive.
9   I want my child to be able to defend himself.
12   I want my child to be aggressive.
16   I want my child to fight for his rights.

ETHICAL VALUES

20   I want my child to have a good sense of values.
23   I want my child to be truthful.
24   I want my child to have a good code of ethics.
29   I want my child to have a sense of right and wrong.
30   I want my child to be responsible.

APPENDIX B
BEHAVIOR OBSERVATION RECORD

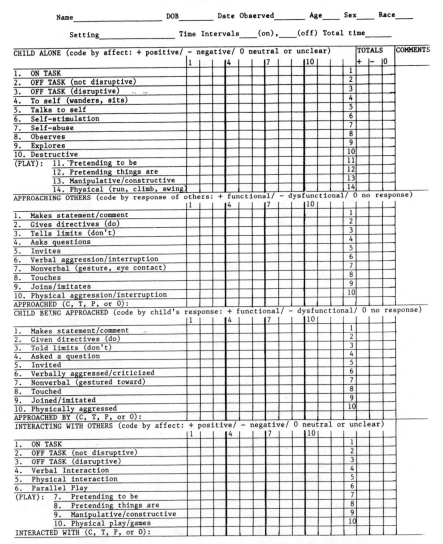

Name_____ DOB_____ Date Observed_____ Age____ Sex____ Race____

Setting_____ Time Intervals____(on),____(off) Total time_____

CHILD ALONE (code by affect: + positive/ − negative/ 0 neutral or unclear)													TOTALS + − 0	COMMENTS
	1		4		7		10							
1. ON TASK													1	
2. OFF TASK (not disruptive)													2	
3. OFF TASK (disruptive)													3	
4. To self (wanders, sits)													4	
5. Talks to self													5	
6. Self-stimulation													6	
7. Self-abuse													7	
8. Observes													8	
9. Explores													9	
10. Destructive													10	
(PLAY): 11. Pretending to be													11	
12. Pretending things are													12	
13. Manipulative/constructive													13	
14. Physical (run, climb, swing)													14	

APPROACHING OTHERS (code by response of others: + functional/ − dysfunctional/ 0 no response)

	1		4		7		10							
1. Makes statement/comment													1	
2. Gives directives (do)													2	
3. Tells limits (don't)													3	
4. Asks questions													4	
5. Invites													5	
6. Verbal aggression/interruption													6	
7. Nonverbal (gesture, eye contact)													7	
8. Touches													8	
9. Joins/imitates													9	
10. Physical aggression/interruption													10	

APPROACHED (C, T, P, or 0):

CHILD BEING APPROACHED (code by child's response: + functional/ − dysfunctional/ 0 no response)

	1		4		7		10							
1. Makes statement/comment													1	
2. Given directives (do)													2	
3. Told limits (don't)													3	
4. Asked a question													4	
5. Invited													5	
6. Verbally aggressed/criticized													6	
7. Nonverbal (gestured toward)													7	
8. Touched													8	
9. Joined/imitated													9	
10. Physically aggressed													10	

APPROACHED BY (C, T, P, or 0):

INTERACTING WITH OTHERS (code by affect: + positive/ − negative/ 0 neutral or unclear)

	1		4		7		10							
1. ON TASK													1	
2. OFF TASK (not disruptive)													2	
3. OFF TASK (disruptive)													3	
4. Verbal Interaction													4	
5. Physical interaction													5	
6. Parallel Play													6	
(PLAY): 7. Pretending to be													7	
8. Pretending things are													8	
9. Manipulative/constructive													9	
10. Physical play/games													10	

INTERACTED WITH (C, T, P, or 0):

Observed by: 1987 by Nova University Family Center

ACKNOWLEDGMENTS

The authors extend a special thanks to Suzan Tanner and Marguerite Vasquez-Gil for their time spent in data collection, data analyses, and compiling information for this chapter. In addition, we are grateful to Wendy Masi, Jeanne Montie, and Suzanne Gregory for their help in reviewing and preparing the final manuscript.

REFERENCES

Azar, S. J., & Rohrbeck, C. A. (1986). Child abuse and unrealistic expectations: Further validation of the Parent Opinion Questionnaire. *Journal of Consulting and Clinical Psychology, 54* (6), 867–868.

Bousha, D. M., & Twentyman, C. T. (1984). Mother–child interactional style in abuse, neglect and control groups: Naturalistic observations in the home. *Journal of Abnormal Psychology, 93,* 106–114.

Bugental, D., Blue, J., Cruzcosa, M. (1989). Perceived control over care-giving outcomes: Implications for child abuse. *Developmental Psychology, 25,* 532–539.

Burgess, R. L., & Conger, R. D. (1978). Family interaction in abusive neglectful & normal families. *Child Development, 49,* 1163–1173.

George, C., & Main, M. (1979). Social interactions of young abused children: Approach, avoidance, and aggression. *Child Development, 50,* 306–318.

Goodnow, J. J. (1988). Parents' ideas, actions, and feelings: Models and methods for developmental and social psychology. *Child Development, 59,* 286–320.

Hoffman-Plotkin, D., & Twentyman, C. T. (1984). A multimodel assessment of behavioral and cognitive deficits in abused and neglected preschoolers. *Child Development, 55,* 794–802.

Howes, C., & Espinosa, M. P. (1985). The consequences of child abuse for the formation of relationships with peers. *Child Abuse and Neglect, 9,* 397–404.

Iverson, T. J., & Segal, M. (1986). *The behavior observation record.* Unpublished manuscript, Nova University.

Iverson, T. J., Tanner, S. L., & Segal, M. (1987). *Assessing abused and neglected children's social interactions with the Behavior Observation Record.* Unpublished manuscript, Nova University.

Jacobson, R. S., & Straker, G. (1982). Peer group interaction of physically abused children. *Child Abuse and Neglect, 6,* 321–327.

Kinard, E. M. (1980). Emotional development in physically abused children. *American Journal of Orthopsychiatry, 50,* 686–696.

Larrance, D. T., & Twentyman, C. T. (1983). Maternal attributions and child abuse. *Journal of Abnormal Psychology, 92,* 449–457.

Mash, E. J., Johnston, C., & Kovitz, K. (1983). A comparison of mother–child interactions. *Journal of Clinical Child Psychology, 3,* 337–346.

Miller, S. A. (1988). Parents' beliefs about children's cognitive development. *Child Development, 59,* 259–285.

Oldershaw, C., Walters, G. C., & Hall, D. K. (1986). Control strategies and noncompliance in abusive mother–child dyads: An observational study. *Child Development. 57,* 722–730.

Reid, J. B., Kavanagh, K., & Baldwin, D. V. (1987). Abusive parent perceptions of child problem behaviors: An example of parental bias. *Journal of Abnormal Psychology, 15,* (3), 457–466.

Reid, J. B., Taplin, P. S., & Lorper, R. A. (1981). A social interactional approach to the treatment of abusive families. In R. Stuart (Ed.), *Violent behavior: A social learning approach to prediction, management and treatment* (pp. 83–101). NY: Brunner Mazel.

Reidy, T. J. (1977). The aggressive characteristics of abused and neglected children. *Journal of Clinical Psychology, 33,* 1140–1145.

Segal, M. (1985). A study of maternal beliefs and values within the context of an intervention program. In I. E. Sigel (Ed.), *Parental belief systems: The psychological consequences for children* (pp. 271–286). Hillsdale, NJ: Lawrence Erlbaum Associates.

Spinetta, J. J., (1978). Parental personality factors in child abuse. *Journal of Consulting and Clinical Psychology, 46,* 1409–1414.

Trickett, P. K., & Kuczynski, E. (1986). Children's misbehaviors and parental discipline strategies in abusive and nonabusive families. *Developmental Psychology, 22,* 115–123.

Trickett, P. K., & Susman, E. J. (1988). Parental perceptions of child-rearing practices in physically abusive and nonabusive families. *Developmental Psychology, 24,* (2), 270–276.

IV Focus on Model Building of Parent Cognition

12 Parents' Ideas, Children's Ideas: Correspondence and Divergence

Jacqueline J. Goodnow
Macquarie University

Psychologists, along with sociologists and anthropologists, are often interested in the conditions that influence the extent to which an older and a younger generation share the same views. The basis of interest is sometimes a large-scale concern with "cultural reproduction" and sometimes a more microanalytic concern with parent–child dyads and the nature of socialization within the family. In this chapter, I note some proposals from both "macro" and "micro" analyses, paying particular attention to gaps in what is known or considered.

As a way of structuring the material, I start with a particular model of how correspondence or its lack comes about (the model proposed by Cashmore and Goodnow in 1985) and then consider a number of additions. These additions are of two kinds. One set consists of methodological points. As people from Cronbach (1955) to Acock (1985) have pointed out, research on cross-generation similarities is studded with methodological and inferential pitfalls. The other set has more to do with the dynamics of transmission. These points have to do with the significance of shared ideas to parents and children, and with the extent to which parents allow a child either to accept part of a message or to select from a set of positions that a parent finds acceptable or at least tolerable. They also have to do with the impact of the ways in which a parental message is delivered and with the need to consider a further form of correspondence: namely, between the ideas held by parents and those held by adults in the larger community.

These additions reflect two sources. One consists of discussions of transmission by anthropologists and sociologists, material that reinforced for me the importance of considering methods of delivery and the nature of correspondence between the viewpoints of individual parents and the viewpoints of others in the community (Goodnow, 1990). The other source consists of research in an area that has presented a number of challenging phenomena. This is the area of ideas about household work — an area where parents and children often hold strong (and divergent) views — views about who should do particular pieces of work, how they should be done, and why the work is worth doing. The examples I choose often come from this research, sometimes from work now reported (Goodnow & Delaney, 1989; Goodnow & Warton, 1991; Warton & Goodnow, 1991), and sometimes from work in progress. The issues contained in these examples, however, apply to any content area.

A FIRST MODEL

This model arose from asking parents (mothers and fathers) and their 12- to 14-year-old children for their ideas about a number of issues: the importance of various characteristics for children to acquire (e.g., being neat, obedient, independent, curious, interested in other people), the importance of various "rules to live by" (e.g., "if at first you don't succeed, try and try again," or "there are no prizes for coming second"), the kinds of jobs the child should aim for, and the sources of success in a variety of school subjects. A quick review of several features of the study serves to describe the data base for the model. The review also serves as a summary of issues seen at that time by ourselves and others as needing to be considered in research on correspondence.

The first two features have to do with what one means by correspondence. They are essentially methodological:

1. *A distinction was drawn between absolute and relative correspondence.* Suppose, for instance, that parents and children are asked to indicate their level of agreement or disagreement with statements about gender stereotypes. The two generations could be different in the absolute ratings they give, but correspond well when one considers relative positions. The most egalitarian of parents, for instance, could have the most egalitarian of children, even though the children may be, in absolute terms, more or less egalitarian than the parents.

2. *A distinction was drawn between "actual" and "perceived" correspondence.* In the case of actual correspondence, the two generations do share the same ideas. In perceived correspondence, they think they share, but may in fact hold divergent views. The distinction may be tapped by asking informants not only to state their views but also to answer questions, or fill in ratings, as they think the other person would. Unless otherwise noted, we

shall use "correspondence" to mean "actual correspondence." The distinction, one should note, is not purely methodological. As Furstenberg (1971) pointed out, parents may wish to perceive correspondence as higher than it actually is and adolescents may have an interest in seeing that parents remain in that blissful state, and therefore withhold or disguise the information that might lead to reconsideration.

An additional set of features to the original study had more to do with dynamics, in the sense that these features stemmed from hypotheses about factors that might affect correspondence:

1. *The content areas varied* in the likelihood of parents having made their message explicit, a feature relevant to the expectation that the degree to which a parental message is overt, as against needing to be inferred, will influence the child's awareness of parents' views.

2. *The sampling covered both parents,* a feature relevant to the expectation that the degree of agreement between parents will influence the child's awareness or acceptance of a parental viewpoint.

3. *The sampling included a variation in ethnicity.* For half the sample, both parents and children were born in Australia. For the other half, the children were born in Australia but the parents were born in Italy and had emigrated. The inclusion of this feature arose from the need to ask whether correspondence stems from direct family transmission or from both generations being part of a common culture.

What were the elements of the model that this study then gave rise to? It was labeled a "two-process model," with one process regarded as consisting of the perception of the original message, and the other as its acceptance or rejection. A lack of correspondence, for instance, may arise if:

1. *The parent's message is not accurately heard by the child.* This possibility could have two sources. The child may not be able to absorb a message that others (e.g. older observers) would regard as clear, or the parental message might not have been made explicit. The latter possibility seemed to us to be of special interest. How often, for instance, do parents say explicitly that it is important to be curious, to ask questions, or to have a good sense of humor? They may place a high value on such qualities but nonetheless leave the child in a position where this value needs to be inferred. Under such circumstances, the child may attribute to the parent a position similar to his or her own (assumed similarity) or the opposite of his or her own (assumed difference). The most common response by the adolescents in the Cashmore and Goodnow (1985) study was assumed similarity. We had expected that the assumption of difference might as

readily prevail but in fact that was not the case, perhaps influenced by the families all being volunteers for the study, with both parents and children agreeing to take part and perhaps inclined toward positive views of family relationships.

2. *The parent's message is accurately heard, but is not accepted.* This type of pattern prevailed when the content dealt, for instance, with the kinds of jobs a child should aim for or, a case of particular clarity, with the importance of being "neat" and "obedient." On the former score (jobs) children were aware of their parents' high hopes but were themselves more modest in their expectations. On the latter (being neat and obedient), children felt they knew exactly where their parents stood (they actually rated their parents as caring more about these qualities than their parents rated themselves as caring), but the children themselves gave these qualities low ratings for importance.

As that brief description of possibilities may suggest, a major component of the model was the proposal that the two processes differed in the extent to which they were influenced by various conditions. The accuracy of perceptions was seen as influenced mainly by conditions having to do with "information": for instance, the clarity, explicitness, or redundancy of the parental message. To take one example from the results, agreement between parents (a form of redundancy) was correlated with the accuracy of perception but not with the degree of agreement. In contrast, the likelihood of acceptance was seen as influenced primarily by conditions that are more motivational or affective in quality. Teenagers and parents, for example, have different degrees of interest in a child's obedience and neatness. They also have a different kind of interest in the occupations that children may take up. Parents may indulge in a little fantasy and a few grandiose hopes. Children, who are the ones required to act, may well need to be more restrained. The distinction was not intended to be completely hard and fast. Affective conditions such as vested interests or a lack of warmth in the parent–child relationship, for instance, may well influence the accuracy of perception as well as a readiness to reject parental messages, inclining the child toward tuning out or selecting only some parts of the message. The points we wished to emphasize were that correspondence or divergence could come about in more than one way and that one should consider any proposed condition for its possibly differential effect on perception and acceptance.

What then remained to be done? We were relatively content with the way that the model fitted our results. We were also pleased to be moving toward a model of correspondence that did not put all its emphasis on problems of comprehension. The situations of particular interest, we felt, were those where the parents' position was accurately known but was nonetheless not agreed with. The attention that this pattern draws to motivational/affective conditions, we were happy to note, fitted well with Bengston and Kuypers' (1971) proposal of a condition they termed "generational stake," a term referring especially to the way that parents may wish to see their children as similar to them whereas the children, at least in adolescence, wish to see themselves as different from their parents. It also fitted well with the argument that Holloway and Hess (1982) offered for differences between parents and children in their attributions for success in school. The higher attribution to effort by children and to talent by parents, they proposed, stemmed from the fact that parents were in the position of observers of events in school, whereas children were in the position of actors with an inevitable difference in the need for attributions that were ego-protective.

Nonetheless, we certainly saw the model as far from final, and in the time since 1985 the need for some additions has begun to make itself felt. As noted earlier, I break them into two sets. One deals with some implications for method. The other (the larger set) deals with several conceptual expansions to the model. In the order in which I take them up, these expansions deal with (a) the significance of correspondence, (b) the assumption of single messages with a yes–no acceptance by children, (c) methods of delivery, and (d) building an interactive picture of transmission. In all sections, my goal is both to lay out the form that an addition might take and to indicate how it would lead to new ways of doing research or new research questions. The final section summarizes the modifications that these additions make to our understanding of the perception and acceptance of parental messages.

SOME METHODOLOGICAL ADDITIONS

I concentrate on two aspects. The first has to do with ways of tapping a variable such as "vested interests." If one suspects that these interests contribute to correspondence or its lack, how may they be tapped (and varied) so that their effects may be studied? The second has to do with ways of achieving variance in both parents' ideas and children's ideas. That state, needed for any statistical comparison, is especially necessary in research on cross-generation comparisons, because a lack of variance exacerbates a pervasive problem: namely, the difficulty often incurred in choosing among the several possibilities that could account for results. Both types of problem call for attention to the ways in which they may be met by particular choices of subjects and content areas.

Tapping Vested Interests

The primary approach is by way of varying the content areas. To start with, we need content areas where parents are likely to have made their positions explicit. If there is then a lack of correspondence, it will not be because children have been left in doubt about where their parents stand. Within such content, we then need to find topics that are likely to elicit differential vested interests among both parents and children. How may we locate such topics?

The choice of content areas in Cashmore and Goodnow (1985) was based on informal knowledge. That is, we knew from everyday experience that parents and children often disagree about the importance of being "neat" and "obedient." Smetana (1988a, 1988b) offered two further steps. One consists of asking parents and adolescents to recall occasions of actual disagreement during the weeks prior to interview. The other consists of asking for views about issues that are "multifaceted": that is, they contain issues of both parents' rights and children's rights. Smetana (1988a, 1988b) asked, for instance, who should make the rules about the child's use of the telephone, choice of dress, choice of friends, or cleaning up one's room. Both approaches appear highly likely to bring out content where each person is aware of the other's position (an aspect that Smetana also checked directly) but where differential interests lead to a lack of correspondence.

Achieving Variance

The ideal is a situation where there is variance among parents and among children. The problem is to find ways of making this happy event likely to occur, with the choice made preferably before the study begins.

One way to bring this about is suggested by Collins' (in press) approach to the views that parents and children have of one another. In essence, he chooses an age span (early to late adolescence) where one of the two parties (the child) is exhibiting rapid change, and therefore the views of the other (the parent) may easily become out-of-phase. The out-of-phase state may arise either by way of a time lag (the adolescent is changing faster than the parent's perceptions are) or by way of running ahead (the parent expects very rapid and consistent changes on the grounds that the child is now "a teenager, practically an adult"). Either possibility provides the variance needed to allow Collins to ask questions about the signals of change that parents pick up, and about the perceptions or expectancies that are most likely to be out-of-phase in a time lag fashion rather than on the basis of running ahead. A further set of questions looks forward in time. If teenagers are followed in a longitudinal study, Collins asked, would parents who display lag at the start of a child's entry into puberty exhibit signs of a catch-up? And, as that realignment of ideas occurs, do parent and child consider that the quality of the relationship has improved?

A second way to promote variance is by looking toward both the content area and the age group. Suppose, for instance, that we have begun to look toward ideas about work in households as an area where messages are likely to be explicit and differential vested interests are involved. There will be little gained by asking Anglo-Saxon parents whether children should make a contribution to the work of a household. All (or almost all) of them will say "yes." We would be better off with questions about whether children should be paid for household jobs, or whether any money given to children should be kept quite separate from tasks. This is an issue where there is already data indicating considerable variance among parents in England (Newson & Newson, 1976) and Australia (Goodnow, 1987). It is, moreover, one of the rare areas where we know that the variance among parents is not attributable to social class. In Newson and Newson's (1976) sample, the issue of whether children should receive money for household jobs splits each of their five socioeconomic groups in similar fashion.

A content area such as money for jobs would then supply variance on the parent's side. What shall we do about variance on the children's side? Suppose we choose the easiest condition to work with, namely the child's age. There is little point in choosing an age where the child's inability to understand the parental message gives rise to no variance. The ideal is an age span within which the issue is easily understood but that nonetheless yields differences between ages and, ultimately, some variance within an age group. So far, I have found no alternative to the actual sampling of several age groups on some specific issues. (In other words, we are not well enough informed about the bases of age differences to be sure of a priori judgments). An example is the procedure Pamela Warton and I are currently using to locate age groups for research on correspondence related to the score of work "for love" or "for money." We now know, for example, that third graders hold opinions about money for jobs that are different from those of their parents and from those of children in Grades 6 or 9. To their parents' surprise, third graders regard it as reasonable to be paid both for washing the car and for making one's bed. Sixth and ninth graders are like their parents. They distinguish between the two jobs (money is OK for the car, but not for the bed: Warton & Goodnow, 1991). The difference appears to be based on the younger children not yet having had the opportunity to hear the parent's distinctions. Although most of them receive some pocket money, few appear to have raised with their parents the issue of extra money for extra jobs. As a result, the statements and practices that make clear what one is paid for and what one is not have not yet been part of their experience.

The information about age differences, it may be noted, does more than tell us where an age difference exists. It also suggests that if one wishes to locate an age range where a parent's position about money has been made very clear to the child, but the child still does not agree, then Grade 3, within Australia at least, is not the optimal choice. Later ages should be more rewarding. That is in fact turning out to be the case in our current research on whether 14- and 18-year olds consider it reasonable that siblings pay one another to take over their jobs, on an occasional or fairly regular basis. This practice many teenagers regard as reasonable while being at the same time very much aware that their parents would hold a different view (Warton & Goodnow, 1990).

SOME CONCEPTUAL ADDITIONS

These four additions are of different kinds. The first (attention to the significance of correspondence) provides a means of bringing affect more strongly into a picture of message delivery and reception. The notion of "vested interests" offers one route into affect, but direct attention to degrees of significance (occasions when correspondence matters or not) promises to do so more fully. Degrees of significance also have the effect of pushing one to ask: Which kinds of message are most likely to be significant?

The second addition, like the first, is concerned with the possibility that parents convey to their children not only the surface content of a message but also information about the kind of response a child should make. In this case, however, the parent presents an array of alternatives from which a child may choose and signals not simply how important it is to accept the parental message but also which alternatives are preferred. The parent may express, for instance, an interest in a child ideally becoming an engineer, lawyer, or physician, preferably not an accountant, rock musician, or film maker, and under no circumstances a taxi-driver, nurse, or secretary. In effect, the message may be in the form of alternatives, with some of these marked "highly preferred," and others tagged as "tolerable," "barely acceptable," or "out of the question." This type of possibility changes not only our view about the nature of a parental message, it also means that we need an expanded view of what "acceptance" may mean. It can no longer, for instance, be thought of only in terms of the yes–no acceptance of a single message. Acceptance may also take the form of a child's selecting, or appropriating, from a range of options that a parent holds out.

The third addition (attention to methods of delivery) is in some ways an expansion again upon the earlier description of the characteristics of parental messages. Where before we had noted such aspects of delivery as the clarity or explicitness of statements, now I would add concern with whether a message is delivered by way of words or practices without words, with drama or in matter-of-fact fashion, by discounting divergent positions or by heavily underlining one's own. In considering all these variations, I would retain a concern with the impact of using various methods of delivery but add questions about why a parent might choose one method of delivery rather than another.

The fourth and final addition has to do with ways of building a more interactive picture than the notion of message transmitted–message noted/accepted may suggest. These interactive steps have to do with considering a more active part for children, with exploring what happens when people become aware of divergence, and with giving attention to interactions not only within the family but also between members of the family and the larger community. As noted earlier, in all sections I give space not only to spelling out the nature of an addition but also to presenting some indications of the kind of research that could follow.

Conceptual Addition 1: The Significance of Correspondence to Parents and Children

In the material covered so far, I have commented several times on the need for content that parents and children care about: content that rules out the possibility that correspondence, or its lack, arises from indifference on one or both sides.

Those comments, however, ignore a question I have come to see as critical: namely, When do parents care about correspondence? Is "ideational compliance" always their goal?

The literature on correspondence, or *intergeneration agreement* as it is often termed, frequently makes it appear that parents (and researchers) care only for correspondence as an outcome. Anything else is a sign of failure on the part of parents. As a parent, however, I may hope to see the next generation hold different values, surpass me, take a different orientation to life, set different goals from those that I or my generation set. In effect, the goal may sometimes be divergence rather than agreement.

How can we explore variations in significance and their bases? As a starting point, I have looked for cases where parents show low or high affect when presented with divergence. This is on the grounds that variations in significance should be linked to variations in the affective response to correspondence or its lack.

Divergence and a Lack of Upset Among Parents. Parents might avoid being upset by divergence by assuring themselves that children will change. Indications that more may be involved come first from Smetana's (1988a, 1988b) analysis of differences in opinion between parents and adolescents. Within her sample were families that reported differences in opinion, without major problems ensuing. Such families led Smetana (1988a) to propose a distinction between "disagreement" and "conflict." She also reported that disagreement without conflict is most likely to arise when both parents and children use sophisticated reasoning processes, even though these may lead to different positions.

One way to account for such a result is to argue that the parents in these families place a higher value on the shared approach to a problem than they do on the difference in the conclusion drawn. Parents have perhaps said to themselves, "Well, X has learned to think well" or "I'm pleased to see X being thoughtful." They are then able to tolerate the difference in the conclusion drawn, regarding the signs of good reasoning as an indication that the child has absorbed the larger message — "Whatever you do, think!"

This notion of messages that "count for more" or are "larger" could also make sense of mothers' comments on the times when they do not push for acceptance of a particular household message, such as the mother who says, "He's terrible about doing anything in the house and his room is a pigsty, but he'll work for hours with his father outside, without being asked, so I don't worry so much about the rest." This mother's statement is reasonable if we assume that the "larger" message in her case has to do with the importance of making a willing contribution, and that the lesser message has to do with this contribution being of a particular kind, namely inside the house. One can well imagine a similar position being taken by the parents of the student activists that Block (1972) studied. Those students diverged from their parents in the causes to which they were committed. They shared with them, however, a quality of commitment: a belief that, whatever the activities in which one became involved, one should not be halfhearted.

Divergence and the Presence of Upset.   To take things a little further, let us take a case where parents (mothers in this instance) do report strong feelings about a difference in viewpoint between themselves and their children. The example comes from mothers' comments when asked about "low moments" in their dealings with children over household tasks (Goodnow & Delaney, 1989).

Many of these low moments came from occasions when children displayed an acceptance of one parental message but not of another. A mother asks a child, for instance, to put away some spread out toys. These are in her way as she attempts to clean up and they need to be cleared from the floor before a family game can begin. The child responds with the argument that "They're not mine," or "I didn't take them out." Now this response does display an awareness, and a use, of one parental message: namely, a message to the effect that "people should clean up after themselves." The same child, however, may happily leave a mother to clean up after him or her, so that at best the acceptance of the rule is partial. More seriously, the child's argument appears to run counter to other maternal messages. It violates, for instance, the message that "you should be willing to do what I ask of you" ("especially when I ask so little"). It violates also the message that the mother's need (the things are in her way) or the needs of others in the family (everyone is now being delayed) should have precedence over whether X on this occasion was the direct cause of the job needing to be done.

Higher- and Lower-order Messages?   Both types of case suggest that parents have "small" and "large" messages, implying the presence of some hierarchical order. The difficulty is that research on parents' ideas has so far given little attention to such differences among messages: attention either to ways of thinking about possible hierarchies or to ways of locating the place of a particular idea in relation to others.

I start with the first problem, asking if there are some distinctions in the literature that would clarify differences among messages in terms of level of generality. As it turns out, there are some available distinctions, offered by Wertheim (1975) in an analysis of family rules, and by Mancuso and Lehrer (1986) in an analysis of mothers' reprimands.

Wertheim (1975) started from a view of families as systems regulated by rules. She labelled some rules as "ground rules" (e.g., "If family member X is out, his job is done by Y."). At a higher level of generality are "meta-rules" (e.g., "How the house runs is everyone's responsibility."), and "meta-meta rules" (e.g., "Your responsibilities are only to your family, you have no obligations to strangers."). Wertheim's (1975) distinction prompts one to wonder whether parents are more likely to be upset by the violation of a higher- or lower-order rule, although this consequence of hierarchical order was not her concern. Her concern lay instead with the effect of a hierarchy being present. A clear hierarchy within rules, she argued (rules consistent with one another and containing an understandable structure) promotes harmony in family relationships. In contrast, one variety of "adaptively deficient systems would . . . be likely to have few rules. These could be expected to be global in character, interconnected loosely or not at all" (p. 294).

The distinctions proposed by Mancuso and Lehrer (1986) have to do with parental reprimands. They referred to the place of a reprimand in a hierarchy of generality. The child who calls his or her sibling "a jerk," for instance, may evoke from the mother a reprimand that contains no elaboration of the underlying rule (e.g., "Stop that") or one that refers to rules of varying degrees of generality (e.g., "That's not the kind of language we use in this house," or "Brothers and sisters should be nice to one another."). The ideal outcome is described as one where the child comes to understand (and presumably agree with) not only the parent's specific commands but also the "implicative structure about the rule" (Mancuso & Lehrer, 1986, p. 75).

The distinctions proposed by both Wertheim (1975) and by Mancuso and

Lehrer (1986) are both based on their sense of what makes good order out of a variety of rules or reprimands. What still needs to be done?

One needed step is the location of ways to determine differences in level. It might be feasible, for instance, to ask parents to place a variety of messages in a hierarchical order or, more naturalistically, to note the times when they use phrases of the kind, "as long as." Parents say, for example, "I don't mind if you don't go to university, as long as you get a decent job," "I don't mind your having sex while you're young as long as you don't get anyone pregnant," "I don't mind what you think to yourself as long as you do not start an argument every time your grandparents come to visit." "As long as" appears to signal the message that has the higher level of generality.

The second step needed is to check whether parental concern is proportional to place in a hierarchy of generality. The notion of such a link is appealing. One word of caution needs to be added, however. When a child is young, I may be content with a simple observance of a ground-rule: "Don't bite other people," or "Put your dirty clothes in the laundry basket." At a later age, I may expect to find some understanding of a larger rule (e.g., "You can't expect other people to pick up after you.") and I may phrase my dissatisfaction in more general terms (e.g., "I wasn't put here on earth to pick up after you."). At a still later age, when I have set my heart on the understanding of a higher-order rule, I may be especially dismayed by "good" behavior for the "wrong" reason, feeling—to adapt the phrase that T. S. Eliot placed in the mouth of Thomas à Becket—that "the greatest treason" is "to do the right thing for the wrong reason." We simply do not know at what ages, in what areas, or on what bases, parents will prefer or will settle for correspondence with a lower-order versus a higher-order rule. We need, in short, research that asks who cares about a lack of correspondence, when they do so, and why.

Two final points finish this section on the significance of correspondence. One has to do with the value of adding attention to parents' attributions for the nonobservance of a cared-about message. Parents, for instance, are known to be more upset when they feel a violation of their expectations is the result of the child's disposition ("just a mean child") than to some more changeable aspect of the child or the situation: the child's capacity to understand, for instance, or the nature of his or her peer group (Dix & Grusec, 1985; Dix, Ruble, Grusec, & Nixon, 1986).

The second has to do with children rather than parents. We would clearly do well to ask children not only about the content of a parent's position but also about its significance to a parent: "How upset would you be if . . . ?" This aspect of knowledge may be more critical to the quality of parent–child relationships than detailed knowledge of parental content in itself. We would, I suggest, also do well to ask children when they themselves are most concerned by a difference in viewpoint. Are children more concerned by differences that can be interpreted as signs of a parent being "old fashioned," or by differences that they see as signs that they are "not understood, not known, not respected"? One should expect both generations to display age effects. I suggested earlier that, as children grow older, parents may be expected to become less happy with good deeds done out of some mechanical routine or fear of punishment rather than out of the hoped-for generosity and awareness of the needs of others. As children grow older, they may also come to expect, from parents, agreement on the "big things"—on the perception of the child as trustworthy, for example—with differences about the "little things" expected to count for far less.

Conceptual Addition 2: A Single Message?

This addition, as noted earlier, is a further look at both the nature of parental messages and at the concept of "acceptance." It seems reasonable to argue first of all that acceptance is not simply present or absent, but occurs in varying degrees. A particular degree of acceptance may in fact be part of a parent's goal. I may, for instance, at times insist that children come to know, and accept, every part of the parental message but settle at other times for a less than total acceptance or even for anything that falls short of complete and open rejection.

I now go beyond degrees of acceptance and propose that parents deliver more than one message, even within the one content area. To use two proverbs as an example, parents may offer both the view that "he who hesitates is lost" and that one should "look before you leap." It is this plurality of views—with one viewpoint being the more prominent at one time, and the alternate at another—that is the essence of Mugny and Carugati's (1985) emphasis on the "plurality" of parents' views about the nature of intelligence. It is possible, for example, to hold at one time two definitions of intelligence (regarding it as both abstract and social in nature) and two hypotheses about its base (regarding it as both genetic and experiential in its source).

As it turns out, plurality is a theme that often occurs in anthropologists' analyses of cultural themes or cultural models (see, for instance, Holland & Quinn, 1987). Goodnow and Collins (1990, chapter 4) describe several of these analyses. I choose one offered by Salzman (1981). In Salzman's phrase, each culture has a "dominant" and a "recessive" message (a "majority" and an "alternative" view) on almost any issue, giving prominence to one but keeping both alive and, within limits, allowing people to choose or endorse one rather than the other. Alternative education, alternative medicine, minority political groups are examples. Some specific messages may be censored or outlawed, but there is a range of positions from which a person may choose and still remain an acceptable member of society. The individual may need to wear the label of "odd" or "eccentric" but he or she remains a member of the group.

Suppose we apply that type of possibility to parents. It quickly becomes apparent that parents also deliver pluralistic messages to their children. They do indicate that some viewpoints are optimal: These are the ones that "I would most like you to hold." They also indicate that some other viewpoints are feasible or tolerable whereas others are "going too far." These last forms of disagreement are those where a parent "draws the line," and treats the difference in position as no longer one of degree but of kind. In Valsiner's (1984) terms, in the interactions between parents and children there are "zones of promoted behavior," "zones of tolerated behavior," and "zones of forbidden behavior."

If we think of parents as holding such views, then our understanding of how correspondence comes about, and of what counts as correspondence, changes. The child now needs to acquire a sense not only of the content of a parental message and of the degree of importance this holds for the parent, but also some sense of the range of alternatives that a parent may accept. The process becomes less one of acceptance–rejection than of choice or appropriation from among the alternatives. The nature of satisfaction with a child's agreement may also change. The "good child" presumably makes a choice that is within the parent's set of tolerable positions. The "difficult" or "dismaying" child may, in contrast, be the one who, in the words of a friend of mine, displays "that adolescent sensitivity for the jugular": that awareness of the least acceptable option, the most obnoxious position, the behavior that truly marks a difference from one's parent and peels off the veneer of permissiveness.

Would such a view of process alter the research we do? To me, it suggests that what we need to know, from parents, is the extent to which parents find a particular opinion or practice optimal, tolerable, or "beyond the pale." We also need to ask whether children make the same distinctions, and are aware of their parents' distinctions. It seems likely, for instance, that they may be more aware of a parent's "bottom line" than of the difference between a parent's most preferred and next-preferred area of agreement. We should, in short, not see the endorsement of a viewpoint as neatly scaled in equal steps from "agree" to "disagree" but as being somewhat grey through the points of agreement and then clear and sharp on what is strongly disagreed with. This is the point of view that Pamela Warton and I are attempting to put into practice in the course of asking about working "for love" or "for money." We are considering, for instance, not simply what parents agree or disagree with, but what they would find optimal, acceptable as a last resort, and unacceptable under any circumstances. (The same type of approach, one should note, is advocated by Joan Grusec for the analysis of parents' views about methods of socialization [personal communication] and that she, Janice Gentle, and I are attempting to put into practice in the course of considering parents' ideas about disciplinary methods.)

Conceptual Addition 3: Methods of Delivery

I now take up an aspect of the bases to correspondence that received relatively little attention in Cashmore and Goodnow's (1985) working model. That model did consider one aspect of delivery: namely, the likelihood that a message had been made explicit (e.g. "be neat") as against needing more to be inferred (e.g., the importance of being "creative").

There are, however, many other ways in which the delivery of messages may vary. We need to consider the variations that occur, the conditions that lead parents to use one method rather than another, and the possible impact of several methods on the occurrence of varying degrees of actual or perceived correspondence.

Let me note at the start that it may not be easy to determine the impact of particular methods. That word of caution comes from a study by John Antill at Macquarie (Antill, 1987, 1988). Antill has been concerned with actual agreement between generations in sex-role attitudes. His study compared the views of parents with the views of their 10- to 12-year-old sons and daughters about appropriate activities for men and women. He also asked about parent's practices, ranging from the kinds of sports or school subjects they encouraged to the way the children's household work is arranged. The underlying concern is with the possibility that children come to agreement with their parents by way of a particular sequence. Parents' ideas about gender give rise to particular practices, and it is from these that children abstract or construct views similar to those of their parents.

To date, however, the burden of the results is that the best predictor of the children's views consists of the parents' views. Adding information about practices does not improve the prediction to any sizeable degree. The result does not invalidate the importance of practices (there may be others that count). It does suggest, however, that it may be no simple task to determine what it is that parents do or say that influences children's views.

Antill's results led me to look more carefully at the ways in which parents convey their positions, asking: What methods of delivery have been noted? Why might variations occur in the way a message is conveyed? And what effects might these variations have? Material relevant to these questions is organized in the following text in terms of distinctions among methods of delivery. For this material, it may be noted, I have—as earlier—taken the term *message* from Shweder (1982) who used it, in the form of "cultural messages," to describe differences among cultures, especially in the domain of moral issues. It is a helpful metaphor, as the implication is quickly drawn of there being a variety of ways in which people "get their message across."

For a sense of the variety of delivery methods that may be used, I take a number of examples from interviews dealing with ideas about household work (interviews for Goodnow, 1987; Goodnow, Bowes, Dawes, Warton, & Taylor, 1991; Goodnow & Delaney, 1989), supplemented by material from some other observations of the way parents mark for their children a parental viewpoint.

Explicit Statements.   Parents may convey a message through explicit statements. A mother may, for example, say "You shouldn't ask for money after you've just done something nice for me; it spoils the favor." Or: "You should talk about money before you do a job, not afterwards." Both statements emerged in answers to a question: "Have you ever had the experience of a child doing something for you and then suggesting that it was worth, say, 20 cents or some other sum?" Two thirds of the mothers of 9- to 11-year-olds said "yes" and reported that they proceeded to explain why this was not a good way to approach the issue (Goodnow, 1987). The statements were highly explicit, but without strong affect. I am led to suggest that such statements occur mainly in response to the violation of a rule that is recognized as complex or unfamiliar, or that may require the spelling out of some new procedural script.

Vague Statements.   The words by which a message is delivered need not be the parent's own. As many a feminist has noted, a message about sex roles is conveyed by every reading primer that starts with "Look, Jane, look; see Dick run." Nor perhaps do they always need to be explicit. Starting from a feeling that explicitness and clarity were always good and useful qualities for a message to have (a residue from a conventional information-processing approach), I have been struck by the frequency with which parents make apparently vague and ambiguous statements. "You should be helpful," "We're a family," "The maid didn't come today," "What do you think you are—a king?," "This is a home, not a hotel": These are just some of the many that I have begun to hear others (and myself) use. Their use seems to have two bases. In some cases, explicit words are not easy to find. It is not easy, for instance, to spell out in words the implications of "We're a family." It is easier to recognize when some boundary has been crossed, and then to say "That's not the way a family works." In other cases, however, there appears to be a preference for ambiguity, perhaps because it leaves room for negotiation or because the parents' main intention is to draw attention to the emotional significance of the situation rather than to the legalistic nature of the rule.

One kind of ambiguous statement that attracts my particular attention takes the form "they're not asked to do much" or "they don't have any work to do, but I do expect them to be willing if they're asked," especially when these statements occur in families where outside coders score the children as doing a fair amount (11% of the sample in the Goodnow & Delaney, 1989, study). Another, less frequent, takes the form of references to whether or not the child "cares." The extreme case is probably the mother who described herself as saying to a child who was reluctant about household jobs: "What can be the matter? Don't you want to be helpful?" Such statements leave what the child is expected to do in a very rubbery state, and—by turning the issue into one of "willingness"—quickly move the reluctant child into a position of guilt in a way that a more straightfor-wardly managerial style on the mother's part would be less likely to do. Discussion turns away from, say, whether and when the job needs to be done and toward the moral area of "helpfulness," "willingness," or "car-ing," where disagreement is a major issue and debate highly unlikely.

Practices Without Words. Even without words, messages may be conveyed by everyday practice. The person served first at the table or given the best pieces of the food clearly has a star place in the family. To step outside our own research, New (1988) described the practice, in the Italian village families she observed, of waking up a sleeping baby when visitors come: no tiptoeing to protect the infant's sleep. This type of practice, along with the subordination of children's activities to family meal times, she saw as helping to mark the place of the child in the family, with the family coming first. Duveen and Lloyd (in press) described in similar terms the way teachers underline the significance of gender by having boys and girls form separate lines for coming into a school, or sit in separate sections of the classroom.

From the area of children's household work, I can draw few clear examples of practices without words. Most of the parents we have inter-viewed seem to find, or to feel, that children require some comment or explanation on the way work should be done. That more may be involved, however, is suggested by a mother who took a "no words" approach to objects such as schoolbags being immediately put away in the child's room and not left elsewhere in the house. "I don't want to argue about it," she said, "I don't want to have to say anything, or explain why it has to be done. I want it all to be just like breathing, to be so automatic that she will feel uncomfortable if she doesn't do it, even if she doesn't know why." Her main technique, one may note, was the use of affect when the norm was violated—horror and stunned surprise when things were out of place: how could this be?—plus her own total observance of everything being in its proper place.

Displays of Affect. One of the striking features of parent–child inter-actions has to do with the way affect provides a way of delivering a message: the look of horror when a child licks the butter knife, the look of embarrassment when he or she asks "private" questions in "public" places. I am particularly intrigued by occasions when mothers make deliberate use of affect, and do so in dramatic fashion. "Every now and then," in the words of one, "I go into my fishwife act" (Goodnow & Warton, 1991). Why would such a technique be used to convey a mother's position about the performance of household jobs? It is as if a message has to be marked not only for its content but also for the importance of its being attended to. The drama marks the information as critical. The mothers, in effect, are making it very clear that a particular behavior is serious, that the mother *does* care, even if the child is not fully clear as to why this should be so. Their behavior is actually nicely in line with D'Andrade's (1981) argument that socializing agents, in any society, pass on not only information about skills but also information about *which* skills or which knowledge must be acquired if one is to be regarded as a competent member of society. Drama, then, may be not so much a way of conveying content as a way of marking the importance of an area. It is, I suspect, particularly likely to be used when, in the midst of a barrage of parental messages, there is some risk of the receiver "turning off" or "tuning out" and needing to be jolted into careful listening. We do not yet know, however, if that is the goal of mothers. Nor do we know about the impact of dramatic displays, although one of these may lie in a child's becoming aware that certain areas are "touchy" long before he or she understands why they are so.

Protection from Outside or Competing Messages.   This method is reminiscent of Furstenberg's (1971) proposal that one of the conditions likely to diminish acceptance of a parental message is the presence of competing information from peers. The method appears in a variety of forms: from monitoring a child's friends ("keeping them away from the wrong kinds of friends") to discounting the value of the messages that cannot be screened out ("What would they know?"). The form we have seen most often used, in the context of household work, consists of arguing for the individuality of every family and the irrelevance of other people's views or practices: "I don't care how things are done in Joey's house or Helen's house – this is the way they are done here."

Some General Possibilities Underlying the Choice of Medium and its Effects.   Are there some general considerations that give rise to the use of one form of delivery rather than another? Of the three I propose, the first has to do with an underlying view of the child. Two views have appeared for centuries in philosophical discussions about ways to produce good citizens. One view regards people as needing mainly to be enlightened. A citizenry given information, provided with a rationale, will act maturely. The other view regards people as needing to be socialized. Rationales may be provided but they need to be accompanied by reinforcement and it is the reinforcement that is primary, providing an affective sense of right and wrong even before a child can understand a verbal rationale.

The second consideration has to do with an underlying view of the competition: that is, of what may militate against one's message being heard or accepted (e.g., the child's disposition, a competing peer group, media images, community practices, etc.).

The third has to do with the goal of any communication. Is the aim one of transmitting information as effectively as possible? Or, as Higgins (1981) argued in his discussions of the "communication game," is there an underlying concern with the nature of the relationship? A parent's concern with the impact of a method of delivery may be with the impact not simply on the child's comprehension or agreement but, and this may be the more important, on the general nature of the relationship. That last consideration is suggested especially by the ways in which adults may cloak their sense of a difference in viewpoints between themselves and a partner. The surface message, for instance, is likely to be in the form "I am fussy," "I have a thing about . . ." rather than "you really are a slob" or "how can you live with things so dirty?" The underlying message—the attribution of "sloppiness" to the other—may still be heard, but there is at least the option of agreement on the surface message and, with that, an avoided risk to the relationship. Perhaps parents are not so careful in their statements to children, but in all relationships there are probably times when a clear mutual knowledge of each other's position is not an asset.

Conceptual Addition 4:
Building an Interactive Model

In studies of transmission, it is easy to give pride of place to effects that flow from parents to children. In principle, we all now accept the view that effects are bidirectional. Children influence parents and parents influence children. Going beyond agreement with the principle, however, building an interactive picture, is a step less easily taken.

A first move toward doing so consists of giving children an active part in the exchange between generations. This could take several forms. One is contained in the proposal (Conceptual Addition 2) that children may choose or appropriate one of the options parents provide rather than simply receiving or rejecting a parental message. Active also is the possibility that it is children who prompt a parent's expression of ideas (rather than only the parent who decides that a child is "ready"). The explicit statements about money that were noted earlier provide a concrete example. Statements about "spoiling the favor" or "asking about money first" were prompted by the child's action (doing a job first and then suggesting that the job was worth a certain amount of money). Still more active, of course, is the situation where a child's expression of a viewpoint different from the parent's leads to a change in the parent's viewpoint or to some compromise between the two. This is the kind of interaction that appears to account, for instance, for Allesandri and Wozniak's (1987) finding of a higher correspondence between the ideas of fathers and adolescents (ideas about the child) than between fathers and preadolescents. Adolescents, it seems, bring their divergent views more forcibly to fathers' attention.

A second move consists of considering the actions of both generations when a divergence of opinions becomes explicit or threatens to surface. (I am bypassing the equally important aspect of the views each generation holds about acceptable ways to monitor for divergence.) This represents a major gap in research. We know very little about the variety of ways in which adults and children respond to a divergence of opinions, or even to the discovery that they hold similar views: not the position all adolescents or young adults hold as their dearest wish. We also know little about the conditions under which people turn a blind eye to a difference, paper over the cracks, propose a compromise, or put extra effort into persuading the other party to change their position. For some responses, we can make a guess. I noted earlier, for instance, one maneuver by adults toward each other, namely an attempt at influence by attributing the source of difference to a flaw in oneself (e.g., "I have a thing about dirty stoves, clean bathrooms, well-ironed shirts") rather than to a flaw in the other. This maneuver appeals to the assumption that people who care for one another should respect each other's foibles or eccentricities, and closes off any discussion about rationality or the actual need for the work to be done. The goal appears to be not so much an immediate agreement in opinions, but agreement on the actions that should now be taken (with perhaps the hope that agreement on opinions or standards will follow). Overall, the topic of response to divergence — and of the understanding that parents and children of various ages have of the meaning of particular responses such as "compromise" — seems both to call for additional attention and to offer a particularly promising research route for the analysis of conflict and for developing an interactive picture of correspondence.

The third and last move proposed has to do with shifting the interactive concern away from the immediate family and toward some inclusion of the larger community. The world outside the family may be invoked by either children or parents in the course of responding to a divergence in viewpoint ("Everyone at school thinks it's OK."; "Nobody in their right mind would hold that view"). The point to which I particularly wish to draw attention has to do with the extent to which there is correspondence between any particular parent or pair of parents and the adult world that surrounds them.

Why should one pay attention to this form of correspondence and to this new set of interactions? A first argument for doing so comes from observations about parents' own interest in the ideas of others. Parents are often interested in what other parents do or say: a phenomenon Pamela Warton and I have noted especially in current interviews about pocket money. This has turned out to be an attractive topic in the recruiting of parents and we have been intrigued to note that parents are less interested in knowing why the research is being done than in knowing other families' practices and principles. The interest appears to be based sometimes on the wish to collect counterarguments (e.g., "You're getting a lot more than some") but more often on a genuine willingness to consider change in the light of what others do and say. Advice about ways to treat one's children may not be readily accepted (a study by Keller, Miranda, & Gauda, 1984 is a rare example of parents' views about advice from other parents), but there is—at least on some issues—an alertness to others' practices and opinions. Just as we have asked about the circumstances under which children are alert to parents' opinions, we now need to ask about the circumstances under which parents are alert to those of friends, neighbors, or "experts."

A second argument for considering a parent's interactions with others outside the family lies in the way these interactions are likely to alter the parent's investment of effort in getting a message across to children. In a world where the child receives constant messages about the importance of gender differences, for instance, I may see no need to add my own voice to any special extent. The "cumulative voice" of the community, to coin a phrase, may be counted upon to convey the message. I may, in fact, use my own voice as a way of moderating the impact of the community's message. When the outside world cannot be counted upon to deliver an acceptable message, however, then parental effort seems likely to be increased. In the words of one mother, "I wouldn't go on and on about the importance of being decent if we lived in a better neighborhood, but around here you really have to work at it." "Working at it" in this case has a clear link to the parent's perception of there being little chance of her viewpoint being echoed and reinforced by others.

The third and final argument has to do with our understanding of the outcomes, for children, of parents' agreements with others. Deal, Halverson, and Wampler (1989), for instance, reported that a child's level of adjustment is predicted not only by agreement between a father and mother but also by the extent to which these parents are in agreement with the views held by the majority of the sample. The processes by which this outcome comes about are not yet clear, but the data certainly direct attention to interactions between parents and the community. Directing attention to the same issue are also data on the accuracy with which children perceive parents' opinions. In the Cashmore and Goodnow (1985) study, accuracy was higher among the children of immigrants than among the locally born, apparently because the former have the greater opportunity to observe a difference between one's own parents and other members of the community. In effect, correspondence and divergence within the family may not be all that matters.

CONCLUDING COMMENTS

I have proposed a number of methodological considerations that influence the way one proceeds in exploring similarities and differences across generations. More broadly, I have also suggested several conceptual additions. It is on the latter that, in these concluding comments, I concentrate.

I do so by returning to the original "two-process model" (Cashmore & Goodnow, 1985), with its emphasis on accounting for how a child may come to hold views like or unlike those of its parents. From the original model, I argue for keeping the notion of two processes: the perception of the other's position, and the acceptance or rejection of it.

The first rounding out would then be to what is perceived. In addition to the surface content of a parent's message, I have proposed, children come to perceive the significance of a message to a parent, together with the presence of tolerated degrees of acceptance, options, limits, bottom lines, and possible alternatives. Moreover, children seldom stop at the perception of a particular message. They also perceive implications to a message, with many of these having to do with the disposition of the parent and the state of the parent–child relationship. They base both the specific and the general perceptions not only on what is officially said or done but also on a parent's method of delivery, method of monitoring, and ways of responding to the presence or to the lack of correspondence.

The second rounding out is to the notion of acceptance/rejection. The child's response, I now propose, needs to be considered in terms that are less yes–no in quality (terms that suggest that "compliance" is the issue) and more in terms of negotiating: choosing among options and appropriating some while rejecting others, aiming for a tolerable level of divergence while avoiding confrontation over a parent's "absolute bottom line," or perhaps even seeking that bottom line so that divergence will come out into the open. Influencing that response, I suggest, are perceptions not only of the parent (including the parent's power or capacity to influence one's views) but also comparisons of the parent with others: comparisons that take into account, for instance, the degree of respect that others give to a parent's views or the degree to which a parent seems out of line with the views that others hold.

Both forms of rounding out suggest a number of new research questions that one might direct toward children and toward a comparison of their perceptions and positions with those of parents'. There is no need, however, to restrict one's focus to children. I now propose, for instance, increased attention to the conditions that influence parents' ratings of some messages as more significant than others, parents' views about the nature and importance of the opinions of other adults, and parents' choices of particular methods of delivery, methods of monitoring for divergence, and ways of responding to the signs of an imminent or present divergence in viewpoints. As such research expansions take place, I argue, we shall move toward a more complete understanding of cross-generation similarity and divergence than is currently the case.

ACKNOWLEDGMENTS

My knowledge on this topic began with Judith Cashmore's selection of it as a PhD project. Since the PhD, her research focus has shifted to the study of children's experiences in court, covering both children's understanding and adults' perceptions of children's competence. I have continued to benefit, however, from her comments on the general topic of inter generation agreement. Her comments on this draft, together with those from a Macquarie research group (alphabetically, Jennifer Bowes, Jackie Crisp, Rosemary Leonard, Laurel Maddison, and Pamela Warton) are warmly acknowledged. Financial support for the preparation of the chapter came from the Australia Research Council.

REFERENCES

Acock, J. K. (1985). Parents and their children: The study of intergenerational influence. *Sociology and Social Research, 68,* 151–171.

Allesandri, S. M., & Wozniak, R. H. (1987). Parental beliefs about the personality of their children and children's awareness of those beliefs: A developmental and family constellations study. *Child Development, 58,* 316–323.

Antill, J. K. (1987). Parents' beliefs and values about sex roles, sex differences, and sexuality: Their sources and implications. In P. Shaver & C. Hendrick (Eds.), *Sex and gender: Review of personality and social psychology* (Vol. 7, pp. 294–328), Beverly Hills CA: Sage.

Antill, J. K. (1988, September). *Sex-role orientations in parents and children.* Paper presented at meetings of the Australian Psychological Society, Hobart, Tasmania.

Bengston, V. L., & Kuypers, J. A. (1971). Generational difference and the development stake. *Aging and Human Development, 2,* 249–260.

Block, J. H. (1972). Generational continuity and discontinuity in the understanding of societal rejection. *Journal of Personality and Social Psychology, 22,* 333–345.

Cashmore, J. A., & Goodnow, J. J. (1985). Parent–child agreement on attributional beliefs. *International Journal of Behavioural Development, 9,* 191–204.

Collins, W. A. (in press). Parent–child relationships in the transition to adolescence: Continuity and change in interaction, affect, and cognition. In R. Montemayor, G. Adams, & T. Gullotta (Eds.), *Advances in adolescent development* (Vol. 2). Beverly Hills CA: Sage.

Cronbach, L. J. (1955). Processes affecting scores on "understanding of others" and "assumed similarity." *Psychological Bulletin, 52,* 177–193.

D'Andrade, R. G. (1981). The cultural part of cognition. *Cognitive Science, 5,* 179–195.

Deal, J. E., Halverson, C. F., & Wampler, K. F. (1989). Parental agreement on child-rearing orientations: Relations to parental, marital, family, and child characteristics. *Child Development, 60,* 1025–1034.

Dix, T. H., & Grusec, J. (1985). Parent attribution processes in the socialization of children. In I. E. Sigel (Ed.), *Parental belief systems: The psychological consequences for children* (pp. 201–233). Hillsdale, NJ: Lawrence Erlbaum Associates.

Dix, T. H., Ruble, D., Grusec, J., & Nixon, S. (1986). Social cognition in parents: Inferential and affective reactions to children of three age levels. *Child Development, 57,* 879–894.

Duveen, G. M., & Lloyd, B. (in press). An ethnographic approach to social representations. In G. Breakwell & D. Cantor (Eds.), *Empirical approaches to the study of social representations.* Oxford: Oxford University Press.

Furstenberg, F. F., Jr. (1971). The transmission of mobility orientation in the family. *Social Forces, 49,* 595–603.

Goodnow, J. J. (1987, April). *The distributive justice of work.* Paper presented at meetings of Society for Research in Child Development, Baltimore.

Goodnow, J. J. (1990). Using sociology to extend psychological accounts of cognitive development. *Human Development, 33,* 81–107.

Goodnow, J. J., Bowes, J., Dawes, L., Warton, P. M., & Taylor, A. (1991). Would you ask someone else to do this task? Parents' and children's views of household requests. *Developmental Psychology, 27,* 818–828.

Goodnow, J. J., & Collins, W. A. (1990). *Development according to parents. The nature, sources, and consequences of parents' ideas.* Hillsdale, NJ: Lawrence Erlbaum Associates.

Goodnow, J. J., & Delaney, S. (1989). Children's household work: Task differences, styles of assignment, and links to family relationships. *Journal of Applied Developmental Psychology, 10,* 209–226.

Goodnow, J. J., & Warton, P. M. (1991). The social bases of social cognition: Interactions about work and their implications. *Merrill-Palmer Quarterly, 37,* 27–58.

Higgins, E. T. (1981). The "communication game": Implications for social cognition and persuasion. In E. T. Higgins, C. P. Herman, & M. P. Zanna (Eds.), *Social cognition: The Ontario Symposium* (Vol. 1, pp. 343–392). Hillsdale, NJ: Lawrence Erlbaum Associates.

Holland, D., & Quinn, N. (Eds.). (1987). *Cultural models in language and thought.* Cambridge: Cambridge University Press.

Holloway, S. D., & Hess, R. D. (1982). Causal explanations for school performance: Contrasts between mothers and children. *Journal of Applied Developmental Psychology, 3,* 319–327.

Keller, H., Miranda, D., & Gauda, G. (1984). The naive theory of the infant and some maternal attitudes: A two-country study. *Journal of Cross-Cultural Psychology, 15,* 165–179.

Mancuso, J. C., & Lehrer, R. (1986). Cognitive processes during reactions to rule violation. In

R. D. Ashmore & D. M. Brodzinsky (Eds.), *Thinking about the family: Views of parents and children* (pp. 67–93). Hillsdale, NJ: Lawrence Erlbaum Associates.

Mugny, C., & Carugati, F. (1985). *L'intelligence au pluriel: Les répresentations sociales de l'intelligence et de son developpment.* Coussett: Editions Delval.

New, R. S. (1988). Parental goals and Italian infant care. In R. A. Levine, P. M. Miller, & M. M. West (Eds.), *Parental behavior in diverse societies* (pp. 51–64). San Francisco: Jossey-Bass.

Newson, J., & Newson, E. (1976). *Seven years old in an urban environment.* London: Allen & Unwin.

Salzman, P. C. (1981). Culture as enhabilmentis. In L. Holey & M. Stuchlik (Eds.), *The structure of folk models* (pp. 223–256). London: Academic Press.

Shweder, R. A. (1982). Beyond self-constructed knowledge: The study of culture and morality. *Merrill-Palmer Quarterly, 28,* 41–69.

Smetana, J. G. (1988a). Adolescents' and parents' conceptions of parental authority. *Child Development, 59,* 321–335.

Smetana, J. (1988b). Concepts of self and social convention: Adolescents' and parents' reasoning about hypothetical and actual family conflicts. In M. Gunnar & W. A. Collins (Eds.), *Minnesota Symposia on child development* (Vol. 21, pp. 79–122). Hillsdale, NJ: Lawrence Erlbaum Associates.

Valsiner, J. (1984). Construction of the zone of proximal development in adult–child joint action: The socialization of meals. In B. Rogoff & J. Wertsch (Eds.), *Children's learning in the zone of proximal development* (pp. 65–76). San Francisco: Jossey-Bass.

Warton, P. M., & Goodnow, J. J. (1991). The nature of responsibility: Children's understanding of "your job." *Child Development, 62,* 156–165.

Warton, P., & Goodnow, J. J. (1990, July). *For love or for money: Practices and ideologies related to household tasks.* Paper presented at meetings of the Australian Developmental Society, Perth, Western Australia.

Wertheim, E. S. (1975). The science and typology of family systems: Further theoretical and practical considerations. *Family Process, 14,* 285–309.

13

Parenting on Behalf of the Child: Empathic Goals in the Regulation of Responsive Parenting

Theodore Dix
University of Texas at Austin

Effective parents are sensitive and responsive to children. Although conceptions of parental sensitivity and responsiveness vary, these qualities recur in one guise or another in most analyses of why some children develop more favorably than others. An impressive volume of research has demonstrated the importance of responsive parenting to child development. Compared with children of unresponsive parents, children of responsive parents develop better socially. They form more secure attachments with their parents (Ainsworth, Bleher, Waters, & Wall, 1978; Belsky, Rovine, & Taylor, 1984; Crockenberg, 1981; Smith & Pederson, 1988), are more cooperative with adults (Maccoby & Martin, 1983; Parpal & Maccoby, 1985), are more socially attentive and engaging (Brazelton & Tronick, 1980; Field, 1977), and display greater general social competence (Bakeman & Brown, 1980; Baumrind, 1989; Clarke-Stewart, 1973). Children of responsive parents also develop better cognitively. They explore and engage objects better (Ainsworth, 1979; Goldberg & Easterbrooks, 1984; Jennings, Harmon, Morgan, Gaiter, & Yarrow, 1979), are more active, persistent, and competent during problem solving (Skinner, 1986; Sroufe, 1979; Sroufe & Waters, 1977), and have greater general cognitive ability (Bakeman & Brown, 1980; Baumrind, 1989; Bournstein, 1989; Lyons-Ruth, Connell, & Zoll, 1989). They are more advanced than other children in language development (Clarke-Stewart, 1973) and more mature in their play (Jennings et al., 1979). Lack of responsiveness, furthermore, characterizes parenting in a variety of dysfunctional families from which children are known to be at risk for serious cognitive and behavioral problems (Lyons-Ruth, Connell, & Zoll, 1989; Crittenden & Ainsworth, 1989).

Given these findings, it is surprising that so little is known about why responsive parenting occurs and about the skills and processes that comprise it. Why are some parents more responsive than others, and why are parents more responsive on some occasions than on others? The thesis of this chapter is that responsive parenting reflects parental empathy. It occurs because parents develop affectional ties that make outcomes related to children's well-being critically important to them. When children's immediate well-being is important, parents organize interactions with children so that empathic goals and concerns are achieved; that is, they seek outcomes that children want. This has cognitive consequences: Seeking outcomes that children want causes parents to try to understand whether children are pleased or displeased with events, to infer why children are reacting as they are, to figure out which outcomes children want, and to assess how outcomes desired by children can be obtained. Empathic goals also have affective consequences: They make parents more likely to experience empathic emotion. When seeking outcomes that children want, parents are likely to become joyous, sad, concerned, and irritated, not simply when events affect them directly, but when events affect their children. These empathic emotions motivate responsive parenting. They urge parents to act on behalf of the child. This chapter examines the potentially critical role empathic goals play in organizing sensitive, responsive parenting and in promoting the healthy development of children.

GOAL REGULATION
IN PARENT–CHILD INTERACTION

Psychologists have long recognized that the goals and purposes that people bring to social interaction organize behavior and psychological functioning (Hull, 1943; Lewin, 1935; Miller, Galanter, & Pribram, 1960; Tolman, 1932; see Pervin, 1989). As a result, goal constructs have been central to diverse theories of behavior (e.g., Atkinson, 1964; Bandura, 1986; Carver & Scheier, 1985; Kuhl & Beckmann, 1985; Mischel, 1973; Rotter, 1954; Schank & Abelson, 1977). A number of models of parenting fall within the goal-regulation tradition (Dix, 1991; Emmerich, 1969; Kuczynski, 1984; Maccoby & Martin, 1983). These models emphasize processes such as those depicted in Fig. 13.1. In this simple, four-step, goal-regulation model, it is assumed that (a) implicitly or explicitly, parents are attempting to achieve particular *goals* or outcomes during interactions with children (Step 1); (b) they select and initiate *plans* or sequences of behaviors that they think will achieve those goals (Step 2); (c) they continually *appraise* events so that they have sufficient understanding and control to achieve their goals (Step 3); and (d) they experience positive emotion when their goals are promoted and

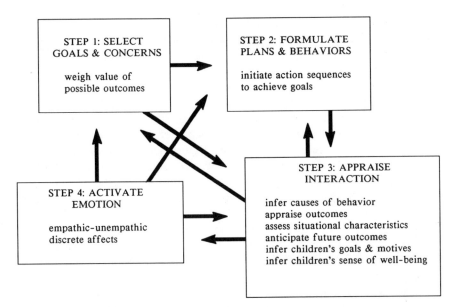

FIG. 13.1   A goal-regulation model of parenting.

negative emotion when their goals are blocked (Step 4). These emotions then promote maintenance or change in parents' goals, plans, and behaviors. Thus, goals are central organizing constructs that are presumed to guide cognition, affect, and behavior. They influence how parents process information, which emotions they experience, and which courses of action they consider (see Pervin, 1989; Sorrentino & Higgins, 1986).

An Example of Goal-Regulation in Parenting

Consider a simple goal-regulation analysis of a father's interaction with his baby daughter. The father begins with an empathic goal, *helping the baby have fun* (Step 1), and a plan to achieve that goal, *bouncing the baby on his knee* (Step 2). He monitors the baby's eye contact, facial expressions, and motor activity to determine whether his plan is indeed pleasureable for the baby (Step 3). When the baby shows signs of disinterest, the father infers that his goal is not being accomplished (Step 3). He feels slightly disappointed (Step 4) and adjusts his plan in the hope that his goal may yet be achieved (Step 2). When the baby begins to cry, the father feels concern (Step 4) and changes his goal to, *remove the baby's discomfort* (Step 1). He initiates a new plan—perhaps, picking the baby up or feeding her (Step 2)—and appraises its effects (Step 3). When she stops crying as he begins to feed her, he feels relief (Step 4) and, therefore, completes his feeding plan (Step

2), while continuing to monitor the baby's vocal, facial, and bodily movements for signs of discomfort or inattention (Step 3).

The speed and thoroughness with which the baby's needs are met depend on which goal the father is attempting to promote. Had he begun with the unempathic goal, *to converse with my friend while watching the baby,* he would have devoted less time and attention to monitoring the baby's vocal and facial cues and would have felt emotions that depended more on the flow of conversation than on the baby's behavior. When the baby began to cry, he might have selected those plans that would not simply pacify her, but that would divert the least time and attention from his conversation. Goal-regulation models imply that daily parenting entails countless scenarios like this, each involving goals and concerns that parents want to promote, plans of action that parents think will promote them, emotional and behavioral adjustments that reflect appraisals of whether plans are successful, and changes in goals and plans as interactions proceed. Because goals define the primary criteria of value in an interaction, they determine that aspect of the interaction that parents are attempting to understand and control, whether and how strongly parents react emotionally, and toward what ends parents direct their subsequent behavior. Whether the goal-regulation process leads to interactions that promote child development depends on whether children's wants and needs are adequately represented in parental goal structures (Dix, 1991). To promote child development, parents must organize interactions with children around goals that, when achieved, secure outcomes beneficial to children.

Types of Parental Goals and Concerns: Self, Empathic, and Socialization Goals

What goals and concerns do parents attempt to promote during interactions with children? Although there is little data with which to answer this question, few can doubt that parents' goals and concerns are numerous, diverse, and multifaceted. They include inclinations toward and away from stimuli that are inherently pleasant or aversive, such as infants' smiles and cries. They reflect general values about how children should act, for example, that children should be honest, independent, considerate, and hard working. Parents' goals also reflect their desires to complete countless concrete plans of action, such as to finish the shopping, to get children ready for school, to relax and read a book, or to have children finish their school work. Which of these diverse goals or concerns parents are attempting to promote at any moment controls significant aspects of parenting.

An important dimension of parents' goals is whether they are intended to benefit parents or children. Although in practice this can be difficult to determine, in many interactions outcomes valued by parents are clearly not valued by children. Parents often seek *self-oriented goals:* They seek to clean the house, converse with friends, read books, or get children to bed early, because achieving these goals makes parents' lives easier or more pleasant. There is, of course, nothing wrong with this. Making money, developing friendships, and achieving countless other self-oriented goals must occur if parents' lives and the lives of their children are to run smoothly. Yet, if they are to be effective as parents, they cannot orient their interactions with children exclusively around self-oriented goals. They also must meet *child-oriented goals:* They must teach, comfort, discipline, and play with children, because these acts, although at times difficult for parents, are necessary if children are to be happy and to develop favorably. To some degree, organizing daily behavior and activity around children's wants and needs is simply part and parcel of being a parent. Children are immature and dependent on parents. They are often unable to meet their own wants and needs, they have difficulty delaying gratification of their desires, and they often are unable to modify their wishes in ways that take parents' wants and needs into account. Yet, the extent to which parents adopt self- versus child-oriented goals probably differs considerably from situation to situation and from parent to parent.

Two specific types of child-oriented goals may have different effects on how interactions with children are organized. First, goals can be child-oriented because they are *intended to achieve outcomes that children want.* I call these *empathic goals* because the parent is attempting to understand the child's perspective and to facilitate outcomes the child will experience as desirable. Interactions focused on play, comfort, and teaching often reflect empathic goals. Other child-oriented goals may *benefit children, but will not necessarily please them.* I call these *socialization goals.* Parents often impose on children rules or expectations that they think will promote children's learning or development. For the child's benefit, parents require children to help, share, and act politely even when children do not want to act in these ways. Interactions involving parental discipline and control often reflect socialization goals. Whereas empathic goals are intended to improve the child's lot as the child experiences it, socialization goals are intended to improve the child's lot as the parent experiences it. Neither self, empathic, nor socialization goals is necessarily preferable; rather, at different times, each must be achieved.

ANTICIPATING OUTCOMES AND COORDINATING INTERACTIONS: THE VALUING PROCESS IN GOAL SELECTION

Daily parenting can be characterized as successive attempts by parents to select and promote countless self, empathic, and socialization goals. At any moment this requires that parents make decisions about which outcomes to seek and which plans of action to select (Steps 1 & 2). These decisions are complex. Parents must coordinate their goals and plans with the goals and plans of their children. They must weigh the importance of various wants and needs that both they and their children have. Then, to promote selected goals, they must elicit behavior from children that enables their plans to succeed. To be on time for work, parents must get children fed and dressed; to converse with friends, they must be sure children can play quietly and independently. Because parents and children each control important outcomes that accrue to the other, their interactions are said to be characterized by interdependence (see Kelley, 1979; Kelley & Thibaut, 1978). If parents and children are to attain their interaction goals harmoniously, they must continually coordinate their plans and behaviors so that outcomes satisfactory to both can be cooperatively achieved (Dix, 1991).

Figure 13.2 depicts how the co-occurrence of particular parent and child behavior controls the outcomes each might obtain in one situation (see Kelley, 1979, and Kelley & Thibaut, 1978, for a thorough analysis of interdependence matrices). The figure represents one simplified set of interdependencies for a situation in which a boy pleads with his mother to stay up past his normal bedtime so that he can watch a special television program. For our purposes, the mother is seen as having two primary options: She can acquiesce or she can refuse. The child in turn can respond by being either cooperative or resistive. The numbers within each cell represent *outcome values:* the value for parent (P) and child (C) of the outcomes that would result were the behaviors corresponding to that particular cell to co-occur. The matrix suggests that for this particular parent and child, were the parent to refuse and the child to resist, the result

Parent Behavior

		Acquiesce	Refuse
	Cooperate	P = -1 C = +3	P = +2 C = -2
Child Behavior	Resist	Null Set	P = -3 C = -3

FIG. 13.2   Sample matrix of outcome values when a child asks for something from a parent.

would be undesirable to both (-6 for the dyad). Were the parent to refuse and the child to cooperate, on the other hand, the result would be on balance favorable for the parent ($+2$, the child does what the parent wants), but unfavorable for the child (-2, the child gets the parents' approval, but cannot watch the television program). Were the parent to acquiesce and the child to cooperate, the result would be favorable for the child ($+3$, he can stay up to watch the show), but unfavorable for the parent (-1, pleasure at seeing the child's happiness, but displeasure at setting a bad precedent and at having an additional hour of child-care responsibilities). This analysis suggests a basis for parents' goal selection, Step 1 of the model: Parents select goals on the basis of the value they anticipate, both to themselves and their children, from the outcomes possible in an interaction.

Conceptualizing parent–child interaction in terms of outcome values and interdependencies highlights the importance of compatibility between the goals and plans of parents and the goals and plans of their children (Dix, 1991; Maccoby & Martin, 1983). If parents adopt goals and behaviors that are compatible with those of their children, coordination of interaction is straightforward. Parents and children act in consort to achieve mutually desired outcomes. If the goals of parents and children are incompatible, however, coordination is more difficult. Incompatibility means that the behaviors that will achieve the parents' goal will result in failure to achieve the child's goal. Such incompatibility is an essential component of conflict. As Peterson (1983) wrote, conflict is, *"an interpersonal process that occurs whenever the actions of one person interfere with the actions of another"* (p. 365). Because incompatibility causes both parent and child to anticipate or experience goal frustration, it increases negative affect and often induces attempts by parents and children to influence the other to adopt, or at least not undermine, their ongoing plan. If the outcomes that children seek are valued highly and are incompatible with those that parents seek, children often will resist parents' attempts to channel interactions toward parental goals. Thus, interdependence theory characterizes the valuing process underlying selection of interaction goals and emphasizes that parents must coordinate their goals and behaviors with those of their children.

There ought to be close correspondence between parents' interaction goals and the outcome values they hold during particular interactions. Parents ought to select interaction goals likely to obtain outcomes of high positive value and to prevent outcomes of high negative value. To do this, parents must weigh the importance of the self, empathic, and socialization goals relevant to the situation at hand. Faced with a boy who wants to stay up late to watch television, for example, a parent might have outcome values for self-oriented concerns that are negative (e.g., parent loses relaxation time), outcome values for socialization concerns that are negative (e.g., bedtimes rules and routines are disrupted), and outcome values for empathic concerns that are positive (e.g., the parent values the child's joy at getting to watch the program). Thus, final outcome values such as those in Fig. 13.2 are actually composites of multiple outcome values reflecting multiple parental concerns. Interactions can be relevant simultaneously to different self, empathic, and socialization goals, as well as to multiple self goals or to multiple socialization goals. Thus, to select interaction goals, parents assess how potential acts will affect the multiple concerns they have in the interaction. They need not do this deliberately or consciously; rather, the valuing process underlying their behavior is probably intuitive and automatic in most instances.

EMPATHIC GOALS, VALUES, AND EMOTIONS

This valuing process, and particularly the degree to which it is empathic, may determine whether parents are responsive to children. In terms of interaction matrices, empathy reflects the value parents place on outcomes, not to themselves, but to their children as experienced by their children. In other words, *empathic outcome values are values that parents place on achieving outcomes that their children experience as desirable.* Given that higher outcome values should correspond with stronger emotional reactions when those outcomes are promoted or blocked, empathic parents will experience stronger emotions than will unempathic parents when outcomes important to their children occur. Because empathic emotions motivate parents to improve the child's sense of well-being, they may be critical to responsive parenting.

This analysis is consistent with research on empathy outside the domain of parenting. Empathy is frequently defined as the tendency to experience events from another's point of view, that is, to feel sympathetic emotions when significant outcomes occur to others (Barnett, 1987; Batson, Duncan, Ackerman, Buckey, & Birch, 1981; Eisenberg & Strayer, 1987; Feshbach, 1987; Hoffman, 1982; Stotland, 1969). That empathic emotion promotes responsive social behavior is a view widely endorsed by psychologists (see Eisenberg & Mussen, 1989; Hoffman, 1982; Batson et al., 1981). Empathic processes are thought to have evolved in humans specifically because the interpersonal ties and altruistic behaviors they promote increase the viability of the species. It has even been argued that empathic abilities first appeared in humans to promote parenting: "the capacity to empathize has evolved from the capacity of mammals to provide nurturant parenting for their young (MacLean, 1982; Panksepp, 1986). Animals who empathize are more likely to be sensitive to their offsprings' needs and thus insure their survival (Eisenberg & Mussen, 1989, p. 38)." Considerable research outside the domain of parent–child interaction has shown that, whether conceptualized as an enduring or momentary variable, empathic affect promotes prosocial behavior. In a recent review, Eisenberg and Mussen concluded that "empathy and sympathetic concern are critical factors mediating prosocial actions (Eisenberg & Mussen, 1989, p. 133)."

It is surprising, therefore, that empathy has been examined only rarely by scholars interested in child rearing. Despite empathy's importance to a number of theoretical accounts of effective parenting (see Feshbach, 1987; Goldstein & Michaels, 1985), neither parents' understanding of their children's feelings and perspectives nor parents' emotional responses to those feelings and perspectives has been widely studied empirically. What research there is suggests that, when assessed as a stable individual difference variable, empathy does predict variables that are related to investment in children, affective sensitivity to children's behavior, and parenting behavior related to responsiveness. When watching videotapes of infants crying and smiling, for example, women high in empathy become more physiologically aroused, report stronger emotions, and think crying infants are in greater need than do women low in empathy (Wessenfeld, Whitman, & Malatesta, 1984). Thus, highly empathic women appear to be more sensitive to affective signals from infants than are unempathic women. Although empathy has not been related specifically to the responsiveness of parental behavior, mothers who are high in empathy do interact with their children during laboratory tasks in ways one would expect to be associated with responsive parenting. Empathic mothers are more involved, more positive, and less negative with their children than are unempathic mothers (Feshbach, 1987). Low maternal empathy, furthermore, is associated with dysfunctional parenting. Mothers from abusive and high-risk families score lower on measures of empathy than do mothers from normal families (Feshbach, 1987; Letourneau, 1981). In fact, there is some evidence that empathy mediates the impact of stress on abusive parenting. High levels of stress are associated with abusive maternal behavior only among mothers who score low on measures of empathy (Letourneau, 1981). Finally, maternal empathy predicts favorable outcomes in children. Unempathic mothers are more likely than empathic mothers to have children who are low in self-control and who exhibit internalizing and externalizing behavior problems (Feshbach, 1987). Thus, although research has not examined relations between empathy and responsive parenting directly, related evidence shows that maternal empathy predicts desirable parenting and favorable child behavior.

Figure 13.3 displays the outcome values an empathic and an unempathic mother might hold were her son to ask to stay up past his bedtime. Upon seeing her son's joy at being given permission to watch the show, the empathic mother would experience empathic pleasure. All other things

		Parent Behavior: Unempathic			Parent Behavior: Empathic	
		Acquiesce	Refuse		Acquiesce	Refuse
	Cooperate	P = 0 C = +3	P = +2 C = -2		P = +2 C = +3	P = +1 C = -2
Child Behavior	Resist	Null Set	P = -3 C = -3		Null Set	P = -4 C = -3

FIG. 13.3   Sample outcome values of an empathic and an unempathic parent.

being equal, her outcome values within cells corresponding to parental acquiescence would be more positive (+2) than the outcome values of an unempathic (0) mother. Similarly, the empathic mother would feel empathic displeasure at her son's disappointment over being refused permission to watch the show. All other things being equal, she would have more negative values in parental refusal cells (+1, −4) than would an unempathic mother (+2, −3), for whom the child's disappointment is relatively unimportant. Thus, empathic outcome values push parents toward children's wishes. They make the cell *parental refusal–child resist* more aversive for empathic parents and the cell *parent acquiesce–child cooperate* more positive. Outcome matrices make graphic the role that empathic concerns play in parenting. Adopting empathic concerns promotes compatibility between parents' goals or concerns and those of their children. It reduces parent–child conflict and promotes cooperative courses of action. Empathic concerns also insure that children's wants are influential in interactions in which children often have limited power. Although parents who are frequently empathic will not always seek outcomes that please their children, they nonetheless should give weight to their children's reactions more than do unempathic parents. Their parenting, in other words, should depend to a greater extent on the effects outcomes are thought to have on their children's subjective well-being. *All other things being equal,* the parent who has empathic goals and emotions is more likely to be motivated to do as the child wants.

All other things, however, are rarely equal, and in practice even highly empathic parents often do not prefer actions that please their children. This is true for two primary reasons. First, most parents recognize that to behave exclusively to actualize children's goals leads to parenting that is painfully shortsighted. Children lack the knowledge and competence to establish goals that will maximize their own well-being and development. As a result, parents often adopt self or socialization goals that conflict with acting to please children. In many interactions children's concerns are simply less important than parents' self or socialization concerns. At times when parents place high value on self or socialization goals that conflict with the goals of children, even empathic parents prefer courses of action that do not please their children. In fact, it can be because they so strongly value their children's well-being that parents apply considerable pressure to resistant children to insure that socialization goals are met.

Second, even empathic parents act contrary to children's wishes when they disagree with children, not about which outcomes should be sought, but about which outcomes are likely to occur. Consider a 4-year-old girl and her father deciding whether she should ride a roller coaster at an amusement park. The father refuses because he infers that the girl will become frightened; he is acting to avoid his daughter's fear, an empathic goal. His daughter insists, however, that she will not become afraid, that she will enjoy it. Here parent and child are in conflict not because their goals conflict — both are acting to promote the daughter's well-being — but because they disagree on which outcome will occur if a given plan is followed. Many parent–child conflicts are of this kind. Parents forbid children to engage in many activities because they fear that their children will get hurt or will become bored, upset, or overly excited — fears that children often do not share. These are conflicts because parents anticipate outcomes that have not occurred and, thus, that need not be outcomes children also anticipate.

Because the outcomes implied by self, empathic, and socialization goals need not differ, it will frequently be difficult to determine which goal parents in fact are seeking. Interdependence theory emphasizes that in close relationships outcomes beneficial for one partner are often beneficial for the other as well. Furthermore, empathic and socialization goals are often compatible; children often want outcomes that are also good for their well-being and development. Yet, there are also times when differing goal orientations lead to important differences in how parents feel and act, and it is then that the relative value to parents of self- and child-outcomes imply differences in the responsiveness of parent behavior. By definition, these are times when different outcomes satisfy different goal orientations; when there is conflict among what children want, what parents want for children, and what parents want for themselves. At these times the sensitivity and responsiveness of parents is most clearly observed and the importance of empathy most clearly seen. Will the parent be sensitive to children's wants and needs when effort or sacrifice is required? In these situations empathic parents, who place high value on their child's concerns, ought to be more responsive to the child's position in the interaction than are unempathic parents.

SITUATIONAL DETERMINANTS OF SELF,
EMPATHIC, AND SOCIALIZATION GOALS

So far I have discussed goal orientations as individual difference factors. This is how goal and value variables have typically been conceptualized in the child-rearing literature (Holden & Edwards, 1989; Schaefer & Bell, 1958; Stolz, 1967; see also Read & Miller, 1989). Yet, the outcomes parents value differ, not only from parent to parent, but from situation to situation (see Kuczynski, 1984). Situations differ in the degree to which outcomes likely to occur in those situations are both *relevant* and *important* to self, empathic, and socialization goals. Consider three situations: (a) A mother leaves her 2-year-old son at a day-care center, (b) a 5-year-old boy is defiant with his mother, and (c) a 7-year-old girl becomes excited when she succeeds at riding a bicycle by herself. Leaving children at child-care centers usually has negative value for parents' empathic concerns (i.e., they feel empathic distress for the child), negative value as well for parents' socialization concerns (i.e., they think the child would be better raised at home), but positive value for parents' self-concerns (i.e., parents' economic viability). This act, thus, is relevant to all three types of goals and is common because parents think its implications for self-concerns are more important than its implications for child concerns. In contrast, the 7-year-old's learning to ride a bicycle is irrelevant to most self-concerns, but has positive value for both empathic concerns (i.e., parents are joyous for her) and socialization concerns (e.g., bicycle riding facilitates children's motor development, independence, and self-esteem). Children's defiance, on the other hand, is highly relevant and important to socialization goals; it violates a strongly held value that children be respectful. Defiance is less relevant to self concerns (although it can interfere with immediate parental plans) and is irrelevant to empathic concerns (although parents could sympathize with the child's anger or frustration). Of course, outcome values vary widely from parent to parent and, as a result, lead to goals that differ widely across parents in some situations. In many situations, however, parents adopt the same goals because the outcomes possible in those situations have clear implications for widely shared values.

An important hypothesis concerning the situational determinants of parents' goals and outcome values is that self-outcomes increase in value and child outcomes decrease in value the more stress parents are experiencing (Dix, 1991; Forehand, McCombs, & Brody, 1987; Maccoby & Martin, 1983). Figure 13.4 depicts interdependence matrices that reflect this hypothesis for our target situation, a boy asking his mother for permission to stay up past his bedtime. These matrices suggests that during goal selection (Step 1) stressed parents value outcomes in the cell *parent*

	Parent Behavior: Normal		Parent Behavior: Under Stress	
	Acquiesce	Refuse	Acquiesce	Refuse
Cooperate	P = 0 C = +3	P = +2 C = -2	P = +2 C = +3	P = +1 C = -2
Resist	Null Set	P = -3 C = -3	Null Set	P = -4 C = -3

Child Behavior (row label, left of Cooperate/Resist)

FIG. 13.4   Changes in outcome values that might occur with stress.

acquiesce–child cooperate less than do nonstressed parents because stressed parents, for example, place less value on the child outcome *getting to watch the show* and more value on the parent outcome *having an additional hour of child-care responsibility.* In the cell *parent refuse–child resist,* the stressed parent may experience the resulting discord as more aversive (self-outcome) than does the nonstressed parent, although the stressed parent may also experience the child's disappointment as less negative (child outcome). The effects of other situational variables can also be conceptualized in terms of changes in the value parents place on potential outcomes. Had the child stayed up past his bedtime on the two previous nights, for example, the parent's value for the socialization goal *enforce clear rules about bedtime* might increase, and the parent's value for the empathic goal *permit activities that bring my child joy* might decrease.

This conceptualization suggests how an important problem within traditional research on parenting can be addressed. Because child-rearing values are usually thought to be stable and general, they are typically assumed to operate in the same way in all situations. Yet, data have been difficult to reconcile with this view (see Holden & Edwards, 1989). Parents who endorse particular child-rearing values often fail to behave in accord with them. Mothers often show no clear value-consistent responding from one moment to the next, but, instead, vary their behavior markedly from situation to situation and from child to child (Bell & Chapman, 1986; Grusec & Kuczynski, 1980). By recognizing that parents bring multiple concerns to most situations and that specific situations have different potentials for satisfying these concerns, one no longer expects parents' behavior to reflect any specific belief or value in any given situation. Rather, some values will take priority in some situations, others in other situations. Whether a parent's behavior corresponds to a particular child-rearing value ought to depend on whether parents believe the outcomes possible in a situation both are relevant to that value and are more important to that value than to other relevant values.

GOALS IN THE REGULATION
OF ONGOING PARENTING PROCESSES

Exactly how will activation of interaction goals, particularly empathic goals, influence parenting? Although almost no research has addressed this question (although see Kuczynski, 1984), findings from experimental and social psychology suggest that goals organize a number of basic adaptive processes.

Goals in the Regulation of Parent Cognition

First, goals and values orient and organize parent cognition. The literature on goals and social cognition (see Pervin, 1989; Srull & Wyer, 1986; Trzebinski, 1989; Zukier, 1986) suggests that goals sensitize people to goal-relevant information and lead them to allocate processing time and attention to goal-relevant inference. Goals provide frames of reference that determine how action sequences are comprehended and how social information is organized, stored, and retrieved from memory. This work suggests that the appraisal component of ongoing behavioral regulation (Step 3) may be guided by the goals parents' seek during interactions with children.

Self, empathic, and socialization goals may sensitize parents to different information and activate different types of inference. When empathic goals are important, parent cognition is oriented toward the experiences of children more than when empathic goals are unimportant. To promote empathic goals, parents need to understand the child's subjective reactions to events. They need to monitor children's facial, vocal, and postural cues; infer children's thoughts, feelings, and reactions; and anticipate the impact that possible turns of events might have on the child's sense of well-being. This cognitive attunement to the impact events are having on children may regulate important aspects of parent cognition. First, it may alter monitoring and attention. Strong empathic concerns may lead parents to scan environments for factors likely to affect children's well-being and may increase their sensitivity to children's expressions of affect, to children's bids for attention, and to other information indicative of children's sense of well-being. Second, empathic goals may influence how parents define events. A child's whining may be seen as an expression of discomfort when empathic goals are primary, but as an interruption when self-goals are primary. Third, empathic goals may determine when and about what inferences are made. Attribution research suggests that parents will search for the causes of behavior primarily when behavior violates active goals and expectations or when parents think they lack sufficient control to achieve their purposes (Pittman & D'Agostino, 1989; Wong & Weiner, 1981). Thus, when empathic goals are active, parents will initiate attributional processing primarily when events influence children's sense of well-being, that is, when children express discomfort or are unexpectedly pleased by a turn of events. Fourth, once processing is activated, empathic goals may bias judgment toward particular conclusions. Because children's thoughts, feelings, and points of view are highly accessible when empathic goals are active, parents at these times may make more benign attributions for children's behavior (Dix & Grusec, 1985; Dix, Reinhold, & Zambarano, 1990). Research suggests that, when people perceive events from the perspective of another, they make attributions for others' behavior that are similar to the attributions others make for their own behavior (Storms, 1973); that is, parents' attributions for negative child behavior will be more situational and less dispositional when empathic concerns are strong than when they are weak. Thus, compared with unempathic parents, empathic parents may attribute children's undesirable behavior more to frustrations, disappointments, and limitations that reflect the situation than to negative dispositions in the child (see Dix, Ruble, Grusec, & Nixon, 1986; Dix, Ruble, & Zambarano, 1989). Placing high value on self and socialization goals should induce comparable biases; that is, self-goals should orient cognition toward information and inference relevant to self-concerns, and socialization goals should orient cognition toward information and inference relevant to socialization goals.

Consider again a father interacting with his baby daughter. When his goal is empathic, *to make the baby happy,* he is attuned to cues indicative of the baby's pleasure or displeasure and insensitive to the conversation of others in the room. When the baby's crying violates his active goal, he appraises why the baby is crying. In part because empathic concerns are strong, he infers that crying reflects the baby's discomfort and is not something the baby intends or controls. He, therefore, feels empathic concern and wishes to remove the baby's discomfort. He invokes a new goal, *to get the baby to stop crying,* and based on his analysis of why the baby is crying, he initiates a series of plans until one is successful. All of the cognitive components of this simple action sequence—from monitoring and attention to causal appraisal and response evaluation—depend on the father's goals and his plans for achieving them. Were he to place low value on the baby's comfort or had he been late for an important appointment, he might have experienced the baby's crying as interference rather than discomfort, might have attributed it to the baby's difficult and overly sensitive temperament, might therefore have become angry rather than empathically concerned, and might have activated behavior less oriented toward alleviating the baby's discomfort than toward getting to his appointment on time. Note that the cognition of parents with empathic goals is biased toward information needed for sensitive, responsive caregiving. Empathic goals sensitize parents to signs of children's pleasure or distress, activate anticipation of outcomes likely to affect children's sense of well-being, and orient appraisal toward determining the causes of children's pleasure and pain.

Goals in the Regulation of Parental Affect

Goals and the plans invoked to achieve them may regulate not only cognition but emotion (Step 4). People experience positive emotions when they infer that events are supporting their interaction goals and negative emotions when they infer that events are blocking their interaction goals (Berscheid, 1983; Dix, 1991; Frijda, 1986; Izard, 1984; Mandler, 1984; see Goodnow, 1988). Emotions then promote maintenance or realignment of interactions so that goals can be achieved. Which emotion is aroused depends on appraisals of how and why plans are being promoted or blocked and on parents' beliefs about whether they can control subsequent outcomes (Bugental & Cortez, 1988; Bugental & Shennum, 1984; Dix et al., 1986; Dix, Ruble, & Zambarano, 1989; see Frijda, 1986; Ortony, Clore, & Collins, 1988; Roseman, 1984). Anger occurs, for example, when parents infer that children have disrupted parental plans intentionally, anxiety occurs when parents infer that uncontrollable harm is about to befall them or their children, appreciation occurs when parents infer that children have sacrificed to promote parental plans. Emotion is strong when events affect goals or plans that are highly valued, that reflect the investment of considerable time and energy, and that allow for few alternate plans for achieving them (Srull & Wyer, 1986). Thus, parents' emotions with children reflect appraisals of how children's behavior is affecting ongoing goals and plans, of why children are engaging in that behavior, and of parents' ability to influence children so that parents' goals are promoted.

Parents who differ in the values they place on self, empathic, and socialization goals will experience different emotions with children. When parents place high value on empathic goals, their emotions will reflect how events are influencing their children's sense of well-being. When parents place high value on socialization goals, their emotions will reflect the extent to which children's behavior conforms to the socialization rule at issue. When parents place high value on self-goals, their emotions will reflect the extent to which children's behavior promotes or blocks their active self-goal. Thus, some emotions will be common when parents adopt one goal, but uncommon when parents adopt another. For example, sympathy is fundamentally empathic. It occurs only when empathic goals for children have been violated. Anger at children, on the other hand, is almost always unempathic. It occurs when parents infer that children are intentionally blocking self or socialization goals. Anxiety, joy, and other emotions occur in each goal orientation, although their causes, objects, and implications for action depend on which goal is primary. Potential harm to children elicits anxiety that is child-directed and that mobilizes action to prevent or minimize that harm; being late for an important appointment elicits anxiety that is self-directed and that mobilizes action to get children ready to go quickly. In fact, the same child behavior can elicit different emotions if performed when different goal orientations are in force. If her active goal is empathic, a mother will feel joy when her delighted son is loud and rambunctious; if her active goal is *to finish a report before lunch,* she may instead become irritated.

Because empathic emotion activates and organizes attempts to promote children's wants and needs, it is critical to sensitive, responsive parenting. Without strong empathic affect, parents may respond with insufficient intensity or coherence when children need parents' help, may show poor involvement in activities that are primarily child-oriented, and may fail to develop diverse and effective action sequences for handling children's wants and needs (Dix, 1991). Given the importance of positive affect for eliciting children's attention and enthusiasm (Sroufe, Schork, Motti, Lawroski, & LaFreniere, 1984), parents who fail to experience empathic pleasure may have difficulty interacting with children in ways children find compelling. Parents described in the literature as emotionally unavailable, disengaged, or neglectful may experience empathic emotion with children that is insufficient to organize effective caregiving (Dix, 1991).

Empathic emotion may be a key element of parenting dimensions that are favorable for child development. Of the six dimensions Maccoby (1980b) emphasized in her review of the literature, four appear to have a significant empathic component:

1. Almost by definition, parental *warmth* involves empathy. It is frequently the expression of joy when children are pleased and the expression of concern when children are upset. In fact, some scholars consider warmth a component of responsive parenting (e.g., Goldberg & Easterbrooks, 1984; Lyons-Ruth, Connell, & Zoll, 1989).

2. *Reasoning and communication* involve empathy because they are the means parents use to learn about the child's position in an interaction and to communicate their own. Were the child's wishes unimportant, parents' could act unilaterally; reasoning would often be unnecessary.

3. Empathic affect may also play a role in parental *restrictiveness.* Parents often restrict children for empathic reasons, that is, because they anticipate harm to the child. Although such restrictiveness is often neces-

sary, highly anxious parents, as if they are overly empathic, fear adverse consequences in activities that are safe, even beneficial, for children, and, thus, they constrain children unnecessarily. Parents also restrict children because they lack empathy. They place greater value on their own desires for quiet, order, or minimal effort than on the child's desires for play, stimulation, and exploration. Or they place greater value on cleanliness, obedience, and other socialization goals than on the child's wishes in an interaction. Thus, in interactions that involve restrictiveness, the value that parents place on the child's wishes in the interaction (i.e., empathic outcome values) is critical.

4. Finally, empathic concern may defuse parents' impulses to use arbitrary, harsh, and *punitive discipline* (Feshbach, 1989). Anticipating or perceiving children's frustration and pain can induce powerful empathic emotions that interfere with the self-oriented emotions that can motivate harsh and arbitrary discipline.

In short, because they direct parenting toward goals children seek, empathic emotions minimize parent–child conflict, promote cooperative decision making, determine whether parents restrict children, and interfere with destructive emotions and discipline practices.

Goals in the Regulation of Parents' Response Evaluation and Selection

Empathic goals may bias not only parents' appraisals and emotions at input, but also their selection of responses at output. A basic assumption of goal-regulation approaches is that people choose actions that they think will achieve their goals (Step 2). The goals that parents seek may influence the repertoire of response options they activate and the decision rules they use to decide which option is preferred. To date, the action sequences parents associate with particular goals and the rules that govern their evaluation and selection have not been studied.

Activating self, empathic, and socialization goals may lead parents to consider different parenting responses. Empathic goals may increase sensitive, responsive parenting by channeling response generation and selection toward behaviors likely to increase the child's sense of well-being. Consider a mother driving to a wedding with an agitated son who is urging her to stop the car for a break. If she values the empathic goal *to help my child feel less agitated,* she is likely to consider actions that will calm or interest a bored child. She might consider stopping the car for a rest, giving the child a toy, playing a game, singing a song, expressing sympathy for the child's plight, or some combination of these responses. On the other hand, if she places high value on the self-goal *to stop my child's whining,* and low value on outcomes desired by the child, she might consider a different, although overlapping, set of actions. Although she still might consider stopping the car or giving the child a toy, she now might consider as well threatening punishment or using other techniques that would achieve the self goal *to stop the child's whining,* but not the empathic goal *to help the child feel less agitated.* The high value empathic parents place on outcomes children desire should make them less willing than unempathic parents to achieve self outcomes at high cost to the child. Empathic parents will search for responses that handle children's concerns to some degree even if self goals take priority. The mother in our earlier example might allow the child to stay up late to watch a special television show — which meets the parent's empathic goal — but make an agreement that the child complete all bedtime preparations prior to the show — which minimizes adverse effects on the parent's self and socialization goals. Problem solving of this kind is likely to lead to response generation and selection that is responsive to children's concerns and therefore that elicits children's dissatisfaction and resistance less often.

EMPATHY AND DYSFUNCTIONAL PARENT-CHILD RELATIONSHIPS

Over time parents and children develop mutual expectations and means for handling their interdependencies that in healthy relationships enable the outcomes they receive as a dyad to exceed those they could obtain alone (cf. Kelley, 1979; Kelley & Thibaut, 1978). Healthy relationships require empathy. They require that people feel emotion when significant outcomes occur to their partner, that they act on those emotions to benefit their partner, and that they expect such benefit to be returned when future outcomes of importance require the cooperation of their partner. Their partner does not exploit their weaknesses, does not act to harm them intentionally, often acts voluntarily to benefit them, and reciprocates compromise and fairness. Over time, the partner's welfare and time together are valuable in themselves. The outcome matrices that characterize interactions in such relationships would contain high empathic outcome values. Each partner values outcomes that benefit the other, chooses joint courses of action that consider both their own and their partner's wishes, and often values joint activities more than solitary ones.

Relationships develop differently in dysfunctional parent-child dyads, and empathic processes may be an important component of that difference (Dix, 1991; Feshbach, 1989). Aversive interactions may gradually erode the extent to which parents feel joy at their children's happiness and concern at their children's distress. In terms of outcome matrices, parents and children in distressed relationships probably do not place high value on outcomes important to their partners and therefore experience less empathic affect. In the interaction depicted in Fig. 13.2, the child's joy at being allowed to watch a special television show or dejection at being refused would be less important to parents in distressed relationships. This would result in disparity in the outcome values of parents and children for particular joint courses of action, conflict therefore in the goals each seeks, and a low probability that either will act to support the goals of the other. Each learns that their wishes exert little control over their partner, and they come to expect, therefore, that their partner will not act on their behalf. Thus, both must use coercive means to achieve their goals. From the perspective of interdependence theory, one would say that distressed partners use fewer joint outcome transformations (Kelley, 1979): They maximize joint outcomes less and individual outcomes more than do partners in healthy relationships. Furthermore, because their interactions are frequently acrimonious, they develop lower positive and higher negative values for any joint course of action, causing them to avoid joint activity. If their resentment becomes chronic and intense, they might even come to value outcomes that hurt, frustrate, or disappoint the other. These individualistic, competitive goal and value orientations would influence how information is processed, which emotions are experienced, and which courses of action are considered. Thus, distressed relationships may be characterized by an absence of the mutual empathic concern that normally promotes trust, compromise, coordination of behavior, and enjoyment of joint activity.

More than other conceptions of dysfunctional family process (e.g., Patterson, 1982), this view stresses the breakdown of positive bonds and interactions. Although dysfunctional family interactions certainly involve anger and dysphoria, the erosion of empathy and affection may also be critical (see Burgess & Conger, 1978; Lorber, Felton, & Reid, 1984; Wolfe, 1985). In an interesting critique of Patterson's coercion theory, Maccoby (1980a) argued that, although the theory explains well how parents stabilize and increase coercive behavior in children, it fails to account adequately for why some children are coercive in the first place. Although coercive behavior is common among even normal children early in life, as Patterson (1982) emphasized, it is usually replaced by more mature forms of influence as language and other social skills emerge. Parental empathy may promote this development. When parents are empathic, children's wishes are anticipated. Children often feel no need to influence parents. When influence is necessary, direct requests, positive signs of interest, and other prosocial forms of influence work. In contrast, when parents place low value on the outcomes that children seek, coercion can be the only effective form of influence. Coercion may emerge, not simply because it works, but because unempathic parents make it necessary. From such parents children fail to learn social role-taking skills, expectations that others reciprocate cooperative behavior, and the value of cooperative motives, dispositions, and actions. Altering coercive relationships may require instilling behaviors that benefit the other, attributions and expectations that promote cooperative possibilities (cf. Dix & Lochman, 1990; Larrance & Twentyman, 1983), and coordinated interactions that each member finds rewarding.

EMPATHIC GOALS AND VALUES: THE PSYCHOLOGICAL CONSEQUENCES FOR CHILDREN

What are the effects on children of parents adopting or failing to adopt empathic goals? I suggest five areas in which empathic parenting might have important consequences for children.

First, by steering interactions toward outcomes that children want, parental empathy minimizes parent–child conflict. It increases the likelihood that parents and children will act cooperatively to seek compatible goals. Although conflict is not always bad for children, when chronic and intense it is associated with child abuse, with noncompliance and aggression, and with other unfavorable developmental outcomes (Emery, 1982; Maccoby, 1980b; Radke-Yarrow, Richters, & Wilson, 1988). Empathy may not only reduce the occurrence of conflict, it may promote conflict resolution when conflict occurs. Because empathic parents value their children's sense of well-being, they resolve conflict in ways that consider children's interests. In contrast, when parents do not value outcomes children desire, they may dominate children, resolving conflicts by maximizing self, but not child, outcomes. There may be costs to controlling children in this way, including anger and resentment in children, low motivation to comply with parents, and acquisition by children of coercive forms of influence.

Second, parental empathy often channels parenting toward meeting the legitimate needs of children. Although frequently parents must seek outcomes children do not seek, few doubt that effective parenting requires that parents support many of children's ongoing concerns. Healthy development requires that children have opportunities for diverse forms of play, for interaction with other children, for involvement in neighborhood and community activities, for comfort and support from adults, and for innummerable other experiences that children actively seek from one moment to the next. Parents who place low value on the outcomes children seek often will undermine the legitimate strivings that constitute children's self-socialization. In contrast, when caregivers have a strong interest in promoting outcomes children seek, children get the assistance, resources, and emotional support that healthy development requires.

Third, empathic processes build parent–child relationships that are fulfilling and beneficial to children's development. Children develop trust, affection, and a receptivity to parental influence when parents understand and show concern for their interests, sacrifice to promote those interests, and handle innummerable daily interactions so that children's interests are promoted (Maccoby & Martin, 1983). Parenting that is responsive to children's desires may motivate children to seek parental approval, may minimize children's resentment and reactance during interactions involving parental influence, and therefore may enable empathic parents to have greater influence with less assertion of power than do unempathic parents. Although few studies have examined empathy's role in the formation of parent–child bonds, empathy is probably one component of the sensitive infant care associated with secure parent–infant attachment (Ainsworth et al., 1978) and of the warm, communicative parenting associated with the development of social and cognitive competence in early childhood (Maccoby, 1980b).

Fourth, because empathy is fundamental to sensitive social relationships, empathic parenting teaches children invaluable social skills (Fabes, Eisenberg, & Miller, 1990). During interactions with empathic parents, children see valued adults inferring and giving weight to others' points of view and negotiating plans of action that benefit all members of the interaction. Although imposing rules for cooperative behavior also contributes to the development of social competence, parents cannot simply impose interpersonal sensitivity; surely they must practice it (cf. Maccoby, 1980b; Rosenhan, Fredericks, & Burrows, 1968).

Fifth, empathic parenting facilitates the development in children of a sense of competence and control. Many researchers have emphasized that children need to feel that they can control events if they are to initiate and persevere in social and cognitive activities (Maccoby, 1980b). Parental empathy promotes this sense of control because it leads parents to help children control events that children cannot control by themselves. Children of empathic parents thus should achieve outcomes they seek at higher rates than do children of unempathic parents. Of course, interactions that promote parents' empathic goals are not the only interactions that contribute to children's sense of competence. Socialization goals also structure children's environments so that children can predict and control events (Maccoby, 1980b). Yet, when children are young, their control over events is mediated so often by parents that it is difficult to see how their sense of competence could emerge without parents working on their behalf.

It is important to stress that, although empathic care giving usually benefits children, this is not always the case. Were parents to act invariably as their children want, their parenting would be shortsighted and indulgent. Parents who put trivial child needs above important parent needs undermine their own well-being and thus, indirectly, their child's as well. Furthermore, to socialize sharing, helping, and other prosocial behaviors, parents must impose rules that require children to act in ways they do not want to act. Research demonstrates that parents who exert little control and make few demands for mature behavior have children low in social and cognitive competence (Baumrind, 1971; Maccoby, 1980b). Parents who are unable to endure children's protestations so that reasonable rules can be enforced have children who are noncompliant and aggressive (Patterson, 1982). Effective parenting requires a balance between what children want (empathic goals), what children need (socialization goals), and what parents want and need (self goals).

SUMMARY AND CONCLUSIONS

This paper develops a goal-regulation model of parenting with emphasis on how empathic goals influence parenting processes. I have proposed that parents' interaction goals reflect an intuitive valuing process that weighs the value that outcomes possible in an interaction have for multiple parental concerns. Empathic goals reflect the value parents place on outcomes children want and may be critical to responsive parenting. Empathic goals lead to information processing oriented toward understanding events from the child's perspective; to emotional reactions that are tied to outcomes children receive, rather than to outcomes parents receive; and, to generation and selection of parenting behaviors aimed at improving the child's sense of well-being. Empathic cognition, emotion, and response evaluation are primary components of responsive parenting because they are the means whereby, despite children's limited power and competence, their needs get represented and effectively handled. Parental empathy results in children's wants and needs being potent determinants of parenting processes and behavior.

Although the role of empathic parenting in children's development is at this point speculative, the proposals advanced here are consistent with considerable research in social and developmental psychology. They point to the importance of understanding how and why parents and children come to value outcomes that occur to the other and of exactly how the goals that those values imply influence ongoing social processes. They highlight as well the expectations that parents and children develop of each other and the cooperative and interdependent nature of their interactions. To operate effectively, parents and children must act to benefit the other. They must come both to experience the value of their relationship and to value the joint outcomes it promotes. If parental competence is to be understood, knowledge is needed of the conditions that promote empathy and that lead parents and children to cooperate for their mutual benefit. Knowledge is needed as well of the conditions that erode empathy and that lead parents and children to consistently undermine the concerns of the other.

REFERENCES

Ainsworth, M. D. S. (1979). Infant–mother attachment. *American Psychologist, 34,* 932–937.

Ainsworth, M. D. S., Blehar, M. C., Waters, E., & Wall, S. (1978). *Patterns of attachment.* Hillsdale, NJ: Lawrence Erlbaum Associates.

Atkinson, J. W. (1964). *An introduction to motivation.* Princeton, NJ: Van Nostrand.

Bakeman, R., & Brown, J. V. (1980). Early interaction: Consequences for social and mental development. *Child Development, 51,* 437–447.

Bandura, A. (1986). *Social foundations of thought and action: A social cognitive theory.* Englewood Cliffs, NJ: Prentice-Hall.

Barnett, M. A. (1987). Empathy and related responses in children. In N. Eisenberg & J. Strayer (Eds.), *Empathy and its development* (pp. 146–162). New York: Cambridge University Press.

Batson, C. D., Duncan, B. D., Ackerman, P. Buckey, T., & Birch, K. (1981). Is empathic emotion a source of altruistic motivation? *Journal of Personality and Social Psychology, 40,* 290–302.

Baumrind, D. (1971). Current patterns of parental authority. *Developmental Psychology Monographs, 4* (1, Pt. 2).

Baumrind, D. (1989). Rearing competent children. In W. Damon (Ed.), *Child development today and tomorrow* (pp. 349–378). San Francisco: Jossey Bass.

Bell, R. Q., & Chapman, M. (1986). Child effects in studies using experimental or brief longitudinal approaches to socialization. *Developmental Psychology, 22,* 595–603.

Belsky, J., Rovine, M., & Taylor, D. G. (1984). The Pennsylvania infant and family development project, III: The origins of individual differences in infant–mother attachment. *Child Development, 55,* 706–717.

Berscheid, E. (1983). Emotion. In H. H. Kelley, E. Berscheid, A. Christensen, J. H. Harvey, T. L. Huston, G. Levinger, E. McClintock, L. A. Peplau, & D. A. Peterson (Eds.), *Close relationships* (pp. 110–168). New York: W. H. Freeman.

Bornstein, M. H. (Ed.). (1989). *New Directions for Child Development: Vol. 43. Maternal responsiveness: Characteristics and consequences.* San Francisco: Jossey-Bass.

Brazelton, T. B., & Tronick, E. (1980). Preverbal communication between mothers and infants. In D. R. Olson (Ed.), *The social foundation of language and thought* (pp. 299–315). New York: Norton.

Bugental, D. B., & Shennum, W. A. (1984). "Difficult" children as elicitors and targets of adult communication patterns: An attributional–behavioral transactional analysis. *Monographs of the Society for Research in Child Development, 49,* Serial No. 205.

Bugental, D. B., & Cortez, V. L. (1988). Physiological reactivity to responsive and unresponsive children as moderated by perceived control. *Child Development, 59,* 686–693.

Burgess, R. L., & Conger, R. D. (1978). Family interaction in abusive, normal, and neglectful families. *Child Development, 49,* 1163–1173.

Carver, C. S., & Scheier, M. F. (1985). A control system approach to the regulation of action. In J. Kuhl & J. Beckmann (Eds.), *Action control* (pp. 237–265). New York: Springer-Verlag.

Clarke-Stewart, K. A. (1973). Interactions between mothers and their young children: Characteristics and consequences. *Monographs of the Society for Research in Child Development, 38* (6–7, Serial No. 153).

Crittenden, P. M., & Ainsworth, M. D. S. (1989). Child maltreatment and attachment theory.

In D. Cicchetti & V. Carlson (Eds.), *Child maltreatment* (pp. 432–463). New York: Cambridge University Press.

Crockenberg, S. (1981). Infant irritability, maternal responsiveness, and social support influences on the security of mother–infant attachment. *Child Development, 52,* 857–865.

Dix, T. (1991). The affective organization of parenting: Adaptive and maladaptive processes. *Psychological Bulletin, 110,* 3–25.

Dix, T., & Grusec, J. E. (1985). Parent attribution processes in the socialization of children. In I. E. Sigel (Ed.), *Parental belief systems: The psychological consequences for children* (pp. 201–234). Hillsdale, NJ: Lawrence Erlbaum Associates.

Dix, T., & Lochman, J. E. (1990). Social cognition and negative reactions to children: A comparison of mothers of aggressive and nonaggressive boys. *Journal of Social and Clinical Psychology, 8,* 418–438.

Dix, T., Reinhold, D. P., & Zambarano, R. J. (1990). Mothers' judgment in moments of anger. *Merrill Palmer Quarterly, 36,* 465–486.

Dix, T., Ruble, D. N., Grusec, J. E., & Nixon, S. (1986). Social cognition in parents: Inferential and affective reactions to children of three age levels. *Child Development, 57,* 879–894.

Dix, T., Ruble, D. N., & Zambarano, R. J. (1989). Mothers' implicit theories of discipline: Child effects, parent effects, and the attribution process. *Child Development, 60,* 1373–1391.

Eisenberg, N., & Mussen, P. H. (1989). *The roots of prosocial behavior in children.* New York: Cambridge University Press.

Eisenberg, N., & Strayer, J. (1987). Critical issues in the study of empathy. In N. Eisenberg & J. Strayer (Eds.), *Empathy and its development* (pp. 3–13). New York: Cambridge University Press.

Emery, R. E. (1982). Interparental conflict and the children of discord and divorce. *Psychological Bulletin, 92,* 310–330.

Emmerich, W. (1969). The parental role: A functional–cognitive approach. *Monographs of the Society for Research in Child Development, 34*(8, Serial No. 132).

Fabes, R. A., Eisenberg, N., & Miller, P. A. (1990). Maternal correlates of children's vicarious emotional responsiveness. *Developmental Psychology, 26,* 639–648.

Feshbach, N. D. (1987). Parental empathy and child adjustment/maladjustment. In N. Eisenberg & J. Strayer (Eds.), *Empathy and its development* (pp. 271–291). New York: Cambridge University Press.

Feshbach, N. D. (1989). The construct of empathy and the phenomena of physical maltreatment of children. In D. Cicchetti & V. Carlson (Eds.), *Child maltreatment* (pp. 349–373). New York: Cambridge University Press.

Field, T. (1977). Effects of early separation, interactive deficits, and experimental manipulations on infant–mother face-to-face interaction. *Child Development, 48,* 763–771.

Forehand, R., McCombs, A., & Brody, G. H. (1987). The relationship between parental depressive mood states and child functioning. *Advances in Behavioral Research and Therapy, 9,* 1–20.

Frijda, N. H. (1986). *The emotions.* New York: Cambridge University Press.

Goldberg, W. A., & Easterbrooks, M. A. (1984). Role of marital quality in toddler development. *Developmental Psychology, 20,* 504–514.

Goldstein, A. P., & Michaels, G. Y. (1985). *Empathy: Development, training, and consequences.* Hillsdale, NJ: Lawrence Erlbaum Associates.

Goodnow, J. J. (1988). Parents' ideas, actions and feelings: Models and methods from developmental and social psychology. *Child Development, 59,* 286–320.

Grusec, J. E., & Kuczynski, L. (1980). Direction of effect in socialization: A comparison of the parents versus the child's behavior as determinants of discipline techniques. *Developmental Psychology, 16,* 1–9.

Holden, G. W., & Edwards, L. A. (1989). Parental attitudes toward child rearing: Instruments, issues, and implications. *Psychological Bulletin, 106,* 29–58.

Hoffman, M. L. (1982). Development of prosocial motivation: Empathy and guilt. In N. Eisenberg (Ed.), *The development of prosocial behavior* (pp. 281–313). New York: Academic Press.

Hull, C. L. (1943). *Principles of behavior.* New York: Appleton-Century-Crofts.

Izard, C. E. (1984). Emotion–cognition relationships and human development. In C. E. Izard, J. Kagan, & R. B. Zajonc (Eds.), *Emotions, cognition, and behavior* (pp. 17–37). Cambridge: Cambridge University Press.

Jennings, K. D., Harmon, R. J., Morgan, G. A., Gaiter, J. L., & Yarrow, L. J. (1979). Exploratory play as an index of mastery motivation. *Developmental Psychology, 15,* 386–394.

Kelley, H. H. (1979). *Personal relationships: Their structures and processes.* Hillsdale, NJ: Lawrence Erlbaum Associates.

Kelley, H. H., & Thibaut, J. W. (1978). *Interpersonal relations: A theory of interdependence.* New York: Wiley-Interscience.

Kuczynski, L. (1984). Socialization goals and mother–child interaction: Strategies for long-term and short-term compliance. *Developmental Psychology, 20,* 1061–1073.

Kuhl, J., & Beckmann, J. (1985). *Action control: From cognition to behavior.* New York: Springer-Verlag.

Larrance, D. T., & Twentyman, C. T. (1983). Maternal attributions and child abuse. *Journal of Abnormal Psychology, 92,* 449–457.

Letourneau, C. (1981). Empathy and stress: How they affect parental aggression. *Social Work, 26,* 383–389.

Lewin, K. (1935). *A dynamic theory of personality.* New York: McGraw-Hill.

Lorber, R., Felton, D. K., & Reid, J. B. (1984). A social learning approach to the reduction of coercive processes in child abusive families: A molecular analysis. *Advances in Behavior Research and Therapy, 6,* 29–45.

Lyons-Ruth, K., Connell, D. B., & Zoll, D. (1989). Patterns of maternal behavior among infants at risk for abuse. In D. Cicchetti & V. Carlson (Eds.), *Child maltreatment* (pp. 464–493). New York: Cambridge University Press.

MacLean, P. D. (1982, May). *Evolutionary brain roots of family, play, and the isolation call.* Paper presented at the annual meeting of the American Psychiatric Association, Toronto.

Maccoby, E. E. (1980a). Commentary and reply. In G. R. Patterson, Mothers: The unacknowledged victims. *Monographs of the Society for Research in Child Development, 45,* (5, Serial No. 186).

Maccoby, E. E. (1980b). *Social development: Psychological growth in the parent–child relationship.* New York: Harcourt, Brace, Jovanovich.

Maccoby, E. E., & Martin J. A. (1983). Socialization in the context of the family: Parent–child interaction. In P. H. Mussen (Series Ed.) & E. M. Hetherington (Vol. Ed.), *Handbook of child psychology: Vol. 4. Socialization, personality, and social development* (4th ed., pp. 1–101). New York: Wiley.

Mandler, G. (1984). *Mind and body: The psychology of emotions and stress.* New York: W. W. Norton.

Miller, G. A., Galanter, E., & Pribram, K. H. (1960). *Plans and the structure of behavior.* New York: Holt & Company.

Mischel, W. (1973) Toward a cognitive social learning reconceptualization of personality. *Psychological Review, 80,* 252–283.

Ortony, A., Clore, G. L., & Collins, A. (1988). *The cognitive structure of emotions.* New York: Cambridge University Press.

Panksepp, J. (1986). The psychobiology of prosocial behaviors: Separation distress, play, and altruism. In C. Zahn-Waxler, E. M. Cummings, & R. Iannotti (Eds.), *Altruism and aggression: Biological and social origins* (pp. 19–57). New York: Cambridge University Press.

Parpal, M., & Maccoby, E. E. (1985). Maternal responsiveness and subsequent child compliance. *Child Development, 56,* 1326–1334.

Patterson, G. R. (1982). *Coercive family process.* Eugene, OR: Castilia.

Pervin, L. A. (1989). *Goal concepts in personality and social psychology.* Hillsdale, NJ: Lawrence Erlbaum Associates.

Peterson, D. R. (1983). Conflict. In H. H. Kelley, E. Bersheid, A. Christensen, J. H. Harvey, T. L. Huston, G. Levinger, E. McClintock, L. A. Peplau, & D. A. Peterson (Eds.), *Close relationships* (pp. 360–396). New York: W. H. Freeman.

Pittman, T. S., & D'Agostino, D. R. (1989). Motivation and cognition: Control deprivation and the nature of subsequent information processing. *Journal of Experimental Social Psychology, 25,* 465–480.

Radke-Yarrow, M., Richters, J., & Wilson, W. E. (1988). Child development in a network of relationships. In R. A. Hinde & J. Stevenson-Hinde (Eds.), *Relationships within families: Mutual influences* (pp. 48–67). Oxford: Oxford University Press.

Read, S. J., & Miller, L. C. (1989). Interpersonalism: Toward a goal-based theory of persons in relationships. In L. A. Pervin (Ed.), *Goal concepts in personality and social psychology* (pp. 415–472). Hillsdale, NJ: Lawrence Erlbaum Associates.

Roseman, I. J. (1984). Cognitive determinants of emotion: A structural theory. In P. Shaver (Ed.), *Review of personality and social psychology (Vol. 5): Emotions, relationships, and health* (pp. 11–36). Beverly Hills: Sage.

Rosenhan, D., Fredericks, F., & Burrows, A. (1968). Preaching and practicing: Effects of channel discrepancy on norm internalization. *Child Development, 39,* 291–301.

Rotter, J. B. (1954). *Social learning and clinical psychology.* Englewood Cliffs, NJ: Prentice-Hall.

Schaefer, E., & Bell, R. (1958). Development of a parent attitude research instrument. *Child Development, 29,* 339–361.

Schank, R. C., & Abelson, R. P. (1977). *Scripts, plans, goals, and understanding.* Hillsdale, NJ: Lawrence Erlbaum Associates.

Skinner, E. A. (1986). The origins of young children's perceived control: Mother contingent and sensitive behavior. *International Journal of Behavioral Development, 9,* 359–382.

Smith, P. B., & Pederson, D. R. (1988). Maternal sensitivity and patterns of infant–mother attachment. *Child Development, 59,* 1097–1101.

Sorrentino, R. M., & Higgins, E. T. (1986). *Handbook of motivation and cognition.* New York: Guilford Press.

Sroufe, L. A. (1979). Socioemotional development. In J. D. Osofsky (Ed.), *Handbook of infant development* (pp. 462–516). New York: Wiley.

Sroufe, L. A., & Waters, E. (1977). Attachment as an organizational construct. *Child Development, 48,* 1184–1199.

Sroufe, L. A., Schork, E., Motti, F., Lawroski, N., & LaFreniere, P. (1984). The role of affect in social competence. In C. Izard, J. Kagan, & R. Zajonc (Eds.), *Emotions, cognition, and behavior* (pp. 289–319). New York: Cambridge University Press.

Srull, T. K., & Wyer, R. S., Jr. (1986). The role of chronic and temporary goals in social information processing. In R. M. Sorrentino & E. T. Higgins (Eds.), *Handbook of motivation and cognition* (pp. 501–549). New York: Guilford.

Stolz, L. (1967). *Influences on parent behavior.* London: Tavistock Publications.

Storms, M. D. (1973). Videotape and the attribution process: Reversing actors' and observers' points of view. *Journal of Personality and Social Psychology, 27,* 165–175.

Stotland, E. (1969). Exploratory investigations of empathy. In L. Berkowitz (Ed.), *Advances in experimental social psychology* (Vol. 4, pp. 271–314). New York: Academic Press.

Tolman, E. C. (1932). *Purposive behavior in animal and men.* New York: Appleton-Century-Crofts.

Trzebinski, J. (1989). The role of goal categories in the representation of social knowledge. In L. A. Pervin (Ed.), *Goal concepts in personality and social psychology* (pp. 363–411). Hillsdale, NJ: Lawrence Erlbaum Associates.

Wessenfeld, A. R., Whitman, P. B., & Malatesta, C. Z. (1984). Individual differences among adult women in sensitivity to infants: Evidence in support of an empathy concept. *Journal of Personality and Social Psychology, 46,* 118–124.

Wolfe, D. A. (1985). Child-abusive parents: An empirical review and analysis. *Psychological Bulletin, 97,* 462–482.

Wong, P. T., & Weiner, B. (1981). When people ask "why" questions and the heuristics of attributional search. *Journal of Personality and Social Psychology, 40,* 650–663.

Zukier, H. (1986). The paradigmatic and narrative modes in goal-guided inference. In R. M. Sorrentino & E. T. Higgins (Eds.), *Handbook of motivation and cognition* (pp. 465–502). New York: Guilford Press.

14 Family Representations of Development

Arnold J. Sameroff
Brown University
Bradley Hospital

Barbara H. Fiese
Syracuse University

Discussions of development have varied in their emphasis on the contributions that the early characteristics of the child and characteristics of the environment make to later behavior. One of the major shortcomings in such presentations is an inadequate conceptualization of the environment. Bronfenbrenner and Crouter (1983) traced the history of empirical investigations of the environment and showed how theoretical limitations have placed limits on the sophistication of research paradigms. The goal of this presentation is to expand upon our understanding of the child's environment and especially its dynamic regulatory function in development.

Traditional attempts to understand development have been based on stable models of child development. In these views, if a child is doing well or poorly early in life, he or she would be expected to continue to do well or poorly later on. As an example, children who were identified early in life as being at developmental risk from biological circumstances, such as birth complications, were thought to have generally negative behavioral outcomes later in life. On the contrary, longitudinal research in this area has demonstrated that the majority of children suffering from such biological conditions did not have intellectual or social problems later in life (Sameroff & Chandler, 1975). On the other hand, early interventionists believed that getting children to perform well early in life would lead to them performing well throughout childhood. The early childhood education movement as exemplified in the Head Start program was designed to improve the learning and social competence of children during the preschool years with the expectation that these improvements would be maintained into later life. However, follow-up research of such children has found that although there were reduced rates of grade retention and need for participation in special education programs and improved maternal attitudes toward school performance (Lazar & Darlington, 1982), only minimal intellectual gains were maintained into adolescence (Zigler & Trickett, 1978).

In both domains early characteristics of the child were frequently overpowered by factors in the environmental context of development. Where family and cultural variables have fostered development, children with severe perinatal complications have been indistinguishable from children without complications. When these variables have hindered development, children from good preschool intervention programs developed social and cognitive deficits.

In this chapter we expand upon the traditional views of development to produce an integrated model incorporating characteristics of the child's behavior, their biological underpinnings, and their environmental regulation. We begin by describing studies that dissect the environment into community, family, and parental factors. These factors are described in terms of regulatory codes that influence the course of each child's development. Special attention is devoted to family codes to differentiate the way families think about themselves, the represented family, and the way families behave together, the practicing family (Reiss, 1989).

Environmental Risk

Research aimed at identifying representative risk factors in the development of cognitive and socioemotional competence have implicated family mental health and especially social class as major candidates (Broman, Nichols, & Kennedy, 1975; Golden & Birns, 1976; Werner & Smith, 1982). Efforts to understand developmental outcomes must be based on an analysis of how families that vary on dimensions such as social class differ on the characteristics that foster or impede psychological development in their children.

In the Rochester Longitudinal Study (RLS) we and our colleagues also found social class and parental mental health to be associated with developmental risk (Sameroff, Seifer, & Zax, 1982). The RLS is a study of the development of several hundred children from birth through early adolescence assessing environmental factors as well as the cognitive and social competence of the children. We decided to subdivide the global variable of social class to see if we could identify factors more directly connected to the child which acted as environmental risks. These factors range from proximal variables like the mother's interaction with the child, to intermediate variables such as the mother's mental health, to distal variables such as the financial resources of the family.

Although causal models have been sought in which singular variables uniquely determine aspects of child behavior, a series of studies in a variety of domains have found that, except at the extremes of biological dysfunction, it is the *number* rather than the *nature* of risk factors that are the best determinants of outcome. Parmelee and Haber (1973) found this to be true for neurological factors in samples of infants with many perinatal problems, Rutter (1979) for family factors in samples of children with many psychosocial problems, and Greenspan (1981) for both biological and family factors in multirisk families.

When the sample of children in the RLS were 4 years old we assessed a set of 10 environmental variables that are correlates of SES but not equivalents (Sameroff, Seifer, Barocas, Zax, & Greenspan, 1987). We then tested whether poor cognitive development in our preschool children was a function of low socioeconomic status (SES) or the compounding of environmental risk factors found in low-SES groups. The 10 environmental risk variables were as follows:

1. A history of maternal mental illness.
2. High maternal anxiety.
3. A parental perspectives score derived from a combination of measures that reflected rigidity in the attitudes, beliefs, and values that mothers had in regard to their child's development.
4. Few positive maternal interactions with the child observed during infancy.
5. Head of household in unskilled occupations.
6. Minimal maternal education.
7. Disadvantaged minority status.
8. Reduced family support.
9. Stressful life events.
10. Large family size.

When these risk factors were related to socioemotional and cognitive competence scores, major differences were found between those children with few risks and those with many. In terms of intelligence, children with no environmental risks scored more than 30 points higher than children with 8 or 9 risk factors (see Fig. 14.1).

These data support the view that IQ scores for 4-year-old children are multidetermined by variables in the social context, but the possibility exists that poverty may still be an overriding variable. To test for this possibility, two additional analyses were completed. The first analysis was to determine if there were consistencies in the distribution of risk factors, that is, were there always the same factors present? The second analysis was to determine if the relation between high risk and lower intelligence was to be found in high- as well as low-SES families.

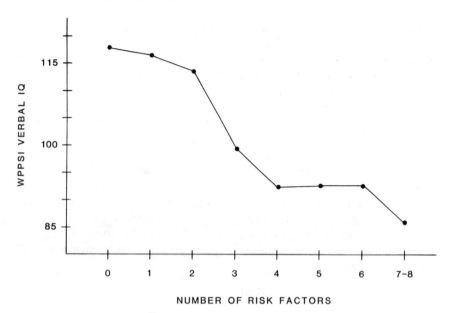

FIG. 14.1   Effects of multiple-risk scores on pre-school intelligence (Sameroff et al., 1987).

For the first type of analysis, the data from the families that had a moderate score of three, four, or five risk factors were cluster analyzed. The families fell into five clusters with different sets of high-risk conditions which are listed in Table 14.1. Different combinations of factors appear in each cluster. Cluster 2 has no overlapping variables with Clusters 3, 4, or 5. Minority status is a risk variable in Clusters 3, 4, and 5, but does not appear in Clusters 1 or 2. Despite these differences in the specific risks among families, the mean IQs were not different for children in the five clusters, ranging from 92.8 to 97.7. Thus, it seems that it was not any single variable but the combination of multiple variables that reduced the child's intellectual performance. If this is the case, it is unlikely that a universal single factor will be found that explains either good or bad developmental outcomes for children. In every family situation a unique set of risk or protective factors will be related to how the children turn out.

For the second analysis, the sample was split into high- and low-SES groups and the effect of increased number of risks was examined within each social class group. The effects of the multiple risk score were as clear within SES groups as well as for the population at large. The more risk factors the worse were the child outcomes for both high- and low-SES families.

These analyses of the RLS data were attempts to elaborate environmental risk factors by reducing global measures, for example, SES, to component

TABLE 14.1
Cluster Analysis of Families with Moderate
Multiple-Risk Scores (Sameroff et al., 1987)

Cluster	Risk Factor
1	Mental health
	Family support
	Mother education
	Anxiety
2	Mother–infant interaction
	Mental health
	Anxiety
3	Family support
	Minority status
4	Mother education
	Minority status
	Occupation
5	Parental perspectives
	Minority status
	Mother education

social and behavioral variables. We were able to identify a set of risk factors that were predominantly found in lower SES groups, but affected child outcomes in all social classes. Moreover, no single variable was determinant of outcome. Only in families with multiple risk factors was the child's competence placed in jeopardy. In the analyses of intellectual outcomes none of the children in the low multiple-risk group had an IQ below 85, whereas 24% of the children in the high multiple-risk group did.

The multiple pressures of environmental context in terms of amount of stress from the environment, the family's resources for coping with that stress, the number of children that must share those resources, and the parents' flexibility in understanding and dealing with their children all play a role in the fostering or hindering development of child intellectual and social competencies.

Environmental Continuity

Within the RLS our attention has been devoted to the source of continuities and discontinuities in child performance. We recently completed a new assessment of the sample when the children were 13 years of age (Sameroff, Seifer, Baldwin, & Baldwin, 1989). We were especially interested in those children from multiple-risk families who had managed to overcome early difficulties and reach normal or above average levels of intellectual or socioemotional competence. We were very disappointed to find little evidence of these resilient or invulnerable children. When we recreated our multiple risk score at age 13 we found the same powerful relationship between environmental adversity and child behavior: Those children with the most environmental risk factors had the lowest competence ratings.

The typical statistic reported in longitudinal research is the correlation between early and later performance of the children. We too found such correlations. Intelligence at 4 years correlated .72 with intelligence at 13 years, and the social competence scores at the two ages correlated .43. The usual interpretation of such numbers is that there is a continuity of competence or incompetence in the child. Such a conclusion cannot be challenged if the only assessments in the study were of the children. In the RLS environmental as well as child factors were examined. We were able to correlate environmental characteristics across time as well as child ones. We found that the correlation between environmental risk scores at the two ages was .76, as great or greater than any continuity within the child. Those children who had poor family and social environments at 4 still had them when they were 13 and probably would continue to have them for the foreseeable future. Whatever the child's ability for achieving high levels of competence, it was severely undermined by the continuing paucity of environmental support. Whatever the capabilities provided to the child by individual factors, it is the environment that limits the opportunities for development.

The importance of the regulatory function of parents became clear when we examined discontinuities in our data. We expected that children from demographically high-risk families would be below average in cognitive achievement. This was true for the majority of such children, but we were able to identify a small group (20%) who were doing better than average on their cognitive outcome scores (Baldwin, Baldwin, Sameroff, & Seifer, 1989). When we searched among our measures to find the factors that permitted these children to do better than their peers, we found differences in the attitudes and practices of their parents. A pattern of restrictiveness with little democracy, clarity of rules, and emotional warmth characterized the parents in these families. The parents had constructed a safe family environment in which their children could develop in the midst of the social chaos that typified their neighbors. The environment was modified to foster development rather than hinder it.

Regulatory Systems in Development

What kind of theory would be necessary to integrate our understanding of internal and external influences on development? It must explain how the individual and the context work together to produce patterns of adaptive or maladaptive functioning and relate how such past or present functioning influences the future.

Just as there is a biological organization, the genotype, that regulates the physical outcome of each individual, there is a social organization that regulates the way human beings fit into their society. This organization operates through family and cultural socialization patterns and has been postulated to compose an "environtype" analogous to the biological genotype (Sameroff, 1985; Sameroff & Fiese, 1990). The environtype is composed of subsystems that not only transact with the child but also transact with each other. Bronfenbrenner (1977) provided the most detailed descriptions of environmental organizations that influence developmental processes within categories of microsystems, mesosystems, exosystems, and macrosystems.

For our present purposes we restrict the discussion to levels of environmental factors contained within the culture, the family, and the individual parent. Developmental regulations at each of these levels are carried within codes: the cultural code, the family code, and the individual code of the parent. These codes regulate cognitive and socioemotional development so that the child ultimately will be able to fill a role defined by society. They are hierarchically related in their evolution and in their current influence on the child. The experience of the developing child is partially determined by the beliefs, values, and personalities of the parents, partially by the family's interaction patterns and transgenerational history, and partially by the socialization beliefs, controls, and supports of the culture. To summarize the overall model of developmental regulation, the child's behavior at any point in time is a product of the transactions between the phenotype (i.e., the child), the environtype (i.e., the source of external experience), and the genotype (i.e., the source of biological organization; see Fig. 14.2).

Adolescence is a good example of how the behavior of the child is an amalgam of biological, social, and personality factors (Petersen, 1988). Although the period is usually associated with biological changes in hormone production, in different cultures sexual behavior can begin years before the hormonal changes or years after. Furthermore, the child during this period must make sense of internal biological changes with or without the assistance of social explanations. In addition, the community will vary in the relation between biological changes and the age-graded timing of social transitions such as the move from elementary to middle and junior high school or puberty rites. Among the Masi, for example, children who range in age from 7 to 14 years make the transition into adulthood as one cohort.

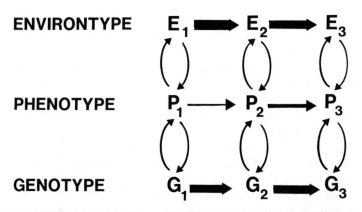

FIG. 14.2   Regulation model of development with transactions among genotype, phenotype and environtype (Sameroff, 1985).

THE ENVIRONTYPE

Traditional research on child development has emphasized the child's utilization of biological capacities to gain experience and the role of experience in shaping child competencies, but there has been far less attention to how that experience is organized. Indeed, the organization of experience is explicit in the great amount of attention given to curriculum development and behavior modification plans, but far less attention is given to the implicit organization of experience found in the environtype.

Individual Code of the Parent

There is clear evidence that parental behavior is influenced by the family and social context. When operating as part of a family, the behavior of each member is altered (Parke & Tinsley, 1987), frequently without awareness of the behavioral change (Reiss, 1981). However, there is also no doubt that individuals bring their own contribution to family interactions. The contribution of parents is determined much more complexly than that of young children, given the multiple levels that contribute to their behavior. The individualized interpretations that each parenting figure imposes on social and family practice are to a large extent conditioned by each parent's past participation in his or her own family's coded interactions, but they are captured uniquely by each member of the family. These individual influences further condition each parent's responses to his or her own child. Main and Goldwyn (1984) identified adult attachment categories that reflect parents' encoding of their interpretation of their attachment to their own parents. What is compelling about these adult attachment categories is that they operate across generations and are predictive of the attachment categories of the infant. In fact, these maternal representations have been better predictors of infant behavior than observational measures of the mother's actual interactions with the child.

In the RLS one of the 10 risk factors we identified was called "parental perspectives." This factor was a composite of three scales, the Sameroff & Feil (1985) Concepts of Development Questionnaire (CODQ), the Kohn (1969) Parental Values Scale, and the Schaefer and Bell (1958) Parent Attitude Research Instrument (PARI). When the children in the study were 4 years old, their mothers completed all three scales and when they were 13 years old their mothers completed the CODQ and the Kohn scales. One would think that there would be a great deal of plasticity in parent attitudes, beliefs, and values across the 9-year intervening period. In fact, there was not. When the 4- and 13-year measures were intercorrelated all the coefficients were in the 60s, all highly significant (see Table 14.2).

The stability of risk factors like low occupational and educational level, the things people do with their lives, is not terribly surprising. However, the stability of beliefs and values, the things people think about, is surprising. Both kinds of stability emphasize the importance of assessments of context as major regulators of how parents deal with children. It is important to recognize the parent as a major regulating agency, but it is equally important to recognize that parental behavior is itself embedded in social and family regulatory contexts. Culture is one of these regulatory contexts (Goodnow, 1988).

Cultural Code

The ingredients of the cultural code are the complex of characteristics that organize a society's child-rearing system and that incorporate elements of

TABLE 14.2
Correlations Between Parent Perspective Measures Using CODQ, Kohn Conformity Factor, and PARI Authoritarianism Scale at 4 Years and CODQ and Kohn Scales at 13 Years (Sameroff et al., 1989)

| | | 13-Year Assessment | |
		CODQ	Kohn
4-year assessment	CODQ	.65	.49
	Kohn	.56	.62
	PARI	.66	.66

socialization and education. These processes are embedded in sets of social controls and social supports. They are based on beliefs that differ in the amount of community consensus ranging from mores and norms to fads and fashions (Sameroff & Fiese, 1990). It would be beyond the scope of this paper to elucidate the full range of cultural regulatory processes that are potentially relevant to intervention efforts. As a consequence, only a few points are highlighted to clarify the dimensions of the cultural code.

Many common biological characteristics of the human species have acted to produce similar developmental agendas in most cultures. For example, in most cultures formal education begins between the ages of 6 and 8 when most children have reached the cognitive ability to learn from such structured experiences (Rogoff, 1981). However, there are historical and cross-cultural differences where changes in child behavior are emphasized or ignored. For example, informal education can begin at many different ages depending on the culture's attributions to the child. Some middle-class parents have been convinced that prenatal experiences will enhance the cognitive development of their children and consequently begin stimulation programs during pregnancy, whereas others believe it best to wait until the first grade before beginning formal learning experiences. Such examples demonstrate the variability of human developmental contexts, and the openness of the regulatory system to modification.

One of the major contemporary risk conditions toward which many intervention programs are directed in the United States is adolescent pregnancy. Although for certain young mothers pregnancy is the outcome of individual factors, for a large proportion it is the result of a cultural code that defines maturity, family relationships, and socialization patterns with adolescent motherhood as a normative ingredient. As Furstenberg, Brooks-Gunn, and Morgan (1987) pointed out, the current life-course perspective on families attributes the timing of marriage and childbearing to the interplay between personal, social, economic, and cultural beliefs about age-appropriate behavior.

Family Code

Just as the cultural code regulates the fit between individuals and the social system, family codes organize individuals within the family system. Family codes serve as guidelines for parental behavior in assigning roles, expressing emotions, and establishing rules of conduct. As in the cultural code, the family code is not synonymous with any one set of behaviors. Rather, family organization is coded along dimensions of beliefs, group practices, and interaction patterns.

Over the past 20 years a great deal of effort has been directed toward identifying patterns of parent–child interaction that may contribute to child outcome (for reviews see Clarke-Stewart, 1988; Parke & Tinsley, 1987). Although issues of cause and effect have been addressed through sophisticated mathematical methodologies such as sequential analyses (e.g., Bakeman & Gottman, 1986; Sackett, 1979) and structural equation modeling (e.g., Bentler, 1987; Patterson, 1986), direct influences rarely account for a large proportion of the variance related to child outcome. A consistent finding has been that global aspects of the environment such as SES regularly account for some of the variance (e.g., Sameroff et al., 1987) and microanalytic factors such as interaction patterns also account for some of the variance (Clarke-Stewart & Herey, 1981; Field, 1987). We propose that an intermediary between the cultural influences and individual interaction patterns are a series of factors which make up the family code.

The family regulates the child's development through a variety of processes that vary in their degree of articulation and practice (Reiss, 1989). Families have *paradigms* that regulate how information is received by the family and are in operation when the family is together as a group. Families create *myths* which exaggerate roles within the family but are not topics open for discussion. Families tell *stories* that transmit values and orientations to other family members and anyone else who will listen. Families practice *rituals* which prescribe roles and ascribe meaning to family interactions. Family paradigms and myths cannot be reported as such by individual members and only come into play when two or more family members are together. Family rituals are most easily accessible for report and their practice can be described by most individual members of the family. Family stories are intermediate to rituals and paradigms being transmitted through narratives but are also dependent on the context or presence of other family members. The four components of the family code are constrained by the cultural code while being sensitive to the individual code. The cultural code provides the family with broad guidelines for permissible behaviors and cultural values. The cultural code is interpreted by the family to maintain its own unique identity. Cultural codes may decree the observance of certain religious events, yet it is the family code that regulates who will attend, what roles individuals will play, and the relative symbolic significance for the family. The family code is also sensitive to the individual code, incorporating differences among its members into the regulatory system. A temperamentally difficult child may elicit different family stories than an easygoing child. Likewise, a depressed parent may adhere to family myths markedly different than a more healthy parent.

Although the empirical data documenting the family code is sparse, we now describe some aspects of the code as well as present initial findings from a research program aimed at empirically demonstrating the relation between the family code and parent–child interaction patterns and child outcome.

Assuming that child outcome is the result of a dynamic transactional process, the family code accounts for multiple influences on child development within the family context. Explicit rules, observed interactions, inferred emotions, and shared beliefs all play a part in the family code. Family codes may be passed down across generations but are also regulated by the developmental status of the family. Families with young infants may be too busy with daily caretaking responsibilities to find time for meaningful family rituals. As children can become more active participants in family activities and establish their role in the family structure, the family code expands with the developmental progress of the family. The family code is not a set of stable enduring characteristics but is an evolving regulatory system. Different empirical strategies are called for in unearthing the components of the family code. Each component also implies different forms of intervention (Sameroff & Fiese, 1990).

Family Paradigms

Family paradigms are beliefs that the family holds about the social world that can only be inferred from observations of family process (Reiss, 1981). Paradigms organize the behavior of family members in their attempts to deal with social institutions and individuals outside of the family unit. Paradigms reside within the family unit and are not considered characteristics of any one individual family member. They operate by filtering information through group processes.

Reiss (1981) provided evidence for family paradigms through a family card-sorting procedure. Families differ in the ways in which they participate in the task. Some families are quick to solve the problem, relying on one expert in the family to dictate the solution. Other families take longer in solving the problem deriving sophisticated sorting procedures based on solutions provided by multiple members of the group. Still other families complete the task only after each individual member has provided a separate solution. The family subtypes differ in how members seek alliances within the family and how information is to be shared outside of the family unit. These characteristic styles of processing information have been shown to be related to how families respond to treatment in group settings and make decisions within the family (Reiss, 1981).

Family paradigms are the least articulated component of the family code. The importance of family paradigms is that they are manifested in family interactions, including how children are incorporated into group processes. The normal or disturbed behavior of children must to some degree be interpreted as an outgrowth of the family paradigm (Reiss, Oliveri, & Curd, 1981).

Family Myths

Family myths are beliefs that have a strong influence on family process. They may highlight family roles but myths are not readily recountable by family members. Family myths are not open for discussion, nor are they readily recognized as distortions (Ferreira, 1963). Myths may have a traumatic origin and frequently have a strong affective component (Kramer, 1985).

Some family myths help to regulate role definitions. For example, a traditional family may consider the mother as unable to handle professional responsibilities of the work world despite the fact that she can balance the family checkbook and organize a busy household. Subtle aspects of a particular role may become inflated and incorporated into the myth. For example, a handicapped child may be treated as the youngest sibling despite birth order or chronological age. A myth develops in which chronological age is ignored and roles are assigned based on the newly created myth.

Family myths frequently provide a sense of continuity across generations. Individual family members carry with them their own beliefs and interpretations of their family of origin experiences and family heritage. Wamboldt and his colleagues (Wamboldt & Reiss, 1989; Wamboldt & Wolin, 1989) proposed that family myths influence mate selection and marital satisfaction and may even be changed through the marriage. They found that when new couples are faced with the task of defining for themselves what their newly created family will be like, they include beliefs about their parents' marital relationships. Individuals who describe their family of origin experiences as primarily positive and rich may also choose mates who have had similar family of origin experiences. This type of couple has the least amount of conflict around defining relationships and is prepared to create their own family definition based on satisfactory experiences. Other individuals, however, may recall their family of origin experiences as less optimal and define their family of origin as rejecting and cold. If the marital partners are unwilling to recognize that their marriage need not perpetuate their parent's mistakes, they are wedded to their family myth. However, it is possible for an individual to be "rescued" from a family of origin myth by pairing with another individual with a healthier background. A crucial factor is whether their is a deliberate choice to change the myth (Bennett, Wolin, Reiss, & Teitelbaum, 1987).

Within the framework of mate selection and family myths, the marital dyad becomes an important influence on child outcome. Previous research has demonstrated that levels of marital satisfaction are directly related to child adaptation (Deal, Halverson, & Wampler, 1989; Goldberg & Easter-brooks, 1984; Howes & Markman, 1989). The relation between marital satisfaction and child outcome may be regulated in part by the family of origin myths that each individual spouse brings to the marital relationship.

Family Stories

A third component of the family code that can be articulated by family members is family stories. They may contribute to the family code by emphasizing values and highlighting roles. Family stories can be told and heard by multiple members of the family.

These stories provide a context in which children learn family roles as well as family values across generations. In particular, the content of family stories may be important in studying how values are transmitted in the family (Fiese & Sameroff, 1989; Reiss, 1989). Bruner (1986) proposed that narratives and stories offer a unique perspective in studying the cultural context of child development. According to Bruner (1986) "narrative deals with the vicissitudes of human intentions" (p. 16). Family stories include the range of goals necessary to incorporate the child into the family and cultural system. Story-telling and narratives by their very nature organize experience in a way that will fit with the storyteller's understanding of the world (Sarbin, 1986) and identity (McAdams, 1989). In this regard, family stories provide a form of regulation that is influenced by the individual personality and experiences of the storyteller. Stories of a parent's childhood may transmit to the child what the parent considers important lessons of growing up as well as affective modifiers of salient childhood experiences.

The relation between the thematic content of family stories and parent--child interaction patterns was examined in a sample of mother and toddler pairs observed during a free-play period (Fiese, 1990b). Following the free-play period the mother was asked to tell her child a story "about when you were a little girl, when you were growing up." The mothers' stories were coded for thematic content along dimensions of play, affiliation, nurturance, rejection, and achievement. Mothers who told more affiliative, nurturant, and playful stories about their childhood engaged in more turn-taking and reciprocal interactions than mothers who told stories that included themes of rejection or achievement. Turn-taking was positively related to themes of play and nurturance and negatively related to themes of rejection. Low levels of engagement were positively related to themes of achievement. In general, mothers who told more playful or affiliative stories of their childhood tended to engage in more reciprocal forms of interaction with their toddlers. However, mothers who told stories of their childhood that included themes of rejection or achievement tended to be less engaged overall and when they did interact with their toddler they tended to be more intrusive and directive.

Family stories may be a pathway for transmitting family of origin experiences to younger generations. The parent's representations of their family system may regulate, in part, how parents interact with their children. One explanation may be that there is a direct path between recollections of childhood experiences and parent–child interactions. The recollection of childhood experiences also includes recollections of how people interact with each other. It may be that replicas of interactions are recalled and enacted across generations. Therefore parents who were treated in a nurturant way remember nurturant interactions and repeat similar patterns with their children. According to this line of interpretation, models of relating are recalled in memory and transmitted through family stories and interaction patterns. The recurrence of maladaptive interaction patterns across generations tends to support this social modeling interpretation (Belsky, 1980).

A different interpretation could be based on characteristics of the contemporary context. The type of story that a parent chooses to tell his or her child could be based in part on their own childhood experiences but also filtered through his or her current experiences as a parent with a particular child. The developmental status of the child, the context in which the stories are recalled, and the individual characteristics of the child may serve as elicitors for certain experiences to be recounted. A child who is constantly in trouble may hear more family stories about when his or her parents were in trouble. A child who is shy and withdrawn may receive words of encouragement from a parent who tells a family story of bravery and courage. If family stories provide a format for imparting lessons and values then it would be reasonable to predict that different themes would predominate according to context.

In addition, there may be a developmental shift in the kind of stories parents tell children. Mothers of 8- to 12-year-old boys told stories of their childhood that included themes of overcoming obstacles and facing adversity. These themes were not evident in the stories told to toddlers. From this dynamic perspective, family stories are adjusted to meet the demands of the family. Although family stories may provide a link across generations, the connection is paired with the demands of the contemporary family. Thematic content may be related to interaction patterns in a more indirect way than through social modeling. A general sensitivity to the developmental demands of the child in the family context may be related to more sensitive interaction patterns overall. Parents who are sensitive to the needs of their children may tell family stories that meet those needs as well as interact in ways that are sensitive to their child's behavior. Further empirical efforts are warranted to determine the contextual nature of family stories.

Family Rituals

Family rituals are the most self-aware aspects of the family code (Bossard & Boll, 1950). Family rituals may range from highly stylized religious observances such as first communion or bar mitzvahs to less articulated daily interaction patterns such as the type of greeting made when someone returns home. Rituals mark the beginning and end of life within a family but also regulate behavior on a daily basis. Families can easily identify ritual practices they hold as well as describe the routines they perform on a daily, weekly, or annual basis (Fiese & Kline, 1990; Wolin, Bennett, & Jacobs, 1988). Rituals are practiced by the whole family and are frequently documented. They may be times for taking photographs, exchanging gifts, or preserving mementos. The content of family rituals includes symbolic information as well as important preparatory phases, schedules, and plans. Rituals serve a regulatory function by assigning roles and providing meaning to family interactions.

The role of family rituals in regulating dysfunctional behavior has been most clearly demonstrated in families of alcoholics (Bennett, Wolin, Reiss, & Teitelbaum, 1987; Wolin, Bennett, Noonan, & Teitelbaum, 1980). In a study of married children of alcoholic parents certain aspects of family rituals were identified as protective factors which guarded against the children becoming alcoholics. Children who came from families that were able to preserve family rituals, such as distinctive dinner and holiday routines, were less likely to become alcoholics themselves. Wolin and his colleagues speculated that rituals provide stability for dysfunctional families (Wolin, Bennett, & Jacobs, 1988).

Family rituals have been demonstrated to be related to a variety of developmental outcomes as well as serve a protective function for children from alcoholic families. A self-report measure of family rituals was developed by Fiese and Kline (1990) to extend the interview research of Wolin, Bennett, and Jacobs (1988). This Family Ritual Questionnaire (FRQ) is a 56-item forced-choice questionnaire designed to assess degree of family rituals in seven settings: dinner time, weekends, vacations, annual celebrations, special celebrations, religious celebrations, and cultural traditions; along eight dimensions: occurrence, roles, routines, attendance, affect, symbolic significance, continuation, and deliberateness. The items from the dinnertime scale are presented in Fig. 14.3.

The respondent chooses the statement that is most like his or her family and then decides if the statement is really true or sort of true for his or her family. The FRQ evidences good psychometric properties with Chronbach alphas ranging from .71 to .87 for settings and .58 to .79 for dimensions (see Fiese & Kline, 1990, for a more complete description of the psychometric properties of the FRQ).

DINNER TIME

Think about a typical dinner time in your family.

For our family really true	sort of true				For our family sort of true	really true
—	—	1. Some families regularly eat dinner together.	**BUT**	Other families rarely eat dinner together.	—	—
—	—	2. In some families everyone has a specific role and job to do at dinner time.	**BUT**	In other families people do different jobs at different times depending on needs.	—	—
—	—	3.In some families dinner time is flexible. People eat whenever they can.	**BUT**	In other families everything about dinner is scheduled; dinner is at the same time every day. —		—
—	—	4.In some families,every one is expected to be home for dinner.	**BUT**	In other families you never know who will be home for dinner.	—	—
—	—	5. In some families people feel strongly about eating dinner together.	**BUT**	In other families it is not that important if people eat together.	—	—
—	—	6. In some families dinner time is just for getting food.	**BUT**	In other families dinner time is more than just a meal; it has special meaning.—		—
—	—	7.In some families dinner time has always been and always will be a regular family event.	**BUT**	In other families dinner time has changed over the years as children grow up and schedules change.	—	—
—	—	8. In some families there is little planning around dinner time.	**BUT**	In other families dinner time is planned in advance.	—	—

FIG. 14.3   Items from dinnertime scale of Family Ritual Questionnaire (Fiese & Kline, 1990).

In the initial study, using the FRQ with college students, the level of ritualization in the family was related to the child's feelings of security and belongingness as measured through a self-report of adolescent attachment to the family, the Inventory of Parent and Peer Attachment (Armsden & Greenberg, 1987). There was a significant positive correlation between adolescent attachment and family rituals (Fiese & Kline, 1990). More specifically, the symbolic and affective qualities associated with family rituals were positively related to adolescent attachment. However, the ascription of roles and routines was found to be negatively related to the attachment outcome. Results from this first normative study on family rituals and adolescent outcome were suggestive of separate dimensions within family rituals.

In a second study, using a larger sample of college students (Fiese, 1990a), the FRQ was factor analyzed and two distinct dimensions of family rituals were found: a ritual meaning factor and a ritual routine factor. The family ritual *meaning* factor included the dimensions of occurrence, attendance, symbolic significance, affect, and deliberateness. The family ritual *routine* factor included the dimensions of roles and routines. The two factors were differentially related to measures of child outcome. The meaning factor was negatively related to a measure of anxiety, the Malaise Inventory (Rutter, Graham, & Yule, 1970), and positively related to self-esteem, the Multidimensional Self-Esteem Inventory (O'Brien & Epstein, 1988). The routine factor was not significantly related to anxiety or self-esteem.

To follow up on the Wolin et al. studies of the intergenerational transmission of alcoholism, a secondary set of analyses was conducted on college students who reported problematic drinking in their family of origin. Students who scored 6 or above on the Children of Alcoholics Test (CAST; Jones, 1983) were considered children of alcoholics. The children of alcoholics' anxiety scores were compared to the remainder of the sample according to high or low levels of meaning associated with family rituals. Children of alcoholics who reported low levels of family ritual meaning had significantly higher anxiety scores than children of alcoholics who reported high levels or children of nonalcoholic families regardless of family ritual meaning level (see Fig. 14.4).

The results of the college student study are in accordance with the findings of Wolin and Bennett (Bennett, Wolin, Reiss, & Teitelbaum, 1987; Wolin, Bennett, & Jacobs, 1988), who sampled self-identified children of alcoholics. Taken together, these results suggest that when meaning is ascribed to family rituals children have lower levels of anxiety. Moreover, this effect is especially significant in alcoholic families. Wolin and Bennett demonstrated that children of alcoholics who recount family rituals that are deliberately different from those in their families of origin are less likely to become alcoholic themselves.

In the college student sample using the FRQ, children of alcoholics who reported more meaning associated with their family rituals reported lower levels of anxiety. Children of alcoholics who reported low levels of meaning appeared to be the most vulnerable to developing anxiety symptoms.

Family rituals may contribute to the family code by providing meaning to patterned interactions. Although it is probable that a certain amount of routine and regularity would have to exist in order for rituals to have a powerful influence, it is apparently the meaning associated with family

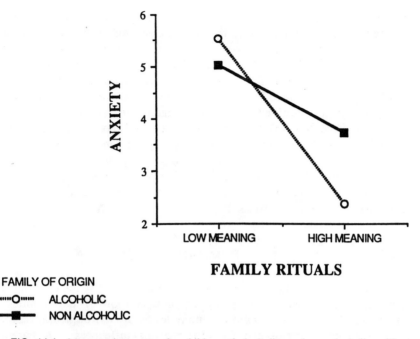

FAMILY OF ORIGIN

·······O······· ALCOHOLIC

——■—— NON ALCOHOLIC

FIG. 14.4   Mean anxiety scores for children of alcoholics and non-alcoholics with high and low Family Ritual Questionnaire meaning factor scores (Fiese, 1990a).

rituals that is significantly related to child outcome. Sociologists have pointed out that when cultures create rituals, the symbolic quality of patterned interactions transforms a routine into a ritual (Moore & Myerhoff, 1977). For the family it may be the meaning associated with routine interactions that transforms momentary interactions into central features of family process and organization.

Consolidating the Family Code

Four aspects of the family code have been presented. Although each component has been presented as distinct, as part of the family system each aspect may influence the other. Future research will focus on how paradigms, myths, stories, and rituals interact with each other to form the family code. Greater specificity is needed in identifying crucial dimensions of the family code for child outcome. It has been demonstrated that family rituals may serve a protective function, family stories may transmit roles and values, myths perpetuate role assignment, and paradigms selectively process information in a group setting. The source of the family code appears to be linked to intergenerational processes. Family myths, rituals, and stories are frequently established in previous generations and passed to the younger generation as a way to regulate behavior in the contemporary family. Yet, the transmission does not appear to be unidirectionally linked and thus may be malleable. The power of the family code is not only its ties to the past but also its ability to be adapted by the contemporary family. Families that are bounded by past generations and are unable to learn from past mistakes are destined to repeat maladaptive family codes. Other families, however, are able to create their own family code through creating healthier marriages, providing different interpretations to family myths, and creating new family stories responsive to the next generation. The points at which a family can create new codes without sacrificing the integrity of past generations may point to a better understanding of intergenerational family processes.

SUMMARY

We began by describing the inadequacy of models that focus on singular causal factors for either the study or manipulation of developmental outcomes. We went on to elaborate many levels of environmental factors that regulate child development from the proximal influences of the parents to the distal effects of culture and class. The family was presented as a major force in its dual role of protecting the child from environmental perturbations but also shaping the child to fit social expectations.

All of these factors were incorporated into a regulatory model provided through the evolution of living systems that incorporates feedback mechanisms between the child's personality and regulatory codes. These environmental and genetic codes are the context of development. By expanding our understanding of this regulatory system at the level of the individual parent, the family, and the community, we may be able to obtain a much better grasp on the process of development.

REFERENCES

Armsden, G. C., & Greenberg, M. T. (1987). The inventory of parent and peer attachment: Individual differences and their relationship to psychological well-being in adolescence. *Journal of Youth and Adolescence, 16,* 427–453.

Bakeman, R., & Gottman, J. M. (1986). *Observing interaction: An introduction to sequential analysis.* Cambridge: Cambridge University Press.

Baldwin, A. L., Baldwin, C., Sameroff, A. J., & Seifer, R. (1989, April). *Protective factors in adolescent development.* Paper presented at the biennial meetings of the Society for Research in Child Development, Kansas City, MO.

Belsky, J. (1980). Child maltreatment: An ecological integration. *American Psychologist, 35,* 320–335.

Bennett, L. A., Wolin, S., Reiss, D., & Teitelbaum, M. A. (1987). Couples at risk for alcoholism transmission: Protective influences. *Family Process, 26,* 111–129.

Bentler, P. M. (1987). Drug use and personality in adolescence and young adulthood: Structural models with nonnormal variables. *Child Development, 58,* 65–79.

Bossard, J. J. S., & Boll, E. (1950). *Ritual in family living.* Philadelphia: University of Pennsylvania Press.

Broman, S. H., Nichols, P. L., & Kennedy, W. A. (1975). *Preschool IQ: Prenatal and early developmental correlates.* Hillsdale, NJ: Lawrence Erlbaum Associates.

Bronfenbrenner, U. (1977). Toward an experimental ecology of human development. *American Psychologist, 32,* 513–531.

Bronfenbrenner, U., & Crouter, A. C. (1983). The evolution of environmental models in development research. In W. Kessen (Ed.), *Handbook of Child Psychology: Vol. 1. History, theories, and methods* (pp. 357–414). New York: Wiley.

Bruner, J. (1986). *Actual minds, possible worlds.* Cambridge, MA: Harvard University Press.

Clarke-Stewart, K. A. (1988). Parents' effects on children's development: A decade of progress? *Journal of Applied Developmental Psychology, 9,* 41–84.

Clarke-Stewart, K. A., & Hevey, C. M. (1981). Longitudinal relations in repeated observations of mother-child interaction from 1 to 2½ years. *Developmental Psychology, 17,* 127–145.

Deal, J. E., Halverson, C. F., & Wampler, K. S. (1989). Parental agreement in child-rearing orientations: Relations to parental, marital, family, and child characteristics. *Child Development, 60,* 1025–1034.

Ferreira, A. J. (1963). Family myth and homeostasis. *Archives General Psychiatry, 9,* 457–463.

Field, T. M. (1987). Affective and interactive disturbances in infants. In J. Osofsky (Ed.), *Handbook of infant development* (2nd ed., pp. 972–1005). New York: Wiley.

Fiese, B. H. (1990a). *Dimensions of family rituals: The interplay between meaning and routine.* Unpublished manuscript.

Fiese, B. H. (1990b, April). *Family stories: Mothers' stories of their childhood and relation to mother–toddler interaction in a free-play setting.* Presented at the International Conference on Infant Studies, Montreal.

Fiese, B. H., & Kline, C. A. (1990). *Development of the Family Ritual Questionnaire.* Unpublished manuscript.

Fiese, B. H., & Sameroff, A. J. (1989). Family context in pediatric psychology: A transactional perspective. *Journal of Pediatric Psychology, 14,* 293–314.

Furstenberg, F. F., Brooks-Gunn, J., & Morgan, S. P. (1987). *Adolescent mothers.* Cambridge: Cambridge University Press.

Goldberg, W. A., & Easterbrooks, M. A. (1984). The role of marital quality in toddler development. *Child Development, 20,* 504–515.

Golden, M., & Birns, B. (1976). Social class and infant intelligence. In M. Lewis (Ed.), *Origins of intelligence: Infancy and early childhood* (pp. 299–351). New York: Plenum.

Goodnow, J. J. (1988). Parents' ideas, actions, and feelings: Models and methods from developmental and social psychology. *Child Development, 59,* 286–330.

Greenspan, S. I. (1981). *Psychopathology and adaptation in infancy and early childhood: Clinical infant reports No. 1.* Hanover, NH: University Press of New England.

Howes, P., & Markman, H. J. (1989). Marital quality and child functioning: A longitudinal investigation. *Child Development, 60,* 1044–1051.

Jones, J. W. (1983). The Children of Alcoholics Screening Test: A validity study. *Bulletin of the Society of Psychologists in Addictive Behaviors, 2,* 155–163.

Kohn, M. L. (1969). *Class and conformity: A study in values.* Homewood, IL: Dorsey.

Kramer, J. (1985). *Family interfaces: Transgenerational patterns.* New York: Brunner/Mazel.

Lazar, I., & Darlington, R. (1982). Lasting effects of early education: A report from the consortium for longitudinal studies. *Monographs of the Society for Research in Child Development, 47* (Whole No. 195).

Main, M., & Goldwyn, R. (1984). Predicting rejection of their infant from mother's representation of her own experience: Implications for the abused and abusing intergenerational cycle. *Child Abuse and Neglect, 8,* 203-217.

McAdams, D. P. (1989). The development of a narrative identity. In. D. M. Buss & N. Cantor (Eds.), *Personality psychology: Recent trends and emerging directions* (pp. 160-174). New York: Springer-Verlag.

Moore, S. F., & Myerhoff, B. G. (1977). *Secular ritual.* Amsterdam, The Netherlands: Van Gorcum.

O'Brien, E. J., & Epstein, S. (1988). *Multidimensional Self-Esteem Inventory.* Odessa, FL: Psychological Assessment Resources, Inc.

Parke, R. D., & Tinsley, B. J. (1987). Family interaction in infancy. In J. Osofsky (Ed.), *Handbook of infant development* (2nd ed., pp. 579-641). New York: Wiley.

Parmelee, A. H., & Haber, A. (1973). Who is the at-risk infant? *Clinical Obstetrics and Gynecology, 16,* 376-387.

Patterson, G. R. (1986). Performance models for antisocial boys. *American Psychologist, 41,* 432-444.

Petersen, A. C. (1988). Adolescent development. In M. R. Rosenzweig & L. W. Porter (Eds.), *Annual review of psychology* (Vol. 39, pp. 583-607). Palo Alto: Annual Reviews Inc.

Reiss, D. (1981). *The family's construction of reality.* Cambridge, MA: Harvard University Press.

Reiss, D. (1989). The represented and practicing family: Contrasting visions of family continuity. In A. J. Sameroff & R. N. Emde (Eds.), *Relationship disturbances in early childhood* (pp. 191-220). New York: Basic Books.

Reiss, D., Oliveri, M. E., & Curd, K. (1981). Family paradigm and adolescent social behavior. In H. D. Grotevant & C. R. Cooper (Eds.), *Adolescent development and the family: Vol 22. New Directions for Child Development.* (pp. 77-91). San Francisco: Jossey-Bass.

Rogoff, B. (1981). Schooling and the development of cognitive skills. In H. C. Triandis & A. Heron (Eds.), *Handbook of cross-cultural psychology: Developmental psychology* (Vol. 4, pp. 233-294). Boston: Allyn & Bacon.

Rutter, M. (1979). Protective factors in children's responses to stress and disadvantage. In M. W. Kent & J. E. Rolf (Eds.), *Primary prevention of psychopathology: Vol. 3. Social competence in children* (pp. 49-74). Hanover, NH: University Press of New England.

Rutter, M., Graham P., & Yule, W. (1970). *A neuropsychiatric study in childhood.* London: Heinemann/SIMP.

Sackett, G. P. (1979). The lag sequential analysis of contingency and cyclicity in behavioral interaction research. In J. Osofsky (Ed.), *Handbook of infant development* (pp. 623-649). New York: Wiley.

Sameroff, A. J. (1985, August). *Can development be continuous?* Paper presented at Annual Meeting of American Psychological Association, Los Angeles.

Sameroff, A. J., & Chandler, M. J. (1975). Reproductive risk and the continuum of caretaking casualty. In F. D. Horowitz, M. Hetherington, S. Scarr-Salapatek, & G. Siegel (Eds.), *Review of child development research* (Vol. 4, pp. 187-244). Chicago: University of Chicago Press.

Sameroff, A. J., & Feil, L. (1985). Parental concepts of development. In I. Sigel (Ed.), *Parental belief systems: The psychological consequences for children* (pp. 83-104). Hillsdale, NJ: Lawrence Erlbaum Associates.

Sameroff, A. J., & Fiese, B. H. (1990). Conceptual issues in prevention. In D. Schafer, I. Philip, & N. Enzer (Eds.), *Prevention of mental disorders, alcohol use and other drug use in children and adolescents* (pp. 25-53). OSAP Prevention Monograph No. 2. Rockville, MD: Office for Substance Abuse and Prevention.

Sameroff, A. J., Seifer, R., Baldwin, A. L., & Baldwin, C. (1989, April). *Continuity of risk from childhood to adolescence*. Paper presented at the biennial meetings of the Society for Research in Child Development, Kansas City.

Sameroff, A. J., Seifer, R., Barocas, B., Zax, M., & Greenspan, S., (1987). IQ scores of 4-year-old children: Social–environmental risk factors. *Pediatrics, 79,* 343–350.

Sameroff, A. J., Seifer, R., & Zax, M. (1982). Early development of children at risk for emotional disorder. *Monographs of the Society for Research in Child Development, 47* (7, Serial No. 199).

Sarbin, T. R. (1986). The narrative as a root metaphor for psychology. In T. R. Sarbin (Ed.), *Narrative psychology: The storied nature of human conduct* (pp. 3–21). New York: Praeger.

Schaefer, E. S., & Bell, R. Q. (1958). Development of a parental attitude research instrument. *Child Development, 29,* 339–361.

Wamboldt, F. S., & Reiss, D. (1989). Defining a family heritage and a new relationship identity: Two central tasks in the making of a marriage. *Family Process, 28,* 317–335.

Wamboldt, F. S., & Wolin, S. J. (1989). Reality and myth in family life: Changes across generations. In S. A. Anderson & D. A. Bagarozzi (Eds.), *Family myths: Psychotherapy implications* (pp. 141–166). New York: Haworth Press.

Werner, E. E., & Smith, R. S. (1982). *Vulnerable but invincible: A longitudinal study of resilient children and youth.* New York: McGraw-Hill.

Wolin, S. J., Bennett, L. A., & Jacobs, J. S. (1988). Assessing family rituals. In E. Imber-Black, J. Roberts, & R. Whiting (Eds.), *Rituals and family therapy* (pp. 230–256). New York: Norton.

Wolin, S. J., Bennett, L. A., Noonan, D. L., & Teitelbaum, M. A. (1980). Disrupted family rituals: A factor in the intergenerational transmission of alcoholism. *Journal of Studies of Alcohol, 41,* 199–214.

Zigler, E., & Trickett, P. K. (1978). IQ, social competence, and evaluation of early childhood intervention programs. *American Psychologist, 33,* 789–799.

V   Focus on Cultural Perspectives of Parent Cognition

15 Parental Ethnotheories in Action

Sara Harkness
Charles M. Super
The Pennsylvania State University

The relationship between beliefs and behavior has been an elusive one in both psychology and anthropology. As suggested elsewhere in this volume, a central question that has heretofore been neglected in the study of parental beliefs is what difference they make in parental behavior that is relevant to children's developmental outcomes. In anthropology, the theoretical relationship between beliefs and behavior has also been problematic, as illustrated by recent critiques of classical anthropological studies of other cultures in which thinking and action were represented as harmoniously integrated (e.g., Mead, 1928; Freeman, 1983). Cognitive anthropological studies of cultural models have tended to avoid systematic behavioral observation because, as D'Andrade (1984) argued, "the external signs, the public events, are too elliptical to serve as a good place to begin the search for organization and structure" (p. 105). Nevertheless, there is increasing recognition of the intimate connections between beliefs and behavior in the formulation of cultural models as goals for action (D'Andrade & Strauss, in press).

In this chapter, we outline a new approach to the understanding of how child development is culturally shaped, with particular attention to the central role of parental ethnotheories. This approach is a further elaboration of the "developmental niche," a theoretical framework for understanding the cultural regulation of the child's micro-environment (Harkness & Super, in press-b; Super & Harkness, 1986). Briefly, the developmental niche is conceptualized in terms of three components: (a) the physical and social settings in which the child lives; (b) culturally regulated customs of child care and child rearing; and (c) the psychology of the caretakers. We have suggested that:

> These three subsystems share the common function of mediating the individual's experience within the larger culture. Regularities in the subsystems, as well as thematic continuities from one culturally defined developmental stage to the next, provide material from which the child abstracts the social, affective, and cognitive rules of the culture, much as the rules of grammar are abstracted from the regularities of the speech environment. (Super & Harkness, 1986, p. 552)

Here, we pursue the question of exactly how the three components are related to each other, and assign a leading role to parental ethnotheories of child behavior and development (part of the third component of the niche). We view parental ethnotheories of children's intelligence and personality as examples of cultural models that, in the words of Quinn and Holland (1987, p. 6), "frame experience, supplying interpretations of that experience and inferences about it, and goals for action." Following the work of D'Andrade and others (D'Andrade, 1984; D'Andrade & Strauss, in press), we suggest that parental ethnotheories have motivational properties, functioning as goals as well as interpretations of reality for parents. We observe that parental ethnotheories are embedded in the experiences of daily life that parents have with their own children at particular ages, as well as being derived from the accumulated cultural experience of the community or reference group. We depart from a more deterministic view of the origins of parental ethnotheories in the socioeconomic structure of parental life, however, in asserting that the assumptions and values in ethnotheories themselves provide a frame of reference within which parents make decisions about how to socialize their children. In this view, parental ethnotheories are expressed in the ways that parents assign their children to different kinds of physical and social settings; this is particularly evident when one examines developmental trends in children's settings of daily life. Finally, we propose that many customs of child rearing function as instantiations of parental ethnotheories and thus are of special importance in translating parental thinking into action that has developmental consequences. To illustrate this approach, we draw from our research on parents and children in rural Kenya and metropolitan America.

THE RESEARCH SETTINGS

The research reported here was carried out in two communities: a Kipsigis settlement in western Kenya, which we studied in the early 1970s, and a sample of middle-class American families in the Boston area in the 1980s. The Kipsigis community of Kokwet was the locus of a 3-year field study involving many aspects of child development and family life (Harkness, 1977, 1988; Harkness, Edwards, & Super, 1981; Harkness & Super, 1983, 1988, in press-a, in press-b, in press-c; Super & Harkness, 1981, 1986). As part of a larger panel of East African communities that were studied under the direction of the Whitings (see Whiting & Edwards, 1988), Kokwet has contributed to our understanding of cultural patterns of child rearing in that part of the world (Harkness & Super, 1991, in press-a, in press-c; Super & Harkness, 1981, 1986). The more recent American study focused on parental ethnotheories of child behavior and development – their sociocultural origins and implications for development (Harkness, 1990; Harkness & Super, in press-c; Harkness, Super, & Keefer, in press).

The community of Kokwet is located in the western highlands of Kenya, where it enjoys a temperate climate protected by altitude (6,300 ft) from the worst of tropical diseases. Consisting of 54 households established on land repatriated from the British at national independence in 1963, Kokwet at the time of fieldwork was a relatively prosperous farming community. As a government-sponsored "settlement scheme," the community was intentionally modern in some respects, such as the use of European-type cows for commercial milk production and the marketing of agricultural produce from household plots of about 20 acres each. This very prosperity, however, had enabled the community to maintain some traditional aspects of social organization and lifestyle. At the time of field research, most of the fathers and virtually all of the mothers had little or no schooling. Few fathers worked away from the homesteads at salaried jobs. Division of labor within the household followed the traditional pattern of men in charge of large livestock, ploughing, and harvesting, and women primarily responsible for the hand-done agricultural tasks (hoeing, weeding, and picking small crops), as well as the many chores of the household, including carrying water from the nearby river for cooking and washing, gathering firewood for the cooking fire, and, of course, preparation of food. In this setting, polygynous families had the functional advantage of more hands to do the household chores; and all hands, even the small hands of children, were needed to accomplish the many tasks to be done. Families thus tended to be large (with eight or more children the cultural norm), and children were expected to help out both in household chores and in the care of younger siblings from early childhood on.

Families in the American sample were recruited through the Cambridge Center of the Harvard Community Health Plan, a large health maintenance organization in the Boston area. Thirty-six families participated in the study, divided into three cohorts based on the age of the focal child at entry into the study: newborn, 18 months, and 36 months (further divided by sex and sibling order of the child). Each family participated in the study over the course of 18 months, with data collection cycles occurring every 6 months. The residences of the Cambridge parents included the city itself as well as the surrounding suburbs. All families were middle or professional class, intact families with healthy children. All fathers were employed, and care of the children was done mainly by mothers and hired baby-sitters or day-care providers. Families tended to be small, ranging from one to three children all born within a few years of each other. Thus, given the selection for early childhood in the sample, these were "young" families in terms of the ages of the children, although many of the parents were in their 30s and 40s. The parents were virtually all American-born and the great majority were of European background. They were all committed parents, interested enough in the daily lives and progress of their children to agree to participate in a study that made real demands of their time over a period of a year and a half. It is notable in this context, however, that of all the parents who were invited to participate in the study (based primarily on the age, gender, and health of their children), about three-quarters agreed to participate and all these remained with the study throughout its duration. In the Cambridge sample, then, we have a set of optimally functioning families in terms of health and stability, but they are not highly self-selected.

PARENTAL CONCEPTS OF CHILDREN'S INTELLIGENCE AND PERSONALITY

A central feature of parental ethnotheories in both Kokwet and Cambridge is a set of concepts about what could be generally glossed as children's "intelligence" and "personality." These are framed very differently in each cultural setting however, as shown by analyses of descriptive words and phrases that parents in each setting used to talk about children.

Kokwet Parents

Our first step in exploring Kipsigis concepts of the child was in a discussion and advisory group organized with six mothers of Kokwet (Super, 1983). We asked the women what words they used to talk about children between 3 and 10 years old. About 20 words and phrases emerged as important ones, and we further clarified their meanings through detailed inquiry with 11 particularly helpful informants, including 3 men.

Six conceptual clusters were identified from this ethnographic inquiry:

1. There is a large group of concepts referring to a child's helpfulness and obedience. Important root words are *ng'ekonda* ("disobedience," often used in the negative: *Ma mi ng'ekong lakwet,* or, "The child is not disobedient"); *kiptekisiot* ("respectful"); and *ingeleliot* ("rude"). There are also several phrases derived from words relating to domains we might separate more in English, such as *Kararon ng'alekyik,* literally "He/she talks nicely," indicating politeness; *kaseit,* derived from the word *kase,* to understand, meaning a child who understands quickly what is to be done and does it, hence translated by native speakers as "obedient"; and several other cognitively oriented phrases. Also belonging in the helpful–obedient cluster is *ne toche chi tugul,* or "(the child) who welcomes/entertains everyone." Although in literal translation this sounds like a social skill, it is often said to mean "respectful and obedient."

2. Second in both number of phrases and in discussion generated is a cluster of concepts close to Euro-American notions of cognition and intelligence. *Ng'om* is the central word when referring to children. Although *ng'om* is universally translated as "intelligent," elaboration of its use reveals a strong component of "responsibility" as well. One informant illustrated the word as follows:

"For a girl who is *ng'om,* after eating she sweeps the house because she knows it should be done. Then she washes dishes, looks for vegetables [in the garden], and takes good care of the baby. When you come home, you feel pleased and say: "This child is *ng'om.*" Another girl may not even clean her own dishes, but just go out and play, leaving the baby to cry. For a boy, if he is *ng'om,* he will watch the cows, and take them to the river without being told. He knows to separate the calves from the cows and he will fix the thorn fence where it is broken. The other boy will let the cows into the maize field and will be found playing while they eat the maize."

A few informants distinguished a separate meaning of *ng'om* for the child who gets good marks in school. This could be specified as *ng'om en sukul* rather than *ng'om en gaa* ("intelligent at home"). The informants stressed, however, that the two meanings (domestic and academic) were not necessarily related, and that a child may do well in school despite often forgetting to do chores at home.

Ng'om is not normally used to refer to adults. Rather, a native speaker is more likely to use *utat,* which has a stronger connotation of "inventive and clever," or sometimes "wise and unselfish." *Kwelat* may also be used, meaning "smart" or "sharp." A man who is *kwelat* dresses smartly and is clever in dealing with his family, although not necessarily educated.

3. A third cluster of words used to talk about children centered on the term *iyanat,* meaning "trustworthy" or perhaps "honest," and related words.

4. Most informants preferred to make a separate category for *mie mukulel,* literally "good-hearted" and usually translated as "loving." A child who is this way, in the words of one informant, "will smile when you say she must wait a little for food, even though she is hungry."

5. *Ng'ololin,* central to the fifth cluster, means "talkative," often with a connotation of "playful" or "cheeky." You leave a visitor in the house for a little time while you go to cook; when you return, the child is sitting there and the visitor says, "Oh, he is *ng'ololin* for he has told me such-and-such." All 4-year-olds are seen to be this way, but if a child is still *ng'ololin* at 9 years, when he is also *ng'om,* then he will use nice words *(Kararon ng'alekyik)* and be polite as well.

6. Bravery, key to the sixth cluster, is an important quality in children as well as adults. Two slightly different meanings of "brave" *(nyigan)* were pointed out. In one case, the child is brave enough to go outside the house at night, or to walk 2 miles to a neighboring village with a message. Second, a child can show bravery when physically punished, or when the lower front teeth are ceremonially removed.

In order to obtain more objective information on the semantic relationships of these words, key concepts were compared for their similarity and then processed for multidimensional scaling. Twelve core adjectives were chosen from the six areas identified through discussion with informants. The 12 words were prepared in a balanced set of triads according to the work of Burton and Nerlove (1976). For example, one triad consisted of *ng'om, kaseit,* and *kiptekisiot* ("intelligent", "obedient," and "respectful"). Twenty-three adult residents of Kokwet (10 female, 13 male) were asked to indicate for each triad which of the two words were most similar in meaning. The similarity ratings were collected through individual interviews, and the pooled results were submitted to the KYST multidimensional scaling program.

The most reasonable scaling solution was found in three dimensions (Figs. 15.1 and 15.2). The first dimension, where *kiptekisiot, ma mi ng'ekong,* and *kaseit* ("respectful," "obedient," and "understanding/ obedient") are at one extreme and *nyigan* and *ng'ololin* ("brave" and "talkative") are at the other, appears to contrast individual assertiveness with social submissiveness. Dimension II reflects a verbal and possible manipulative component, with *ng'om* and *ng'ololin* ("intelligent" and "talkative") at one end and the quiet, more straightforward *nyigan* and *iyanat* ("brave" and "honest") at the other. The third dimension might be labeled "individual quickness versus positive interpersonal attributes," where *kwelat, utat, ng'om,* and *kaseit* ("smart," "clever," "intelligent," and "understanding/obedient") are opposed to *kararon ng'alekyik* and *mie mukulel* ("polite" and "good-hearted").

Kipsigis Concepts of the Child: I vs II

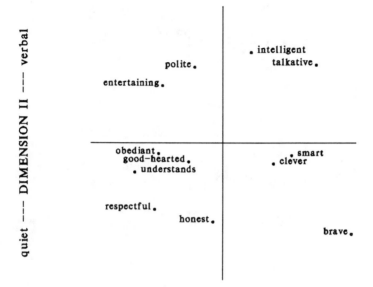

submissive --- **DIMENSION I** --- assertive

FIG. 15.1   KYST scaling of adjectives used to describe children (Dimensions 1 & 2).

In considering the patterns of response in both the informant discussions and triads tests, three features are striking. First is the dominance of the helpfulness/obedience cluster among the terms for describing children's behavior. Of equal importance is the fact that the illustrations that informants provided to talk about the second cluster, glossed as intelligence, are also drawn from the domain of helpful and intelligent behavior. Thus, although "intelligence" is recognized as a verbal, social quality in the abstract, its most salient expression is in the domain of carrying out one's responsibilities at home. In this context, the ability to be helpful without being reminded by an adult emerges as an important marker of intelligence. This expression of intelligence is perhaps the central meaning of the word *ng'om;* it is the unmarked category, in contrast to the marked category *ng'om en sukul,* or "smart in school." Finally, the importance of *ng'om* as a developmental parameter is striking. *Ng'om* is not used to describe adult

Kipsigis Concepts of the Child: I vs III

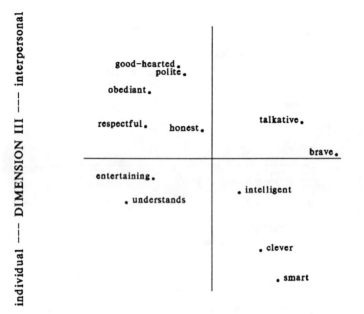

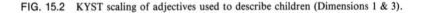

FIG. 15.2   KYST scaling of adjectives used to describe children (Dimensions 1 & 3).

behavior, although it is recognized as very similar to adult cleverness and wisdom; neither is it applied to infants.

Cambridge Parents

Data on the Cambridge parents' concepts of children's personal qualities come from parent interviews. These interviews, which were carried out every 6 months with each couple together, lasted about an hour each and were open-ended in structure, focusing around parents' observations and interpretations of their child's behavior and development at the time. Conversation was aided by parent "diaries," one-page sheets for recording the child's daily routines and parental comments on aspects of the child's behavior (e.g., sleeping, eating, relationships with siblings, current "issues"). We report here some preliminary results from textual analysis of personal descriptors used by parents in a subset of interviews with six different couples. Because these descriptors are derived using a different method from the Kipsigis study and because they refer to children mostly at the lower end of the 3–10 age range or below, caution should be used in comparing the results. Nevertheless, the differences are striking.

The six interviews with the Cambridge parents produced a total of over 70 different words or phrases describing personal qualities in children, mostly referring to the "target" child but also about siblings and children of friends or relatives. The number of descriptors in each interview (not counting repeats of any given term or phrase) varied from 6 to 39, with an average of 16 descriptors for each interview.

Like the Kipsigis terms, the words used by American parents seem to fall rather naturally into a small number of conceptual clusters, but these are very different from the Kipsigis categories. For the American parents, we have identified five categories:

1. The largest group of words and phrases refers to children's cognitive capacities. Words in this cluster include "intelligent" and "smart" as well as "curious," "inquisitive," "imaginative," and "interested." Parents related many different kinds of overt behavior to perceived underlying intelligence. For example, one mother associated "restlessness" and "intelligence" in her 6-month-old baby. In contrast, the parents of a 3-year-old boy attributed his "slowness" in getting mobilized for family errands to the fact that the child was "in his own world," commenting that his mind was "very fast" although physically he was "slow." Intelligence was a quality identified by all the parents in relation to their children and there seemed to be no relationship to age: That is, unlike the Kipsigis parents, the Cambridge parents were ready to attribute intelligence even to young infants. Whereas the Kipsigis ng'om seems to be developmentally bounded, the Cambridge parents used observations on the child's developmental status relative to other children the same age as evidence of intelligence. Thus, words such as "advanced" or "way ahead" were indicators of cognitive capacities, whether manifested in social behavior, the acquisition of language, or motor skills.

2. Second-largest in number of terms produced was a cluster referring to children's independence and self-reliance. Children who had this quality were said to have a "focused personality" or a "sense of themselves." This kind of child could "make choices" and "play by himself." Children who were independent might also be "rebellious" and "defiant." The qualities of independence and self-reliance were closely related to desirable cognitive capacities in that children who were independent, could make choices and

entertain themselves were seen as well-equipped to learn about the world around and assimilate this knowledge to their own goals.

3. The third cluster of terms refers to desirable social qualities and their opposites, many related to the "independence" cluster. Parents described their children as "comfortable with others" (especially in new situations), "confident," or "well-adjusted." Contrasted to this were children who were "shy," "reserved," or "attached" (especially to the mother).

4. A fourth set of descriptors were affective, describing qualities that were mostly positive but more importantly, suggested parental perception of their child as a unique individual. One couple produced 22 such descriptors to refer to a 6-month-old baby girl, including "serious," "fierce," "sweet," "feminine," "passionate," and having "a powerful personality."

5. Finally, most parents also described their children in relation to ease of care, using such words as "flexible," "adaptable," "easy," or in contrast "difficult." It is noteworthy that only in this context did parents use the word "good" to refer to a child. Sometimes the desirable qualities within this cluster were contrasted to the culturally valued quality of "independence"; as one mother ruefully remarked, "At times I sort of wish he'd be a little more submissive and listen to his mom."

The contrasts between the Kokwet and Cambridge parents' concepts of children's intelligence and personality show how parental concepts are embedded in culturally structured events or situations. The Kokwet informants define "intelligence" in terms of responsible and autonomously motivated completion of household chores; the Cambridge parents find evidence of their child's intelligence in performance of a memory game at a birthday party, or a child's interest in words and letters in books or on TV. Although parental ethnotheories are grounded in everyday experience shared by parents and children, parents are not simply the enactors of a previously written and externally directed cultural script. Rather, parents are the active constructors of culture in the ways that they organize children's daily lives, and this function becomes particularly evident as we review developmental trends in children's routine activities.

SETTINGS OF CHILDREN'S DAILY LIVES

The settings of children's daily lives in Kokwet and Cambridge were of course radically different in many ways. The Kokwet children were members of large families in a semi-traditional community of farmers and pastoralists in East Africa, whereas the Cambridge children were born into small middle- and professional-class families in an urban post-industrial society. Whereas most of the Kokwet children could expect to complete primary school while continuing to help with the family farms, the Cambridge children were being raised with the expectation of higher education and individualistic professional careers. Even the health parameters of life for children in the two settings were markedly different: Whereas most families in Kokwet had experienced the loss of at least one child early in life, children in the Cambridge families, and their parents, could normally expect to live long and healthy lives.

We focus here on how these general environmental differences translate into differences in the physical and social settings of children's lives in the two cultures. Following the work of B. Whiting (1980), we recognize the role of parents in assigning children to settings involving different activities, locations, and participants as an important dimension of socialization. Here, we examine the allocation of waking time among different activities for infants and young children (through age 6 in Kokwet, through age 4 in Cambridge). For the Kokwet children, the data for making this comparison are "family spot observations," an adaptation of the technique developed by the Munroes (Munroe & Munroe, 1971) for observing social behavior at a given moment in time. In the family spot observations, a research assistant approached the homestead and noted down the activities of all household members who were present, then asked about the location and activities of all others. All families in Kokwet ($n = 64$) were visited in this way approximately ten times between the hours of 9 a.m. to 6 p.m., in a pseudorandomly assigned order, over the course of a couple of weeks (n observations $= 690$). Overall, the family spot observations were spread over a year, in order to capture seasonal variation in activities at the group level. The data for the Cambridge children come from "parental diaries," one-page sheets for keeping track of the study child's daily routines in terms of location, activity, caretaker and others present. The parental diaries were kept by one of the parents (usually the mother) for a week at a time at 6-month intervals over a year and a half, making a total of four sets of diaries for each of the 36 children in the study. Because the times for keeping these diaries were established by the child's birthday, the diaries also cover all seasons as well as ages from early infancy to almost the fifth birthday. We present here the results of two analyses of the diary data: one including all waking time (both day and night), and the other all waking time from 9 a.m. to 6 p.m., corresponding to the Kokwet data.

Kokwet Settings

Table 15.1, showing the proportions of time that the Kokwet children spend in different activities, reflects many aspects of the social ecology of childhood in this cultural setting. The first variable, "baby," indicates physical caretaking (including bathing, holding, soothing, or entertaining)

TABLE 15.1
Child Activities (Percent) by Age: Kokwet

Age in years	0	1	2	3	4	5	6
Baby	73	61	0	0	0	0	0
Eating	16	11	14	8	9	9	8
Trips/away from home	10	17	1	4	2	6	1
Watch/socialize/ be with	1	2	28	26	24	18	12
Play	0	8	42	36	28	25	18
Chores	0	0	15	25	35	40	55
School	0	0	0	0	0	4	6

that is directed only to children in the first 2 years of life, when they are the focus of intensive caretaking attentions. Trends in the variable "eating" also reflect changing feeding patterns related to the child's age: Infants nurse frequently on demand, children in the second and third years of life snack more frequently than older children, and thereafter the amount of time spent in eating seems to level off, corresponding to mealtimes for the rest of the family. During the first 2 years, babies are more likely to be off on trips outside the community, being carried on their mothers' backs in cloth slings (the fact that this is especially common in the second year of life reflects the fact that very young infants are mostly kept at home to protect them from the "evil eye" of strangers). After reaching age 2, children are generally not carried on the mother's back, and remain at home with the other children when the mother must go outside the community for errands. The variable "watch, socialize, 'be with'," which becomes an important component of children's activities starting at age 2 and begins to drop after age 3, captures a transitional stage in children's activities from infancy to early childhood when they are no longer the object of caretaking but not yet old enough to be of much help around the homestead. Children of this age are often found in little groups of siblings and half-siblings, seated together on a cowhide laid out on the ground as they watch the goings-on of the older family members. The main activity of children aged 2 to 3 years, however, is play. Although babies were never coded as "playing" by our Kipsigis research assistants, children aged 2 were observed playing 42% of the time. This activity, like the "sociable" variable, drops off soon thereafter and is replaced by increasing time during which children are observed doing chores. This category becomes the single largest occupier of children's time in Kokwet, using a quarter of it by age 3 and over half by age 6.

The profile of activities for the Cambridge children from infancy through age 4 years, shown in Table 15.2, suggests a different set of interactions between physical growth and development on the one hand and the culturally structured microenvironment on the other. Although the Cam-

TABLE 15.2
Child Activities (Percent) by Age: Cambridge

Age in years	0	1	2	3	4
Eating	29	22	23	20	18
Errand/away from home	10	14	14	17	16
Help/accompany	4	6	6	5	4
Play	38	42	36	35	42
Chores	0	0	0	1	0
TV/books	1	4	9	11	8
Bedtime/bath	9	10	10	10	10
Other	7	3	1	1	0

bridge children's time spent in eating drops after the first year, it remains higher than for the Kokwet children through age 4, reflecting the fact that mealtimes are more organized and elaborate for the Cambridge families than for the Kokwet families. Age trends for the variable "errand, entertainment away from home" also show that the Cambridge children spend a great deal more time than do the Kokwet children on outings or errands with their parents—and, unlike the Kokwet picture, this activity increases with age. The contrast with the Kokwet age trend is based first on the different mode of transport—cars for the Cambridge families, walking for the Kokwet families—and secondly on the fact that Cambridge parents seem to have many consumer-related errands to carry out as well as a full array of outings for the pleasure of the child or the family as a whole. The single greatest contrast between the Cambridge and Kokwet children, however, is in the areas of chores and play. The Cambridge children do virtually no chores (less than 1 percent of the time) at any age within the range recorded here, although they do spend small amounts of time "helping" or "accompanying" others (usually a parent) in the other's chore—for example, "helping" the mother to peel a carrot or fold laundry. The fact that this "helping" activity shows no increase with age, however, indicates that it is not truly an instrumental activity from the parents' point of view. In contrast, the Cambridge children are recorded as "playing" during large amounts of the day from infancy on, up to half the child's daytime hours by age 4. Further, the Cambridge children spend significant amounts of time in two other activities which do not occur at all for the Kokwet children: watching TV or reading books, and bedtime-related activities. These two activities are particularly significant during the evening hours after 6 p.m. (and the TV category also for the time before 9 a.m. in some families). Taken together, the three categories of play, TV/books, and bedtime activities account for over half the child's waking time after the first year of life, with most of the remainder divided between eating and errands or outings (time in daycare is not coded separately here, so is included in the "play" category for the most part).

Differences between activities for children in each culture can be related to the larger ecology of their families, including the structure of parents' work, the nature of household tasks, the availability of both money to spend and things to spend it on. B. Whiting (1980) related parental assignment of children to various settings to the needs of parents themselves, for example, mothers' workloads or needs for sociability. In addition to recognizing the importance of this perspective, we suggest that the exigencies of parents' lives by themselves do not fully explain socialization practices. On one hand, the Kokwet mother who assigns her very young children to do chores will achieve only limited results in terms of the work that is actually accomplished; on the other, the Cambridge mother who does chores herself while the children nap in order to spend time with them in play is undoubtedly adding to her already heavy workload.

For a fuller understanding of the sociocultural origins of parental behavior in structuring their children's daily lives, we find it useful to draw from the concept of parental ethnotheories as being not only representations of what is, but also goals for what is to be attained. From this perspective, it becomes clear that for the Kokwet children, the increase in chores and decrease in play and sociability starting at age 2 are indicators of socialization pressure toward early learning of responsibility and obedience expressed in the household context, or the development of those qualities that Kipsigis parents regard as *ng'om*. Developmental trends for the Cambridge children show no such pressure toward learning to be helpful and responsible at home: As we have noted, performance of chores by these children is so rare that it never even reaches one percent of their time; and the "helping" category is as frequent for toddlers as for older children, suggesting that this is simply a way for the child to be with a parent while the parent carries out some task. Similarly, time spent in bedtime routines does not change for the Cambridge children in the first 5 years of life. Continued parental involvement in bedtime routines indicates that this task is related to much more than just getting the child into bed with clean hands and face and teeth brushed—a task that young children in many cultures might be expected accomplish on their own. In contrast to the Kokwet children, the Cambridge children spend the great majority of their time in play or play-related activities during the first 5 years of life. For consideration of the cultural and developmental significance of practices such as American bedtime routines and the structuring of play, and for the Kipsigis the assignment of chores, we turn to customs of child rearing as the final focus of this chapter.

CUSTOMS OF CHILD REARING

Kipsigis parental expectations and related training are formalized in several customs of child rearing, such as the use of sibling caretakers for babies, and early training for household tasks including gardening, sweeping out the house, and cooking over an open fire. This kind of socialization is supported by a style of parent–child discourse that emphasizes commands over questions, and that does little to elicit speech from the young child, as we have discussed elsewhere (Harkness, 1977, 1988, 1990; Harkness & Super, 1982). Harsh discipline is also considered appropriate for disobedient children. Whiting and Edwards (1988, pp. 94–95) described mothers in East Africa who carry out this style of child rearing as "training mothers," and they described the mothers' beliefs and related customs of child rearing as follows:

> The training mothers in subsaharan Africa believe that responsibility and obedience can and should be taught to young children. They begin teaching household, gardening, and animal husbandry skills at a comparatively early age. The Ngeca mothers we interviewed are typical: They believe that they should train a child to be a competent farmer, herdsman, and child nurse and that a child from age 2 on should be assigned chores that increase in complexity and arduousness with age. They punish their children for failure to perform these tasks responsibly or for stubbornly refusing to do what their elders request of them. They allow much of their children's learning to occur through observation and imitation; only occasionally do they instruct them explicitly. Moreover, mothers seldom praise their children lest they become proud, a trait that is unacceptable. They allow the major rewards for task performance to be intrinsic.

For the Cambridge children, play is a major component of children's activities starting in infancy, and from the parents' perspective it plays an important role in the development of children's cognitive capacities and independence. In this regard, parental organization of (and participation in) children's play activities emerges as a significant custom of child rearing. Thus, the Cambridge parents talked about the importance of play *in certain contexts* or structured in certain ways, as opposed to play simply for amusement. One mother who is also a day-care teacher talked about organizing play for her class of 2-year-olds to "stimulate sensory–motor development," for example using the water table. Another mother expressed concern about whether the quality of play in the mixed-age family day-care setting that her 3-year-old son was attending was adequate:

> Malcolm is exposed to babies through 6-year-olds basically, plus her own kids. He's exposed to a lot and he seems to adapt pretty well. But I think, judging from the interaction that he has with kids around his own age, I think he's ready to go into something else. I think he's a smart kid. I think he needs a little bit of a challenge, not just play, creativeness on his own, but maybe a little bit more. Not forced, but just an opportunity for him.

The mother explained that she wanted to offer her son "opportunities that I think are beneficial, that are kind of playful. So that's what I want for Malcolm and I think some kind of nursery school . . . . "

Interestingly, another mother stressed the importance of staying at home and playing alone for her son, as a means of developing imagination and self-reliance:

> . . . we suddenly realized that it's only recently that everybody is shipping their kids out. I like having Alex at home, but I also sort of believe in it in terms of what—I guess I think that if children are at home, even if they're bored and they don't socialize as much—first of all, they'll learn to socialize in good time—but that they build up self—their ability to amuse themselves, which I think is the number one gift you can give a human being for the rest of their life. He may go through a week where he's sort of bored and hanging on me and picking fights with me. The rest of the time, for months on end, he is occupying himself and has an incredible imagination and inventing things and talking about things. I just think that if little teeny kids are with other kids all day long, they just don't develop that kind of original self-reliant mind if they have a tendency in that direction.

Although one mother wanted to send her son to nursery school whereas the other wanted to keep hers at home, both shared a concern about the quality of play interaction between the child and others as it relates to the development of culturally valued aspects of intelligence and independence. Parents assign themselves an important role in this regard as playmates and teachers. This role was outlined by a father even as he mocked other parents who, in his opinion, overdid the "quality time" idea with their children:

> They need some of that one-on-one interaction. But a lot of the time they seem perfectly comfortable to explore in their own light. You have to give them some of the tools to do it—I listen to people at work where both parents have to work. It seems they descend on the kid like a ton of bricks. Here's this greatest new idea and you're going to learn it come hell or high water. And I'm not sure that that's quality time from the child's point of view . . . I think in some ways the quality time aspect is being around the kid enough to sense when he is changing and when you have to sort of roll with the punches and keep their intellectual stimulation going.

The Cambridge parents' talk about their children's play and their own roles in this context relates to a series of customary practices, including "special time" or "quality time," bedtime routines, fathers' involvement in play with children, parental organization of visits to museums as well as arrangement of play with peers, and even the choice of nursery school or day care. Although these practices each relate to different specific activities, they share the common property of expressing similar underlying parental ethnotheories of child behavior and development, centering around cognitive capacities and independence. Customs of child care and child rearing can thus usefully be regarded as *instantiations* of parental beliefs that both represent the beliefs to the parents themselves and provide a means for parents to convey their beliefs to their children.

PARENTAL ETHNOTHEORIES AND CHILD DEVELOPMENT

In this chapter, we have discussed the role of parental ethnotheories as they contribute to the organization of settings of everyday life for children and as they are expressed in customs of care. These three elements — ethnotheories, settings, and customs — together function as the "developmental niche" to mediate the individual's developmental experience within the larger culture. As we suggested elsewhere (Super & Harkness, 1986), the three components of the niche function together as a system, with homeostatic mechanisms that promote consonance among them. In this chapter, we have pursued further the question of exactly how the three components are related to each other through the beliefs and behavior of parents, and have assigned a more powerful role to parental ethnotheories than has been previously attributed in anthropological thinking. In particular, we draw attention to developmental trends in children's everyday activity settings as indicators of parents' developmental goals, and to customs of child care as instantiations of parental ethnotheories.

The developmental results of differing parental ethnotheories and their expression in the organization of settings of daily life and customs of childrearing in Kokwet and Cambridge is that children's competence in the culturally marked areas is accelerated, whereas development in other domains lags if indeed it is even recognized. Thus, it is customary in Kokwet for children as young as 5 years old to take care of infants without the immediate supervision of an adult. A 3-year-old boy can drive cows from the garden, and an 8-year-old girl can cook an entire dinner for the family over an open fire. These same children do poorly in a simple cognitive test that involves retelling a story to an adult tester (Harkness & Super, 1982). The Cambridge children, on the other hand, may be highly precocious verbally, in some cases speaking in full sentences by the age of 2 according to their parents. These children become adept at imaginative play and at competing for the attention and praise of parents and other adults. Typically, however, these children will also frustrate their parents by slow developmental progress in relation to household responsibilities.

In discussing both cross-cultural differences and developmental trends in settings and customs of child care, we have sought to identify regularities in the learning environments of children that have important influences on the pace and quality of development in several areas. Although many variations in the specifics of these may be found both among and within families in each culture, we suggest that they are overwhelmed by the regularities that exist at the cultural level. Our assumption that the child's learning is drawn from these regularities is analogous to Bates' (1991) argument that regularities in the child's speech environment provide the basis for language learning, even though they may not be obvious if one looks at a series of imperfect examples of language input. From this perspective, the description of settings of daily life for children and the identification of customs of care may both provide access to processes through which parental theories are put into action.

ACKNOWLEDGMENTS

This research was supported in part by grants from the National Science Foundation, the William T. Grant Foundation, the Spencer Foundation, the National Institute of Mental Health, and the Carnegie Corporation of New York. All statements made and opinions expressed are the sole responsibility of the authors.

REFERENCES

Bates, E. (1991, April). Language acquisition in the 1990s. In R. Vasta (Chair) *Setting a path for the 1990s: Some goals and challenges.* Symposium conducted at the biennial meeting of the Society for Research in Child Development, Seattle, WA.

Burton, M. L., & Nerlove, S. B. (1976). Balanced designs for triad tests. *Social Science Research, 5,* 247–267.

D'Andrade, R. G. (1984). Cultural meaning systems. In R. A. Shweder & R. A. LeVine (Eds.), *Culture theory: Essays on mind, self, and emotion* (pp. 88–119). Cambridge, England: Cambridge University Press.

D'Andrade, R. G., & Strauss, C. (Eds.). (in press). *Human motives and cultural models.* Cambridge, Cambridge University Press.

Freeman, D. (1983). *Margaret Mead and Samoa: the making and unmaking of an anthropological myth.* Cambridge, MA: Harvard University Press.

Harkness, S. (1977). Aspects of social environment and first language acquisition in rural Africa. In C. Snow & C. Ferguson (Eds.), *Talking to children: Language input and acquisition* (pp. 309–316). Cambridge, England: Cambridge University Press.

Harkness, S. (1988). The cultural construction of semantic contingency in mother–child speech. *Language Sciences, 10,* 53–67.

Harkness, S. (1990). A cultural model for the acquisition of language: Implications for the innateness debate. In C. H. Dent & P. G. Zukow (Guest eds.), Special Issue: The idea of innateness: Effects on language and communication research. *Developmental Psychobiology, 23,* 727–740.

Harkness, S., Edwards, C. P., & Super, C. M. (1981). Social roles and moral reasoning: A case study in a rural African community. *Developmental Psychology, 17,* 595–603.

Harkness, S., & Super, C. M. (1982). Why African children are so hard to test. In L. L. Adler (Ed.), *Cross-cultural research at issue* (pp. 145–152). New York: Academic Press.

Harkness, S., & Super, C. M. (1983). The cultural construction of child development: A framework for the socialization of affect. *Ethos, 11,* 221–231.

Harkness, S., & Super, C. M. (1988). Fertility change, child survival, and child development: Observations on a rural Kenyan community. In N. Scheper-Hughes (Ed.), *Child survival: Anthropological perspectives on the treatment and maltreatment of children* (pp. 59–70). Boston: D. Reidel.

Harkness, S., & Super, C. M. (1991). East Africa. In J. M. Hawes & N. R. Hiner (Eds.), *Children in historical and comparative perspective: An international handbook and research guide* (pp. 217–240). New York: Greenwood Press.

Harkness, S., & Super, C. M. (in press-a). Shared child care in East Africa: Sociocultural origins and developmental consequences. In M. Lamb, K. Sternberg, C.-P. Hwang, & A. Broberg (Eds.), *Child care in context: Cross-cultural perspectives.* Hillsdale, NJ: Lawrence Erlbaum Associates.

Harkness, S., & Super, C. M. (in press-b). The "developmental niche": A theoretical framework for analyzing the household production of health. *Social Science and Medicine.*

Harkness, S. & Super, C. M. (in press-c). The cultural foundations of fathers' roles: Evidence from Kenya and the U.S. In B. Hewlett (Ed.), *The father–child relationship: Anthropological perspectives.* New York: Aldine.

Harkness, S., Super, C. M., & Keefer, C. H. (in press). Learning to be an American parent: How cultural models gain directive force. In R. G. D'Andrade & C. Strauss (Eds.), *Human motives and cultural models.* Cambridge, England: Cambridge University Press.

Mead, M. (1928). *Coming of age in Samoa.* New York: Freeman.

Munroe, R. H., & Munroe, R. L. (1971). Household density and infant care in an East African society. *Journal of Social Psychology, 83,* 3–13.

Quinn, N., & Holland, D. (1987). Culture and cognition. In D. Holland & N. Quinn (Eds.), *Cultural models in language and thought* (pp. 3–42). Cambridge, Cambridge University Press.

Super, C. M. (1983). Cultural variation in the meaning and use of children's "intelligence." In J. B. Deregowski, S. Dziurawiec, & R. C. Annis (Eds.), *Expiscations in cross-cultural psychology.* Lisse, The Netherlands: Swets & Zeitlinger.

Super, C. M., & Harkness, S. (1981). The infant's niche in rural Kenya and metropolitan America. In L. L. Adler (Ed.), *Cross-cultural research at issue* (pp. 247–255). New York: Academic Press.

Super, C. M., & Harkness, S. (1986). The developmental niche: A conceptualization at the interface of child and culture. *International Journal of Behavioral Development, 9,* 545–569.

Whiting, B. B. (1980). Culture and social behavior: A model for the development of social behavior. *Ethos, 8,* 95–116.

Whiting, B. B., & Edwards, C. P. (1988). *Children of different worlds: The formation of social behavior.* Cambridge, MA: Harvard University Press.

16

Parental Belief Systems Under the Influence: Social Guidance of the Construction of Personal Cultures

Cynthia Lightfoot
State University of New York at Plattsburgh

Jaan Valsiner
University of North Carolina

Contributors to this volume are taking part in an important movement to link children's development to broader familial, cultural, and historical systems. Parental belief systems are particularly intriguing in this context because they are assembled at the crossroads of everyday experiences of parents and the "expert advice" that is circulated through social communication channels.

The goal of this chapter is to analyze the foundations and the processes by which culturals guide the construction of parental beliefs. It is meant to complement the other contributions to this volume that more specifically address the issues of beliefs as intrapsychological phenomena. Instead, we try to make sense of the interpersonal nature of parents' belief systems. First, we consider different ways in which social suggestions might impact the development of parental beliefs. The context of construction of parental beliefs is the history of the culture. Culture is always a heterogeneous entity that entails a variety of meanings, cultural models, and their encodings in the human physical environment. We present some historical evidence of ideological diversity and inconsistency within the American culture that is reflected in social suggestions to adults about child-related issues. Finally, we analyze a set of suggestions for parents in the 1980s that were encoded into commercial advertisements published in a popular magazine for parents. It is demonstrated that the co-constructionist perspective on parental beliefs can be applied to social suggestions emanating from the advertisements.

PARENTAL ROLES AND BELIEF SYSTEMS, AND THEIR STUDY

Psychologists and anthropologists have long maintained that social and cultural systems of meaning are not fixed and absolute, but vary according to individual points of view. Reality is construed differently according to variations in developmental status, life history and events, and intrapsychic conflicts (Scheibe, 1970). This basic tenet of psychological development is predicated upon the open–systemic nature of all developing systems, and creates a major theoretical difficulty for contemporary empiricistic psychology. Specifically, a conflict exists between the need for conceptualizing the "context dependency" of psychological phenomena, and the context-eliminating theoretical traditions that psychology has been built upon (Valsiner, 1987, chapter 5). Hence, a gulf exists between the levels of theory and empirical work; static conceptions of society and culture remain implicit in empirical work that generally defines "culture" as a homogeneous entity shared by all (or at least most) of its members. Recent appeals have been made for explicitly addressing the relational and public nature of parental psychology (Goodnow & Collins, 1991). These should include a call for rethinking the meaning of "effects" that parental belief systems might have on children's development.

What Are "Effects" in Psychology?

The concept of "effect" is one of the most widely used, but poorly defined, conceptual tools in contemporary psychology. Part of the difficulty stems from the extension of statistical jargon (e.g., "effects" of "independent variables" that are discovered post-factum with statistical analysis packages) to general theoretical reasoning. Thus, the empirical finding of differences between the contrasted conditions enter the process of inductive generalization by which some of the "variables" that have been observed to "have an effect" become elevated to the level of theoretical concepts, and acquire surplus meaning as a result of this process. Thus, the reasoning of the investigator inadvertently shifts from *descriptive* uses of the term "effect" to implicitly *causal-explanatory* uses. The concepts that are thus labeled as "having effect" may become assigned to a class of "causes" — for instance, child psychologists remain tempted to isolate different abstract classes of "causes" of development — nature versus nurture, genes versus environment — or "context" (e.g., context effects).

This inductive derivation of causes that are detected by their effects has produced a large pool of concepts to which causal attributions are made. It follows the mind-set of linear causality *(A* causes *X)* that is inductively applied in the research process: If a contrast between *A* and non-*A* leads to the corresponding contrast in the results *(X* vs. non-*X),* then *A* causes *X.*

Alternatively, we may want to consider a second general approach to effect — any effect is always interactive, because it emerges *in the course of interaction* between different parts of a holistic system. All effects in this case become side-products of a system — no effect can be attributed solely to a cause that exists beyond the systemic relations. If *A* and *B* constitute a system that generates an effect *X,* then neither *A* nor *B* can be said to cause *X,* but a description of the interdependence between *A* and *B* gives us the explanation of the emergence of the effect *X.* From this point of view, parental beliefs cannot have direct effects on the behavior of parents. Neither can the latter have such effects on children's development. However, as parts of the parental psychological system, beliefs are linked systemically with parental actions, and different forms of that link may have different consequences for the life-world of developing children.

Parental Co-Construction of Beliefs

It is obvious that only the second approach to effects fits the goals of research in developmental psychology where the organism's active role in the (co)construction of its development is a basic axiom. "Co-construction" (see also Wozniak, 1986) reflects the culturally guided construction (and reconstruction) of higher psychological processes that organize a person's life. Although the individual is active in this process, the personal construction of psychological instruments and knowledge is guided by the cultural world in which the person lives. That cultural world, however, is not uniform — it is filled with a variety of specific persons who set themselves a variety of goals in their interaction with one another. A person's system of beliefs reflects the variability present in his or her social world.

Beliefs are a good example of semiotically coded higher psychological functions that are constructed and internalized with cultural guidance (see Valsiner, 1988, 1989). The socially communicated meanings (and exchanged cultural artifacts) constitute the collective culture that provides material for constructing a personal culture. Thus, belief systems that exist within a collective culture do not have an effect in the sense of being copied directly (or appropriated) by individuals. Instead, they constitute resources from which active persons construct their own (personal) belief structures. Obviously, the resources of the collective culture are biased in ways that direct persons to construct their personal belief systems in some generic ways, rather than others. Nevertheless, individually unique belief systems are results of the construction process, based on the beliefs embedded in social suggestion complexes. These complexes—loosely organized structures of social expectations that circulate in the social discourse of the time—can tie together many heterogeneous beliefs, and present those to individuals in ways that become linked with their existing intrapersonal knowledge and belief systems.

Parental beliefs are assembled by coordinating inductive and deductive logics. Inductive knowledge emerges from personal child-rearing experiences, whereas deductive knowledge is based on meanings and values maintained in the collective culture. When adults become parents, they also become active participants in the collective cultural organization of their parenting roles. One input to the organizational process consists of social suggestions communicated by other parents, teachers, pediatricians, counselors, mass media, and so forth. Parents act on these suggestions in a variety of ways, accepting, rejecting, and modifying them. Thus, their parental roles develop in the form of personal cultures, where their role-based actions are linked with their personal cultural "sense" of those actions. Beliefs here serve as mental organizers of the kinds of actions (but not necessarily specific ways of acting) that the parents are likely to undertake.

The realm of parental beliefs encompasses a multitude of social suggestions communicated by the collective culture at particular points in time. For example, the "landscape" of social suggestions presented to North American parents in the 1980s is likely to differ from previous decades. Furthermore, the suggestions may be considered *complexes*—structured entities consisting of particular beliefs and facts that may be hierarchically organized (see Sigel, 1985). Social suggestion complexes, which are negotiated on the interpersonal plane of communication, become reorganized at the intrapersonal level; they provide the raw material for communicating about parenting, and for constructing personal cultures.

However, the ways in which a person's cognitive system handles the social suggestion complexes are variable, and the idea that persons simply *appropriate* (accept, take over) the social suggestions is a narrow model of the complex ways in which persons relate to their social surroundings. Borrowing a metaphor from modern medicine, we could speak of the social suggestion complexes as carriers of "collective cultural viruses" (in the form of affect-laden meanings) meant to infect or penetrate personal belief systems (systems of personal sense). Their success, however, depends on whether the individual's personal culture in its present state is susceptible to such influence, or whether it contains psychological "antibodies" or conflicting beliefs (that had emerged during previous experiences), that block or neutralize the "attack." As we elaborate later, social suggestion complexes vary in intensity and forcefulness, and several strategies are available for coping with them.

Diversity of Ideas in the Collective Culture:
The North American Case

A variety of sources substantiate the claim that shared cultures are ideologically heterogeneous, and permit a wide range of often inconsistent personal beliefs. For example, in an anthropological study of a small American rural community, West (1945) documented inconsistencies regarding beliefs about class structure. People claimed, "This is *one* place where ever'body is equal. You don't find no classes here." Nonetheless, community members provided highly reliable accounts of a differentiated class structure in which "people know their place." Furthermore, West observed that children are socialized, by parents and peers alike, to express beliefs of both equality and class hierarchy. Scheibe (1970) compiled evidence of belief inconsistencies from several other sources, and argued that it is fruitless to worry over which belief is *the* belief. Rather, the lesson to be learned is that belief systems should be conceptualized in light of the different interactional (social and cultural) realities in which they operate. The work presented here proceeds from this general perspective. Any collective culture is naturally heterogeneous, and provides different (at times contradictory) foundations for the construction of personal cultures.

The notion of cultural heterogeneity is not widespread in cultural anthropology or cross-cultural psychology. Most analyses of North American ideologies focus on homogeneity rather than diversity, but they provide a convenient point from which to trace divergences. Hogan and Elmer (1978), for example, enumerated several consistent ideological beliefs that define the American way of life. These include: *rationalism* (the belief that the highest form of human activity is thinking and knowing); *individualism* (the belief that society is a mere association of separate and self-directed individuals); and *liberalism* (the belief that people are inherently competent and rational in pursuing their individual interests and goals) (see Morris, 1956, and Kluckhohn, 1961, for similar analyses). Hogan and Elmer argued that the peculiarly American norm of competitive individualism undergirds these beliefs, and contrasted it with collectivism—"the usual lot of mankind" (p. 484). Terrence Ball (1983) made a similar distinction when he portrayed the designers of the American political system as reactionaries bent on dispelling collectivist notions of culture. According to Ball, the principle of self-interest animated the very engineering of America; it was the first government to constitutionally sanction the pursuit of private interests.

The individualism–collectivist distinction has been useful for framing a variety of cultural differences in human behavior and development. Dien (1982) emphasized the distinction in his account of cultural differences in moral reasoning. Comparing Chinese and American performances on

Kohlberg's dilemmas task, he argued that Western cultures socialize human autonomy, rationality, and individual responsibility—all derivative of an individualistic ideology, and all characteristic of Kohlberg's higher levels of moral reasoning. Eastern cultures, in contrast, rely on the belief in the individual as morally obliged to maintain group harmony and to subordinate self-interest to the interests of the group. According to Dien, the collectivistic orientation is responsible for "lower" levels of reasoning found typically in Eastern cultures. A similar case has been made for culture-specific conceptions of mental health, and behavioral manifestations of psychiatric disorders (e.g., Draguns, 1974; Kleinman, 1980). The people of Taiwan, for example, are socialized to suppress personal affect, as befits their collectivist ideology; the group is given status above the psychological state and point of view of the individual. It is no coincidence, argued Kleinman (1980), that 70% of clinically depressed Taiwanese patients initially complained of physical symptoms (e.g., weight loss, loss of energy) whereas their American counterparts complained of affective symptoms (e.g., *feeling* depressed).

Although individualism seems to pervade the American way of life, affecting behaviors as diverse as moral reasoning and mental illness, Coleman (1941) cautioned against excluding oppositional features in assertions about American culture and character. The feature of democracy, for example, is usually hailed as an American institution. It encompasses ideas regarding human equality, intolerance of class and social distinctions, universal suffrage, and so on. Yet, Coleman argued, most of the founding fathers followed the aristocratic ideal, and the social and economic stratification in modern United States typifies an autocracy more than a democracy. Coleman presented evidence for ideological ambivalence in a number of other areas as well. On the intellectual front, he discussed widely held American beliefs regarding the power of knowledge and education. These he countered with the charge that a "strong frontier tradition" continues to scorn intellectual achievement, "that our standards of scholarship are low and our teachers poorly trained, that we lack respect for teachers, that our thinking is external, that we seek information instead of knowledge, that our glorified "education for the masses" is superficial, that our business world looks with disdain on academic theory" (Coleman, 1941, p. 493). Other ideological conflicts included those between political passion and apathy, freedom of expression and censorship, deference to authority and independence. Harking back to Scheibe, it appears that core conflicts in American belief systems assume different forms in different social, cultural, and historical contexts. This perspective is consistent with the idea that development is culturally constrained and co-constructed (Valsiner, 1987, 1988, 1989). The whole range of *possible* beliefs in the ideological sphere includes subregions of oppositions (and denials of oppositions) that the collective culture promotes for its self-definition. Thus, the widespread emphasis on the "independence" of North Americans that may be reflected in different accounts can be seen as collective culture's self-promotion of one of the opposites (independence), and denial of the other (dependence) (Winegar, Renninger, & Valsiner, 1989).

The relationship between the range of culturally acceptable ideas and the promotion of particular ideas within that range varies according to the individual's place in history, in his or her current life cycle, the socioeconomic hierarchy, and so forth. So, for example, vocational and academic careers are both acceptable in Western cultures, but may be promoted differently for individuals from different social classes or age cohorts. Likewise, "contradictory" beliefs in freedom of expression and censorship may be promoted differently depending on the source of the message (artist or pornographer), or the intended recipient (adult or child). In more general terms, a culture's accounting of its own history is always selectively constrained to emphasize some of its aspects, and suppress others.

Ideological Diversity Around Children: History of Culture

The full corpus of ideas available in a collective culture at any given time is necessarily heterogeneous. Historical analyses tell an interesting story about the infusion of ideological conflicts into beliefs about children and childhood. Most suggest that social and cultural ambivalences toward the young disappear when placed in historical perspective. Taken separately, the analyses are convincing; inconsistent beliefs become separated by time and are attributed to historical trends rather than coexistent conflicts. But superimposed, conceptual fluctuations documented in certain areas seem to shift in opposite directions from those documented in other areas, and the idea that changing belief systems correspond directly to changing cultural ideologies loses force. The alternative position is that historical fluctuations in belief systems represent a change of focus within a range of ideological possibilities, some of which are inconsistent, and may reflect unresolved conflicts regarding children and the nature of their development.

An obvious place to look for cultural changes in conceptions about children is in cultural artifacts. Art historians have noted that prior to the 20th century children were portrayed as miniature adults (e.g., Humm, 1978). The idea that childhood has special significance, or constitutes an unique period in the life cycle was absent entirely from early American art. The concept of the miniature adult was expressed in children's adult-like body proportions, their elegant and fine clothing, their stiff and self-composed countenance, and the serious-minded activities that they were shown to engage in. At the turn of the century, however, children were painted differently. They became depicted in ways suggestive of their mischievous and playful nature. The change in artistic convention was related to general attitude transformations. Prior to the 20th century, a belief in obedience and subservience to authority (parents and God) prevailed. Children were expected to conform to the same rigid strictures set down for adults. Clergy advised parents to suppress their children's impulses, which were considered dangerous, and to enforce submissiveness early on in order to lay a foundation for moral and virtuous character development. In the late 1800s, however, a more benevolent view of children emerged which granted tolerance on account of their natural naivete and innocence.

Kett's (1977) historical analysis of the American educational system provides evidence for a similar shift in conceptions about children, but in the opposite direction. In the early 1800s, for example, independence and initiative in youth were valued, and education was presumed to take place in the natural course of daily activities. By the 1840s, the lackadaisical attitude toward educating the young was replaced by the assumption that "internalization of moral restraints and the formation of character were more likely to succeed in planned, engineered environments than in casual ones" (Kett, 1977, p. 112). Shortly thereafter, compulsory education laws were introduced, and toward the end of the century concerted efforts were made to enforce obedience and dependency. Indeed, Kett described schools and youth groups of the time as "paramilitary-like" in aim and method.

In addition to teaching compliance, institutions were meant to isolate and protect the young from the more offensive aspects of adult life—dirt, crime, economic, and political concerns, and so on. Paradoxically, close supervision, expectations for compliance, and disengagement from adult affairs and concerns were considered preparatory for the assumption of adult roles. Such a sequestered and extended initiation was considered the ideal context for training independence, initiative, and leadership skills. Kett commented on this paradox by suggesting that institutions concealed the vagaries, contradictions, and pleasures of adult life so that adolescents might build the "character" necessary to keep themselves "pure" and "untempted" (Kett, 1977, p. 253).

Historical analyses of how children are depicted in art, and of the evolution of formal education, support the view that ideological conflicts do not always disappear from one moment in history to another. Instead, it seems that cultural ideologies permit a range of often contradictory beliefs, a subset of which are explicitly promoted at given points in time. However, the ideas that are not promoted actively at a given time need not be absent in the collective culture, but merely underemphasized. Perceived changes in belief systems, then, reflect changes of focus or interest, rather than conceptual revolutions.

Social Suggestions to Parents

Inconsistency and conflict in collective-cultural beliefs is particularly well represented in literature addressed to parents from child care specialists whose expert status marks them symbolically as sources of ideas that should be taken seriously by parents. Hence the potential relevance of experts in the co-construction of parental beliefs.

Clark Vincent (1951) undertook an analysis of articles published from 1890 to 1949 in popular child-care magazines. He focused on changing conceptions regarding breast versus artificial feeding of infants, and disciplinary (i.e., scheduling) practices. Throughout the years surveyed, child-care experts advised mothers to breast-feed their infants, although Vincent noted that the rationale shifted somewhere around 1920 from a concern with infant health and mortality to a concern with the psychological loss suffered by the infant from having the breast withheld, which was presumed to create "distance" between mother and child. Regarding disciplinary practices, in 1890 all of the articles addressing the issue of scheduling recommended that the child's activities be loosely structured. In 1920, however, all of them recommended tight scheduling. So, across the two areas of feeding and scheduling, conceptual shifts occurred in the 1920s, but in opposite directions: The infant's needs became emphasized in the area of feeding, but became subordinated to the mother's needs in the area of scheduling.

Martha Wolfenstein (1953) conducted a similar survey but traced historical fluctuations in the child-care literature to temporally enduring ideological conflicts regarding children's impulses. She surveyed articles appearing between 1914 and 1951 in various editions of *Infant Care,* a widely circulated child-care publication. In the first period, 1914–1921, most articles addressed the dangers of the child's autoerotic impulses — masturbation and thumb-sucking in particular. At this time, parents were advised to vigorously suppress these activities, lest they become uncontrollable and seriously impair future growth and development. As they were most likely to occur while in bed, it was recommended that children's hands and feet be bound to inhibit genital stroking and thumb-sucking. Mechanical restraints were available commercially, including a cuff that could be put on the arms to prevent bending the elbows, and would thus inhibit self-stimulation.

During the second period, 1929–1938, the focus shifted from the dangers of autoerotism to the dangers of the child's domination. Strict scheduling, especially during weaning and bowel training, was considered ammunition against the child's struggle for control.

Another shift occurred between 1942 and 1945. Autoerotism became even less an issue. Now the child's basic urge was one of exploration, and genital play and thumb-sucking were considered incidental to the need to discover one's self and environment. Experts advocated mildness and gentleness in all areas, but the concern with domination continued, albeit in a different form. Now it was believed that meeting children's demands would make them less domineering in the future. The pendulum swung back in the 1950s — mildness continued to be recommended, but the rationale had changed in step with beliefs about domination. Mildness became a strategy for avoiding parent–child struggles for control, which the parent would surely lose.

Wolfenstein (1955) related changing beliefs about child-care practices to conflict regarding the nature of children's impulses. The conflict concerned the relationship between what is *enjoyable* for the child, and what is *good* for the child. At the turn of the century, the enjoyable was considered deleterious. This was reflected not only in advice to suppress autoerotic behavior, but in attitudes toward play. Early on, it was considered excessively exciting and thus dangerous. Later, however, the opposition between pleasant and good was dissolved, but this was accomplished by denying the infant's autoerotic impulses, and replacing them with exploratory drives. At this time, play became associated with motor development and exercise (Frost & Wortham, 1988, reached a similar conclusion based on their analysis of the relationship between conceptions of play and the evolution of American playgrounds).

As time went on, play became not only good, but obligatory. It was fused with all other "serious" activities, and parents were advised to make mealtime fun, toilet training enjoyable, and so forth. Wolfenstein (1955) referred to the infusion of fun into all areas of health and development as the "fun morality" and linked it to the increasing mixing of work and play in American culture. In a recent analysis of parent-oriented journals *(Parents' Magazine* and *Infant Care,)* Kathryn Young (1990) demonstrated inconsistencies in the advice for parents in 1955–1984. In the area of cognitive development, parents are given a basically maturationist message of the competent infant experimenting with the world, but in the domain of language development the emphasis has been on the relevance of social interaction between adult and the baby (increasingly emphasizing the role of fathers as important for healthy infant development). If one tries to generalize about the history of advice to parents, it is clear that experts are driven less by the latest empirical advances than the culturally defined fashion of the times. It is equally clear that cultural conceptions of childhood are meaningfully linked with experts' advice, and parents' felt obligations, to handle children in specific ways.

The Nature of "Fun Morality": Fusion Without Integration

Since the 1950s we can see proliferation of "fun"-linked thinking about everyday life in the United States. This "fun morality," according to

Wolfenstein, does not reflect a synthetic solution to the opposition between work and play. Analogous to the early 1900s arm cuff, the "fun morality" represents a modern redressing of ancient puritanical defenses against impulses. In her words:

> This defense would consist in diffusion, ceasing to keep gratification deep, intense, and isolated, but allowing it to permeate thinly through all activities — Instead of the image of the baby who has fierce pleasures of autoeroticism and the dangerous titillation of rare moments of play, we get the infant who explores his world, every part of whose extent is interesting but none intensely exciting, and who may have a bit of harmless play thrown in with every phase of the day's routine. (Wolfenstein, 1955, p. 175).

Thus, instead of channeling pleasure to a few domains of "leisure," the collective culture organizes the *fusion* of pleasure with *any* activity in which the person is involved. As many activities of children are embedded in competitive settings, "fun" can become a target of competition (who has the most of it?). Likewise, one would expect that social suggestions meant for parents are encoded in such a way that the need for "fun" becomes used as a vehicle for promoting other cultural objectives.

In order to find out more about the collective-cultural direction of parental belief systems, we turned our attention to the contents of commercial advertisements published in a magazine oriented toward parents. The primary goal of these advertisements is to have parents buy things, and to this end, advertisements communicate cultural ideas that have been carefully selected to enhance the appeal of their products. We examined *Parents Magazine* of the mid-1980s. Material was collected from issues published in the even-numbered months (i.e., February, April, June, August, October, December) of 1983, 1985, and 1987. All full-sized commercial advertisements of products intended specifically for children's use and consumption were selected for analysis. Advertisements for general household products (e.g., laundry detergent), or products intended for the entire family (e.g., soup), were excluded.

Each advertisement was coded for the age of the child portrayed (or the age group for which the product was intended: infant/toddler, preschooler, school-aged, mixed ages), whether or not the product was described explicitly as promoting growth or development, the area of functioning the product was intended to impact (motor coordination, physical structures of the body, safety, social relationships, emotions, creativity). Finally, the type of product that was promoted was coded (books, soft and cuddly toys, manipulative toys, clothing, games, computers, audio- and videotapes, food and medicine, diapers and lotions). Reliability between an investigator and a trained coder was calculated to be 81% (agreements divided by agreements plus disagreements). Given the goals of the present study, differences between the 3 years were not considered interesting (and were modest, according to statistical tests), and data were summed across years for the analyses.

Summary of Coded Advertisements

Frequency distributions of different codes for 728 advertisements are shown in Table 16.1. It can be seen that most products were intended for infants and toddlers, followed by preschoolers, school-aged children, and finally, children of mixed ages. Regarding the growth promotion variable, Table 16.1 indicates that less than one third of the advertisements made explicit statements about the growth-promoting potential of their product. The remaining advertisements made no statement regarding this issue, or claimed that the product would maintain current levels of growth or development (e.g., would "meet the changing needs" of the child).

From the data it was possible to discover combinations of different codes (for example—between impact area and product type). We looked at those patterns that occurred in at least 5% of the advertisements. Typically,

TABLE 16.1
Frequencies and Percentages of Categories Coded in *Parents Magazine*

			Frequency	*Percent*
	infant/toddler		337	46.3
	preschooler		201	27.6
Age	school-aged		105	14.4
	mixed ages		85	11.7
		Total	728	100.0
	yes		212	29.1
Growth promotion	no		516	70.9
		Total	728	100.0
	emotion		95	13.0
	safety, health, hygiene		286	39.3
Impact area	emotion and cognition		93	12.8
	emotion and safety, health		45	6.2
		Total	519	71.3
	diapers, soaps, lotions		154	21.2
	food and medicine		191	26.2
Product type	clothes		80	11.0
	manipulatives		124	17.0
	books		47	6.5
		Total	596	81.9

emotion and cognition advertisements were for products claimed to be both fun and educational. Advertisements for products that combined emotion with safety, health, and hygiene included "fun foods," superhero underwear and other "fun clothing," and colorful toothpaste that makes brushing "fun."

It is also interesting to note which categories did not occur, or occurred infrequently. Social skills were represented in only 13 advertisements. Also noteworthy by virtue of their relative absence were advertisements for products claimed to impact the cognition area alone (i.e., without also impacting emotion). There were only 14 such instances. Likewise, motor coordination and functioning was given little emphasis (18 instances).

Highlights of the more interesting summary findings are as follows:

- *Age/growth promotion:* A higher proportion of products intended for preschoolers were claimed to promote growth, compared to products aimed at other age groups. Most of these were "school readiness" products.
- *Age/impact area:* Most infant and toddler products (70.4%) were claimed to impact safety, health, and hygiene; those for preschoolers were fairly evenly distributed among the three areas of emotion, emotion and cognition, and safety, health, and hygiene; those for school-aged children (77.5%) and children of mixed ages (65.3%) were evenly distributed between the two areas of emotion and safety, health, and hygiene.
- *Age/product type:* Diapers, soaps, and lotions accounted for 45% of the products intended for infants and toddlers; 83% of the preschooler products were evenly distributed among food and medicine, manipulatives, and books; food and medicine products accounted for 52% of advertisements directed at school-aged children and 44% of advertisements directed at children of mixed ages.
- *Growth promotion/impact area:* Virtually all advertisements that made explicit statements about the growth-promoting potential of the product claimed to impact the hybrid category of emotion and cognition. Typically, these advertisements claimed that the product would stimulate a "love of learning" (or reading, mathematics, etc.).
- *Growth promotion/product type:* A proportion of advertisements for all product types claimed to promote growth, but this was particularly true for the book and manipulative toy categories; 88.1% of all book advertisements made growth-promotion statements, as did 41.5% of all manipulative toy advertisements.

The foregoing survey of child product advertisements indicates that parents are exposed to a wide variety of products intended to impact a gamut of domains. The organized link between age and product type was evident. Safety, health, and hygiene products, for example, were more common in infant and toddler advertisements. Clearly, parents of infants are expected to be particularly concerned with providing a safe and healthy environment: nutritious foods comfortable and flame resistant clothing, nontoxic objects to chew on, clean and rash-free bottoms. In contrast, parents of preschoolers are expected take on a new concern—that of preparing the child for school. Indeed, there were twice as many advertisements for preschool educational products compared to school-aged educational products. This is due, presumably, to the fact that the location of learning, and the obligation to educate, has shifted from the home to the school.

Social Suggestions for Individual Active Autonomy

Our survey results can also be compassed by the individualistic–collectivistic distinction made by Hogan and Elmer, and others. The emphasis on individual thinking and knowing, in contrast to collectivistic ideals, was apparent in the number of advertisements for educational products compared to those portrayed as impacting social relationships. In fact, of the 13 advertisements for social relationship products, only one showed a child socially engaged with another *person*. The remainder proclaimed that the child would enter a social relationship with the *product* (usually a soft and cuddly one). That the individualistic focus is promoted by the advertisements is evident also from the depiction of parents' roles. Parents were portrayed as rational agents with an important role to play in planning their children's development:

> *FREE* YOUR CHILDREN. Video game machines *do little more than trap your* children in an *unproductive, limited* world. It's not that playing games is bad. It's just that *there's a whole lot more to life than blasting space monsters.* That's why your children need the [brandname computer]. The [brandname computer] is a full function, affordable home computer that *frees* them *to explore* whole new worlds. *Thousands of programs* are available to help your children prepare *for anything* from a third-grade math test to college boards. And they can gain serious computing skills while doing it. A comforting thought, because according to one estimate, by the time your children are ready to enter the job market, three out of four occupations will be computer related. In fact, *studies suggest* that students who get computer aided instruction tend to be more motivated and score higher in the basic disciplines like math, science, and English. The [computer] can also introduce your children to *the finer things in life*—like art and music. The [computer] even *beats* video game machines on their home ground, by offering kids a selection

of *hundreds more* games than all video game machines combined. Games that are *educational, informative — and a whole lot of fun.* So, don't let your children *get trapped. Free* them with the [computer name]. (italics added)

This example links the needs of the child's future (undoubtedly a relevant aspect in parental thinking) to the contrast between *freedom* and *control* (being captured by "unproductive" computer games). The mastery emphasis is apparent in the suggestion that parents can prevent their children from being "trapped," and that they are in power to "free them" and prepare them for a future in a computer dominated world (filled with achievement and "fun").

We find also that Wolfenstein's "fun morality" has inundated modern commercial advertisements. Virtually none promoted a product on the basis of its educational value alone. Instead, products that were claimed to increase academic skills — teach reading, numbers, prepare the child for school, and so forth — did so in the context of teaching the child that "learning is fun." Apparently, learning, in and of itself, is not sufficient to promote a product. Instead, it must be made fun and enjoyable. One advertisement boasted parenthetically: "(And your child won't even know he is learning)." It is assumed that from the child's point of view, play is paramount, and learning incidental. But media communications to parents, sometimes presented in the form of an inside joke, belie a different belief system. Between adults, educating the young is given high priority. The prevailing belief, however, is that the success of educational efforts lies in how well they are disguised as play.

The infusion of fun into "serious" activities was evident not only in the domain of learning and intellectual development, but also in the area of safety, health, and hygiene. Food needs to be more than nutritious, dental care needs to accomplish more than the prevention of tooth decay. These things should also be fun and enjoyable for children. Again, adults are assumed to "know better": "Now there's a cereal with the taste, the crunch and the fun your children want. And what you want for them — good, sound nutrition." So, as Wolfenstein (1955) argued, the opposition remains between what is pleasurable and what is developmentally advantageous. Were it otherwise, parent and child points of view on this issue would not be so clearly demarcated. Furthermore, the two opposites (nutritional value and "fun") remain nonintegrated into one, although such synthesis could in principle be used. Instead, advertisers make clear distinctions between how they want parents versus children to perceive the value of their products. Parents are meant to see serious, no-nonsense intentions — cleanliness, nutrition, education. Children, on the other hand, are expected to be protected from this reality; we allow them the illusion that they are simply having fun.

INTERPERSONAL COMMUNICATIONS AND INTRAPERSONAL BELIEFS

As we argued earlier, parental beliefs are personal constructions. They are organized collectively by individuals who are assuming the role of parent, and by cultural beliefs and ideologies communicated in the form of social suggestions. Although social suggestions emanate from a variety of sources and assume a variety of source-specific forms, our concern here was with advertisements for child-related products.

Parental beliefs are the psychological "products" of the cultural communication process. As such, they mediate between the collective culture at large, and the developing personal cultures of their children. As we elaborated before, the individual psychological consequences of social suggestion complexes can be likened to individual physical consequences of viral infections. The existing belief structure of parents is the base to which incoming social suggestions are related, transformed or rejected.

Let us chart out a hypothetical process of how parental belief systems might handle child-linked product advertisements. Consider the following advertisement for Superhero underwear in which a mother is depicted holding two children on her lap, with Spider-Man and Superman images in the background. One of the children holds a handwritten message — "Mom, you're our real hero" — and the text of the advertisement reads:

TEAM UP WITH THEIR FAVORITE CHARACTERS AND YOU'LL BE THE HERO. When you buy [brand name] boys' briefs and [brand name] underwear sets, you'll be a big hero with your kids. Because every time your boys put on our quality [company name] decorated underwear, you are giving them all the fun and excitement of changing into their favorite characters, like Superman, Thundercats, Spider-Man and many more. All at an affordable price. So team up with their favorite characters and you'll come out a hero.

This social suggestion complex emphasizes a number of issues. First is the mother's role as an agent in providing her children with special underwear and, thus, fun and excitement. Second is the promise that her children will include her in their fun by identifying her with a class of admired superheroes. Third, it suggests by implication that the children's impersonation of a superhero is an emotionally positive experience for them, and one that the mother can promote. The advertisers presume that the mother has already accepted superheroes as positive images, and her role is defined in terms of facilitation: In exchange for providing this avenue to fun and excitement, she is granted social status equal to that of a superhero. This complex is a good example of the construction of "independent dependence" (Winegar, Renninger, & Valsiner, 1989) of parental belief systems —

it is suggested to the parents that they are free to participate in the given relation (child–superheroes) in a specified way (promoting it), rather than in any other ways.

The dialectic of assimilation/accommodation is an appropriate framework for explaining the social co-construction of internalized communicative messages. While assimilating the social suggestion complex, the parent reorganizes it into a different one. At the same time, the existing belief structure is reorganized to accommodate the restructured message. This can be accomplished in a number of ways, four of which are described next, and only one of which resembles simple compliance (see a similar discussion of effects of war toys in Wegener-Spoehring, 1989). We call these varied ways of handling this social suggestion complex "strategies"—without assuming that the use of these strategies needs to be conscious.

Strategies of Co-construction of Parental Beliefs

The compliance strategy would be the one desired by the advertisers. In their best of all worlds, parents should rush into shops to buy the underwear, after accepting all (or some) of the parts of the social suggestion complex. So, some mothers understand the message in ways that link up with previous beliefs: "Superheroes are good"; "taking roles helps children to develop." From that background, the newly constructed connection between the advertised product and "role-impersonation" or "good superheroes" (i.e., "this underwear allows my child to play superhero more easily") can be integrated into the existing belief structure. Similarly, another parent may focus on the parent's active role, and link the advertised underwear into another belief structure (e.g., the coordination of beliefs "parents must do their best to help the child to develop" *and* "parents must be the primary reference figures for children" *and* "children like to impersonate superheroes"). The belief in the beneficial role of the underwear may be integrated into the belief system in yet another connection— with an emphasis on how parents can win their children's appreciation by purchasing special underwear. What we see here is the *multiplicity* of ways in which the *same* social suggestion complex becomes internalized by different parents, still resulting in the same action/outcome.

The transfer strategy is probably the widest class of ways in which social suggestion complexes are processed by their recipients. It involves dissipating the original suggestion complex and integrating its different parts into different belief structures that exist concurrently. Thus, for instance, the advertisement presented in this case may provide facilitative or reorganizing influences to belief structures that exist in parallel: (a) "superheroes are good for the child"; (b) "mothers play an active role in facilitating child development"; and (c) "role impersonation is good for development." Thus, transferring the social suggestion to any of these belief structures may result in a parent buying new superhero *toys* (but *not* underwear) for the child (transfer of the assimilated/accommodated complex part to a structure that leads to action in an adjacent area of purchases). Also, the same parent may more firmly believe in the active role of the mother in children's games, and buy and promote the use of *educational toys* (extension of the "active parenting role" belief in a different content area). And, in another context, the mother may promote children's impersonation of figures that have nothing in common with the superheroes (extension of the advertised impersonation idea to another content area). It is obvious that from the perspective of the advertisers of the underwear, this "effect" upon the parental belief system (leading to action) does not fit with their desired goals (and is a "non-effect" in that narrow sense). At the same time, the social suggestion complex used in the advertisement actually had a latent effect on the parents' beliefs, and actions.

Third, the class of *counteraction strategies* indicates the realm of opposite effects (to those desired by the communicator) resulting from the internalization of the message. Suppose that the parent has a strong preexisting belief in the "ill effects of superheroes for the development of children." Quite expectably, the advertisement may be discarded exactly because of the superhero connection. Or, with a negativistic twist, the parent may actively decide not to purchase goods produced by the given company, as it promotes the detested connection (albeit only imaginary) with superhero play. Or another parent may accept the belief of "positive role of superhero play for children," but the suggested idea that she "needs to team up" with these figures may go contrary to the existing beliefs, and would thus block the expected effects of the ad. Again, the social suggestion complex effectively reorganizes parental belief systems, but in ways that are contrary to the goals of the communicators.

Finally, we should not neglect the immense capability of human beings for purposefully forgetting or neutralizing communicative messages. *Neutralization strategies* include those that *block* the very assimilation/accommodation of the messages at the outset. The parent's preexisting belief structures may dismiss the whole social suggestion complex as irrelevant. So, for instance, a general belief that "product advertisers are tricksters who cannot be believed" may be sufficient to neutralize all three suggestions of the advertisement (parent's active role, impersonation as beneficial in play, superheros as positive figures), even if at a lower level of the belief structure each of these three beliefs exist with positive connotations (e.g., "Yes, of course, superheroes are good images, and it helps my child in development if the child impersonates positive heroes, and certainly I should be the best I can for my child, but all these advertisements are lies anyway").

Interparental Variability In Belief Structures

It is important to recognize that the particular hierarchy of beliefs constructed from media suggestions may vary from one individual to another. A higher-order belief for one individual may be a lower-order belief for another, or entirely irrelevant. Here is an advertisement for manipulative toys that stands out in stark contrast to the bulk of school-readiness advertisements for similar products:

> Give your child a better world. A world of excitement without violence. Adventure without cruelty. Where heros are still brave and kind. That's the fascinating world of (brandname) playsets. Classic, European-designed play environments that stretch your child's imagination to the universe and beyond. Isn't this the world you want for your child?

This particular "play environment" may be appealing to some parents as a direct consequence of its advertised promotion of a violence-free world. Other parents, however, might consider it unlikely that their preschool-aged children would develop such utopian ideals from block and figure play. On the other hand, these same parents might consider the toy set appropriate for developing imagination and creativity. In contrast, other parents may be drawn to a highly similar playset produced by a different company because the blocks are shown as material for constructing blockades and the figures are called "action figures." In short, the different individual belief structures of parents are being taken into account in advertisements by concatenating a number of (usually positively flavored) beliefs into (limited) advertisement space. Still, the advertisers know the general scope of the field of ideas that parents might find attractive. As a curious demonstration of an ad that violates these expectations, let us modify the last one and judge how well it might be received:

> Give your child a better world. A world of excitement and violence. Adventure and cruelty. Where heros are still brave and mean. That is the fascinating world of (brandname) playsets. Classic, Libyan-designed play environments that force your child's imagination to defend what's right. Isn't this the world you want for your child?

This "advertisement" would sell few playsets, but it illustrates the ideas expressed in this chapter. The collective culture provides a range of possible beliefs that can be concatenated in different structural forms by the communicators, who hope that these message complexes trigger desired effects in a large number of recipients. Beliefs that may be feasible in one historical period (for instance, during a period of war), may be "off limits" in another time. The emotional response of the recipients is anticipated accordingly—the evocation of neutralization or counteraction strategies is meant to be minimized by the communicators. Of course, it is the recipients who actually co-construct the effects of social suggestions in their belief systems.

CONCLUSIONS

As with any social role, the role of parent is guided by social institutions that function to ensure the internalization of role-relevant values, meanings, and action plans. Individuals, however, do not passively appropriate cultural roles, but pursue and construct them actively, in conjunction with their emerging role belief system, and their experiences acting within it. Thus, parental belief systems are under the influence of role beliefs and expectations communicated by other adults, and experiences acting with children.

Commercial advertisements in parent-oriented literature constitute a goal-directed framework in which products are made attractive through their association with carefully selected cultural beliefs. We have suggested a few ways in which individual parents might interpret such media messages according to their prevailing and evolving beliefs about parenting and children's development. Our argument that social suggestions are construed differently by different parents holds equally for the effects parental suggestions are presumed to have on children. For example, a parent might purchase the European-designed play environment with the idea of promoting beliefs about a kinder and gentler world. The child, however, (dressed in superhero underwear) may use the playset for enacting favorite scenes from Batman. But, alternatively, he may introduce innovations by enacting scenes from other socially available events, or ignore the underwear design altogether. Collective-cultural guidance of parents' beliefs involves the participation of parents; likewise, the guidance of child development by the parents' personal cultures requires the developing children's active contribution. As a result, any effect of a collective-cultural message upon parental belief structures is a reconstruction of the message in a new form, which (if transmitted further to the child) can have further effect that goes beyond the original social suggestion. This position implies quasi-determinate linkage between both the collective culture and parental beliefs, and between parental beliefs and children's construction of their personal cultures. An effect in development is merely the (social) provision of raw materials for the person's construction of oneself; what exact structure of the self is erected on the basis of that effect can be determined only in terms of the general direction of development, not its specific outcome (see Valsiner, 1987). We hope our analysis has demonstrated that in placing social suggestions in a historical–cultural context and viewing them as instruments in the never-ending process of culture reconstruction, we gain access to a broader view of belief systems that impact the socialization of children in North America and elsewhere.

ACKNOWLEDGMENTS

We are grateful to Patty Clubb for help in coding the advertisements. The editors of this volume provided helpful and insightful comments on the previous version of this chapter.

REFERENCES

Ball, T. (1983). The ontological presuppositions and political consequences of a social science. In D. Sabia & J. Wallulis (Eds.), *Changing social science* (pp. 31–51). Albany: State University of New York Press.

Coleman, L. (1941). What is American? A study of alleged American traits. *Social Forces, 19,* 492–499.

Dien, D. (1982). A Chinese perspective on Kohlberg's theory of moral development. *Developmental Review, 2,* 331–341.

Draguns, J. (1974). Values reflected in psychopathology: The case of the Protestant ethic. *Ethos, 2,* 115–136.

Frost, J., & Wortham, S. (1988). The evolution of American playgrounds. *Young Children, July,* 19–28.

Goodnow, J., & Collins, W. A. (1991). *Development according to parents: The nature, sources, and consequences of parents' ideas.* London: Lawrence Erlbaum Associates.

Hogan, R., & Elmer, N. (1978). The biases in contemporary social psychology. *Social Research, 45,* 478–534.

Humm, R. (1978). *Children in America: A study of images and attitudes.* Atlanta: The High Museum of Art.

Kett, J. (1977). *Rites of passage.* New York: Basic Books.

Kleinman, A. (1980). *Patients and healers in the context of culture: An exploration of the borderland between anthropology, medicine and psychiatry.* Berkeley: University of California Press.

Kluckhohn, F. (1961). *Variations in value orientations.* Evanston, IL: Row, Peterson & Co.

Morris, C. (1956). *Varieties of human value.* Chicago: University of Chicago Press.

Scheibe, K. (1970). *Beliefs and values.* New York: Holt, Rinehart & Winston.

Sigel, I. (1985). A conceptual analysis of beliefs. In I. Sigel (Ed.), *Parental belief systems: The psychological consequences for children* (pp. 341–375). Hillsdale, NJ: Lawrence Erlbaum Associates.

Valsiner, J. (1987). *Culture and the development of children's action.* Chichester: Wiley.

Valsiner, J. (1988). Ontogeny of co-construction of culture within socially organized environmental settings. In J. Valsiner (Ed.), *Child development within culturally structured environments: Vol. 2. Social co-construction and environmental guidance in development* (pp. 283–297). Norwood, NJ: Ablex.

Valsiner, J. (1989). *Culture and human development.* Lexington, MA: D.C. Heath & Co.

Vincent, C. (1951). Trends in infant care ideas. *Child Development, 22,* 199–209.

Wegener-Spoehring, G. (1989). War toys and aggressive games. *Play and Culture, 2,* 35–47.

West, J. (1945). *Plainville, U.S.A.* New York: Columbia University Press.

Winegar, L. T., Renninger, K. A., & Valsiner, J. (1989). Dependent-independence in adult–child relationships. In D. A. Kramer & M. J. Bopp (Eds.), *Transformation in clinical and developmental psychology.* New York: Springer-Verlag.

Wolfenstein, M. (1953). Trends in infant care. *American Journal of Orthopsychiatry, 23,* 120–130.

Wolfenstein, M. (1955). The fun morality. In M. Mead & M. Wolfenstein (Eds.), *Childhood in contemporary cultures* (pp. 168–178). Chicago: University of Chicago Press.

Wozniak, R. (1986). Notes toward a co-constructive theory of the emotion-cognition relationship. In D. J. Bearison & H. Zimiles (Eds.), *Thought and emotion: Developmental perspectives* (pp. 35–64). Hillsdale, N.J.: Lawrence Erlbaum Associates.

Young, K. T. (1990). American conceptions of infant development from 1955 to 1984: What the experts are telling parents. *Child Development, 61,* 17–28.

17

Child Competence and Developmental Goals Among Rural Black Families: Investigating the Links

Gene H. Brody
Zolinda Stoneman
University of Georgia

This chapter describes a project in which members of our laboratory staff observed and interviewed rural Black families to find out why, despite their difficult circumstances, many of these children grow up competent rather than succumbing to the effects of their environments. Our project is an unusual one because very little work has been done on Black family dynamics, particularly among rural populations. Through our work we intend, therefore, to help fill this gap in the literature, as well as to provide a basis for intervention by specifically identifying those family strengths that help rural Black parents to rear successful children.

Rural Black families' difficulties and deprivation have been well documented. Data suggest that many of the 1 million Black families who live in the rural south are faced with adverse environmental conditions and are at risk for such factors as unemployment, low wages, and low educational levels, as well as substandard housing and high infant and maternal mortality rates (Coward & Smith, 1983). In the state of Georgia, illiteracy rates are particularly high among Black citizens, and those rural counties with largely Black populations also have the lowest adult education levels (Gabriel, 1986). Failure to complete high school, and school failure in general, are particularly serious problems for Georgia's Black rural children. Economically, the poverty rate among the state's Black rural families exceeds 41%.

Given these conditions, knowledge of those aspects of family life that help these families to cope with such severely and chronically stressful lives is important. Nevertheless, scant information is available concerning any aspects of these families' lives, particularly concerning their dealings with

415

their children. Little is known about Black parents' developmental goals —
the behaviors, skills, and attitudes they want to foster in their children,
toward which the children are socialized. Allen (1985) conducted one of the
few studies in this area, but her sample was limited to urban families with
adolescent boys. Other studies, performed 20 to 60 years ago, were focused
primarily on covariation between developmental goals and social class
(Duvall, 1947; Kohn, 1969; Lynd & Lynd, 1929; Miller & Swanson, 1958).
Although the more recent conceptual and methodological work of Sigel and
his colleagues (Sigel, 1985) has provided substantial direction to researchers
investigating the role of parental beliefs in fostering child competence
among urban White families, no such systematic studies have been conducted among rural Blacks. Work focused on urban Black families provides
no better background, because this literature is more often theoretical than
empirical (see Clark, 1983).

The most relevant information concerning the developmental goals of
southern rural Black families with school-aged children can be found in
Young's (1970, 1974) ethnographic work. In her rich descriptions of life in
a southern rural community, Young synthesized a set of developmental
goals central to the socialization of rural Black children, which more recent
scholars often have cited as their basis for proposing similar constructs.
These goals include:

1. *self-independence,* including strong self-esteem, individuality, assertiveness, and persistence in the face of frustration (Allen, 1985;
   Ogbu, 1985; Peters, 1976; Peters & Massey, 1983);
2. *obedience,* tempered with an enjoyment and valuing of the child's
   spirited challenges to authority and testing of adult rules and limits
   (Allen, 1985; Peters & Massey, 1983);
3. an *interpersonal focus,* characterized by an orientation toward
   persons and social relationships rather than toward objects or the
   physical environment;
4. a *prosocial orientation,* which includes sharing, helping, cooperat-
   ing, and assuming responsibility for the well-being of younger, less
   able children (accompanied by an acceptance of aggression as a
   legitimate technique for solving problems) (Ogbu, 1985; Peters &
   Massey, 1983);
5. skills in *evaluating social situations* and the ability to influence
   situations and persons to achieve desired goals, rather than unquestioning compliance with conventional rules and standards of conduct (Ogbu, 1985); and
6. *autonomy/self-responsibility* (Ogbu, 1985). Other writers have
   defined an additional strong goal common to Black parents from

all social and economic strata, *success in school* (Allen, 1985; Grant, 1979).

These goals may contribute to the resilience, as described by Garmezy (1976, 1981) and by Rutter (1979), that characterizes many Black rural children despite their environmental difficulties, helping them to mature into emotionally healthy, competent individuals despite the seemingly great odds against them. Such positive outcomes can be further understood through an examination of the more general aspects of southern Black rural families' functioning. These families often display considerable strength despite great hardship, an attribute central to understanding their children's adaptability. Reliance on family and extended kin networks has supported Blacks through economic adversity and multiple social transitions. These strong family patterns arose from the Southern plantation system, and continued as Blacks became farmers on small plots of land and as they later responded to the transition from an agrarian to an industrial society (Day, 1982). In relations between kin and family members, reciprocity and mutual responsibility are expected and child-rearing responsibilities are shared (Day, 1982).

From the available literature, therefore, we discovered that a number of rural Black children do not succumb to the ill effects of poverty, but grow up to be capable adults. We further suspected that the strengths of the Black family, its supportive kin network, and parenting goals such as those that Young (1970, 1974) identified, may influence these children's resilience. From this preliminary information we formulated a research project designed to empirically identify those family strengths, parenting goals, and socialization practices that are associated with children's development of competence.

Our research plan is tailored to the characteristics of our sample in two ways. First, we included family caregivers outside the nuclear family in our sample. Shimkin, Lonie, and Frate (1978) found that many Black rural families are extended, interconnected kinship networks that provide economic and instrumental assistance and cooperation, nurturance and socialization, and a cultural identity. Wilson (1986) therefore suggested that the appropriate unit of analysis in the study of Black family processes is the extended kin network rather than the nuclear family. Second, as members of a minority group, rural Black children must function effectively both within their own culture and in the larger society; this often necessitates their adjustment to two sets of norms. Because of this, we evaluated the children's performance both in their own social group (as assessed by their parents, family caregivers, and adult acquaintances) and in the larger society (as assessed by their teachers).

Our specific research questions involve the examination of the following family characteristics for their association with child outcomes: families' endorsement of competence-producing goals for their children, the socialization of these goals through effective parenting practices, and agreement among family caretakers on these goals and practices. The families' goals represent their expectations for their children, the socialization practices employed will make it either easier or more difficult for the child to achieve the family's goals, and agreement among caretakers helps the child to attain the goals by presenting a clear and consistent set of expectations to follow.

To test our questions we are recruiting a sample of rural Black families in the state of Georgia, with the assistance of state agencies, pastors of Black churches, and other contacts in the Black community. To enhance rapport and cultural understanding, Black students from a variety of majors at the University of Georgia are serving as home visitors to collect data from the families. At the conclusion of the project we plan to have 80 families in the sample from nonmetropolitan counties in Georgia, as defined by the U.S. Bureau of the Census. Although such counties may include urbanized areas with populations of 20,000 or more (United States Department of Agriculture, 1986), we only selected subjects from rural areas with populations of less than 2,500. Only those counties in which 25% or more of the population is Black are being sampled, in order to insure that a viable Black community exists in the area. In these counties consistent and enduring ties with the local Black community and strong intergenerational relationships exist. Families live on land they inherited from tenant farmers, with several families clustering on one parcel of land and extended family members occupying several nearby landholdings (V. Ashley, personal communication, April 7, 1987). As a result, family members have been known to travel daily to nearby counties for employment in order to avoid relocating (V. Ashley, personal communication, April 7, 1987).

All families in the sample include at least one child. The parents are married and living together in the home; they are the biological parents of the target child, who must be 10 to 11 years old. About half the children in our current sample are male, and about half are female. Because we are examining family processes underlying competence, rather than difficulty, among rural Black children, those selected for inclusion in the study will not have been referred for services such as special education programs or mental health treatment. They will be performing at grade level, and will not have been enrolled in compensatory preschool programs such as Head Start; this will control for potential confounds due to the programs' impact on child competence. This limitation should not significantly affect our ability to recruit children, because few eligible preschoolers are actually enrolled in compensatory educational programs (Orthner, 1986).

Table 17.1 presents a breakdown of the mothers' and fathers' social status

TABLE 17.1

Percentage of Mothers and Fathers in Each Hollingshead Occupational Category ($N = 39$)

	Unemployed	Menial Service Workers	Unskilled Workers	Machine Operators and Semi-Skilled Workers	Skilled Manual Laborers, Craftsmen	Clerical and Sales Workers	Technicians, Semi-Professionals	Managers	Administrators, Lesser Professionals	Professionals
Mothers	.13	0	.05	.46	.08	.05	.13	.05	.05	0
Fathers	.11	.02	0	.47	.26	.03	.03	.03	.03	.03

according to criteria developed by Hollingshead. Sixty percent of the mothers and of the fathers are classified into four categories: unemployed, menial services workers, unskilled workers, and machine operators/semi-skilled workers. In many families, one or both spouses work two jobs, and mothers and fathers often work different shifts; although this scheduling may make it more likely that at least one parent will be at home with the child, the parents consequently spend a minimal amount of time at home together. Such long working hours are apparently necessary to provide for the families' needs, given the low wages that the parents earn.

From the beginning we wanted to involve community leaders in the decision-making process of our study, to help them feel a part of the project and make them comfortable referring potential participants. We wanted them to share in this effort and benefit from it, so that they would not perceive it as one more government program imposed on them by the majority culture. In addition, we were concerned about accurately assessing the population we were to study. Most instruments used to evaluate family processes and individual outcomes have been developed for use with, and standardized on, White, middle-class families. Accordingly, we did not know whether the available measures would provide a valid portrayal of family dynamics among disadvantaged rural Blacks. We addressed these concerns through the formation of focus groups comprised of rural Black community members.

The communities from which we recruited study participants are served by two state agencies housed on the University of Georgia campus. The Energy Education Program (EEP) and the Expanded Food and Nutrition Education Program (EFNEP) employ rural community members as peer agents who visit their neighbors' homes as educators and advocates in areas such as application for energy assistance, energy conservation, and basic nutrition. These agents are themselves Black parents, representative of the families to be included in our study. The staffs of the state agencies contacted these peer agents to see whether they would be interested in spending a day on the University of Georgia campus to assist us in our research effort. Some of the peer agents invited other rural Black community leaders to attend, and some of the supervisors from the agencies participated. The final group included 40 people from throughout Georgia.

We explained our project to the focus group and asked for their feedback. The community members enthusiastically endorsed our hypotheses, affirmed our decision to employ Black students as home visitors, and encouraged us to go forward with the study. We next addressed two measurement issues, the first of which concerned the best way to structure videotaped family interactions.

The group members expressed reservations about our plan to videotape the families. They believed that families would not participate in the study if videotaping were included because they would feel suspicious about the uses to which the tape would be put. The group did suggest that, if videotaping were attempted, it should be made as nonthreatening as possible by not recording any interactions involving financial concerns or other sensitive information. In addition, we presented them with a list of activities in which families have been videotaped in our other projects, and asked them to indicate the ones to which they believed the families in the present study would be most receptive. The group indicated that game playing would be acceptable, so we incorporated it into the study.

In past projects, we have found videotaping of family interactions to be essential for close study of the relationships under consideration. The observational data gleaned from the tapes provides an objective record of family interaction that is a vital supplement to the subjective self-report data we collect in our multimethod studies. We videotape interactions instead of coding them live because our previous work has shown that subjects behave in a more socially conventional manner when an observer is in the room than they do when alone with a camera that they tend to forget, that subjects—especially children—attempt to interact with the live observer, which distracts them from their interactions with each other, and that live observers can have difficulty in recording all the behaviors that occur during rapid or emotionally charged interactions. Videotapes thus provide an archive against which coding can be checked to ensure that the interactions are accurately recorded in full detail.

For these reasons, we decided to attempt videotaping of the family interactions despite the focus group's cautions. We realized, however, that if the families did in fact find the taping to be unacceptably disruptive, we would have to change our procedures to accommodate their needs. In order to make this procedure as acceptable as possible to the families in the sample, during the first home visit the student visitors clearly explained the videotaping procedure, why it was to be used, and what the tape would be used for, strongly emphasizing its confidentiality. During this visit the students also gave particular attention and effort to establishing rapport and putting the family at ease, a process that was emphasized throughout the entire project. In actual practice, the focus group's concerns did not materialize. The majority of the participating families freely cooperated with the taping, and only two families dropped out of the study because of it.

The second measurement issue concerned the validity, for use with rural Black families, of the self-report instruments that we planned to use in the study. In order to establish a measure of the instruments' propriety, we presented them one at a time to the group. We explained and discussed each instrument's measurement purpose, after which each member read the instrument and suggested wording changes that would make the questions more comprehensible to our sample. Each group member then rated each instrument on a five-point Likert scale ranging from (1) *not appropriate* for rural Black families through (3) *appropriate* to (5) *very appropriate.* Those instruments that attained a mean rating of at least 3.5 were retained.

As with the videotaping issue, our concerns about the propriety of the instruments for rural Black families largely were not supported. Most of the instruments presented no validity problems for the members of the focus group. They did indicate that too many instruments were included, a problem that would be addressed later during pilot testing. Some of the individual items in the instruments were reworded for simplicity and clarity according to group members' suggestions, and a few were eliminated as irrelevant to rural Blacks.

After we received the input from the focus group, we conducted pilot studies with six families to enable the student visitors to practice their home visit procedures, refining any that did not operate smoothly. As did the focus group members, the student visitors reported that too many self-report instruments were included, requiring too much time for the family members to complete them. Accordingly, we prioritized the instruments and included in the final study only those that we considered essential to obtain the information we needed.

PROCEDURES

Home Visits

Student visitors are assigned to families in teams of two, one male and one female, in order to give both parents in the family someone with whom they can identify and to whom they can comfortably relate. During home visits the male researcher therefore focuses primarily on the father and the female researcher on the mother and child, although both researchers work with all family members during the course of the visit.

The research team's first contact with the family takes place during a phone call, in which they confirm the time of the home visit that has been scheduled by the supervising staff and obtain directions to the home. Warmth, courtesy, and the establishment of rapport are high priorities during this conversation and the home visits. Visitors are instructed to show courtesy and respect to the family members at all times; for example, they ask permission before setting up activities in particular areas or moving any furniture. Because of the sensitivity that the subject families may feel about being assessed, the researchers emphasize the confidentiality of the information that is being gathered. We have taken even more care than is usual in our projects in reassuring the participants about this issue, and have taken the additional measure of identifying data by number only, not by the families' names. This extra consideration has been especially important in such areas as videotaping and requesting information from the child's school.

Three home visits, each lasting 2 to 3 hours, are made to each family, arranged as close to a week apart as the family's schedule will allow. During the first visit, continuing to establish rapport and placing the family at ease are the primary goals. During this visit the parents complete the consent forms, which the researchers carefully explain to make sure they understand them. Demographic information is collected, and extended family members who have responsibility for the target child's care or frequent contact with the child are identified. If the extended family caretaker is not present during the home visit, a separate visit is scheduled to the caretaker's home to collect self-report information. The families are also given a form which they can use to refer other families who may be interested in study participation.

At the beginning of each visit the parents and target child, as well as any other family members or friends who may be present, are invited to play a ring toss game as a warm-up activity. During each visit all children present in the house are served a snack of cookies and punch, in order to give the target child a break and reinforce his or her participation. Data-collection activities that take place at every visit include videotaping of the target child playing the board game "Trouble" (Gilbert Industries) with one or both of the parents. We have used this particular activity extensively in our research on sibling and parent–child relations, because we have found it to be both understandable and interesting to children in the age ranges with which we have worked. In addition, self-report questionnaires are administered to each parent and the target child in an interview format. Each interview is conducted privately between the family member and a researcher, with no other family members present or able to overhear the conversation. At no time during the presentation of the self-report instruments do the visitors assume that a family member can read. This literacy concern is one reason the questionnaires are presented in an interview format; in addition, our previous research indicates that this format helps subjects become comfortable, increases their rapport with the home visitor, and reduces their feelings of suspicion. When responses to a Likert scale are required, the family member is shown a card with a series of dots in graduated sizes that correspond to the magnitude of the responses from which he or she is to choose, and is asked to indicate his or her feelings using the dots on the card. The following instruments that are germane to the purposes of this chapter were included in the interview battery.

Rank Order of Parental Values. We revised M. L. Kohn's (1977) Rank Order of Parental Values into an eight-item listing of desired child attributes: to be respectful, to be independent, to be well-educated, to be happy, to have self-respect, to be well-behaved and well-mannered, to be responsible, and to be honest. These items were based on Young's (1970, 1974) ethnographic research in which she identified those goals that she perceived to be central to the socialization of rural Black children. Each parent and family caretaker was asked to designate the value he or she considered to be most important, then to indicate the second most valued attribute out of the remaining list.

Beliefs About Child's School Longevity. Each parent and family care-taker was asked to indicate how far they believed the target child would go in school, selecting from the answers, *to graduate from high school, to go to vocational school, to have some college, to graduate from college,* and *to go to graduate or professional school.*

Beliefs About Age at Marriage. Each parent and family caretaker was asked the age, in years, that he or she considered the youngest at which the target child should marry. We included the latter two items because Furstenberg, Brooks-Gunn, and Morgan (1987) found parents' beliefs that their children will stay in school, as well as adolescents' postponement of marriage, to be associated with more positive and fewer negative experiences in the children's lives.

During the third home visit, the parents and the target child were each interviewed privately concerning the influences that they believe determine whether or not a child from a poor family will be successful in life. After the researchers confirmed each member's willingness to discuss his or her answers with the others, the family met together to discuss the topic on videotape. The family's responses to this particular question provide us with their direct perspective on the subject we are investigating.

Teacher Assessments

In order to enable us to collect the data needed to evaluate the child's functioning in the majority culture, the parents' informed consent letter includes space for them to provide the name and location of the target child's school, as well as to grant permission for the teacher to complete assessments about the child. These instruments are mailed to the teachers with a cover letter, a copy of the signed consent form, and a stamped return envelope. Follow-up phone calls were made and letters were sent if questionnaires had not been returned after 2 weeks. The following information was collected from the child's school.

Teacher's Rating Scale (TRS) of Child's Actual Competence. The TRS (Harter, 1982) is a 28-item instrument used for children in Grades 3 through 9, on which the teacher rates each item on a scale indicating the extent to which the item applies to the child. The TRS includes four subscales: *cognitive,* which deals mainly with school performance; *social,* which assesses peer-related interpersonal issues; *physical,* which focuses on doing well in sports and games; and *perceptions of general self-worth.* Harter (1982) provided internal consistency and test–retest reliability information.

Revised Behavior Problem Checklist (RBPC). On the RBPC (Quay & Peterson, 1983), the teacher indicates on a 3-point scale whether each of 89 problem behaviors are for the target child *not a problem (or no opportunity to observe),* a *mild problem,* or a *severe problem.* Although six subscales can be derived from the checklist, we are only examining two at present: *conduct disorder* (22 items) and *anxiety–withdrawal* (11 items).

Parents' School Involvement. The teachers completed, separately for mothers and fathers, a scale designed to indicate the degree of each parent's involvement at school. They indicated, on a 5-point scale ranging from *not very involved* to *very involved,* the degree of the parents' participation in school activities. The teachers also reported whether or not they had met the parents, whether the parents had visited the school, and whether the parents attend parent–teacher conferences.

Grades. The home visitors recorded the target child's latest grades in reading, math, and language arts from a copy of his or her last report card, and assigned grade-point values ranging from 5 for an A to 1 for an F.

After each visit the family was given $20; those families who completed all three visits without a cancellation were given an extra $20 at the end of the third visit. Compensating families for their time and participation is routine for us in our studies, as an acknowledgment of the value of our subjects' time and effort; we did not institute this practice in this study in response to the subject families' poverty.

PRELIMINARY RESULTS

The videotaped interactions featuring the parents and child playing "Trouble" and the family discussion are currently being coded, and should yield information in the near future. From the self-report data, we have begun to investigate two aspects of our research question: the goals that parents and family caretakers have for their children, and the relationship of these goals

TABLE 17.2
Percentage of Mothers, Fathers, and Relatives that Endorsed Each
Developmental Goal (N = 39)

Goal: To Be	Mother	Father	Relative
Respectful	.23	.36	.62
Independent	.10	.06	.09
Well-educated	.26	.61	.32
Happy	.26	.14	.15
Self-respecting	.41	.22	.15
Well behaved/mannered	.18	.06	.24
Responsible	.05	.17	.09
Honest	.49	.36	.32

to teacher-assessed child competence. In the discussion that follows we present only those results that were statistically significant.

Parents' and Caretakers' Goals

The goals listed in this section were the first or second choices of the majority of respondents in each category in terms of importance for their children. Mothers selected *to have self-respect* and *to be honest* as their primary goals, fathers selected *to be well educated,* and family caretakers selected *to be respectful* (See Table 17.2). Thus, different adults in the child's life appear to have different goals for his or her development, thus placing multiple demands on the child's behavior.

The Goals in Relation to Teacher Assessments

Mothers.   Mothers who selected *to have self-respect* as an important goal were more involved with the child's school, and the child had higher grades. The children of those who selected *to be respectful* had lower grades (See Table 17.3).

Fathers.   When fathers endorsed *to be respectful* as an important developmental goal, teachers rated the child lower on cognitive competence,

TABLE 17.3
Correlations Between Maternal Developmental Goals and Child Competence

Maternal Measures	School Involvement	Reading Grade	Math Grade	Language Arts Grade
To be respectful		− .44	− .52	− .44
To have self-respect	.47	.44	.44	.41

physical competence, and global self-esteem, and higher on conduct disorders and anxiety–withdrawal. Teachers also gave lower ratings in cognitive and physical competence and global self-esteem when fathers endorsed *to be well-behaved*. The farther that the father believed the child should go in school, the more competent the teacher perceived the child to be and the more school-involved he or she rated the father to be. Finally, the older that the father believed the child should be at marriage, the higher were the teacher's assessments of cognitive, social, and physical competence (See Table 17.4).

Family Caretakers.   Caretakers' endorsement of the developmental goal *to be well-educated* was associated with higher assessments from teachers of cognitive competence, physical competence, and global self-esteem, lower assessments of anxiety, and higher grades. Their endorsement of *to be well-behaved* was related to lower teacher ratings on cognitive competence, social competence, and global self-esteem, to lower grades, and to higher ratings on conduct disorders and anxiety–withdrawal. Caretakers' selection of *to be responsible* was associated with lower teacher assessments of cognitive, social, and physical competence and general self-worth, and with higher assessments of anxiety. Finally, the higher the age at which the family caretaker believed the child should marry, the higher were the teacher's assessments of the child's social and physical competence, and the lower were the assessments of his or her anxiety (see Table 17.5).

CONCLUSIONS

In this chapter we described a project designed to inform us about the factors that produce competence among impoverished rural Black children, in both their own and the majority culture, despite the stresses they encounter in their environments. We explored ways of relating to families in this group that will make them comfortable in participating in our research. The planning and consideration that have gone into this effort have begun to produce results, as we have gathered preliminary data about the issue under examination.

In general, the endorsement of developmental goals that are concerned with obedience and respect for authority appear to be associated with lower teacher evaluations of competence, higher levels of conduct and anxiety problems, and lower academic achievement. Mothers' endorsement of developmental goals that address individual development, such as self-respect, as well as family caregivers' endorsement of education-related goals, were associated with academic achievement.

Because we assessed the developmental goals and beliefs of three adult

TABLE 17.4

Correlations Between Paternal Development Goals and Beliefs and Teachers' Assessments of Competence

Paternal Measures	Cognitive Competence	Social Competence	Physical Competence	Global Self-Esteem	Conduct Disorders	Anxiety/ Withdrawal	School Involvement
To be respectful	-.52		-.40	-.57	.43	.45	
To be well behaved	-.44	-.57	-.50	-.38			
How far child will go	.46	.56	.42	.50	-.47	-.72	
Youngest age to get married	.45	.45	.52			-.36	.42

TABLE 17.5

Correlations Between Family Caregiver's Developmental Goals and Beliefs and Teachers' Assessments of Competence

	Cognitive Competence	Social Competence	Physical Competence	Global Self-Esteem	Conduct Disorders	Anxiety/ Withdrawal	School Involvement	Reading Grade	Math Grade	Language Arts Grade
To be respectful	-.43		-.47	.53		-.46		.50	.50	.51
To be well behaved	-.64	-.39		-.59	.45	.39		-.65	-.61	-.67
How far child will go	-.42	-.41	-.49	-.42		.39	.42			
Youngest age to get married		.33	.35			-.46				

429

family members, this study provides a description of associations that is more complete and representative than if, for example, we had confined data collection to mothers only. The availability of the father and family caretaker data illustrated that the developmental goals and beliefs of more than one adult in the child's life are associated with different areas of functioning. These data will provide the starting point for further analyses addressing the contribution of developmental goals and beliefs to child outcomes.

Albeit a first step, we have presented a glimpse of the processes involved in determining the relationships of developmental goals and beliefs to child outcomes for rural Black families. In future work we will continue to refine our research practices to reliably assess these families as we address such issues as rearing practices that actualize developmental goals, convergence in rearing practices among adult family members and its impact on these goals, and the influences of family relationships on rearing practices and child outcomes.

REFERENCES

Allen, W. R. (1985). Race, income, and family dynamics: A study of adolescent socialization processes and outcomes. In M. B. Spencer, G. K. Brookins, & W. R. Allen (Eds.), *Beginnings: The social and affective development of black children* (pp. 273–292). Hillsdale, NJ: Lawrence Erlbaum Associates.

Clark, R. M. (1983). *Family life and school achievement: Why poor Black children succeed or fail.* Chicago: University of Chicago Press.

Coward, R. T., & Smith, W. M. (1983). *Family services: Issues and opportunities in contemporary rural America.* Lincoln, NE: University of Nebraska Press.

Day, K. Y. (1982). Kinship in a changing economy: A view from the Sea Islands. In R. L. Hall & C. B. Stack (Eds.), *Holding onto the land and the Lord: Kinship, ritual, land tenure, and social policy in the rural South* (pp. 11–24). Athens, GA: University of Georgia Press.

Duvall, E. (1947). Conceptions of parenthood. *American Journal of Sociology, 52,* 193–203.

Furstenberg, F. F., Jr., Brooks-Gunn, J., & Morgan, P. (1987). *Adolescent mothers in later life.* New York: Cambridge University Press.

Gabriel, R. (1986). *Report to the Kellogg Task Force on the learning society.* Unpublished manuscript, University of Georgia, Athens.

Garmezy, N. (1976). The experimental study of children vulnerable to psychopathology. In A. Davids (Ed.), *Child personality and psychopathology: Current topics* (Vol. 2, pp. 171–216). New York: Wiley.

Garmezy, N. (1981). Children under stress: Perspectives on antecedents and correlates of vulnerability and resistance to psychopathology. In A. I. Rabin, J. Aronoff, A. M. Barclay, & R. A Zucker (Eds.), *Further explorations in personality* (pp. 196–269). New York: Wiley.

Grant, A. H. (1979). *New perspectives on rural society.* Boulder, CO: Westview Press.

Harter, S. (1982). The perceived competence scale for children. *Child Development, 53,* 87–97.

Kohn, M. (1969). *Class and conformity: A study in values.* Homewood, IL: Dorsey Press.

Kohn, M. (1977). *Social competence, symptoms, and underachievement in childhood: A longitudinal perspective.* Washington, DC: Winston.

Lynd, R. S., & Lynd, H. M. (1929). *Middletown: A study in contemporary American culture.* New York: Harcourt, Brace.

Miller, D., & Swanson, G. (1958). *The changing American parent.* New York: Wiley.

Ogbu, J. U. (1985). A cultural ecology of competence among inner-city Blacks. In M. B. Spencer, G. K. Brooking, & W. R. Allen (Eds.), *Beginnings: The social and affective development of Black children* (pp. 139–154). Hillsdale, NJ: Lawrence Erlbaum Associates.

Orthner, D. (1986). *Children and families in the south: Trends in health care, family services, and the rural economy.* Prepared statement for a hearing before the U.S. House of Representatives Select Committee on Children, Youth, and Families. *Washington, DC: U.S. Government Printing Office.*

Peters, M. (1976). *Nine Black families: A study of household management and childrearing in Black families with working mothers.* Unpublished doctoral dissertation, Harvard University.

Peters, M. F., & Massey, G. C. (1983). Chronic vs. mundane stress in family stress theories: The case of Black families in White America. *Marriage and Family Review, 6,* 193–218.

Quay, H. C., & Peterson, J. (1983). A dimension approach to behavior disorder: The revised behavior problem checklist. *School Psychology Review, 12,* 244–249.

Rutter, M. (1979). Protective factors in children's responses to stress and disadvantage. In M. W. Kent & J. E. Rolf (Eds.), *Primary prevention of psychopathology: Vol. 3. Social competence in children* (pp. 352–389). Hanover, NH: University Press of New England.

Shimkin, D., Lonie, G. L., & Frate, D. A. (1978). The Black extended family: A basic rural institution and a mechanism of urban adaptation. In F. B. Shimkin, E. M. Shimkin, & D. A. Frate (Eds.), *The extended family in Black societies* (pp. 25–148). The Hague: Mouton.

Sigel, I. (1985). A conceptual analysis of beliefs. In I. Sigel (Ed.), *Parental belief systems: The psychological consequences for children.* Hillsdale, NJ: Lawrence Erlbaum Associates.

United States Department of Agriculture. (1986). Social and economic characteristics of the population in metro and nonmetro counties, 1970–1980. *Rural Development Research Report,* No. 58.

Wilson, M. N. (1986). The Black extended family: An analytical consideration. *Developmental Psychology, 22,* 246–258.

Young, V. H. (1970). Family and childhood in a Southern Negro community. *American Anthropologist, 72,* 269–288.

Young, V. H. (1974). A Black American socialization pattern. *American Ethnologist, 1,* 415–431.

VI Focus on a Methods Issue

18 The Belief–Behavior Connection: A Resolvable Dilemma?

Irving E. Sigel
Educational Testing Service

For those of us who study parent beliefs as predictors of parent actions, the success rate for uncovering robust findings between stated beliefs and overt actions has been disappointing. Although it seems reasonable to contend that what a person believes guides his or her action, the empirical data do not provide the kinds of information that support this conviction. The question is: Why is the task so difficult?

The aim of this chapter is to address the problem of weak belief–behavior relationships, identify some of the issues involved, and offer some potential solutions. The material for this discussion is based on a series of studies conducted at Educational Testing Service (ETS) over the past decade.

The studies we have done over the last decade have been directly concerned with the examination of the belief–action connection. We have demonstrated some relationships between parents' stated beliefs about how children develop knowledge and the strategies parents employed in "teaching" their children. These results have been modest at best (McGillicuddy-DeLisi, 1982). The findings do, however, lend some credence to the contention that beliefs are indeed sources of influence on parent teaching actions. It is these findings that pose the challenge of whether to reject reported relationships as spurious and due to a convergence of chance factors with minimal validity, or accept them as significant markers whose power can be enhanced by improved conceptualization and/or research strategies. Rather than rejecting the connection outright at this time, we prefer to investigate possible sources of difficulty with particular interview techniques and parent–child interactions in a teaching context. In this way we might discover regularities and irregularities that lead to new ways of studying the problem of belief–behavior linkage, with the hope that such analyses will enhance the predictive power and the understanding of parents' beliefs in relation to their actions. The rationale for such an approach at this time is based on the assumption that actions are derived to a significant degree from internal mental states, along with other external sources of influence. From a common sense point of view, it seems reasonable to hold that how parents regard and interact with their children reflects their beliefs and values.

To be sure, some research has sought to investigate the relationship between parent beliefs or their analogues such as ideas, attributions, attitudes, and the like to developmental outcomes for children *without* attending to the intervening parent actions that may have influenced the child outcomes. (See Goodnow & Collins, 1990, and Miller, 1988, for a discussion of these issues.) Studies of this type have not attended (either by design or by accident) to identification of parent actions that serve as conduits between parent intentions and child effects. The omission of the intervening parental actions as sources of influence on the child precludes efforts of defining linkages between parents' ideas or beliefs and their behaviors, which must complete the chain of events experienced by the child. How else is the child to engage the parent unless the parent acts in ways that communicate parental wishes, expectations, understandings to the child? These overt parent actions provide a concrete manifestation of his or her mental event. It is from these observable actions that the child comes to learn the parents' intentions regarding his or her activity. We believe that analyses of parent actions in relation to beliefs will therefore shed light on the child's cognitive, social, and emotional course of development.

The model that my colleagues and I have developed does emphasize the role of parent actions, holding that parent actions have psychosocial roots that reflect sociocultural perspectives as well as idiosyncratic ones. In a sense, the parent integrates the external and the internal sources of influence which serve as guides to action.

To provide the overall context from which the subsequent discussion follows, we present the conceptual base, the research procedures, and the variables identified in our studies. Then we describe our findings, indicating the belief–action connections. Finally, we offer some explanations for the findings and offer some suggestions for future research that, we believe, will increase information concerning the linkage between parent beliefs and parent teaching actions.

BACKGROUND OF THE PROJECT

The goal of the project was the study of the development of children's representational competence, that is, the child's understanding and use of symbolic thought. Two background variables were chosen as underpinnings of such development: parents' teaching behaviors and parents' beliefs about children's acquisition of representational systems. The beliefs were hypothesized as predicting the teaching strategies, and the combination of beliefs and teaching strategies theoretically affect the development of representational competence of the children. The model is interactive. The children's response to a parent's teaching strategy would also be a source of influence on the parents' belief and/or behavior (McGillicuddy-DeLisi & Sigel, 1982; Sigel, 1982; Sigel & McGillicuddy-DeLisi, 1984; Sigel, McGillicuddy-DeLisi, & Johnson, 1980; Sigel, Stinson, & Flaugher, 1991; Sigel, Stinson, & Kim, in press; Stinson, 1989). The hypothesized relationships between beliefs, behaviors, and child outcomes are derived form distancing theory are as follows: The parental beliefs, or constructions about children, are seen as a source of teaching strategies called *distancing behaviors*— behaviors that place mental operational demands on the child to separate self from the ongoing present. These strategies were found to influence children's representational abilities (Sigel, 1982; Sigel et al., 1991).

Sample

The initial project involved 240 families, 120 with preschool children who were communication handicapped and their 120 nonhandicapped controls. The project discussed in this chapter is a follow-up study with a subsample of the same children about 5 years later—38 of the children originally diagnosed as communication-handicapped and 40 noncommunication-handicapped children. The 40 families with noncommunication-handicapped children are the target group for this chapter. They are intact families who are White, middle-class, college educated, and employed in professional and managerial occupations and include both parents of the children. They were all Americans, of different ethnic and religious backgrounds.

Research Procedures

Beliefs. The interview was the method of choice for ascertaining parents' beliefs and teaching strategies. An observation of parents engaged in teaching their child a task was the basis of ascertaining parents' overt action. We were interested in determining what strategies the parent would use with particular types of events, and why the strategies were selected. We wanted a sample of events that is shared within most families. To accomplish these objectives we constructed an interview using thematic vignettes dealing with four major knowledge domains that we believe cover basic knowledge domains. These are: *physical knowledge, social* (interpersonal) *knowledge, moral knowledge,* and *self* (intrapersonal) *knowledge.*

The first three domains are based on Piaget's epistemological categorization, the fourth is our own view of an important life domain. We defined each of these domains as follows: *Physical knowledge* refers to the physical universe of space, time, and distance, as well as ways of determining physical dimensionality; *social knowledge* refers to knowledge of social rules (such as for aggression) dealing with social conflict; *moral knowledge* refers to matters of right and wrong, for example, cheating and stealing; and *self-knowledge* refers to how the child comes to know about his or her inner feelings and emotional state.

In pilot work with parents we were advised to keep the vignette simple and not to get bogged down in too much detail so the situation would not become too particularized. We accepted this idea and created simple statements for each knowledge domain. The 12 vignettes were created to present a sample of situations that parents of young children would most likely face in their everyday social interactions. We constructed three vignettes in each area with a clear theme and with only essential details (see Table 18.1 for a prototype example).

Each vignette was read to the parent, and a series of probe questions was asked. The rationale for each question was based on methodological concern for the order effects of the belief question and the strategy question (What would you do?). We found that asking the parent to give the strategy first and then probing for the belief provided a context in which to elicit the belief. In this way we expected to get a connection between belief and self-report of one's behavior. The answer to this question would reveal what the parent believes as to how the child learns in that specific context. The strategy was context specific. We thought it would be indicative of a more general belief.

Each parent was administered the interview which was recorded on an

TABLE 18.1
Example of a Vignette from the Parent Belief Interview with Probes

Measurement

(Child's name) comes to you with a yardstick and asks you how many cubic meters of water your bathtub could hold. You want him/her learn about measurement.	
Strategy I:	What would you do or say to help (child) learn about measurement, what words would you use?
	What words or actions would you use?
Construct I:	HOW do you think (your strategy) will help him/her learn about measurement?
	Knowing HOW (child) learns, HOW do you think (your strategy) will help him/her learn about measurement?
Child Construct:	How do you think (child's name) will eventually learn about measurement?
General Construct:	How do you think most children eventually learn about measurement?

audiotape. The interviewer also coded the parents' responses on the spot, using a coding system that had been developed using a pilot set of interviews. Reliability estimates were based on independent scoring of 20% of the interviews by a second coder who was unacquainted with the respondent. Thus, they were not biased by the observed behavior of the respondent. An average agreement of 94% was obtained. Reduction of categories was necessary because low frequency occurred in some categories. Through statistical and logical analysis four belief categories were identified: *Cognitive processes, direct instruction, positive feedback,* and *negative feedback,* which included 88% of the parent responses (see Table 18.2 for definitions). The remaining 12% included categories that occurred within each interview rarely.

In this section we focus on only two belief categories: *cognitive processes* and *direct instruction.* These two belief constructs comprise over half of the parent statements concerning sources of children's knowledge. In addition, from the point of view of the theory in which this research effort is embedded, these two types present the most important domains. The reason for their significance is that cognitive process beliefs refer to the emphasis on thinking and reasoning as bases for children's learning, and direct instruction refers to the learning by being told, lectured at, and being the recipient of adult instruction. In effect, these two beliefs are antithetical, as the former reflects a belief in the child as an active thinker and in the latter the child is considered to be a passive recipient. (See Sigel, 1982, for a description of the model of the larger project.)

In addition, parents were asked how they would handle each situation presented in the vignettes. Their proposed strategies were scored as representing either *distancing, rational authoritative, direct authoritative, negative feedback* (substitute), or *positive reinforcement* (see Table 18.3). It should be kept in mind that all of these categories of strategies were derived from self-reports of parents, and observed behaviors were assessed in a different context.

TABLE 18.2
Definitions of Beliefs from the Parent Belief-Strategy Interview

Cognitive Processing (CP):	Belief that a child learns through using his/her imagination and figuring things out on his/her own, weighing the consequences, comparing, reconstructing, proposing alternatives, evaluating, inferring, synthesizing, anticipating, empathizing, or speculating.
Direct Instruction (DI):	Belief that a child learns from instructions, explanations, advice, or guidance.
Positive Feedback (PF):	Belief that a child learns through receiving affirmation of or approval for his/her behavior.
Negative Feedback (NF):	Belief that a child learns through receiving punishment for or an adverse reaction to his or her behavior.

TABLE 18.3
Definitions of Teaching Strategies from the Parent Belief–Teaching
Strategy Interview

Distancing (DS):	When a parent demands that the child think or reason by separating self from the ongoing concrete situation to transcend the ongoing present by seeking alternatives or anticipating outcomes or reconstructing past experiences. Usually expressed in the form of a question.
Rational Authoritative (RA):	When a parent provides explanations; gives reasons with commands or information ("because" may be implied).
Direct Authoritative (DA):	When a parent gives a direct order, statement of a fact, or rule.
Positive Reinforcement (PR):	When a parent bribes or gives a privilege.
Negative Reinforcement (NR):	When a parent punishes or deprives a child.

Behavioral Observations. In addition to the interview, each parent-and-child pair (mothers and fathers separately) were brought into a room with a one-way mirror. The parent was asked to teach his or her child to tie knots (e.g., square knot, bow line) using a model as a guide. These interactions were videotaped and coded subsequently for the type of teaching strategy used. Teaching strategies are conceptualized in terms of the mental operational demand the parent makes for the child to think or reason in solving a problem. Three levels of mental operational demands (MODs) were identified: high, middle, and low.[1] Mental operational demands are distancing strategies that place a cognitive demand on the child to separate self mentally (distance) from the ongoing present so that the child is stimulated to reconstruct past events, and/or anticipate the future, and/or assume alternative perspectives on the present (see Table 18.4 for definitions). All of these strategies are presumed to stimulate representational thinking and have been linked empirically to children's memory, language, and imaginal performance (Sigel, 1982). These MODs are theoretically linked to beliefs in that high MODs require children to engage in representational thinking and are therefore based on the view of the child as an active thinker and processor of information. Low MODs do not encourage the child to take an active role in the process. Quite the contrary: they are assumed to encourage a passive, dependent role. Structuring, although not a MOD, functions like an authoritative strategy expressing high control.[2]

---

[1]Middle-level MODs were excluded from this analysis because of low frequency.

[2]The distancing concept in the interview is identical to the MOD in the observation. The parents' use of low-level strategies was so infrequent that we created a general distancing category. The observations, however, allow for finer distinctions. I do not believe that this seriously affected the data analysis.

TABLE 18.4
Definitions of the Observed Mental Operational Demands Used in
Observations

High-Level Distancing MOD:	Demands that are abstract, open; allow alternatives; activate evaluative and inferential cognitive processes. Also demands that activate representational thinking, but are still dependent on some observable evidence. The process activated involves specific information (somewhat concrete, somewhat focused) in order to produce a response. The demand on the other person is to evaluate, infer, resolve conflict, generalize, transform, plan, propose alternatives, conclude, reconstruct, sequence, compare, and/or combine/classify.
Low-Level Distancing MOD:	Demands that are focused, concrete, closed; require minimal representational thinking and do not allow for debate. The demand on the other person is to label, describe, demonstrate, and/or observe.
Structuring:	Defining or facilitating the task at hand or an aspect of it. Telling the other what to do and explaining the reasons why, or demonstrating how to do it, in order to move the task along. Setting the rules of the activity, or of the task, and defining the limits of it. Any utterance by the parent that aims at managing the child's behavior, whether or not task related.

Initial Data Analysis

A series of analyses was done to search for the relationship between beliefs and distancing behaviors. It was expected that beliefs in cognitive processes would relate to use of high and medium MODs in the teaching situation and to distancing strategies proposed as ways to handle situations in the interview. Beliefs in direct instruction were expected to relate to authoritative-type proposed strategies in the interview and in the teaching situation. Correlations and regression analyses yielded weak relationships which were surprising and disappointing to say the least. We did find relationships between parents' teaching behaviors and children's cognitive outcomes as well as between beliefs and cognitive outcomes. What was inconclusive were the connections among the beliefs, behaviors, and child outcomes (Sigel, Stinson, & Flaugher, in press; Sigel et al., 1991). The question to be addressed deals with these linkages.

Approaches to Understanding the Limited Relationship of Belief to Behavior. To understand the lack of findings in these various types of correlations we began to explore the interview responses as an initial step. This was done in two ways, first by examining different aspects of the interview content and second by identifying the strategies presented for each vignette.

It will be recalled that we constructed four content areas comprised of three items each, which were represented in the initial interview. We subjected these initial data to a confirmatory factor analyses. A varimax rotation of parent statements yielded three categories with the moral social beliefs forming one category, physical knowledge forming the second factor, and interpersonal knowledge forming the third. The results of this analysis yielded factor loadings from .76 to .95 for the moral social domain (five items) .78 to .95 (three items) on the interpersonal, and .72 to .94 for the physical knowledge domain (three items.)

It will be recalled that for each vignette parents were given a series of probes concerning their beliefs about how they would learn the topic in the question, followed by what strategies the parents would use to help the child learn about that topic. For example, in a vignette depicting the child's not being truthful about going directly home from school, the interviewer initially asked the parent what he or she could do to teach the child not to lie (predicted strategy). Then the parent is asked: "How do you think (parent's strategy) helps your child learn to be truthful?" Beliefs about particular sources of development were then summed within each content area as well as aggregated across situations. Frequencies were placed over total possible responses for conversion to proportional values (e.g., mean percentages). These proportions may thus be considered an intensity index reflecting the strength of the parent's beliefs within a particular domain. Only one belief statement per probe was accepted by the interviewer who instructed parents to focus on their primary belief when multiples were offered. Both the specific and general orders of beliefs were coded in the same manner using the designated statements from prior studies. The belief codes that are target in this discussion are *cognitive processing* and *direct instruction*. For the purposes of this chapter, these are sufficient to demonstrate the message I am presenting.

Behavior–Belief Analysis for Particular Beliefs

We had originally assumed that for each belief construct referred to by a parent, a predicted strategy would correspond to that construct of development. That is, if a parent posited that children acquire knowledge by thinking and reasoning, he or she would be likely to propose a distancing strategy to handle the situation presented in the vignette. In addition, we assumed that such a parent would be likely to use high MODs when teaching the child the rope task. Thus we hypothesized that beliefs about development would relate to both predicted strategies and observed behaviors. This reasoning did not take the different domains into account.

However, when we discovered the low and nonsignificant correlations between beliefs and behaviors, we began a detailed analysis of strategies associated with each belief type. In the absence of one-to-one correspondences between developmental constructs and predicted/actual teaching behaviors, we asked, "What are the different types of teaching behaviors that parents propose/use when they believe that children develop through cognitive processing of information?"

Two types of individual scores were computed: (a) a percentage score for each belief category using aggregate numbers of beliefs per interview, and (b) the percentage of specific beliefs within domains. Each of these scores was used in all of our analyses.

As for the observations, we used only the data from the knot-tying task because that task provided considerable variability in strategy use. We coded each of the utterances made by the parent yielding a frequency of utterances in each of the categories. Using the total number of verbal and nonverbal interactions as the denominator, we used the number of utterances in each strategy category as the numerator, thereby creating an individual's percentage score on each observational category. These scores were used in all of our subsequent computations.

RESULTS

Correlations between beliefs and self-reported predicted strategies are presented first, followed by correlations between beliefs and observed teaching behaviors. Finally, correlations between self-reported strategies and observed behaviors are examined. These presentations include examinations of aggregate scores as well as examination of the belief–behavior relationships within the particular domains of physical knowledge, self-knowledge and social-moral knowledge. Finally, a belief-self-reported analysis is presented demonstrating the heterogeneity of reported strategies within particular belief categories.

Obtained Relationships Between Beliefs and Self-Reported Strategies Within the Interview. Examination of Table 18.5 reveals significant relationships between parents' stated beliefs about developmental constructs and parents' predicted strategies. Mothers and fathers who believe that children acquire knowledge through their own acts of thinking and reasoning (cognitive processing) tend to hold that distancing strategies should be used to teach the child. More didactic and authoritative strategies are advocated by parents when they believe that children learn through direct instruction. Note that for both mothers and fathers, there is a significant negative correlation between beliefs in direct instruction and

TABLE 18.5
Correlations Between Selected Parents' Beliefs and their Self-Reported
Teaching Strategies

| | Parent Beliefs | | | |
| | Mothers | | Fathers | |
Self-Reported Teaching Strategies	Cognitive Processing	Direct Instruction	Cognitive Processing	Direct Instruction
Distancing	.72***	− .60***	.77**	− .37*
Rational authoritative	.02	.31*	− .23	.44**
Direct authoritative	− .60***	.56***	− .17	.22

Note. The correlations are one-tailed tests. $N = 40$.
*$p < .05$; **$p < .01$; ***$p < .001$.

reports of parental distancing strategies. This indicates that beliefs in direct instruction not only correspond to directive or "telling" strategy preferences (especially for mothers), but essentially preclude the use of distancing teaching strategies in the parents' reports.

A similar pattern emerges for mothers and fathers. When parents think that their children learn knowledge in a particular domain through cognitive processing, they are likely to propose distancing as a strategy of choice, and they are less likely to propose direct authoritative strategies (see Tables 18.6 and 18.7). When they propose direct instruction as a belief, direct authoritative strategies are predicted. Distancing strategies are less likely to be preferred strategies the more parents posit direct instruction as a source of children's knowledge. These relations hold across domains, and the findings are consistent with the theory that holds that cognitive processes would be expressed via distancing and direct instruction would be expressed via authoritative types of strategies. The relationships hold for the three domains and are relatively consistent for both mothers and fathers. Note, however, that belief about the source of knowledge in one domain does not necessarily predict reported strategies in another domain. That is, parents who posit cognitive processing as a source of physical knowledge are likely to predict distancing for situations that involve physical principles, but there is no relationship between such beliefs and how parents propose handling intrapersonal or moral-social situations.

Relationship Between Reported Beliefs and Observed Behaviors.   Now we move to the critical area, the degree to which the parent's belief about developmental constructs relates to his or her actual behavior during the teaching situation. This relationship has formed the cornerstone of our research project. The obtained correlations coefficients are presented in

TABLE 18.6

Correlations Between Mothers' Beliefs and Their Self-Reported Teaching Strategies by Knowledge Domains

	Mothers' Beliefs					
	Cognitive Processing			Direct Instruction		
Self-Reported Teaching Strategies	Physical Knowledge	Intrapersonal	Moral/Social	Physical Knowledge	Intrapersonal	Moral/Social
Distancing						
Physical knowledge	.77***	.34*	.48**	−.49**	−.16	−.30*
Intrapersonal	.11	.61***	.21	−.39**	−.50***	−.08
Moral/social	.19	.18	.68***	−.26	−.19	−.47**
Rational Authoritative						
Physical knowledge	.01	.09	−.21	.18	−.06	.23
Intrapersonal	−.01	−.03	.01	−.04	.27*	.18
Moral/social	−.02	.11	.07	.15	.01	.30*
Direct Authoritative						
Physical knowledge	−.48**	−.29*	−.23	.44**	.06	.10
Intrapersonal	−.08	−.47**	−.09	.36*	.32*	−.03
Moral/social	−.27*	−.32*	−.51***	.23	.30*	.58***

Note. The correlations are one-tailed tests. N = 40.
*p < .05; **p < .01; ***p < .001.

TABLE 18.7
Correlations Between Fathers' Beliefs and Their Self-Reported Teaching Strategies by Knowledge Domains

Self-Reported Teaching Strategies	Fathers' Beliefs					
	Cognitive Processing			Direct Instruction		
	Physical Knowledge	Intrapersonal	Moral/Social	Physical Knowledge	Intrapersonal	Moral/Social
Distancing						
Physical knowledge	.43**	.11	.18	-.26	-.09	-.27*
Intrapersonal	.44**	.63***	.27*	-.31*	-.29*	.04
Moral/social	.34*	.27*	.76***	-.12	-.03	-.33*
Rational Authoritative						
Physical knowledge	-.34*	-.01	.14	.11	.09	-.07
Intrapersonal	-.23	-.19	-.22	.30*	.24	.30*
Moral/social	-.11	-.02	-.23	.04	.08	.52***
Direct Authoritative						
Physical knowledge	-.02	.11	-.13	.11	-.02	.25
Intrapersonal	-.14	-.08	-.01	.17	.14	-.08
Moral/social	-.07	.11	-.36*	-.04	-.14	.38***

Note. The correlations are one-tailed tests. $N = 40$.

*$p < .05$; **$p < .01$; ***$p < .001$.

Table 18.8. The aggregate score for mothers' and fathers' beliefs in cognitive processes yielded nonsignificant correlations of .25 and .24 respectively with the use of high-level MODs. However, mothers' use of direct instruction relates to structuring, which is as expected. The negative relation between high-level distancing and beliefs in direct instruction for fathers is consistent with the theory. These results are consistent with prior reports of low, sometimes significant, relationships between such beliefs and observed behaviors (Sigel et al., 1991).

There is some increase in the number of correlation coefficients that reach level of significance when each of the three domains of knowledge and actual teaching behaviors during the rope task are considered (as presented in Table 18.9). For example, beliefs in cognitive processes expressed when the parent discussed physical knowledge of the child were related to the use of high level MODs by both mothers and fathers ($rs = .31$ and .30, $p < .05$, respectively), but were not related significantly for self-knowledge. Thus, the relationship between beliefs and behaviors may exist within domains as the parents may have developed different types of explanations for children's behaviors in the different domains.

In sum, mothers' and fathers' beliefs do reflect some modicum of relationship between what they believe in and what they say they will do. The relationships are stronger for beliefs in cognitive processing than for direct instruction—at least for mothers. Mothers' beliefs in direct instruction relate to their structuring behavior but this is not the case with fathers.

Relationships Between Self-Reported Strategies and Observed Strategies.
The question addressed in this section is: What is the relationship between what parents say they do to help children learn in the interview and what they do in the actual teaching situation? Table 18.10 shows the correlations for fathers and for mothers between self-reported teaching actions and the

TABLE 18.8
Correlations Between Parents' Beliefs and their Observed Teaching Strategies

| | Parent Beliefs | | | |
| | Mothers | | Fathers | |
Observed Teaching Strategies	Cognitive Processing	Direct Instruction	Cognitive Processing	Direct Instruction
Distancing				
High MOD	.25	− .22	.24	− .34*
Low MOD	− .06	− .11	.07	.09
Structuring	− .25	.27*	.08	.07

Note. The correlations are one-tailed tests. $N = 40$.
*$p < .05$.

TABLE 18.9

Correlations Between Beliefs and their Observed Reported Teaching Strategies by Knowledge Domains for Mothers and for Fathers

Observed Teaching Strategies	Cognitive Processing			Direct Instruction		
	Physical Knowledge	Intrapersonal	Moral/Social	Physical Knowledge	Intrapersonal	Moral/Social
	Mothers' Beliefs					
Distancing						
High MOD	.31*	.05	.23	-.14	-.03	-.26
Low MOD	-.11	.08	-.10	.04	-.13	-.13
Structuring	-.20	-.24	-.18	.22	.11	.22
	Fathers' Beliefs					
Distancing						
High MOD	.30*	.11	.16	-.37*	-.02	-.27*
Low MOD	.01	.04	.09	.17	.07	-.01
Structuring	-.01	-.08	.19	.03	.04	.07

Note.   The correlations are one-tailed tests. $N = 40$.

*$p < .05$.

TABLE 18.10
Correlations Between Observed and Self-Reported Teaching Strategies

Self-Reported Teaching Strategies	Observed Teaching Strategies					
	Mothers			Fathers		
	Distancing		Structuring	Distancing		Structuring
	High MOD	Low MOD	One Level	High MOD	Low MOD	One Level
Distancing	.31*	.09	-.27*	.10	.01	.07
Rational Authoritative	-.25	-.06	.04	-.02	.29*	-.08
Direct Authoritative	-.09	-.19	.17	-.15	-.39*	.25

Note. The correlations are one-tailed tests. $N = 40$.
*$p < .05$; **$p < .01$.

use of mental operational demands. The correlations reported in Table 18.10 reveal some consistency between self-report and outcomes, although the correlations tend to be low. Mothers' reports of distancing relate significantly to the use of high-level MODs.

Analysis of the relationships within the three knowledge domains (see Table 18.11) indicates that, for mothers, distancing behaviors on the knot task are related to their reported strategies in hypothetical situations involving physical principles. There is some consistency here. For fathers, predicted distancing behaviors were also related to high MODs during the rope task, but reported strategies for vignettes involving other knowledge issues were also related to their teaching behavior during the rope task. A negative relationship is obtained with distancing and the use of low-level mental operational demands for the mothers who use distancing in the physical knowledge domain. When the parents' strategies are examined across domains, there is some consistency between mothers' reports of distancing and their actual use in the knot-tying task (see Table 18.11). Further, the reported use of distancing relates negatively with structuring. For fathers, the obtained correlations are ambiguous. Significant relationships were found for rational authoritative strategies and low MODs in the intrapersonal as well as the physical knowledge domains. These strategies are structurally similar to low MODs inasmuch as they involve an elaboration or an explanation of a directive, whereas direct authoritative is an unqualified and unjustified directive. The task demands of the knot task involve physical principles such as spatial relations and measurement, which are also involved in the interview items dealing with acquisition of physical knowledge. These similarities may account for the correlation between the responses to the interview items and the observed behaviors.

In sum, the relationships between self-reported strategies and behavior are weak, but, where they are found, they are consistent with the theory. It is that which inspires us to try to understand why this is the case. The analysis that we describe next asks the question: Do parent beliefs have a common set of actions that define that belief? In essence, we know from the correlations that there is no one-to-one correspondence between beliefs and behaviors, but we demonstrate specifically what the array of strategies is.

The Array of Beliefs Subsumed Within a Belief Category.   Having gone through the process of data analyses just described, we asked whether the belief variable signified similar strategies. For example, if one believed in cognitive processing, there should be a high probability that the belief would be instantiated similarly for all those holding that belief. To test this idea, and working with the four major belief categories (cognitive processing, direct instruction, positive feedback, and negative feedback) we identified the strategies used by each participant who stated a belief in a

TABLE 18.11

Correlations Between Observed and Self-Reported Teaching Strategies by Knowledge Domains for Mothers and Fathers

	Observed Teaching Strategies					
	Mothers			Fathers		
	Distancing		Structuring	Distancing		Structuring
Self-Reported Teaching Strategies	High MOD	Low MOD	One Level	High MOD	Low MOD	One Level
Distancing						
Physical knowledge	.34*	.04	−.21	.35*	−.07	−.40**
Intrapersonal	.16	.21	−.33*	−.08	−.08	.11
Moral/social	.18	.01	−.11	.05	.10	.21
Rational Authoritative						
Physical knowledge	−.30*	.10	.14	.04	.39**	−.22
Intrapersonal	−.06	−.16	−.10	.06	.35*	.04
Moral/social	−.12	−.08	−.11	−.11	−.06	−.03
Direct Authoritative						
Physical knowledge	.01	−.11	−.03	−.25	−.19	.12
Intrapersonal	−.15	−.15	.19	.01	−.15	.15
Moral/social	−.04	−.12	.15	−.05	−.40**	.21

Note. The correlations are one-tailed tests. $N = 40$.
*p < .05; **p < .01.

449

particular category. Initial analyses of the interview protocols revealed that an array of strategies were presented for each of the beliefs. We also examined the variability within each domain. Within each belief category we identified the strategies associated with the belief (see Fig. 18.1 and 18.2). For example, as depicted in Fig. 18.1 across all domains for mothers, 45% of the beliefs of this group was cognitive processing, 23% direct instruction, and 10% positive feedback. Within each of these belief categories a spread of strategies is found. For cognitive processing 60% of the strategies are distancing, 13% are positive reinforcement, 8% are rational authoritative, and so on. Inspection of the diagram reveals that for direct instruction, most of the strategies are authoritative of some type, whereas for cognitive processing, distancing is the highest frequency. The distancing category is found essentially with the cognitive processing belief. A second finding of interest is that the frequency of beliefs varies with domains.

To summarize, it is clear that beliefs as assessed in this study may be expressed in more than one type of act. Although some beliefs tend to be predominantly expressed in a particular way (e.g., cognitive processing and distancing), there is no rational basis for expecting one-to-one correspondence. Such variations in the belief–behavior connection are due not only to the context in which the belief is assessed, but also to sample characteristics (e.g., gender differences between parents). These findings preclude a strong, consistent belief–behavior connection.

DISCUSSION

The impetus for undertaking the type of analysis presented here was to gain further understanding of why the relationship between parents' beliefs regarding their children's knowledge acquisition and their teaching strategies was not as strong and consistent as expected. The initial hypothesis was that what parents believed about children's acquisition of representational competence would influence their teaching strategies which in turn would affect children's competence.

Because the findings were not as strong as expected, it seemed reasonable to reflect on why this was the case because the basic notion seemed reasonable both then and now. (See Sigel et al., 1991; Sigel, Stinson, & Kim, in press, and Sigel & McGillicuddy-DeLisi, 1984, for details of the larger project.)

The analysis presented in this chapter provides some of the insights gained into the source of the often discussed problem of the relationship between beliefs and actualization of beliefs into action (Miller, 1988).

First, it must be kept in mind that the beliefs of interest in this study are

Mothers

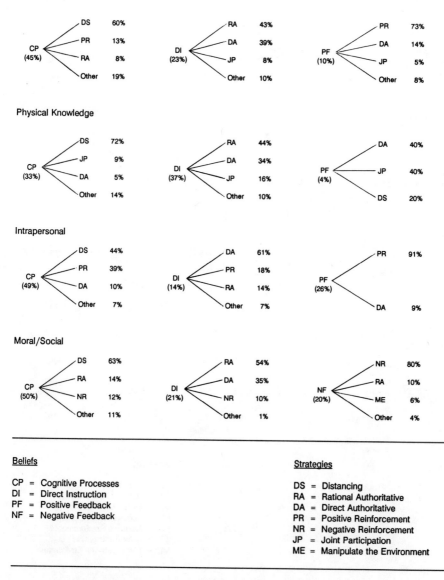

FIG. 18.1 Mothers' belief to behavior response patterns on the parent belief construction communication strategy interview ($N = 40$).

Fathers

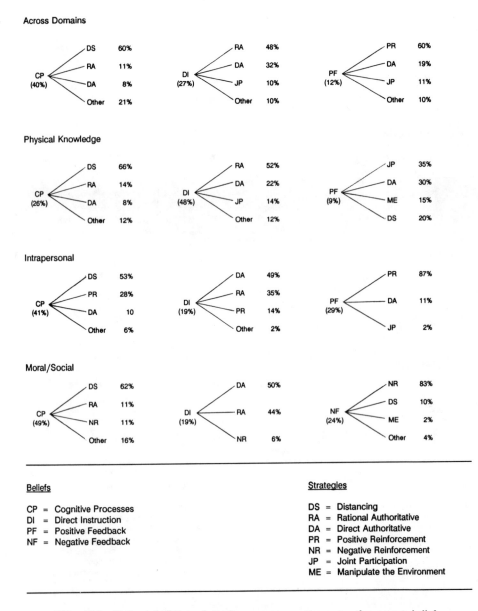

FIG. 18.2 Fathers' belief to behavior response patterns on the parent belief construction communication strategy interview (*N* = 40).

limited to how children acquire social, moral, physical, and self knowledge. The original view was that parents' beliefs are general and transcend specific knowledge domains. A related question had to do with parent activity expressing that particular belief. The thought was that the belief would be expressed in ways consistent with the belief. For example, if a parent believes that children learn through direct instruction, authoritative, directive strategies would be used.

The results presented in this chapter were contrary to the expectations. Beliefs regarding knowledge acquisition are in part contingent on the knowledge domains; the beliefs are expressed in different ways, that is, there is no one-to-one correspondence between a held belief and its instantiation. Finally, the belief–behavior connection is found most often when the belief and the behavior expressing it share a common context, as in the case of the self-report (Eccles, Harold, Wigfield, Yoon, Aberbach, & Doan, 1991; Kochanska, Kuczynski, & Radke-Yarrow, 1989). Let me elaborate briefly on each of the points.

The initial assumption that tapping a sample of hypothetical situations in significant knowledge domains was compromised by the domains. By aggregating across the interview, significant domains differences were masked. Thus, understanding of parents' belief structure required decomposing the interview into relevant domains. Inspection of Figs. 18.1 and 18.2 demonstrates this fact. Thus, it is clear that in studying the beliefs of parents relative to knowledge acquisition, aggregation across domains can be misleading.

The fact that parents' reported strategies relate more consistently to their beliefs may be because the self-reported strategy was contextually related to hypothetical situations, whereas the observed teaching situation was unrelated. The latter case, suggests that strategies are not generalized but are context or task dependent. Further, it may be the case that the parent's behavioral strategies are also context dependent, so that had the actual teaching task been similar in content or structure to the interview vignette, better relationships might have been found. In this context it is worth pointing out that upon reviewing Tables 18.7 through 18.10, the reader will note that neither beliefs nor self-reported behaviors relate to observed behavior to the same degree as self-reported strategies relate to beliefs. These results lead me to suggest an operating principle to increase the relationship between beliefs and behavior. The greater the overlap between the knowledge domain of the belief and the task to be taught or learned, the greater will be the relationship. However, it should be kept in mind that even when using that principle, parent's self-reports of strategies and actual behaviors may differ for those holding the same belief. If that principle is coupled with a conceptualization of a relationship to be predicted in advance, and then relevant antecedents are defined, greater correspondence is possible (Sigel, 1986; Sigel & Hoffman, 1956). The difficulties reported here may not only be due to the types of interview method used, but also to the parents' general views of the nature of children's learning, a topic we did not address. In addition, the parents' own learning history in the domain under study is often overlooked as a source of their beliefs and teaching strategies. This is clearly demonstrated in a Vermont study of the relationship between mothers' epistemological development and their communication strategies. It was found that the level of knowing was an important feature of the way the mothers communicated with their children. These mothers came from an impoverished rural environment (Monsey, Bond, Belenky, Weinstock, & Burgmeier, 1991). These parents are not experts in the knowledge domain in question nor are they educators in the formal sense. Consequently, they rely on their personal experiences regarding specific knowledge acquisition. This finding is also a reflection of the fact that beliefs can be expressed in a variety of ways. It may well be the case, in general, that parents have a variety of strategies available which, from their point of view, are not contradictory. Rather, they reflect strategy, that is, the parents have a repertoire of teaching tools which become available as the situation and the task dictate. This perspective is analogous to the notion that individuals possess a variety of mental tools or actions to solve problems where the tool of choice is defined in part by the task and the setting. The parent–child interaction can be viewed also as a problem-solving situation requiring the parent to dip into his or her mental tool kit for ways to interact with his or her child. (See Tulviste in Wertsch, 1991, pp. 96–97, for a discussion of the concept.)

Although there may be a preponderance of use of some strategies in some areas, for example, distancing, there are enough variations within domains to account for the low predictability of a belief to child outcome. It seems that the linkage between belief–behavior and teaching behavior will be improved when one takes into account the knowledge domain in which the belief is instantiated.

In addition to the complexities I have described that create prediction difficulties, there are other factors, not incorporated in this study, that may play an important role. It is beyond the scope of this chapter to deal with them in detail (see Goodnow & Collins, 1990). Succinctly put, however, in addition to knowledge domain and context differences, beliefs are multi-determined, reflecting demographic, sociocultural, and personal factors that coalesce to influence the quality of the parent–child interaction, both in its dyadic nature as well as in the context of the family.

In this chapter I have highlighted only one issue among many that must be addressed as we unravel the knotty, challenging problems in coming to understand the role that parents' ideas or beliefs play in their lives as well as in the lives of their children.

SUMMARY AND CONCLUSIONS

In this chapter I have addressed the issue of the relationships between parents' beliefs regarding children's knowledge acquisition, the parents' expression of these beliefs in two settings: the interview and an interactive teaching situation. The results of the analyses of parents' responses to hypothetical situations yielded greater consistency than their behavior in teaching their children a task. However, the parents' beliefs and their activities are attenuated by knowledge domain and the task, and the gender of the parent. Influences of a demographic, sociocultural, and psycholog-, ical nature should be addressed to begin to close the gaps in our knowledge of the role parents' beliefs play in influencing their behavior. Increasingly, the coherence between the content of the belief and the task to be taught, along with the identification of the relevant demographics, sociocultural, and psychological factors, should improve our understanding of the underlying bases for parents' actions with their children (Goodnow & Collins, 1990).

ACKNOWLEDGMENTS

Part of the research reported in this chapter was supported by the National Institute of Child Health and Human Development Grant No. R01-HD10686 to Educational Testing Service, National Institute of Mental Health Grant No. R01-MH32301 to Educational Testing Service, and Bureau of Education of the Handicapped Grant No. G007902000 to Educational Testing Service.

My thanks to Ann McGillicuddy-DeLisi for her thoughtful editorial comments, to Myung-In Kim for his preparation of the statistical material, and to Linda Kozelski for her thorough preparation of the manuscript for publication.

REFERENCES

Eccles, J. S., Harold, R., Wigfield, A., Yoon, K. S., Aberbach, A., & Doan, C. F. (1991, April). *Influences on, and consequences of, parents' beliefs regarding their children's abilities and interests.* Paper presented at the meeting of the Society for Research in Child Development, Seattle, WA.

Goodnow, J. J., & Collins, W. A. (1990). *Development according to parents: The nature, sources, and consequences of parents' ideas.* Hillsdale, NJ: Lawrence Erlbaum Associates.

Kochanska, G., Kuczynski, L., & Radke-Yarrow, M. (1989). Correspondence between mothers' self-reported and observed child-rearing practices. *Child Development, 60,* 56–63.

McGillicuddy-DeLisi, A. V. (1982). The relationship between parents' beliefs about development and family constellation, socioeconomic status, and parents' teaching strategies. In L. M. Laosa & I. E. Sigel (Eds.), *Families as learning environments for children* (pp. 261–299). New York: Plenum.

McGillicuddy-DeLisi, A. V., & Sigel, I. E. (1982). Effects of the atypical child on the family. In L. A. Bond & J. M. Joffe (Eds.), *Facilitating infant and early childhood development* (pp. 197–233). Hanover, NH: University Press of New England.

Miller, S. A. (1988). Parents' beliefs about children's cognitive development. *Child Development, 59,* 259–285.

Monsey, T. V. C., Bond, L. A., Belenky, M. F., Weinstock, J. S., & Burgmeier, P. T. (1991, April). *The relationship between mothers' epistemological perspectives and their communication strategies with their young children.* Paper presented at the meeting of the Society for Research in Child Development, Seattle, WA.

Sigel, I. E. (1982). The relationship between parents' distancing strategies and the child's cognitive behavior. In L. M. Laosa & I. E. Sigel (Eds.), *Families as learning environments for children* (pp. 47–86). New York: Plenum.

Sigel, I. E. (1986). Reflections on the belief–action connection: The aftermath of a research program on parental belief systems and teaching strategies. In R. D. Ashmore & D. M. Brodzinsky (Eds.), *Thinking about the family: Views of parents and children* (pp. 35–65). Hillsdale, NJ: Lawrence Erlbaum Associates.

Sigel, I. E., & Hoffman, M. L. (1956). The predictive potential of projective tests for nonclinical populations. *Journal of Projective Techniques, 20,* 262–264.

Sigel, I. E., & McGillicuddy-DeLisi, A. V. (1984). Parents as teachers of their children: A distancing behavior model. In A. D. Pellegrini & T. D. Yawkey (Eds.), *The development of oral and written language in social contexts* (pp. 71–92). Norwood, NJ: Ablex.

Sigel, I. E., McGillicuddy-DeLisi, A. V., & Johnson, J. E. (1980). *Parental distancing, beliefs and children's representational competence within the family context* (ETS RR 80-21). Princeton, NJ: Educational Testing Service.

Sigel, I. E., Stinson, E. T., & Flaugher, J. (in press). Family processes and school achievement. In R. Cole & D. Reiss (Eds.). *How do families cope with chronic illness?* Hillsdale, NJ: Lawrence Erlbaum Associates.

Sigel, I. E., Stinson, E. T., & Flaugher, J. (1991). Socialization of representational competence in the family: The distancing paradigm. In R. J. Sternberg & L. Okagaki (Eds.), *Directors of development: Influences on the development of children's thinking* (pp. 121–144). Hillsdale, NJ: Lawrence Erlbaum Associates.

Sigel, I. E., Stinson, E. T., & Kim, M-I. (in press). Socialization of cognition: The distancing model. In K. W. Fischer & R. Wozniak (Eds.), *Specific environments: Thinking in contexts.* Hillsdale, NJ: Lawrence Erlbaum Associates.

Stinson, E. T. (1989). *Parental ideology: Implications for child academic achievement and self-concept.* Unpublished doctoral dissertation, The University of Pennsylvania.

Wertsch, J. V. (1991). *Voices of the mind: A sociocultural approach to mediated action.* Cambridge, MA: Harvard University Press.

Author Index

Subject Index